EMPIRICALLY BASED PLAY INTERVENTIONS FOR CHILDREN

EMPIRICALLY BASED PLAY INTERVENTIONS FOR CHILDREN

Edited by Linda A. Reddy,

Tara M. Files-Hall,

and Charles E. Schaefer

American Psychological Association, Washington, DC

Published by
American Psychological Association
750 First Street, NE
Washington, DC 20002
www.apa.org

To order
APA Order Department
P.O. Box 92984
Washington, DC 20090-2984
Tel: (800) 374-2721; Direct: (202) 336-5510
Fax: (202) 336-5502; TDD/TTY: (202) 336-6123
Online: www.apa.org/books/
E-mail: order@apa.org

In the U.K., Europe, Africa, and the Middle East, copies may be ordered from
American Psychological Association
3 Henrietta Street
Covent Garden, London
WC2E 8LU England

Typeset in Goudy by Page Grafx, Inc., St. Simons Island, GA

Printer: Sheridan Books, Ann Arbor, MI
Cover Designer: Anne Masters, Washington, DC
Technical/Production Editor: Gail B. Munroe

The opinions and statements published are the responsibility of the authors, and such opinions and statements do not necessarily represent the policies of the American Psychological Association.

Library of Congress Cataloging-in-Publication Data
Empirically based play interventions for children / Linda A. Reddy, Tara M. Files-Hall, and Charles E. Schaefer, editors.— 1st ed.
    p. cm.
  Includes bibliographical references and index.
  ISBN 1-59147-215-6
1. Play therapy. I. Reddy, Linda A. II. Files-Hall, Tara M. III. Schaeffer, Charles E. IV. Title.

RJ505.P6E567 2005
618.92'891653—dc22

2004019035

British Library Cataloguing-in-Publication Data
A CIP record is available from the British Library.

Printed in the United States of America
First Edition

To my parents,
Thomas Joseph and Gerri Mary Reddy
Linda A. Reddy

To my husband, Erik M. Hall,
and my parents, Edward and Karen Files
Tara M. Files-Hall

To my wife, Anne Weldon Schaefer
Charles E. Schaefer

CONTENTS

CONTRIBUTORS

Tanya Atamanoff is a doctoral student in the clinical psychology program at Fairleigh Dickinson University. Her clinical and research interests include child and adolescent disruptive behavior disorders, substance abuse, and group-based intervention. She received her BA (1999) in psychology from New York University and her MA (2004) in clinical psychology from Fairleigh Dickinson University, Teaneck, New Jersey.

April K. Bay-Hinitz is in private practice in Reno, Nevada. Her clinical interests include psychotherapy and psychological evaluations with children, adults, and families. She has additional specialties in brief treatment of traumatic stress and child custody evaluations. Her research focuses on children and game play and its effects on their behavior. She earned her BA (1986) and her PhD (1991) in clinical psychology from the University of Nevada, Reno.

Elizabeth Schmelzer Benisz completed her doctorate in clinical psychology at Fairleigh Dickinson University and predoctoral internship at the University of Medicine and Dentistry of New Jersey in 2003. Her clinical and research interests include psychological assessments, developmental delays, disruptive behavior disorders, early intervention, and child abuse and neglect. She received her BA (1996) in psychology from Yeshiva University in New York City and her MA (2000) and PhD (2003) in clinical psychology from Fairleigh Dickinson University, Teaneck, New Jersey.

Dania Braunstein is a doctoral student in the clinical psychology program at Fairleigh Dickinson University. Her clinical and research interests include neuropsychological assessment, play therapy, and psychotherapy with children, adolescents, and families. She obtained her BA in psychology from

Cornell University (1997) and her MA (2003) in clinical psychology from Fairleigh Dickinson University, Teaneck, New Jersey.

Stephen P. Demanchick is a doctoral student in the counselor education program at the University of Rochester. His clinical and research interests include child-centered play therapy, supervision, and group therapy. He received his MSEd (2002) in counselor education from the State University of New York College at Brockport. He is also a nationally certified counselor.

Erika D. Felix has research interests in school bullying and sexual harassment, family violence, school-based prevention programs, and program evaluation. She received her BA (1996) in psychology from the University of Southern California and her MA (1999) and PhD (2002) in clinical psychology from DePaul University.

Tara M. Files-Hall completed her predoctoral internship in clinical child psychology at St. Luke's Roosevelt Hospital Center in New York and her postdoctoral fellowship in the School District of Hillsborough County, Florida. Her clinical and research interests include disruptive behavior disorders, play therapy, early intervention, family–school assessment and intervention, group-based intervention, consultation, and program development and evaluation. She has published and presented several papers on the utility and efficacy of play-based interventions and behavioral treatments for children with attention-deficit/hyperactivity disorder (ADHD). She received her BA (1997) in psychology from the University of Central Florida and her MA (2000) and PhD (2003) in clinical psychology from Fairleigh Dickinson University, New Jersey. She maintains her private practice in Sarasota, Florida, and is employed as a school psychologist in Tampa, Florida.

Yvonne Hauch is a doctoral student in the clinical psychology program at Fairleigh Dickinson University. Her clinical interests include working with children, adolescents, and families within a systemic and multicultural perspective. Her research interests include treatment outcome research for children with ADHD. She obtained her BA (1997) in psychology at Rutgers University, her MA (2000) in developmental psychology from Teachers College, Columbia University, and her MA (2003) in clinical psychology from Fairleigh Dickinson University, Teaneck, New Jersey.

Amy D. Herschell is completing a research fellowship in child psychiatry with a concentration in treatment dissemination and services research at Western Psychiatric Institute and Clinic, University of Pittsburgh School of Medicine. Her research focuses on treatment of early onset conduct disorders and child physical abuse as well as implementation of evidence-based treatments in community settings. She received her BA (1995) in psychology from Westminster College and her MA (1999) and PhD (2003) in clinical psychology from West Virginia University.

Melissa R. Johnson is a pediatric psychologist at WakeMed in Raleigh, North Carolina, with a clinical faculty appointment at the University of North Carolina School of Medicine. Her major clinical interests include hospitalized and chronically ill infants, children, and adolescents; high-risk infant follow-up; and child abuse and neglect. Her research focuses on premature infant behavior and development, as well as attachment and temperament issues. She received her BA (1975) in psychology from Duke University and PhD (1980) in clinical psychology from the University of North Carolina at Chapel Hill.

Deborah B. Johnson is the director of community services at Children's Institute, Inc., the national director of the Primary Mental Health Project, and a senior clinical associate at the University of Rochester. Her major research interests include the Primary Mental Health Project, the National Development and Dissemination of Community-Based Collaboratives: Building Coalitions Based on Community Needs, the changing roles of school-based mental health professionals, and effecting system change to improve education and mental health programs for children. Dr. Johnson is also a nationally certified school psychologist. She received her BA (1975) from the University of California, Davis, and MS (1979) in school psychology from California State University, Chico.

Sheryl H. Jones is currently working at Children's Institute, Inc., with the Pre-K Primary Project and with Program Development. At this time, her interest is focused on preventive mental health interventions for prekindergarten children. She received her BS (1981) in medical dietetics and nutrition from the University of Illinois, MS (2001) in information technology from Rochester Institute of Technology, and PhD (1995) in clinical psychology from Northwestern University.

Sarina Kot is employed as a psychologist at British Columbia's Children's Hospital in Vancouver. She provides psychological assessments and short-term intervention for children referred to the hospital child protection team for abuse and neglect. Her clinical interests focus on play therapy and child abuse and neglect. She received her BA (1985) in social work from the University of Hong Kong and her MA (1990) and PhD (1995) in counseling from the University of North Texas.

Jennifer L. Kreimer is a certified child life specialist at WakeMed Day Surgery Center in Raleigh, North Carolina. Her clinical and research interests are focused on trauma and grief issues and stress, coping, and support systems for the hospitalized child. She received her BS (1988) in therapeutic recreation from Eastern Michigan University and MS (1998) in counselor education from North Carolina State University.

Cheryl B. McNeil is an associate professor of psychology in the child clinical program at West Virginia University. Her clinical and research interests are focused on program development and evaluation, specifically with regard to abusive parenting practices and managing the disruptive behaviors of young children in both the home and school settings. She has coauthored two books, *Parent–Child Interaction Therapy* and *Short-Term Play Therapy for Disruptive Children*; a continuing education audio and video package, *Working With Oppositional Defiant Disorder in Children*; and a classroom management program, The Tough Class Discipline Kit. She obtained her BS (1983) in psychology from Louisiana State University and MS (1986) and PhD (1989) in clinical psychology with a child specialization from the University of Florida.

JoAnne L. Pedro-Carroll is director of program development at Children's Institute, Inc., and an associate professor of psychology and psychiatry at the University of Rochester. She is the founder and director of the Children of Divorce Intervention Program, an award-winning prevention program for kindergarten through eighth-grade children dealing with the challenges of family reorganization. Her research interests include the effects of marital adjustment on children and the development, implementation, and evaluation of preventive interventions for children and families experiencing stressful life transitions. She lectures locally and nationally and provides consultation and training to schools, courts, and service organizations. She is the recipient of American Psychological Association's 2001 Award for Distinguished Contributions to Public Service. She earned her BS (1973) in education, MEd (1974) in education from the University of Cincinnati, and an MA (1981) and PhD (1984) in clinical psychology from the University of Rochester.

William A. Rae is a clinical professor and the director of the Counseling and Assessment Clinic at Texas A&M University. His primary clinical interests are externalizing disorders and coping with illness. His research focuses on pediatric psychology and child ethics. He obtained his BA (1970) in psychology from the University of California, Berkeley, and PhD (1975) in counseling psychology from the University of Texas, Austin.

Linda A. Reddy is an associate professor of psychology, founder and director of the Child/Adolescent ADHD Clinic, and former director of the Center for Psychological Services at Fairleigh Dickinson University, Hackensack, New Jersey. She has published two edited books, *Innovative Mental Health*

Interventions for Children: Programs That Work and *Inclusion Practice in Special Education: Research, Theory, and Application*. She has published over 30 book chapters and articles. She specializes in the assessment and treatment of children with disruptive behavior disorders, family–school interventions, test validation, behavioral consultation, play interventions, and treatment outcome evaluation. She maintains her practice in New Jersey. She received her BA (1986) in psychology from Boston University, MA (1989) in educational psychology and PhD (1994) in school psychology from the University of Arizona and postdoctoral research and clinical fellowship at the Devereux Foundation Institute of Clinical Training and Research.

Sally J. Rogers is a developmental psychologist and a professor of psychiatry at the M.I.N.D. Institute, University of California, Davis. She heads a diagnostic team for toddlers and preschoolers with autism at the M.I.N.D. Institute and is the principal investigator of several autism research projects, including a large program of research on autism funded by NICHD called "Definition and Development of the Phenotype in Autism." She has published papers on cognitive development in children with profound mental retardation and on cognitive and social development of blind infants, as well as numerous papers on clinical and developmental aspects of autism. She is also the main author of the Michigan Scales. She received her BA (1969) from Ashland College and PhD (1975) from Ohio State University, with a specialization in mental retardation and developmental disabilities.

Scott D. Ryan is an assistant professor at the Florida State University School of Social Work, where he teaches classes focusing on therapeutic interventions with children and parents. He is also a registered play therapist supervisor (RPT-S). His research focuses on interventions with children, with a specific emphasis on play therapy, as well as on adoptive families. He has presented across the country and consults with agencies on programmatic and evaluative issues. He earned his BSW (1990) from Florida Atlantic University, MSW (1992) from Columbia University, MBA (1995) from Howard University, and PhD (2001) from Case Western Reserve University, with an emphasis on social work practice and research.

Charles E. Schaefer is a professor of psychology and former director of the Center for Psychological Services at Fairleigh Dickinson University, Hackensack, New Jersey. He is the cofounder and Board Member Emeritus of the International Play Therapy Association. Dr. Schaefer is the founder and codirector of the Play Therapy Training Institute in New Jersey. He has published over 40 books and numerous articles and book chapters on play-based interventions. He has over 30 years of experience working with young children and parents. Dr. Schaefer coordinates an annual international play therapy study group in England. He earned his BA from Fairfield University and his MA and PhD in clinical psychology from Fordham University (1967).

Janine S. Shelby is on the clinical faculty at the University of California, Los Angeles (UCLA), in the department of psychiatry, and is in private practice in Santa Monica, California. She holds a diplomate from the American Academy of Experts in Traumatic Stress. She is a consultant for the National Center for Child Traumatic Stress at UCLA. She presents widely to national and international audiences and is a consultant for several international humanitarian organizations. Her specialty area is posttraumatic play therapy. She is president of the Foundation Board for the Association for Play Therapy (APT), the past president of the California branch of the APT, and a registered play therapist supervisor (RPT-S). Dr. Shelby is also the founding director of the Child Trauma Clinic at Harbor-UCLA Medical Center and former clinical director of the Rape Treatment Center at Santa Monica-UCLA Medical Center. Her publications focus on posttraumatic intervention with survivors of traumatic events. She earned her BA (1987) from Samford University, MS (1989) from the University of South Alabama, and PhD (1994) in counseling psychology from the University of Miami. In 1996, she completed a postdoctoral fellowship in child psychology at Harbor-UCLA.

Shelly K. Smith is a third-year doctoral student at the Florida State University School of Social Work. She has worked in the field of child welfare for the past six years, providing services to children in foster care as well as children entering into adoptive families and those that were part of disrupted adoptions. In addition, she is also involved in research through Florida State University, including serving as project director for a play therapy program for adoptive families. She received her BSW (1999) from the University of Georgia and MSW (2000) from Florida State University.

Craig Springer completed his doctorate in clinical psychology at Fairleigh Dickinson University (2004) and predoctoral internship at the Jewish Child Care Association in Pleasantville, New York. His clinical interests include working with children and adolescents with behavioral, social, and emotional needs, as well as parent training. His research interests include evaluating treatment adherence as it relates to treatment efficacy for young children with ADHD. He obtained his BA (1998) in psychology at New York University and MA (2002) and PhD (2004) in clinical psychology at Fairleigh Dickinson University.

Jeremy R. Sullivan is a doctoral candidate at Texas A&M University and is completing his predoctoral internship at Cypress-Fairbanks Independent School District, Houston, Texas. His clinical interests include internalizing problems and coping skills interventions. His research focuses on ethical decision making and adolescent development. He obtained his BS (1998) in psychology from Sam Houston State University.

Ashley Tyndall-Lind is the director of clinical and professional services at Genesis Women's Shelter in Dallas, Texas, and an adjunct professor at the University of North Texas. She is a Licensed Professional Counselor Supervisor, a Registered Play Therapist Supervisor, and a National Certified Counselor. Her research focuses on domestic violence and trauma recovery. She earned her BA (1991) in psychology from Louisiana State University, MS (1993) in counseling psychology from Loyola University, and PhD (1999) in counseling from the University of North Texas.

Risë VanFleet is a psychologist and the president of the Family Enhancement and Play Therapy Center, Inc., in Boiling Springs, Pennsylvania, an independent practice and professional training center specializing in play therapy, filial therapy, and family therapy. She is also a registered play therapist–supervisor. She is a past president of the Association for Play Therapy. Her clinical interests focus on play–filial interventions for families experiencing chronic illness, trauma, and attachment difficulties. Her research focuses on applications of filial therapy to different populations. She has written numerous books, chapters, and articles about filial therapy and is featured on several educational videos. She is a popular conference speaker who has trained thousands worldwide in play therapy and filial therapy. She received her BA (1975) in psychology and chemistry from the University of Pennsylvania, MA (1978) in clinical–community psychology from Indiana University of Pennsylvania, and PhD (1985) in human development and family studies from Pennsylvania State University.

Ginger R. Wilson is a doctoral student at the University of Nevada, Reno (UNR) in the behavior analysis program. She is currently the assistant director of the UNR Early Childhood Autism Program. Her research focuses on child pathology, specifically autism and other developmental disorders; parent and teacher training; and gambling behavior. She earned her BS (1999) in psychology from South Dakota State University and MA (2002) in behavior analysis from UNR.

FOREWORD

SUE C. BRATTON

Which treatments work best for specific childhood disorders has long been debated among mental health professionals; however, only recently have children's mental health needs and treatment efficacy received national attention. The number of children experiencing emotional and behavioral problems severe enough to impair normal functioning is growing at an alarming rate. The most recent U.S. Surgeon General's report on children's mental health emphasized the critical need for early intervention and prevention-focused, empirically validated treatments designed to respond to the distinct needs of children.[1]

Play-based interventions are uniquely responsive to children's developmental needs and therefore are widely used by practitioners to treat a broad range of social, emotional, and behavioral problems in their young clients. Play not only promotes optimal growth and development; it also provides children with a nonthreatening means of bridging the gap between their experiences and cognitive understanding, thereby providing opportunities for insight, learning, problem solving, coping, and mastery. In spite of its popularity among practitioners, play therapy has not received widespread acceptance from the scientific community and has often been criticized for a lack of an adequate research base to prove its efficacy. Not only are child therapists ethically bound and accountable to their clients to provide the most effective interventions; they are also under increasing pressure from third-party payers, school administrators, the legal community, and consumers to provide proof of treatment efficacy.

During the past 2 decades, play therapy researchers have responded to the demand for stronger empirical support, which has resulted in a growing

[1]U.S. Public Health Service. (2000). *Report of the Surgeon General's Conference on Children's Mental Health: A national action agenda.* Washington, DC: Author.

body of well-designed outcome research demonstrating the efficacy of play-based interventions with various populations.[2] Two recent meta-analyses focused on the efficacy of play therapy interventions and gave much-needed validation to this growing field.[3] Although these studies support the overall effectiveness of play therapy, they do not provide answers regarding which approach works best for each disorder. An overall weakness of individual research studies that promote play therapy's efficacy is inadequate descriptions of theory and methods, which prevent the practitioner or researcher from replicating the treatment. The field is sorely in need of a useful and comprehensive resource of proven, theoretically sound play therapy interventions that are described in sufficient detail for the reader to use in practice.

Reddy and her colleagues have responded to this critical need by creating the first book that focuses exclusively on empirically based play interventions. They have created a user-friendly reference of innovative, developmentally responsive, play-based interventions that are proven clinically effective with a variety of populations and childhood disorders. Each program featured in this text is theoretically grounded and designed to be implemented in multiple settings. In addition, many of the interventions featured in this text are time-limited, requiring 10 weeks or less of treatment. A major strength of this book is its organization and ease of use. The editors organized chapters into four main sections, differentiating between empirically based interventions aimed at prevention and those targeted for specific disorders. Also, review chapters on broader substantive areas are included. Although they focus on the outcome research that supports each program's efficacy, the chapter authors also provide clearly stated objectives, theoretical and developmental rationale for the intervention, required materials and training, and salient treatment components. In addition, they offer recommendations for clinical use and ongoing evaluation in sufficient detail that should allow the reader to replicate the program with other populations or settings.

This book marks a significant contribution to the field of child therapy and related disciplines as it is the first of its kind to focus exclusively on empirically based play interventions. Although scientifically proving the effectiveness of any therapeutic intervention is essential to its acceptance as a viable treatment, disseminating the information in a format that is useful to practitioners, educators, researchers, and the public is critical to its clinical utility and widespread use. Reddy and her colleagues have accomplished that in a well-organized, accessible work.

---

[2]Bratton, S., & Ray, D. (2000). What the research shows about play therapy. *International Journal of Play Therapy, 9*(1), 47–88.

[3]LeBlanc, M., & Ritchie, M. (2001). A meta-analysis of play therapy outcomes. *Counseling Psychology Quarterly, 14*(2), 149–163; Ray, D., Bratton, S., Rhine, T., & Jones, L. (2001). The effectiveness of play therapy: Responding to the critics. *International Journal of Play Therapy, 10*(1), 85–108.

EMPIRICALLY BASED

PLAY INTERVENTIONS

FOR CHILDREN

1

ANNOUNCING EMPIRICALLY BASED PLAY INTERVENTIONS FOR CHILDREN

LINDA A. REDDY, TARA M. FILES-HALL, AND
CHARLES E. SCHAEFER

Play is a universal behavior of children that has been documented since ancient times (Janssen & Janssen, 1996; Lowenfeld, 1939). It is estimated that by 6 years of age, children are likely to have engaged in more than 15,000 hours of play (Schaefer, 1993). The benefits of play for healthy cognitive development (Bornstein & O'Reilly, 1993; Piaget, 1962), language development (Lyytinen, Poikkeus, & Laakso, 1997; McCune, 1995; Tamis-LeMonda & Bornstein, 1994), social competence (Howes & Matheson, 1992; Parten, 1932), and physical development (Pellegrini & Smith, 1998) have been well established. Play has the power not only to aid in normal child development but also to help alleviate emotional and behavioral difficulties. For over six decades, play therapy has been recognized as the oldest and most popular form of child therapy in clinical practice (Association for Play Therapy, 2001; Parten, 1932). Play-based assessment and intervention approaches are routinely taught in masters and doctoral level training programs across the country. The Association for Play Therapy

(2001) defined play therapy as "the systematic use of a theoretical model to establish an interpersonal process wherein trained play therapists use the therapeutic powers of play to help clients prevent or resolve psychosocial difficulties and achieve optimal growth and development" (p. 20).

In recent years, clinicians and researchers have sought to identify the specific elements inherent in play that make it a therapeutic agent for change. Among the major therapeutic powers (also termed *therapeutic factors*) that have been described are its communication power (children naturally express their conscious and unconscious thoughts and feelings better through play than by words alone); its teaching power (clients attend and learn better when play is used to instruct); its abreaction power (clients can relive past stressful events and release the associated negative emotions in the safe environment of the play world); and its rapport-building power (clients tend to like therapists who are playful and fun-loving). A comprehensive listing of the 14 therapeutic factors of play is presented by Schaefer (1993).

Each of the well-known schools of play therapy (i.e., client-centered, cognitive–behavioral, family, and psychodynamic) emphasizes one or more of the curative powers of play. The prescriptive–eclectic school of play therapy (Kaduson, Cangelosi, & Schaefer, 1997) advocates that play therapists become skilled in the use of numerous therapeutic powers and differentially apply them to meet the individual needs of clients. Despite a strong theoretical foundation, some have questioned the clinical utility and efficacy of play interventions (e.g., Lebo, 1953; Reade, Hunter, & McMillan, 1999). The main criticism of play interventions has been that the field in general lacks rigorous research designs and data-analytic methods (Phillips, 1985). Research in this area is often based on anecdotal reports or case study designs and includes limitations seen in the psychotherapy outcome literature (e.g., lack of control or alternative treatment groups, small sample sizes, limited or no generalizability of findings to natural settings; LeBlanc & Ritchie, 1999).

Over the past two decades, well-designed controlled play intervention studies have emerged. Two meta-analytic studies have examined the effectiveness of play therapy with children (e.g., LeBlanc & Ritchie 1999; Ray, Bratton, Rhine, & Jones, 2001). LeBlanc and Ritchie's meta-analysis included 42 experimental studies, dated from 1947 to 1997. The studies used came from multiple sources, including journals, dissertations, and unpublished studies. Studies selected included control or comparison group designs and sufficient data and statistical information. The average age of the children in the studies was 7.9 years; no child was older than 12 years of age. Play therapy yielded an overall positive effect size of .66, reflecting that play therapy has a moderate treatment effect. The authors also investigated the specific characteristics of treatment that related to outcome success.

Two factors that significantly related to outcome were parental involvement in the children's therapy and the duration of therapy. Studies that involved the parent as a therapist resulted in an effect size of .83 (i.e., large positive treatment outcome), compared with an effect size of .56 (i.e., moderate positive treatment outcome) for studies that did not involve parents. Treatment outcome appears to improve with a sustained treatment regimen. Several factors not related to outcome were noted, such as the type of presenting problem, the treatment context (group vs. individual), and the age and gender of the participants.

Ray and her colleagues conducted a meta-analysis that included 94 experimental studies, dated from 1940 to 2000. The studies included were journal articles, dissertations, or unpublished studies. Each study included a control or comparison group design and pre–post measures. The child participants ranged in age from 3 to 16 years old, with a mean age of 7.1. Results revealed that play therapy yielded an overall effect size of .80 (i.e., large positive treatment outcome). Characteristics of treatment associated with outcomes were explored, such as the influence of different play therapy theoretical models on outcomes. Studies were coded as follows: (a) 74 studies were coded as humanistic–nondirective play therapy, (b) 12 studies were behavioral–directive play therapy, and (c) 8 were not coded because of a lack of information. The humanistic–nondirective category demonstrated a slightly larger effect size (ES = .93) than the behavioral–directive category (ES = .73); however, the authors caution that this difference is likely influenced by the disproportionate number of studies in the two categories. When comparing the effect of general play therapy with filial play therapy, it was found that the filial therapies exhibited a greater effect (ES = 1.06) than general play therapies (ES = .73). Similar to LeBlanc and Ritchie's (1999) findings, routine parental involvement in treatment was a significant predictor of outcome (p = .008). Likewise, the treatment context (i.e., individual vs. group), whether the population was clinical versus analog, and the age or gender of participants were found to be unrelated to outcome.

Collectively, the two meta-analytic studies revealed that play interventions have moderate to large positive effects (ES = .66 to .80) on outcomes. Play interventions appear to be effective for children across treatment modalities (group, individual), age groups (3 to 16 years), gender, referred versus nonreferred populations, and treatment orientations (humanistic–nondirective, behavioral–directive). Thus, these reviews provide evidence for the clinical utility and efficacy of play interventions with children and families. However, a compilation of innovative, well-designed, and empirically supported play interventions and reviews of the outcome literature had yet to be published in one text. This book serves as the first published text of empirically validated play interventions for children.

THE PURPOSE
OF THIS BOOK

In an era of cost-containment and outcomes, the need to provide empirical evidence of the effectiveness of an intervention is increasingly important to the general acceptance of that intervention by practitioners, third-party payers, and consumers. As a result of managed behavioral health care, professionals are being pressured to use well-established, theoretically based, and flexible interventions (Reddy & Savin, 2000).

The goal of this book is to offer scholars and practitioners a unique clinical reference that presents evidence-based and maximally useful play interventions for a variety of child populations and settings. This book illustrates the usefulness of both directive and nondirective approaches. To meet the needs of both practitioners and researchers, each chapter includes clinical theory and observations, as well as research data. Our selection of intervention programs was guided by 11 principles. We identified programs that

- included well-defined treatment components and processes;
- offered innovative treatment options;
- are guided by developmental theory;
- demonstrated clinical effectiveness;
- are adaptable for a variety of settings and appropriate for prevention or intervention;
- included ongoing, comprehensive outcome assessment approaches;
- offered structured or time-limited treatments;
- are tailored to the developmental level of the child;
- targeted behaviors or competencies in children or parents;
- identified and assessed quantifiable behavioral goals; and
- included varied treatment agents such as psychologists, psychiatrists, nurses, physical therapists, occupational therapists, social workers, teachers, or parents.

Seven of the intervention programs in this book meet the guidelines set forth by the American Psychological Association's Task Force on Promotion and Dissemination of Psychological Procedures (Chambless, 1995). Criteria for probably efficacious psychosocial interventions for childhood disorders include "(a) two studies showing the intervention more effective than a no-treatment control group (or comparison group) OR (b) two studies otherwise meeting the well-established treatment criteria (I, III, IV), but both are conducted by the same investigator, or one good study demonstrating effectiveness by these same criteria, OR (c) at least two good studies demonstrating effectiveness but flawed by heterogeneity of the client samples, OR (d) a small series of single case design studies (i.e., less than three) otherwise meeting the well-established treatment criteria (II, III, IV)" (Chambless, 1995, p. 22). Our selection of programs does not signify a special status or ranking, nor do we suggest that our choice of programs is exhaustive. Other excellent programs do exist that meet our criteria.

We invited four distinguished contributors to critically review the outcome literature on one well-known model (i.e., filial therapy) and three intervention approaches for children with internalizing disorders. A description of each is included below.

We present the information in four parts: Empirically Based Play Prevention Programs, Empirically Based Play Interventions for Internalizing Disorders, Empirically Based Play Interventions for Externalizing Disorders, and Empirically Based Play Interventions for Developmental Disorders and Related Issues. The chapters include a description of the theoretical basis and objectives of the play intervention, key treatment ingredients and processes, outcome studies supporting the effectiveness, replication, and transportability of the intervention to other settings and populations, and a recommended evaluation approach for clinical practice.

Part I presents three empirically based play prevention programs. Prevention interventions reduce the social, emotional, behavioral, and developmental difficulties faced by children and also prevent the early onset of more severe and costly disorders. In chapter 2, Johnson, Pedro-Carroll, and Demanchick discuss a well-researched school-based preventative play intervention program, the Primary Mental Health Project (PMHP). PMHP, established in 1957, targets primary school-age children at risk for adjustment difficulties and has been implemented in over 2,000 schools worldwide. Under supervision, paraprofessionals are trained in child-centered play therapy principles and skills so they can conduct individual play sessions. Outcome evaluations of PMHP reveal that the children demonstrate significant improvements in adjustment in both the short and the long term. In chapter 3, Kot and Tyndall-Lind present intensive play-based therapy, a short-term crises intervention model (i.e., 2 weeks or less of treatment) for children temporarily living in a domestic violence shelter. Based on child-centered play therapy theory, this approach requires professionals with advanced play therapy training to conduct daily play therapy for individual children or with sibling groups, when appropriate. This intervention is effective in reducing children's distress related to witnessing violence between parents and to adjustments caused by changes in residence. In the final chapter in this part, Pedro-Carroll and Jones present a school-based prevention program that targets the needs of children of divorce. The Children of Divorce Intervention Program (CODIP) is implemented by specially trained and supervised mental health professionals and paraprofessionals. Developmentally sensitive, play-based activities within a group context are used to help children address the stressful changes that divorce often brings. There is strong evidence for CODIP's effectiveness in reducing the stress of divorce on children and in improving their social, emotional, and school adjustment in the short and long term.

Part II includes three chapters on play interventions for children with internalizing disorders. In chapter 5, Shelby and Felix propose an innovative intervention model, posttraumatic play therapy, for children with symptoms of posttraumatic stress disorder. The authors integrate directive and nondirective procedures to create a prescriptive approach for responding to the unique needs of traumatized children. The type and intensity of symptoms, as well as developmental factors, guide trained professionals in tailoring treatments for individual children. In chapter 6, Johnson and Kreimer present a critical review of guided fantasy play interventions for chronically ill children. Grounded in analytic and cognitive theory, this approach can be implemented by trained professionals to uniquely address the needs of chronically ill children related to the effects and ongoing stress of their experience. In the final chapter of Part II, Rae and Sullivan present a time-limited approach to implementing play interventions for hospitalized children. The authors critically review the outcome literature on play-based interventions for this population. Based on client-centered, humanistic principles, this approach reduces the psychological distress related to children's illnesses and hospitalization. It is designed for professionals trained in nondirective play therapy procedures who are familiar with pediatric medical disorders.

Part III presents empirically based play interventions for children with externalizing disorders. This group of interventions uses a variety of therapeutic agents, including professionals, teachers, parents, and paraprofessionals in treatment delivery. In chapter 8, Reddy and her colleagues provide a detailed description of the Child Attention Deficit Hyperactivity Disorder (ADHD) Multimodal Program (CAMP), an empirically supported intervention that treats the social and behavioral needs of young children diagnosed with ADHD. Grounded in social learning theory and behavioral principles, this developmental, skill-based program uses developmentally appropriate games to improve social skills, self-control, and anger/stress management within a 10-week, structured group format. Parents receive concurrent group training focused on behavioral management techniques in the home, school, and community. Behavioral consultation services are also offered to each child's parent(s) and teacher. Research on evaluations of CAMP reveals significant improvements in parents' functioning and child behavior, both at home and in school. In chapter 9, Herschell and McNeil offer a highly informative overview of parent–child interaction therapy (PCIT), a well-researched intervention designed to treat young children exhibiting externalizing behavior problems. Based on developmental theory, social learning theory, behavioral principles, and traditional play therapy procedures, PCIT is a structured, time-limited model focused on training parents as therapeutic agents of change. Trained therapists use in vivo coaching methods to help parents enhance their child behavior management. Research on PCIT reveals significant improvement in child and parent outcomes. Bay-Hinitz and Wilson present the final intervention in this part, a cooperative games intervention. This empirically supported intervention for aggressive preschool children uses teacher-directed cooperative board games and other cooperative activities to reduce aggressive behavior. This intervention requires minimal training and can be used by parents, mentors, and paraprofessionals.

Part IV presents empirically based interventions for developmental disorders and related issues. Unique to the interventions featured in this part is a focus on the value of play in the healthy development of children. In chapter 11, Rogers presents the Denver model, a well-researched, school-based daily play intervention program effective in facilitating the development and growth of young children with autism spectrum disorders. The Denver model is grounded in developmental theory and emphasizes the importance of symbolic, interpersonal, and cognitive aspects of play in the development of children with autism. Children who have participated in this program exhibit significant improvements in symbolic play and affective, reciprocal exchanges during play with their parents. In chapter 12, Van Fleet, Ryan, and Smith offer an impressive review of the outcome literature on filial therapy. Filial therapy has been found to be effective in treating a wide range of child and family behavior problems through strengthening the parent–child attachment. This approach focuses on enhancing the relationship between parent and child, rather than on the behavior of concern. Under supervision, parents are trained in child-centered play therapy procedures and conduct weekly play sessions with their children.

In the final part, Files-Hall and Reddy provide a synthesis of the current outcome research on play interventions and offer new models for designing play interventions and outcome assessment approaches. A thoughtful discussion of future directions for research and training is presented.

It is our hope that this reference of innovative, well-designed, and empirically based play interventions illustrates to the reader the range of play prevention and intervention programs for children. We express our appreciation to all the contributors, who were fully committed to ensuring that this book represents a timely, scholarly, and comprehensive presentation of their programs. Furthermore, it is our hope that this book serves as a springboard for future program development and research in the area.

REFERENCES

Association for Play Therapy. (2001, June). Play therapy. *Association for Play Therapy Newsletter, 20*, 20.

Bornstein, M. H., & O'Reilly, A. (Eds.). (1993). *New directions for child development:*

The role of play in the development of thought (Vol. 59). San Francisco: Jossey-Bass.

Chambless, D. L. (1995). Training in and dissemination of empirically-validated psychological treatments: Report and recommendations. *The Clinical Psychologist, 48*(1), 3–24.

Howes, C., & Matheson, C. (1992). Sequences in the development of competent play with peers: Social and social pretend play. *Developmental Psychology, 28,* 961–974.

Janssen, R. M., & Janssen, J. J. (1996). *Growing up in ancient Egypt.* London: Rubicon Press.

Kaduson, H., Cangelosi, D., & Schaefer, C. E. (1997). *The playing cure: Individualized play therapy for specific childhood problems.* Northvale, NJ: Jason Aronson.

LeBlanc, M., & Ritchie, M. (1999). Predictors of play therapy outcomes. *International Journal of Play Therapy, 8*(2), 19–34.

Lebo, D. (1953). The present status of research on nondirective play therapy. *Journal of Consulting Psychology, 17,* 177–183.

Lowenfeld, M. (1939). The world pictures of children: A method of recording and studying them. *British Journal of Medical Psychology, 18,* 65–101.

Lyytinen, P., Poikkeus, A. M., & Laakso, M. L. (1997). Language and symbolic play in toddlers. *International Journal of Behavioral Development, 21*(2), 289–302.

McCune, L. (1995). A normative study of representational play in the transition to language. *Developmental Psychology, 21,* 198–206.

Parten, M. B. (1932). Social participation among preschool children. *Journal of Abnormal and Social Psychology, 27,* 243–269.

Pellegrini, A. D., & Smith, P. K. (1998). Physical activity play: The nature and function of a neglected aspect of play. *Child Development, 69,* 577–598.

Phillips, R. (1985). Whistling in the dark?: A review of play therapy research. *Psychotherapy, 22,* 752–760.

Piaget, J. (1962). *Play, dreams, and imitation in childhood.* New York: Norton.

Ray, D., Bratton, S., Rhine, T., & Jones, L. (2001). The effectiveness of play therapy: Responding to the critics. *International Journal of Play Therapy, 10*(1), 85–108.

Reade, S., Hunter, H., & McMillan, I. (1999). Just playing . . . is it time wasted? *The British Journal of Occupational Therapy, 62,* 157–162.

Reddy, L. A., & Savin, H. (2000). Designing and conducting outcome studies. In H. A. Savin & S. S. Kiesling (Eds.), *Accountable systems of behavioral health care* (pp. 132–158). San Francisco: Jossey-Bass.

Schaefer, C. E. (1993). *The therapeutic powers of play.* Northvale, NJ: Jason Aronson.

Tamis-LeMonda, C. S., & Bornstein, M. H. (1994). Specificity in mother–toddler language play relations across the second year. *Developmental Psychology, 30,* 283–292.

I

EMPIRICALLY BASED PLAY PREVENTION PROGRAMS

2

THE PRIMARY MENTAL HEALTH PROJECT: A PLAY INTERVENTION FOR SCHOOL-AGE CHILDREN

DEBORAH B. JOHNSON, JOANNE L. PEDRO-CARROLL, AND STEPHEN P. DEMANCHICK

His name is Zach, he is 7 years old, and he is in the first grade. His oldest sister is Courtney, age 16, followed by Susan, who is 13, and then by John, who is 10. He is a bright student but has difficulty paying attention, is often out of his seat, and doesn't finish his work. Zach interrupts others and seeks to be the center of attention. In October of first grade, his teacher says he has difficulty in two general areas: task orientation and peer social skills. Zach is then referred to Primary Project, a school-based program designed to prevent school adjustment difficulties and foster children's social and emotional well-being. Zach is one student who will benefit from the Primary Mental Health Project.

Primary Project, which began in 1957, is a program that borrows from the theoretical underpinnings of child-centered play and has been widely disseminated to over 2000 elementary schools throughout the world.

Estimates of the number of young school-aged children who have emotional or behavioral maladjustment that requires intervention range from 8% to 22% (Tuma, 1989; U.S. Department of Health and Human Services, 1999). Children with early school adjustment problems are at greater risk of dropping out of school (Ensminger & Slusarick, 1992) and are more likely to be among the 25% to 50% of teenage youth at moderate to high risk for delinquency, substance abuse problems, teenage pregnancy, and other problems of adolescent and early adult development (Weissberg, Caplan, & Harwood, 1991). Patterns of school failure often begin in the first 3 years of school; research on potential dropouts indicates that characteristics associated with such outcomes can often be identified early (Rotheram, Armstrong, & Booraem, 1982). Risk factors associated with delinquency and drug abuse are also evident in the early grades (Hawkins, Jishner, Jenson, & Catalano, 1987). This growing body of research strongly suggests the critical importance of providing positive early school experiences to young children. If a child's life experience can be fortified at an early age, this support will help him or her as the child grows older.

THE THERAPEUTIC ELEMENTS OF PLAY

There are numerous advantages to play-based approaches to working with young children, most notably the universal, intrinsic appeal of play as a natural way to communicate and safely explore their world. Play enables children to communicate when words are unavailable, inaccessible, or not readily understood. Play provides an opportunity for adults to share the child's inner world on the child's terms and at the child's pace. This approach is at the heart of the Primary Mental Health Project model: developing a trusting, therapeutic relationship in which the child feels safe to express and explore feelings, deal with stressful experiences, and perhaps master challenges.

Within the theoretical constructs of Carl Rogers' (1942, 1951) client-centered therapy theory, Virginia Axline (1947, 1969) postulated nondirective or self-directive play therapy that builds on Rogers's concept that individuals are constantly striving, seeking need fulfillment, and self-actualizing. Because a child's experiences and perceptions of the environment result in an understanding of reality, the child's adjustment is in direct proportion to the ability of the environment to meet the child's needs. Internal conflicts and maladaptive behavior arise as the child begins to fulfill needs missing from the environment. Axline posited that in an optimal environment such as the playroom, the exposure to empathy, implementation of structured limits, and acceptance by the therapist allows the child to reduce his or her conflict with the environment. This resulting decrease in inner conflict facilitates the child's self-actualization, growth, development, and the release of blocked

...when needed, Primary Project's training and intervention plan relies on seven key practices that each child associate must use to achieve success. They are (a) creating a caring relationship; (b) providing a safe environment; (c) establishing the core conditions of empathy, genuineness, and unconditional positive regard (Rogers, 1957); (d) engaging the child in child-centered play; (e) providing limits in play; (f) using active listening to facilitate the child's emotional growth; and (g) supporting child associates by facilitating supervisory sessions with a school mental health professional. Primary Project believes that the most important practice that helps children become better adjusted to school rests with the child associate's ability to create a warm and caring relationship with the child, which allows the child associate to provide a physically and emotionally safe environment. It is important to note that the child associate does not provide therapy to the child. However, Cowen et al. (1996) suggest that the child associate evoke and work with the naturally therapeutic elements of a warm and trusting relationship to help the maladjusted child become better adjusted to the school culture.

THE PRIMARY MENTAL HEALTH PROJECT

Simply put, the Primary Project is a prevention program designed to help young children adjust to the stresses of the school environment. Primary Project seeks to enhance and maximize children's school adjustment and other related competencies and to reduce social, emotional, and school adjustment difficulties from preschool through third grade. It is intended for children with evident or incipient school adjustment problems in the mild to moderate range, not for children with already crystallized, serious dysfunction. Carefully selected and trained paraprofessionals (child associates) provide timely, effective help to children who are just beginning to show adjustment difficulties. Play is the primary mediator for children. What may be viewed as a simple construct, however, is one that has evolved and been refined over the course of 45 years.

Schools are important settings for implementing preventive interventions for several reasons. First, it is estimated that 70% to 80% of mental health services received by children are provided in schools (Burns et al., 1995). Young children are frequently referred for mental health services because they have difficulty adjusting to the school environment (e.g., classroom behavior expectations, peer relationships). Although some prevention programs are targeted primarily for children while in school, others are targeted primarily for the adults (e.g., teachers) and the environment (e.g., classroom management). These have also been shown to be important elements in supporting children's healthy development. Targeting multiple systems of children's development by simultaneously enhancing children's competence and promoting effective behavior interactions across school and home settings was identified as a key characteristic of effective school-based prevention programs (Greenberg, Domitrovich, & Bumbarger, 2001).

Primary Project is one program that is targeted primarily for children, within the context of school, and using school-based staff. The school mental health professional who supervises the program is also part of the school structure and therefore has a natural consultative relationship with teachers and school administration. Those factors promote the building of "ownership" of the prevention program by an individual school, including teachers and administrators. "Buy-in" and ownership by teachers promotes successful referrals to families and high levels of participation.

Key Treatment Ingredients

Primary Project has been developed around five structural components, each of which contributes to the program's success:

- focus on young children,
- early screening and selection,
- use of paraprofessionals to provide direct services to children,
- role change of the school-based mental health professional, and
- ongoing program evaluation.

Primary Project targets children who are beginning to show signs of early adjustment difficulties. This targeted population is depicted schematically in Figure 2.1. Although this figure appears to represent four "discrete" levels of adjustment, those levels are in fact more continuous than discrete. The figure first conveys the notion that most children (those in the lower section of the triangle) are adequately adjusted to school and do not need Primary Project services. Next, it depicts a group of children in whom mild to moderate school adjustment problems are evident—students like Zach. Zach is doing well academically compared to most students, but his teacher says that he doesn't seem to fit in with others. This is the type of child for whom

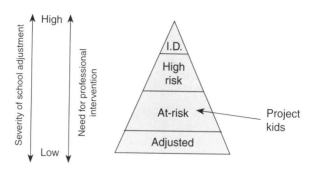

Figure 2.1. Primary Mental Health Project's target population.

Primary Project services are most appropriate. The third group has more difficulties and is ordinarily served by school mental health professionals. The top group, by far the smallest, depicts children already identified with specific diagnoses (e.g., seriously emotionally disturbed, behavior disorder, depressed) who are, or should be, receiving help through the school's special education system or from clinical mental health professionals.

Systematic screening of all children in the target age groups facilitates consideration of *all* children for participation in Primary Project. It is particularly helpful in differentiating children who can benefit most from a prevention program and those in need of more intensive help. Screening also focuses on behaviors that relate most closely to later school difficulties. (See Program Services for a more complete description.)

Use of Paraprofessionals to Provide Intervention Services

Primary Project uses carefully selected and trained paraprofessionals (referred to as child associates) to provide direct services to children identified through the screening process. The child associates work under the direct supervision of certified school mental health professionals (e.g., school psychologists, social workers, or counselors).

The program seeks to identify qualified adults for the paraprofessional role from within the local community. Although logic suggests that adults within a community can often provide optimal services to children that are compatible with their cultural and racial values and goals, it is not an absolute. Child associates are central to the effectiveness of any local program. Their ability to enter into a meaningful relationship with children is can see 10 to 15 children in a week and have sufficient time for participation in training, supervision, and completion of necessary documents related to program implementation. Many schools have two part-time associates who see a combined 50 to 60 children in a school year.

The mental health professional provides clinical supervision, training, and oversight of the Primary Project. Her or his clinical skills can be redirected to work with the children most in need of more intensive intervention. As a result, the impact of the work is geometrically expanded to include a larger number of children.

Ongoing program evaluation is an important tool to improve the quality of the program and understand its impact on children. Evaluation can and should be conducted regularly and should include both process and outcomes.

Program Services Screening and Selection

The process of child selection begins with procedures to screen all children within the target grades to identify those who would benefit from Primary Project. Children experiencing adaptive or interpersonal problems such as mild aggression, acting-out, shyness, anxiousness, withdrawal, and learning behaviors that interfere with educational progress in school are typical Primary Project children. Children may be identified and referred to Primary Project via formal and informal processes such as the use of behavior rating scales (teacher or child completed), observation, or referral.

The screening process begins with a collection of information four to six weeks after school starts, which allows time for children to "settle in" to their new environment. For kindergarten children, screening is often deferred for a few months to allow the children's behavior to stabilize after their first school experiences.

Targeted teachers in classrooms complete a standardized screening measure, typically the AML-R (Acting-out, Moody, Learning Difficulties–Revised; Cowen et al., 1996) for each child in the class. All items are rated on a 5-point frequency of occurrence scale and are summed to yield factor and total scores. AML-R norms provide individual adjustment profiles for all children in targeted classrooms in three domains: Aggressive Behaviors; Learning Problems; and Anxious–Withdrawn Behaviors. Predictive validity of the AML-R has been demonstrated using independent teacher ratings of children's behavior and other independent indicators of school adjustment (e.g., achievement; Cowen et al.).

Children's scores can thus be related to an appropriate reference group and a rough initial index of their adjustment status can be determined. AML-R results can be viewed as a "snapshot in time" and should be used in conjunction with other information regarding the children.

Systematic use of the AML-R, Child Rating Scale (CRS; Hightower et al., 1987), or similar measures is one key element in Primary Project's mass-screening procedures. Beyond this early focused step, screening is an ongoing, open process. Throughout the year, and across school years, teachers and other school personnel function as observers whose concerns about children can be raised at any time with the Primary Project team.

In addition to being identified as at-risk based on screening, additional independent information (e.g., observation, teacher and parent input, children's self-report) is used to better understand the needs of the child. Screening may also include observation of a child working on structured classroom activities. This provides an opportunity to see how the child interacts with peers and adults. What a child is doing during this time is less important than how he or she interacts with others.

Selection and Assignment Conferences

Relevant screening data are reviewed during "assignment conferences." These usually start in mid-October and are conducted in ways that best fit the school's operating procedure. Primary Project staff, participating teachers, and other relevant school personnel review the information assembled, create composite sketches of children's school adjustment, and identify children who seem most appropriate for Primary Project services.

In essence, the assignment conference seeks to assess the child's current adjustment (competencies and problems) from pertinent perspectives and on that basis develop a mutually agreed upon plan to address the child's needs. By the end of the process, children from all classes have been reviewed and those appropriate for Primary Project referred. As part of this process, some children may be referred for further evaluation or outside services.

Parent Permission

After children have been identified for participation in Primary Project and agreed on by the Primary Project team, written parental consent for the child's participation is obtained.

Establishing Intervention Goals and the Intervention Process

After children are identified and permission is received, classroom teachers complete the Teacher–Child Rating Scale 2.1 (T-CRS) prior to the start of services (Perkins & Hightower, 2002). The T-CRS is a behavior rating scale designed specifically for use by teachers to assess children's school behaviors. It consists of 32 items that assess four primary domains of a child's socioemotional adjustment.

1. Task orientation: A child's ability to focus on school-related tasks.
2. Behavior control: A child's skill in adapting and tolerating limits imposed by the school environment or by the child's own limitations.
3. Assertiveness: A child's interpersonal functioning and confidence in dealing with peers.
4. Peer social skills: A child's likeability and popularity among peers and how well the child interacts with peers.

An adjustment profile for each child is used to establish intervention goals in collaboration with the child's classroom teacher, the school mental health professional, and the child's parent. Program goals include a dual focus on enhancing competencies and addressing problems. For example, goals for an individual child might include enhancing peer social skills, decreasing the child's aggression through the development of prosocial means of anger expression (e.g., anger identification, developing language for feelings), and increasing frustration tolerance.

Zach was identified during the traditional screening process. His parents were aware that he was having difficulty in school and worked to support him at home. They stayed in contact with his teacher during the first weeks of school and were not surprised when she called to suggest that he participate in "Special Friends" (the local name for the project).

WORKING WITH CHILDREN THROUGH EXPRESSIVE PLAY

All aspects of Primary Project support the building of a positive therapeutic relationship between the child associate and the child. After initial training and after the children are selected to participate through the screening and selection process, child associates begin to see children regularly. Children are typically scheduled for one 30-minute, one-to-one session per week for one to two school semesters, depending on the child's needs and the program goals for that child. Child associates meet with children in specially equipped playrooms that provide age and culturally appropriate activities for children. For example, toys and materials in a playroom may include various types of art supplies, such as crayons, markers, paints and construction paper, family dolls, a doll house, action figures, a sand table, building blocks, Legos, and so on. The main purpose of toy selection is to enable children to have as many opportunities to be expressive as possible. Thus, the playroom provides a safe, welcoming, and facilitative environment in which the child and adult can interact.

In a Primary Project session, the child typically sets the pace of the interaction; the child associate supports, reflects, and empathizes with the child. Occasionally, the child associate may direct the child toward his or her goals; however, self-directed, expressive play is the primary activity of the child. Because the Primary Mental Health Project is primarily driven by a theoretical grounding in child-centered play therapy, it is fundamental that the child is able to lead, uncover, and work with troubling thoughts and emotions as the process unfolds. However, there are instances when the child associate may want to capitalize on a particular moment to build skills in a particular area of need. Exact, scripted session descriptions are not possible to convey because each child brings his or her uniqueness into the playroom; however, expressive symbolic play should be the focus. Further, these sessions are supported through weekly supervision of the child associate by a school mental health professional.

The child associate is an active participant in the relationship; the child determines the intensity of participation. Child associates have to be flexible in the playroom—they have to enter into the child's play, but not be simply a playmate. It is okay for a child to direct the child associate in the role she or he wants the associate to take on, within reasonable limits.

After a child has participated in Primary Project for one school semester, conferences are scheduled to assess the child's progress in meeting program goals. Parents may be invited to attend these meetings. Decisions are made regarding the extent to which goals have been reached, and whether goals need to be changed. If program goals are met, graduation from the program is planned.

Zach followed the traditional pattern of a child participating in Primary Project. He spent time each week with "Thoothan," known to others as Susan. Susan had worked in Primary Project for 5 years and was well respected by the school faculty and parents. Her "playroom" was down the hall from his classroom and Zach readily went there when it was his time. For Zach, this became a safe place where for 30 minutes a week he would have the undivided attention of an adult. Within four to five weeks his teachers reported that he was beginning to settle down in class and interact more appropriately with peers. His attention-seeking behaviors were reduced. At home, he gloated at dinner that he got to "play" at school with Susan. For Zach, one of four children in a hectic, active household with both parents working as educators, the day began early and ended late. During the year he participated in Primary Project, the children in his family attended three different schools; one sibling was in full day special education because of a developmental delay. The chaos in Zach's life continued in school, where he was in a large class of high-achieving students. Zach was trying desperately to find his niche. Primary Project gave him the opportunity to unwind and obtain individual attention. His play was not aggressive; rather, during his first few sessions, he seemed scattered, going from activity to activity. Within a few weeks, he settled down and engaged Susan in his play. Similar patterns were observed in the classroom.

SUPERVISION AND TRAINING
OF CHILD ASSOCIATES

Great care is taken to hire child associates with skills and characteristics that provide effective helping services for children, and training is intended to build on these positive qualities. Orientation and initial training activities are *focused* and *time-limited*. The specifics depend in part on the background experiences and needs of the child associates. Training is designed to impart information and skills that facilitate work with children in a school environment and to clarify basic procedures and intervention strategies.

For the Primary Project program, necessary support has always included supervision of the associates by mental health professionals, beginning with the entrance of a child associate into the program and continuing until each associate separates from the Primary Project. Supervision is a developmental process for each child associate.

Primary Project recognizes two major areas of supervision in work with child associates: child-centered and child associate-centered supervision. Child-centered supervision relates to the individual children the associates see and reviews the work with the children, helps in understanding the children's words, and offers specific direction to associates about their weekly work with the children. Associate-centered supervision focuses on each associate by exploring his or her developing understanding of mental health, children's adjustment issues, and how the work is affecting him or her. This supervision includes advice and guidance for each associate as he or she evolves in this role both emotionally and cognitively.

GRADUATION FROM PRIMARY PROJECT

Most children will exit from Primary Project as a natural course of events. Occasionally, some children will transition to more intensive helping services. Whatever the case, a clear transition is important. Approximately 3 weeks prior to termination, the process of saying goodbye begins.

Susan had told Zach that he would come to see her for 12 to15 sessions. Around the eighth session, it was felt that he had met the goals of the project and he was reminded that his time with Susan would soon end. Zach used his final sessions engaged in play similar to that of previous weeks. Susan reminded him at each of the final sessions exactly how many more times Zach would be coming to see her. A final conference was held, this time with Zach's father; Zach's progress was described by the teacher and Susan. All agreed that his time in Special Friends had a positive impact on his classroom behavior. Although behavioral changes at home were not observed, his father told the team that Zach was more excited about going to school than he had been earlier in the school year.

Evaluating Student Progress

Children's progress in Primary Project is measured formally. A child's progress is discussed through ongoing supervision and, in the case of group supervision, with other child associates. It is also shared with the classroom teacher and some programs incorporate a "teacher progress report." Formal progress is routinely measured by changes in the T-CRS. To measure children's behavior change, pre- and postassessments are conducted.

At the conclusion of Zach's time in Primary Project, his teacher completed the T-CRS, and the school psychologist completed a summary report. The goal of increasing task orientation was met and Zach was more appropriately engaged in school. Analysis of the final rating scale showed positive change in both task orientation and peer social skills.

OUTCOME EVALUATION

There is general consensus among experts that Primary Project is an exemplary practice, a conclusion based on the evidence available from decades of evaluation and research. In 1984, the National Mental Health Association awarded Primary Project the Lela Rowland Prevention Award as the outstanding prevention program (Cowen & Hightower, 1989). Four years later, Primary Project was reviewed by the New York State Education Department and was the first program designated a validated program under New York State's Sharing Successful Programs. The section of Clinical and Child Psychology section I of Clinical Psychology Division of Child Youth and Family Services of the American Psychological Association awarded Primary Project the "Model Program in Service Delivery in Child and Family Mental Health" in 1993. Seymour B. Sarason stated, regarding *School-Based Prevention for Children at Risk: The Primary Mental Health Project* (1996),

This book describes the history, rationale, implementation and out-comes of the longest, most carefully researched, prevention-oriented program in American psychology and education. Not only has this pro-gram been refreshingly successful, but it has been adopted in hundreds of schools in the United States and abroad. [book jacket]

Primary Project was highlighted as an exemplary practice in *Primary Prevention Works* (Albee & Gullotta, 1997), in *Successful Prevention Programs for Children and Adolescents* (Durlak, 1997), and in *Establishing Preventive Services* (Weissberg, Gullotta, Hampton, Ryan, & Adams, 1997). The U.S. Surgeon General's Report on Mental Health (U.S. Department of Health and Human Services, 1999) recognized Primary Project as one of the five exemplary research-based prevention programs in the nation for enhancing children's mental health. In 2000, Safe and Drug Free Schools of the U.S. Department of Education named Primary Project a Promising Program.

Research on Primary Project started when Primary Project started; it has been a continuing, essential part of the program's fabric ever since. Tests of Primary Project's effectiveness as a prevention program have used several evaluation designs. Each of these evaluation designs has strengths (methodological or ecological) that provide complementary evidence about program efficacy (Cowen et al., 1996), including a composite evaluation for seven consecutive annual cohorts (Weissberg, Cowen, Lotyczewski, & Gesten, 1983). Primary Project's research effort has considered elements beyond outcomes, such as factors that relate to good and poor school ad-justment, specific program elements, and the relationship between the associate-child and associate-supervisor (Cowen et al., 1996; Cowen & Hightower, 1989).

EVALUATION OUTCOME

These primary evaluation designs and their major findings are de-scribed below.

Controlled Studies

In a study by Duerr (1993), approximately 600 children from 18 school sites were randomly assigned to immediate intervention or delayed treat-ment groups. Using standard comparison techniques for this design, chil-dren who received Primary Project services showed statistically significant decreases in adjustment problems such as lower aggression, fewer learning problems, and increased social–emotional competencies (e.g., frustration tolerance, peer relations), compared with those awaiting services. Another evaluation of the Primary Project model also used a wait-control design and a 3-month follow-up evaluation (Nafpaktitis & Perlmutter, 1998). In this study, statistically significant differences were found between children in an immediate intervention group and those in a wait-list control group. Statistically significant results indicate a decline in teacher ratings of learning problems and shy–anxious behaviors and an increase in task orientation and peer social skills. Improvements in both behavior problems and competencies placed children within a range of functioning exhibited by non-referred peers. These gains were maintained at a three-month follow up, based on teacher ratings (Nafpaktitis & Perlmutter, 1998).

Comparison Designs

Winer-Elkin, Weissberg, and Cowen (1988) compared adjustment between children receiving Primary Project services and comparably at-risk children in schools without Primary Project services and tracked their adjustment over time. Their study compared (a) children in the Primary Project model who received an average of twenty-five 40-minute contacts over a 5- to 6-month period and (b) comparison children with similar initial adjustment status identified in non-Primary Project schools. After one school year, Primary Project-served children were shown to have decreases in adjustment problems and increases in adaptive competencies compared to comparison children. These results were statistically significant.

Longer Term Follow-Up of Primary Project Children

Chandler, Weissberg, Cowen, and Guare (1984) evaluated 61 urban children, seen 2 to 5 years earlier in the Primary Project model, with 61 matched to the Primary Project sample by gender, grade level, and current teacher. Adjustment ratings by children's current classroom teachers confirmed that children seen in the Primary Project model had maintained their initial adjustment gains 2 to 5 years later.

Primary Project was introduced into several elementary schools in community school district 4, in the East Harlem section of New York City. This district, consisting of approximately 60% Hispanic and 30% African American children, is characterized by high rates of poverty, unemployment, health problems, teen pregnancy, and drug use. The implementation of the Primary Project model for kindergarten to third grade children in school district 4 was evaluated over a 4-year period. Results showed that participating children had more positive school adjustment (e.g., fewer adjustment problems, greater competencies) after 1 year in the program (Meller, Laboy, Rothwax, Fritton, & Mangual, 1994). Moreover, children's self-ratings of adjustment showed statistically significant increases in rule compliance, school interest, peer acceptance, and decreased anxiety (Meller et al., 1994).

Ongoing Site-Based Evaluations

Evaluations of Primary Project program sites in New York and California included comparison of children's classroom adjustment problems and competencies at time of referral, and at graduation from the program. Through this method, an ecologically valid assessment of children's adjustment status in large numbers of school sites is possible. During the 1997–1998 school year, evaluation of children in New York State Primary Project included over 1,500 children in 50 schools. These Primary Project sites provided more than 15,000 preventive-focused contacts to children. Overall, 82% of these children had adjustment problems prior to referral that placed them at "high" or "moderate high" risk. Mental health professionals reported that 60% of children in Primary Project showed reductions in aggressive behavior and improved social skills, and 50% displayed better academic performance (Hightower, 1998).

REPLICATION AND TRANSPORTABILITY

The Primary Project model has been described in numerous publications including peer-reviewed journals and books. Primary Project's development and evaluation were summarized in *School-Based Prevention for Children at Risk: The Primary Mental Health Project* (Cowen et al., 1996), published by the American Psychological Association. A second comprehensive source of information about the Primary Project model and how it can be implemented and evaluated is found in the *Primary Project Program Development Manual* (Johnson, 2002). The key structural components of Primary Project allow for adaptation to the local district or sites, while retaining the flexibility to meet the uniqueness of the individual setting. This makes Primary Project applicable to a broad range of children and communities.

Primary Project model programs have been successfully established in 120 school districts across New York state. At the national level, centralized networks of programs based on Primary Project in over 1,000 school districts (Cowen, Hightower, Johnson, Sarno, & Weissberg, 1989) have been established in the following states: California (Primary Intervention Program); Connecticut (Primary Mental Health Project); Hawaii (Primary School Adjustment Program); Maine (Healthy Learners Initiative); Washington (Primary Intervention Program); Florida; Minnesota; Texas; Vermont; and Michigan. In two states, California and Connecticut, specific legislation that includes the key structural components has been chaptered with accompanying budget support. In California, the Primary Project is coordinated through the department of Mental Health through the Early Mental Health Initiatives; in Connecticut, Hawaii, Maine, New York, and Washington, through the departments of Education.

Support to districts and sites interested in implementing a Primary Project are available through multiple venues, including consultation, training, program materials, and internship opportunities. Program materials include *School Based Prevention for Children at Risk: The Primary Mental Health Project* (Cowen et al., 1996); *The Primary Project: Program Development Manual* (Johnson, 2002); *Behind These Young Faces: The Primary Mental Health Project* (Children's Institute, 1995); *Screening and Evaluation Measures and Forms: Guidelines* (Children's Institute, 2002); *Supervision of Paraprofessionals in School-Based Programs* (Mijangos & Farie, 2001); *T-CRS Examiner's Manual* (Perkins & Hightower, 2002).

On-site consultation and support is available through Children's Institute program consultants; a listing of training programs is available for state and local personnel who have successfully implemented local programs. Additional training videos have been developed and are available for loan from Children's Institute.

In each state, as well as at each school site, replication of the Primary Project is dependent on the ability to meld the five key structural components of the program with the goals and objectives of the site. A process for implementing a Primary Project at a local site is outlined in *Best Practices for Adopting a Prevention Program* (Hightower, Johnson, & Haffey, 1995).

To ensure that a Primary Project is implementing a "true" Primary Project, a school site may apply for national certification. Specific criteria are available to determine whether a Primary Project program has implemented a model with fidelity to the program concepts. A designation of Primary Project National Certification is applied for a 3-year period to programs that meet these criteria. Schools that apply for certification must pass a site review conducted by a Primary Project consultant. The certification committee also examines each school's ability to meet the following requirements: systematic screening and review of children; length of participation of children in the program; selection and training of child associates; consistent supervision; appropriate space for the program within a school building; administrative support; program evaluation; active teacher and support staff; and community support.

CONCLUSION

Primary Mental Health Project (Primary Project) is a time-tested early intervention program that helps young children adjust to school during the early years. It has been refined over the past 45 years into a model that is transferable across settings and with children from varied backgrounds and homes. Programs with the strongest results adhere to the five key components, with particular emphasis on high quality child associates who receive systematic training and support from quality mental health professionals.

The importance of child-centered play is woven throughout ongoing training for child associates.

Zach is now in middle school. He remembers his time with Susan and occasionally sees her in the community. He talks about the time he got to just "play" at school. He is doing well academically and socially. He has found his pace and place in the home and at school.

REFERENCES

Albee, G. W., & Gullotta, T. P. (1997). *Primary prevention works.* Thousand Oaks, CA: Sage.

Axline, V. M. (1947). *Play therapy.* Boston: Houghton Mifflin.

Axline, V. M. (1969). *Play therapy* (Rev. ed.). New York: Ballantine Books.

Burns, B. J., Costello, E. J., Angold, A., Tweed, D., Dalene Stangl, E., Farmer, M. Z., & Erkanli, A. (1995). Children's mental health service use across service sectors. *Health Affairs, 14,* 147–159.

Chandler, C., Weissberg, R. P., Cowen, E. L., & Guare, J. (1984). The long-term effects of a school-based secondary prevention program for young maladapting children. *Journal of Consulting and Clinical Psychology, 52,* 165–170.

Children's Institute. (1995). *Behind these young faces: The Primary Mental Health Project* [Video]. Rochester, NY: Children's Institute.

Children's Institute. (2002). *Screening and evaluation guidelines.* Rochester, NY: Children's Institute.

Cowen, E. L., & Hightower, A. D. (1989). The Primary Mental Health Project: Thirty years after. In R. E. Hess & J. DeLeon (Eds.), *The National Mental Health Association: Eighty years of involvement in the field of prevention* (pp. 225–257). New York: Haworth Press.

Cowen, E. L., Hightower, A. D., Johnson, D. B., Sarno, M., & Weissberg, R. P. (1989). State level dissemination of a program for early detection and prevention of school maladjustment. *Professional Psychology, 20,* 513–519.

Cowen, E. L., Hightower, A. D., Pedro-Carroll, J. L., Work, W. C., & Wyman, P. A. (1996). *School-based prevention for children at risk: The Primary Mental Health Project.* Washington, DC: American Psychological Association.

Cowen, E. L., Trost, M. A., Lorion, R. P., Dorr, D., Izzo, L. D., & Issacson, R. V. (1975). *New ways in school mental health: Early detection and prevention of school maladaptation.* New York: Human Sciences Library.

Duerr, M. (1993). *Early mental health initiative: Year-end evaluation report.* Chico, CA: Duerr Evaluation Resources.

Durlak, J. A. (1997). *Successful prevention programs for children and adolescents.* New York: Plenum Press.

Ensminger, M. E., & Slusarick, A. L. (1992). Paths to high school graduation or dropout: A longitudinal study of a first-grade cohort. *Sociology of Education, 65,* 95–113.

Greenberg, M. T., Domitrovich, C., & Bumbarger, D. (2001). The prevention of mental disorders in school-aged children: Current state of the field. *Prevention and Treatment, 4*, 1–59.

Hawkins, J. D., Jishner, D. M., Jenson, J. M., & Catalano, R. F. (1987). Delinquents and drugs: What the evidence suggests about prevention and treatment programming. In B. S. Brown & A. R. Mills (Eds.), *Youth at high risk for substance abuse* (DHHS Publication No. ADM 87–1537, pp. 81–131). Rockville, MD: National Institute on Drug Abuse.

Hightower, A. D. (1998). *Primary Project annual report to the New York State Education Department.* Rochester, NY: Children's Institute.

Hightower, A. D., Johnson, D. B., & Haffey, W. G. (1995). Best practices in adopting a prevention program. In A. Thomas & J. Grimes (Eds.), *Best practices in school psychology III* (pp. 311–323). Washington, DC: National Association of School Psychologists.

Hightower, A. D., Work, W. C., Cowen, E. L., Lotyczewski, B. S., Spinell, A. P., Guare, J. C., & Rohrbeck, C. A. (1987). The child rating scale: The development of a socioemotional self-rating scale for elementary school children. *School Psychology Review, 16*, 239–255.

Johnson, D. B. (2002). *The Primary Mental Health Project: Program development manual.* Rochester, NY: Children's Institute.

Meller, P. J., Laboy, W., Rothwax, Y., Fritton, J., & Mangual, J. (1994). *Community school district four: Primary Mental Health Project, 1990–1994.* New York: Children's Institute Technical Report Series.

Mijangos, L. B., & Farie, A. M. (2001). *Supervision of paraprofessionals in school-based programs.* Rochester, NY: Children's Institute.

Nafpaktitis, M., & Perlmutter, B. F. (1998). School-based early mental health intervention with at-risk students. *School Psychology Review, 27*, 420–432.

Perkins, P. E., & Hightower, A. D. (2002). *T-CRS 2.1: Teacher-child rating scale examiner's manual.* Rochester, NY: Children's Institute.

Rogers, C. R. (1942). *Counseling and psychotherapy: New concepts in practice.* Boston: Houghton Mifflin.

Rogers, C. R. (1951). *Client-centered therapy: Its current practice, implications, and theory.* Boston: Houghton Mifflin.

Rogers, C. R. (1957). The necessary and sufficient conditions of therapeutic personality change. *Journal of Consulting Psychology, 21*, 95–103.

Rotheram, M. J., Armstrong, M., & Booraem, C. (1982). Assertiveness training in fourth- and fifth-grade children. *American Journal of Community Psychology, 10*, 567–582.

Tuma, J. M. (1989). Mental health services for children: The state of the art. *American Psychologist, 44*, 188–189.

U.S. Department of Health and Human Services. (1999). *Mental health: A report of the Surgeon General.* Rockville, MD: U.S. Department of Health and Human Services, Substance Abuse and Mental Health Services Administration,

Center for Mental Health Services, National Institutes of Health, National Institute of Mental Health.

Weissberg, R. P., Caplan, M., & Harwood, R. L. (1991). Promoting competent young people in competence enhancing environments: A systems-based perspective on primary prevention. *Journal of Consulting and Clinical Psychology, 59*, 830–841.

Weissberg, R. P., Cowen, E. L., Lotyczewski, B. S., & Gesten, E. L. (1983). The Primary Mental Health Project: Seven consecutive years of program outcome research. *Journal of Consulting and Clinical Psychology, 51*, 100–107.

Weissberg, R. P., Gullotta, T. P., Hampton, R. L., Ryan, B. A., & Adams, G. R. (1997). *Establishing Preventive Services* (Vol. 9). Thousand Oaks, CA: Sage.

Winer-Elkin, J. I., Weissberg, R. P., & Cowen, E. L. (1988). Evaluation of a planned short-term intervention for school children with focal adjustment problems. *Journal of Clinical Child Psychology, 17*, 106–115.

3

INTENSIVE PLAY THERAPY WITH CHILD WITNESSES OF DOMESTIC VIOLENCE

SARINA KOT AND ASHLEY TYNDALL-LIND

Acts of violence between members of the same family are an age-old phenomena. Research on the topic of family violence has greatly expanded public knowledge about the antecedents and consequences of abusive behavior within the home; however, a full understanding of prevention and treatment remains incomplete. Responses to child maltreatment have gained public and political attention, yet the issue of children witnessing violence at home remains unaddressed by many governing bodies. Most states continue to allow unsupervised visitation with an abusive parent, even if there is documented evidence of extreme violence by the abuser toward his or her intimate partner. This appears to be a testimony to the lack of understanding regarding the risks for children that are associated with experiencing or witnessing violence.

This chapter provides an overview of the dynamics of domestic violence, with a specific emphasis on the impact and treatment of child witnesses of domestic violence. An empirically validated play therapy intervention specifically designed to address issues related to the dynamics of domestic violence is introduced. Also, methods of intensifying treatment for children that seek time-limited, yet in-depth, emotional and psychological support are proposed. Finally, treatment generalizability and related research will be reviewed.

EFFECTS OF DOMESTIC VIOLENCE ON CHILDREN

The environment in which children are raised has a profound effect on overall adjustment and ability to cope with daily stressors. Families entrenched in a pattern of violence endure a cycle of violent interactions that fluctuate in intensity on a daily basis. The battering cycle has three distinct phases: the tension building phase, the acute battering incident, and the calm, loving respite. The pattern varies in time and intensity and is perceived as fairly unpredictable by those who experience the violence. Minimization and denial of the danger involved in violent episodes are common coping mechanisms demonstrated by those being abused as well as by the children who witness the incidents. Additionally, families affected by domestic violence demonstrate extreme feelings of hopelessness, helplessness, and intense anxiety associated with isolation. All these mechanisms foster the continuation of the violent family dynamic (Walker, 2000).

The emotional and behavioral effects of witnessing domestic violence are heavily documented in the literature. Children who witness domestic violence demonstrate more externalizing problems (aggression, hyperactivity, and conduct problems); internalizing behavioral problems (anxiety, social withdrawal, and suicidal ideation); total behavior problems (school problems, excessive screaming, clinging behaviors, and less social competence); and somatic complaints (headaches, bed-wetting, disturbed sleeping, failure to thrive, vomiting, and diarrhea). Child witnesses of domestic violence also tend to show more symptoms of depression, temperamental problems, less empathy, and lower verbal, cognitive, and motor abilities (e.g., Campbell & Lewandski, 1997; Fantuzzo et al., 1991; Holden & Ritchie, 1991; Hughes, Parkinson, & Vargo, 1987; Hughes, Vargo, Ito, & Skinner, 1991; Jaffe, Wolfe, & Wilson, 1990; Jaffe, Wolfe, Wilson, & Zak, 1986; Johnson et al., 2002, Jouriles, Murphy, & O'Leary, 1989; Wolfe, Jaffe, Wilson, & Zak, 1985).

As a short-term effect, children who witness domestic violence often experience psychic trauma. This can be conceptualized as a direct repercussion of witnessing events that involve a high degree of threat to personal safety of the child or a loved one and create feelings of intense fear and helplessness (e.g., Erel, Margolin, & John, 1998; Frick-Helms, 1997). In many cases, the magnitude and nature of stressful events observed by child witnesses of domestic violence are significant enough to warrant a diagnosis of posttraumatic stress disorder. With immediate supportive treatment, the short-term effects can be resolved without longstanding psychological ramifications. However, some children struggle to overcome the exposure to family violence for a lifetime.

As a long-term effect, 30 percent of children raised in violent homes demonstrate violence within their adult relationships (Kaufman & Zigler, 1987). The theory of intergeneration transmission of violence relies on the assumption that observing physical violence in the home provides children with a model for learning aggressive behavior and suggests that they receive support when aggression is used as a resolution for difficulties (Hampton, Gullotta, Adams, Potter, & Weissberg, 1993; Jaffe et al., 1990). According to this theory, when a child who has grown up in a violent home becomes a parent, the cycle continues and becomes compounded by attempts to cope with a traumatic upbringing, current violence, and ineffective, distracted parenting.

USE OF PLAY THERAPY FOR
CHILD WITNESSES OF DOMESTIC VIOLENCE

Careful consideration is required for selecting appropriate therapy for child witnesses of domestic violence. Alternatives for verbal expression are particularly important for children exposed to domestic violence, as they have been taught to maintain the secret of violence.

Play Therapy

A primary goal of play therapy with child witnesses of domestic violence is to help establish a corrective therapeutic relationship that optimizes trust, safety, and mutual respect, thereby enhancing the child's opportunity to accurately integrate denied and distorted traumatic material. Behavioral change is contingent on the change of self-perceptions and an accurate assimilation of parental discord into the self-structure. This can only occur when there is a decreased perception of threat to the self (e.g., Axline, 1955; Mearns & Thorne, 1988; Rogers, 1955, 1961; Tyndall-Lind, 1999b). Any relationship that is incongruent with the child's existing self-perception causes the child to question core beliefs that reinforce maladaptive relational patterns (Carey, 1997). The therapeutic setting in the playroom provides the child with the opportunity to evaluate perceptions of past events and the associated emotional attitudes in a nonthreatening environment (Rogers, 1955).

In play therapy, toys are used both as children's primary method of communication and as a tool to create a feeling of safety. Toys help children fully communicate thoughts and feelings. Toys also provide a means for children to explore new behaviors and restructure and redefine their world (Axline, 1969). Children may engage in reality play and use the toys to play out actual events to which they have been exposed; or they may use the toys to demonstrate a thematic representation of their subconscious concerns. Frick-Helms (1997) implemented a child-centered individual play therapy intervention with child witnesses of domestic violence. Detailed case studies supported play therapy as a beneficial intervention because it allowed "children to re-enact the traumatic event, remember and feel the feelings that accompanied the event, and restructure it in such a way as to provide meaning for the event" (p. 86).

It is not uncommon for child witnesses of domestic violence to be preoccupied with issues related to safety, control, and conflict. Many child witnesses appear to be preoccupied with safety and self-preservation, which is believed to be representative of high levels of anxiety pertaining to obtaining safety from the perpetrator (Kot, 1995). This is acted out in the playroom by engaging in elaborate play themes that revolve around shielding oneself from harm and gaining mastery and control over an otherwise frightening situation (Tyndall-Lind, 1999a). Elaborate play with weapons or shields and the creation of secret, protected hiding places for themselves and for the toys that represent themselves are healing rituals that occur in the playroom. These types of play behaviors allow children to restructure their reality to experience control and psychological safety, thereby decreasing high levels of anxiety (Frick-Helms, 1997). The symbolic use of toys as an extension of self is clearly exemplified by the following case example.

Tony, a 7-year-old boy, was exposed to extreme domestic violence. Several attempts to gain safety by residing with friends and relatives had failed as the abuser located Tony and his family. Tony's family subsequently sought protective care in a domestic violence shelter. At the shelter, Tony presented with extreme anxiety and used his play therapy hour to engage in anxiety reducing protective play. This involved the creation of a "super durable metallic tank" that had special protective powers. The metallic tank had the ability to withstand all violent attacks from dinosaurs and magical destructive demons. It was even able to withstand nuclear bombs. In addition to the protective powers of this tank, there was a secret hiding place under "ten tons" of sand on the side of a mountain in the desert. No one was allowed to know where the tank went to rest every night; however, on a daily basis the metallic tank retrieved all the soldiers who were honored members of its force (i.e., his brother) and retreated to this secret hiding place. Tony's play served to reduce the overwhelming anxiety that he was experiencing regarding his safety at the shelter and his own ability to protect himself. Additionally, the play created a feeling of safety, control, power, and resolution during a time of intense vulnerability and fear (Tyndall-Lind, 1999a).

By using symbolic play, the child is able to gain psychic distance, which reduces anxiety enough to allow the replay and reorder of more intense traumatic events. Therapeutic progress can be seen as the child makes a variety of changes to the actual scenario by re-enacting the traumatic events, demonstrating his or her capacity to view the victimization and family violence from a variety of perspectives and thereby gaining an understanding of how these events may have occurred. Increased personal objectivity can occur as the child manipulates the toys as an objective observer of the traumatic event, rather than as a victim. Mastery is a primary healing component of the play therapy process. This is accomplished when the child moves from the role of a victim to the role of control bearer by identifying with various play characters within the scenario. Mastery assists the child in reincorporating a positive self-concept that extends beyond the relationship with the primary caregiver (Friedman, 1983; Gil, 1991; Perez, 1987).

Ultimately, increased personal awareness yields new behavioral responses, and the child learns to own behaviors rather than depersonalize them (Axline, 1955; Rogers, 1955, 1961). Children from violent families often feel powerless and vulnerable to environmental circumstances. Through play therapy, they can access feelings associated with personal control, and they can more easily internalize new coping skills (Landreth, 1991). Armed with advanced coping skills, the child then has the opportunity to self-evaluate and engage more fully in the healing process (Rogers, 1955, 1961).

Intensive Play Therapy: Use of Time and Frequency

In an effort to extend and intensify the effectiveness of play therapy, therapists are encouraged to reconsider the traditional methods of intervening with at-risk children. Positive therapeutic results have been demonstrated with a variety of populations simply by increasing the frequency of counseling (e.g., Hoffman & Rogers, 1991; Hunter, 1993; Kot, 1995; Kot, Landreth, & Giordano, 1998; Leavitt, Gardner, Gallagher, & Schamess, 1998; Tyndall-Lind, 1999a; Tyndall-Lind, Landreth, & Giordano, 2001). It is difficult to say how rapidly children integrate new material and how readily they can alter patterns that are ingrained in the ego. Predictable elements introduced into the child's environment on a daily basis have the potential to have a profound impact on the developing psyche. Daily treatment of children who have been exposed to extreme trauma may combat negative consequences of violent stressors encountered in the home by balancing the frequency of negative family messages with positive therapeutic messages. By conceptualizing therapeutic interventions in this manner, consideration given to the time between sessions is an essential element of the therapeutic process. Intensive therapy with adults originated in the late 1960s with marathon group sessions that maximized therapeutic effectiveness by offering treatment interventions lasting 24 to 48 hours. These extended encounters were believed to be effective because the length of the sessions led to weakened ego defenses, rapid trust building, and increased truthfulness.

The marriage of play therapy with daily treatment serves to protect a child who has limited ego strength by providing the child with the opportunity to work through external difficulties as they arise. It allows the child to be exposed to a healthy, supportive environment on a daily basis (Tyndall-Lind & Landreth, 2001). The nonverbal nature of play therapy avoids potential revictimization by allowing the child to work through extremely traumatic events without being challenged to communicate these confusing events to an adult (Terr, 1990). Additionally, when the time between sessions is collapsed, both the child and the therapist have a better recollection of symbolic content in previous sessions. This enhances appropriate therapist responses and provides conditions for improved thematic continuity and progress.

Intensive Play Therapy:
Use of Sibling Relationship

When evaluating the components of treatment that maximize therapeutic intensity and results, it is important to consider that domestic violence occurs within the family context and that therapeutic interventions that readily access the experience of family and social difficulties have a more direct route to the source of the problem. Sibling play therapy incorporates the dynamics of group therapy, play therapy, and family therapy to create an intensely dynamic intervention. Pairing children from the same family who have been exposed to a similar degree of family violence in a therapeutic setting expedites the speed at which core issues can be tapped into. Siblings tend to create a pseudofamily in which they are able to create or re-create family interactions without relying on the generalizability from the therapeutic arena to the family environment. Individual play therapy gives the child only one avenue for a positive relational experience and that is between the therapist and the child. Although the therapist–child relationship is often a healing one, the child must internalize experiences and generalize them to the family context, which has vastly different dynamics.

Within the context of sibling play therapy, the therapist often serves as a representation of the parent figure. During play therapy sessions, the child is able to experience acceptance and nurturing, thereby restructuring the child's perception of the parental role. Clarification of the parent–child dynamic relationship is of key importance, given the theory of intergenerational transmission of family violence. The therapeutic alliance that occurs between the child and the clinician can be used as a powerful tool for therapeutic change. During the therapeutic hour, the clinician may play the role of a caring parent, which introduces an alternative view of potential family dynamics and allows the child to redefine acceptable parental behaviors.

Intensive sibling play therapy provides child witnesses with an open forum in which they can openly express what occurred within the family, thus breaking feelings of isolation and secrecy established in the home. Although individual play therapy addresses this issue by helping the child feel safe with the therapist, it does not directly assist family members to become more open about the domestic violence. Individual play therapy leaves the child with the difficult risk of expressing "taboo topics" without the safety of the therapeutic environment. In sibling play therapy, the therapist is available to mediate between potentially harmful interchanges and to protect the nurturing environment of the playroom when the children risk expression.

Siblings also experience more rapid results because of their preexisting relationships, which allow them to immediately explore difficult issues because of their shared bond and mutual understanding of what has occurred in their home (Tyndall-Lind, 1999a). In individual play therapy or in non-sibling play therapy, the child lacks the advantage of having a partner who has an assumed knowledge of previous events. This process circumvents the child's need to develop enough trust with the therapist to "tell their story." When engaging in sibling play therapy, the therapist does not necessarily need to know the factual details of what the children are working on together for the experience to have intense therapeutic value.

APPLICATION OF INTENSIVE PLAY THERAPY MODEL

Two studies that considered the characteristics of child witnesses of domestic violence were developed to test the hypothesis that an increase in treatment frequency, coupled with the use of play therapy as an intervention strategy, maximizes positive therapeutic gains. In 1995, Kot found that children who received individual play therapy for 12 consecutive days showed significant gains in self-concept and decreases in externalizing behavior problems. A comparative study conducted by Tyndall-Lind in 1999 found that the use of sibling play therapy in a similar treatment format resulted in an increase in positive self-concept, a decrease in externalizing behavior problems, a decrease in aggressive behaviors, and a decrease in anxious–depressed behaviors.

Key Treatment Ingredients

It is believed that the studies described above yielded significant results because of the incorporation of several key factors that maximized treatment outcome: (a) a brief intervention from intake to termination; (b) collapsed time between therapeutic sessions; (c) use of an appropriate space for treatment; and (d) adequate therapist training.

Paying attention to the time between sessions is essential. Because of the transient nature of families struggling with domestic violence issues, completion of treatment within a two- to three-week period increases the chances that children will receive enough treatment to enhance existing coping mechanisms and work through traumatic material. To allow for maximal treatment exposure, children receive one play therapy session per day for four to five days a week, over a period of approximately 2 to 3 weeks (a total of 12 sessions). The length of session may range from 30 to 60 minutes, depending on the age of the child, the available schedule of the therapist, and the number of children in the group.

Additionally, a designated play therapy area is needed for consistency and predictability; however, where space is limited, the play therapy area may take the form of a rolling cart that holds toys. The cart can be opened during play therapy sessions and closed at other times to allow the shared space to be used for other purposes. The area should be equipped with different categories of toys, such as family toys, scary toys, aggressive toys, expressive toys, and pretend–fantasy toys. Provisions should be made to incorporate toys that can facilitate therapeutic exploration of common domestic violence events. Many children coping with domestic violence have witnessed police interventions and emergency medical assistance for the injured. Handcuffs, weapons, police puppets or dolls, doctor kits, and ambulances are helpful toys for child witnesses of domestic violence.

Play therapists trained at the master's level in a mental health related field such as counselling, social work, or psychology have the appropriate skills to conduct play therapy sessions. Sibling play therapy requires a therapist with additional skills and expertise because of the increased need to monitor potentially aggressive sibling behavior, to ensure environmental safety, and to prevent a replication of the dysfunctional family dynamics.

Although session structure plays a major role in the facilitation of the process, there is no statistical evidence that outcome is affected by the number of children present in treatment or the chosen clinical orientation. Therefore, factors other than treatment effect may guide format choice. In individual play therapy, one child participates in the play session. In sibling play therapy, 2 to 4 siblings are included. The age difference between or among siblings may be greater than what is usually acceptable for group play therapy. However, because of the sibling relationship, the greater age gap of up to four or five years does not seem to be an obstacle. The nondirective or the child-centred approach in the play therapy is a treatment style that readily offers core relational conditions as its foundation; however, the theoretical approach used during sessions does not appear to be a determining factor for treatment effectiveness. Therefore, other approaches might also be used.

Research Design

In an attempt to design a comparison study, Kot (1995) and Tyndall-Lind (1999a) closely matched all parameters in sample selection and data collection. Kot gathered data specific to intensive individual play therapy and Tyndall-Lind gathered data specific to intensive sibling play therapy. Both studies used the same control group.

Data were collected in domestic violence shelters in the Dallas–Fort Worth area. Typical shelter services provided for children, in addition to the treatment intervention, included age appropriate educational groups and case management. The shelters used in the studies maintained a time-limited stay of approximately four to six weeks. The environment of the shelter outside of treatment time was similar to a home setting, with communal space and ample opportunity for the children to interact with each other in a variety of contexts.

Children from 4 to 10 years of age residing in domestic violence shelters were provided with the option to participate in the studies, with informed consent from the legal guardian. All children were eligible for the study, regardless of the severity or lack of severity in their clinical presentation. Many of the children exhibited a range of behavioral difficulties, such as aggression, parental defiance, poor boundaries, parentification, lack of social skills, nightmares, bed-wetting, increased anxiety, extreme withdrawal, and overdependence on parents and strangers. Participants reflected a full range in clinical presentations from minimal symptoms to diagnostically significant difficulties, including posttraumatic stress disorder and major depressive episode. Most behavioral presentations of those who participated in the studies were seen as typical of children coping with displacement from their homes as well as with family crisis or domestic violence.

The dropout rates in intensive individual play therapy and in intensive sibling play therapy were consistently significant and reflect the transient nature of this population. Those who dropped out typically left the shelter for alternate living arrangements. In the intensive individual play therapy group, of the 40 children who originally participated, 22 completed the study and 18 left the shelter before completion (45% dropout rate). In the intensive sibling play therapy group, of the 20 children recruited to participate in sibling play therapy, 10 completed the study (50% dropout rate).

Children received either individual play therapy (experimental group) or sibling play therapy (comparison group) for 12 sessions within a two- to three-week period, or no treatment (control group). The experimental group, comparison group, and control group were very similar in their mean ages, at 6.9, 6.2, and 5.9, respectively. The gender distribution was similar, with all three groups having slightly more girls. The treatment groups almost matched in ethnicity; however, there was a greater difference in ethnicity between the treatment groups and the control group. The experimental group was 46% Caucasian, 27 % African American, and 27% Hispanic; the comparison group was 60% Caucasian, 20 % African American, and 20% Hispanic; and the control group was 70% African American, 15% Caucasian, and 15% Hispanic.

Variables and Measures

The Joseph Preschool and Primary Self-Concept Screening Test (JPPSST; Joseph, 1979) was used to measure the self-concept of each child by using pictures to stimulate responses from the child. The JPPSST uses two sets of gender-specific pictures depicting polar opposite positive and negative situations. For example, one card depicts a child alone in a corner whereas the other card depicts a group of children playing together. The examiner asks the child to identify which situation in each set of pictures is most like him- or herself. The JPPSST is appropriate for use with children ranging in age from 3 years 6 months to 9 years 11 months.

The Child Behavior Checklist (CBCL; Achenbach, 1991) was used to measure behaviors of a child as reported by his or her parents. The following CBCL scales were used to measure the effects of intensive individual play therapy: Internalizing Behavior Problems, Externalizing Behavior Problems, and Total Behavior Problems. The same scales were used to measure the effects of intensive sibling play therapy; however, the following subscales were also used: Withdrawn, Anxious–Depressed, Somatic Complaints, Social Problem, Thought Problem, Attention Problem, Aggressive Behavior, and Delinquent Behavior.

Procedure

Prior to intensive play therapy sessions, mothers of the children in the individual play therapy group, sibling play therapy group, and control group completed the CBCL and the children completed the JPPSST. The children in the individual play therapy group and the sibling play therapy group received 12 sessions of play therapy within a period of two to three weeks. The playrooms were equipped with play materials, as outlined by Landreth (1991). Play therapy was provided by two master's and three doctoral level counsellors who were specifically trained in play therapy.

Children in all three groups also participated in the regular shelter programs of educational and recreational group sessions. Sessions focused on family violence awareness, sexual abuse prevention, identifying feelings, and developing self-esteem. Group activities included arts and crafts, paper and pencil worksheets, and outdoor activities.

Following the completion of 12 play therapy sessions or at the end of two weeks for the control group, the posttest battery of instruments were administered to the experimental and control groups. Posttesting procedures followed the same guidelines used in pretesting.

Results

Analysis of covariance (ANCOVA) was used to test the significance of the differences between groups on self-concept and behavior. In each case, the posttest specified in each of the hypotheses was used as the dependent variable and the pretest as the covariant. ANCOVA was used to adjust the means on the posttest on the basis of the pretest, thus statistically equating the individual play therapy, sibling play therapy, and control groups.

In a comparison of the individual play therapy group with the control group, the individual play therapy group scored significantly higher in posttest self-concept scores: $F(1, 22) = 48.96$, $p < .001$. The mothers of the children in the individual play therapy group reported at posttest that their children exhibited significantly fewer Externalizing Behavior Problems: $F(1, 22) = 4.39$, $p < .05$, and fewer Total Behavior Problems: $F(1, 22) = 9.56$, $p < .01$ as measured by the Child Behavior Checklist. Results did not reach significance for Internalizing Behavior Problems.

In a comparison of the sibling play therapy group with the control group, the sibling play therapy group scored significantly higher in posttest self-concept scores: $F(1, 21) = 8.91$, $p < .001$. The mothers of the children in the sibling play therapy group reported at posttest that their children exhibited significantly fewer Externalizing Behavior Problems: $F(1, 21) = 13.71$, $p < .01$ and fewer Total Behavior Problems: $F(1, 21) = 11.67$, $p < .01$ as measured by the Child Behavior Checklist. In addition, the mothers of the children in the sibling play therapy group reported at posttest that their children exhibited significantly fewer Aggressive Behaviors: $F(1, 21) = 11.01$, $p < .01$ and Anxious–Depressed Behavior: $F(1, 21) = 5.04$, $p < .05$. Results did not reach significance in Internalizing Behavior Problems.

In a comparison of the sibling play therapy group with the individual play therapy group, no significant differences were found in the scores between the two treatment groups.

Discussion

The results of the studies demonstrate the effectiveness of individual play therapy and sibling play therapy with child witnesses of domestic violence in improving self-concept, reducing Externalizing Behavior Problems, and reducing Total Behavior Problems. Additionally, sibling play therapy is shown to be effective in reducing Aggressive Behavior and Anxious–Depressed Behavior.

The improvement in self-concept may have a more profound impact on total coping than on simply reducing problematic behaviors because self-concept is at the core of a child's social–emotional development. DeMaria and Cowden (1992) suggest that changes in self-concept must be achieved indirectly, through the child's experiences, activities, and environment, thus allowing the child to experience him- or herself in a new way. In turn, the child has the chance to create new beliefs about his or her potential and abilities. This concept is particularly important when applied to child witnesses of domestic violence, because it implies that the actual process of engaging in therapeutic play behaviors may challenge messages conveyed in the family about the child's right to be valued. Therefore, the long-term results of improved self-concept potentially include breaking the intergeneration cycle of violence and replacing it with a new understanding of self that incorporates self-respect and positive relational patterns.

When interpreting the discrepancy between Externalizing Behavior Problems and Internalizing Behavior Problems, it should be noted that the children's behaviors were rated by their mothers. In interpreting the lack of significant change for the Internalizing Scale for both treatment interventions, one should consider the possible insensitivity of the mothers to changes in the children's internalizing behaviors. The mothers in the study were in a state of crisis and might have been less sensitive to the children's Internalizing Behavior Problems of withdrawal, anxiety, depression, and somatic complaints. Externalizing Behavior Problems, such as aggression and delinquency, are more visible and usually require attention and intervention by the mothers. However, within the Internalizing Scale, it seems that children who struggle with depression and anxiety are noticed more readily by their mothers than children struggling with withdrawal and somatic complaints, again because of the need for intervention by the caregiver. This may be the reason for a statistical significant reduction in anxious–depressed behavior for the sibling play therapy group, despite the insignificant difference at posttest on the overall Internalizing Behavior Problems scores.

In view of the similar results in the effectiveness of individual and sibling play therapy, the choice of using individual play therapy or sibling play therapy seems to be naturally guided by the family composition. The availability of age-appropriate sibling pairs or groups is a prerequisite for providing sibling play therapy. In determining the most appropriate intervention for siblings, one should consider the additional benefits of sibling play therapy such as the preexisting sibling bond and shared experience of witnessing domestic violence, which expedites the therapeutic process. However, of equal importance is an evaluation of the dynamics of the preexisting sibling bond and the overall health of the relationship. The therapist must be equipped to ensure physical and emotional safety for the siblings and prevent replication of dysfunctional family dynamics.

Although individual and sibling play therapy are both viable treatment alternatives for this population, it is worth noting several statistical trends in the comparison of results from both interventions. Given a larger sample size, these trends may have shown more statistical power. Intensive individual play therapy showed more positive change than intensive sibling group play therapy on the Attention Problems subscale of the CBCL at posttest. Those who participated in intensive sibling play therapy showed more positive change than children who participated in intensive individual play therapy on the following subscales: Total Behavior Problems, Internalizing Behaviors, Externalizing Behaviors, Anxious–Depressed, Aggressive

Behavior, Delinquent Behavior, Somatic Complaints, Social Problems, and Withdrawn Behavior. The implications associated with these trends are helpful in assisting clinicians to optimize treatment plans for varied presenting issues. Overall, intensive sibling play therapy seems well suited for social and emotional difficulties. However, intensive individual play therapy may be better suited for children coping with attention and concentration issues such as Attention Deficit Disorder. Placing highly distractible children in a treatment dyad may be counterproductive.

Also, when evaluating the results of the research, one should not overlook the potential impact that residing at the shelter has on the child's overall well-being. More specific, to understand the improvement in Total Behavior Problems, one should consider that residing in a violent home causes extreme emotional distress severe enough to result in a broad spectrum of negative behaviors (Jaffe et al., 1990). After the mother and child move to the shelter, they are no longer exposed to an extreme degree of violent activity, which may result in a positive effect on emotional and behavioral adjustment. However, it should be noted that the Control Group showed an increase in Total Behavior Problems as measured by the CBCL posttest. This suggests that although environmental change may be a factor in overall adjustment, residence in a shelter is not a salient enough factor to account for the degree of change observed in children who received play therapy.

TREATMENT GENERALIZABILITY

A review of the literature provides a limited number of studies on the use of play or group play therapy for child witnesses of domestic violence. There is a lack of quantitative research related to play therapy and domestic violence.

Related Research

The following reflects a recent increase in interest focused on reporting treatment interventions for children exposed to family violence. It is unfortunate that because of the many complications associated with conducting research with this population, most of the studies are qualitative in nature.

Huth-Bocks, Schettini, and Shebroe (2001) examined the effectiveness of group play therapy for preschoolers exposed to domestic violence. The 14 one-hour group therapy sessions were held in a Head Start Program facility. The group was limited to six child participants and was facilitated by two therapists. The format followed for each session included a warm-up exercise about feelings, followed by structured activities and ending with unstructured free play. General techniques used in the structured part of the group included storytelling, the use of puppets or dolls in role-play situations, and the use of "stimulus" pictures. Unstructured play was used as a therapeutic group technique to communicate with the young children and enable them to work through emotional difficulties. There were not sufficient data available to conduct a quantitative analysis of the process; however, qualitative data suggest that the group had a positive impact on the participants. Teachers and parents noted that the children improved in their ability to verbally express their feelings and that they displayed fewer behavior problems.

A play-based family therapy approach was developed by Van Meyel (1999) to treat children under five years of age who had experienced domestic violence, in conjunction with their mothers. The interventions included unstructured play, structured play, and nurturing play. The therapist's role was to facilitate interactions and activities between mothers and children, with the aim of increasing the children's self-esteem, sense of mastery around problem solving, and understanding of safety and responsibility. Conclusions drawn from the use of these interventions included that providing preschoolers with an opportunity to express their perceptions about domestic violence was an important step toward repairing cognitive distortion and presenting strategies to manage anger, anxiety, and intrusive memories.

Webb (1999) found that individual play therapy was effective in reducing externalizing behavior problems for "Michael," a 4-year-old client who witnessed domestic violence. As a result of his experience, Michael displayed severe aggression. Webb noted that the early play therapy treatment allowed Michael to reenact and play out his experience of aggression and helplessness. The therapist validated his feelings symbolically through play and helped him work through loss issues related to his parents' divorce and the resulting disruption in paternal visitation. Follow-up contact was made with Michael's mother 12 years after the original course of treatment, and Michael was found to be doing very well.

Robinson (1999) reviewed a case study of "Charlie," a 10-year-old boy in individual play therapy whose crisis emerged five years after witnessing marital violence. After witnessing domestic violence at age five, Charlie lived in a domestic violence shelter, experienced the hostile separation and divorce of his parents, and relocated with his mother to another home. Charlie had been doing well both academically and behaviorally until his father was granted visitation rights when Charlie was 10 years old. After Charlie returned home from a summer visit with his father, violent behaviors at home as well as withdrawn behaviors at school were noted. Charlie's mother reported that his attacking behaviors provoked, for her, frightening memories of her ex-husband's abuse. According to Robinson, Charlie's symptoms rekindled unresolved family conflicts, demonstrating how trauma can be expressed years later as a disorder in behavior, emotion, and family interaction.

Robinson primarily used an individual nondirective play therapy approach. Charlie used his play therapy time by setting up battle scenes to express his need to destroy, conquer, and control his world. In the first conjoint session with Charlie and his mother, Robinson intervened strategically to decrease their fighting at home. Charlie's behaviors at home began to improve; however, treatment was prematurely terminated following the second conjoint session that explored the family's experiences with the father. Robinson reviewed the case in the areas of assessment, engagement, treatment planning, and nondirective versus directive interventions. This case study provided insight into how difficult it is to manage and treat a complex case of domestic violence in which the mother has also been traumatized.

REPLICATION AND TRANSPORTABILITY

One unique feature of the intensive play therapy model is the availability of daily or almost daily therapy to children at their residence. Offering therapy at a child's location eases the problem of scheduling with adult caregivers and reduces time conflicts resulting from transportation difficulties. This model can be used in other types of residential settings, such as pediatric hospitals, inpatient child psychiatry units, temporary shelters after a disaster, foster care homes, treatment centers for adult substance abuse that allow children to stay with their parents, and therapeutic summer camps for children. In addition, settings such as schools and therapeutic day care, which children attend for four to five days a week, may be considered.

Intensive play therapy may also be carried out by trained parents. Using the filial therapy model, parents may be trained to conduct play sessions with their children. The traditional model of instructing parents to conduct weekly play sessions can be modified to include daily sessions by the parent if the situation calls for this modification (Smith, 2002).

RECOMMENDATIONS FOR OUTCOME EVALUATION IN CLINICAL PRACTICE

In addition to relying on formal research, the evaluation of interventions in everyday clinical practice is essential in guiding the therapist to deliver the most appropriate service for each child. Policy makers can also be guided by the outcome of the evaluation of clinical practice to appropriately design and fund programs based on empirical research.

Children's functioning should be considered in outcome evaluation efforts. The accomplishment of treatment goals, children's behavior, trauma symptoms, self-concept, and long-term functioning in social, emotional, and academic dimensions are important outcome measures. In day-to-day clinical practice, there may be limitations in staff time, budget (for the purchase of assessment instruments), and parents' availability to complete assessment instruments. The use of treatment plans or goals and the evaluation of accomplishment of the goals at the end of treatment are considered a viable gauge of treatment effectiveness. If rating scales for children's behavior are used, they should be chosen for good psychometric qualities as well as user friendliness. Additionally, consideration should be given to the high level of maternal stress that may skew results. The Parenting Stress Index (Abidin, 1995) may be used to measure the stress experienced by mothers. Teachers' ratings or shelter workers' ratings of children's behavior may also be considered. Older children's self-report rating of their own behavior is another source of information. The Behavior Assessment System for Children (BASC) by Reynolds and Kamphaus (1998) has a wide range of beneficial applications. The self-report scale of the BASC is suitable for children 8 to11 years old and for youngsters 12 to 18 years old. To measure trauma symptoms, older children can complete a self-report measure on trauma symptoms. The Trauma Symptom Checklist for Children (Briere, 1996) is suitable for those 8 to 16 years old.

The above mentioned instruments measure immediate treatment outcomes. Long-term follow up is challenging because of the transient nature of the families. In everyday clinical practice, if even a small fraction of the children receiving intensive play therapy treatment are available for tracking, longer-term outcome measures can be used. The knowledge gained from studying these children's long-term emotional and behavioral functioning may further enlighten practitioners in the field.

CONCLUSION

Children experience significant sequelae from witnessing domestic violence. Finding and using effective interventions for child witnesses of domestic violence is a key to restoring mental health and well-being in these children. As a result of the transience and instability in families of child witnesses of domestic violence, traditional once-a-week therapy sessions may not impact these vulnerable children. The format of intensive, high-frequency treatment within a period of two to three weeks for each child provides a viable alternative. Gaining more information about potential interventions and their impact on this population is an essential element to breaking the cycle of violence. Although case studies and other qualitative measures provide useful information on this topic, both quantitative research and follow-up research have the potential to dramatically affect what is known about providing quality care to child witnesses of domestic violence.

REFERENCES

Abidin, R. R. (1995). *Parenting Stress Index* (3rd ed.). Odessa, FL: Psychological Assessment Resources.

Achenbach, T. M. (1991). *Manual for the child behavior checklist–4–18 and 1991 profile*. Burlington: University of Vermont, Department of Psychiatry.

Axline, V. (1955). Group therapy as a means of self-discovery for parents and children. *Group Psychotherapy, 8,* 152–160.

Axline, V. (1969). *Play Therapy* (Rev. ed.). New York: Ballantine Books.

Briere, J. (1996). *Trauma symptom checklist for children: Professional manual.* Odessa, FL: Psychological Assessment Resources.

Campbell, J. C., & Lewandski, L. A. (1997). Mental and physical effects of intimate partner violence and women and children. *Psychiatric Clinics of North America, 20,* 353–374.

Carey, A. L. (1997). Survivor revictimization: Object relations dynamics and treatment implications. *Journal of Counseling and Development, 75,* 357–365.

DeMaria, M., & Cowden, S. (1992). The effects of child-centered group play therapy on self-concept. *The International Journal of Play Therapy, 1*(1), 53–67.

Erel, O., Margolin, G., & John, R. (1998). Observed sibling interaction: Links with marital and the mother–child relationship. *Developmental Psychology, 34,* 288–298.

Fantuzzo, J. W., DePaola, L. M., Lambert, L., Martino, T., Anderson, G., & Sutton, S. (1991). Effects of interparental violence on the psychological adjustment and competencies of young children. *Journal of Consulting and Clinical Psychology, 59,* 258–265.

Friedman, D. (1983). A self-psychology perspective. *Association for Play Therapy Newsletter, 2*(3), 6–8.

Frick-Helms, S. (1997). "Boys cry louder than girls": Play therapy behaviors of children residing in a shelter for battered women. *International Journal of Play Therapy, 6,* 73–91.

Gil, E. (1991). *The healing power of play.* New York: Guilford Press.

Hampton, R. L., Gullotta, T. P., Adams, G. R., Potter, E. H, & Weissberg, R. P. (Eds.). (1993). *Family violence: Prevention and treatment.* Newbury Park: Sage.

Holden, G. W., & Ritchie, K. L. (1991). Linking extreme marital discord, child rearing, and child behavior problems: Evidence from battered women. *Child Development, 62,* 311–327.

Hoffman, J., & Rogers, P. (1991). A crisis play group in shelter following the Santa Cruz earthquake. In N. B. Webb (Ed.), *Play therapy with children in crisis: A casebook for practitioners* (pp. 379–395). New York: Guilford Press.

Hughes, H. M., Parkinson, D. D., & Vargo, M. (1987). Witnessing spouse abuse and experiencing physical abuse: A "double whammy"? *Journal of Family Violence, 4,* 197–209.

Hughes, H. M., Vargo, M. C., Ito, E. S., & Skinner, S. K. (1991). Psychological adjustment of children of battered women: Influences of gender. *Family Violence Bulletin, 7,* 15–17.

Hunter, L. (1993). Sibling play therapy with homeless children: An opportunity in the crisis. *Child Welfare, 72*(1), 65–74.

Huth-Bocks, A., Schettini, A., & Shebroe, V. (2001). Group play therapy for preschoolers exposed to domestic violence. *Journal of Child and Adolescent Group Therapy, 11,* 19–34.

Jaffe, P., Wolfe, D., & Wilson, S. (1990). *Children of battered women.* Newbury Park, CA: Sage.

Jaffe, P., Wolfe, D., Wilson, S., & Zak, L. (1986). Family violence and adjustment: A comparative analysis of girls' and boys' behavioral symptoms. *American Journal of Psychiatry, 143,* 74–77.

Johnson, R. M., Kotch, J. B., Catellier, D. J., Winsor, J. R., Dufort, V., Hunter, W., et al. (2002). Adverse behavioral and emotional outcomes from child abuse and witnessed violence. *Child Maltreatment: Journal of the American Professional Society on the Abuse of Children, 7,* 179–186.

Joseph, J. (1979). *Joseph preschool and primary self-concept screening test.* Chicago: Stoelting Co.

Jouriles, E. N., Murphy, C. M., & O'Leary, K. D. (1989). Interpersonal aggression, marital discord, and child problems. *Journal of Consulting and Clinical Psychology, 57,* 453–455.

Kaufman, J., & Zigler, E. (1987). Do abused children become abusive parents? *American Journal of Orthopsychiatry, 57,* 186–192.

Kot, S. (1995). Intensive play therapy with child witnesses of domestic violence (Doctoral dissertation, University of North Texas, 1995). *Dissertation Abstracts International, 56,* 3002.

Kot, S., Landreth, G., & Giordano, M. (1998). Intensive child-centered play therapy with child witnesses of domestic violence. *International Journal of Play Therapy, 7*(2), 17–36.

Landreth, G. L. (1991). *Play therapy: The art of the relationship.* Muncie, IN: Accelerated Development.

Leavitt, K., Gardner, S., Gallagher, M., & Schamess, G. (1998). Severely traumatized siblings: A treatment strategy. *Clinical Social Work Journal, 26*(1), 55–70.

Mearns, N., & Thorne, B. (1988). *Person-centered counseling in action.* Beverly Hills, CA: Sage.

Perez, C. (1987). A comparison of group play therapy with individual play therapy for sexually abused children (Doctoral dissertation, University of Northern Colorado, 1987). *Dissertation Abstracts International, 48,* 3079.

Reynolds, C. R., & Kamphaus, R. W. (1998). *The behavioral assessment for children.* Circle Pines, MN: American Guidance Service, Inc.

Robinson, R. (1999). Unresolved conflicts in a divorced family: Case of Charlie, age 10. In N. B. Webb (Ed.), *Play therapy with children in crisis* (pp. 272–293). New York: Guilford Press.

Rogers, C. (1955). *Client-centered therapy.* Boston: Houghton Mifflin.

Rogers, C. (1961). *On becoming a person.* Boston: Houghton Mifflin.

Smith, N. R. (2002). A comparative analysis of intensive filial therapy with intensive individual play therapy and intensive sibling group play therapy with child witnesses of domestic violence (Doctoral dissertation, University of North Texas, 2001). *Dissertation Abstracts International, 62,* 2353.

Terr, L. C. (1990). *Too scared to cry: Psychic trauma in childhood.* New York: Harper & Row.

Tyndall-Lind, M. A. (1999a). A comparative analysis of intensive sibling group play therapy and intensive individual play therapy with child witnesses of domestic violence (Doctoral dissertation, University of North Texas, 1999). *Dissertation Abstracts International, 60,* 1465.

Tyndall-Lind, M. A. (1999b). Revictimization of children from violent families: Child-centered theoretical formulation and play therapy treatment implications. *International Journal of Play Therapy, 8*(1), 9–25.

Tyndall-Lind, M. A., & Landreth, G. L. (2001). Intensive short-term group play therapy. In G. Landreth (Ed.), *Innovations in play therapy: Issues, process, and special populations* (pp. 203–215). Philadelphia: Brunner-Routledge.

Tyndall-Lind, A., Landreth, G., & Giordano, M. (2001). Intensive group play therapy with child witnesses of domestic violence. *International Journal of Play Therapy, 10*(1), 53–83.

Van Meyel, R. (1999). Play-based family therapy: A systemic model for the treatment of preschool children who have witnessed woman abuse. *Journal of Systemic Therapies, 18,* 32–43.

Walker, L. E. (2000). *The battered woman syndrome* (2nd ed.). New York: Springer Publishing Company.

Webb, N. B. (1999). The child witness of parental violence: Case of Michael, age 4, and follow up at age 16. In N. B. Webb (Ed.), *Play therapy with children in crisis* (pp. 49–73). New York: Guilford Press.

Wolfe, D. A., Jaffe, P., Wilson, S. K., & Zak, L. (1985). Children of battered women: The relation of child behavior to family violence and maternal stress. *Journal of Consulting and Clinical Psychology, 53,* 657–665.

4

A PREVENTIVE PLAY INTERVENTION TO FOSTER CHILDREN'S RESILIENCE IN THE AFTERMATH OF DIVORCE

JOANNE PEDRO-CARROLL AND SHERYL H. JONES

This chapter describes the use of semistructured play in the Children of Divorce Intervention Program (CODIP), a developmentally based, preventive intervention for children of divorce. The goals, objectives, and key components of the intervention and implementation process are described, as are a number of outcome studies that provide a solid evidence base for the program's effectiveness. Implications for replication and transportability in various settings are also discussed.

RATIONALE FOR PLAY-BASED PREVENTIVE INTERVENTIONS

Advocates of prevention efforts have provided a compelling rationale for allocating resources toward the promotion of wellness rather than trying to contain difficulties once they become chronic and entrenched (Albee, 1983; Cowen, 1991; Durlak & Wells, 1997; Pedro-Carroll, 2001). Many prevention programs designed to promote children's social and emotional well-being use play as an integral part of the intervention. Given its instrumental role in development and its natural appeal to children, play has been the main component of many therapeutic and preventive interventions for children (Kazdin, 1990; Phillips, 1985). The Primary Mental Health Project (PMHP), a school-based program designed to prevent school adjustment problems in young children, has used play as a central component since the program's inception in 1957. The PMHP's longevity is supported by an extensive body of research documenting its effectiveness (Cowen, Hightower, Pedro-Carroll, Work, & Wyman, 1996). Several other investigators have reported the successful use of play in preventive interventions. Bay-Hinitz, Peterson, and Quilitch (1994) used cooperative games in play therapy and found a decrease in aggressive behaviors in 4- and 5-year-old children. Children of alcoholics or substance abusing parents responded well to a play-based intervention and demonstrated increased competencies and reductions in behavioral problems (Springer, Phillips, Phillips, Cannady, & Kerst-Harris, 1992). Play-based preventive strategies were also effective in reducing anxiety in hospitalized children (Rae, Worchel, Upchurch, Sanner, & Daniel, 1989).

Puppets and noncompetitive games are essential tools in play-based interventions. The Children of Divorce Intervention Program (CODIP) makes extensive use of these tools to achieve program objectives with children of different ages. Puppets and games are used to engage children, enable them to safely express feelings, learn information, and practice new skills. Puppet play is also used as a displacement technique that is especially effective for young children dealing with emotionally charged issues such as parental divorce (Kalter, 1990; James & Myer, 1987). The purpose of this displacement technique is to represent the child's distress about a situation or behavior problem, demonstrate alternate ways of effective coping, and when appropriate, show a reassuring or positive outcome to the underlying difficulties (Kalter). Empirical studies have also supported puppets or dolls as a valuable tool (e.g., Chittenden, 1942; McCarthy, 1998).

Games are a natural part of children's play, especially when they reach school age and begin to play more games with rules (Rubin, Fein, & Vandenberg, 1983). By adolescence, the participation in games with rules declines and is replaced with more time alone or talking and spending time with peers (Larson & Verma, 1999; Rubin et al., 1983). The Children of Divorce Intervention Program incorporates games in groups for all ages, except for the early adolescent group, which focuses more on role-playing and group interaction activities. Others have described the use of games in child-focused interventions and play-based activities, including its use with children who have witnessed domestic violence (Crockford, Kent, & Stewart, 1993), or who have emotional and behavioral problems (Johnson et al., 1998). In addition to studies on CODIP, empirical studies have indicated that games are effective as a play therapy technique for children with specific problems, such as those with learning disabilities (Utay & Lampe, 1995) or whose parents have recently divorced (Burroughs, Wagner, & Johnson, 1997).

Collectively, these studies provide a substantial evidence base for the benefits of play-based interventions for children dealing with stressful life experiences. The next section considers the particular stresses that parental divorce poses for children and protective factors shaping children's adjustment.

PARENTAL DIVORCE
AS A STRESSOR

From a child's perspective, few life changes are as unwelcome as their parents' separation or divorce. Except in situations of domestic violence or intense, protracted conflict in which divorce provides an effective release from its toxic effects, most children experience family reorganization as a series of undesirable changes over which they feel powerless. There is substantial variation in children's long-term reactions to divorce; however, in the early stages, most children of all ages experience considerable distress. Sadness, anxiety, anger, guilt, confusion, loyalty conflicts, and yearning for the absent parent are common early reactions (Clulow, 1990; Hetherington, Stanley-Hagan, & Anderson, 1989; Oppawsky, 1991; Pedro-Carroll, 2001). Research on children's long-term outcomes indicates that although some children fare well, the individual and societal costs of divorce for some children can be profound and enduring; these include higher rates of high school dropout, earlier marriage, out-of-wedlock childbirth, and disruption of their own marriages (McLanahan & Bumpass, 1988; Wallerstein & Blakeslee, 1989; Werner & Smith, 1992).

Although some earlier studies were not as well-designed as later studies, recent research using more rigorous techniques has demonstrated small but significant negative effects of divorce on children (Amato & Keith, 1991; Hoyt, Cowen, Pedro-Carroll, & Alpert-Gillis, 1990; Zill, Morrison, & Coiro, 1993). These studies show increased rates of conduct, depression, and school adjustment problems among children of divorce. However, it is important to note that a significant proportion of children function well in the long-term. The variability in children's outcomes highlights the fact that long-term difficulties are not inevitable and underscores the need to identify factors that mediate children's adjustment to parental divorce over time (Pedro-Carroll, 2001). The next section considers the role of protective factors in children's postdivorce adaptation and the implications of those findings for developing preventive interventions for children of divorce.

FACTORS PREDICTING RISK AND RESILIENCE IN CHILDREN OF DIVORCE

Research on children and divorce has historically focused more on risk factors for negative outcomes than on protective factors that influence positive outcomes (Emery & Forehand, 1994). Although more research is needed to identify pathways to wellness following divorce, individual child, family, and extrafamilial factors have been identified that offer important information for designing preventive interventions. In this chapter, we focus only on those factors that are modifiable and applicable to preventive interventions for children (see Table 4.1).

Individual Factors

Coping with unwanted, uncontrollable, and often unexpected life-altering experiences can be enormously challenging, if not overwhelming. Studies have identified a number of individual factors that are related to the quality of children's adjustment to divorce. Self-blame, misconceptions, and inaccurate attributions increase the risk of more difficulties for children (Kurdek & Berg, 1983, 1987). Conversely, preventive interventions that focus on developing effective coping styles, clarifying misconceptions, framing realistic appraisals of control, and providing accurate attributions for parental problems have been shown to relate to better adjustment in school-aged children (Alpert-Gillis, Pedro-Carroll, & Cowen, 1989; Pedro-Carroll & Alpert-Gillis, 1997; Pedro-Carroll, Alpert-Gillis, & Cowen, 1992; Pedro-Carroll, Sutton, & Wyman, 1999; Stolberg & Mahler, 1994).

TABLE 4.1
Protective Factors Identified in Research on Children and Divorce

Individual factors	Family factors	Extrafamilial factors
Realistic appraisal of control	Protection from interparental conflict	Supportive relationship with positive adult models
Accurate attributions	Psychological well-being of parents	Support network: family, school and community
Active coping style	Solid, supportive parent–child	Evidence-based preventive relationships interventions providing support and skills training
Effective coping skills	Authoritative parenting; household stability and structure	

Similarly, active coping that involved problem solving and positive thinking (Sandler, Tein, & West, 1994) increased children's feelings of confidence in their ability to cope (Sandler, Tein, Mehta, Wolchik, & Ayers, 2000) and led to greater resilience among children. These studies demonstrate the importance of incorporating effective coping strategies into interventions for children and the solid potential that well-designed programs have for reducing risk and building social and emotional competencies.

Children of Divorce Intervention Program: Theoretical Underpinnings

Clinical aspects of the Children of Divorce Intervention Program are shaped by developmental theory, which focuses on age-based reactions to parental divorce and intervention approaches tailored to children's developmental characteristics. This is a preventive intervention based on theories of resilience that suggest that wellness can be promoted by protective factors that provide supportive scaffolding for children experiencing difficult times (Vygotsky, 1978). As developmental psychopathologists have noted, children's adjustment is influenced by changes over time as conditions, environments, and life events unfold (Cicchetti, 1989; Masten, 1989). This view suggests a bilateral proposition that just as wellness can erode under adverse conditions, so can it be enhanced by nurturing conditions and protective processes such as supportive, evidence-based interventions. The key is to foster supportive outreach and reduce risk across systems that affect children, including schools, courts, communities, and families. This cumulative protection across systems is intended to provide a foundation on which children can effectively navigate challenges (Masten & Coatsworth, 1998). Wyman, Sandler, Wolchik, and Nelson's (2000) concept of *cumulative competence promotion and stress protection* underscores the ways in which preventive interventions such as CODIP can be fortified by using an organizational–developmental model of resilience. Central features of this model include (a) enhancing protection from the negative impact of adverse experiences such as parental conflict and divorce, and (b) facilitating the child's mastery of healthy developmental milestones. CODIP is also based on a transitional-events model that emphasizes the stressful challenges and changes associated with marital disruption for families (Felner, Farber, & Primavera, 1983; Sandler, Braver, & Gensheimer, 2000). These stressors are posited to influence postdivorce adjustment through mediating factors such as children's individual resources, effective coping strategies, accurate appraisals and attributions of divorce-related events, and the availability of social support.

> CODIP is a school-based, selective preventive intervention program, built on the assumption that timely intervention for children of divorce can offer important short- and long-term benefits. The primary goals are to *create a supportive group environment in which children can freely share*

experiences, establish common bonds, clarify misconceptions, and acquire skills that enhance their capacity to cope with the stressful changes that divorce often poses. (Pedro-Carroll, 1997, p. 217)

From our earliest experiences developing this program for children of different ages, it was clear that even an empirically derived, carefully developed intervention with a rigorous research design would fail miserably if not embedded in play-based activities that have intrinsic appeal for children. CODIP began with an initial intervention for fourth- to sixth-grade suburban children of divorce modeled after the Children's Support Group (CSG; Stolberg & Garrison, 1985). Like the Children's Support Groups, CODIP groups included semistructured, interactive play-based activities geared to the developmental characteristics of 9- to 12-year-olds. The positive results of that early pilot (Pedro-Carroll & Cowen, 1985) led to subsequent adaptations of the program model for children of different ages and sociodemographic backgrounds. Four separate versions of the CODIP model have been developed for children of different grade levels: kindergarten and first; second and third; fourth through sixth, and seventh through eighth grade.[1] Different play-based techniques have been developed to match the clinical profile and developmental needs of each age group, and to promote the specific objectives of the intervention. Semi-structured play is used extensively with younger children, whereas creative writing and activities reflecting mastery motivation are geared to older school age youth. Thus, each subsequent adaptation for an additional age group has been built on their age-related needs and play practices.

The Group Model

All CODIP programs use a group modality for several reasons. Although limited support services in the schools are one reason for doing so, there are more basic and important justifications. Parental divorce alters children's lives profoundly. Despite record high divorce rates, many children of divorce feel alone and different as a result of their family circumstances. One important potential benefit of a group format is that it offers children support and comfort by virtue of sharing experiences and feelings with peers who have been through similar experiences; children learn that they are not alone at a time when it feels as if everything in their life is changing. The group format also provides natural opportunities for exchanging information on common divorce-related issues and for clarifying common misconceptions about divorce.

One of the most comforting aspects of group interaction comes from mutual support for shared experiences. Children who have gone through

---

[1]Copies of the CODIP manuals for different age groups are available by contacting JoAnne Pedro-Carroll at the Children's Institute, 274 North Goodman Street, Suite D103, Rochester, New York 14607.

common stressful experiences are more credible to peers than those who have not had that experience. A child who fears, deep down, that he or she is responsible for the breakup of her or his parents' marriage can find comfort and relief from the words of a peer with exactly the same feelings—more so than from the intellectual assurances of an adult. Furthermore, a group format provides the opportunity for children who are further along in the process of adjusting to divorce to serve as credible coping models for those in the early stages of adjusting to family changes.

Moreover, in CODIP's later, structured, skill acquisition meetings, the group format offers children opportunities to learn about others' efforts to solve problems, deal with anger, disengage from loyalty conflicts, and effectively manage day-to-day challenges. Thus, children learn from each other's successes and setbacks. The group format also includes discussion and role-playing in an engaging and active format that provides opportunities for acquiring and practicing important coping skills.

Group Leaders

The success of CODIP depends on the commitment and clinical skills of group leaders. The group leader's sensitivity and ability to establish a trusting environment, to encourage children's involvement in group activities, and to express feelings all contribute to the development of a cohesive group. The leader's ability to deal comfortably with emotionally laden issues sets a basic tone and climate for the group. CODIP groups are generally co-led, ideally by both a man and woman. The two leaders share task and process roles. This arrangement allows children to observe firsthand a positive, cooperative, cross-gender adult relationship. Because most CODIP groups are mixed-gender groups, this arrangement also offers children a positive, same-sex adult role model. The availability of two leaders also facilitates responses to sensitive issues, nonverbal cues, and behavior management problems. What one leader may miss in the midst of group interaction, the other can address.

CODIP leaders are selected more for their interest, skills, and sensitivity than for training in any specific discipline. In practice, leaders have included psychologists, social workers, and nurses; guidance counselors; principals and teachers; graduate trainees in mental health fields; and a trained paraprofessional teamed with a mental health professional. Leaders have four to five 2-hour, weekly training sessions before the program begins, and $1^{1}/_{2}$-hour training–supervision meetings every other week while it is in process. The initial training sessions provide information about the impact of divorce on parents and children, age-related reactions of the target age group to parental divorce, factors that shape children's adjustment to parental divorce over time, and group leadership and facilitation skills. Supervisory meetings review clinical and programmatic aspects of the prior week's meetings, including what went well and what problems were experienced; provide opportunities to problem solve and modify curriculum materials or management strategies; and preview the following week's curriculum.

Developmental Factors

Despite individual differences, children's age and developmental level appear to be the most salient factors shaping initial responses to marital disruption. Developmental stage profoundly influences a child's dependence on parents and peers, perceptions of the family changes, as well as their coping and defensive strategies. Thus, CODIP's structure (e.g., duration of sessions) and content (e.g., therapeutic approach) are tailored to the developmental characteristics of the target population.

Group size, duration of the sessions, and length of the program are predicated on the developmental characteristics of the four age groups. For example, with older children, one-hour group sessions spaced over 12 to 14 weeks has worked effectively. By contrast, 45-minute weekly sessions with smaller groups of four to five children distributed over 12 to 16 weeks is more appropriate for younger children.

Program content is also tailored to variations in reactions that divorce predisposes in children of different ages. For example, issues of loyalty conflicts, anger, and feelings of stigma and isolation are predominant responses among 9- to 12-year-old youngsters; intense sadness, confusion, guilt, and fears of abandonment are prominent among 6- to 8-year-olds (Wallerstein & Kelly, 1980). Therefore, such differing clinical profiles indicate the need to shape the central themes and focal issues of interventions to the special attributes of particular age groups. The next section outlines how specific program objectives are translated into developmentally tailored, play-based activities for children.

PROGRAM OBJECTIVES

1. Foster a Supportive Group Environment

Social support is a fundamental underpinning of the CODIP group process. Contact with peers who have had similar experiences helps reduce children's feelings of isolation and promotes a sense of camaraderie and trust. Creating an atmosphere in which children can share experiences and feel that what they say will be respected and kept confidential is a major objective from the first session to the last.

Depending on the age range, different techniques are used within the group process to foster supportive interactions and a sense of belonging. In the first few sessions, fourth to sixth grade students choose a name for their group and create a group banner and special symbol that remains in the room for the duration of the meetings. The process of choosing a name is often one that fosters an early sense of connectedness and common bonds among group members. The names children have selected for their groups reflect themes of support, solidarity and feelings about families, including "Forever Family," "The Confidential Group," "Kids Helping Kids," "K.I.C.S.—Kids Incorporated in Caring and Sharing," and "Kids' Union."

Younger children (kindergarten through third grade) are introduced to the purpose of the group through "get acquainted" games and puppet play. Semistructured puppet play is used extensively to promote program goals and objectives with young children. As discussed above, puppet play is a valuable displacement technique that helps children understand feelings and learn strategies for dealing with the many challenging aspects of their parents' divorce (Kalter, 1990).

Thus, in the first session with young children, after leaders and members have introduced themselves, a shy puppet hesitantly emerges, apprehensive and unsure what to expect from the group. In our experience, young children love to be asked to help, so group leaders request their assistance in helping the puppet (who is their age, and whose parents are recently separated) to feel accepted and more comfortable with the group. They typically respond with suggestions ("Let's tell him our names, and what we'll be doing in our group"; "Let's give him or her a name") and reassurances ("I wasn't sure what the group would be like so I sort of feel like he does"). As group discussion continues and members share common likes and dislikes, favorite games, foods, and TV shows, the puppet also shares many of those interests and takes on the role of group mascot. When important topics such as confidentiality and coping skills are discussed, the puppet takes an active role in sharing feelings, problems, ideas, and solutions.

2. Facilitate Identification and Appropriate Expression of Feelings

The stressful changes associated with parental divorce cause complex feelings that are difficult for children to identify and understand. Young children are especially vulnerable to being overwhelmed because of their limited cognitive understanding, verbal skills, and coping strategies. Accordingly, an important program objective is to enhance children's ability to identify and appropriately express a range of emotions. However, leaders must carefully balance the need for children to express their feelings while moderating the dose of emotionally-laden material with more neutral experiences in a nonthreatening, play-based format. Thus, group process is sequenced so that early sessions emphasize the universality, diversity, and acceptance of all feelings before divorce-related issues are introduced.

A variety of play techniques are used to help children identify a range of emotions, including the interactive use of books, pictures of facial expressions, feelings charades, a feelings telegram, and a feelings "grab bag" game. In this game, children take turns choosing cards depicting various emotions, and silently act out the emotion while group members guess the feeling and share a time when they too felt that way. The group puppet actively participates in this activity, sharing times when she or he had a similar feeling or experience as a group member. An important element of this game involves helping children learn techniques for self-soothing when they're distressed.

These games have multiple objectives, including helping to (a) develop empathy through an awareness and sensitivity to nonverbal signs of how another person feels; (b) expand children's "emotional vocabulary" with a label for a variety of emotions (e.g., frustrated, proud, embarrassed, excited, confused, loving); (c) promote children's understanding of the universality of emotions (e.g., "even the President has times when he feels afraid or worried"); (d) emphasize that all feelings are acceptable ("All feelings are OK, but all behaviors are not."); puppet play is used to convey the message that "Tenderheart" (the group puppet) is not bad if she feels angry, but it's not OK for her to hit someone when she is angry; and (e) increase children's awareness that feelings can change and learn healthy ways to help themselves feel better when they are upset.

Sometimes during the game, a reticent child may need support and encouragement from the group. When 7-year-old "Jenny" drew a "proud" card, she was baffled and unable to think of a time she felt that way. With the aid of supportive modeling by the leaders, group members (and the puppets) pointed out her strengths (e.g., good at drawing and math; kind to others). "Jenny" beamed at these affirmations and commented that she was proud to be a part of the group.

Promote Accurate Understanding of Divorce-Related Concepts and Clarify Misconceptions

One of the tasks inherent in this objective is helping children separate their worst divorce-related fears from reality. Young children are especially vulnerable to fears of abandonment and may worry that if the marital bond could dissolve, they too might be left behind. Therefore, clarifying misconceptions is an important aspect of preventive interventions for children of divorce. Magical thinking, partially a function of young children's egocentrism, also leaves them vulnerable to feelings of guilt and responsibility for restoration of the intact family. Hopes and wishes for reconciliation run high, as one child commented: "I pray every night that they won't get a divorce." Confusion and misconceptions relating to the reasons for the marital conflict include troublesome self-blame. "They broke up because of me . . . I could hear my name come up over and over when they fought." Clarifying such damaging misconceptions requires a gradual process to increase the child's ability to separate adult responsibilities from child concerns. Through structured puppet play and the interactive use of books, the concept is conveyed that *Divorce Is a Grown-Up Problem* (Sinberg, 1978), not one caused or fixed by children. "Daring Dinosaurs," a board game developed specifically for CODIP, contains cards that reflect misconceptions children often have about the reasons for family problems, with opportunities for group discussion and puppet play to clarify common reasons for self-blame. (This game is described in more detail later in this chapter.)

For many children in our groups, explaining an absent parent's lack of involvement in their lives is a central issue. When children have infrequent contact with a parent, their search for explanations for the parent's absence may lead them to internalize the belief that they are somehow defective and not lovable enough. Through group discussion, puppet and doll play, and interactive use of books such as *Dinosaur's Divorce* (Brown & Brown, 1986), the message is conveyed that sometimes parents feel too upset or guilty to stay in touch with their children, but that is in no way a reflection of the child's worth. Group leaders actively guide group discussion and puppet play to increase children's ability to attribute adult problems to external factors, rather than internal child attributes. The goal of these activities is to restore diminished self-esteem and break the link between a parent's departure and other adult issues and the child's fantasized unlovability.

Teach Relevant Skills to Enhance Children's Competence and Capacity to Cope

Although the support and solidarity that comes from sharing common experiences is important for children, enhancing coping skills is an equally essential component of this intervention model. Training in prosocial skills such as problem solving, communicating effectively, dealing with anger, and asking for help and support is accomplished over a number of sessions. A variety of games and play techniques are used to encourage practice, acquisition, and eventual generalization of skills.

Teaching coping skills helps prepare group members to deal effectively with the multiple life changes that children of divorce are often expected to take in stride. Developing a repertoire of coping skills helps reduce the stress and confusion inherent in the divorce process and enables children to gain control over a situation in which they initially may have felt helpless. A key element of social problem-solving training involves helping children gain realistic perceptions of control, e.g., teaching children to differentiate between problems that they *can* and *cannot* control. That distinction is instrumental in helping children master the psychological task of disengaging from interparental conflicts and redirecting their energies into age appropriate pursuits (Wallerstein, 1983). Coping skills training in a group context has the additional benefit of facilitating supportive, cohesive group interactions. Members are often eager to offer suggestions and feedback to peers. In turn, they are comforted by an awareness that they are not alone with their problems.

Interpersonal communication and problem-solving skills are presented over several sessions, using interactive games and activities to learn and practice new skills. Through games and puppet play, young children are drawn into discussions of problem scenarios and various solutions. They are taught to "stop and think" in these situations (e.g., "You want to watch your favorite show on TV, but your brother wants to watch something else. What can you do?"). In this way, they are eased naturally into learning relevant problem-solving skills and applying them to personal problems. A team-based "tic-tac-toe" game helps children learn to generate alternate solutions, evaluate their consequences, and choose the most appropriate solutions to problems. Puppet play is used to depict common divorce-related problems such as loyalty conflicts. Group members then actively participate in generating alternate solutions to help the puppets deal effectively with those problem scenarios. Play-based activities such as the "red light–green light game" help children differentiate between solvable (green light) and unsolvable (red light) problems. When faced with an unsolvable (red light) problem, children are encouraged to disengage from that uncontrollable problem and spend their time instead on age-appropriate activities.

Enhance Children's Perceptions of Self and Family and Reinforce Coping Skills

This final integrative unit emphasizes positive qualities of children and families. Children in the midst of stressful life changes often feel different and defective (e.g., "If I were a better kid, my parents would have stayed together"). Several self-esteem building exercises are used to highlight their positive qualities, including a "you're a special person" activity. In this exercise, all children receive written feedback from peers and leaders about their unique qualities and special contributions to the group. Children enjoy this exercise; some keep their "special person" card long after the group ends.

Building children's competencies and coping skills are so essential to the CODIP intervention that the board game called the "Daring Dinosaurs" (formerly called "Kids Are Special People") was specially designed to foster children's sense of self-efficacy and assess children's progress in understanding divorce-related issues and developing skills. The game is one of several therapeutic techniques used in the program and is designed to review feeling words and concepts, family and divorce-related issues, social problem-solving, communication, and anger control skills, and to promote self-awareness and self-esteem.

The game cards ask questions about children's thoughts and beliefs (e.g., "Do you believe you can make your parents get back together?"); their feelings (e.g., "How do children feel when their parents fight?"); and show ways to self-soothe when feeling upset (e.g., "Act as though you are feeling lonely. Name two things you could do to feel better."). If a child cannot answer a question, other children or the group puppet are invited to help. The content of the cards covers most of the topics explored in previous sessions. However, to reflect the unique experience of individual groups, blank cards are included with the game. Leaders can write individualized cards to reflect problems, situations, or feelings specifically discussed in their groups. Leaders are encouraged to "stack the deck" so that the most relevant cards for the children in their group are placed on top.

To consolidate skills and reinforce key program objectives with older youngsters, a popular CODIP activity is the WKID-TV "panel of experts" on family changes. Children take turns as members of a panel of experts on divorce and field questions from the "audience" (i.e., the other group members). This activity (a) underscores common problems of children dealing with divorce; (b) further clarifies misconceptions about divorce; (c) provides practice in solving personal problems; (d) highlights problems that *can*, and *cannot*, be controlled; (e) diversifies suggestions for coping with difficult problems; and (f) enhances children's sense of competence and self-esteem by emphasizing the fact that they have indeed acquired skills for resolving problems and insights about divorcing families that can help others. Sample questions from this activity include "What are some things kids worry about when their parents separate?" and "My parents still fight even though they're divorced; what can I do to solve this terrible problem?" Children offer spontaneous solutions to the problems posed, often with wit, wisdom, and understanding. A few examples include the following advice:

For Parents

- Don't give us everything we want just to get us to like you more than our other parent.
- Be honest with us. Tell us if you're getting a divorce, but please, spare us the gory details.
- Don't use us as bullets. Don't fight in front of us. Don't say, "Your Dad is an idiot." Don't ask us if Mom is dating.
- Let us know that it's OK to love both of you. Don't make us choose between the two of you.
- Let us know that you love us. Even if we act like we already know, tell us again.

For Other Kids

- Just remember, it's not your fault that your parents are splitting up, even if you did laugh when your Dad told that joke about your Mom.

- Find someone you can trust to talk to. Sometimes you just need to let it all out.
- Remember that there are some things—like your parents' divorce—that you can't change. Spend your time on things that make you happy instead.
- If your parents start to date or get married again, it doesn't mean they will stop loving you.

REPLICATION AND TRANSPORTABILITY

CODIP has been disseminated to over 500 schools around the world. Although CODIP is primarily school-based, it is a transportable model that has been adapted successfully to other settings, including mental health centers, family nurturing centers, private practitioners' offices, and court-connected services for children. CODIP has been translated into French and successfully implemented in Quebec, in a program called "entramis" (Mireault, Drapreau, Faford, Lapointe, & Clotier, 1991). The model can be applied to different populations in urban, suburban, and rural settings. A new holistic health approach combines CODIP services with medical care and well-child visits in urban pediatric clinics. Pediatric practitioners are often the first professionals to identify initial warning signs of stress in children that warrant additional supportive services and early intervention. As they discuss the child's health status during pediatric visits, they are trained to identify children who may benefit from a preventive intervention such as CODIP; parents of these children are referred to an educational program designed to help them reduce the stress of a breakup on their children (Pedro-Carroll, Nakhnikian, & Montes, 2001). Children's support groups can be provided at clinics, neighborhood community centers, and after-school care programs. Program facilitators are trained to link families with additional supportive services and remain available to families for supportive "booster sessions" after the program ends.

CODIP has recently been designated a national "Model Program" by SAMHSA (Substance Abuse and Mental Health Services Administration), a branch of the U.S. Department of Health and Human Services. Information about CODIP and other programs that have undergone careful evaluation and met criteria for effectiveness is listed on their Web site for those seeking to adapt a program for their community (http://www.modelprograms. samhsa.gov).

We find it useful to implement CODIP in new settings with a relatively brief meeting to describe the program to relevant mental health professionals. As they are the people most likely to be conducting the program, their interest and commitment is an essential precondition for beginning the program. At sites where professionals express interest in CODIP, follow-up meetings are held with administrators to obtain formal approval and establish preliminary contracts outlining how the program works.

After initial need and contract issues are resolved, the recruitment of program participants can begin. We send letters on school letterheads describing the program to all parents at the targeted grade levels. The letter includes a consent form. An informational meeting is held at the site for parents who wish to learn more about the program. There the coordinator describes the program's goals, provides an overview of its activities, and responds to parents' questions.

Occasionally, even with parental consent, a child may initially resist getting involved in CODIP. In such cases we explain to the parent that the child's hesitation is understandable because not all children know what to expect from the groups; we then request permission to meet with the child to explain how the program works. These steps are intended to give parents and children an accurate picture of the program and thus to facilitate informed decisions about participating. Children are free to withdraw from the program at any time; however, less than 1% have ever chosen to do so. Before the program begins, leaders meet individually with all children to welcome them, provide further information about the groups, and answer their questions.

To qualify for CODIP, a child must (a) be within the targeted age range; (b) have parents who at one time lived together and are now separated; (c) have written parental consent; and (d) be capable of functioning adequately in a group (i.e., show no evidence of serious aggressive behaviors or severe emotional problems that warrant more intensive services). These selection criteria are important. Sometimes there are pressures to include children who are not appropriate for the group. The inclusion of such children can be frustrating for all parties if managing the child's inappropriate behavior, rather than the program's central divorce-related objectives, becomes the major focus. In other words, CODIP is designed as a preventive intervention, not as intensive group therapy for serious emotional difficulties.

OUTCOME EVALUATION

CODIP has been evaluated extensively to assess its effectiveness with children of different ages and sociodemographic backgrounds. Since its inception in 1982, eight separate studies have been conducted, including a two-year follow up documenting the program's enduring benefits (Pedro-Carroll et al., 1999). Some of the key information and results are summarized in Tables 4.2 and 4.3, and a brief summary follows.

Research on the initial program with fourth- to sixth-grade suburban children, using a delayed treatment control group design, assessed CODIP's efficacy on the children's adjustment from four perspectives: parents,

TABLE 4.2
Overview of Factors Measured in Outcome Evaluation Studies on Children
of Divorce Intervention Program

Age, SES group, and citation	Data source(s) and timing	Results
Suburban 4th, 5th, and 6th graders (Pedro-Carroll & Cowen, 1985; Pedro-Carroll, Cowen, Hightower, & Guare, 1986)	Teachers Parents Group leaders Children Pre–post measurements	Changes in risk factors ↓ problem behaviors ↓ anxiety (children) Changes in protective factors ↑ school-related and social competencies ↑ home adjustment (e.g., better communication, more able to express feelings, more age-appropriate behavior, and better able to deal with problem situations) ↑ adjustment to family changes ↑ group-based peer interaction ↑ acceptance and understanding of changes in their families (children)
Urban 2nd and 3rd graders 4th, 5th, and 6th graders (Alpert-Gillis, Pedro-Carroll, & Cowen, 1989; Pedro-Carroll, Alpert-Gillis, & Cowen, 1992)	Multiple input sources Pre–post measurements	Changes in risk factors ↓ anxiety ↓ divorce-related concerns Changes in protective factors ↑ home and school adjustment ↑ social competencies ↑ prosocial peer interactions
2nd and 3rd graders (Sterling, 1986)	Pre–post measurements	Key components Support component alone without coping skills training not as effective 16 weekly sessions more effective than twice a week for 8 weeks with young children
Kindergarten and 1st graders (Pedro-Carroll & Alpert-Gillis, 1997)	Teachers Group leaders Parents Children Pre–post measurements	Changes in risk factors ↓ school-related problem behaviors (teachers) Changes in protective factors ↑ school-related competencies ↑ accurate attributions for the divorce ↑ coping skills ↑ being able to talk about deal with divorce-related feelings ↑ getting along with peers ↑ ability to deal with feelings ↑ positive feelings about self and family

continues

TABLE 4.2 *(Continued)*

Age, SES group, and citation	Data source(s) and timing	Results
Kindergarten and 1st graders (Pedro-Carroll, Sutton, & Wyman, 1999)	Teachers Parents Follow up at 2nd and 3rd grade (2 years after program)	Gains had endured at 2-year follow-up compared with divorce control participants Changes in risk factors ↓ school problems ↓ worries about family visits ↓ to school health office Changes in protective factors ↑ school competencies ↑ adjustment to family changes ↑ positive feelings about self and family ↑ coping skills ↑ ability to express feelings appropriately
7th and 8th graders (Pedro-Carroll, Sutton, & Black, 1993)	Parents Group leaders Participants Pre–post measurements	↑ overall adjustment ↑ ability to cope effectively with family changes ↑ ability to express feelings, manage anger, solve interpersonal problems, and differentiate between controllable and uncontrollable problems ↑ strategies for disengaging from parent conflict and refocusing on age-appropriate activities ↑ friendship formation, anger control, and communication effectiveness ↑ hopes and expectations for the future (for personal responsibility, interpersonal relationships, staying out of trouble, and having people care about them)

Note. SES = socioeconomic status.

teachers, group leaders, and the children themselves. From all four perspectives, the program children improved significantly compared with matched controls randomly assigned to a delayed treatment condition (Pedro-Carroll & Cowen, 1985). A replication study with different group leaders and different schools confirmed these initial findings (Pedro-Carroll, Cowen, Hightower, & Guare, 1986).

Encouraging results from those early studies promoted extension of CODIP to children of different ages and sociodemographic backgrounds. These next steps included adaptations of CODIP for second- to third-grade and for fourth-, fifth-, and sixth-grade urban children. Evaluations of these new programs confirmed the improvements in adjustment previously reported for suburban samples (Alpert-Gillis et al., 1989; Pedro-Carroll et al., 1992). Overall, these data, involving multiple input sources, demonstrated

TABLE 4.3
Statistics on Outcome Evaluation Studies on Children of Divorce Intervention Program

Study	Age/SES	Rater	Constructs measured	N/df	Effect Size[a]	Relevant statistics[b]	p
Pedro-Carroll and Cowen, 1985	4th, 5th, and 6th graders/ suburban	Teacher	Behavior problems	72	-.99	$F = 23.75$	<.001
		Parent	Competencies	40	.68	$F = 19.69$	<.001
		Child self-report	Child maladjustment		-1.19	$F = 21.92$	<.001
		Group leader	Anxiety		-.36	$F = 5.40$	<.02
			Perceived competence			$F = 6.44$	ns
			Coping skills				<.001
Pedro-Carroll, Cowen, Hightower, and Guare, 1986	4th, 5th, and 6th graders/ suburban	Teacher	School adjustment	132	.73	$F = 2.22$	<.05
		Parent	Child's adjustment	54	.79	$F = 6.87$	<.01
		Child self-report	Anxiety			$F = 18.58$	<.001
		Group leader	School engagement			$F = 4.04$	ns
			Locus of control			$F = 7.67$	ns
			Behavior problems				<.001
			Coping skills				<.001
Alpert-Gillis, Pedro-Carroll, and Cowen, 1989	2nd and 3rd graders/ urban	Teacher	Behavior problems	185		$F = 0.89$	ns
		Parent	Competencies	50		$F = 4.96$	<.01
		Child self-report	Child's adjustment			$F = 11.12$	<.001
		Group leader	Adjustment to divorce			$F = 11.92$	<.001
			Coping skills			$t = 8.37$	<.001

Study	Sample	Source	Measure	df	Effect size	F	p
Pedro-Carroll, Alpert-Gillis, and Cowen, 1992	4th, 5th, and 6th graders/ urban	Teacher	Behavior problems	2, 157	.44	$F = 1.97$	.14[c]
			Competencies	2, 157	-.50	$F = 2.54$	.08[d]
		Parent	Child's adjustment	2, 153	.18	$F = 15.88$	.001
		Child self-report	Anxiety	2, 170	-.18	$F = 4.79$	.01
			Family adjustment	2, 169	.46	$F = 6.15$	.003
			Adjustment to divorce	1, 83	.47	$F = 9.40$	.003
Pedro-Carroll and Alpert-Gillis, 1997	Kindergarten and 1st graders	Teacher	Behavior problems	2, 95		$F = 9.41$	.001
		Parent	Competencies	2, 95		$F = 7.00$	.002
		Child self-report	Child's adjustment	2, 80		$F = 6.41$	.003
		Group leader	Family adjustment	2, 92		$F = 11.90$	.001
			Coping skills	37		$F = 7.85$	.001
Pedro-Carroll, Sutton, and Wyman, 1999	Kindergarten and 1st graders 2-year follow-up	Teacher[d]	Behavior problems	77	-1.57	$F = 4.04$	<.01
		Parent	Competencies		1.28	$F = 5.41$	<.001
		Child self-report	Child's adjustment		0.78	$F = 1.68$	.15
		School records	Child's divorce coping		1.15	$F = 14.23$	<.001
			Family adjustment		0.75	$F = 4.23$	<.01
			Anxiety		-1.82	$F = 17.85$	<.001
			Frequent nurse visits		-1.35	$\chi^2 = 16.02$	<.01

Note. SES = socioeconomic status.

[a]Effect sizes are for the experimental group compared with the control group (see original article for statistics on experimental group compared with the nondivorce control group).

[b]F values reflect multivariate analyses of variance with all three groups: experimental/in program group, children of divorce control group, children in nondivorced families control group.

[c]There were significant predifferences (i.e., at pretest, the divorce control group was rated by teachers as higher functioning than the experimental group).

[d]Teachers were blind to condition.

improved home and school adjustment for CODIP children, reductions in their anxiety and divorce-related concerns, and gains in their social competencies. Collectively, these studies demonstrated that the program model could be modified effectively for young children and for low-income populations for whom divorce is but one of many stressors.

A further challenge for CODIP was to identify key program components and practices that accounted for positive outcomes (Grych & Fincham, 1992). As noted earlier, CODIP rests on two essential components: providing support and teaching coping skills. Others have also found these components effective with children of divorce (Stolberg & Mahler, 1994). Sterling's (1986) evaluation of CODIP for second- and third-graders included a components analysis assessing the effectiveness of a program with and without an emphasis on social problem-solving (SPS) and coping skills. Sterling found that the support alone (i.e., no SPS) condition was less effective than the full program with a coping skills component. She also found that 16 weekly sessions for this group yielded more positive outcomes with young children than a twice-weekly, 8-week program format. Those results provided a useful foundation for the later adaptation of CODIP for very young (5- and 6-year-old) children. Evaluation of the CODIP program for kindergarten to first-grade children again provided multisource evidence of the program's effectiveness (Pedro-Carroll & Alpert-Gillis, 1997).

The positive findings cited above reflect children's adjustment status when the program ended. Pedro-Carroll, Sutton, and Wyman (1999) assessed the stability of these outcomes over a 2-year follow-up period. New teachers, blind to children's initial group status, rated CODIP children as having significantly fewer school problems and more competencies than comparison children. Parent interview data showed that their improvements at home and in school endured over the 2-year period. These results demonstrate that CODIP provided skills and benefits that enhanced children's resilience and healthy adjustment over time.

An evaluation of a pilot CODIP program for seventh and eighth graders (Pedro-Carroll, Sutton, & Black, 1993) again reflected the perspectives of parents, leaders, and children. Although findings from this study are tempered by relatively small sample sizes, agreement about important gains for participants was again found across diverse perspectives. A further finding of special interest for this age group was the significant improvement in participants' hopes and expectations for the future—a finding with implications for choices and decisions that shape their lives. Such self-views facilitate responsible decision making and the formation of trusting, enduring, satisfying relationships. In this context, Wyman, Cowen, Work, and Kerley (1993) found that the presence of positive future expectations among 10- to 12-year-old, highly stressed urban children related to resilient outcomes 3 years later. Such views functioned as a protective factor in reducing the negative effects of major life stressors.

Practitioners wishing to implement CODIP groups in a clinical setting could evaluate the effectiveness of the intervention by using many of the child- and parent-focused measures in the studies described above, including assessments of children's anxiety, coping skills, attitudes and beliefs about divorce, parent–child relationships, and other variables known to relate to children's risk and resilience in the aftermath of parental divorce.

CONCLUSION

This chapter summarizes an empirically validated, play-based preventive intervention for children of divorce. Marital disruption is a well-documented stressor for families and affects millions of children in this country. The risks that these stresses pose for children's long-term adjustment are equally well established. However, long-term social and emotional difficulties are not inevitable outcomes. The extent to which risk and protective factors influence children's adjustment over time and the availability of supportive scaffolding from the child's family and environment have a large affect on the outcome.

Preventive interventions that incorporate support and competence enhancement hold promise for reducing the stress of a breakup on children and fostering their resilience and healthy development. The intervention model described here, the Children of Divorce Intervention Program, uses play as an integral component of the intervention model to foster a safe, trusting environment in which children can share experiences and acquire essential coping skills. Although it is primarily a school-based program, the play-based activities described in this chapter can be applied in individual and group work with children in various professional and community settings.

Program evaluation over the years has established a solid evidence base for CODIP's effectiveness in reducing the stress of a breakup on children and enhancing their social, emotional, and school adjustment. At a time when millions of children are grappling with stressful disruptions in family relationships, effective preventive interventions offer much-needed support and the potential for fostering children's resilience and healthy development.

REFERENCES

Albee, G. W. (1983). The argument for primary prevention. In H. A. Marlowe & R. B. Weinberg (Eds.), *Primary prevention: Fact or fallacy* (pp. 3–16). Tampa: University of South Florida.

Alpert-Gillis, L. J., Pedro-Carroll, J. L., & Cowen, E. L. (1989). Children of Divorce Intervention Program: Development, implementation, and evaluation of a program for young urban children. *Journal of Consulting and Clinical Psychology*, 57, 583–587.

Amato, P. R., & Keith, B. (1991). Consequences of parental divorce for children's well-being: A meta-analysis. *Psychological Bulletin, 110,* 26–46.

Bay-Hinitz, A., Peterson, R. F., & Quilitch, H. R. (1994). Cooperative games: A way to modify aggressive and cooperative behaviors in young children. *Journal of Applied Behavior Analysis, 27*(3), 433–446.

Brown, L. K., & Brown, M. (1986). *Dinosaur's Divorce.* New York: The Atlantic Monthly Press.

Burroughs, M. S., Wagner, W. W., & Johnson, J. T. (1997). Treatment with children of divorce: A comparison of two types of therapy. *Journal of Divorce and Remarriage, 27*(3–4), 83–99.

Chittenden, G. E. (1942). An experimental study in measuring and modifying assertive behavior in young children. *Monographs of the Society for Research in Child Development, 7*(1), pp. iii–87.

Cicchetti, D. (1989). Developmental psychopathology: Some thoughts on its evolution. *Development and Psychopathology, 1,* 1–4.

Clulow, C. F. (1990). Divorce as bereavement: Similarities and differences. *Family & Conciliation Courts Review, 28*(1), 19–22.

Cowen, E. L. (1991). In pursuit of wellness. *American Psychologist, 46,* 404–408.

Cowen, E. L., Hightower, A. D., Pedro-Carroll, J. L., Work, W. C., & Wyman, P. A. (1996). *School-based prevention for children at risk: The Primary Mental Health Project.* Washington, DC: American Psychological Association.

Crockford, M., Kent, G., & Stewart, N. (1993). Play friendly and safe: A therapeutic group model for young children (5–8 years old) who have witnessed wife assault. *Journal of Child and Youth Care, 8*(3), 77–86.

Durlak, J. A., & Wells, A. M. (1997). Primary prevention mental health programs for children and adolescents: A meta-analytic review. *American Journal of Community Psychology, 25,* 115–152.

Emery, R. E., & Forehand, R. (1994). Parental divorce and children's well being: A focus on resilience. In R. J. Haggerty, L. R. Sherrod, N. Garmezy, & M. Rutter (Eds.), *Stress, risk and resilience in children and adolescents* (pp. 64–99). Cambridge, MA: Cambridge University Press.

Felner, R. D., Farber, S. S., & Primavera, J. (1983). *Transitions and stressful life events: A model for primary prevention.* New York: Pergamon Press.

Grych, J. H., & Fincham, F. D. (1992). Interventions for children of divorce: Towards greater integration of research and action. *Psychological Bulletin, 111,* 434–454.

Hetherington, E. M., Stanley-Hagan, M., & Anderson, E. R. (1989). Marital transitions: A child's perspective. *American Psychologist, 44,* 303–312.

Hoyt, L. A., Cowen, E. L., Pedro-Carroll, J. L., & Alpert-Gillis, L. J. (1990). Anxiety and depression in young children of divorce. *Journal of Clinical Child Psychology, 19,* 26–32.

James, R. K., & Myer, R. (1987). Puppets: The elementary school counselor's right or left arm. *Elementary School Guidance & Counseling, 21,* 292–299.

Johnson, C. V., Riester, A. E., Corbett, C., Buehler, A., Huffacker, L., Levich, I., et al. (1998). Group activities for children and adolescents: An activity group therapy approach. *Journal of Child & Adolescent Group Therapy*, 8(2), 71–88.

Kalter, N. (1990). *Growing up with divorce*. New York: Macmillan.

Kazdin, A. E. (1990). Psychotherapy for children and adolescents. *Annual Review of Psychology*, *41*, 21–54.

Kurdek, L. A., & Berg, B. (1983). Correlates of children's adjustment to their parents' divorce. In L. A. Kurdek (Ed.), *New directions in child development: Vol. 19. Children and divorce* (pp. 47–60). San Francisco: Jossey-Bass.

Kurdek, L. A., & Berg, B. (1987). Children's beliefs about parental divorce scale: Psychometric characteristics and concurrent validity. *Journal of Consulting and Clinical Psychology*, *55*, 712–718.

Larson, R. W., & Verma, S. (1999). How children and adolescents spend time across the world: Work, play, and developmental opportunities. *Psychological Bulletin*, *125*, 701–736.

Masten, A. S. (1989). Resilience in development: Implications of the study of successful adaptation for developmental psychopathology. In D. Cicchetti (Ed.), *Rochester Symposium on Developmental Psychopathology: Vol. 1.* (pp. 261–294). Hillsdale, NJ: Erlbaum.

Masten, A. S., & Coatsworth, J. D. (1998). The development of competence in favorable and unfavorable environments: Lessons from research on successful children. *American Psychologist*, *53*, 205–220.

McCarthy, G. (1998). Attachment representations and representations of the self in relation to others: A study of preschool children in inner-city London. *British Journal of Medical Psychology*, *71*(1), 57–72.

McLanahan, S., & Bumpass, L. (1988). Intergenerational consequences of family disruption. *American Journal of Sociology*, *93*, 130–152.

Mireault, G., Drapreau, S., Faford, A., Lapointe, J., & Clotier, R. (1991). *Evaluation of an intervention program for children of separated families* (in French). Quebec, Canada: Department of Community Health at the Hospital of the Infant Jesus.

Oppawsky, J. (1991). The effects of parental divorce on children in West Germany: Emphasis: From the view of children. *Journal of Divorce and Remarriage*, *16*(3–4), 291–304.

Pedro-Carroll, J. L. (1997). The Children of Divorce Intervention Program: Fostering resilient outcomes for school-age children. In G. W. Albee & T. Gullotta (Eds.), *Primary prevention works* (pp. 213–238). Thousand Oaks, CA: Sage.

Pedro-Carroll, J. L. (2001). The promotion of wellness in children and families: Challenges and opportunities. *American Psychologist*, *56*, 993–1004.

Pedro-Carroll, J. L., & Alpert-Gillis, L. J. (1997). Preventive interventions for children of divorce: A developmental model for 5- and 6-year-old children. *Journal of Primary Prevention*, *18*, 5–23.

Pedro-Carroll, J. L., Alpert-Gillis, L. J., & Cowen, E. L. (1992). An evaluation of the efficacy of a preventive intervention for 4th–6th grade urban children of divorce. *Journal of Primary Prevention*, *13*, 115–130.

Pedro-Carroll, J. L., & Cowen, E. L. (1985). The Children of Divorce Intervention Project: An investigation of the efficacy of a school-based prevention program. *Journal of Consulting and Clinical Psychology, 53*, 603–611.

Pedro-Carroll, J. L., Cowen, E. L., Hightower, A. D., & Guare, J. C. (1986). Preventive intervention with latency-aged children of divorce: A replication study. *American Journal of Community Psychology, 14*, 277–290.

Pedro-Carroll, J. L., Nakhnikian, E., & Montes, G. (2001). Assisting children through transition: Helping parents protect their children from the toxic effects of ongoing conflict in the aftermath of divorce. *Family Court Review, 39*, 377–392.

Pedro-Carroll, J. L., Sutton, S. E., & Black, A. E. (1993). *The Children of Divorce Intervention Program: Preventive outreach to early adolescents—final report.* Rochester, NY: Rochester Mental Health Association.

Pedro-Carroll, J. L., Sutton, S. E., & Wyman, P. A. (1999). A two-year follow-up evaluation of a preventive intervention program for young children of divorce. *School Psychology Review, 28*, 467–476.

Phillips, R. D. (1985). Whistling in the dark?: A review of play therapy research. *Psychotherapy, 22*(4), 752–760.

Rae, W. A., Worchel, F. F., Upchurch, J., Sanner, J. H., & Daniel, C. A. (1989). The psychosocial impact of play on hospitalized children. *Journal of Pediatric Psychiatry, 14*, 617–627.

Rubin, K. H., Fein, G. C., & Vandenberg, B. (1983). Play. In P. H. Mussen (Ed.), *Handbook of child psychology* (4th ed., pp. 693–774). New York: Wiley.

Sandler, I. N., Braver, S. L., & Gensheimer, L. K. (2000). Stress: Theory, research, and action. In J. Rappaport & E. Seidman (Eds.), *Handbook of community psychology* (pp. 187–214). Dordrecht, Netherlands: Kluwer Academic/Plenum Publishers.

Sandler, I. N., Tein, J. Y., Mehta, P., Wolchik, S. A., & Ayers, T. (2000). Perceived coping efficacy and psychological problems of children of divorce. *Child Development, 74*(4), 1097–1118.

Sandler, I. N., Tein, J., & West, S. G. (1994). Coping, stress, and psychological symptoms of children of divorce: A cross-sectional and longitudinal study. *Child Development, 65*, 1744–1763.

Sinberg, J. (1978). *Divorce is a grown-up problem.* New York: Avon Books.

Springer, J. F., Phillips, J. L., Phillips, L., Cannady, L. P., & Kerst-Harris, E. (1992). CODA: A creative therapy program for children in families affected by abuse of alcohol or other drugs. *Journal of Community Psychology, OSAP Special Issue*, 55–74.

Sterling, S. E. (1986). *School-based intervention program for early latency-aged children of divorce.* Unpublished doctoral dissertation, University of Rochester, NY.

Stolberg, A. L., & Garrison, K. M. (1985). Evaluating a primary prevention program for children of divorce: The Divorce Adjustment Project. *American Journal of Community Psychology, 13*, 111–124.

Stolberg, A. L., & Mahler, J. (1994). Enhancing treatment gains in a school-based intervention for children of divorce through skill training, parental involvement, and transfer procedures. *Journal of Consulting and Clinical Psychology, 62,* 147–156.

Utay, J. M., & Lampe, R. E. (1995). Use of a group counseling game to enhance social skills of children with learning disabilities. *Journal for Specialists in Group Work, 20*(2), 114–120.

Vygotsky, L. S. (1978). *Mind in society: The development of higher psychological processes.* Cambridge, MA: Harvard University Press.

Wallerstein, J. S. (1983). Children of divorce: Stress and developmental tasks. In N. Garmezy & M. Rutter (Eds.), *Stress, coping and development in children* (pp. 265-302). New York: McGraw-Hill.

Wallerstein, J. S., & Blakeslee, S. (1989). *Second chances: Men, women, and children a decade after divorce—who wins, who loses, and why?* New York: Ticknor & Fields.

Wallerstein, J. S., & Kelly, J. B. (1980). *Surviving the breakup: How children and parents cope with divorce.* New York: Basic Books.

Werner, E. E., & Smith, R. S. (1992). *Overcoming the odds: High risk children from birth to adulthood.* Ithaca, NY: Cornell University Press.

Wyman, P. A., Cowen, E. L., Work, W. C., & Kerley, J. H. (1993). The role of children's future expectations in self-system functioning and adjustment to life-stress. *Development and Psychopathology, 5,* 649–661.

Wyman, P. A., Sandler, I. N., Wolchik, S. A., & Nelson, K. (2000). Resilience as cumulative competence promotion and stress protection: Theory and intervention. In D. Cicchetti, J. Rappaport, I. Sandler, & R. Weissberg (Eds.), *The promotion of wellness in children and adolescents* (pp. 133–184). Washington, DC: Child Welfare League of America Press.

Zill, N., Morrison, D. R., & Coiro, M. J. (1993). Long-term effects of parental divorce on parent–child relationships, adjustment, and achievement in young adulthood. *Journal of Family Psychology, 7,* 91–103.

II

EMPIRICALLY BASED PLAY INTERVENTIONS FOR INTERNALIZING DISORDERS

5

POSTTRAUMATIC PLAY THERAPY: THE NEED FOR AN INTEGRATED MODEL OF DIRECTIVE AND NONDIRECTIVE APPROACHES

JANINE S. SHELBY AND ERIKA D. FELIX

Drenica is a memory now; the city of my birth.
The streets are barren; the wind is still.
No one has survived.
I am all that's left now; everyone is dead.
My new mother is Kosova and my father is the flag.

Merita, age 9

The girl repeated her song several times while staring blankly at the other Kosovar refugees. "She will sing but she will not speak a word," whispered the Albanian relief worker about Merita. *"The streets are barren. The wind is still."* Merita's recitation was rote, her face devoid of emotion. *"No one has survived. I am all that's left now."* Apart from her song, Merita did not speak. What happened in Kosovo, called Kosova by the ethnic Albanian Kosovars, was too devastating to articulate, yet too powerful to leave unspoken. She could not stop remembering; she could not stop trying to forget. As if in compromise to her conflicting desires for both silence and voice, Merita sang.

Merita sang of the soldiers who stormed her home in search of ethnic Albanian Kosovars to murder and terrorize. In her Albanian village, she

We offer heartfelt thanks to Christopher M. Layne and Michael Tredinnick, who played enormous roles in envisioning, supporting, and editing this chapter.

had witnessed the sexual mutilation, physical assaults, and kidnapping of her family members. Merita had somehow managed to slip away from the attackers, only to be detained by more enemy troops in a nearby town. The soldiers forced Merita onto a bus already overcrowded with other Kosovars. After the bus had mechanical problems, the Kosovars took the opportunity to flee. Merita spent two days walking with the other refugees to the safety of Albania. With each new, horrific realization of danger and loss, Merita's childhood retreated to the recesses of her awareness, rendering every present moment a growing figment of someone else's nightmare. For two weeks, Merita had been in the refugee camp; for two weeks she had been singing.

"My *new mother is Kosova*," she sorrowfully intoned again. Another child tried in vain to get Merita to play. "My *father is the flag*," was Merita's only response. Later, the Albanian relief workers, a Kosovar social worker, and an author of this chapter (Janine Shelby) met to discuss Merita's plight. By the light of the stars, the relief workers deliberated how to intervene with the young survivor. At the heart of the discussion lay an oft-debated question: After such extreme traumatic stressors, do children like Merita benefit from telling or playing out the traumatic events they endured? That is, given many children's avoidance of trauma-related themes and dissociation reactions, is it therapeutic to direct the child to engage in trauma-focused activities? Conversely, do children like Merita benefit more from nondirective, present-focused, support-oriented interventions that emphasize current coping skills and strengths?

In the distance, Merita began her song again. The workers paused in collective empathy. "How can I help her?" pleaded one of the social workers, who was also a Kosovar refugee. "I can't bear to hear that song again. Please teach me how to help her."

This chapter is written in response to the plea of the Kosovar social worker and to all those who seek to help traumatized children. Throughout the history of child trauma therapy, the specifics of *how* to intervene have often been debated. The result has been a general lack of consensus regarding both what standard practice is and how to deliver it. It is generally agreed that posttraumatic treatment for children usually involves a "mixture of cognitive–behavioral, supportive, and psychodynamic psychotherapy" (Amaya-Jackson & March, 1995, p. 290), but we know of no empirically supported framework that combines these three approaches. There is also a growing consensus that "the era of generic therapies is over" (Fonagy, 1998, p. 133) and that global techniques should be modified for each disorder (Fonagy, 1998; Schaefer, 2001). Notwithstanding the call to tailor treatments to specific disorders, precisely how treatments should be individually modified for children has not been well articulated.

As described below, a number of empirically validated treatment techniques (e.g., cognitive–behavioral therapy) have emerged during the last decade. Much of the focus of these recent studies has been directed toward one fundamental issue: Whether directive, trauma-focused approaches are preferable to nondirective therapeutic, support-oriented approaches (see Bonner, Walker, & Berliner, 2003; Cohen & Mannarino, 1996, 1998; Deblinger, McLeer, & Henry, 1990; Deblinger, Lippmann, & Steer, 1996). Additional focus has been directed toward the role of parental involvement in treatment, and whether it provides greater benefits compared to individual treatment alone (e.g., Cohen & Mannarino, 1993; Deblinger, et al., 1990; LeBlanc & Ritchie, 1999). Though the presence of specific therapeutic techniques and approaches does offer clinicians a broader array of evidence-based options for intervention, more information is needed to systematically integrate these distinct techniques into a comprehensive framework to fit the complex needs of young trauma survivors. For example, Cohen, Mannarino, Berliner, and Deblinger (2000) have argued that more research is needed to determine whether specific symptoms respond better to specific components of intervention; why some children do not respond well to trauma-focused cognitive–behavioral interventions; and how to identify those young survivors.

In this chapter, we introduce posttraumatic play therapy (PPT), which was developed as an evidence-informed framework that seeks to integrate these diverse components into a coherent and practical set of guidelines for therapists. PPT is designed to help clinicians maximize their effectiveness by providing strategies for selecting, tailoring, blending, and applying effective treatments or components of posttraumatic treatment for children. In the remainder of this chapter, we outline and discuss various components of effective treatment based on a PPT perspective. We first review the long-debated issue undergirding all posttraumatic therapy with children by examining the advantages and limitations of both directive and nondirective treatment approaches. Next, we describe the essential components of PPT (i.e., parental involvement, developmentally sensitive intervention, and specific techniques). We then chart the PPT framework, which provides evidence-informed practical guidelines for therapists working with young survivors. Following this description, we discuss the transportability of the PPT framework to various populations and comment more broadly on methods and considerations for successful exportation of effective treatments from research to community settings. We conclude by reviewing several tools with which to conduct outcome assessments of young trauma survivors.

DIRECTIVE, TRAUMA-FOCUSED VERSUS NONDIRECTIVE, SUPPORT-ORIENTED TREATMENT

Below we will review the advantages and limitations of both directive, trauma-focused and nondirective, support oriented therapies.

Directive, Trauma-Focused Play Therapy

The advantages and limitations of this method have been well described in the literature. These findings are outlined and explored in this section.

Advantages of Directive Play Therapy for Trauma Treatment

Directive techniques have been demonstrated to be effective both immediately after treatment and one year posttreatment (Cohen & Mannarino, 1996, 1997, 1998; Saywitz, Mannarino, Berliner, & Cohen, 2000). In fact, trauma-focused cognitive–behavioral therapy (CBT) was classified as a well-supported, efficacious treatment by Saunders, Berliner, and Hanson's (2003) guidelines for treating child physical and sexual abuse. Indeed, of the 24 treatments reviewed, trauma-focused CBT was the only treatment given this highest designation.

In recent years, several comparisons between directive and other approaches (e.g., nondirective, support-oriented, or combined nondirective–psychodynamic treatment) have been undertaken both for traumatized children (Bonner et al., 2003; Cohen & Mannarino, 1996, 1997, 1998; Deblinger et al., 1990; Deblinger et al., 1996; Kendall, 1994; Saigh, 1989; Saywitz et al., 2000) and traumatized adults (Foa & Rothbaum, 1998; Kilpatrick, Veronen, & Resick, 1982). In general, the literature supports the use of directive, trauma-focused therapy over nondirective, support-oriented techniques to reduce most child trauma symptoms. A notable exception is Bonner and colleagues, who found no significant therapy outcome differences among children exhibiting sexually inappropriate behavior who were treated in either a CBT group or a combined psychodynamic–nondirective group. More broadly, behavioral methods were found to be superior to nonbehavioral methods in therapy for children with a variety of disorders (Weisz, Weiss, Alicke, & Klotz, 1987). Although the preponderance of studies favor CBT, it should also be noted that CBT-oriented researchers have conducted the great majority of the existing comparative research.

In addition to its demonstrated effectiveness, directive treatment offers several advantages over other methods. One chief advantage is a relatively rapid change in targeted signs and symptoms; many models have a duration of fewer than 20 sessions. From a practical perspective, directive therapy techniques often have manualized instructions, are relatively easy to understand and use, and offer standardized intervention protocols.

Limitations of Directive Play Therapy for Trauma Treatment

Current evidence suggests that directive treatment approaches may reduce symptoms but may not be sufficient to address other problem areas (e.g., mistrust or lack of confidence). In addition, some trauma survivors simply dislike directive, trauma-focused techniques (Bryant & Harvey, 2000). In one study of adult sexual assault survivors (Kilpatrick et al., 1982), the comparison group had to be discontinued because not a single victim selected the directive, exposure-based treatment. Clearly, if survivors in common clinical settings reject directive techniques, those techniques will have limited use outside the research setting. Directive approaches usually require that clients focus on the traumatic event, despite the presence of avoidance symptoms characteristic of posttraumatic stress disorder (PTSD). The use of some directive techniques may unwittingly discourage clients (e.g., those experiencing severe avoidance or dissociation symptoms) from seeking assistance. Further, directive trauma-focused interventions may not be appropriate for survivors manifesting certain symptoms, such as dissociation. Rather, recent treatment recommendations specify that in cases involving extreme dissociation, exposure treatments should be avoided (Bryant & Harvey, 2000; Putnam, 1997).

Nondirective Play Therapy With Children

The advantages and limitations of nondirective play therapy have not been as well described in the literature as those for directive trauma-focused treatment. Below, we will outline the key findings for this method.

Advantages of Nondirective Play Therapy for Trauma Treatment

Despite the popularity and long tradition of nondirective play therapy, only recently have well-controlled studies emerged to support its use. Most notably, Ray, Bratton, Rhine, and Jones's (2001) meta-analysis revealed large effect sizes for play therapy involving both nondirective and cognitive–behavioral methods, with the nondirective therapy showing the greatest effect size. In individual studies, some evidence supports the use of nondirective play therapy over no treatment. For example, in a study of 8- to 12-year-old Taiwanese earthquake survivors, Shen (2002) randomly assigned 30 children to either a child-centered play therapy treatment condition or a no-treatment control condition. The group that received treatment showed reduced anxiety, but not depression symptoms, 2 weeks posttreatment. Research studies that generally support the use of directive over nondirective treatment have found no significant differences between treatments on measures of social competence in groups of traumatized preschoolers (Cohen & Mannarino, 1996, 1997, 1998).

Nondirective play therapy for young trauma survivors holds a number of intuitive advantages over more directive methods. Anecdotal evidence provided by many experienced clinicians suggests that nondirective play therapy is a gentle approach that generally feels satisfying to the child (Axline, 1947; Guerney, 2001; Landreth, 1991). The in-session focus on relationship, rather than on trauma, may pose less risk of elevating the child's anxiety. As a result, children in nondirective play therapy may be less likely to develop an aversion to therapy or to have experiences in the process of treatment that make them feel uncomfortable. In cases in which a child replays the traumatic event without prompting, the self-initiated posttraumatic play may be advantageous over therapist-directed posttraumatic play by providing the perception of increased control over content, pacing, and mode of expression and exploration. In addition, the nondirective approach may provide therapeutic benefits in nonpathological areas such as increased assertiveness, trust, insight, abreaction, and esteem (Saywitz et al., 2000).

Limitations of Nondirective Play Therapy for Trauma Treatment

Currently, the primary limitation of nondirective play therapy is the limited empirical support for the method compared with directive treatment. This limited empirical support has led a number of experts to conclude, as did Cohen and Mannarino (1993), that there is no empirical evidence that long-term, nondirective play therapy holds any significant advantage over cognitive–behavioral approaches in treating the symptoms of abused children.

Attempts by nondirective play therapists to address these conclusions have been hindered by methodological constraints and a general shortage of well-controlled studies of nondirective play therapy. Even Ray and colleagues' (2001) meta-analysis, which concluded that nondirective therapies showed a greater effect size than directive methods, is not without potential weaknesses that suggest the need for caution in interpreting its conclusions. Specifically, several studies of directive play therapy with children were not included in the analysis (e.g., Cohen & Mannarino 1996, 1997, 1998; Deblinger et al., 1990; Deblinger et al., 1996; Deblinger, Steer, & Lippmann, 1999) because of conservative criteria used to select studies involving play therapy methods (specifically, included studies involved methods specifically labeled as *play therapy* or clinicians identified as *play therapists*). Excluding such studies from the meta-analysis resulted in a disproportionate number of studies in the nondirective group ($n = 74$) compared with the cognitive–behavioral group ($n = 12$). These selection criteria consequently restricted the analysis to a minority of all published CBT outcome studies that include play therapy methods. In addition, several studies included in the meta-analysis found that nondirective play therapy benefited children with conditions such as schizophrenia and mental retardation (e.g., Bratton & Ray, 2000), although the use of nondirective therapy for these disorders has been widely refuted in contemporary research. It is, therefore, not clear whether these inclusionary and exclusionary criteria were sufficiently rigorous and balanced to warrant Ray et al.'s primary conclusion that nondirective play therapy is superior in effectiveness to directive methods.

Other disadvantages of nondirective play therapy warrant consideration. For example, some children refrain from addressing the traumatic event when doing so would likely benefit them. Also, children may need directed relief from repetitive posttraumatic play that lacks resolution and positive affect (e.g., Merita's repetitive song). Further, some children have access to mental health services for only a limited time, which necessitates brief and efficient intervention methods.

It should be noted that the effectiveness of nondirective play therapy may simply be more difficult to demonstrate. For example, a number of positive growth outcomes often targeted by nondirective methods (e.g., improved social skills and self-concept, making or deepening friendships, improved grades, self-efficacy expectations, self-concept, or other non-pathological areas of functioning) are more difficult to assess and often go unexamined in research studies (Saigh, Mroueh, Zimmerman, & Fairbank, 1995; Saywitz et al., 2000).

In light of these observations, PPT seeks to draw on the strengths of both directive and nondirective approaches to provide an integrative framework for symptom-specific techniques. We describe the essential components of PPT and delineate a framework for selecting and applying evidence-informed intervention strategies below.

POSTTRAUMATIC PLAY THERAPY: INTEGRATION AND GUIDANCE FOR THERAPISTS

This framework offers therapists a variety of evidence-informed clinical techniques. Many interventions we describe are designed to influence more than one symptom category. For practical reasons, we categorize the interventions with respect to both their directive–nondirective nature and the symptoms they target. Although most trauma-focused interventions are also directive, these two domains are not identical, given that some directive interventions are not trauma-focused (e.g., relaxation skills training), and some nondirective interventions are also trauma-focused (e.g., a child's self-initiated posttraumatic repetitive play). To use the framework described here (see Figure 5.1), the therapist first identifies the client's predominant symptom or problem area, and then follows the prescriptive chart to locate recommended interventions or recommended readings that are matched to the area of concern.

In the remainder of this chapter, we review and provide reference citations for treatment literature that will assist clinicians in making evidence-informed decisions and choices regarding which treatment models and strategies should be matched with specific client symptoms, problems, and strengths. Notably, several studies cited herein also appear in Saunders' et al. (2003) useful review of the child trauma treatment literature, which rates

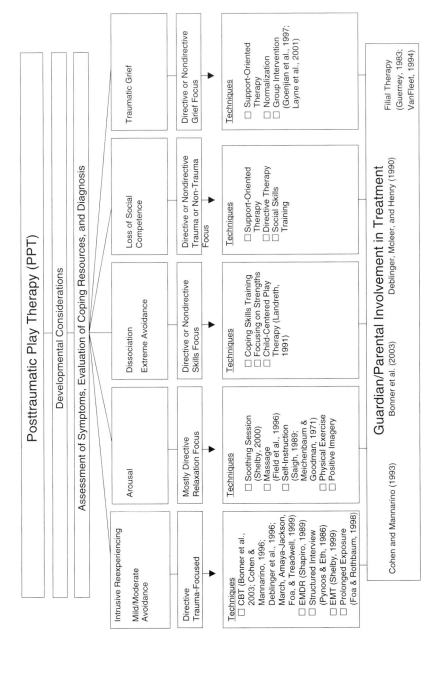

Figure 5.1. Posttraumatic play therapy flow chart.

several popular treatments along a continuum from "efficacious" to "harmful" and provides detailed statistical information. We therefore restrict our review of these studies to those findings of greatest clinical relevance (paired with a reference for interested readers to the Saunders et al. review); we also review more statistical data in conjunction with the clinical implications of those studies not included in Saunders' review.

KEY TREATMENT INGREDIENTS

Below are some of the central components related to treatment outcome, such as adult caretaker involvement in the treatment, developmentally sensitive intervention, and assessment and diagnosis.

Parental Involvement in the Treatment

Mounting research evidence indicates that parental or caretaker involvement in the child's therapy is a critical part of child trauma treatment, given that children's trauma symptoms are related to family functioning, parental reactions, and social support (Cohen & Mannarino, 1993, 1998; Deblinger, Stauffer, & Steer, 2001; Silverman & La Greca, 2002; Vernberg, 2002). In their models for treating sexually abused children, both Cohen and Mannarino (1993) and Deblinger et al. (1990) found that parental involvement in treatment was related to improved child outcome. In fact, LeBlanc and Ritchie (1999) concluded from their meta-analysis that, regardless of the therapeutic approach used (i.e., directive or nondirective), interventions involving parents were important to the success of play therapy. Similarly, Bonner and colleagues (2003) found no therapy outcome differences between groups of successfully treated children with hypersexual behavior whose parents received collateral parent group therapy. These studies emphasize how critical parental involvement is to effective treatment for children. For manualized treatment involving nonoffending parents of sexual abuse survivors, see Bonner and colleagues (2003), Cohen and Mannarino (1993), and Deblinger et al. (1990).

Developmental Tailoring

Children's developmental stage affects their ability to understand and benefit from some treatments (Nader, 2001; Saywitz et al., 2000; Shelby, 2000; Vernberg, 2002; Vernberg & Johnston, 2001) because children have different symptoms, cognitive abilities, and coping skills across different developmental eras. These differences provide ample reason to adapt interventions to each child's developmental level. Yet most treatment techniques described in the child trauma literature are not presented with detailed developmental modifications. Shelby described a model for developmentally sensitive child posttraumatic therapy, specifying differences in cognitive capacities, coping patterns, symptoms, and interventions across childhood and adolescence. James (1989) presented a framework for developmentally sequenced treatment in which the child's maturing interpretations of the traumatic event are a focus of treatment. Nader also prescribed modifications incorporating play for posttraumatic therapy with younger children.

Assessment and Diagnosis

In the PPT framework, the therapist is called on to accurately recognize not only the symptoms of PTSD, acute stress disorder (ASD), and dissociation, but also the common issues of childhood trauma. Although traumatic grief, mistrust, and loss of social competence are not included in the *DSM–IV–TR* (American Psychiatric Association, 2000), as part of the PTSD criteria, their frequent occurrence has been noted by clinicians and researchers working with this population (Herman, 1992; Putnam, 1997). These symptom categories appear in our PPT Framework as areas of clinical focus (see Figure 5.1). During the assessment phase, the therapist must also assess the child's coping resources.

Therapist Training

The PPT framework requires therapists who use it to be comfortable and adept in implementing both directive and nondirective modes of treatment, with both children and their guardians. The specific training needs of the therapist will depend on the therapist's competencies and the specific issues of the client. Some of the techniques we describe below (e.g., eye movement desensitization and reprocessing) require specific training and certification to practice the method. Other techniques (e.g., prolonged exposure or Pynoos & Eth's [1986] child interview) involve less specific training requirements. For some techniques (e.g., structured play therapy or empathic listening), play therapists with mental health training may not need additional preparation.

Length of Treatment

The techniques we present below range in length from single sessions to long-term treatment. The PPT framework is a symptom, rather than calendar-based, treatment guide. Therefore, the length of treatment varies depending on the unique symptom profile, history, exposure, coping resources, and other factors of each child. Traumatized children often present with several serious symptoms that affect their functioning. In these cases, the treatment begins with the symptom that is most detrimental or of greatest concern to the child or caregiver. After sufficient progress is made in one area, additional goals can be sequentially targeted.

SYMPTOMS AND EMPIRICALLY-SUPPORTED INTERVENTIONS

The hallmark symptoms of posttraumatic distress are reviewed below. Additional areas of posttraumatic difficulty (i.e., loss of social competence or interpersonal functioning, and traumatic grief) are also discussed.

Intrusive Reexperiencing

Flashbacks, nightmares, repetitive play, and other forms of intrusive reexperiencing have long been thought to result from physiological attempts to organize and integrate the trauma experience (Horowitz, 1976). As victims integrate their traumatic memories, intrusive reexperiencing is believed to decline. Thus, the treatment of choice for intrusive reexperiencing is trauma-focused intervention aimed at posttraumatic integration. Several techniques described here illustrate the use of directive, trauma-focused approaches to alleviate intrusive reexperiencing.

Pynoos and Eth Interview

The Pynoos and Eth (1986) interview is a semistructured intervention to assist children in their retelling of a traumatic event. Children are asked to draw a picture, tell a story about their picture, and then describe the event in a slow, step-by-step fashion while remembering all of their sensory experiences. Children describe the worst moment, explore revenge fantasies, describe fears and symptoms, and give a critique of the interview. The therapist provides psychoeducation and reframing of the child's bravery.

This technique was used following the 1988 Armenian earthquake across two to four sessions with a small group of children, in combination with classroom discussions and relaxation training. Pre–post posttraumatic and depressive symptoms were measured in both the experimental and no-treatment control groups. Results indicated that trauma symptoms significantly decreased among treated children and increased among nontreated children (Nader, 2001). Further analyses revealed that depressive symptoms remained constant for the treatment group, but increased for the nontreated group.

Eye Movement Desensitization and Reprocessing

Shapiro (1989) proposed eye movement desensitization and reprocessing (EMDR) as a method for helping survivors reprocess a traumatic event.

Though survivors are not asked to describe the entire incident, they begin the intervention by holding the traumatic image in mind. Numerous studies have shown EMDR's efficacy for the treatment of adults, but only a few preliminary studies suggest that EMDR is efficacious for young trauma survivors (Greenwald, 1994; Puffer, Greenwald, & Elrod, 1998). In Greenwald's case study, five Hurricane Andrew survivors with PTSD, from 4- to 11-years-old, were administered one or two sessions of EMDR. Pre–post mother's ratings of children's symptoms reflected significant reductions that held at a four-week follow-up. EMDR was given the "supported and acceptable treatment" designation in Saunders et al.'s (2003) review of common childhood post-traumatic treatments.

Cognitive–Behavioral Treatment of Childhood Sexual Abuse

Cohen and Mannarino (1993, 1996) merged cognitive–behavioral techniques with traditional play therapy methods, such as art techniques and puppet and doll play, to make their approach developmentally appropriate for young victims of sexual abuse. Specifically, the authors propose a treatment protocol addressing (a) safety education; (b) assertiveness training; (c) identification of appropriate versus inappropriate touching; (d) attributions regarding the abuse; (e) ambivalent feelings toward the perpetrator; (f) regressive and inappropriate behaviors; and (g) fear and anxiety. Interventions include cognitive reframing, thought-stopping, positive imagery, contingency reinforcement programs, parent training, and problem solving. They view interventions with the nonoffending parent as integral to treatment success.

Cohen and Mannarino (1996, 1997, 1998) found that their directive, trauma-focused therapy was superior to nondirective, support-oriented therapy for reducing most symptoms among young sexual assault survivors. In a study of 67 randomly assigned preschool children, the authors (1996) compared 12 sessions of nondirective supportive therapy (NST) to CBT for sexual abuse victims. The NST group showed no significant changes; however, the CBT group showed significant symptomatic improvement. These findings remained at a 1-year follow up (Cohen & Mannarino, 1997). In addition, 12 NST participants were removed from the study because of sexually inappropriate behavior. When given CBT, six of these children were treated successfully.

Deblinger et al. (1990) propose a treatment model similar to Cohen and Mannarino's that incorporates coping skills training, gradual exposure, and sexual abuse education and prevention skills. The authors make traditional CBT techniques child friendly by using dolls, drawing, reading, poetry, and singing to reinforce treatment goals. The model also involves the nonoffending parent in the treatment process. Deblinger and colleagues found that CBT involving either the young survivor alone or with the child and parent was more effective in reducing PTSD symptoms than a treatment-as-usual community comparison group both at posttreatment and at a 2-year follow-up (Deblinger et al., 1996, 1999). On the basis of these findings, both treatments have been designated as "well-supported and efficacious" (Saunders et al., 2003).

Experiential Mastery Technique

The experiential mastery technique (EMT; Shelby, 1997) is designed to help young children achieve a developmentally appropriate sense of mastery over feared stimuli. Children are first asked to draw pictures of whatever frightens them most (e.g., marauding troops who invade and burn a village). Second, they are encouraged to express their feelings to their drawings (e.g., "I don't like you because you set my house on fire"). Third, the children are instructed to do whatever they wish to the drawings to express a sense of mastery over their fears (e.g., scribbling over, ripping up).

Although EMT is a simple and brief intervention, very young children in particular may benefit from such techniques, which are designed to restore a developmentally appropriate sense of mastery and control over their environment. Developmental psychologists argue that an overestimated sense of control may facilitate the healthy development of young children by helping to buffer against the adverse effects of the many failures and disappointments characteristic of childhood (Bjorkland & Green, 1992). By extension, children who are robbed of a sense of mastery by overwhelming traumatic events may benefit psychologically from developmentally sensitive interventions that seek to restore a previously held, naïve overestimation of their ability to predict and control their worlds.

Shelby (1999) investigated the effectiveness of EMT as a tool for crisis intervention with 56 young trauma survivors following Hurricane Andrew. The children, from 3- to 8-years-old, were randomly assigned to either the EMT treatment plus condition, or treatment as usual in an American Red Cross setting. Specifically, both groups of children completed the standard-issue Red Cross therapeutic coloring book, which was designed to elicit feelings and memories of the storm. Immediately following the completion of the coloring book, children were randomly assigned to receive either manualized EMT or to a no-treatment group that played a board game. Children in the EMT condition reported significantly less fear of the storm on a fear thermometer ($p < .008$). However, parent reports of children's symptoms on the PTSD Reaction Index (Frederick, 1985) revealed no significant differences between groups. The treatment gain reported by the children in the EMT as compared to the treatment-as-usual condition was highly significant at a 3-day follow-up ($p < .0005$).

CBT for Survivors of Single Incident Stressors

The CBT model empirically supported by March, Amaya-Jackson, Murray, and Schulte (1998) is a 14-session, graded exposure model designed for use with child and adolescent survivors of a single-incident disaster. The initial support for the use of this technique was a case study of 14 young people (March et al., 1998). Subsequently, March and colleagues (March, Amaya-Jackson, Foa, & Treadwell, 1999) treated 17 distressed school students (with 14 completing); of these, 12 were PTSD negative at post-treatment and at a 6-month follow-up. Treatment consisted of assessment, psychoeducation, muscle relaxation, positive self-talk, and coping skills training. Later sessions assist the survivor through retelling his or her story (e.g., a videotape replay technique), narrative exposure, imaginal exposure, in vivo exposure, exposure-based methods to process the worst moment, and training to "boss back" PTSD.

Structured Play Therapy

Structured play reenactment and mastery has also been used to treat traumatized children (Gil, 1996; Shelby, 1997) and to involve adults in hopeful play. Trauma-focused play therapy, as developed by Gil to include elements of psychodynamic and nondirective play, was rated by Saunders et al. (2003) as a "promising and acceptable treatment." A structured play therapy method was used in Merita's refugee camp to help children express their experiences and to obtain a sense of mastery over their fears. The clinicians designated three areas of the refugee camp to represent the three cities from which the refugees had been expelled. Children were encouraged to describe their experiences and to show what happened to their towns through play reenactment in their model "cities." The clinicians carefully monitored the anxiety level of each child to ensure that the children remained within a therapeutic working range of arousal. Following the children's demonstrations, the therapists encouraged the children to return to their destroyed "homes" and change the damaged "cities." As some of the children began to discuss rebuilding their "towns," the therapists rallied enthusiasm. By the end of the day, the entire refugee camp, including adults, was participating in the "rebuilding" of the model cities. One therapist joked that CNN should report, "Three Kosovar cities were rebuilt today without anyone ever leaving the camp in Albania."

Avoidance

As children retell or replay traumatic events in safe conditions, they can potentially reduce their avoidance of trauma-related behaviors and activities associated with the traumatic event (e.g., in Merita's case, fear of talking about the war). Posttraumatic therapy techniques designed to reduce avoidance aim to teach victims that trauma-related stimuli can be recalled without overwhelming anxiety and fear (Foa & Rothbaum, 1998). While using these methods, it is critical that therapists monitor children's distress levels (e.g., clinical observation, self-reported fear thermometers) to ensure that the children remain within tolerable anxiety levels. Otherwise, replaying traumatic events in the session might reinforce the child's fear that the traumatic event is too disturbing to be remembered. Some children have such extreme avoidance symptoms that they cannot comfortably participate in play or discussion of the traumatic event. For these children, nondirective play therapy is recommended, at least until their capacity to tolerate and manage intense emotions increases.

Prolonged Exposure

In Prolonged Exposure (Foa & Rothbaum, 1998), an empirically validated treatment for adult trauma (Foa, Rothbaum, Riggs, & Murdock, 1991), victims both retell the details of the traumatic event over several sessions and engage in desensitization of the avoided stimuli. The first component of treatment entails repeated exposure in which clients engage in detailed retelling of the traumatic event. In the second component, clients rank–order their fears, from least to most. They then complete weekly homework assignments to engage in two or three of the least feared or avoided activities. After clients successfully engage in least feared activities, they are asked to engage in the more feared items on the list.

CBT techniques that target avoidance symptoms can be made more child friendly by drawing a life-sized person on butcher paper who will be the "focus" of treatment. The person is aptly named; for example, "Frightened Fred." Fred describes his feared activities, writes or draws each fear on an index card, and then ranks the cards from least to most feared. In addition to some of the client's actual fears, some comical items should be named that do not mimic the child's fears. For example, the young survivor might tell the therapist that Fred is frightened of trauma-related stimuli. The therapist then adds comical items to Fred's fear list, such as the fear of his own big toe, baby dolls, or french fries. The therapist and the child can engage in laughter-ridden demonstrations of Fred encountering french fries fearfully or looking down at his toe and becoming distressed. The therapist and child teach Fred coping skills before taking Fred on field trips to engage in his feared activities. When the child reports minimal fear during the session, the therapist might then accompany or train the parent to accompany the child during in vivo exposure homework assignments without Fred.

Arousal

Soothing Sessions

Traumatized children often need help to calm themselves. Parents can help reduce children's arousal symptoms by providing "soothing sessions" (Shelby, 2000) several times each day. Rocking, singing, simply saying "shhhh," holding infants on their sides or stomachs, and giving young children something to suck are all useful methods to comfort young survivors. In addition, therapeutic massage (Field, Seligman, Scafidi, & Schanberg, 1996) has also been found to reduce arousal in traumatized children and infants. Field et al. (1996) randomly assigned 60 elementary-school-age survivors of Hurricane Andrew to a massage therapy or video control condition. Children receiving massage reported less anxiety and depression, evidenced lower physiological signs of distress, and were observed to be more relaxed than the children in the control group.

Cognitive–Behavioral Techniques

Flooding techniques paired with relaxation were found to be effective in a quasi-experimental analysis of 8 traumatized youth with a mean age of 11 years (Saigh & Fairbank, 1995). Similarly, Self-Instruction (Meichenbaum & Goodman, 1971) has been widely used with modifications for children. This technique was used with Merita to help her return to Kosova when the war ended. She first identified her physical sensations, emotions, and self-talk in response to the thought of returning to Kosova. Merita reported sensing tightness in her throat, feeling afraid, and saying to herself, "terrible things are going to happen." The social worker made this technique more child friendly by constructing an imaginary village from cardboard to represent Merita's hometown. The social worker helped Merita practice deep breathing and positive self-statements, such as "I am scared, but I will get through this," as they walked through the imaginary village. Initially, the therapist reminded Merita to both breathe deeply and verbalize the positive statements aloud. Ultimately, the child engaged in silent self-talk. A neighbor was trained to assist Merita in vivo as she practiced her new skills on her return to Kosova.

Dissociation or Extreme Avoidance

For those who experience significant dissociation or pronounced avoidance, exposure-based techniques are not recommended (Bryant & Harvey, 2000; Putnam, 1997). Anecdotally, many therapists who have encouraged survivors with marked dissociation or extreme avoidance to retell the traumatic event find that the survivors often decompensate, dissociate, or withdraw from treatment. The emerging bioneurophysiological theories of PTSD (Flannery, 2001; Rothschild, 2000; Spiegel, 1997) suggest that some survivors may have undergone chemical and structural changes that hinder them from organizing and accessing memories through regular mechanisms. In light of this, it is recommended that treatment for those who have marked dissociative tendencies or extreme avoidance may benefit more from reminders of safety, a focus on coping, or a positive therapeutic relationship (e.g., child-centered play therapy; Landreth, 1991) than from exposure-based techniques (Putnam, 1997).

Loss of Social Competence and Faith in Others

Some traumatized children, particularly those who have been chronically abused, may be affected as much by their difficulty developing and maintaining trusting relationships as by traditional PTSD symptoms (Gil, 1996; Herman, 1992). For them, the traumatic event may teach that people cannot be trusted (Janoff-Bulman, 1992). Both nondirective and directive play designed to enhance the therapeutic relationship has the potential to restore children's stolen sense of self-direction and trust in others. In fact, Putnam (1997) noted that "therapy with maltreated individuals is always concerned with trust and never moves very far from this basic issue" (p. 281).

Traumatic Grief

Traumatic grief, unlike ordinary bereavement, exists when the experience of a traumatic death significantly interferes with normal grief processes (Cohen, Mannarino, & Greenberg, 2002; Pynoos, 1992). Interventions targeting traumatic grief reactions are designed to reduce distress reactions associated with the traumatic nature of the death that intrude into normative grief processes and to promote positive accommodation to the loss. Recent manualized treatments provide clinicians with evidence-based tools with which to intervene with grieving children (Cohen et al., 2001; Layne, Saltzman, & Pynoos, 2003; Saltzman, Layne, Steinberg, & Pynoos, in press).

Goenjian et al. (1997) manualized a brief, time-limited intervention for children that specifically addressed grief following an earthquake in Armenia. Their model included the following: (a) reconstructing trauma narrative, normalizing posttraumatic stress reactions, and addressing maladaptations; (b) identifying and coping with traumatic reminders; (c) coping with stress in a proactive manner and social support; (d) developing bereavement skills (e.g., by holding a nontraumatic mental image of the deceased person and by learning how to tolerate reactivity to reminders of loss); and (e) identifying missed developmental opportunities, developing goals in compromised areas of functioning, and enhancing prosocial efforts.

This model was elaborated on in a pre–posttreatment open trial treatment evaluation study conducted with war-exposed Bosnian adolescents by Layne and colleagues (2001). The authors studied 55 Bosnian adolescents, age 15- to 19-years-old, who participated in a school-based trauma–grief-focused group treatment program. The treatment protocol was based on five therapeutic foci, including traumatic experiences, reminders of trauma and loss, bereavement and the interplay of trauma and grief, posttraumatic adversities, and developmental progression. Participation in trauma–grief-focused group psychotherapy was associated with significant reductions in posttraumatic stress, depression, and grief symptoms between pre- and post-treatment.

Some losses are so horrendous that directive techniques seem woefully inadequate without a parallel focus on the supportive, therapeutic relationship. In these situations, perhaps *remaining with* rather than *doing something with* the survivor is among the most important interventions. As nondirective play therapists have long professed, bearing witness may be a powerful intervention in its own right. As a poignant example, Mrs. Barani, a woman from Merita's village, grieved the deaths of all five of her children, including a newborn. Mrs. Barani was seen wandering aimlessly through the camp, repetitively voicing an unspeakable and unanswerable plea: "How can all of my children be dead?" In the early days following her tragedy, there were no answers to comfort her and no interventions that could change her feelings about her children's deaths. During this phase, the therapist's role was to *listen* as one human being fully sharing the pain of another. Mrs. Barani's children were not resurrected, but her tragic story was spoken, heard, and deeply felt. It is interesting that Mrs. Barani insisted that one of the authors (Janine Shelby) had been present during her flight from Kosava to Albania. "You were there when we crossed over the border, weren't you? I would know your eyes anywhere." The survivor insisted, "You were there watching on the worst night of my life." To experience this devastating loss alone, bereft of a supportive witness, may have been so agonizing that inserting the psychologist into her recollection made the experience somehow more tolerable. Eventually, this woman assumed parental responsibilities for Merita and the two returned to Kosova to rebuild something of the lives they had once lived. Years later, word came from Kosova that the two were doing well, had located several family members, and were pleased with the birth of Mrs. Barani's daughter, whom they nicknamed "NATO." Grasping hope for these once-unimaginable futures is part of what posttraumatic interventions seek to promote. Indeed, whether directive or nondirective, part of the therapist's role in helping survivors through their grief is to hold fast to hope for a future that survivors often do not initially see.

REPLICATION AND TRANSPORTABILITY

In recent years, the distinction between *efficacy* and *effectiveness* studies has been made in discussions of the transportability of treatment (Hibbs, 1998). Efficacy studies demonstrate that the benefits from a fairly standardized treatment are due to the treatment rather than to chance or other factors. These studies are generally conducted in laboratory settings under highly controlled conditions. In these circumstances, the participants may not represent typical clients, those administering the treatment may not represent typical therapists, and the laboratory setting may not be similar to the usual clinical setting. As a result, some studies with demonstrated *efficacy* may not be *effective* in common clinical settings. Although we strived to select techniques for PPT with both efficacy and effectiveness, some techniques within the framework have not yet been shown to be transportable to common clinical settings. As the previously described Kilpatrick and colleagues study (1982) illuminates, exposure-based treatments with demonstrated efficacy might not be effective for some trauma survivors who may find the very idea of the treatment extremely aversive. As research clarifies the clinical differences among survivors of various types of trauma (e.g., sexual abuse vs. physical abuse vs. motor vehicle accidents), more light will be shed on which distinct treatment techniques are indicated for children who have survived particular kinds of trauma (La Greca, Silverman, Vernberg, & Roberts, 2002).

In summary, this preliminary framework is a first-phase tool to assist therapists match the child's symptoms to therapeutic interventions across multiple and diverse settings, such as clinics, disaster sites, schools, and hospitals.

RECOMMENDATIONS FOR OUTCOME EVALUATION

Outcome assessment is an important issue that cannot be adequately dealt with in this chapter. As Layne and associates (in press) have observed, comprehensive assessment of the effects of trauma must include a full range of variables, including markers of risk for trauma exposure, etiological factors, intervening variables (especially vulnerability and protective processes), and a broad spectrum of positive and negative outcome variables, preferably adopting longitudinal designs, to clearly depict the manner in which the surrounding ecology influences children's lives following traumatic events.

When assessing the effects of trauma, multiple factors should be considered: (a) the purpose of the assessment (i.e., what are the referring questions, and for what purposes will the results be used?); (b) practical–logistical and material issues (e.g., time constraints; ability to attend repeated assessment sessions; availability of testing materials); (c) careful consideration of ways in which outcome data might be detrimental to victims (e.g., risk for misinterpretation by caregivers; in forensic settings, the likelihood that treatment gains might be used to downplay the magnitude of children's mental suffering); (d) the degree to which formal assessment procedures are appropriate for survivors (e.g., many survivors have pressing material needs and limited resources in the acute aftermath of trauma; the presence of physiological hyperarousal or avoidance symptoms; the local culture's prohibitions on the direct assessment of undesirable traits such as depression, family discord, or sexual abuse); and (e) difficulties associated with oft-observed discrepancies between adult and child reports of children's posttraumatic experiences (e.g., disagreement between parent–teacher–child reports of the child's exposure to traumatic experiences, posttraumatic distress reactions, and psychosocial functioning in school, peer relationships, and family relationship domains); and (f) monitoring ongoing response to treatment through children's self-report, adult observational reports, and direct clinical observation.

CONCLUSION

It is unfortunate to note that advances in theory and methods for assessing child and adolescent trauma victims often lag 5 to 10 years behind similar advances made with adult populations. This poses a particular challenge for child and adolescent theoreticians and clinicians, who must either extrapolate downward from adult methods, taking pains to make such adaptations developmentally relevant; or rely on ingenuity, practical experience, cultural wisdom, and at times sheer luck to create effective and innovative approaches.

In light of these circumstances, any chapter that presumes to offer cutting edge recommendations relating to methods for intervening with traumatized children must do so with the caveat that such recommendations are based on a markedly incomplete and evolving knowledge base (see Saunders et al., 2003). By integrating a variety of treatment techniques from both directive and nondirective approaches, the PPT framework allows clinicians to blend a variety of empirically supported, symptom–problem-focused intervention strategies to provide the best treatment possible under a broad array of treatment settings.

It is our earnest hope that the PPT framework described in this chapter constitutes an effective response to the heartfelt and perplexing question, "How can I help these children?", posed by mental health workers in countless places around the world. More than is perhaps the case in any other branch of mental health program development, it falls to us as trauma treatment developers to humbly acknowledge that our most valuable teachers are our clients themselves: children, like Merita, who entrust to us their songs, their histories, their feelings, and their hopes. With these words, we remember *their* eyes.

REFERENCES

Amaya-Jackson, L., & March, J. S. (1995). Posttraumatic stress disorder. In J. S. March (Ed.), *Anxiety disorders in children and adolescents* (pp. 276–299). New York: Guilford Press.

American Psychiatric Association. (2000). *Diagnostic and statistical manual of mental disorders* (4th ed.). Washington, DC: Author.

Axline, V. M. (1947). *Play therapy*. New York: Ballantine Books.

Bjorkland, D. F., & Green, B. L. (1992). The adaptive nature of cognitive immaturity. *American Psychologist, 47*, 46–54.

Bonner, B. L, Walker, C. E., & Berliner, L. (2003). *Children with sexual behavior problems: Assessment and treatment—Final report.* [On-Line]. Retrieved from http://w3.ouhsc.edu/ccan/page10.html

Bratton, S., & Ray, D. (2000). What the research shows about play therapy. *International Journal of Play Therapy, 9*, 47–88.

Bryant, R. A., & Harvey, A. G. (2000). *Acute stress disorder: A handbook of theory, assessment, and treatment.* Washington, DC: American Psychological Association.

Cohen, J. A., & Mannarino, A. P. (1993). A treatment model for sexually abused preschoolers. *Journal of Interpersonal Violence, 8*, 115–131.

Cohen, J. A., & Mannarino, A. P. (1996). A treatment outcome study for sexually abused preschool children: Initial findings. *Journal of the American Academy of Child & Adolescent Psychiatry, 35*, 42–50.

Cohen, J. A., & Mannarino, A. P. (1997). A treatment study for sexually abused preschool children: Outcome during a one-year follow up. *Journal of the American Academy of Child & Adolescent Psychiatry, 36*, 1228–1235.

Cohen, J. A., & Mannarino, A. P. (1998). Interventions for sexually abused children: Initial treatment outcome findings. *Child Maltreatment, 3*, 17–26.

Cohen, J. A., Mannarino, A. P., & Greenberg, T. (2002). Childhood traumatic grief: Concepts and controversies. *Trauma, Violence & Abuse, 3*, 307–327.

Cohen, J. A., Mannarino, A. P, Berliner, L., & Deblinger, E. (2000). Trauma-focused cognitive–behavior therapy: An empirical update. *Journal of Interpersonal Violence, 15*, 1203–1223.

Cohen J. A., Greenberg, T., Padlo, S., Shipley, C., Mannarino, A. P., & Deblinger, E. (2001). *Cognitive–behavioral therapy for childhood traumatic grief.* Unpublished treatment manual, Drexel University College of Medicine, Pittsburgh, PA.

Deblinger, E., Lippmann, J., & Steer, R. (1996). Sexually abused children suffering posttraumatic stress symptoms: Initial treatment outcome findings. *Child Maltreatment, 1*, 310–321.

Deblinger, E., McLeer, S. V., & Henry, D. (1990). Cognitive–behavioral treatment for sexually abused children suffering posttraumatic stress: Preliminary findings. *Journal of the American Academy of Child & Adolescent Psychiatry, 29*, 747–752.

Deblinger, E., Stauffer, L. B., & Steer, R. A. (2001). Comparative efficacies of supportive and cognitive–behavioral group therapies for young children who have been sexually abused and their nonoffending mothers. *Child Maltreatment, 6*, 332–343.

Deblinger, E., Steer, R. A., & Lippmann, J. (1999). Two-year follow-up study of cognitive–behavioral therapy for sexually abused children suffering posttraumatic stress symptoms. *Child Abuse & Neglect, 23*, 1371–1378.

Field, T., Seligman, S., Scafidi, F., & Schanberg, S. (1996). Alleviating posttraumatic stress in children following Hurricane Andrew. *Journal of Applied Developmental Psychology, 17*, 37–50.

Flannery, R. B. (2001). *Posttraumatic stress disorder: The victim's guide to healing and recovery.* New York: Crossroad Publishing.

Foa, E. B., & Rothbaum, B. O. (1998). *Treating the trauma of rape: Cognitive–behavioral therapy for PTSD.* New York: Guilford Press.

Foa, E. B., Rothbaum, B. O., Riggs, D., & Murdock, T. (1991). Treatment of posttraumatic stress disorder in rape victims: A comparison between cognitive–behavioral procedures and counseling. *Journal of Consulting and Clinical Psychology, 59*, 715–723.

Fonagy, P. (1998). Prevention, the appropriate target of infant psychotherapy. *Infant Mental Health Journal, 19*, 124–150.

Frederick, C. J. (1985). Children traumatized by catastrophic situations. In R. S. Seth & R. S. Pynoos (Eds.), *Post-traumatic stress disorder in children* (pp. 71–99). Washington, DC: American Psychiatric Press.

Gil, E. (1996). *Treating abused adolescents.* New York: Guilford Press.

Greenwald, R. (1994). Applying eye movement desensitization and reprocessing (EMDR) to the treatment of traumatized children: Five case studies. *Anxiety Disorders Practice Journal, 1*, 83–97.

Goenjian, A. K., Karayan, I., Pynoos, R. S., Minassian, D., Najarian, L. M., Steinberg, A. M., et al. (1997). Outcome of psychotherapy among early adolescents after trauma. *American Journal of Psychiatry, 154*, 536–542.

Guerney, L. (1983). Introduction to filial therapy: Training parents as therapists. In P. A. Keller & L. G. Tirr (Eds.), *Innovations in clinical practice: A source book* (Vol. 2, pp. 26–39). Sarasota, FL: Professional Resource Exchange.

Guerney, L. (2001). Child-centered play therapy. *International Journal of Play Therapy, 10*, 13–32.

Herman, J. (1992). *Trauma and recovery: The aftermath of violence—From domestic abuse to political terror.* New York: Basic Books.

Hibbs, E. D. (1998). Improving methodologies for the treatment of child and adolescent disorders: Introduction. *Journal of Abnormal Child Psychology, 26*, 1–6.

Horowitz, M. J. (1976). *Stress response syndromes.* New York: Jason Aronson.

James, B. (1989). *Treating traumatized children: New insights and creative interventions.* New York: Free Press.

Janoff-Bulman, R. (1992). *Shattered assumptions: Toward a new psychology of trauma.* New York: Free Press.

Kendall, P. C. (1994). Treating anxiety disorders in children: Results of a randomized clinical trial. *Journal of Consulting and Clinical Psychology, 62*, 100–110.

Kilpatrick, D. G., Veronen, L. J., & Resick, P. A. (1982). Psychological sequelae to rape: Assessment and treatment strategies. In D. M. Dolays & R. L. Meredith (Eds.), *Behavioral medicine: Assessment and treatment strategies* (pp. 473–479). New York: Plenum Press.

La Greca, A. M., Silverman, W. K., Vernberg, E. M., & Roberts, M. C. (2002). Children and disasters: Future directions for research and public policy. In A. M. La Greca, W. K. Silverman, E. M. Vernberg, & M. C. Roberts (Eds.), *Helping children cope with disasters and terrorism* (pp. 405–423). Washington, DC: American Psychological Association.

Landreth, G. L. (1991). *Play therapy: The art of the relationship.* Muncie, IN: Accelerated Development.

Layne, C. M., Pynoos, R. S., Saltzman, W. R., Arslanagic, B., Black, M., Savjak, N., et al. (2001). Trauma–grief-focused group psychotherapy: School-based postwar intervention with traumatized Bosnian adolescents. *Group Dynamics: Theory, Research, and Practice, 5,* 277–290.

Layne, C. M., Warren, J. S., Saltzman, W. S., Fulton, J., Steinberg, A., & Pynoos, R. S. (in press). Contextual influences on posttraumatic adjustment: Retraumatization and the roles of revictimization, posttraumatic adversities, and distressing reminders. In L. A. Schein, H. I. Spitz, G. M. Burlingame, & P. R. Muskin (Eds.), *Group approaches for the psychological effects of terrorist disasters.* New York: Haworth Press.

Layne, C. M., Saltzman, W. R., & Pynoos, R. S. (2003). *Trauma–grief-focused group psychotherapy manual for adolescents.* Unpublished treatment manual, University of California, Los Angeles.

LeBlanc, M., & Ritchie, M. (1999). Predictors of play therapy outcomes. *International Journal of Play Therapy, 8*(2), 19–34.

March, J., Amaya-Jackson, L., Foa, E. B., & Treadwell, K. (1999). *Trauma-focused coping treatment of pediatric posttraumatic stress disorder after single-incident trauma.* Unpublished protocol.

March, J., Amaya-Jackson, L., Murray, M., & Schulte, A. (1998). Cognitive–behavioral psychotherapy for children and adolescents with posttraumatic stress disorder following a single-incident stressor. *Journal of the American Academy of Child and Adolescent Psychiatry, 37,* 585–593.

Meichenbaum, D. H., & Goodman, J. (1971). Training impulsive children to talk to themselves: A means of developing self-control. *Journal of Abnormal Psychology, 77,* 115–126.

Nader, K. (2001). Treatment methods for childhood trauma. In J. P. Wilson & M. J. Friedman (Eds.), *Treating psychological trauma and PTSD* (pp. 278–334). New York: Guilford Press.

Puffer, M. K., Greenwald, R., & Elrod, D. E. (1998). A single session EMDR study with twenty traumatized children and adolescents. *Traumatology, 3*(2). Retrieved from http://www.fsu.edu/~trauma/v3i2art6.html

Putnam, F. W. (1997). *Dissociation in children and adolescents: A developmental perspective.* New York: Guilford Press.

Pynoos, R. S. (1992). Grief and trauma in children & adolescents. *Bereavement Care, 11,* 2–10.

Pynoos, R. S., & Eth, S. (1986). Witness to violence: The child interview. *Journal of the American Academy of Child Psychiatry, 25,* 306–319.

Ray, D., Bratton, S., Rhine, T., & Jones, L. (2001). The effectiveness of play therapy: Responding to the critics. *The International Journal of Play Therapy*, *10*, 85–108.

Rothschild, B. (2000). *The body remembers: The psychophysiology of trauma and trauma treatment*. New York: Norton.

Saigh, P. A. (1989). The use of an in vitro flooding package in treatment of traumatized adolescents. *Journal of Developmental and Behavioral Pediatrics*, *10*, 17–21.

Saigh, P. A., & Fairbank, J. A. (1995, November). The effects of therapeutic flooding on the memories of child–adolescent PTSD patients. In J. D. Bremner (Chair), *Memory and cognition in PTSD*. Symposium conducted at the annual meeting of the International Society of Traumatic Stress Studies, Boston, MA.

Saigh, P. A., Mroueh, A., Zimmerman, B., & Fairbank, J. A. (1995). Self-efficacy expectations among traumatized adolescents. *Behavior Research and Therapy*, *33*, 701–705.

Saltzman, W. R., Layne, C. M., Steinberg, A. M., & Pynoos, R. S. (in press). Trauma–grief-focused group psychotherapy with adolescents. In L. A. Schein, H. I. Spitz, G. M. Burlingame, & P. R. Muskin (Eds.), *Group approaches for the psychological effects of terrorist disasters*. New York: Haworth Press.

Saunders, B. E., Berliner, L., & Hanson, R. F. (Eds.). (2003, January 15). *Child physical and sexual abuse: Guidelines for treatment*. Charleston, SC: National Crime Victims Research and Treatment Center.

Saywitz, K., Mannarino, A. P., Berliner, L., & Cohen, J. A. (2000). Treatment for sexually abused children and adolescents. *American Psychologist*, *55*, 1040–1049.

Schaefer, C. (2001). Prescriptive play therapy. *International Journal of Play Therapy*, *10*, 57–73.

Shapiro, F. (1989). Efficacy of the eye movement desensitization procedure in the treatment of traumatic memories. *Journal of Traumatic Stress*, *2*, 199–223.

Shelby, J. S. (1997). Rubble, disruption, and tears: Helping young survivors of natural disaster. In H. Kaduson, D. Cangelosi, & C. Schaefer (Eds.), *The playing cure*. Northvale, NJ: Jason Aronson.

Shelby, J. S. (1999, November). *Crisis intervention with children following Hurricane Andrew*. Poster session presented at the annual meeting of the International Society for Traumatic Stress Studies, Miami, FL.

Shelby, J. S. (2000). Brief therapy with traumatized children: A developmental perspective. In H. Kaduson & C. Schaefer (Eds.), *Short-term play interventions* (pp. 69–104). New York: Guilford Press.

Shen, Y. J. (2002). Short-term group play therapy with Chinese earthquake victims: Effects on anxiety, depression, and adjustment. *International Journal of Play Therapy*, *10*, 43–63.

Silverman, W. K., & La Greca, A. M. (2002). Children experiencing disasters: Definitions, reactions, and predictors of outcomes. In A. M. La Greca, W. K. Silverman, E. M. Vernberg, & M. C. Roberts (Eds.), *Helping children cope with disasters and terrorism* (pp. 11–33). Washington, DC: American Psychological Association.

Spiegel, D. (1997). Trauma, dissociation, and memory. In R. Yehuda & A. C. McFarlane (Eds.), *Annals of the New York Academy of Sciences: Vol. 821. Psychobiology of posttraumatic stress disorder* (pp. 225–237). New York: New York Academy of Sciences.

VanFleet, R. (1994). *Strengthening parent-child relationships through play.* Sarasota, FL: Professional Resource Press.

Vernberg, E. M., & Johnston, C. (2001). Developmental considerations in the use of cognitive therapy for PTSD. *Journal of Cognitive Psychotherapy, 15,* 223–237.

Vernberg, E. M. (2002). Intervention approaches following disasters. In A. M. La Greca, W. K. Silverman, E. M. Vernberg, & M. C. Roberts (Eds.), *Helping children cope with disasters and terrorism* (pp. 55–72). Washington, DC: American Psychological Association.

Weisz, J. R, Weiss, B., Alicke, M. D., & Klotz, M. L. (1987). Effectiveness of psychotherapy with children and adolescents: A meta-analysis for clinicians. *Journal of Consulting and Clinical Psychology, 55,* 542–549.

6

GUIDED FANTASY PLAY
FOR CHRONICALLY ILL CHILDREN:
A CRITICAL REVIEW

MELISSA R. JOHNSON AND JENNIFER L. KREIMER

THEORETICAL BASIS AND OBJECTIVES

Guided fantasy play and the closely related phenomenon of guided imagery stems from roots in both analytic and cognitive studies in children. The analytic tradition, particularly that of C. J. Jung, has presented much clinical material (J. Singer, 1973), but little empirical data, on the use of fantasy and imagination to access the unconscious for creative problem solving. The more cognitively-oriented traditions have viewed the capacity to form internal "pretend" representations as a skill (J. L. Singer, 1973) that can be encouraged and actually taught, and have sought to encourage both child and adult patients to manipulate them in playful and potentially constructive ways. Singer maintains that the tendency to generate and manipulate imagery is a personality trait that has some constitutional and temperamental roots but is also influenced by environmental (particularly parental) encouragement and modeling, and that children with this trait may cope better with boredom, isolation, anger, and other stressors.

This chapter discusses the theoretical and empirical basis for the use of guided fantasy play with chronically ill children, reviews relevant empirical research, and provides creative clinical examples of the use of this technique. It also suggests ways to evaluate the effectiveness of this intervention in clinical settings.

There is a small but growing empirical literature on the use of these capacities in psychotherapy (Johnson, 1999). This literature is difficult to interpret because there is no standardized terminology to describe the process of assisting, supporting, and guiding children to use their capacity for fantasy and imagination in playful ways as a means of coping better with the issues that confront them. Terms such as guided fantasy, guided imagery, relaxation–imagery, self-induced mental imagery, hypnosis, and storytelling have all been used to describe similar or closely related activities (Langley, 1999). D. G. Singer (1993a, 1993b, 1994) offers a taxonomy of imagery-based psychotherapeutic techniques, as well as clinical examples of their use in therapy for children with a range of difficulties, including trauma, anxiety, and depression. Several of the categories she describes, particularly guided affective imagery, mind play, and relaxation therapy, fit closely with the models under discussion. Zeltzer and LeBaron (1986) offered straightforward definitions that may be useful in discussions of the application of these activities therapeutically. They define imagery as "pictures created in one's mind" and fantasies as "the stories created by the self-manipulation of these images in the internal theater of the mind" (p. 195).

In addition to definitional issues, doing research on the use of a process such as guided fantasy play, where so many of the phenomena of interest are internal, is challenging. Dean (1990) analyzed the developmental aspects of the formation of mental images from both Piagetian and cognitive psychological perspectives and concluded that "the study of mental imagery development is still in its infancy (or perhaps preoperational) stage" (p. 141). However, her review supports the position that the formation and manipulation of internal images is an important cognitive capacity that begins early in childhood and develops in elaboration and complexity over time.

An ingenious approach to demonstrating the power and potential clinical significance of playful fantasy activity in children was published by Lee and Olness (1996). The researchers asked children to think about pleasurable but quiet activities first, and then imagine themselves doing an exciting physical activity such as a sport. Consistent changes, assessed using paired t tests and repeated measures analysis of variance, were obtained in pulse rate, skin temperature, and electrodermal activity at the $p < .001$ level; the authors concluded that "deliberate changing of mental imagery by children results in immediate autonomic changes" (p. 327).

RELEVANCE TO CHILDREN
WITH CHRONIC ILLNESS

Children with chronic illness have a range of psychological needs that may be met by guided fantasy play and related techniques (Johnson, Whitt, & Martin, 1987). Several different goals and purposes have been described in the literature, all of which relate to increasing coping and decreasing stress.

The first of these goals are relaxation and anxiety reduction. Chronically ill children face a number of sources of ongoing stress, including the direct and indirect effects of their illness, uncertainty about outcome, and frequent exposure to novel, often unpleasant events. Therefore, techniques that reduce anxiety and achieve improved levels of physical as well as psychological relaxation are important.

The second goal, pain reduction, includes assistance in handling both chronic disease-related pain and acute pain from the disease or from necessary diagnostic or therapeutic interventions. A number of approaches containing a significant imagery component have been described, generally including a significant hypnotic element (Olness & Kohen, 1996).

The third goal is the opportunity to engage in play activities that substitute for the release and pleasure found in the gross-motor physical activities that may be restricted because of the child's illness. An additional goal is to have an impact on the disease process itself, through imagery that relates to physiologic and immune functions or through relaxation activities that affect physiology.

Finally, guided fantasy has been used to help children deal with the many issues of loss that they face, including actual and potential loss of function, independence, and lifespan. LeBaron and Zeltzer (1985) emphasized the need to weave the guided fantasy component of the intervention seamlessly into the overall relationship that the therapist builds with the patient.

Several authors have suggested additional reasons why guided fantasy play may be of particular importance for children with chronic illness. Johnson et al. (1987) proposed that the limitations on mobility resulting from many chronic illnesses may increase the importance of play activities that are purely cognitive as opposed to physical in nature. Zeltzer and LeBaron (1986) speculated that because so much of the process of experiencing a disease and treatment is not under a child's control, she or he wishes to exert control whenever possible, such as in fantasies.

Much of the published clinical and empirical material on guided fantasy and guided imagery that has been applied to chronically ill children includes interventions that either contain many components of hypnosis or are clearly labeled as hypnosis. Numerous clinicians believe that the labels given to these techniques are not as important as their components, and researchers also tend to be inclusive as they work to define and differentiate the techniques they are using. Kohen (1997) offers an example of how he presents his hypnotic interventions to asthmatic children in a way that illustrates this issue beautifully.

> You know, some call this imagery or visualization, some call it hypnosis, some call it imagination or daydreaming, some call it biofeedback, and I don't really care what you call it, because what is really important is that you learn how to do it pretty fast and that you can use it to help your asthma. (p. 178)

Zeltzer and LeBaron (1982) grappled with this issue in their research comparing hypnotic and nonhypnotic techniques for work with pediatric cancer patients; their "hypnosis" intervention fit closely with the guided fantasy intervention model, whereas for the "non-hypnosis" group, they used deep breathing, distractions, and practice sessions, but "the use of imagery or fantasy was strictly avoided" (p. 1033). Olness and Kohen (1996) offer a wealth of clinical guidelines and examples for the use of hypnotherapy with children, with much emphasis on the chronically ill child; many of their examples contain a major component of guided fantasy. Their suggestions for hypnotic inductions include visual, auditory, and multisensory imagery, such as favorite places, animals, flower gardens, activities, cloud gazing, television or movie fantasies, the flying blanket, and imaginary movements such as bicycling, sports, and playground activities. Although their induction strategies contain other elements, it is clear that the guided fantasy component is often key to achieving the deeply relaxed, highly focused state of consciousness that they seek in hypnotic work and is in itself a part of the therapeutic intervention. These illustrations support the inclusion of many hypnotic approaches described in the literature in this discussion of empirically supported guided fantasy play in therapy; they also point out the futility of trying to create rigid boundaries between hypnotic and nonhypnotic techniques when discussing guided fantasy.

KEY TREATMENT INGREDIENTS

At the most basic level, the key treatment ingredients for guided fantasy with children are playfulness and the child's own imaginative capacity. Play is a central part of a child's life. The natural ability of most children to use their imaginations and join in make-believe play makes guided imagery and fantasy particularly well suited for them. With the guidance and participation of adults—professionals, trained parents, or assistants—this natural skill and tendency can be used to facilitate relaxation and distraction, which may lead to pain reduction and other benefits (Marin-Hertz, Thurber, & Patterson, 2000). Marin-Hertz and colleagues also note that guided imagery takes slightly different forms with younger children than with adolescents because younger children may be more interactive; however, the results can be equally effective. They advocate its use with children as young as toddler-age.

The degree of structure and the relative contributions of the child and therapist can be quite variable. Ott (1996) emphasizes the importance of the child's input and the linking of the imagery with the specific developmental challenges faced by the individual child. LeBaron and Zeltzer (1985) present clinical material demonstrating that for some children and adolescents, the therapist's respect for the child's autonomy and avoidance of approaches that appear to be mind control are very important. Belsky and Khanna (1994) actively incorporate control by the child into their imagery; for example, the child is given the option of driving a car, boat, plane, or train, and is invited to be the expert on the function of all the buttons in the traffic control room. Research has also shown that prepared or standardized material can be used effectively, at least for anxiety reduction, when administered by parents (Johnson et al., 1987).

Because of the flexibility of this technique and how readily it can be incorporated into other modalities and everyday play activities, there are no rigid guidelines outlining the number of sessions needed. Most research studies used a limited and often semi-standardized number of sessions, although a few explored the utility of one or two sessions in crisis situations. Children were frequently taught guided fantasy and encouraged to use it in other settings. The authors had positive experiences using the technique for fifteen minutes awaiting the start of a radiology study and as an integral part of long-term therapy that also used other, multiple modalities.

One of the advantages of guided fantasy is that minimal resources are required for its use. A reasonably quiet setting and enough time to connect with the child are all that are needed. Although a quiet room and comfortable chair, bed, or cushion on the floor are helpful, it is possible to incorporate it into conversations taking place in fairly busy waiting areas in medical settings, even bustling intensive care units. The therapist's primary tool is his or her voice, along with an understanding of the child's interests, concerns, developmental level, and personality. If the therapist elects to use existing guided visualizations and fantasies that have been published (deMille, 1967/1981; Garth, 1991, 1992, 1994) or to record sessions and provide the child with tapes, then a few inexpensive items would be needed (e.g., paperback books, a tape recorder).

An important question is who can appropriately assist children with guided fantasy. Depending on the goals and approaches used in various situations, the amount of training and preparation varies. As Zeltzer and LeBaron (1982) point out, "formal training with hypnosis per se is not necessary to tell a frightened child an exciting story or to help a child remember the details of a favorite TV program" (p. 1035). On the other hand, ongoing support of chronically traumatized children clearly falls into the realm of advanced clinical practice; in addition, it should be noted that guided imagery to help children handle procedures can place large demands on the clinician's time, particularly if the clinician helps the child practice beforehand and also supports the child through procedures (Chen, Joseph, & Zeltzer, 2000).

A number of the studies evaluated the effectiveness of guided fantasy as part of hypnotherapy. Clearly, it is not recommended that parents or untrained professionals engage in efforts to induce trances in children or to otherwise actively attempt hypnosis. However, the therapeutic elements of guided fantasy alone seem to have sufficient value for the technique to be used by parents if they are given materials to use and appropriate instruction and support (e.g., coaching, modeling, and practice with the experimenter; Johnson et al., 1987; Pederson, 1994). Kohen and Wynne (1997) included parents in the imagery exercises they used to facilitate relaxation in their asthmatic patients. They also provided teaching about their techniques to allow the parents to eventually become the facilitators of their children's self-hypnosis activities.

In addition, there are a number of clinical references to the successful use of guided imagery and fantasy in medical settings by pediatric nurses and child life specialists (Rusy & Weisman, 2000; Kachoyeanos & Friedhoff, 1993), the professionals most widely available to children in medical settings.

REVIEW OF OUTCOME STUDIES

Empirical studies that use guided fantasy or imagery as a key intervention component with chronically ill children are examined in this chapter. Studies that use guided fantasy or imagery in a primarily hypnosis-based context are also briefly reviewed.

Little research is available on guided fantasy play alone as the major treatment intervention. A study that does meet this criterion focused on the applicability of a relatively standardized guided fantasy play technique. The authors compared the effectiveness of this technique with a structured play attention–control condition in children with and without chronic illness (Johnson et al., 1987). There were 13 children in four cells, for a total of 56 subjects. The intervention was the daily use of a book (deMille, 1967/1981) that provided a series of playful, pleasant fantasy sequences. These were read aloud to the children by their parents, who were able to choose the optimal time of day for the reading and had flexibility in selecting the most appealing sequences for their children. Anxiety ratings were obtained before and after the two-week intervention; both the assessments and the training for parents in the use of the techniques took place in the home. The chronically ill children in the treatment condition experienced declines significant at the $p < .01$ level in their anxiety ratings to levels similar to the healthy children; those in the attention–control condition maintained their previously elevated anxiety level, as assessed using analysis of covariance. Parents and children reported finding the intervention enjoyable and practical as a home-based intervention. Since the publication of this study, several other books providing a range of appealing and intriguing guided fantasy materials have become available, thus increasing the choices available to therapists and parents (Garth, 1991, 1992, 1994).

Another study using guided imagery along with other cognitive–behavioral techniques demonstrated significant pain reduction in 13 children with chronic juvenile rheumatoid arthritis (Walco, Varni, & Ilowite, 1992). The authors noted that the difference between pre- and postintervention pain scores, assessed by t tests, was significant at the $p < .0001$ level and also clinically significant with an effect size of 1.77 and posttreatment pain levels near zero. Although this study did not use a control group, it did provide 6- and 12-month follow-up data demonstrating continued statistically and clinically significant pain decrement and improved activity. The treatment package consisted of eight sessions, during which children were taught progressive relaxation, meditative breathing, and guided imagery. The children were encouraged to imagine themselves having an enjoyable and pain-free experience in scenes they selected. The therapist encouraged experimentation with other scenes to maintain a high level of interest. In addition, the children were taught to use images that were metaphorically related to the pain experience and could be altered to increase comfort.

Labbé and Ward (1990) conducted a small study that targeted muscle contraction headache pain with a combination of biofeedback and guided imagery. A multiple-baseline across subjects design was used with two adolescent patients who had histories of severe headaches for several years. Both patients achieved dramatic reduction in reported headaches (significance tests not reported, but baseline average headache scores declined from 0.40 and 0.30 in the two subjects to zero for the last several weeks of treatment), which was maintained at 6-month and 1-year follow-up. However, the study did not differentiate the effects of the biofeedback from that of the guided imagery.

Migraine headache pain was the target of a study that used multiple interventions, including a number of cognitive–behavioral coping strategies and imagery (McGrath et al., 1992). A total of 87 adolescent migraine patients were assigned to a placebo control group, a clinic treatment program, or a group that received the same information and instructions as the treatment group but through a self-administered book–tape program supported by weekly phone and mail contacts. The two treatment groups were equally effective in reducing headache symptoms (using repeated measures analysis of variance, a group-by-time effect was found significant at the $p < .001$ level), with the self-administered package being less costly. The guided imagery component was only one part of a lengthy package. However, the success of this research in demonstrating the usefulness of self-administration of such interventions makes this study of interest to those using related therapies in chronically ill children.

Several other studies have demonstrated the potential for guided imagery and related techniques to impact illness processes directly, even in relatively high-risk groups. Castes et al. (1999) worked with 35 children with asthma from a small Venezuelan island who also had the added immune burden of intestinal parasites. In addition to conventional treatment, the experimental group received a psychosocial package that included education, self-esteem workshops, and a relaxation-guided imagery component. This component included the instruction to create mental images directly related to the disease processes seen in asthma, which was supervised daily. Results, examined with repeated measures ANOVA, included significant decreases in the experimental group in asthmatic episodes (at the $p < .01$ level) and inhaler use (at the $p < .003$ level), as well as improvements in several measures of immune system function.

Another research effort used similar techniques in a different population to directly impact an infectious disease process. This study examined the utility of guided mental imagery and stress management techniques to reduce symptoms of upper respiratory infections in children with a history of frequent (10 or more a year) infections. These children had also been found to have higher than usual numbers of stressful life events and psychological vulnerability (Hewson-Bower & Drummond, 2001). The authors hypothesized that because stress appears to increase susceptibility to colds and flu (perhaps by decreasing concentrations of secretory immunoglobulin A), the use of stress management and relaxation techniques might affect the immune system and thus reduce occurrence of illness. The children in the study received individual and group interventions in both general cognitive–behavioral stress management, problem-solving techniques, and a relaxation procedure using vivid visualization of an enjoyable journey to a favorite place. They were also asked to visualize increasing immune system proteins and germ-fighting activity. After four weeks of training, clinically and statistically significant (using analysis of variance with planned contrasts, $p < 0.01$) decrements in symptomatic days were achieved, along with an increase in the presence of secretory immunoglobulin A in the two treatment groups ($p < .05$). The design of the study made it difficult to separate the effectiveness of the guided imagery from that of other stress management interventions. However, the authors specified some characteristics of their intervention that were consistent with similar efforts, including a focus on making the image of the child's preferred scenes as rich, vivid, and detailed as possible. Another interesting feature of this intervention was the use of a relaxation–suggestion practice audiotape at home between sessions that emphasized both breathing and vivid imagery.

Respiratory function was also affected in a small pilot study of self-hypnosis in children with cystic fibrosis (Belsky & Khanna, 1994). These authors conceptualized the hypnosis as "an intervention that introduces metaphors designed to strengthen the child's metaphor, belief, or construct of him- or herself and the illness" (p. 283). They used a structured intervention that included a car and driver metaphor that contained vivid images related to better lung function and to mastering a task. The standardized induction was taped, and the five children in the experimental group were encouraged to listen regularly at home. The experimental group demonstrated improvement in several measures of psychological well-being, as well as in lung function. Specifically, using Mann Whitney U tests on change scores, improvements favoring the experimental group were found for Locus of Control and Health Locus of Control at the $p = .001$ level, Self-Concept at the $p = .003$ level, and Trait Anxiety at the $p < .004$ level.

Guided imagery played a major role in a study exploring ways to help children with leukemia cope with painful procedures (Kazak et al., 1996). This study randomized 92 children to either a pharmacologic-treatment only group or a combined group that received pharmacologic and psychological intervention. The psychological intervention consisted of training parents to work with their children in an individualized way during the procedures. Most children age 6 and older used guided imagery similar to those used in other studies, including visiting special places, such as an enchanted forest. Counting and breathing techniques were also used. Extensive observational and questionnaire data were collected. Both mothers and nurses reported a reduction in procedural distress in the combined intervention group, found to be significant at the $p < .03$ and $p < .05$ levels, respectively, using repeated measure analyses of covariance. It was clear to these authors that the parents themselves benefited from the opportunity to be helpful to their children, which is consistent with the observations of other authors using parent-administered guided imagery approaches.

Pediatric cancer patients also benefited from a hypnotic intervention that decreased anticipatory nausea and vomiting in children receiving chemotherapy and decreased their need for antiemetic medication (Jacknow, Tschann, Link, & Boyce, 1994). The 10 children in the treatment group were taught self-hypnosis techniques that encouraged the active use of their imaginations, with involvement of all the senses to develop fantasies about special experiences and adventures. Although the intervention was labeled hypnosis, progressive relaxation was used only for the older children. The younger group started with the suggestion to think about being in a favorite place or doing a favorite activity, and then were offered further suggestions about using the imagination when the child was "observed to be in a relaxed state" (p. 260). Thus the boundary between hypnosis and nonhypnotic guided fantasy–imagery was even more blurred in this particular study. The children were encouraged to practice twice a day. Follow-up of the children indicated that most practiced once every three days, but it also revealed that many children spontaneously used the techniques to help themselves deal with other unpleasant aspects of their treatment, such as procedure pain. This study was further strengthened by the use of random assignment to either the self-hypnosis group or to an attention–control condition offering an equivalent amount of supportive time with the same therapist. Results were based on one-tailed paired t tests with p values less than .05 accepted as significant and confirmed with nonparametric Wilcoxon tests, which yielded the same significance levels.

Another study used more classic self-hypnosis to help children with leukemia deal with the pain of bone marrow aspirations (Liossi & Hatira, 1999). The authors compared this modality with nonhypnotic cognitive–behavioral therapy and with standard therapy (lidocaine injection only) with 10 children in each group. The hypnotic intervention included progressive relaxation, positive visual imagery, and specific hypnotic suggestions around various forms of analgesia and anesthesia. The cognitive–behavioral intervention included relaxation, breathing, and cognitive restructuring, with the avoidance of any imagery techniques. Both psychological approaches were effective in reducing the amount of pain that the children reported, but the hypnotized group had less anxiety and observed distress (using Wilcoxon Matched-Pairs Signed-Rank Tests with p values ranging from .005 to .012). The authors noted that this effect was achieved even though the treatments occurred several days before the actual procedure, for methodological reasons; they suggested that the techniques would have been even more effective if the therapist could be present with the child during the bone marrow aspiration. This is supported by an older study that used a technique labeled as hypnotic by the author (Kuttner, 1988) and reported on in children ages 3 to 6. In this study, the therapist told the child his or her favorite story during the actual painful procedure while interweaving information about the procedure and suggestions about coping into the story and telling the story in a lively and flexible way. Kuttner gave such a broad definition of hypnosis in children that it appears that any child who is fascinated and absorbed in an interaction would be labeled as hypnotized. This study compared this approach with nine children to a distraction group with eight children and to a control group of eight children who received standard treatment. It was necessary to covary for the very different initial baseline distress scores. Results from the analysis of covariance, significant at the $p < .05$ level, indicated that the "favorite story" resulted in the most marked decrease in distress behaviors in the shortest time period.

REPLICABILITY AND TRANSPORTABILITY

Because this intervention is so positive and builds on children's natural tendencies, it can be applied in many settings in which chronically ill children are seen, as well as to children with other clinical issues.

The research just presented includes children in inpatient settings, in outpatient clinics during visits for the care of their illness, in outpatient visits specifically set up for the purposes of psychological support, and in the home. The authors have also used the technique with children receiving preparation prior to surgery, in postoperative care, and in support groups for bereaved children. The dental clinic is another promising setting for the application of guided imagery for both relaxation, fear reduction, and pain control. Another group in the medical setting with distinct but related issues includes children who have experienced major physical trauma, such as from automobile crashes or serious sports injuries. The authors have clinically found guided fantasy helpful in dealing with the dual issues often facing these children: the direct posttraumatic symptoms they experience and the need to cope with pain, procedures, and body alterations.

Outside the medical setting, several other groups of children may derive particular benefit from guided fantasy, although there is minimal empirical support for its use with these populations. Several experienced therapists have noted that children and adolescents who have experienced sexual abuse or other forms of inflicted trauma may derive great benefit from carefully planned and structured guided fantasies that allow them to safely recall their trauma and gain mastery over the overwhelming emotions connected with it (Gil, 1996). James (1989) used a variety of guided fantasy techniques focusing on mastery of trauma, including abuse and both natural and man-made disasters. An older but classic reference (Oaklander, 1988) offered a wonderfully creative range of guided fantasy techniques in a variety of clinical applications. Although these authors do not present controlled empirical data, their techniques have stood the test of time and offer multiple ideas and clinical examples of techniques similar to those that have been demonstrated to be effective in research.

RECOMMENDATIONS FOR OUTCOME EVALUATION
IN CLINICAL PRACTICE

The literature offers little guidance for clinicians seeking to evaluate the effectiveness of their use of these techniques in practice. It is important to maintain an open mind as one assesses outcome, because in the authors' experience children's responses can be deceptive. It is often clear from multiple sources of information when these approaches are effective. When the child is engaged and focused on the guided fantasy, their bodies visibly relax, their breathing becomes more regular, and their facial expressions appear focused, whether or not their eyes are closed. They tolerate discomfort more easily and report less pain or fear. When asked to provide their own fantasy details, they are able to do so readily. Children frequently ask for more stories or more "pretend time." Other children spontaneously inform the therapist of the new fantasy they developed on their own between sessions. Parents report that their children have returned to the techniques they have learned with the therapist between visits. Medical staff may mention observing increased cooperation or improved mood in the child. In such situations, the clinician can be assured that the child is deriving benefit. However, the authors have had experiences, particularly with young adolescents, when they noted relatively muted responses to guided fantasy sessions and concluded that the child had not derived much benefit, only to discover that the child described his or her positive memory of the experience several years later. Therefore, it is recommended that clinicians begin with careful observation of the child's mood, interest, participation, and stress behaviors. Clearly, if the child demonstrates ongoing distress or lack of interest, or appears unable to engage and focus on the interaction, another approach may be more beneficial. However, it is important not to give up too quickly, because the approach may represent a new experience for the child and adequate time to learn such a novel behavior may be important. In addition, there are children who are unable to use the techniques under times of greatest stress or pain but still benefit from experiences with guided fantasy to improve their ability to cope with the less drastic, but still significant, daily stresses of hospitalization or chronic illness. Ultimately, the therapist's most important tool in clinical practice is sensitive observation in the context of a positive and trusting relationship.

CLINICAL APPLICATIONS

No review of this topic would be complete without detailed examples of some creative clinical techniques used by the researchers. In addition, those interested in adopting this approach can benefit from the ideas offered by those who have published clinical techniques that they have found valuable.

It is apparent from reviewing outcome data that the actual techniques used vary on a number of dimensions. A key dimension is the person who actually guides the fantasy. As mentioned earlier, some approaches use only professional therapeutic staff, including psychologists, physicians, child life specialists, and nurses; others train or support parents to provide the imagery and guidance for the child. In general, programs that conceptualize their intervention as containing all the elements of clinical hypnosis tend to be administered by medical or mental health professionals; programs that offer more general imagery and fantasy play activities use a wider range of providers, including parents.

Another important dimension is the degree of individualization versus standardization. The availability of well-developed guided fantasy resources, such as those by deMille (1967/1981) and Garth (1991, 1992, 1994), is a benefit in terms of providing options in situations where the parent or other nonprofessional is the most appropriate "therapist" for the child. In addition, they provide a valuable resource for therapists who are looking for creative options to share with children who do not require them to reinvent material each time they work with a child. On the other hand, the opportunity to weave a child's own experience, interests, and preferences into an individualized fantasy experience can be a powerful and especially effective resource for children facing particularly challenging situations. As demonstrated above, the literature provides support for both approaches.

With these thoughts in mind, the following are examples of imagery techniques used in published studies with children that emphasize the range of creative ideas that have been found to be helpful and consider the goal for which each was undertaken.

In a preschool asthma education program, a script was used to help children relax and to counteract the tightening of the respiratory muscles that are often involved in an asthmatic attack. The script involved a story about a magical fairy named "Twinkle" who is invited inside the children's bodies to bring feelings of health. With her magic wand, she can touch tight muscles, causing them to loosen and relax (Kohen & Wynne, 1997).

The second goal mentioned for the use of imagery with chronically ill children is that of pain reduction. When using hypnotic techniques with children and adolescents with cancer during bone marrow aspirations and lumbar punctures, Zeltzer and LeBaron (1982) found that imagery techniques needed to be adapted to the child and situation to help the child stay involved in the imaging process. They state that "the method used to help children become involved in their imaginations was to weave exciting stories filled with humor, adventure, surprises, and magic, with each story designed spontaneously based on knowledge of the child, her or his family, and the child's level of anxiety" (p. 1035). They share the example of a child who loved bubble gum using the image of riding in a bubble gum car. The child also enjoyed jokes, so they told jokes while riding in the car. This car was equipped with "magic air conditioning" that "anesthetized" his hip during bone marrow aspirations. In another study, Zeltzer and LeBaron (1986) offered examples of children using images of eating favorite foods, walking with a pet, or watching favorite television programs.

Walco et al. (1992) present specifics of some imagery they used for pain management in a study of juvenile rheumatoid arthritis. The children were asked to "imagine themselves in a scene previously experienced as pain free . . . then to invoke images that represented a metaphor for the sensory pain experience and then to alter the metaphor and thus the perception of pain" (p. 1076). For example, if the pain was experienced as a hot sensation, the child may incorporate the image of a blowtorch on that part of the body and actively work in the imaging to extinguish it. They also used the idea of children assigning color to their painful sites, then visualizing those areas or colors shrinking and vanishing. They had older children visualize a pain switch and use it to turn down or block painful messages from transmitting. This teaching technique includes providing some education about the functioning of the nervous system and incorporating this knowledge into the images.

Other examples of the use of fantasies to cope with pain include imaging the painful part of the body as being detached and possibly floating out by itself. The child can imagine blowing the pain out of his or her body into a cloud or bubble and allowing it to float away or just leaving it all far behind by escaping on a magic carpet ride to a desirable place (Solomon, Walco, & Robinson, 1998).

Other fantasy and imagery techniques have been used in helping children cope with issues of loss, including their own impending deaths. In their work with pediatric cancer patients, LeBaron and Zeltzer (1985) used a relatively unstructured approach in which they encouraged the children to develop and focus on significant personal images. "Children were usually invited simply to let pictures come into their minds. As the child's imagination developed scenes and stories, these images portrayed important themes which had not previously been exposed in purely verbal communication" (p. 252). They found that some children were able to detach from life as they previously experienced it, and that as this process occurred, the significance of previously important images changed. They noted that though familiar topics were often of greatest interest and utility, at other times exotic fantasies that took them far away from their current reality provided freedom and tranquility. One example was of a remote beach scene with images of marine life and the child imaging him- or herself as a seagull, free of the constraints of life, settling gently into a nest high above this tranquil place (LeBaron & Zeltzer, 1985).

For some seriously ill children, fantasy images were used that allowed the patient to explore what they still wished to do or achieve to bring meaning to their lives. The authors note that

> adolescents who are so helpless that they require assistance to move from their beds or to go to the toilet can explore future plans and realize goals in a symbolic form, thereby experiencing some of the independence and creativity which has been denied them during their medical treatment. For children who have withdrawn into apathy and helplessness, the expression of wishes and desires and the exercise of independence through imagery may, by themselves, create new excitement and interest. Such fantasies, as they develop, can result in a renewal of the child's energy

and motivation to live longer or at least more fully, rather than passively giving way to death. (LeBaron & Zeltzer, 1985, p. 257)

These authors cited a case in which the communication opened up by the guided fantasies allowed one adolescent patient to express a longing for a motorcycle, a desire that was shared with his father, along with appropriate support and interpretation. This allowed the boy and his father to share a joyful activity together and strengthen their relationship shortly before the boy's death.

For other children, images involving themes of transition and metaphors of death were found to decrease anxiety. Some children imagined themselves with family in a new and reassuring way. Religious imagery also brought comfort to some children, even if they had rejected religious concepts on a cognitive level. This imagery was found to appear spontaneously as an integral part of the fantasies shared by some children (LeBaron & Zeltzer, 1985).

CONCLUSION

In conclusion, guided fantasy and imagery is a powerful technique in its own right and forms an important part of other valuable modalities. Hypnotherapy, relationship-based talk therapies, cognitive–behavioral therapies, and play therapy approaches all can benefit from the incorporation of guided fantasy. The natural tendency of children to use fantasy in their daily lives and the strong motivation that chronically ill children often possess to feel better and enjoy life, make it particularly appropriate for this population. Its flexibility and applicability by professionals and parents working with these children, as demonstrated by a small but significant body of research, recommend it for consideration by those offering psychosocial support and treatment to children affected by chronic illness.

REFERENCES

Belsky, J., & Khanna, P. (1994). The effects of self-hypnosis for children with cystic fibrosis: A pilot study. *American Journal of Clinical Hypnosis, 36*(4), 282–292.

Castes, M., Hagel, I., Palenque, M., Canclones, P., Corao, A., & Lynch, N. R. (1999). Immunological changes associated with clinical improvement of asthmatic children subjected to psychosocial intervention. *Brain, Behavior, and Immunity, 13*, 1–13.

Chen, E., Joseph, M. H., & Zeltzer, L. K. (2000). Behavioral and cognitive interventions in the treatment of pain in children. *Acute Pain in Children, 47*(3), 513–525.

Dean, A. L. (1990). The development of mental imagery: A comparison of Piagetian and cognitive psychological perspectives. *Annals of Child Development, 7,* 105–144.

deMille, R. (1981). *Put your mother on the ceiling: Children's imagination games.* Santa Barbara, CA: Ross-Erikson. (Original work published 1967)

Garth, M. (1991). *Starbright: Meditations for children.* New York: HarperCollins.

Garth, M. (1992). *Moonbeam: A book of meditations for children.* Blackburn, Australia: HarperCollins.

Garth, M. (1994). *Sunshine: More meditations for children.* North Blackburn, Australia: HarperCollins.

Gil, E. (1996). *Treating abused adolescents.* New York: Guilford Press.

Hewson-Bower, B., & Drummond, P. D. (2001). Psychological treatment for recurrent symptoms of colds and flu in children. *Journal of Psychosomatic Research, 51,* 369–377.

Jacknow, D. S., Tschann, J. M., Link, M. P., & Boyce, W. T. (1994). Hypnosis in the prevention of chemotherapy-related nausea and vomiting in children: A prospective study. *Developmental and Behavioral Pediatrics, 15*(4), 258–264.

James, B. (1989). *Treating traumatized children: New insights and creative interventions.* Lexington, MA: Lexington Books.

Johnson, M. R. (1999). Imagery—A tool in child psychotherapy. In C. E. Schaefer (Ed.), *Innovative psychotherapy techniques in child and adolescent therapy* (2nd ed., pp. 77–107.). New York: Wiley.

Johnson, M. R., Whitt, J. K, & Martin, B. (1987). The effect of fantasy facilitation on anxiety in chronically ill and healthy children. *Journal of Pediatric Psychology, 12*(2), 273–283.

Kachoyeanos, M. K., & Friedhoff, M. (1993). Cognitive and behavioral strategies to reduce children's pain. *Maternal and Child Nursing, 18,* 14–19.

Kazak, A. E., Penati, B., Boyer, B. A., Himelstein, B., Brophy, P., Waibel, M. K., et al. (1996). A randomized controlled prospective outcome study of a psychological and pharmacological intervention protocol for procedural distress in pediatric leukemia. *Journal of Pediatric Psychology, 21*(5), 615–631.

Kohen, D. P. (1997). Teaching children with asthma to help themselves with relaxation/mental imagery. In W. J. Matthews & J. H. Edgette (Eds.), *Current thinking and research in brief therapy: Solutions, strategies, narratives* (Vol. 1, pp. 169–191). New York: Brunner/Mazel.

Kohen, D. P., & Wynne, E. (1997). Applying hypnosis in a preschool family asthma education program: Uses of storytelling, imagery, and relaxation. *American Journal of Clinical Hypnosis, 39*(3), 169–181.

Kuttner, L. (1988). Favorite stories: A hypnotic pain reduction technique for children in acute pain. *American Journal of Clinical Hypnosis, 30*(4), 289–295.

Labbé, E. E., & Ward, C. H. (1990). Electromyographic biofeedback with mental imagery and home practice in the treatment of children with muscle-contraction headache. *Developmental and Behavioral Pediatrics, 11*(2), 65–68.

Langley, P. (1999). Guided imagery: A review of effectiveness in the care of children. *Pediatric Nursing, 11*(3), 18–21.

LeBaron, S., & Zeltzer, L. K. (1985). The role of imagery in the treatment of dying children and adolescents. *Developmental and Behavioral Pediatrics, 6*(5), 252–258.

Lee, L. H., & Olness, K. N. (1996). Effects of self-induced mental imagery on autonomic reactivity in children. *Developmental and Behavioral Pediatrics, 17*(5), 323–327.

Liossi, C., & Hatira, P. (1999). Clinical hypnosis versus cognitive–behavioral training for pain management with pediatric cancer patients undergoing bone marrow aspirations. *International Journal of Clinical Hypnosis, 47*(2), 104–116.

Marin-Hertz, S. P., Thurber, C. A., & Patterson, D. R. (2000). Psychological principles of burn wound pain in children II: Treatment applications. *Journal of Burn Care & Rehabilitation, 21*(5), 458–472.

McGrath, P. J., Humphreys, P., Keene, D., Goodman, J. T., Lascelles, M. A., Cunningham, S. J., et al. (1992). The efficacy and efficiency of a self-administered treatment for adolescent migraine. *Pain, 49,* 321–324.

Oaklander, V. (1988). *Windows to our children.* Highland, NY: The Center for Gestalt Development.

Olness, K., & Kohen, D. P. (1996). *Hypnosis and hypnotherapy with children* (3rd ed.). New York: Guilford Press.

Ott, M. J. (1996). Imagine the possibilities! Guided imagery with toddlers and preschoolers. *Pediatric Nursing, 122*(1), 34–38.

Pederson, C. (1994). Ways to feel comfortable: Teaching aids to promote children's comfort. *Issues in Comprehensive Pediatric Nursing, 17,* 37–46.

Rusy, L. M., & Weisman, S. J. (2000). Complementary therapies for acute pediatric pain management. *Pediatric Clinics of North America: Acute Pain in Children, 47*(3), 589–599.

Singer, D. G. (1993a). Fantasy and visualization. In C.E. Schaefer (Ed.), *The therapeutic power of play* (pp. 189–221). Northvale, NJ: Jason Aronson.

Singer, D. G. (1993b). *Playing for their lives: Helping troubled children through play therapy.* New York: Free Press.

Singer, D. G. (1994). Imagery techniques in play therapy with children. In J. Hellendoorn, R. van der Kooij, & B. Sutton-Smith (Eds.), *Play and intervention* (pp. 85–97). Albany: State University of New York Press.

Singer, J. (1973). *Boundaries of the soul.* Garden City, NY: Anchor Press.

Singer, J. L. (1973). *The child's world of make-believe: Experimental studies of imaginative play.* New York: Academic Press.

Soloman, R., Walco, G., & Robinson, R. M. (1998). Pediatric pain management: Program description and preliminary evaluation results of a professional course. *Developmental and Behavioral Pediatrics, 19*(3), 193–195.

Walco, G. A., Varni, J. W., & Ilowite, N. T. (1992). Cognitive–behavioral pain management in children with juvenile rheumatoid arthritis. *Pediatrics, 89*(6), 1075–1079.

Zeltzer, L., & LeBaron, S. (1982). Hypnosis and nonhypnotic techniques for reduction of pain and anxiety during painful procedures in children and adolescents with cancer. *The Journal of Pediatrics, 101*(6), 1032–1035.

Zeltzer, L. K., & LeBaron, S. (1986). Fantasy in children and adolescents with chronic illness. *Developmental and Behavioral Pediatrics, 7*(3), 195–198.

7

A REVIEW OF PLAY INTERVENTIONS FOR HOSPITALIZED CHILDREN

WILLIAM A. RAE AND JEREMY R. SULLIVAN

According to recent statistics, approximately 6.4 million children are hospitalized in the United States each year. About 80% of these children are either under 1 year old (4.5 million) or over 14 years old (.5 million). Of the remaining children and young adolescents hospitalized, the mean length of stay in the hospital is between 3.2 to 4.5 days (Healthcare Cost and Utilization Project, 2000). Hospital-based therapeutic play programs are designed for those children between 3- and 13-years-old who could benefit from a psychosocial play intervention. However, the use of therapeutic play interventions would be considered appropriate for only a portion of children in this age range. The limited applicability of these interventions occurs for several reasons. Because of the recent decline in the length of hospital stays, many children remain hospitalized for only short periods of time (e.g., 1 day). Of the children who are hospitalized for a longer period of time (e.g., more than 3 days), many are extremely ill and may not benefit from a play therapy intervention. The remaining children represent a heterogeneous group with varying acute or chronic illnesses and are undergoing a range of medical procedures. Although therapeutic play programs are applicable to only a select group of hospitalized children each year, such programs have great potential to enhance the psychological well-being of these children and their families.

Therapeutic play programs with hospitalized children involve two specific elements. In the first element, the child must process his or her feelings related to the experience of hospitalization. Children often have a sense of disruption and intrusion about being hospitalized. Children are placed in an environment that, unlike home, can be interpreted as unfamiliar, intrusive, and hostile. For example, many adults working in a hospital setting profess to be helpful to the child, but young children in particular do not always understand how these adults can put them though painful, intrusive medical procedures that do not appear to be "helpful." The second element involved in hospital-based play programs is the opportunity for the child to process feelings concerning the physical illness itself (e.g., anxiety about the course of the disease or recovery from injury, distress about loss of functioning, worry about separation from parents). In an era of managed care, a child typically is not hospitalized unless the child is seriously ill or requires significant medical assessment and intervention. A pediatric hospitalization represents an attempt to deal with a serious medical condition that could not be adequately dealt with on an outpatient basis.

It is important to note that not all children manifest pathological symptoms of emotional or psychological distress as a result of their hospital or illness experience. Most normal children do not experience significant psychopathology as the result of pediatric hospitalization (Wallander & Varni, 1992). In fact, some children may benefit from hospitalization in that the child is able to master internal states (e.g., anxiety) and learn that they can cope with stressful separation from parents and invasive, painful medical procedures (e.g., Rae, 1981; Siegel & Conte, 2001).

A therapeutic play program represents an attempt to prepare a child psychologically for the untoward effects of hospitalization and illness. Therapeutic play is one of several methods designed to help a child cope with a potentially harmful pediatric hospitalization. Other methods of preparation for hospitalized children may include providing information, increasing familiarity with the hospital environment, preparing parents, providing emotional support to the family, developing trust, and providing coping strategies (Elkins & Roberts, 1983; Hunsberger, Love, & Byrne, 1984). These traditional preparation programs for children undergoing elective surgery or hospitalization are common in pediatric hospital settings and have been shown to be effective at ameliorating untoward emotional reactions (Harbeck-Weber & McKee, 1995; Siegel & Conte, 2001). In contrast, therapeutic play interventions are especially useful with children who may be unable or unwilling to express attitudes, fears, or feelings verbally and directly (Ellinwood & Raskin, 1993), and who may not be able to benefit from a traditional preparation program.

The purpose of this chapter is to describe a therapeutic play program for hospitalized children. First, the theoretical basis and objectives of the intervention is described, followed by a discussion of the key treatment ingredients of the intervention. Next, the empirical basis for the effectiveness of the program is illustrated, and the replicability of the program in other settings is considered. Finally, issues regarding the evaluation of this kind of program are outlined. Although the terms "play therapy" and "therapeutic play program" are used interchangeably throughout this chapter, we recognize that the focused, short-term therapeutic play program described here is very different from long-term play therapy.

THEORETICAL BASIS AND OBJECTIVES

Hospitalization in a medical–surgical setting is believed to be a stressful and potentially harmful experience for children and families. Although a clear-cut causal relationship between pediatric hospitalization and maladaptive psychological functioning has not been empirically established, numerous authors have cogently argued that pediatric hospitalization can adversely impact a child's psychological development (Golden, 1983; Harbeck-Weber & McKee, 1995; Rae, 1981, 1982; Siegel & Conte, 2001). Common sources of distress for the hospitalized child include the unfamiliar and potentially threatening nature of the hospital environment; separation from parents; pain and discomfort associated with medical procedures; fear of bodily harm and death; loss of autonomy; and parental distress and anxiety (Golden, 1983; Petrillo & Sanger, 1980; Poster, 1983; Wishon & Brown, 1991).

Harbeck-Weber and McKee (1995) reviewed the research on preparation for hospitalization as well as the effects of chronic illness in children, and identified five factors that can influence the outcome of preparation. First, previous negative experiences with hospitalization are associated with the need for more extensive preparation. Second, the child's coping style also affects the outcome. For example, a child who copes by avoiding information about his or her illness may do worse when confronted with medical information than a child who actively seeks out medical information. Third, the timing of the intervention with the child may affect the outcome. Fourth, a parent may influence the child's coping because the parent's own emotional status can influence the child's emotional status. That is, parents who are very anxious about the child's illness or hospitalization can communicate their distress to their child, which in turn can cause the child to feel anxious. Finally, the developmental level of the child affects how the child conceptualizes his or her hospitalization or illness. Interventions congruent with the developmental skills of the child have been more effective than approaches that have not taken development into account. In general, younger children tend to be at greater risk for developing behavioral and emotional problems during and after hospitalization (Siegel & Conte, 2001).

A distinction can be made between medical preparation and medical play. Medical play can occur either before or after a procedure and provides information to the child while also allowing the child to process and express his or her feelings with regard to the procedure or event. In contrast, medical preparation occurs before the medical procedure and primarily serves an information-giving function (Bolig, Yolton, & Nissen, 1991). McCue (1988) noted that medical play sessions always involve medical themes or play with medical equipment. Preparation interventions, on the other hand, primarily attempt to educate the child and may or may not involve actual play. Inherent in this distinction is the difference in the role of the therapist. Preparation interventions that include a play component entail the therapist providing information to the child while also facilitating play with certain medically themed objects and thus may be seen as therapist-directed. Medical play interventions, with their greater emphasis on emotional expression, give greater control to the child with regard to both the objects that are used during play and the content of the play sessions and place great importance on the therapist–child relationship. Thus, medical play interventions may be seen as more child-directed than preparation interventions, although degrees of adult direction within both types of interventions may vary widely.

Although the distinction between medical play and preparation interventions is useful to make, there also exists some overlap between the two definitions. For example, a medical play intervention could also be considered a preparation intervention if the intervention occurs before the medical procedure, focuses on providing information, focuses on processing and expressing emotions, and allows the child some freedom in determining the direction of therapy. Indeed, this combination of play and preparation appears to be a common version of the hospital-based play intervention. This chapter will focus on medical play, preparation, and unstructured play interventions in which the content and process of the play sessions may be seen as at least somewhat child-directed, as opposed to completely therapist-directed.

Bolig, Fernie, and Klein (1986) theorized that unstructured or child-directed play in the hospital setting provides more opportunity for the child to develop a sense of competence, internal locus of control, and mastery than structured medical play and preparation interventions. Unstructured play allows children to assume different roles (e.g., the medical professional instead of the patient) and determine the outcome of events. More structured interventions are primarily concerned with providing information and reducing anxiety and distress associated with specific illnesses and treatment procedures, thereby giving the child less opportunity for creativity and control in determining the content of sessions.

Medical play interventions can take several forms. McCue (1988) presented four categories of medical play: role rehearsal–role reversal medical play; medical fantasy play; indirect medical play; and medical art. According to McCue's classification, role rehearsal–role reversal play involves the child assuming the role of medical professional and performing medical procedures on dolls or stuffed animals using actual medical equipment. This type of play may be used to prepare a child for an upcoming medical procedure or to help the child process his or her feelings after a medical procedure has been performed. Medical fantasy play also involves medical themes and situations but does not involve the use of actual medical equipment. Children use more common and neutral play materials to engage in fantasy and medical role-play, thereby avoiding the initial anxiety that children may feel toward actual medical equipment. As children become more comfortable during medical fantasy play, they may progress to the use of actual medical equipment during play, thereby engaging in the more direct role rehearsal–role reversal play.

In contrast to role rehearsal–role reversal and fantasy play, indirect medical play does not typically involve fantasy or role-play and may be considered more structured than the other types of medical play. Indirect medical play purports to facilitate familiarization and education with regard to medical procedures and the hospital environment. This type of play may involve puzzles, games, and other activities that have a medical theme. The indirect approach may be especially appropriate when the therapist wishes to provide information and develop a meaningful relationship with children who are severely ill, noncommunicative, anxious, or otherwise unwilling or unable to participate in more active and unstructured play activities. Finally, medical art activities allow children to use creativity and imagination to express their feelings about the hospital setting, their illnesses, and their treatments. These activities should be child-directed and should focus on process rather than on content or outcome.

Medical play therapy is derived from traditional play therapy techniques. Webb (1995) thoughtfully applied Axline's (1969) principles of play therapy to the context of hospital-based interventions. Several important concepts arise from this work. The development of rapport and of the therapeutic relationship is of special significance as the play therapist represents one of the few people within the hospital setting who is not associated with painful or unpleasant medical procedures. Many children, especially the severely or terminally ill, need a safe and confidential setting in which they can express their fears and emotions without having to be concerned about upsetting or worrying their parents. The therapist must be prepared to process the child's emotions with regard to illness and death, which may present a great challenge to the therapist.

Hospital-based play interventions differ in goals and purposes from traditional play therapy interventions. During a short-term hospitalization the child's play is semistructured, whereas in most common forms of play therapy the child's play is unstructured and child-directed. At the same time, play interventions in the hospital setting do allow the child to decide with what to play, but the therapist influences the content of sessions by providing the child with medically related toys and materials. The therapist's verbalizations and behaviors are not scripted and depend on what the child says or does. In this way, the therapist follows the child's lead (Oremland, 1988). In contrast to traditional forms of play therapy, hospital-based play interventions focus primarily on preparation for specific medical procedures or events as well as on helping the child cope with untoward feelings about the hospitalization or illness.

Play is seen as a method by which a child can master his or her environment and cope with the stressful effects of hospitalization. Furthermore, hospital-based play programs are believed to help the child gain a sense of control within a stressful environment. In this stressful context, therapeutic play may serve to give the child a sense of normalcy and familiarity, as play is associated with the normal daily life of the child outside the hospital (Petrillo & Sanger, 1980). General play interventions have been credited with providing the child with a sense of mastery, as he or she can manipulate the process and outcomes of situations through play, thereby changing his or her role from that of passive observer to one of active participant (Cooper & Blitz, 1985). With regard to play interventions within a health care context, supervised play with syringes and other medical equipment may give the child a sense of mastery over the threatening environment and may reduce anxiety and fears associated with medical equipment and procedures (Klinzing & Klinzing, 1987; Petrillo & Sanger, 1980). Further, play activities provide a context in which children can make decisions and feel in control, which, intuitively, would be adaptive for children who may have little control over their illness or over what happens to them in the hospital (Bolig et al., 1986; Klinzing & Klinzing, 1987; Webb, 1995).

Therapeutic play in a medical environment helps the child understand the reasons for her or his hospitalization. The child's capacity to conceptualize the meaning of her or his illness or the hospitalization may be viewed as following a Piagetian developmental progression (Wadsworth, 1984). In the preoperational stage, children tend to understand illness in terms of a sensory phenomenon (e.g., stomachache) or in terms of magical thinking (e.g., "I took the toy and I got sick"). The illness is often seen as the result of human action (e.g., "I ate the sucker"). In the concrete operational stage, children tend to understand illness as being the result of contamination (e.g., germs), which usually is believed to be caused by some kind of direct internal process (e.g., swallowing). In the formal operational stage, children or adolescents view illness in terms of a generalized, relative, or abstract notion of physiological functioning; the phenomena of illness and health are generalized to basic concepts of physical susceptibility or weakness. The child's ability to understand illness and hospitalization has been summarized elsewhere (e.g., Thompson & Gustafson, 1996). It is sufficient to note here that a particular child's understanding and conceptualization of her or his illness will depend on the child's level of development, and will influence how the child feels about the illness, as expressed during play therapy sessions.

KEY TREATMENT INGREDIENTS

Several caveats must be provided prior to implementing a therapeutic play program for hospitalized or physically ill children. First, as with any psychological intervention, the person implementing the program must be competent to work with children, pediatric medical disorders, and play interventions. Second, the clinician should take into account empirically supported factors that could influence the outcome of the play intervention. For example, the clinician should consider the previously described factors important to hospitalization preparation programs (e.g., developmental level of the child, previous hospital experience, coping style, timing of intervention, and inclusion of parents; Harbeck-Weber & McKee, 1995). In addition, the clinician must be intimately familiar with the child's history so the play intervention program can be crafted to meet the specific needs of the child. Individual child risk and resilience factors must be considered when shaping the intervention, including premorbid psychological functioning, coping style, invasiveness of medical procedures, length of hospitalization, degree of disability, seriousness of illness, family support and resources, cognitive functioning, temperament, and motivation. The therapeutic play program should not be dished out to each child "cafeteria style"; rather, the program should be based on each child's unique needs.

The therapeutic play program for hospitalized and physically ill children described in this chapter is modeled after the program described and evaluated by Rae, Worchel, Upchurch, Sanner, and Daniel (1989). It is designed as a time-limited, brief intervention because most children are hospitalized only for short periods of time (i.e., a few days). Under certain circumstances, a child may be hospitalized for an extended period of time (e.g., for a bone marrow transplant). In cases of extended hospitalization, the general elements of the program function in the same way. The program is designed to provide daily intervention during pediatric hospitalization. Although not specifically designed for outpatient treatment, the elements of the program could be easily adapted to the needs of a nonhospitalized child who is experiencing adaptation problems regarding illness or medical interventions. Three key treatment ingredients for a treatment program with hospitalized and physically ill children are described below.

Client-Centered Approach

A slightly modified client-centered, nondirective, humanistic approach is the most basic element of the therapeutic play program for hospitalized children. The basic elements of a client-centered, humanistic play therapy approach are well documented elsewhere (see Landreth & Sweeney, 1997; O'Connor, 2000). The client-centered approach uses three essential elements that include unconditional positive regard, empathic understanding, and congruence of feelings (Ellinwood & Raskin, 1993). Bolig et al. (1986) suggested that this approach provides more opportunity for the child to develop an internal locus of control and a sense of competence or mastery because the child can choose to assume different roles during the play sessions.

Axline (1969) developed the basic principles that are used by most play therapists who use a child-centered approach. The first principle requires that the therapist develop a warm, supportive relationship with the child. The child is unconditionally accepted for who he or she is, without qualification. The therapist's duty is to create a permissive atmosphere within the therapeutic relationship in which the child is free to express his or her feelings. By reflecting feelings back to the child, the therapist helps the child understand his or her feelings and develop insight. Within this philosophy, the therapist only puts limitations on the child necessary to secure the therapy in the real world and to help the child become aware of the social responsibility involved in the relationship with the therapist.

Although these elements are generally consistent with the play therapy program for hospitalized children, Axline (1969) posited two other principles that require a slight modification. First, she stated that because therapy is a gradual process, the therapeutic intervention should not be rushed or hurried. This may not be possible in the therapeutic play program because the therapeutic intervention is time-limited, corresponding to the child's hospitalization. During a brief hospitalization there is not time to allow the child's feelings to unfold gradually. Second, she stated that the child's behaviors or conversation should never be directed because the child has the capacity to solve his or her problems and make appropriate choices. Although we believe this to be the case in most therapy situations, within a therapeutic play program for hospitalized children there is some allowance for the therapist giving direction to the client.

Within this program, the child may be cautiously and carefully invited to talk about his or her illness or hospitalization. In the same way, the child should be invited to play with hospital equipment or toys. Because of the brief time involved in the intervention, this cautious invitation can have the benefit of "priming the pump" for catharsis about the illness or hospitalization. In addition, being mildly directive allows the therapist to talk about the child's coping style, misconceptions, and cognitive distortions. As in all settings, psychologists or therapists working with pediatric patients in the hospital setting must function within the limitations of their place of work; therefore, hospital-based play interventions are necessarily brief and the direction of sessions is shared by therapist and child.

Focus on Mastery and Coping

Within the context of this modified client-centered approach, the therapist helps the child cope with her or his illness and hospitalization by mastering negative emotions. Because of the time-limited nature of the intervention, the therapist gently exposes the child to potentially distressing material during the therapeutic play program. This exposure takes place with the play materials, play activities, and verbal content of the interaction between the therapist and the child. The therapist is very careful to be attuned to the child's emotional status to ensure she or he is not emotionally overwhelmed, as that could be countertherapeutic. The therapist continues to provide unconditional positive regard and empathic understanding within a supportive relationship. As the child experiences negative emotions about the hospitalization or illness, the therapist helps the child process these feelings and provides an atmosphere within which the child's coping strategies can emerge. Within this context, the child can also process feelings concerning separation from family and friends.

The major goal of the therapeutic play intervention is to facilitate coping. Two categories of children's coping have been hypothesized (Miller, Sherman, Combs, & Kruus, 1992). In the first method, coping is conceptualized in terms of specific coping methods (e.g., self-talk, distraction). This micro-level coping is seen as consisting of numerous, distinct coping techniques used by the child. In the second method, coping is conceptualized in terms of global coping methods (e.g., approach-avoidance, defensiveness). This macro-level coping is seen as consisting of a single, global coping approach used by the child. Both methods are probably used simultaneously by children and would be addressed in any therapeutic play program with hospitalized children.

Miller et al. (1992) have extensively reviewed the empirical literature on children coping with medical stressors and have described the relationship between coping and adaptation. First, children tend to adapt better when they prepare for a stressful event and are able to master it. Second, children tend to do better if they seek out threat relevant information and are able to actively cope with the stressor. Third, children who are less emotionally defended and are more open also tend to adapt more positively. Finally, children who use psychological defenses of intellectualization, intellectualization with isolation, or a mixed pattern tend to cope more adaptively with stressors (Miller et al., 1992).

Although it is acknowledged that coping with hospitalization and illness involves a number of divergent components, these results are consistent with the use of a child-centered, mastery focused play therapy approach during hospitalization. Therapeutic play provides a platform for the therapist to gently introduce the child to stressful hospital-based or procedure-based equipment in a nonthreatening, supportive therapeutic environment in which the child can master his or her emotions. The therapeutic relationship provides an atmosphere in which defensiveness is deescalated; as a result, the child is more open to dealing with negative emotions. In addition, during the play intervention the child can be helped to deal with his or her psychological defenses and can be aided in the use of more adaptive cognitive coping strategies. This may require that the therapist confront the child's coping style directly if the child is avoiding important material or information or is using other maladaptive coping strategies.

Mastery and coping are usually achieved by a concurrent combination of therapeutic play techniques and verbal processing (i.e., cognitive–behavioral) techniques. The therapeutic play techniques involve the use of play materials that are selected to facilitate the expression of aggression, fantasies, and fears associated with hospitalization and illness. Often this takes the form of medical or nonmedical play materials. Medical play materials might include medical equipment (e.g., syringe, stethoscope, gauze, bandages) and hospital related representational materials (e.g., doctor puppet, hospital bed, hospital dollhouse). Nonmedical play materials include toys often used in traditional play therapy programs. A variety of toys are helpful, including manipulatives (e.g., clay, drawing materials), family puppets or dolls, dollhouse, vehicles, building materials (e.g., blocks, Legos), and board games. In addition, toys that evoke aggressive play (e.g., dinosaurs, lions) also can be useful. By presenting the child with a variety of play materials, the therapist can maximize the likelihood that the child will find materials appropriate and relevant to the expression of a variety of ideas and feelings. Further, this variety allows the therapist to ease the child into play and discussions specifically related to the hospital and illness, starting with the neutral toys and gradually encouraging play with the medically themed materials.

Parent Support and Involvement

Although not a component of the original study (Rae et al., 1989), parental involvement is seen as crucial to facilitating the child's positive adjustment to hospitalization. LeBlanc and Ritchie (2001) have clearly shown that there is a strong positive relationship between treatment effectiveness of the play intervention and the inclusion of parents in the therapeutic process. Parents can usually help their children emotionally unless they themselves are emotionally stressed by the hospitalization; this may make them psychologically unavailable to their children. Parents may be intimidated by the hospital environment, anxious for their child, financially stressed, and unable to use typical soothing and coping strategies with their child. Parents who support their child can have overall positive effects on the child. Within the therapeutic play program, parents need to understand the meaning of the child's anxiety or distress. The parents must not only be educated about their child's illness and hospitalization, but also must be helped to facilitate appropriate emotional coping. Parental understanding of and involvement with the therapeutic play program with hospitalized children are crucial aspects contributing to the program's success.

REVIEW OF OUTCOME STUDIES

Play therapy has clearly been shown to be an effective overall intervention with children. A plethora of books have been written on the positive therapeutic effects of play (e.g., O'Connor, 2000; O'Connor & Braverman, 1997; Schaefer, 1993; Webb, 1999), but few provide empirical support. In contrast, in a meta-analysis of 42 empirical studies on play interventions, LeBlanc and Ritchie (2001) concluded that the average treatment effect of play therapy was comparable to the treatment effect of non-play interventions (e.g., verbal psychotherapy) with both children and adults. They also concluded that the inclusion of parents in the treatment process seemed to improve the effectiveness of play interventions.

In a review of the effects of play therapy on hospitalized children's distress, Thompson (1985) noted that research on play therapy in hospital settings through the mid-1980s was limited to a few experimental studies. Further, the evidence provided by these studies is limited because of methodological problems (e.g., none of the studies included a condition in which children interacted with an adult in a way other than through therapeutic play). Phillips (1988) later stated that the benefit of play interventions in health care settings was not convincing. He reviewed four areas of play therapy in pediatric settings, including autonomy, mastery, and control; cooperation and communication; coping with anxiety and fear; and learning and information giving. Phillips concluded that with the possible exceptions of reducing anxiety and providing information, the utility of play interventions in child health settings generally has not been supported.

After reviewing the literature on therapeutic play with hospitalized children, we found no methodologically rigorous empirical articles published during the last decade that evaluated medical play programs using the key treatment ingredients discussed above. There are several likely reasons for the paucity of articles in this area. First, children are hospitalized for far shorter periods of time than in decades past. Fifty years ago, it was common for a child to be hospitalized for two or more weeks; however, with the advent of managed care the average length of stay in the hospital is far shorter (Healthcare Cost and Utilization Project, 2000). In fact, many children are hospitalized for only a single day, thus providing fewer opportunities for the children to participate in a therapeutic play program. Second, because most pediatric care is conducted on an outpatient basis, only the most ill or medically involved children are hospitalized. Because of the extent of their incapacity or medical involvement, these children often cannot access a therapeutic play program. Finally, although psychosocial interventions are the duty of all health care professionals in a pediatric inpatient setting (e.g., nurses), there is often little time available to implement such programs. These pragmatic, real world factors may have contributed to the recent lack of interest in conducting empirical evaluations of hospital-based play interventions. Although somewhat dated, the literature reviewed here generally does suggest that hospitalized children can benefit from play therapy interventions.

To determine whether play interventions with hospitalized children are helpful, the literature was reviewed and applied to the criteria for probably efficacious treatments set forth by the American Psychological Association's Task Force on Promotion and Dissemination of Psychological Procedures (1995). One of these criteria specifies that to be efficacious, two studies have to show that the treatment is more effective than a waiting-list control group. It is unfortunate that each study of hospital-based play interventions uses a slightly different treatment approach. At the same time, the literature provides examples of effective play interventions with hospitalized children who are compared with a control group.

In one of the frequently cited studies of play therapy effectiveness, Clatworthy (1981) examined whether a therapeutic play intervention reduced anxiety among hospitalized children. The sample included 114 children between 5 and 12 years of age from two different hospital settings; 55 were randomly assigned to the experimental group, while 59 were assigned to the control group. The intervention consisted of daily, individual therapeutic play sessions that lasted 30 minutes. Play materials included typical toys (e.g., dolls, cars, books, art supplies) as well as hospital equipment; all sessions were conducted by a nurse play therapist. The intervention was described as child-directed, with the therapist providing reflection and interpretation as the child played with materials of his or her choice. Using a pre–post design, anxiety was measured with the Missouri Children's Picture Series (MCPS) at both admission and discharge. On admission, the control and experimental groups scored similarly on the MCPS; at discharge, however, children in the control groups in both hospital settings and across lengths of hospital stay scored higher than children in the experimental groups ($p \le .10$). It is interesting to note that anxiety scores among children in the experimental groups did not decrease following the intervention; rather, scores among children in the control groups increased between admission and discharge. Thus, the group differences in anxiety scores at time of discharge are attributed to increased levels of anxiety among children in the control group; children who received the intervention appeared to maintain their levels of anxiety throughout their hospital stay. The play intervention may not have helped children reduce their anxiety, but it may have helped them to keep their anxiety from increasing.

Rae et al. (1989) conducted an empirical study that attempted to address the limitations of previous research by including random assignment to different treatment conditions. In their investigation, Rae et al. assessed the effects of a therapeutic play intervention on children who were hospitalized for diagnosis and treatment of acute illnesses. Several pre–post measures were used, including the Fear Thermometer, MCPS, Stress Inventory, Zuckerman Adjective Checklist, and Vernon Posthospitalization Behavior Questionnaire. Following the preassessment phase, the 46 participants were randomly assigned to one of four groups or conditions. One group received the therapeutic play intervention, which consisted of nondirective, child-centered play therapy with both medical (e.g., bandages, syringes, stethoscopes) and nonmedical (e.g., dolls, puppets, animals) materials. The research assistant provided verbal support, encouragement, reflection, and interpretation of feelings as the child played with the materials of her or his choosing. The remaining participants were assigned to one of the following conditions: verbal support condition, which consisted of a verbal discussion between the child and the research assistant concerning the child's fears and anxieties, followed by empathic responses by the research assistant; diversionary play condition, in which the child was allowed to play with board games, card games, and puzzles, and in which discussion focused only on nonhospital related information; and control condition, in which the child had no contact with the research assistant other than the pre- and postassessment sessions. The children in the three treatment groups received two 30-minute sessions that were conducted individually in the children's rooms during the course of their hospitalization. Statistical analyses conducted with pre–post data indicated that children in the therapeutic play group reported significantly greater reduction ($p < .01$) in hospital related fears following the intervention than did children in the other three groups. However, children in the therapeutic play group reported a slight increase in somatization, and there were no significant differences between treatment groups based on nurse and parent ratings. Still, the results do suggest that the therapeutic play intervention was statistically significantly more influential in reducing self-reported hospital related fears than diversionary play, verbal support, and no treatment. Further, the study used methodologically sound procedures, such as random assignment to treatment conditions and consistent administration of experimental conditions by the same research assistant.

Other researchers also conducted empirical investigations of hospital-based play interventions during the 1980s and early 1990s. Gillis (1989) evaluated the use of a play therapy intervention with hospitalized children who were immobilized. Immobilized children in the hospital represent a special population in that immobility limits the child's capacity for exploration and physical activity, which may threaten the child's self-esteem and self-concept. Sixty hospitalized participants from 7 to 12 years of age were randomly assigned to an experimental or control group; participants across groups were demographically similar. All participants were immobilized because of their medical conditions or the treatment of these conditions. An adaptation of the Coopersmith Self-Esteem Inventory (SEI) was used to measure children's self-evaluations with regard to peers, parents, school, and interests. The intervention consisted of four sessions of individual assisted play between the child and either the researcher or research assistant. Each play session lasted from 30 to 45 minutes and included child-directed play using art, music, role modeling, and puppets. Unfortunately, the exact nature of the intervention is not clearly specified. Children in the control group received normal care without the intervention. Following the intervention, children in the experimental group reported significantly higher self-esteem on the SEI than children in the control group ($p < .01$).

Fosson, Martin, and Haley (1990) examined the effect of a single 30-minute play session on the anxiety of hospitalized children aged 5 to 9 years. The 50 participants were randomly assigned to either an experimental or comparison group. The experimental group received a 30-minute medical play session in which the child was presented with actual and play medical equipment, in addition to a doll of the same gender as the child. The content of the session included exploration of the medical equipment, needle play, and play medical procedures. Play was facilitated by the recreational therapist, who encouraged the child to express her or his feelings, expressed acceptance of the child's feelings, and provided reassurance. The child often assumed the role of medical professional while performing medical procedures on the doll. The comparison group received a single 20-minute session. During this time, the recreational therapist greeted the child, and the child and therapist spent the remainder of the session watching television together. Both experimental and comparison conditions were administered by the same recreational therapist, and parents usually were present in both conditions. Anxiety was measured in several ways, including reports by parents and nurses, self-report, direct observation, and physiological indices; scores on these various measures were combined to obtain an overall anxiety score. Results of statistical analyses indicated that following the intervention, anxiety among children within the experimental group decreased to a greater extent than anxiety among children within the comparison group. However, this group mean difference was not great enough to reach statistical significance. It is important to note that in this study, child participants were accompanied by a parent throughout the hospitalization experience, which may account for the failure to detect a greater intervention effect. That is, the tendency for both groups to report reduced anxiety following the intervention (or comparison condition) may have been influenced more by parental presence and support than the intervention condition itself. Further, the experimental group received only a single play session, which may not be enough to produce a large effect.

Young and Fu (1988) examined the effects of a needle play intervention on children's perceptions of pain following a blood test. Eighty children, aged 48 to 83 months, participated. Instruments included measures of subjective pain appraisal (child-report) and objective pain appraisal (children's pulse rate, body movements–posture, and vocalization or crying), both of which were completed three different times: before the blood test (to establish baselines that would later be used as covariates), immediately after the blood test, and five minutes after the blood test. Participants were randomly assigned to one of four groups: (a) pre-blood test needle play, (b) post-blood test needle play, (c) pre- and post-blood test needle play, and (d) no needle play. Thus, there were three intervention groups and a control group. For those groups receiving pre-blood test needle play, the intervention consisted of the researcher demonstrating the blood test procedure for the child using a soft doll and medical equipment (e.g., syringe, tourniquet, alcohol swab). This physical demonstration was accompanied by a narrative explanation of the procedure, and the child's questions were answered and misconceptions were corrected. Following the demonstration, the child performed a blood test on the doll and then engaged in unstructured play. After the actual blood test procedure was performed, children in groups (b) and (c) received the post-blood test needle play intervention. Results of statistical analyses indicated that children in the three intervention groups produced pulse rates statistically significantly lower than those produced by children in the control group, based on the assessment conducted 5 minutes after the blood test. Further, children in the pre-blood test play group and post-blood test play group scored statistically significantly lower than children in the control group on the body movements–posture index, indicating that children in the control group displayed more resistant, tense, and restless behaviors following the blood test than did children in the intervention groups. This difference also was based on the assessment conducted 5 minutes after the blood test. No differences in these outcome variables were observed based on the assessment conducted immediately following the blood test. With regard to children's self-reports of pain, no group differences were detected either immediately after or 5 minutes after the blood test, indicating that all four groups reported similar perceptions of pain. Thus, while the intervention did appear to influence children's pulse rates and nervous behaviors, participation in the intervention did not influence children's subjective pain appraisals.

The studies reviewed above suggest that psychosocial play interventions are probably efficacious for hospitalized children (Task Force on Promotion and Dissemination of Psychological Procedures, 1995), particularly regarding decreasing anxiety and hospital-related fears, preventing anxiety from worsening, improving self-esteem, and reducing behaviors indicative of distress. A number of case studies evaluating play therapy interventions in hospital settings also have provided anecdotal support for their effectiveness (e.g., Adams, 1976; Atala & Carter, 1992; Cooper & Blitz, 1985; Landreth, Homeyer, Glover, & Sweeney, 1996; Linn, Beardslee, & Patenaude, 1986).

REPLICATION AND TRANSPORTABILITY

The replicability of the previously discussed hospital-based interventions in nonhospital settings is difficult to determine. Because the therapeutic interventions involved nondirective play, it might be difficult to replicate the therapeutic trajectory. Within the context of hospital-based interventions, different children will present with different fears, coping styles, illnesses or injuries, and resources. Thus, the direction that a child takes within a play therapy session will vary as a function of these and other factors (e.g., temperament, propensity to disclose). In the same way, each study had a slightly different treatment approach. Although common features exist, exact replication might be difficult. At the same time, we suspect that these approaches can be replicated in outpatient clinics and other settings where medically related issues are important. Although not specifically designed for this purpose, the elements of the play interventions could easily be adapted to meet the needs of a nonhospitalized child who is experiencing adaptation problems related to illness, medical interventions, or outpatient treatment.

Although the therapist must be trained in play therapy theory and techniques, other health care professionals might be able to implement aspects of this program. Hospital personnel implementing this kind of program must be trained in the delivery of psychological interventions with children. Clearly, knowledge of childhood medical conditions and diseases and how these conditions can affect the psychosocial development of children is desirable. In fact, child life personnel within many hospital settings routinely conduct similar therapeutic play activities.

RECOMMENDATIONS FOR OUTCOME EVALUATION IN CLINICAL PRACTICE

Given that different interventions attempt to stimulate change in different behaviors or emotions, the constructs that are evaluated will vary according to the targeted emotions or behaviors. On the basis of our literature review, anxiety or fear has been a common area assessed in evaluations of hospital-based play interventions, but outcome also could be evaluated by examining change in other constructs, such as locus of control, knowledge, self-esteem, and communication (Phillips, 1988; Thompson, 1988). The objectives of an intervention should drive how the intervention is evaluated. For example, if a hospital-based play program is developed to reduce general fears and worry, then norm referenced self-report anxiety measures may be used within a pre–post research design. If an intervention is designed to increase knowledge about a particular medical procedure or illness, then questionnaires can be developed to assess increases in such knowledge following participation in the intervention. If the intervention purports to facilitate generalized change in behavioral or emotional functioning (e.g., across home and school settings), then rating scales and anecdotal reports provided by parents and teachers will provide valuable information. Again, evaluation decisions should be based on the purpose of the intervention. Finally, a longitudinal study looking at the long-term positive effects of therapeutic play in hospital settings would be useful in helping to determine the extent to which these interventions may be able to produce change in the psychosocial functioning of hospitalized children over a period of time.

CONCLUSION

Research suggests that therapeutic play programs for hospitalized children can be a useful approach to reducing psychological distress related to the experience of illness and hospitalization. At the same time, Bolig (1990) asserted that trends related to health care may serve to reduce the use of unstructured, child-directed play interventions and increase the use of more structured and directive interventions that relate specifically to the child's illness and associated treatment procedures (e.g., medical play and preparation). In light of these trends, it will be necessary to determine the effectiveness of these directive interventions compared with relatively unstructured interventions such as those described in this chapter.

Phillips (1988) noted that whether play therapy interventions are able to reach their lofty goals regarding the facilitation of children's adjustment to hospitals and medical procedures (e.g., enhancing autonomy, mastery, and control; reducing anxiety and fear) awaits more rigorous empirical support than is currently available. The child health care literature is replete with case studies and anecdotal accounts attesting to the utility of play therapy in hospital settings, in addition to theoretical, conceptual, and position papers. What is needed, however, is a shift from descriptive and anecdotal papers to methodologically sound research. In addition, future empirical research can help identify common treatment components that might work across settings. Hospital-based play interventions hold the potential to make hospitalization less threatening for children, but more convincing data will be needed to communicate the value and importance of these programs to parents and hospital administrators.

REFERENCES

Adams, M. A. (1976). A hospital play program: Helping children with serious illness. *American Journal of Orthopsychiatry, 46,* 416–424.

Atala, K. D., & Carter, B. D. (1992). Pediatric limb amputation: Aspects of coping and psychotherapeutic intervention. *Child Psychiatry and Human Development, 23,* 117–130.

Axline, V. M. (1969). *Play therapy* (Rev. ed.). New York: Ballantine Books.

Bolig, R. (1990). Play in health care settings: A challenge for the 1990s. *Children's Health Care, 19,* 229–233.

Bolig, R., Fernie, D. E., & Klein, E. L. (1986). Unstructured play in hospital settings: An internal locus of control rationale. *Children's Health Care, 15,* 101–107.

Bolig, R., Yolton, K. A., & Nissen, H. L. (1991). Medical play and preparation: Questions and issues. *Children's Health Care, 20,* 225–229.

Clatworthy, S. (1981). Therapeutic play: Effects on hospitalized children. *Children's Health Care, 9,* 108–113.

Cooper, S. E., & Blitz, J. T. (1985). A therapeutic play group for hospitalized children with cancer. *Journal of Psychosocial Oncology, 3*(2), 23–37.

Elkins, P. D., & Roberts, M. C. (1983). Psychological preparation for pediatric hospitalization. *Clinical Psychology Review, 3,* 275–295.

Ellinwood, C. G., & Raskin, N. J. (1993). Client-centered humanistic psychotherapy. In T. R. Kratochwill & R. J. Morris (Eds.), *Handbook of psychotherapy with children and adolescents* (pp. 258–277). Boston: Allyn & Bacon.

Fosson, A., Martin, J., & Haley, J. (1990). Anxiety among hospitalized latency-age children. *Journal of Developmental and Behavioral Pediatrics, 11,* 324–327.

Gillis, A. J. (1989). The effect of play on immobilized children in hospital. *International Journal of Nursing Studies, 26,* 261–269.

Golden, D. B. (1983). Play therapy for hospitalized children. In C. E. Schaefer & K. J. O'Connor (Eds.), *Handbook of play therapy* (pp. 213–233). New York: Wiley.

Harbeck-Weber, C., & McKee, D. H. (1995). Prevention of emotional and behavioral distress in children experiencing hospitalization and chronic illness. In M. C. Roberts (Ed.), *Handbook of pediatric psychology* (2nd ed., pp. 167–184). New York: Guilford Press.

Healthcare Cost and Utilization Project. Agency for Healthcare Research and Quality. (2000). *2000 Hospital Stays for Children Only* [Data file]. Available from HCUPnet Web site, http://www.ahrq.gov/data/hcup/hcupnet.htm.

Hunsberger, M., Love, B., & Byrne, C. (1984). A review of current approaches used to help children and parents cope with health care procedures. *Maternal-Child Nursing Journal, 13,* 145–165.

Klinzing, D. G., & Klinzing, D. R. (1987). The hospitalization of a child and family responses. *Marriage and Family Review, 11,* 119–134.

Landreth, G. L., Homeyer, L. E., Glover, G., & Sweeney, D. S. (1996). *Play therapy interventions with children's problems.* Northvale, NJ: Jason Aronson.

Landreth, G. L., & Sweeney, D. S. (1997). Client-centered play therapy. In K. O'Connor & L. M. Braverman (Eds.), *Play therapy theory and practice: A comparative presentation* (pp. 17–45). New York: Wiley.

LeBlanc, M., & Ritchie, M. (2001). A meta-analysis of play therapy outcomes. *Counseling Psychology Quarterly, 14*, 149–163.

Linn, S., Beardslee, W., & Patenaude, A. F. (1986). Puppet therapy with pediatric bone marrow transplant patients. *Journal of Pediatric Psychology, 11*, 37–46.

McCue, K. (1988). Medical play: An expanded perspective. *Children's Health Care, 16*, 157–161.

Miller, S. M., Sherman, H. D., Combs, C., & Kruus, L. (1992). Patterns of children's coping and short-term medical and dental stressors: Nature, implications, and future directions. In A. M. La Greca, L. J. Siegel, J. L. Wallander, & C. E. Walker (Eds.), *Stress and coping in child health* (pp. 157–190). New York: Guilford Press.

O'Connor, K., & Braverman, L. M. (Eds.). (1997). *Play therapy theory and practice: A comparative presentation*. New York: Wiley.

O'Connor, K. J. (2000). *The play therapy primer* (2nd ed.). New York: Wiley.

Oremland, E. K. (1988). Mastering developmental and critical experiences through play and other expressive behaviors in childhood. *Children's Health Care, 16*, 150–156.

Petrillo, M., & Sanger, S. (1980). *Emotional care of hospitalized children: An environmental approach*. Philadelphia: Lippincott.

Phillips, R. D. (1988). Play therapy in health care settings: Promises never kept? *Children's Health Care, 16*, 182–187.

Poster, E. C. (1983). Stress immunization: Techniques to help children cope with hospitalization. *Maternal-Child Nursing Journal, 12*, 119–134.

Rae, W. A. (1981). Hospitalized latency-age children: Implications for psychosocial care. *Journal of the Association for the Care of Children in Hospitals, 9*, 59–63.

Rae, W. A. (1982). Body image of children and adolescents during physical illness and hospitalization. *Psychiatric Annals, 12*, 1065–1073.

Rae, W. A., Worchel, F. F., Upchurch, J., Sanner, J. H., & Daniel, C. A. (1989). The psychosocial impact of play on hospitalized children. *Journal of Pediatric Psychology, 14*, 617–627.

Schaefer, C. E. (Ed.). (1993). *The therapeutic powers of play*. Northvale, NJ: Jason Aronson.

Siegel, L. J., & Conte, P. (2001). Hospitalization and medical care of children. In C. E. Walker & M. C. Roberts (Eds.), *Handbook of clinical child psychology* (3rd ed., pp. 895–909). New York: Wiley.

Task Force on Promotion and Dissemination of Psychological Procedures. (1995, Winter). Training in and dissemination of empirically validated psychological treatments: Report and recommendations. *The Clinical Psychologist, 48*, 3–24.

Thompson, R. H. (1985). *Psychosocial research on pediatric hospitalization and health care: A review of the literature*. Springfield, IL: Charles C Thomas.

Thompson, R. H. (1988). From questions to answers: Approaches to studying play in health care settings. *Children's Health Care, 16*, 188–194.

Thompson, R. J., Jr., & Gustafson, K. E. (1996). *Adaptation to chronic childhood illness*. Washington, DC: American Psychological Association.

Wadsworth, B. J. (1984). *Piaget's theory of cognitive and affective development* (3rd ed.). New York: Longman.

Wallander, J. L., & Varni, J. (1992). Adjustment in children with chronic physical disorders: Programmatic research on a disability–stress–coping model. In A. M. La Greca, L. J. Siegel, J. L. Wallander, & C. E. Walker (Eds.), *Stress and coping in child health* (pp. 279–300). New York: Guilford Press.

Webb, J. R. (1995). Play therapy with hospitalized children. *International Journal of Play Therapy, 4*, 51–59.

Webb, N. B. (Ed.). (1999). *Play therapy with children in crisis* (2nd ed.). New York: Guilford Press.

Wishon, P. M., & Brown, M. H. (1991). Play and the young hospitalized patient. *Early Child Development and Care, 72*, 39–46.

Young, M. R., & Fu, V. R. (1988). Influence of play and temperament on the young child's response to pain. *Children's Health Care, 16*, 209–215.

III

EMPIRICALLY BASED PLAY INTERVENTIONS FOR EXTERNALIZING DISORDERS

8

CHILD ADHD MULTIMODAL PROGRAM: AN EMPIRICALLY SUPPORTED INTERVENTION FOR YOUNG CHILDREN WITH ADHD

LINDA A. REDDY, CRAIG SPRINGER, TARA M. FILES-HALL,
ELIZABETH SCHMELZER BENISZ, YVONNE HAUCH,
DANIA BRAUNSTEIN, AND TANYA ATAMANOFF

The Child ADHD (Attention Deficit Hyperactivity Disorder) Multimodal Program (CAMP) is an empirically supported intervention program for young children diagnosed with ADHD (8.5 years and younger). CAMP is designed to treat children, parents, and teachers and is conducted in 90-minute, weekly training sessions. Children and their parents are separately and concurrently trained in a group context for 10 consecutive weeks. The children's training group includes behavioral management techniques,

Preparation for this chapter was partially supported by grants 2-022627 and 2-022682 from the Society for the Study of School Psychology and a university faculty research grant awarded to Linda A. Reddy. For information about CAMP contact Linda A. Reddy, PhD, Fairleigh Dickinson University, Department of Psychology, 100 River Road, Teaneck, NJ 07666.

developmentally appropriate games, and skill-based self-control and problem-solving strategies (Reddy, 2000a). Behavioral consultation is provided individually to parents and classroom teachers in the home and at school. Randomized experimental designed studies reveal that completion of the program results in an improvement in parental stress, child behavior problems, internalized distress (i.e., anxiety and depression), and social interactions with peers in the home and school setting. Outcome findings also reveal that the children training component alone results in improvements in child disruptive and aggressive behavior, social skills, and parental stress. The inclusion of parent group training and home–school behavioral consultation provides additive effects on home and school outcomes.

This chapter describes the use of a developmental and skill-based multimodal intervention program for young children diagnosed with ADHD. First, a brief review of the outcome literature with this population and age group is presented. The rationale for and research that supports the use of developmentally appropriate games in children's group training are provided. Second, the theoretical basis, goals, and key treatment elements, as well as implementation processes of each program component, are detailed. Third, outcome research on the effectiveness of this program is described. Finally, the implications for replication and transportability and recommendations for outcome evaluation are offered.

RESEARCH ON EARLY INTERVENTION

The importance of early intervention is paramount with children diagnosed with ADHD (McGee, Partridge, Williams, & Silva, 1991). Grizenko (1997) and Grizenko, Sayegh, and Papineau (1994) found that younger children have greater treatment success and are more likely to maintain treatment benefits than older children. Furthermore, studies indicate that ADHD symptoms are identifiable in 67% of children with ADHD by age 4 and that the disorder can be accurately diagnosed by this age (e.g., Connor, 2002; Lahey et al., 1998). Thus, early diagnosis and treatment can alleviate many of the serious impairments in social and academic settings that are likely to develop if left untreated.

Despite the benefits of early intervention, few investigations evaluated the effects of treatment for young children (i.e., 8 years and younger). To date, there are only 14 investigations with this population and age group. Four of these studies evaluated the effects of stimulant medication (i.e., methylphenidate or dextroamphetamine) on young children with ADHD (e.g., Alessandri & Schramm, 1991; Barkley, 1988; Byrne, Bawden, De-Wolfe, & Beattie, 1998; Musten, Firestone, Pisterman, Bennett, & Mercer, 1997). Stimulant medication is effective in treating some symptoms associated with ADHD in young children. However, symptoms often return after medication has been discontinued (e.g., Greenhill, 1992; Sagvolden & Sergeant, 1998). Rebound effects (i.e., when medication wears off) such as hyperactivity, insomnia, and moodiness and increases in behavioral problems have been found (e.g., Barkley, 1998; Weiss, Jain, & Garland, 2000). Side effects often accompany medication use such as insomnia, appetite suppression, growth suspension, irritability, headaches, abdominal pain, dry mouth, dizziness, and a decrease in sociability (e.g., Barkley, 1997a; Firestone, Monteiro, Pisterman, Mercer, & Bennett, 1998; Klein & Bessler, 1992; Monteiro, Firestone, Pisterman, Bennett, & Mercer, 1997). Moreover, side effects of methylphenidate have been found to be more severe and variable for younger children (i.e., preschool age) than older children (i.e., elementary and middle school age; Firestone et al., 1998). As a result, physicians and parents may delay or avoid the use of medication. Therefore, alternate forms of treatment are warranted.

Eight investigations assessed the efficacy of parent training for young children (i.e., 8 years and younger) diagnosed with ADHD (e.g., Danforth, 1998; Eisenstadt, Eyberg, Bodiford-McNeil, Newcomb, & Funderburk, 1993; Erhardt & Baker, 1990; Pisterman, McGrath, et al., 1989; Pisterman, Firestone, et al., 1992; Sonuga-Barke, Daley, Thompson, Laver-Bradbury, & Weeks, 2001; Strayhorn & Weidman, 1989; Strayhorn & Widman, 1991). Among the eight studies, three provided individual parent training and five provided group parent training. Positive effects on compliance to parental commands, use of positive parenting techniques, increased parental self-efficacy, and reductions in parental stress were found. Collectively, these investigations provide support for the efficacy of parent training for young children with ADHD.

One study evaluated child behavioral interventions for children 8 years and younger diagnosed with ADHD (Hupp, Reitman, Northup, O' Callaghan, & LeBlanc, 2002). This study focused on the sportsmanlike behavior during kickball games of five children in a 3-week (i.e., 15-day) summer program. Two types of behavioral reinforcement schedules were compared: delayed reward and token plus delayed reward on a reversal (ABCBC) research design. Results indicate that the use of tokens with delayed reward increased sportsmanlike behavior for all participants and that the delayed reward condition did not increase sportsmanlike behaviors.

The use of multiple interventions has been shown to be an effective approach for treating children of 7- to 12-years-old with ADHD (e.g., Horn, Ialongo, Greenberg, Packard, & Smith-Winberry, 1990; Pfiffner & McBurnett, 1997; Richters et al., 1995). However, only one study has examined the combined effects of treatment modalities for young children with ADHD (Reitman, Hupp, O'Callaghan, Gulley, & Northup, 2001). In this investigation, the effect of a token economy system and methylphenidate on attention and disruptive behavior for three children attending a 4-week summer treatment program was assessed. Results revealed that stimulant medication alone increased attention and decreased disruptive behavior, and the addition of a token economy system further enhanced the behavioral gains.

To date, research on the combined effects of child and parent group training for children in this population and age group is not available. This chapter outlines a multimodal program that includes child and parent group training, as well as home and school behavioral consultation. Moreover, the program includes a children's group curriculum with developmentally appropriate games (DAGs). The following section presents the benefits of DAGs and the outcome literature that supports its use with children.

BENEFITS OF DAGs

DAGs that are designed to be competency-based and enjoyable to young children can significantly increase motivation and skill development. Interventions are most effective when skills are taught and reinforced in contexts in which children work and play (Barkley, 1998). Group DAGs are a highly effective way to engage ADHD children's interest and motivation while teaching them important skills for the home, school, and playground. Group DAGs provide children with the opportunity to interact naturally with peers and adults and learn appropriate behaviors and skills in the context in which they will be used. DAGs enhance children's socialization through group contact, increase self-confidence through group acceptance, and provide recreational and leisure-time activities (Reed, Black, & Eastman, 1978). Treating children in a natural play group context also increases the likelihood of maintaining and generalizing treatment gains over time (Hoag & Burlingame, 1997).

Research on DAGs

Research has shown that DAGs significantly improve the participation, cooperation, social skills, self-esteem, and visual motor skills of regular education, emotionally disturbed, and perceptually impaired children more than traditional school-based games (Ferland, 1997). For example, Bay-Hinitz, Peterson, and Quilitch (1994) studied the impact of DAGs and competitive games on the participation and cooperative group behavior of 70 preschoolers for 30 minutes per day, 5 days a week, for 50 days. Children who participated in DAGs exhibited more participation and prosocial behavior than those in traditional competitive games. Similar findings were also reported by Orlick (1988). Garaigordobil and Echebarria (1995) examined the effects of a cooperative game program on the social behavior and self-concept of 178 mainstreamed children (6–7 years of age). Twenty-two play sessions that included games designed to enhance children's cooperation, sharing, symbolic play, and feelings of self-worth were implemented. Significant improvements in classroom behavior (e.g., leadership skills, cheerfulness, sensitivity and respect to others, aggression, apathy, and anxiety) were found.

Schneider (1989) compared the effects of DAGs versus free play (i.e., 15–20 minutes per session) on the self-esteem of 36 kindergarten students across 17 sessions. Teacher and child self-reported ratings of self-esteem improved more among students who participated in DAGs than those in free play.

The efficacy of play interventions with children diagnosed as emotionally disturbed has also been investigated by Hand (1986). Two groups of children, 10 to 12 years of age, were systematically observed during recess. One group participated in traditional games where success was defined as the defeat or elimination of others; the other group participated in DAGs three times per week for 16 weeks. Greater reductions in verbal and physical aggression and the use of time-out were found among children in the DAG group.

Reed et al. (1978) investigated the effectiveness of a parent–child group training program for perceptually disabled children, 6 to 12 years of age. Children in the group had few friends, seldom participated in peer group activities, and were verbally and physically aggressive. The program consisted of 1 hour sessions held twice a week for 16 weeks and implemented games that enhanced social skills and perceptual motor abilities (e.g., visual-motor skills, visual acuity, and body awareness). Parent ratings revealed improved peer interactions at home and school, including greater group participation and rule following, and fewer behavior problems.

Few investigations have assessed the efficacy of group DAGs with ADHD children (e.g., Reddy, Braunstein, Hauch, Springer, & Hall, 2002; Reddy, Spencer, Hall, & Rubel, 2001). Group DAGs afford young ADHD children opportunities to learn new skills through participating in structured peer group activities that are behaviorally and cognitively challenging. DAGs are flexible, require minimum equipment, and can be easily modified to meet specific individual, group, or classroom needs.

The following section describes the CAMP, a psychoeducational program for young children with ADHD that includes DAGs.

CAMP

Child Training Group

The first component of CAMP is the ADHD Child Training Group (Reddy, 2000a), which uses DAGs, in part, to train young ADHD children (i.e., 8.5 years and younger). The ADHD Child Training Group is designed to promote three areas: (a) social skills, (b) self-control, and (c) anger and stress management.

Theoretical Basis and Objectives

The children's program is partially based on the seminal work of Bandura's (1973) social learning theory and behavior-deficit model, Goldstein's (1988) skill streaming approach, and Torbert's (1994) cooperative games. Skill development is fostered through the teaching of skill sequences, a set of behavioral procedures designed to enhance social competence in children (McGinnis & Goldstein, 1997; Reddy & Goldstein, 2001). Each skill is broken down into its behavioral steps, which are taught through didactic instruction, symbolic and in vivo modeling, role-playing, behavioral rehearsal, and coaching by adults in a group context. Collectively, the behavioral steps illustrate the implementation of the skill. For example, the skill "using nice talk" would consist of the following behavioral steps: (a) approach the person in a friendly way; (b) use a friendly look; and (c) use a friendly voice.

Skill sequences are taught and reinforced through (a) *modeling*—adult therapists demonstrate behaviors and skills; (b) *role-playing*—guided opportunities to practice and rehearse appropriate interpersonal behaviors; and (c) *performance feedback*—children are frequently praised and provided with feedback on how well they model the therapists' skills and behavior. A number of skill transfer and maintenance-enhancing procedures are used, such as (a) *overlearning*—correctly rehearsing and practicing skills learned over time; (b) *identical elements*—children are trained in real-world contexts (e.g., schools, playground, peer groups) with children and adults with whom they interact on a daily basis; and (c) *mediated generalization*—teaching children a series of self-regulation skills such as self-evaluation, self-reinforcement, and self-instruction. In addition, skill acquisition is taught and reinforced through the implementation of group DAGs.

DAGs are gross motor activities that are based on three principles:

1. Each child has the opportunity to choose to participate at his or her ability level.
2. Opportunities to play and practice skills increase as the DAG proceeds. Elimination of a group member is not possible. As a result, children become more active members of the group and exhibit greater cooperation, cohesion, and problem solving.
3. Children who vary in ability can interact positively with each other (Torbert, 1994).

Group DAGs enhance children's feelings of creativity, accomplishment, autonomy, and positive regard for themselves and others, while teaching them important life skills for work and play (e.g., Reddy et al, 2001;

Torbert & Schneider, 1993). Children who participate in group DAGs share an affiliation through which they can encourage others' growth in positive social interactions (Torbert, 1994). DAGs present cognitive, social, and physical challenges that encourage children to persist and try alternative solutions (Bunker, 1991). For a detailed description of the DAGs used in this curriculum, see Reddy et al. (2001).

Group Sessions

Children's training is run for 90 minutes per session, once per week, for 11 training sessions. The final session serves as a graduation ceremony for the children and parents in the program. A carpeted room that accommodates about 15 people is used. There are approximately 8 to 10 children in each group, and one adult therapist for every 2 children is recommended.

A token economy system is used to monitor and reinforce positive behaviors during each training session. The children are given rewards for following three goals: (a) *follow directions*; (b) *use my words to express my thoughts and feelings*; and (c) *keep my hands and feet to myself*. Children are given one sticker–point for each of the three goals during each group session. A group sticker chart is displayed. At the end of each session, every child is asked to evaluate, with adult assistance, how well he or she achieved each goal during the session. Next, a star for each goal the child attained is placed next to the child's name on the group sticker chart. The child then selects stickers (that correspond with the number of goals attained) and places them in his or her sticker book at the end of each session. The sticker book is given to the child at the program graduation (i.e., session 11).

Time-out is used as a positive self-control technique in the group. Children are instructed that taking a "time-out" is not a punishment, but rather a positive technique for regaining self-control. In this program, children are not placed in time-out for a set period of time (e.g., 60 seconds times the child's age). Instead, children are to remain in time-out until they demonstrate positive control over their hands, feet, and mouth. For example, some children will be in time-out for 45 to 60 seconds, while others may remain in time-out for 2 to 3 minutes. Children are verbally praised for self-initiating time-out and for compliance with adult direction to take time-out. Time-out is modeled by therapists. Children are encouraged to monitor their behavior to self-initiate time-out. The procedure for taking a time-out includes (a) raising your hand; (b) waiting to be called on; (c) requesting a time-out; and (d) taking the "time-out pass" to the time-out chair. A "time-out pass" is used to nonverbally communicate to others that the child is taking a break and needs to be left alone. After a few minutes (i.e., 1 or 2 minutes) in time-out, a therapist approaches the child, validates him or her for taking a time-out, and then helps the child assess whether he or she is ready to return to the group.

Three levels of time-out are used. Level one time-out is designated by a specific chair placed on the far side of the group room. Level one time-out distances the child from being directly involved in the group's activity. Level two time-out is a chair located directly outside of the group room. Level two time-out further distances the child from the group activity and decreases the level of visual and auditory stimulation for the child. Level three time-out is a chair in a separate room. Level three time-out eliminates the visual and auditory stimulation of the group activity. A child is accompanied by a therapist when level two or three time-out is implemented. Children in level two or three time-out are required to return to the group activity gradually by spending a few minutes in each of the successively lower levels of time-out (e.g., the child in level two time-out must go to level one time-out before returning to the group activity).

At the beginning of each session, the group rules (e.g., raise hand before talking) and the group structure (e.g., review of group goals, sticker awards, use of time-out or bathroom passes) are reviewed. As mentioned, children are taught skills through four methods: (a) verbal description, (b) modeling, (c) role-playing, and (d) performance feedback. The behavioral steps for each skill are written on an easel placed in front of the group. Each step is read out loud by a child or therapist and is then explained and discussed. Each skill sequence is role-played in three ways: (a) modeled by two therapists, (b) modeled by a therapist and child, and (c) modeled by two children who are assisted by a therapist. Skills taught are role-played in three social contexts: the home, school, and peer group. During role-plays, children are asked to evaluate whether the role-player demonstrated each skill step correctly.

A therapeutic workbook, "All About Me" is used toward the end of each session. Children answer questions about themselves and their families and draw pictures about hobbies, likes, dislikes, and other personal information. During each group session, the children are directed to complete two pages in their workbooks. They are asked to explain to the group what they drew or wrote. This workbook provides a structured, individual activity for children to share information about themselves in the group. Each session is concluded with reviewing the stickers and points earned.

Curriculum

Several skill sequences and DAGs are included to promote social skills, impulse control, and anger–stress management. The skill topics taught include using nice talk, following directions, sharing with others, helping others, asking for help, identifying and coping with scared, sad, and angry feelings in oneself and others, using self-control, ignoring provocation, managing stress and anger, dealing with boredom, using brave talk (saying no and accepting no), not interrupting others, joining in, dealing with being left out, and being a good sport. Nine DAGs are implemented (see Reddy et al, 2001; Reddy, 2000a).

Training

This program can be implemented by teachers, paraprofessionals, or professionals, with appropriate supervision. Training for the children's training group entails a 6-hour seminar on (a) behavioral, social, and neurocognitive features of ADHD; (b) structure of the group; (c) behavioral techniques to promote positive behavior and group cooperation; (d) implementation of skill sequences and DAGs; (e) time-out procedures; (f) token economy system; and (g) team building among the group therapists. It is recommended that all techniques and group sessions be discussed, modeled, and role-played (for 40 minutes) with the child group therapists prior to each session. In addition, it is helpful to conduct postgroup process sessions (for 30 minutes) with the group therapists to discuss the implementation process and how the children performed during the session.

Concurrently, parents are provided group training. The next section outlines the parent training program used.

Parent Training Group

The second component of CAMP, the parent training group, is designed to provide an intensive parent training and support group experience. A modified version of Barkley's (1997b) parent training program is used.

Theoretical Basis and Objectives

Barkley's program was based, in part, on Hanf's (1969) two-stage program for child noncompliance. First, parents are taught techniques for attending to positive behaviors and ignoring of inappropriate behavior. Second, parents are taught methods for setting clear and effective commands for compliance and use of time-out for noncompliance. The parent training program was based on the work of Forehand and McMahon (1981) and Patterson (1982) and includes developmental theory, social learning, and behavioral principles.

Parents are trained in techniques to promote their children's social and behavioral needs in the home and at school. The five primary objectives of the program are to (a) increase parents' applied knowledge of ADHD and awareness of their child's strengths and weaknesses; (b) teach and systematically maintain the use of behavioral techniques in the home, school, and public places; (c) improve interactions between parents and children; (d) teach parents effective methods for managing their anger and stress; and (e) enhance parents' collaboration with school personnel and knowledge of special education law.

Group Sessions

The parent group runs for 10 consecutive weeks, concurrently with the children's group. The group is held in a large conference room and instruction consists of both lecture and discussion. Handouts outlining behavioral techniques and strategies, as well as homework assignments, are distributed weekly to reinforce concepts and skills taught. Homework assignments are designed to promote parents' skills in implementing techniques that complement their children's training. Parents are encouraged to take notes, ask questions, and provide advice and support to other members of the group. At the conclusion of each session, a brief summary of the skills taught to the children during that session is provided.

Curriculum

The concepts and skills taught in the parent training group build on each other and complement the skills taught in the children's training group. Each session is briefly described below.

Session One. Parents are welcomed to the program and praised for obtaining early intervention services. The program goals and issues of confidentiality are discussed. An overview is given of the social, behavioral, learning, and neurocognitive processes associated with ADHD. The rules, behavioral techniques, and structure of the child training group are described. Parents are encouraged to review their children's performance (on the group sticker chart) in the group at the end of each session. Parents are asked to complete a family weekly schedule and list their family rules for the next session.

Session Two. Family weekly schedules are assessed in the context of factors that affect children's symptoms and parental stress. Parents are encouraged to review their family rules and revise them in behavioral terms. The skill sequence, Giving Effective Commands, is taught with a detailed handout. Parents are asked to practice this skill sequence two times a day for the next session.

Session Three. The Giving Effective Commands homework is reviewed. Parents are then trained on Game Cards, a technique to structure daily routines (e.g., morning or evening routine) and increase parent and child positive interactions. Parents are taught several key concepts in child management (e.g., negative or positive consequences must be immediate, specific, and consistent). A group exercise on the characteristics of parents' "best and worst bosses" is conducted and compared to their own characteristics as parents (i.e., bosses). Parents are trained on Using Positive Attention to promote child compliance. For homework, parents are told to implement the positive attention technique for 10 minutes, twice a day.

Session Four. Previously taught techniques (i.e., homework) are discussed. Parents are encouraged to continue implementing all techniques. The technique, Teaching Your Child to Not Interrupt You, is taught with a detailed handout. Parents are asked to identify and define in behavioral terms two behaviors they wish to improve in their children. An overview of the benefits of a token economy system is presented. Parents are asked to revise their family rules and list privileges their children could earn for the next session. The use of time-out as a positive technique for self-control is introduced. Parents are encouraged to model the use of time-out in the home and told to practice the Teaching Your Child to Not Interrupt You technique once a day until the next session.

Session Five. Homework is reviewed. Steps in designing and implementing a token economy system are presented. Parents are asked to continue to implement the techniques already taught and to begin designing their token economy systems.

Session Six. Homework is reviewed. Plans for token economy systems are presented and revised. Parents are asked to begin implementing their token economy systems at home.

Session Seven. Homework is reviewed. Data on the initial success of the token economy systems are discussed. The benefits and steps for graphing children's performance across time is outlined. As an extension to the token economy system, the technique, Managing Behavior in Public Places is taught. Parents are also taught how to implement Time-out in Public Places. Parents are asked to implement these techniques before the next session. Parents are also encouraged to continue implementing all techniques taught.

Session Eight. After reviewing homework, methods for Managing Parental Stress are presented. For homework, parents are told to implement two stress management techniques during the course of the next week.

Session Nine. Homework is reviewed. Strategies for managing parental anger are introduced. Considerations and strategies for Fostering Positive Peer Relationships through adult supervised, structured, play opportunities are presented. A step-by-step handout is provided. Parents are asked to set up structured "play dates" for their child for the next session.

Session Ten. After reviewing homework, termination is discussed. Strategies for promoting home and school collaboration are outlined. A brief overview of special education laws and regulations is provided.

Training

The parent training program should be implemented by trained professionals who have adequate training in child development, child psychopathology, social learning, behavior modification techniques, and other clinical assessment and interventions with families.

This program includes techniques designed for parents of children with behavioral difficulties who have language or general cognitive functioning above 2 years of age. Professionals must be aware and sensitive to individual child and family differences in training. Behavioral consultation is also provided. The next section briefly outlines the critical ingredients and implementation processes used.

Home and School Behavioral Consultation

The third component of CAMP is the implementation of individual parent and teacher behavioral consultation. Behavioral consultation (BC) is an indirect service delivery model in which the consultant works collaboratively with the consultee (i.e., parent or teacher), who works directly with the client (i.e., child).

Theoretical Basis and Objectives

BC is based on behavioral, systems, and ecological theory (e.g., Bergan & Kratochwill, 1990; Reddy, Barboza-Whitehead, Hall, & Rubel, 2000). BC promotes the examination of antecedents and consequences of behavior to determine variables that influence the frequency, intensity, or duration of the problem behavior. Evaluation of the effectiveness of planned interventions is based on examination of outcome data, serving as a means to determine if goals have been met (Fuchs & Fuchs, 1989).

The BC model includes several features: (a) the consultee is an active participant throughout the problem-solving process; (b) the client is involved to varying degrees in the consultation process; (c) the consultant provides knowledge and skills to the consultee; (d) the model links all stages of the consultation decision making to empirical evidence; (e) problems are described as a discrepancy between existing and desired behaviors; (f) environmental factors impact behavior; and (g) plan effectiveness and goal attainment are emphasized, rather than client deficits (Bergan & Kratochwill, 1990).

Sessions

Parents are assigned the same consultant as their classroom teacher. Consultation is provided separately to parents in their home and to teachers at school. Parents and teachers are encouraged to communicate and collaborate through face-to-face visits, telephone calls, and use of home–school daily notes. On average, four to five consultation sessions are provided to parents, and three to four consultation sessions are provided to teachers.

Behavioral consultation follows four stages that include problem identification, problem analysis, plan (treatment) implementation, and problem evaluation. The first stage, problem identification, entails operationally defining the goals to be achieved, specifying the measures of client performance to be used (e.g., tests, work samples, and naturalistic observations of behavior), establishing and implementing data collection procedures, and determining the discrepancy clause between current performance and desired performance. The second stage, problem analysis, involves choosing and conducting an analysis procedure (i.e., analysis of skills or analysis of conditions), developing plan strategies (i.e., broad action plans) and tactics (i.e., specific procedures, events, and materials to be used), and determining procedures for evaluating performance during plan implementation. The third stage, plan (treatment) implementation, is a two-stage process that involves developing the preparations to carry out the plan and then monitoring the implementation of the plan. In addition, the resources and constraints involved in implementing a specific plan are examined. The fourth stage, problem evaluation, consists of evaluating treatment data and determining whether the goals have been achieved and plans were effective, and conducting postimplementation planning (i.e., strategies and tactics to continue and generalize treatment gains).

Training

BC requires professionals to be knowledgeable and trained in child development, behavioral principles and techniques, consultation methods, and data collection. Coursework and supervised training in consultation are needed.

Outcome studies that support the efficacy of CAMP are presented. The effectiveness of any treatment rests, in part, on the children and families included in a program. Thus, a comprehensive screening is recommended to identify children and parents who would benefit most from a program.

OUTCOME EVALUATION

CAMP has been evaluated across four experimental design studies. In these investigations, five inclusion criteria were used: (a) children were 4.5 to 8.5 years of age; (b) enrolled at a preschool or elementary school; (c) diagnosed with ADHD by a pediatric neurologist, psychiatrist, or psychologist; (d) met the *DSM–IV* criteria for ADHD (American Psychiatric Association, 1994), and (e) exhibited clinically elevated scale scores (1.5 standard deviations above the mean) on several standardized child assessment measures. The three exclusion criteria used were (a) children whose parents were recently separated or in the process of divorce; (b) children who had experienced other significant losses in the past 12 months (e.g., death of sibling, parent); and (c) children who had been sexually or physically abused within the past 18 months. Training took place at Fairleigh Dickinson University's Child and Adolescent ADHD Clinic and at the children's homes and schools.

A multimethod, multisource assessment approach was used to evaluate the effectiveness of CAMP. Parents were asked to complete four measures to assess their children's behavior in the home: Child Behavior Checklist (CBCL; Achenbach & Edelbrock, 1991a), Conners Parent Rating Scale–

Revised (CPRS-R; Conners, Sitarenios, Parker, & Epstein, 1998a), Home Situations Questionnaire–Revised (HSQ-R; DuPaul & Barkley, 1992), and the Social Skills Rating System–Parent Form (SSRS-PF; Gresham & Elliot, 1990). In addition, parents were asked to complete the Parenting Stress Index III (PSI-III; Abidin, 1990) and the Family Efficacy Scale (FES; Reddy, 2000b) to evaluate the impact of treatment on parental stress and efficacy. Teachers were asked to complete four measures to assess children's classroom behavior: Teacher Report Form (TRF; Achenbach & Edelbrock, 1991b), Conners Teacher Rating Scale–Revised (CTRS-R; Conners, 1989; Conners, Sitarenios, Parker, & Epstein, 1998b), School Situation Questionnaire–Revised (SSQ-R; DuPaul & Barkley, 1992), and Social Skills Rating System–Teacher Form (SSRS-TF; Gresham & Elliot, 1990). Assessment instruments were administered in home and at school prior to the start of the program, at program completion, and at 4-month follow-up for three of the four studies.

We evaluated the effectiveness of CAMP by using two approaches. The first approach assessed the statistical or reliable change observed across time periods. To accomplish this, repeated measures analysis of covariances (ANCOVAs) were computed to statistically compare group posttest and follow-up scores after adjusting for baseline scores differences between groups. Preplanned comparisons (i.e., paired t-tests) with Dunn-Bonferonni correction were computed to assess within group effects. The second approach assessed the clinically meaningful effects of CAMP on outcomes in the home and school. The clinical significance was assessed during the course of treatment through three methods: (a) between group effect sizes (Glass, McGaw, & Smith, 1981); (b) within group effect sizes (Smith & Glass, 1977); and (c) Jacobson and Truax's (1991) reliable change index.

In our preliminary investigation, 19 families were randomly assigned to a child training group only condition and the CAMP condition (Reddy, Files, & Rubel, 1999). Children were approximately 6 years of age and predominantly Caucasian boys. Seventy-nine percent of the fathers had bachelor's degrees or beyond. The teachers were female and Caucasian. On average, the teachers had 13 years of teaching experience and had 20 students in their classrooms. CAMP resulted in significant reductions in externalizing behaviors (as measured by the CBCL, CPRS-R, SSRS) in the home at program completion and 4-month follow-up. Gains in social skills were also noted across time. Improvements in parent ratings of self-efficacy and child internalizing problems (i.e., anxiety, depression, withdrawn behavior) were found immediately following treatment and at 4-month follow-up. Modest gains in oppositional and aggressive behavior and social skills were found in the school at program completion and follow-up.

In our second study, the effects of child gender on CAMP were examined (Reddy, Hall, Benisz, Rubel, & Isler, 2000). Eighteen families were randomly assigned within gender to two treatment conditions, a child training group only condition and CAMP. The sample included five boys and four girls in each treatment condition. Children were, on average, 6.5 years old and 88% of the sample was Caucasian. Fourty-four percent of the fathers and 78% of the mothers had bachelor's degrees or beyond. The sample included female Caucasian teachers with approximately 14 years of teaching experience.

Exploratory analyses revealed that both treatment conditions exhibited behavioral improvements (e.g., HSQ-R Factor 1 and 2, CBCL Internalizing and Externalizing Composites) at program completion. However, CAMP participants displayed significantly larger gains in the home than those in the child training group only condition. Some interaction effects of gender by treatment condition were found. For example, females in CAMP exhibited greater reductions in overall psychopathology (e.g., CBCL Total Scale, CPRS-R Total Scale), internalizing distress (e.g., CBCL Internalizing Composite), and externalizing problems (e.g., CBCL Externalizing Composite, CPRS-R Hyperactivity Scale) than males in both treatment conditions and females in the child training only condition.

In our third study, 29 children (21 boys and 8 girls) were randomly assigned to three treatment conditions: (a) a child training group; (b) a child and parent group training; and (c) CAMP (Hall & Reddy, 2002). The average age was 6.3 years. Families were primarily Caucasian and had an annual gross income exceeding $60,000. About 80% of the fathers had bachelor's degrees or beyond. The sample included Caucasian female teachers with 15 years of teaching experience.

Data analytic techniques revealed statistically reliable and clinically meaningful reductions in children's externalizing behavior in the home in all three conditions. Parents reported that their children exhibited less hyperactivity, oppositional, or problem behaviors (e.g., CBCL, CPRS-R). As expected, CAMP participants demonstrated the greatest reduction, followed by participants in the child and parent training group condition and the child training-group only condition. Gains were maintained at 4-month follow-up. Moreover, CAMP teachers reported greater reductions in student externalizing behaviors at program completion and follow-up than those teachers participating in the other two conditions.

Improvements in children's social competence at home and in the classroom were found. In the home, child training group participants exhibited small clinical improvements (i.e., effect sizes ranging from .24 to .27), child and parent training group participants yielded statistically significant and moderate clinical improvements (i.e., effect size of .59), and CAMP participants demonstrated statistically significant and large clinical improvements (i.e., effect sizes ranging from .80 to 1.84). Gains were sustained at follow-up. Generalization of gains to the classroom was noted. All three groups demonstrated statistical and clinical (i.e., ESs ranging from .22 to 1.31) improvements, with the greatest level of generalization to the classroom occurring in CAMP.

Improved parental stress and efficacy were found. All conditions exhibited reductions in parental stress. For example, child and parent training group participants demonstrated statistically significant decreases in total parenting stress on the PSI-III Total Scale, and stress associated with their personal characteristics (e.g., stress related to their competence, spouse, role restriction, health, isolation, depression, and attachment) as measured by the PSI-III Parent Domain. CAMP parents exhibited statistically significant decreases in parental stress associated with their child's characteristics (e.g., stress related to their children's distractibility–hyperactivity, adaptability, demandingness, reinforcement, acceptability, and mood) as measured by the PSI-III Child Domain. At follow-up, gains were maintained for both conditions. Parental efficacy improved for all three conditions. Surprisingly, the child and parent training group condition yielded more gains at program completion and follow-up than CAMP condition. It is possible that CAMP parents felt overwhelmed by the amount of interventions or support rendered to them and therefore perceived themselves as less efficacious.

Children's internalizing behavior was also investigated. At program completion, CAMP children exhibited statistically significant improvements and large positive clinical effects (i.e., effect size of .90) on internalizing behavior. At follow-up, the child training group condition exhibited small clinical improvements (i.e., effect size of .27), the child and parent training group condition had medium clinical improvements (i.e., effect size of .40), and the CAMP condition had large clinical improvements (i.e., effect size of .89).

Jacobson and Truax's (1991) reliable change index was computed to assess the clinical significance of individual treatment-related outcomes at program completion. CAMP families exhibited the greatest percentage of reliable change or reliable change with recovery for all of the measures. Moreover, CAMP families demonstrated the lowest percentage of no change–deterioration on all of the measures.

In our fourth investigation, 50 families were randomly assigned to the three treatment conditions previously mentioned (Reddy et al., 2002). The mean age of the sample was approximately 6.3 years and 41 were Caucasian boys. Maternal and paternal educational levels ranged from less than high school to doctorate level education. Approximately 68% of the fathers had bachelor's degrees or beyond. Teachers were Caucasian females with 14 years of teaching experience. Outcome findings in this investigation were comparable across domain area (e.g., externalizing and internalizing behaviors, social skills, parental stress and efficacy) and informants (i.e., parents, teachers) to those reported in Hall and Reddy (2002). Thus, findings provide further support for the efficacy of CAMP.

REPLICATION AND TRANSPORTABILITY

The replication and transportability of any program is predicated, in part, on the appropriateness of the clinical population and treatment setting used. Comprehensive screening assessments are critical for ensuring the replication and transportability of efficacious programs. The CAMP screening process was used to determine whether children and families are appropriate for the program or would be better served by other forms of treatment.

CAMP was developed to provide intensive psychoeducational training for young children with ADHD, their parents, and classroom teachers. CAMP is a language-based program designed to treat children with ADHD who may have other processing disorders, such as speech–language difficulties, occupational or physical therapy needs (e.g., sensory integration, motor planning, fine–gross motor skills), and learning disabilities. However, this program is not suited for children with limited or no language skills. Because CAMP is a new program, outcome investigations have been limited to a narrow scope of children or families. For example, the four investigations outlined have been conducted with Caucasian, college educated, middle-class families. Thus, it remains unanswered whether CAMP would be equally effective with ADHD children from ethnically diverse, lower middle-class or middle-class families. Moreover, the efficacy of CAMP for ADHD children with histories of physical abuse or general maltreatment is unknown.

CAMP has been implemented at a university-based clinic with consultation services provided in home and at school. An apprenticeship approach was used to train personnel for this program. Doctoral students in the clinical psychology and school psychology programs facilitated the children's training group, parent training group, and consultation services with weekly intensive individual and group supervision. Step-by-step training manuals and protocols were developed for training and dissemination. CAMP can be easily implemented in schools, agencies (e.g., Head Start), or outpatient clinics.

RECOMMENDATIONS FOR OUTCOME EVALUATION IN CLINICAL PRACTICE

As mentioned, a multimethod, multisource assessment approach is advantageous for evaluating the efficacy of CAMP. Given the nature of the program, outcome assessments should include child, parent, and teacher reports of change because each treatment component promotes different outcomes. The outcome evaluation approach outlined in this chapter was intended to offer a comprehensive program assessment for research purposes. Thus, it may not be financially or practically feasible for practitioners to adopt such an outcome approach in the field. It is recommended that practitioners use at least three measures described previously to assess program success (e.g., PSI-III, CPRS-R, CTRS-R, SSRS-PF, SSRS-TF).

Outcome assessment should include the monitoring of treatment integrity from two perspectives: (a) therapists'–trainers' adherence to the program and (b) trainees' adherence to the techniques taught in the program. Trainers' treatment adherence can significantly contribute to variability in outcomes (Gage & Wilson, 2000). Thus, trainers who monitor program implementation are critical. To maintain protocol integrity, trainers in CAMP are required to complete a checklist of each component implemented in the children's training group and parent training group. Moreover, a Consultation Process Form (CPF, Reddy, 1998) was designed to guide and to document consultants' work with parents and teachers.

Measuring trainees' treatment adherence is a critically important addition to outcome assessment. To date, only one study has measured adherence to treatment with children with ADHD (Brown, Borden, Wynne, Spunt, & Clingerman, 1987). Springer and Reddy (2004) asserted that between-session adherence may profoundly impact treatment outcome over and above within-session adherence (as measured by attendance to treatment). For example, whether a client uses the techniques outside of training sessions and how accurately he or she implements these techniques outside of the training sessions may impact the effectiveness and generalizability of gains to natural settings. For this purpose, a Parent Adherence Measure (PAM; Springer & Reddy, 2001) was developed to accompany the parent training group curriculum in CAMP.

CONCLUSION

CAMP, a newly developed program, offers a promising treatment approach for children, parents, and teachers that can be easily replicated and transported to other settings (e.g., school, clinics, or agencies). This program uses play interventions (i.e., DAGs), in part, to promote ADHD children's social and behavioral skills in the context of peer group activities. Given the complexity of ADHD children's social, behavioral, and cognitive needs, play interventions alone cannot serve as the "sole tool" in treating this population. Thus, the success of CAMP program rests on the careful screening and selection of families for the program, sequencing of behavioral interventions, trainer and trainee adherence to the treatment protocol, and comprehensive outcome assessments used.

REFERENCES

Abidin, R. R. (1990). *Parenting Stress Index* (3rd ed.). Charlottesville, VA: Pediatric Psychology Press.

Achenbach, T. M., & Edelbrock, C. (1991a). *Manual for the child behavior checklist/ 4–18 and Revised 1991 child behavior profile.* Burlington: University of Vermont, Department of Psychiatry.

Achenbach, T. M., & Edelbrock, C. (1991b). *Manual for the teacher's report form and 1991 profile.* Burlington: University of Vermont, Department of Psychiatry.

Alessandri, S. M., & Schramm, K. (1991). Effects of dextroamphetamine on the cognitive and social play of a preschooler with ADHD. *Journal of the American Academy of Child & Adolescent Psychiatry, 30,* 768–772.

American Psychiatric Association. (1994). *Diagnostic and statistical manual of mental disorders* (4th ed.). Washington, DC: Author.

Bandura, A. (1973). *Aggression: A social learning analysis.* Englewood Cliffs, NJ: Prentice-Hall.

Barkley, R. A. (1988). The effects of methylphenidate on the interactions of preschool ADHD children with their mothers. *Journal of the American Academy of Child & Adolescent Psychiatry, 27*(3), 336–341.

Barkley, R. A. (1990). *Attention deficit hyperactivity disorder: A handbook for diagnosis and treatment.* New York: Guilford Press.

Barkley, R. A. (1997a). *ADHD and the nature of self-control.* New York: Guilford Press.

Barkley, R. A. (1997b). *Defiant children: A clinician's manual for assessment and parent training.* New York: Guilford Press.

Barkley, R. A. (1998). Attention-deficit/hyperactivity disorder. In E. J. Mash & R. A. Barkley (Eds.), *Treatment of childhood disorders* (2nd ed., pp. 55–110). New York: Guilford Press.

Bay-Hinitz, A., Peterson, R. F., & Quilitch, R. H. (1994). Cooperative games: A way to modify aggressive and cooperative behaviors in young children. *Journal of Applied Behavior Analysis, 27,* 435–446.

Bergan, J. R., & Kratochwill, T. R. (1990). *Behavioral consultation and therapy.* New York: Plenum Press.

Brown, R., Borden, K. A., Wynne, M. E., Spunt, A. L, & Clingerman, M. S. (1987). Compliance with pharmacological and cognitive treatments for attention-deficit disorder. *American Academy of Child & Adolescent Psychiatry, 26*(4), 521–526.

Bunker, L. K. (1991). The role of play and motor skill development in building children's self-confidence and self-esteem. [Special issue: Sport and physical education.] *Elementary School Journal, 91,* 467–471.

Byrne, J. M., Bawden, H. N., DeWolfe, N. A., & Beattie, T. L. (1998). Clinical assessment of psychopharmacological treatment of preschoolers with ADHD. *Journal of Clinical & Experimental Neuropsychology, 20*(5), 613–627.

Conners, C. K. (1989). *Conners rating scales manual.* North Tonawanda, NY: Multi-Health Systems.

Conners, C. K., Sitarenios, G., Parker, J. D., & Epstein, J. N. (1998a). The revised Conners parent rating scale (CPRS-R): Factor structure, reliability, and criterion validity. *Journal of Abnormal Child Psychology, 26*(4), 257–268.

Conners, C. K., Sitarenios, G., Parker, J. D., & Epstein, J. N. (1998b). The revised Conners teacher rating scale (CTRS-R): Factor structure, reliability, and criterion validity. *Journal of Abnormal Child Psychology, 26*(4), 279–291.

Connor, D. F. (2002). Preschool attention-deficit disorder: A review of prevalence, diagnosis, neurobiology, and stimulant treatment. *Journal of Developmental & Behavioral Pediatrics, 23*, S1–S9.

Danforth, J. (1998). The outcome of parent training using the Behavior Management Flow Chart with mothers and their children with oppositional defiant disorder and attention-deficit hyperactivity disorder. *Behavior Modification, 22*(4), 443–473.

DuPaul, G. J., & Eckert, T. L. (1997). The effects of school-based interventions for attention-deficit hyperactivity disorder: A meta-analysis. *School Psychology Review, 26*(1), 5–27.

Eisenstadt, T., Eyberg, S., Bodiford-McNeil, C., Newcomb, K., & Funderburk, B. (1993). Parent–child interaction therapy with behavior-problem children: Relative effectiveness of two stages and overall treatment outcome. *Journal of Clinical Child Psychology, 22*(1), 42–51.

Erhardt, E., & Baker, B. (1990). The effects of behavioral parent training on families with young hyperactive children. *Journal of Behavior Therapy and Experimental Psychiatry, 21*(2), 121–132.

Ferland, F. (1997). *Play, children with physical disabilities, and occupational therapy.* Ottowa, Canada: The University of Ottawa Press.

Firestone, P., Musten, L. M., Pisterman, S., Mercer, J., & Bennett, S. (1998). Short-term side effects of stimulant medication are increased in preschool children with attention-deficit/hyperactivity disorder: A double-blind placebo-controlled study. *Journal of Child and Adolescent Psychopharmacology, 8*(1), 13–25.

Forehand, R., & McMahon, R. J. (1981). *Helping the noncompliant child: A clinician's guide to parent training.* New York: Guilford Press.

Fuchs, D., & Fuchs, L. S. (1989). Exploring effective and efficient prereferral interventions: A component analysis of behavioral consultation. *School Psychology Review, 18*(2), 260–279.

Gage, J. D., & Wilson, L. J. (2000). Acceptability of attention-deficit/hyperactivity disorder interventions: A comparison of parents. *Journal of Attention Disorders, 4*(3) 174–182.

Garaigordobil, M., & Echebarria, A. (1995). Assessment of peer-helping program on children's development. *Journal of Research in Childhood Education, 10*, 63–70.

Glass, G., McGaw, B., & Smith, M. (1981). *Meta-Analysis in Social Research.* Beverly Hills, CA: Sage.

Goldstein, A. P. (1988). *The prepare curriculum: Teaching prosocial competencies.* Champaign, IL: Research Press.

Greenhill, L. L. (1992). Pharmacologic treatment of attention-deficit hyperactivitydisorder. *Psychiatric Clinics of North America, 15*(1), 1–27.

Gresham, F. M., & Elliott, S. N. (1990). *Social skills rating system: Manual.* Circle Pines, MN: American Guidance Service.

Grizenko, N. (1997). Outcome of multimodal day treatment for children with severe behavioral problems: A five-year follow-up. *Journal of the American Academy of Child & Adolescent Psychiatry*, 36(7), 989–997.

Grizenko, N., Sayegh, L., & Papineu, D. (1994). Predicting outcome in a multimodal day treatment program for children with severe behavior problems. *Canadian Journal of Psychiatry*, 39(9), 557–562.

Hall, T. F., & Reddy, L. A. (2002, March). *Therapeutic benefits of child and parent group training and behavioral consultation for young children with ADHD.* Paper presented at the Eastern Psychological Association Conference, Boston, MA.

Hand, L. (1986). *Comparison of selected developmentally oriented low organized games and traditional games on the behavior of students with emotional disturbance.* Unpublished master's thesis, Temple University, Philadelphia, PA.

Hanf, C. A. (1969). *A two-stage program for modifying maternal controlling during mother–child (M–C) interaction.* Paper presented at the meeting of the Western Psychological Association, Vancouver, Canada.

Hoag, M. J., & Burlingame, G. M. (1997). Evaluating the effectiveness of child and adolescent group treatment: A meta-analytic review. *Journal of Clinical Child Psychology*, 26(3), 234–246.

Horn, W., Ialongo, N., Greenberg, G., Packard, T., & Smith-Winberry, C. (1990). Additive effects of behavioral parent training and self-control therapy with attention-deficit hyperactivity disordered children. *Journal of Clinical Child Psychology*, 19(2), 98–110.

Hupp, S., Reitman, D., Northup, J., O'Callaghan, P., & LeBlanc, M. (2002). The effects of delayed rewards, tokens, and stimulant medication on sportsmanlike behavior with ADHD-diagnosed children. *Behavior Modification*, 26(2) 148–162.

Jacobson, N., & Traux, P. (1991). Clinical significance: A statistical approach to defining meaningful change in psychotherapy research. *Journal of Consulting and Clinical Psychology*, 59, 12–19.

Klein, R. G., & Bessler, A. W. (1992). Stimulant side effects in children. In J. M. Kane & J. A. Lieberman (Eds.), *Adverse effects of psychotropic drugs* (pp. 470–496). New York: Guilford Press.

Lahey, B. B., Pelham, W. E., Stein, M. A., Loney, J., Trapani, C., Nugent, K., C., et al. (1998). Validity of *DSM–IV* attention-deficit/hyperactivity disorder for younger children. *Journal of the American Academy of Child & Adolescent Psychiatry*, 37, 695–702.

McGee, R., Partridge, F., Williams, S., & Silva, P. (1991). A twelve-year follow-up of preschool hyperactive children. *Journal of the American Academy of Child & Adolescent Psychiatry*, 30(2), 224–232.

McGinnis, E., & Goldstein, A. P. (1997). *Skillstreaming the elementary school child: New strategies and perspectives for teaching prosocial skills* (Rev. ed.). Champaign, IL: Research Press.

Musten, L. M., Firestone, P., Pisterman, S., Bennett, S., & Mercer, J. (1997). Effects of methylphenidate on preschool children with ADHD: Cognitive and behavioral functions. *Journal of the American Academy of Child & Adolescent Psychiatry*, 36(10), 1407–1415.

Orlick, T. (1988). Enhancing cooperative skills in games and life. In F. L. Smoll, R. Magill, & M. Ash (Eds.), *Children in sport* (pp. 149–159). Champaign, IL: Human Kinetics.

Patterson, G. R. (1982). *Coercive family process*. Eugene, OR: Castalia.

Pfiffner, L. J., & McBurnett, K. (1997). Social skills training with parent generalization: Treatment effects for children with ADHD. *Journal of Consulting and Clinical Psychology, 65* (5), 749–757.

Pisterman, S., Firestone, P., McGrath, P., Goodman, J., Webster, I., Mallory, R., et al. (1992). The role of parent training in treatment of preschoolers with ADHD. *American Journal of Orthopsychiatry, 62*(3), 397–408.

Pisterman, S., McGrath, P., Firestone, P., Goodman, J., Webster, I., & Mallory, R. (1989). Outcome of parent-mediated treatment of preschoolers with attention-deficit disorder with hyperactivity. *Journal of Consulting and Clinical Psychology, 57*(5), 628–635.

Reddy, L. A. (1998). *Consultation process form*. Teaneck, NJ: Fairleigh Dickinson University.

Reddy, L. A. (2000a). *Children's ADHD training group program*. Teaneck, NJ: Fairleigh Dickinson University.

Reddy, L. A. (2000b). *Family efficacy scale*. Teaneck, NJ: Fairleigh Dickinson University.

Reddy, L. A., Barboza-Whitehead, S., Hall, T., & Rubel, E. (2000). Clinical focus of consultation outcome research with children and adolescents. *Special Services in the Schools, 16*(1/2), 1–22.

Reddy, L. A., Braunstein, D., Hauch, Y., Springer, C., & Hall, T. (2002, August). *Randomized trial of three child/parent training groups for ADHD children*. Poster session presented at the American Psychological Association Conference, Chicago, IL.

Reddy, L. A., Files, T. M., & Rubel, E. (1999, August). *Multimodal treatment study for young children with ADHD*. Poster session presented at the American Psychological Association Conference, Boston, MA.

Reddy, L. A., & Goldstein, A. P. (2001). Aggressive replacement training: A multimodal intervention for aggressive children. In S. I. Pfeiffer & L. A. Reddy (Eds.), *Innovative Mental Health Prevention Programs for Children* (pp. 47–62). New York: Haworth Press.

Reddy, L. A., Hall, T. M., Benisz, E., Rubel, E., & Isler, L. (2000). *Effects of gender on a multimodal intervention for young children with ADHD*. Poster session presented at the American Psychological Association Conference, Washington, DC.

Reddy, L. A., Spencer, P., Hall, T., & Rubel, E. (2001). Use of developmentally appropriate games in a child group training program for young children with attention-deficit hyperactivity disorder. In C. Schaefer, A. Drewes, & L. Carey (Eds.), *School based play therapy* (pp. 256–274). New York: Wiley.

Reed, M., Black, T., & Eastman, J. (1978). A new look at perceptual-motor therapy. *Academic Therapy, 14*, 55–65.

Reitman, D., Hupp, S., O'Callaghan, P. M., Gulley, V., & Northup, J. (2001). The influence of a token economy and methylphenidate on attentive and disruptive behavior during sports with ADHD-diagnosed children. *Behavior Modification, 25*(2) 305–323.

Richters, J., Arnold, E., Jensen, P., Abikoff, H., Conners, K., Greenhill, L., et al. (1995). NIMH collaborative multisite multimodal treatment study of children with ADHD: I. Background and rational. *Journal of the American Academy of Child & Adolescent Psychiatry, 34*(8), 987–1000.

Sagvolden, T., & Sergeant, J. A. (1998). Attention-deficit/hyperactivity disorder: From brain dysfunctions to behavior. *Behavioral Brain Research, 94*(1), 1–10.

Schneider, L. B. (1989). *The effect of selected low organized games on the self-esteem of kindergartners.* Unpublished manuscript, Leonard Gordon Institute for Human Development Through Play, Temple University, Philadelphia, PA.

Smith, M., & Glass, G. (1977). Meta-analysis of psychotherapy outcome studies. *American Psychologist, 32,* 752–760.

Sonuga-Barke, E., Daley, D., Thompson, M., Laver-Bradbury, C., & Weeks, A. (2001). Parent-based therapies for preschool attention-deficit/hyperactivity disorder: A randomized controlled trial with a community sample. *Journal of the American Academy of Child & Adolescent Psychiatry, 40*(4), 402–408.

Springer, C., & Reddy, L. A. (2001). *Parental adherence measure.* Teaneck, NJ: Fairleigh Dickinson University.

Springer, C., & Reddy, L. A. (2004). Measuring treatment adherence in behavior therapy: Opportunities for research and practice. *The Behavior Therapist, 27*(4), 1–9.

Strayhorn, J. M., & Weidman, C. S. (1989). Reduction of attention-deficit and internalizing symptoms in preschoolers through parent–child interaction training. *Journal of the American Academy of Child & Adolescent Psychiatry, 28*(6), 888–896.

Strayhorn, J. M., & Weidman, C. S. (1991). Follow-up one year after parent–child interaction training: Effects on behavior of preschool children. *Journal of the American Academy of Child & Adolescent Psychiatry, 30*(1), 138–143.

Torbert, M. (1994). *Follow me: A handbook of movement activities for children.* New York: Prentice Hall.

Torbert, M., & Schneider, L. (1993). *Follow me too.* Menlo Park, CA: Addison Wesley.

Weiss, M., Jain, U., & Garland, J. (2000). Clinical suggestions for management of stimulant treatment in adolescents. *Canadian Journal of Psychiatry, 45*(8), 717–723.

9

PARENT–CHILD INTERACTION THERAPY FOR CHILDREN EXPERIENCING EXTERNALIZING BEHAVIOR PROBLEMS

AMY D. HERSCHELL AND CHERYL B. MCNEIL

Parent–Child Interaction Therapy (PCIT; Eyberg & Calzada, 1998; Hembree-Kigin & McNeil, 1995) is an empirically supported treatment program that was originally designed to treat families with children 2 though 6 years of age who were exhibiting externalizing behavior problems.[1] Conducted in weekly, 1-hour sessions, parents and their child meet with a PCIT therapist for approximately 10 to 14 weeks. Outcome studies have demonstrated that completion of treatment results in increased parent skill, decreased child behavior problems, and generalizations to home and school settings as well as to untreated siblings (see Herschell, Calzada, Eyberg, & McNeil, 2002b for a detailed research review).

---

[1]The term "externalizing behavior" is used to refer to disruptive behavior characteristic of diagnostic criteria for oppositional defiant disorder or conduct disorder (e.g., noncompliance, aggression).

This chapter provides an overview of PCIT by first describing the treatment's theoretical basis and objectives. Next, essential treatment elements and the structure of PCIT are reviewed, as is treatment outcome research. The transportability of PCIT to other populations and settings is also discussed. Recommendations are made for evaluating PCIT in everyday clinical practice. Finally, a case vignette is described to illustrate the application of PCIT.

THEORETICAL BASIS AND OBJECTIVES

Within a Hanf (1969) two-stage model, PCIT blends developmental theory, social learning theory, behavioral principles, and traditional play therapy. Hanf's two-stage operant conditioning model originally was developed to treat problematic interaction patterns of mothers and their young children experiencing multiple handicaps. During the first phase of treatment, mothers were taught to allow their child to lead a play activity while observing and commenting on the child's positive behavior and ignoring inappropriate behavior. In the second phase of treatment, mothers were taught to use clear, direct commands to reward child compliance and to use timeout as a punishment for child noncompliance. Hanf's model also involved coaching parents in vivo with their child. Since its development, the Hanf model has been successfully applied to treating children with externalizing behavior problems by scientist-practitioners including Eyberg (e.g., Eyberg & Robinson, 1982), Forehand (e.g., Forehand, Cheney, & Yoder, 1974), and Pisterman (Pisterman et al., 1989, 1992). Variants of the Hanf model are evident in treatment programs designed to treat children with similar concerning behavior by Barkley (1981), Cunningham (1989), and Webster-Stratton (1981).

Like other Hanf-derived programs, PCIT is conducted in two phases and uses in vivo coaching. However, PCIT can be differentiated from other Hanf-derived programs because of its strong reliance on the teaching of relationship enhancement skills espoused by Axline (1969) to improve the quality of the parent–child relationship (Foote, Eyberg, & Schuhmann, 1998), and its reliance on the developmental psychology literature (Eyberg, Schuhman, & Rey, 1998). For example, developmental psychology has demonstrated a strong relationship between parenting styles and child outcomes (e.g., Azar & Wolfe, 1989; Baumrind, 1995; Franz, McClelland, & Weinberger, 1991; Olson, Bates, & Bayles, 1990; Power & Chapieski, 1986). Informed by this literature, PCIT assists parents in adopting an authoritative parenting style (Baumrind, 1967), which incorporates a young child's dual needs for parental nurturance and limit setting to achieve optimal child outcomes.

PCIT also draws on social learning theory, which asserts that child behavior problems can be inadvertently established and maintained by problematic parent–child relationships (Patterson, 1975; 1976). Patterson's (1982) coercive interaction theory, a transactional model, accounts for the development and maintenance of externalizing behavior problems in young children by maintaining that each member of the parent–child relationship attempts to control the other's behavior through habitual, aversive behaviors. These behaviors create a coercive cycle that is then maintained by negative reinforcement. (See Foote et al., 1998 and Greco, Sorrell, & McNeil, 2001 for more detailed and sophisticated theoretical reviews.) In the second phase of treatment, PCIT assists parents is gaining control over these situations by teaching parents to set consistent and fair limits, to predictably follow through with directives, and to provide reasonable, age-appropriate consequences for child misbehavior within the context of a positive parent–child relationship.

The phases of PCIT emphasize enhancing and balancing specific parenting skills; the same is true of the goals of PCIT. The goals of PCIT for parents are to assist them in establishing and maintaining a secure, nurturing relationship with their child and balancing that positive relationship with healthy, consistent discipline. Goals for children include developing and increasing prosocial behaviors (e.g., using polite words, sharing, taking turns), as well as decreasing inappropriate behavior, particularly noncompliance and defiance (Eyberg & Boggs, 1989). Goals for both parents and children are quantifiable and are measured at each session. Treatment progress is based on how quickly skills are acquired; this is discussed in the following section.

Structure of PCIT

PCIT is conducted in two phases, child directed interaction (CDI) and parent directed interaction (PDI). At the beginning of each phase, parents are taught specific skills in one didactic session. That teaching session involves discussing, providing examples for, and role-playing each skill. It also involves tailoring the skills to meet the individual needs of each child and family, and it provides a valuable opportunity for therapists to continue building rapport with parents. In subsequent sessions, parents are coached in the use of skills using a bug-in-the-ear hearing device and a one-way mirror. A therapist on the other side of the one-way mirror observes the parent–child interaction and provides the parent with specific, immediate, and frequent positive feedback regarding the use of PCIT skills in the interaction via the bug-in-the-ear hearing device (i.e., the therapist "coaches" the parent). If more than one caregiver (e.g., spouse, childcare provider, extended family member) attends sessions, the coaching time is split among them. The caregivers alternate between being coached and joining the therapist behind the one-way mirror to learn through observation.

The skills taught in the first phase of PCIT, CDI resemble traditional play therapy skills but rely heavily on the behavioral principles of strategic attention and selective ignoring. Parents are taught to attend to all appropriate child behavior (e.g., sharing, using manners, playing nicely) and to actively ignore attention-seeking, minor, inappropriate child behaviors (e.g., whining, playing rough with the toys, sassing) through the use of the CDI skills also known as the PRIDE skills. PRIDE skills include using praise (preferably labeled praise), reflection, imitation, description (preferably behavioral descriptions), and enthusiasm and avoiding questions, commands, and criticism. Definitions and examples of each of these skills are provided in Table 9.1.

The skills taught in the second phase of PCIT, PDI, assume that compliance is a key issue to be targeted. It is presumed that if a child will comply with parental directives, the large majority of child misbehaviors can be managed effectively. The PDI skills taught to parents include: differentiating when a command is necessary; giving effective direct commands; evaluating compliance versus noncompliance; and providing appropriate consequences for compliance and noncompliance. Once these skills are mastered, parents are provided information on establishing house rules, managing difficult behavior in public, handling future behavior problems, and knowing when behavior concerns might warrant a future "booster" session. Booster sessions are held after treatment completion if a parent feels the child's behavior has worsened, if a new challenging behavior has developed, or if a parent feels the need for some support. These sessions are conducted much like other PCIT sessions in that they are solution-oriented, involve active parent participation, and focus time on coaching parents.

The length of treatment varies for each family because it is dependent on how quickly the parents master skills and the child's behavior improves to within normal limits on standardized measures of child functioning. On average, one-hour PCIT sessions are conducted weekly for 10 to 14 weeks; however, treatment can be as few as 5 sessions or as many as 25 sessions. These 5 to 25 sessions include (a) a pretreatment assessment of child, parent, and family functioning; (b) assessment feedback; (c) teaching and coaching of CDI skills; (d) teaching and coaching of PDI skills; (e) teaching generalization skills; and (f) posttreatment assessment of child, parent, and family functioning. Also integral to treatment is the parents devoting five to ten minutes a day for play interactions with their child at home. Throughout treatment, homework completion is monitored and its importance is emphasized. Although it might be tempting to omit a phase of treatment or reverse the order of phases, treatment outcome research indicates that both phases are necessary and that CDI should precede PDI to effectively decrease problematic child behavior (Eisenstadt, Eyberg, McNeil, Newcomb, & Funderburk, 1993).

TABLE 9.1
Child Directed Interaction Skills

Skills	Definitions	Examples
Skills to Use		
Praise— Labeled	Any specific verbalization that expresses a favorable judgment on an activity, product, or attribute of the child.	Parent: "I love how you are using such nice manners."
Reflection	A statement that immediately repeats back the child's verbalization.	Child: "My favorite is the Play-Doh." Parent: "Your favorite toy is the Play-Doh. I like the Play-Doh, too."
Imitation	A physical act that mimics or accompanies the activity or behavior in which the child is engaged.	Child: (playing with cars) Parent: (picking up a car) "I'm going to drive my car carefully and gently just like you're driving your cars."
Description— Behavioral	A declarative sentence or phrase that gives a neutral account of the child's activity, product, or attributes.	Child: (playing with farm animals) Parent: "You're feeding the baby chickens."
Enthusiasm	Excitement or interest in the child's activity, product, or attributes.	Child: (completes a Play-Doh mold) Parent: (smiles and speaks in an animated voice) "What a great Play-Doh star you made!"
Skills to Avoid		
Questions	A declarative or reflective comment expressed in question form.	Parent: "What do you think we should play with now?"
Commands— Indirect	An order, demand, or direction for a behavioral response that is implied, nonspecific, or stated in question form.	Parent: "Let's color now."
Criticism	A verbalization that finds fault with the activities, products, or attributes of the child.	Child: (drawing a picture with the grass in red) Parent: "Now you know that isn't right. The grass should be green, not red."

Note. Definitions are adapted from "Manual for the Dyadic Parent-Child Interaction Coding System-II," by S. M. Eyberg, J. Bessmer, K. Newcomb, D. Edwards, and E. Robinson, 1994, *Social and Behavioral Sciences Documents* (Ms. No. 2897).

With the exception of the two didactic sessions conducted at the onset of each phase of treatment, all other sessions involve coaching the parent and are structured the same way. Each coaching session begins with a brief (10 minute) check-in, during which the therapist and parent discuss the week's homework, the child's progress, any evidence of generalization, and any setbacks or concerns that have occurred over the week. Check-ins end with a brief review of which skills the parent already has mastered and which skills will be targeted for improvement during the session. Afterward, the therapist goes behind the one-way mirror and codes a five-minute observation of the parent's current skill level. As we discuss later in this chapter, the behavior observation data collected at each session are an essential element of treatment. Next, parents are coached for 30 minutes. Finally, each session ends with a check-out time, during which the parent and therapist discuss progress made during the session and since treatment began. Also discussed are homework and goals for the following week.

At the end of this chapter, a clinical description of PCIT is included that offers a general treatment synopsis. For detailed clinical reviews and case descriptions using PCIT with children exhibiting externalizing behavior problems, see Hembree-Kigin and McNeil (1995); Eyberg and Calzada (1998); or Herschell, Lumley, and McNeil (2000). For a clinical review and case example of the use of PCIT with a child who experienced physical abuse and exhibited externalizing behavior problems, please see Herschell, Calzada, Eyberg, and McNeil (2002a); or with children who experienced histories of general maltreatment, see Fricker, Ruggiero, and Smith (2005).

KEY TREATMENT INGREDIENTS

Recognizing that each child and family presents with their own set of strengths and challenges, PCIT is tailored to meet their unique, individual needs; however, there are certain elements of PCIT that remain the same for each family. These essential elements are core components that define PCIT and include utilizing parents as active agents of change, applying in-vivo coaching as a primary therapeutic tool, and relying on assessment to guide treatment.

Parents as Agents of Therapeutic Change

Currently considered the treatment of choice for child conduct problems (e.g., Azar & Wolfe, 1989; Brestan & Eyberg, 1998; Kazdin, 1996), behavioral parent training, or parent management training, programs like PCIT recognize that parents play an important role in shaping and maintaining their child's positive and problematic behaviors (e.g., Denham,

Renwick, & Holt, 1991; Dix, Ruble, & Zambrano, 1989; Parpal & Maccoby, 1985). Parents can become effective agents of therapeutic change for their young children. From this perspective, PCIT involves changing the child's behavior through changing parent–child interaction patterns. As previously discussed, parents are actively involved in each session and are taught specific skills to affect their child's positive social, emotional, and behavioral development.

In Vivo Coaching

A hallmark of PCIT is the use of constructive, positive, in vivo coaching. At least 30 minutes of each treatment session is devoted to the therapist's live coaching of parenting skills. Most coaching statements are brief and precise labeled praises or descriptions of the parent's affect on the child. Occasionally, coaching statements include redirection or noncritical correction. This live coaching involves the therapist providing specific, immediate, and frequent feedback to the parent via a bug-in-the-ear hearing device. Feedback is provided on the parent's use of the PRIDE skills as well as other aspects of the parent–child relationship. For example, parents with histories of physically abusing their children often are coached in understanding developmental norms, accurately interpreting child behavior, and remaining calm during discipline interactions, because these often are areas in need of improvement for these families. Just as focusing on the parent–child relationship emphasizes the value of social reinforcement, PCIT therapists use these same principles to shape parent behavior (Borrego & Urquiza, 1998). Therapists continually model positive communication skills with the parent and child in all verbalizations.

Coaching is directive and provides several advantages over less directive teaching methods. First, parent skill acquisition (and thereby child skill acquisition) is hastened because of the immediacy and intensity of feedback provided. Second, coaching allows the therapist to tailor more general PCIT skills, such as the PRIDE skills, to meet the individual needs of the child and parent. Third, therapists are able to correct parents' misapplication of skills before the skills become engrained into the parents' behavioral repertoire.

Use of Assessment to Guide Treatment

Treatment begins with a comprehensive, multimethod assessment that includes structured clinical interviews, parent and teacher rating scales, behavior observation in the clinic and school, and specific measures of parent functioning. Assessment guides clinical decisions regarding the focus and outcome of treatment throughout the treatment process. Comprehensive assessments often are completed at the beginning, middle, and end of treatment, and observational data are collected at each treatment session.

Several assessment instruments have been developed specifically for use in PCIT, including a semistructured interview (Eyberg & Calzada, 1998), the Eyberg Child Behavior Inventory (ECBI; Eyberg & Pincus, 1999), the Therapy Attitude Inventory (TAI; Brestan, Jacobs, Rayfield, & Eyberg, 1999), the Sutter-Eyberg Student Behavior Inventory-Revised (SESBI-R; Eyberg & Pincus, 1999), the Dyadic Parent–Child Interaction Coding System-II (DPICS-II; Eyberg, Bessmer, Newcomb, Edwards, & Robinson, 1994), and the Revised Edition of the School Observation Coding System (REDSOCS; Jacobs et al., 2000). Although each of these measures contributes to a broader understanding of the parent–child dyad, the two assessment tools that are most essential to PCIT are the ECBI and DPICS-II.

The ECBI (Eyberg & Pincus, 1999) is a 36-item parent-report measure of externalizing behavior problems that is appropriate for use with children from 2 to 16 years of age. For each of 36 behaviors, parents are asked to rate how intense and problematic that behavior is for their child. Two scales are derived: an intensity scale, which represents how extreme the child's behaviors are; and a problem scale, which represents how problematic the parent views the child's behaviors to be. This measure takes approximately 10 minutes to complete and provides the clinician with a list of specific child behaviors to target in treatment.

The DPICS-II, a behavior observation coding system (Eyberg et al., 1994), is used in the initial assessment and during a 5-minute segment of each treatment session to measure the quality of the parent–child interaction. Results from data coded at each session are used to assess the parent's treatment progress, to guide coaching and homework assignments, and to monitor progress across sessions. Results also inform the therapist when the family is ready to progress to the second phase of treatment and when the family is ready to end treatment. To advance to the second phase of treatment, parents must give at least 10 behavioral descriptions, 10 reflections (given the opportunity to do so), and 10 labeled praises within a 5-minute coding segment. Also, no more than three verbalizations that are questions, commands, or criticisms may be used during that same time. Definitions and examples from this coding system are included in Table 9.1. After these skills are mastered, parents move on to the second phase of treatment and learn a set of constructive discipline skills. To complete treatment, mastery of the discipline skills also is required. A parent is considered to have mastered the skills if in a 5-minute coding segment, 75% of the directives they give to the child are effective, direct commands, and 75% of the time the parent appropriately follows through with each command. In addition, parents must be able to follow through with all discipline procedures taught.

OUTCOME EVALUATION

Outcome studies examining the efficacy of PCIT have measured variables related to child outcomes and family functioning, immediately, 1 year, 2 years, and up to 6 years after treatment completion. In addition, a large, NIMH-funded study currently is being conducted to examine maintenance of treatment gains 4 to 6 years after treatment completion (Eyberg & Boggs; NIMH Grant RO1 MH-60632). In a recent review of 17 PCIT outcome studies that included 628 children, 368 of whom participated in PCIT, Gallagher (2003) reported that child behavior improvements were statistically significant across all studies. Clinical significance, demonstrated by behavior problems on assessment measures changing from clinically significant ranges (pretreatment) to within normal ranges (posttreatment) was found in 82% (14 of 17) of studies. In a similar way, compliance rate changes have been reported in multiple studies (e.g., Borrego, Urquiza, Rasmussen, & Zebell, 1999; Eisenstadt et al., 1993; Eyberg, Boggs, & Algina, 1995; Eyberg & Robinson, 1982; McNeil, Eyberg, Eisentadt, Newcomb, & Funderburk, 1991; Nixon, Sweeney, Erickson, & Touyz, 2003), and have been reported to change (pre- to posttreatment) from 29% to 43%; 41% to 72%; 21% to 46%; 39% to 89%; 41% to 70% and 64% to 81%, respectively. Of six PCIT outcome studies examining social and emotional functioning (e.g., mood and self-esteem), all have shown pre- to posttreatment statistical and clinical improvement. In addition, studies demonstrate diagnostic changes. For example, Eisenstadt et al. (1993) reported 100% of children meeting diagnostic criteria for a disruptive behavior disorder at pretreatment, in comparison to 15% at posttreatment. All of the children comprising that 15% continued to meet criteria for attention-deficit/hyperactivity disorder, as opposed to oppositional defiant disorder or conduct disorder.

Positive child outcomes have been found to generalize from the controlled clinic setting to the home environment, as well as to school classrooms (Eisenstadt et al., 1993; McNeil et al., 1991; Schuhmann, Foote, Eyberg, Boggs, & Algina, 1998). With no direct classroom intervention and completion of clinic-based PCIT, both parents and teachers reported statistically and clinically significant reductions in the intensity of child behavior problems (Pearson correlation = .78, p = .007 considering pre-minus posttreatment difference scores of parent ECBI and teacher SESBI intensity scores) and increases in classroom compliance rates from 40.7% to 70.4% (McNeil et al., 1991). Study of classrooms has also indicated that generalization may be less promising for hyperactivity, distractibility, and peer relationships. Instead, generalization to the classroom is likely most promising for oppositional and disruptive behavior (McNeil et al., 1991).

Follow-up studies have explored how long treatment gains maintain. Eyberg, Funderburk, Hembree-Kigin, McNeil, Querido, and Hood (2001) found treatment gains in the home setting at 1 and 2 years after completion of treatment. In a small sample of children (n = 10), Funderburk et al. (1998) found classroom improvements maintained up to 1 year, but to a lesser extent at 18-month follow-up. Also, Edwards, Eyberg, Rayfield, Jacobs, and Hood (2001) found that families who dropped out of PCIT looked the same after 1 to 3 years as they had before treatment started. In contrast, families who completed PCIT maintained their gains in both child and family functioning. For children who had completed PCIT 3 to 6 years earlier, Hood and Eyberg (2003) found that child behavior problems were significantly less frequent ($F(2, 44) = 35.69$, $p < .0001$) and problematic ($F(2, 44) = 36.68$, $p < .0001$) for parents than before treatment, and maternal locus of control was significantly more internal ($F(2, 44) = 24.26$, $p < .0001$). In addition, child behavior problems decreased as the length of time from treatment increased. Not only did PCIT treatment gains maintain over 3 to 6 years, but children actually continued to improve, lending support to the durability of treatment over time. Children who have fathers participating in treatment tend to maintain gains better over time than children with nonparticipating fathers (Bagner & Eyberg, 2003).

In terms of family functioning, studies have demonstrated increases in parents' use of reflective listening and praise, decreases in parents' use of sarcasm and criticism with their children, and increases in physical proximity between parents and children after completion of treatment (Eisenstadt et al., 1993; Schuhmann et al., 1998) as measured by behavior observations. It is interesting that, after completion of PCIT with a target child, gains have been found to generalize to untreated siblings, according to parent-report (Brestan, Eyberg, Boggs, & Algina, 1997; Eyberg & Robinson, 1982).

On self-report measures, parents report statistically significant decreases in parenting stress (Eisendstadt et al., 1993), decreases in marital distress (Eyberg & Robinson, 1982), and increases in confidence in their parenting skills (Schuhmann et al., 1998) after completing PCIT. Minnesota Multiphasic Personality Inventory (MMPI) profile scores reveal statistically significant decreases in psychopathology scores as well (Eyberg & Robinson, 1982). Also, parents report high satisfaction with the content and process of treatment (Brestan et al., 1999; Eyberg & Matarazzo, 1980).

Outcome studies have examined the efficacy of PCIT treatment relative to waitlist controls (McNeil, Capage, Bahl, & Blanc, 1999; Schuhmann et al., 1998), normal classroom controls, classroom controls with behavior problems (McNeil et al., 1991), modified treatment groups (Nixon et al., 2003), treatment drop outs (Edwards et al., 2001), and control groups varying in severity of disruptive behavior (Funderburk et al., 1998). Each comparison has demonstrated the superiority of treatment over control conditions. One additional study compared PCIT to a parent group didactic training and found PCIT to be more effective than the parent group didactic training (Eyberg & Matarazzo, 1980).

REPLICATION AND TRANSPORTABILITY

Efforts have been made to systematically extend PCIT to varied populations and settings. In combination with these efforts, care has been taken to ensure that innovative clinical efforts are theoretically grounded and empirically supported.

Using PCIT With Other Populations

PCIT originally was developed to treat children exhibiting behaviors diagnostically consistent with a disruptive behavior disorder (i.e., oppositional defiant disorder, attention-deficit hyperactivity disorder, conduct disorder, or disruptive behavior disorder, not otherwise specified) and their biological parents. However, PCIT has also been successfully applied to children with separation anxiety disorder (Pincus, Choate, Eyberg, & Barlow, in press), developmental delays (Eyberg & Matarrazzo, 1980), chronic illness (Bagner, Fernandez, & Eyberg, 2004), histories of physical abuse (Urquiza & McNeil, 1996; Chaffin et al., 2004), and histories of general maltreatment (Fricker et al., 2002). In addition, depending on the child's home situation, nontraditional caregivers have been incorporated into PCIT, including foster parents, adoptive parents, and kinship caregivers (Fricker et al., in press; McNeil, Herschell, Gurwitch, & Clemens-Mowrer, in press; Urquiza, Timmer, Herschell, et al., in press).

Research and clinical experience suggest that there are certain populations with whom PCIT is less successful. In general, PCIT is less successful with parents who have difficulty in their interpersonal relationships because of extreme psychopathology (e.g., borderline personality disorder, psychotic disorders, substance dependence, major depression). PCIT also appears to be less successful with families currently experiencing *severe* marital discord or extreme family chaos, as well as with children over 7 years of age (Hembree-Kigin & McNeil, 1995).

Transporting PCIT to Other Settings

The traditional, clinic-based model of PCIT has been primarily used in university training centers (e.g., West Virginia University, University of Florida) or university-affiliated medical centers (e.g., Oklahoma Health Sciences Center, University of California, Davis Medical Center). Training in these centers has been conducted with an apprenticeship model. Clinical psychology doctoral students typically conduct co-therapy with more experienced clinicians and receive intensive individual and group supervision. Although this method of training has been effective, a small number of therapists are trained relative to the large number of children and families who could benefit from the intervention. A number of steps have recently been taken to disseminate PCIT more widely. For example, a treatment manual is now available through a major publisher (Hembree-Kigin & McNeil, 1995). Workshops have been conducted at national conferences (e.g., American Psychological Association, Association for Advancement of Behavior Therapy), and trainings conducted at community mental health centers (e.g., CARE Center in Santa Rosa, California; Family Life Center in Columbus, Kansas). Also, Urquiza and colleagues at the University of California, Davis Medical Center have developed a training model and protocol to disseminate PCIT to California community mental health agencies specializing in treating child maltreatment.

Training conducted in community-based mental health centers has involved (a) intensive didactic presentations containing information on PCIT's theoretical basis, assessment, treatment protocol, and session structure; (b) videotape review of relatively straightforward to very complex cases; (c) interactive discussions, modeling, and role-plays; (d) supervision of multiple cases; and (e) continued consultation. Timing of training components and continued consultation have been critical in dissemination success.

Slight modifications to the clinic-based PCIT protocol have been made to transport it to settings where bug-in-the-ear and one-way mirror technologies are unavailable (e.g., medical exam rooms, traditional therapy rooms). Without such technology, PCIT therapists can do "in-room" coaching. This involves structuring the playroom so the parent and child sit side-by-side at an adult sized table with approximately three age-appropriate toys on it. The therapist positions him- or herself slightly behind the parent, on the side opposite to the child. As the parent and child interact, the therapist provides the same intensity and quality of feedback by subtly whispering comments to the parent in the room as would be provided by coaching behind the one-way mirror. Both parents and children are instructed to avoid conversations with the therapist until the coaching part of the session is complete. A preliminary study by Rayfield and Sobel (2000) indicated that this in-room coaching is effective within the larger PCIT protocol.

More substantial modifications have been made to PCIT by adapting it to fit home- and school-based settings. For families with extreme difficulty attending weekly, clinic-based sessions, PCIT therapists have gone to family homes and conducted PCIT with the same treatment and session structure as the clinic-based model, but have used in-room coaching. In addition to using in-home PCIT for families with transportation difficulties, it also has been used in combination with clinic-based services for children with extreme behavior problems or families with low resources, to aid in generalization of skills. Although this home-based strategy is used clinically, no studies have been published about the effectiveness of this approach.

Adaptations also have been made to PCIT to meet the needs of children experiencing disruptive classroom behavior and the needs of their teachers. Querido and Eyberg (2001) developed a model of PCIT delivery for children and families participating in Head Start, thereby targeting low-income families. Several incentives (e.g., provision of transportation, care for siblings during sessions) were added to the traditional clinic-based model to enhance parents' ability to attend sessions. Bahl (1998) also modified PCIT to fit a school setting. Labeled Teacher–Child Interaction Therapy (TCIT), this intervention focuses first on enhancing the teacher–child relationship and later on improving child compliance in preschool classrooms. One case study has been published about this technique (McIntosh, Rizza, & Bliss, 2000), in which TCIT was found to increase positive interactions between the teacher and child, to decrease child disruptive behavior, including noncompliance, and to decrease the teacher's need to issue commands. It is important to note that although these innovations in PCIT are exciting and appear promising, they do not have the same level of empirical support that clinic-based PCIT has acquired.

RECOMMENDATIONS FOR OUTCOME EVALUATION IN CLINICAL PRACTICE

As efforts to disseminate PCIT expand, care should continue to be taken to implement the treatment in a manner consistent with the original PCIT model, including its "essential elements." Assessment of efforts at both client and therapist levels will be important to ensure consistent implementation.

Evaluating Clients' Treatment Progress

As previously mentioned, assessment plays an integral role in PCIT in that all treatment decisions are based on assessment data. Although a comprehensive, multimethod assessment is ideal, it is not always possible. Many community-based centers operate on tight budgets that prohibit the purchase of expensive assessment tools. For such situations, it is recommended that at least two measures be used, the DPICS-II and the ECBI, both of which were described in this chapter. These two measures are central to determining families' progress in treatment, and subsequently, treatment planning.

Evaluating Therapists' Implementation of the Treatment Protocol

The efficacy of empirically supported treatments is based on how these treatments were implemented in treatment outcome studies. Therefore, if therapists implement ESTs, such as PCIT, without regard for treatment integrity, the treatment's effectiveness is unknown. Research by Henggeler,

Melton, Brondino, Scherer, and Hanley (1997) has demonstrated better client outcomes when therapists adhere closely to the treatment protocol, thus supporting the value in evaluating the therapists' integrity with established treatment procedures.

Eyberg and Calzada (1998) have developed treatment checklists for each PCIT session. These checklists are used in university-based training clinics and research centers to ensure that therapists implement PCIT in a consistent manner. They likely would be useful to therapists learning PCIT, as it can be a fairly complex treatment to implement and therapists often have specific questions about each treatment session. Supervisors or researchers might also find these checklists useful, because sessions can be observed or videotaped and coded for inclusion of key treatment components to ensure good treatment integrity.

CASE VIGNETTE

Greg's Head Start teacher approached his mother, Ms. S, after Greg had been in her classroom for slightly over one month. The teacher mentioned her concerns that Greg was noncompliant, disrespectful, aggressive toward other children, and had tried to hurt the classroom pet hamster. Ms. S agreed that Greg's behavior was difficult, but thought that "boys will be boys" and that he would eventually grow out of it. His teacher persisted and pointed out that he was one of the most defiant and aggressive children she had worked with in her 12 years as a preschool teacher. To her, Greg's behavior was a concern, and she recommended that Ms. S take Greg to be seen by a behavioral health specialist.

Evaluation

Because of his teacher's concerns, Ms. S scheduled an appointment for Greg at a local clinic that specialized in evaluating and treating young children. At their first appointment, Ms. S completed several standardized measures, including the Child Behavior Checklist (CBCL), the Eyberg Child Behavior Inventory (ECBI), and the Parenting Stress Index (PSI). She also participated in a clinical interview and a structured behavior observation with Greg that consisted of three 5-minute situations (child-directed interaction, parent-directed interaction, and clean-up), which were coded using the previously described DPICS-II. The therapist also asked for Ms. S's permission to gather information, including the Sutter-Eyberg Student Behavior Inventory-Revised (SESBI), from Greg's Head Start teacher.

From the gathered intake information, the therapist learned that Greg was a 5-year-old Caucasian male who was one of three children. He lived with his biological mother, Ms. S (24 years of age), his biological father, Mr. S (25 years old), and his younger sisters, Emily (3 years) and Carol (7 months). Greg was described as having always been a difficult child to parent. As an infant he cried a lot, was difficult to soothe, and had difficulty eating. As an infant and toddler, Greg experienced light sleep with patterns of awakening in the middle of the night. His sleep recently had improved, but he continued to exhibit a pattern of aggressive, defiant, destructive, and over-active behavior. His aggression often appeared to be targeted at his younger sister, Emily. On different occasions, Greg had thrown rocks at Emily, pushed her to the floor, and sat on her while hitting her repeatedly in the head. He often hurt the slower of the family's two cats by frequently pulling its ears and tail. Ms. S reported that she had some concerns, but because Greg was her first child and a boy, she did not want to overreact. When Greg's teacher approached her with concerns about his behavior, she began to recognize that his behavior was a problem that needed to be addressed.

Standardized assessment measures confirmed that Greg was exhibiting a clinically significant level of disruptive behavior. Ms. S's CBCL T scores were clinically elevated on the Externalizing (T = 80) and Total Problems Scales (T = 85). These scores were consistent with the scores on the ECBI. Ms. S obtained an intensity score of 156 and a problem score of 21, indicating conduct problems. Greg's classroom teacher completed a SESBI-R that indicated an intensity score of 163 and a problem score of 23. During the DPICS-II baseline behavioral observations, Ms. S demonstrated many positive parenting behaviors, including praise, enthusiasm, reflections, and close physical contact with Greg. She also tended to use high levels of questions and commands. In the CDI observations, Ms. S gave 10 praise statements (6 of which were unlabeled), 8 reflective statements, 7 descriptive statements, 15 questions, and 7 indirect commands. Similar patterns were noted during observation of the PDI and clean-up situations. Greg complied with approximately 20% of Ms. S's commands (far less than the normative level of approximately 64%). Considering all the information gathered, the therapist diagnosed Greg with oppositional defiant disorder and recommended that he participate in PCIT with both of his parents.

Child Directed Interaction

Mr. S was unable to attend sessions; however, Ms. S returned the following week to begin PCIT by attending a didactic session with the therapist. During this one-hour meeting, the therapist presented each skill individually (see Table 9.1), provided its description and rationale, and offered examples of the application of each skill to Greg's specific behaviors. Throughout the session, the therapist highlighted Ms. S's strengths, complimented her parenting style, and described how the skills would enhance the strong relationship she and Greg already had, as well as how the skills would be used to improve Greg's behavior. Ms. S was asked and agreed to complete five minutes of homework (i.e., CDI play) with Greg each day. She was given a form for recording her homework completion and noting any questions or behavioral concerns that came up during the play or week.

Ms. S and Greg attended the next session, the first coaching session, together. After a brief explanation and treatment room tour for Greg, the therapist reviewed the completed homework sheet with his mother. Ms. S had completed homework on five out of seven days, and she reported that Greg continued to be defiant and disrespectful. The therapist discussed with Ms. S that behavioral improvements would occur, but would take some time. Ms. S's efforts to complete homework were acknowledged, and the therapist specifically mentioned that this regular homework completion would help Greg's behavior improve more rapidly.

Because Ms. S mentioned that descriptions were difficult for her, she and the therapist decided to work on her increasing behavioral descriptions during the session. After helping Ms. S place the bug-in-the-ear in her ear, the therapist left the playroom and went into the observation room to conduct the 5-minute DPICS-II coding before coaching. This coding indicated that Ms. S had increased her use of labeled praise and slightly decreased commands from the initial assessment. Over the bug-in-the-ear, the therapist highlighted this improvement and focused on assisting Ms. S to increase her use of behavioral descriptions throughout the coaching period. After 30 minutes of coaching, the therapist met with Ms. S and Greg to review the session and a graph depicting Ms. S's use of the PRIDE skills over sessions. Specific homework goals were agreed on for the next week. Ms. S and Greg participated in six additional CDI coaching sessions until Ms. S met mastery criteria for the CDI skills. Each session followed a similar format, including a 10- to 15-minute check-in, a 5-minute behavior observation, 30 minutes of coaching, and a 10-minute review of skill use and homework planning.

Parent Directed Interaction

Similar to the CDI phase of treatment, PDI began with an interactive, didactic teaching session attended by Ms. S alone. During this time, the therapist provided an overview of PDI, described the use of effective, direct commands, and explained how to differentiate child compliance versus noncompliance. Labeled praise was recommended to reward compliance and a structured, time-out procedure was recommended after repeated noncompliance. The therapist reviewed, modeled, and role-played with Ms. S the structured PDI time-out procedure. After this detailed instruction and practice, Ms S. agreed *not* to use the PDI skills with Greg during the next week. Instead, the therapist wanted to coach Ms. S through the procedure the first time she used it so that the therapist could help manage the potentially difficult situation, as well as prevent any procedural errors.

Ms. S. returned the following week with Greg. At the start of this first PDI coaching session, the therapist briefly reviewed the PDI procedure with Ms. S and then through the bug-in-the-ear, coached her on how to explain it to Greg. Ms. S was noticeably nervous, so the therapist took some time to reassure her, reminded her how well prepared she was, how quickly she learned the CDI skills, and noted that the therapist would be there to support her. The therapist's coaching style during this session was directive, proactive, and fast-paced to ensure the child and parent were successful and to prevent any unnecessary escalation in behavior. During the session, Greg experienced three time-outs; however, by the end of the session, he was complying with his mother's direct commands. At the end of the session, the therapist congratulated Ms. S on her perseverance, processed the session with her, emphasized the importance of continuing CDI practice with Greg every day, and recommended 10-minute PDI practice each day.

During the remaining six PDI sessions, Greg's behavior, particularly his compliance, continued to improve and he rarely needed to go to time-out. He also was better able to regulate his emotions during the time-out when they were necessary. Once Greg was more compliant and Ms. S was more confident and skillful, PDI sessions were devoted to practicing real-life situations (e.g., clean-up, coming into the room when asked), establishing "house rules," including Greg's sisters in sessions to practice sharing, and providing in vivo coaching on the use of the PDI skills in public places. Three consultation–coaching sessions were conducted at the Head Start to assist the teacher in implementing a discipline program in the classroom that was similar to the one working in the home.

Treatment Completion

During the fourteenth session, Ms. S demonstrated mastery criteria of both CDI and PDI skills. The therapist asked Ms. S to complete the same standardized measures she completed during the initial evaluation (CBCL, ECBI, and PSI) and asked Greg's teacher to complete the SESBI-R. Ms. S's CBCL T scores were within normal limits on previously elevated scales on both the CBCL and ECBI: CBCL Externalizing (T = 55), CBCL Total Problems Scales (T = 56), ECBI Intensity Score (102), and ECBI Problem Score of 9. Greg's classroom teacher indicated a SESBI-R Intensity Score of 99 and Problem Score of 10. She also included written comments noting the improvement she had seen over time. Ms. S and Greg were invited back to the clinic to attend a graduation session in which Ms. S was presented with a treatment completion certificate and Greg was given an award for good behavior. The therapist asked about their impressions of treatment and reviewed the behavior observations (which had been videotaped) from their initial and final sessions. The therapist highlighted the gains that had been made by pointing out on the videotape notable improvements in both parent skill and child behavior.

CONCLUSION

Since its development to treat externalizing behavior problems in young children, PCIT has been empirically investigated and subsequently modified to incorporate meaningful research findings. In its current state, PCIT is a clinic-based, 10- to 14-week treatment program that assists parents in managing their children's difficult behavior through a dual focus on relationship enhancement and consistent, predictable discipline. The PCIT model has been modified to fit hospital, home, and school settings to improve families' access to treatment, as well as to provide more comprehensive care. All modifications to PCIT have included the treatment's dual focus on relationship enhancement and discipline as well as its three essential elements: targeting parents as agents of therapeutic change, using in vivo coaching, and relying on assessment to guide treatment.

REFERENCES

Axline, V. (1969). *Play therapy*. New York: Ballantine Books.

Azar, S. T., & Wolfe, D. A. (1989). Child abuse and neglect. In E. J. Mash & R. A. Barkley (Eds.), *Treatment of childhood disorders* (pp. 451–489). New York: Guilford Press.

Bagner, D. M., & Eyberg, S. M. (2003). Father involvement in parent training: When does it matter? *Journal of Clinical Child and Adolescent Psychology, 32,* 599–605.

Bagner, D. M., Fernandez, M. A., & Eyberg, S. M. (2004). Parent-child interaction therapy and chronic illness: A case study. *Journal of Clinical Psychology in Medical Settings, 11,* 1–6.

Bahl, A. (1998). *Adapting parent–child interaction therapy to the preschool classroom: A model for effective teacher training*. Unpublished doctoral dissertation, West Virginia University, Morgantown.

Barkley, R. A. (1981). *Hyperactive children: A handbook for diagnosis and treatment*. New York: Guilford Press.

Baumrind, D. (1967). Childcare practices antecedent three patterns of preschool behavior. *Genetic Psychology Monographs, 75,* 43–88.

Baumrind, D. (1995). Child rearing dimensions relevant to child maltreatment. In D. Baumrind (Ed.), *Child maltreatment and optimal care giving in social contexts* (pp. 55–73). New York: Garland Publishing.

Borrego, J., Jr., & Urquiza, A. J. (1998). Importance of therapist use of social reinforcement with parents as a model for parent–child relationships: An example with parent–child interaction therapy. *Child and Family Behavior Therapy, 20,* 27–54.

Borrego, J., Jr., Urquiza, A. J., Rasmussen, R. A., & Zebell, N. (1999). Parent–child interaction therapy with a family at high risk for physical abuse. *Child Maltreatment, 4,* 331–342.

Brestan, E. V., & Eyberg, S. M. (1998). Effective psychosocial treatments for children and adolescents with conduct-disordered behavior: 29 years, 82 studies, and 5272 kids. *Journal of Clinical Child Psychology, 27,* 179–188

Brestan, E. V., Eyberg, S. M., Boggs, S., & Algina, J. (1997). Parent–child interaction therapy: Parent perceptions of untreated siblings. *Child and Family Behavior Therapy, 19,* 13–28.

Brestan, E. V., Jacobs, J., Rayfield, A., & Eyberg, S. M. (1999). A consumer satisfaction measure for parent–child treatments and its relationships to measures of child behavior change. *Behavior Therapy, 30,* 17–30.

Chaffin, M., Silovsky, J. F., Funderburk, B., Valle, L. A., Brestan, E. V., Balachova, T., et al. (2004). Parent–child interaction therapy with physically abusive parents: Efficacy for reducing future abuse reports. *Journal of Consulting and Clinical Psychology, 72*(3), 500–510.

Cunningham, C. E. (1989). A family-systems-oriented training program for parents of language-delayed children with behavior problems. In C. E. Schaefer & J. M. Briesmeister (Eds.), *Handbook of parent training: Parent as cotherapists for children's behavior problems.* New York: Wiley.

Denham, S. A., Renwick, S. M., & Holt, R. W. (1991). Working and playing together: Prediction of preschool social–emotional competence from mother–child interaction. *Child Development, 62,* 242–249.

Dix, T., Ruble, D. N., & Zambrano, R. J. (1989). Mothers' implicit theories of discipline: Child effects, parent effects, and the attribution process. *Child Development, 60,* 1373–1391.

Edwards, D. L., Eyberg, S. M., Rayfield, A., Jacobs, J., & Hood, K. K. (2001). *Outcomes of Parent-child interaction therapy: A comparison of treatment completers and treatment dropouts one to three years later.* Manuscript submitted for publication.

Eisenstadt, T. H., Eyberg, S. M., McNeil, C. B., Newcomb, K., & Funderburk, B. (1993). Parent–child interaction therapy with behavior problem children: Relative effectiveness of two stages and overall treatment outcome. *Journal of Clinical Child Psychology, 22,* 42–51.

Eyberg, S. M., Bessmer, J., Newcomb, K., Edwards, D., & Robinson, E. (1994). Manual for the Dyadic Parent–Child Interaction Coding System-II. *Social and Behavioral Sciences Documents* (Ms. No. 2897).

Eyberg, S. M., & Boggs, S. R. (1989). Parent training for oppositional-defiant preschoolers. In C. E. Schaefer & J. M. Breismeister (Eds.), *Handbook for parent training: Parents as cotherapists for children's behavior problems* (pp. 105–132). New York: Wiley.

Eyberg, S. M., Boggs, S. R., & Algina, J. (1995). Parent–child interaction therapy: A psychosocial model for the treatment of young children with conduct problem behavior and their families. *Psychopharmacology Bulletin, 31*, 83–91.

Eyberg, S. M., & Calzada, E. (1998). *Parent–child interaction therapy: Procedures manual.* Unpublished manuscript, University of Florida, Gainesville.

Eyberg, S. M., Funderburk, B. W., Hembree-Kigin, T. L., McNeil, C. B., Querido, J. G., & Hood, K. K. (2001). Parent–child interaction therapy with behavior problem children: One and two year maintenance of treatment effects in the family. *Child and Family Behavior Therapy, 23*(4), 1–20.

Eyberg, S. M., & Matarazzo, R. G. (1980). Training parents as therapists: A comparison between individual parent–child interaction training and parent group didactic training. *Journal of Clinical Psychology, 36*, 492–499.

Eyberg, S. M., & Pincus, D. (1999). *Eyberg Child Behavior Inventory Sutter Student Behavior Inventory—Revised professional manual.* Lutz, FL: Psychological Assessment Resources.

Eyberg, S. M., & Robinson, E. A. (1982). Parent–child interaction training: Effects on family functioning. *Journal of Clinical Child Psychology, 11*, 130–137

Eyberg, S. M., Schuhmann, E., & Rey, J. (1998). Psychosocial treatment research with children and adolescents: Developmental issues. *Journal of Abnormal Child Psychology, 12*, 347–357.

Foote, R., Eyberg, S. M., & Schuhmann, E. (1998). Parent–child interaction approaches to the treatment of child behavior problems. In T. Ollendick & R. Prinz (Eds.), *Advances in clinical child psychology* (Vol. 20, pp. 125–151). New York: Plenum Press.

Forehand, R. L., Cheney, T., & Yoder, P. (1974). Parent behavior training: Effects on the noncompliance of a deaf child. *Journal of Behavior Therapy and Experimental Psychiatry, 5*, 575–593.

Franz, C. E., McClelland, D. C., & Weinberger, J. (1991). Childhood antecedents of conventional social accomplishments in midlife adults: A 36-year prospective study. *Journal of Personality and Social Psychology, 60*, 586–595.

Fricker, A. E., Ruggiero, K. J., & Smith, D. W. (2005). Parent–child interaction therapy with two maltreated children in foster care. *Clinical Case Studies, 4*(1), 13–39.

Funderburk, B. W., Eyberg, S. M., Newcomb, K., McNeil, C. B., Hembree-Kigin, T., & Capage, L. (1998). Parent–child interaction therapy with behavior problem children: Maintenance of treatment effects in the school setting. *Child and Family Behavior Therapy, 20*, 17–38.

Gallagher, N. (2003). Effects of parent–child interaction therapy on young children with disruptive behavior disorders. *Bridges: Practice-based Research Syntheses, 4*(1), 1–17. Retrieved February 19, 2004, from U. S. Department of Education, Research and Training Center on Early Childhood Development Web site: http://www.evidencebasedpractices.org/bridges/bridges_vol1_no4.pdf

Greco, L. A., Sorrell, J. T., & McNeil, C. B. (2001). Understanding manual-based behavior therapy: Some theoretical foundations for parent–child interaction therapy. *Child and Family Behavior Therapy, 23*(4), 21–36.

Hanf, C. A. (1969). *A two-stage program for modifying maternal controlling during mother–child (M–C) interaction*. Paper presented at the meeting of the Western Psychological Association, Vancouver, Canada.

Hembree-Kigin, T. L., & McNeil, C. B. (1995). *Parent–child interaction therapy*. New York: Plenum Press.

Henggeler, S. W., Melton, G. B., Brondino, M. J., Scherer, D. G., & Hanley, J. H. (1997). Multisystemic therapy with violent and chronic juvenile offenders and their families: The role of treatment fidelity in successful dissemination. *Journal of Consulting and Clinical Psychology, 65*, 821–833.

Herschell, A. D., Calzada, E. J., Eyberg, S. M., & McNeil, C. B. (2002a). Clinical issues in parent–child interaction therapy. *Cognitive and Behavioral Practice, 9*, 16–27.

Herschell, A. D., Calzada, E. J., Eyberg, S. M., & McNeil, C. B. (2002b). Parent–child interaction therapy: New directions in research. *Cognitive and Behavioral Practice, 9*, 9–16.

Herschell, A. D., Lumley, V. A, & McNeil, C. B. (2000). Parent–child interaction therapy. In L. E. Vandercreek (Ed.), *Innovations in clinical practice: A source book, 18*, (pp. 103–120). Sarasota, FL: Professional Resource Press.

Hood, K. K., & Eyberg, S. M. (2003). Outcomes of parent–child interaction therapy: Mothers' reports of maintenance three to six years after treatment. *Journal of Clinical Child and Adolescent Psychology, 32*, 419–429.

Jacobs, J. R., Boggs, S. R., Eyberg, S. M., Edwards, D. L., Durning, P., Quertido, J. G., et al. (2000). Psychometric properties and reference point data for the Revised edition of the School Observation Coding System. *Behavior Therapy, 31*, 695–712.

Kazdin, A. E. (1996). Problem solving and parent management in treating aggressive and antisocial behavior. In E. D. Hibbs & P. S. Jensen (Eds.), *Psychosocial treatments for child and adolescent disorders: Empirically based strategies for clinical practice* (pp. 386–387). Washington, DC: American Psychological Association.

McIntosh, D. E., Rizza, M. G., & Bliss, L. (2000). Implementing empirically supported interventions: Teacher–child interaction therapy, *Psychology in the Schools, 37*, 453–462.

McNeil, C. B., Capage, L. C., Bahl, A., & Blanc, H. (1999). Importance of early intervention for disruptive behavior problems: Comparisons of treatment and wait-list control groups. *Early Education and Development, 10*, 445–454.

McNeil, C. B., Eyberg, S. M., Eisenstadt, T. H., Newcomb, K., & Funderburk, B. W. (1991). Parent–child interaction therapy with behavior problem children: Generalization of treatment effects to the school setting. *Journal of Clinical Child Psychology, 20*, 140–151.

McNeil, C. B., Herschell, A. D., Gurwitch, R. H., & Clemens-Mowrer, L. (in press). Training foster parents in Parent–Child Interaction Therapy. *Education and Treatment of Children*.

Nixon, R. D. V., Sweeney, L., Erickson, D. B., & Touyz, S. W. (2003). Parent–child interaction therapy: A comparison of standard and abbreviated treatments for oppositional defiant preschoolers. *Journal of Consulting and Clinical Psychology, 71,* 251–260.

Olson, S. L., Bates, J. E., & Bayles, K. (1990). Early antecedents of child hyperactivity: The role of parent–child interaction, cognitive competence, and temperament. *Journal of Abnormal Child Psychology, 18,* 317–334.

Parpal, M., & Maccoby, E. (1985). Maternal responsiveness and subsequent child compliance. *Child Development, 56,* 1326–1334.

Patterson, G. R. (1975). *Families: Application of social learning to family life.* Champaign, IL: Research Press.

Patterson, G. R. (1976). The aggressive child: Victim and architect of a coercive system. In E. Mash, L. A. Hamerlynch, & L. C. Handy (Eds.), *Behavior modification and families. I. Theory and research. II. Applications and developments* (pp. 265–316) New York: Brunner/Mazel.

Patterson, G. R. (1982). *Coercive family process.* Eugene, OR: Castalia.

Pincus, D. B., Choate, M. L., Eyberg, S. M., & Barlow, D. H. (in press). Treatment of young children with separation anxiety disorder using Parent–child interaction therapy. *Cognitive and Behavioral Practice.*

Pisterman, S., McGrath, P., Firestone, P., Goodman, J., Webster, I., & Mallory, R. (1989). Outcome of parent-mediated treatment of preschoolers with attention-deficit disorder with hyperactivity. *Journal of Consulting and Clinical Psychology, 57,* 628–635.

Pisterman, S., McGrath, P., Firestone, P., Goodman, J., Webster, I., Mallory, R., et al. (1992). The effects of parent training on parenting stress and sense of competence. *Canadian Journal of Behavioral Science, 24,* 41–58.

Power, T. G., & Chapieski, M. L. (1986). Child rearing and impulse control in toddlers: A naturalistic investigation. *Developmental Psychology, 22,* 271–275.

Querido, J. G., & Eyberg, S. M. (2001, June). *Parent–child interaction therapy with Head Start families.* Poster session presented at the second annual PCIT meeting, Sacramento, CA.

Rayfield, A., & Sobel, A. (2000). *Effectiveness of "in-room" coaching of Parent–child interaction therapy.* Paper presented at the First Annual Parent-Child Interaction Therapy Conference, Sacramento, CA.

Schuhmann, E., Foote, R., Eyberg, S. M., Boggs, S., & Algina, J. (1998). Parent–child interaction therapy: Interim report of a randomized trial with short-term maintenance. *Journal of Clinical Child Psychology, 27,* 34–45.

Urquiza, A. J., & McNeil, C. B. (1996). Parent–child interaction therapy: Potential applications for physically abusive families. *Child Maltreatment, 1,* 134–144.

Urquiza, A. J., Timmer, S. G., Herschell, A. D., McGrath, J. M., Zebell, N. M., Porter, A. L., et al. (in press). Parent–child interaction therapy: Application of an empirically supported treatment to maltreated children in foster care. *Child Maltreatment.*

Webster-Stratton, C. (1981). Videotape modeling: A method of parent education. *Journal of Clinical Child Psychology, 10,* 93–97.

10

A COOPERATIVE GAMES INTERVENTION FOR AGGRESSIVE PRESCHOOL CHILDREN

APRIL K. BAY-HINITZ AND GINGER R. WILSON

The games children play are often overlooked as a powerful tool that can shape a child's behavior. A child's playground, or play environment, is the stage where behaviors are learned, practiced, and tested. When children play games together, the setting becomes structured and the children's behaviors become governed by the contingencies arranged by the game. Hence, the rules of the game exhibit control over the children's behavior.

Play may involve structured and unstructured activities. The type and structure of play materials have been found to be associated with prosocial and antisocial behavior in preschool children (e.g., Boot, 1928; Doyle, 1976; Green, 1933; Quilitch & Risley, 1973; Shure, 1963). Games are a structured form of play and are governed by rules. Games often establish the rules of the interaction and may involve competitive, cooperative, or individual interactions. A competitive interaction is one in which the success of one person requires the failure of others (Kohn, 1983). In contrast, a cooperative interaction requires coordinated efforts of one or more persons so that the success of one can only be achieved with the assistance of others. A third type of interaction, the independently structured activity, differs from both of these. In an independently structured activity, the achievement of one person is unaffected by the achievement of others.

COMPETITIVE ACTIVITIES

A competitive game is designed to create a winner and a loser. The goal is to do better than your opponent and doing best is the optimal outcome. The social or interpersonal skills are minimized, as the game is usually structured to encourage opposition. In some children, opposition comes with aggressive behavior; although aggression may not be part of the game structure, it is a significant effect of competitive games (Bay-Hinitz, Peterson, & Quilitch, 1994). Children are essentially learning how to oppose others. Placed in this context, most children discover that lying, deceiving, or cheating will help them attain the goal of the game, which is to win and have your opponent lose.

Problematic effects of competitive school activities have been identified in numerous studies. Competition has been correlated with decreased academic performance (Kohn, 1983), with greater anxiety (Kernan, 1983), and was found to have an inverse relationship with achievement (Helmreich, Spence, Beane, Lucka, & Mathews, 1985). Sports is the most obvious arena for competitive activities in schools for older children; for younger children, games provide a competitive arena. In a classic study by Sheriff, Harvey, White, Hood, and Sherif (1961), results demonstrated that when 11- and 12-year-old boys were divided into competitive teams for baseball, football, and tug-of-war, there was a generalized increase in hostility and aggressive acts. Similarly, in younger children, exposure to aggressive models during competitive play resulted in increased aggressive behavior (e.g., Hoving, Wallace, & LaForme, 1979; Nelson, Gelfand, & Hartmann, 1969; Rocha & Rogers, 1976). Aggression has also been correlated with competitive recreation in emotionally disturbed children (Phillips, 1981).

Competitive sports and games, by their very nature, involve a potential for aggression. In examining the relationship between competition and aggression, most studies used physically aggressive sports (e.g., football) to represent competition and then measured subsequent aggressive behavior (Quanty, 1976). Other researchers introduced an aggressive model prior to engaging children in competitive play and then measured subsequent aggression (Nelson et al., 1969). In contrast to the aggressive physical tactics that many view as acceptable in competitive sports, aggression in games of younger children is almost always considered problematic.

COOPERATIVE ACTIVITIES

Enhancing social and prosocial behaviors in school environments is of similar importance to reducing aggressive behaviors in the play environment. Cooperative activities have been shown to influence various prosocial behaviors; such benefits have been demonstrated by literally hundreds of studies (Johnson & Johnson, 1975). For example, cooperative instruction enhanced liking of school and teacher (DeVries & Slavin, 1978; Johnson, Johnson, & Scott, 1978), decreased rejection of newly integrated students (Madden & Slavin, 1983), and reduced prejudice and ridicule behaviors (Johnson & Johnson, 1975; Johnson et al., 1978).

A large-scale meta-analysis that reviewed 122 studies from 1924 to 1980 examined achievement data resulting from competitive, cooperative, and individualistic activities (Johnson, Maruyama, Johnson, Nelson, & Skon, 1981). Of the 122 studies, 65 found cooperation produced higher achievement than competition, 8 found the opposite, and 36 found little difference. Thus, the literature on competitive and cooperative activities suggests that beneficial effects are more frequently associated with cooperative activities.

EFFECTS OF COMPETITIVE AND COOPERATIVE GAMES

When a game is a cooperatively structured activity, children report greater enjoyment as compared with competitive games (Orlick, 1981). Orlick reports that after children were exposed to both cooperative and competitive games, two thirds of the boys and all of the girls preferred to play cooperative games. Finlinson, Austin, and Pfister (2000) examined the effects of competitive and cooperative games on negative and positive game time behaviors, as scored by the Child Behavior Checklist (CBCL). The authors reported that cooperative games were shown to be associated with positive behaviors, and negative behaviors were associated with competitive games. The Finlinson and colleagues' study examined game time behavior, whereas a study reported by Lejeune (1995) showed less clear findings when examining the effects of cooperative and competitive games on subsequent free time behavior. Lejeune found similar increases in cooperative behavior as a result of participation in cooperative, as compared to competitive, games; however, all groups showed increased rates of cooperative behavior at the end of the study when compared to initial baseline rates.

Studies of cooperative games with preschoolers have continued to focus on changes in socially desirable behaviors. Provost (1981) reported that children who watched films of other children playing cooperative games showed an increase in their own cooperative behavior following the film. Specifically, 75 preschool children, 2- to 4-years-old, watched children playing several different games (e.g., cooperative musical chairs and musical hugs). A control group was shown animated films. Results indicated that compared to the control group, the treatment condition was significantly more effective in teaching cooperative behaviors.

METHODS OF TREATING AGGRESSION

Interventions aimed at reducing aggressive behaviors in younger children frequently involved manipulations of the conditions of play. Murphy, Hutchinson and Bailey (1983) found that organized games, along with a time-out procedure, significantly reduced the frequency of aggressive acts. Wolfe, Boyd, and Wolfe (1983) found concomitant decreases in the percentage of intervals spent in time-out in children who showed high rates of aggressiveness when teachers reinforced cooperative play. Verbal instruction and a token economy effectively increased cooperative play among these children by 50% over baseline rates. These results suggest that reinforcement of cooperative play had an inadvertent effect on problem behavior that was not specifically targeted.

Aggressive behaviors have also been decreased by altering antecedent conditions in the play environment. Smith (1974) investigated how the availability of toys could affect undesirable behaviors. Results showed a significant decrease in aggression when the number of toys was increased from 15 to 45. In addition, the amount of physical space in the play area was also shown to affect aggression. Boe's study (1977) demonstrated decreases in aggression when the amount of physical space per child was increased.

Other methods for treating aggression include manipulation of reinforcing and punishing consequences. These interventions typically involve a carefully considered individual treatment plan to target decreasing aggression and increasing appropriate social skills. Such interventions include differential reinforcement for alternative behavior (DRA), noncontingent attention (NCR), token economies, time-out, and extinction (EXT). These behavioral strategies have demonstrated success with decreases in aggression; however, they require extensive professional time and involvement in designing a program for one child, followed by the need for additional time to train others to implement the program.

An important consideration when developing a behavior plan is the use of a least restrictive intervention. The sociolegal doctrine of the least restrictive alternative (LRA) suggests therapists should always first try the least restrictive, positive intervention (Green, 1989). Cooperative games as an antecedent intervention are positive, extremely easy to implement into a classroom, require brief teacher training, and pose minimal disturbances to the classroom or play group. Targeted children are not separated from the group for the intervention, nor are they treated differently. Therefore, cooperative game intervention is a least restrictive, positive intervention imposing few, if any, of the negative considerations that other interventions must consider.

KEY TREATMENT INGREDIENTS

The key treatment ingredients for a cooperative games intervention include using cooperatively structured games and activities, assessing for and reducing competitive game exposure, gaining compliance with those involved, and determining the delivering agent.

Description of the Games

Almost any game can be restructured to be a cooperative game. Cooperative board games require that all players work together to move around the board, problem solve, cooperate, share, and help each other reach a common goal. Examples of cooperative board games with their descriptions and where to find them can be found in Appendix 10.1.

Cooperative games that are not board games may also be used. For example, a game of cooperative musical chairs is similar to traditional musical chairs. Children skip around a group of chairs and when the music stops, they must find a chair or share a chair to sit on. In this form of musical chairs, no one is eliminated from the group; chairs are eliminated. When only one or two chairs are remaining (depending on the size of the group), all children are leaning, touching, and sharing a space on a chair for the group to win. This is a great game to play when children seem to be pairing off, forming cliques, or excluding others.

Assessing for Competitive Game Exposure

A thorough assessment of a child's exposure to competitive games and activities at school and home is the first step prior to introducing cooperative games. After competitive games and activities have been identified and removed, cooperatively structured games and activities can replace the competitive games that were eliminated. In those situations in which competitive games were not used, cooperative games and activities are merely added to the schedule or replace activities that were independently structured.

Gaining Compliance

Perhaps the most difficult part of introducing cooperative games to families is convincing the parents how influential games are to their child's behavior. The difference between competitive and cooperative games must be explained. To reduce or eliminate competitive games from a child's environment, the parent must understand its effects on their child. Discuss the adverse effects of competition as mentioned in the research; for example, competition has been correlated with increased fear of failure, decreased academic performance (Kohn, 1983), and greater anxiety (Kernan, 1983), and was found to have an inverse relationship with achievement (Helmreich et al., 1985). Competitive games and competitive activities are associated with a wide variety of problem behaviors, particularly aggressive behaviors.

Some parents may worry that their child needs competitive skills to succeed and to be tough. Although the research does not support this, it is important to attend to the parents' concerns, assuring them that their child will still be acquiring competitive skills in multiple other situations. It is also helpful to educate parents about differences between cooperative skills and passivity. Focusing attention on enhancing a child's social repertoire, which empowers a child and may result in decreased or eliminated aggression, will usually be enough to promote parental compliance.

In addition to educating parents regarding the effects of competition, they must also be educated about cooperative rules and cooperative structure to facilitate compliance. The benefits of cooperative games, such as their effects on a multitude of positive behaviors (notably decreased aggressive behavior), should be discussed. Treatment should also aim to reinforce the behavior of the parents for their compliance with the program.

In school situations, the compliance of educators is the focus. Teachers often need the same explanations that parents require regarding differing game structures. Teachers' compliance will also increase once they begin observing changes and understand that these changes will reduce class aggressiveness on the whole, which in turn will require less teacher discipline.

Changing the rules on children who are familiar with competitive games can be difficult at first. Most children are exclusively exposed to competitively structured games and, given their familiarity with these types of rules, a shift to cooperative games could be resisted. Children, in general, are resistant to change unless they see personal benefit. Therefore, explaining the beneficial impact of this shift on their lives will soften the transition.

Treatment Delivery

With this particular treatment, almost anyone can be the delivering agent. One of the benefits of this treatment is that the delivering agent does not have to be a highly trained clinician because the intervention is not multicomponent or highly complex. After a thorough understanding of cooperative structure and modeling of such understanding, treatment integrity should not be an issue. This intervention is rather simple and highly flexible to many social situations and environmental contexts, such as home, school, and daycare.

If a child is displaying aggressive behaviors at school, then the teacher or aide will most likely be the optimal person to implement treatment. When teachers are part of the observation team, they will need operational definitions for problem and cooperative behaviors that are targeted (see Appendix 10.2). As with parents, training the teachers to be observers often has a therapeutic effect, i.e., increasing their awareness of positive behaviors and thereby increasing the likelihood that good behaviors will be reinforced.

If a child displays aggression solely in domestic situations, then the parents and all family members should participate in the use of cooperative games. Of course, if a child displays aggressive behaviors across all environments, then all persons interacting with the child should be trained on how to manipulate game play. As a rule of thumb, the parents should always be trained and provide subsequent training to all pertinent parties.

Because this treatment intervention is based on skill acquisition in social situations, there is no maximum number of treatment sessions that are needed before discontinuing treatment. In fact, even after subsequent decreases in aggressive behavior and increases in cooperative behavior, this intervention will still be effective in helping the child to acquire further and more advanced social skills as the child ages and the complexity of the games and social situations increases.

OUTCOME EVALUATION

The therapeutic effect of cooperative games in preschool children has been demonstrated by Bay-Hinitz et al. (1994). In this study, behavior problems such as aggression showed dramatic reductions during cooperative game conditions, whereas cooperative behaviors (defined in Appendix 10.2), showed significant increases. These results often generalized to later times, that is, free play conditions.

A Description of the Study

Cooperative games were evaluated with 70 preschool children (4–5 years old). The children were split into four groups, containing an average of 13 children per group. The effects of cooperative games were evaluated in a staggered multiple baseline design with reversal components.

A preschool environment set the stage for the evaluation of cooperative games. All classroom settings included both indoor and outdoor play areas. Outdoor play areas contained playground equipment such as swings and jungle gyms. Indoor play areas contained large desks for group seating that were used for craft activities and lunch. The six teachers were informed of the general procedure of the study and were given a list of cooperative and competitive games. They were instructed how to play the games and how to explain the rules to the class. They were asked to teach and then lead both types of games for 30 minutes each day. Teachers were told to use only the games on the list during any given phase. Changes in treatment conditions were discussed a day prior to implementation.

One to three games were played per 30-minute session. Initially, the teacher introduced the game, explained the rules, and asked who wished to play the game. Once children were familiar with the game, little instruction was needed. Children were not required to be involved in any particular game; they were allowed to leave the games if they wished and could rejoin at any time.

During baseline and free play periods, children were not given instruction on any particular games. They were allowed to play in whatever way they wished. However, cooperative and competitive board games were not available for use at these times. Typical activities included drawing, painting, crafts, and dress-up. The children occasionally gathered for stories or a movie. When games were scheduled in the morning, free-play observations were made during the afternoon. If free play was scheduled in the afternoon, games were played the following morning.

The competitive games used in this research involved activities that pitted the children against each other to determine a winner. Competitive board games consisted of Candy Land®, Chutes and Ladders®, Aggravation®, Double Trouble®, and Children's Trivial Pursuit®. Physical competitive games included musical chairs, Simon says, duck-duck-goose, beanbag balance, and tag.

In this research, cooperative board games included Max®, Harvest Time®, Granny's House®, and Sleeping Grump® (see Appendix 10.1 for game descriptions). Cooperative physical activities, as described in Orlick's *The Second Cooperative Sports and Games Book* (1982), included cooperative musical chairs, balance activities, freeze-defreeze tag, devine, half-a-heart, cooperative musical hugs, and bean bag freeze. Several games were variations of their competitive counterparts, such as the already mentioned cooperative musical chairs

In this study, trained observers sat in the back of the classroom, avoiding eye contact and social interactions with the children. Observers scanned the entire group sequentially, beginning with those on the left side of the room. Instances of the two behaviors were recorded as they occurred; however, no more than one instance of cooperative or aggressive behavior was scored for a given child in any one 30-second interval. Reliability on cooperative behavior ranged from 50% to 100% and averaged 95%. Reliability on aggressive behavior ranged from 0% to 100% and averaged 88%. Teachers were interviewed at the end of the study. They were asked for their opinions on the effects of the games on the children's behavior and the children's preferences or dislikes.

Scores were obtained by dividing the total number of behaviors observed in each session by the number of minutes observed and then by the number of children present (including those who did not participate). Because of the number of children to observe, observers were limited to scoring a maximum of one aggressive or cooperative behavior per child per 30-second interval. A ratio of cooperative to aggressive behavior was obtained by summing the number of aggressive and cooperative behaviors recorded during each session and dividing the number of cooperative behaviors by the total. The ratio is expressed as the percentage of cooperative behavior observed (the percentage of aggressive behavior is the inverse). Behavior during game time and free play periods was examined.

Game Time Behavior

The effects of cooperative and competitive games on the behavior of the children in Group 1 and Group 2 are shown in Figure 10.1. Cooperative behaviors for Group 1 averaged about 80% during baseline and fell to a mix of about 50% cooperative and 50% aggressive behavior when competitive games were introduced. Involving the children in cooperative games raised the level of cooperative behaviors to about 90%, whereas aggressive behaviors averaged less than 9%.

Following the introduction of competitive games, cooperative behavior for Group 2 decreased. When baseline was reintroduced, cooperative behavior increased but was lower (M = 67%) and more variable than during the prior baseline. Variability progressively lessened after the introduction of cooperative games, and cooperation rose to a mean of 84%.

Treatment conditions were counterbalanced for Groups 3 and 4. Figure 10.2 represents the effects of cooperative and competitive games on the behavior of Groups 3 and 4. During cooperative games, cooperative behavior increased to a mean of 86%. Cooperative behaviors decreased following the introduction of competitive games to 37% and an increase in aggressive responses to 63%. When the cooperative condition was reinstated, cooperative behaviors rose to a mean of 86%.

Group 4 showed relatively minimal changes as a result of treatment conditions. The proportion of cooperative behaviors remained high throughout the study. The children's cooperative behavior dropped to 86% during competitive games and rose to a mean of 94% during the final cooperative phase.

Behavior During Free Play

The number of data points between game time and free play does not correspond on a one-to-one basis. Games were not played on some days when free play observations were taken. Also, observer absence occasionally

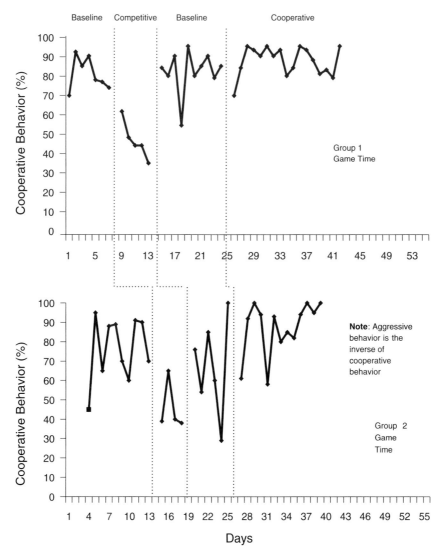

Figure 10.1. Percentage of cooperative behavior during game time for Groups 1 and 2.

prevented free play recording on game days. Free play data thus constitute a sample of behavior measured during particular treatment phases.

Figure 10.3 shows cooperative (and aggressive) behaviors during free play for the children in Groups 1 and 2. Overall, the behavior of Group 1 during free play was very similar to that exhibited during game time. Following a high level of cooperative behavior during baseline (M = 83%), there was a sharp drop after competitive games were introduced (M = 53%).

The behaviors of Group 2 showed more variability during free play and did not reflect changes in treatment conditions as strongly as did those of Group 1. The first baseline showed a mix of 70% cooperative and 30% aggressive behaviors, with little change from this level during competitive games. There was a small increase in cooperative responses in the cooperative games phase, when cooperation averaged 83% and aggression averaged 17%. Despite the relatively small changes in behavior, it should be noted that aggressive responses during this final phase were 57% of the level observed during the first baseline period.

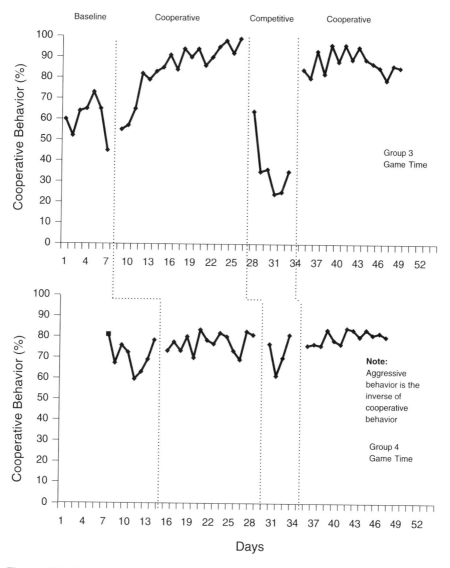

Figure 10.2. Percentage of cooperative behavior during game time for Groups 3 and 4.

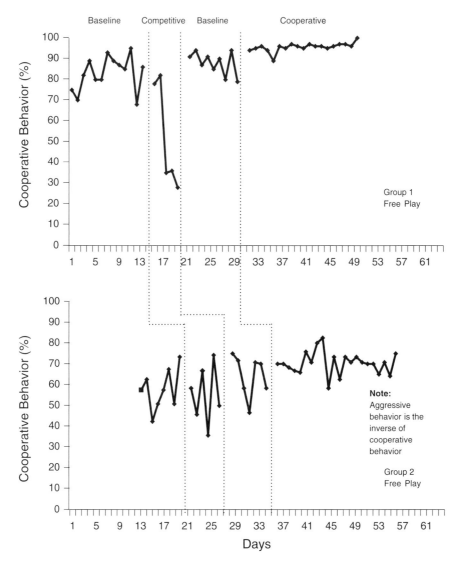

Figure 10.3. Percentage of cooperative behavior during free play for Groups 1 and 2.

As shown in Figure 10.4, the children in Groups 3 and 4 displayed high levels of cooperative behavior during free play. The children in Group 3 showed few changes in behavior from baseline to cooperative games. However, cooperative behaviors dropped from a mean of 89% during the first cooperative game phase to a mean of 73% during competitive games. Cooperation increased to 94% in the final cooperative game phase.

The children in Group 4 displayed high levels of cooperation and low levels of aggression throughout free play. The mean percentage of cooperative play was 97% during the first cooperative game phase, fell to 83% during competitive games, and then rose to 95% in the final cooperative phase. This demonstrates the beneficial effects of cooperative games on subsequent free play times.

Four of the six teachers were available for interviews at the end of the study. Two of the four indicated that the children preferred cooperative games; the other two did not see one type of game preferred over another.

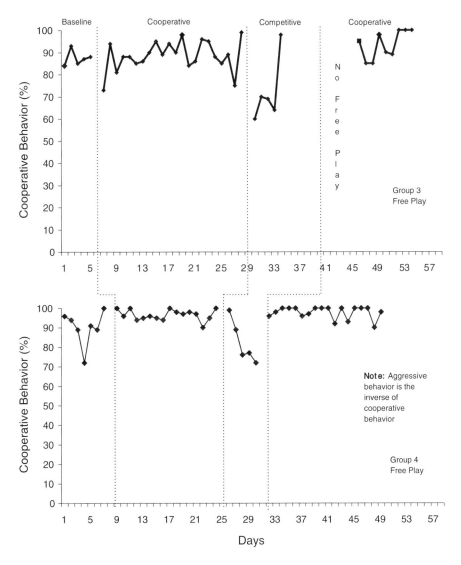

Figure 10.4. Percentage of cooperative behavior during free play for Groups 3 and 4.

Teachers reported that after playing cooperative games, children began devising their own games and often used cooperative rules.

The four groups varied in their responsiveness to cooperative and competitive games. This was true in game time and in later free play periods. The children in all groups displayed fewer cooperative behaviors and more aggressive behaviors in varying degrees when playing competitive games. The children's behavior in Groups 1, 3, and 4 also showed that the type of game played could affect behavior during subsequent free play, even when free play was measured the next day or later.

REPLICATION AND TRANSPORTABILITY

The use of cooperative games as an intervention for aggression can be used in any setting where the child displays aggression. Cooperative games can be used in daycare centers and schools during playtime, or in the classroom as a social skills lesson. In addition, cooperative games can be used in the child's home by setting up game time where all family members are involved. Cooperative games teach the child social skills that may generalize to many different settings and times.

Cooperative games may also be useful for children or adults with disabilities. Aggression is a prevalent problem displayed by many children and adults with disabilities such as autism, mental retardation, Down's syndrome, and other learning disabilities. Cooperative games are a viable treatment for aggression displayed by this population, and may also be useful for those who do not display aggressive behaviors as a method for teaching appropriate social skills.

As defined by the sociolegal doctrine of the least restrictive alterative (LRA), cooperative games may be the ideal intervention for children with disabilities, as these games are minimally intrusive. The LRA principle has evolved in statutes and case law over nearly three decades and states that all citizens should be permitted to live, work, play, learn, and receive services in contexts that are as free as possible of undue constraints on their liberties (Green, 1989). When applied to services for individuals with behavior problems, the LRA doctrine has been interpreted in absolute terms. It is advised that therapists first try the least restrictive, positive intervention, and only after documentation of its ineffectiveness should the therapist consider more aversive, intrusive, or restrictive procedures (Green, 1989).

Cooperative games as an antecedent intervention are among the least restrictive treatments for aggression; as such, they provide many benefits to children, especially children with disabilities. First, this intervention may allow the child with disabilities to remain in the typical classroom, rather than be restricted to a special education classroom. Also, cooperative games as an intervention do not isolate the "problem child" and signal to other children that a particular child is in need of special services; instead, all children are involved in a cooperative game that collaterally decreases aggressive behaviors. In addition, cooperative games can be conducted in the classroom, rather than removing the child with disabilities from the classroom for treatment sessions. Finally, social situations can be very difficult for some children with disabilities and cooperative games provide a context for forced social interactions that are facilitated by a cooperative structure.

RECOMMENDATIONS FOR OUTCOME EVALUATION IN CLINICAL PRACTICE

The recommended evaluation method for cooperative games is observation and self-report. The therapist assigns one or more people to observe the child's aggressive behaviors in differing contexts and have them report any increases, decreases, or differences observed. Another evaluation method is straightforward data collection. The therapist provides the parents or teachers with a data sheet to collect data on the number of times aggressive behaviors occurred during cooperative game play or in various contexts (see Appendix 10.3). It is important to look at the aggressive behaviors in the environment in which they occur to examine changes in behavior across changing environments. Using the parents or teacher in the data collection process not only provides necessary data, but it also promotes changes within the observers, (e.g., increased awareness of subtle behavior changes, a sense of success when observing behavior improvement).

CONCLUSION

Cooperative games are an important treatment option for reducing aggressive behaviors in children. Introducing cooperatively structured activities into a child's environment, whether at home, school, or daycare, promotes a multitude of benefits for the child and her or his playmates. In addition to decreases in aggression, cooperatively structured activities also promote positive internal states, such as a greater sense of acceptance of peers and enjoyment in recreational and academic environments. Cooperatively structured activities create a social milieu with rules that reinforce positive social interactions. Interpersonal relationships formed within the context of these interactions are a major contributor to a child's emotional well-being and developing self-concept. All these benefits translate into a happier child who is disciplined less and positively reinforced more.

Using cooperatively structured play as a treatment will benefit all playmates, not just the targeted child. Because this treatment is not a specific individualized plan, no child is singled out from the rest of the class.

This advantage is particularly useful with disabled individuals because it is a minimally restrictive intervention and provides the least interference in classroom settings. Other advantages noted in school settings are the need for minimal teacher instruction and time. Parents can be used as the primary person in charge of follow-up and can assist the teacher in instituting new activities. This approach allows the professional to withdraw once the program has been initiated and evaluated as successful. The teachers and parents are then free to work together and produce their own successes.

Competitively structured activities seem to live on despite clear negative findings from research. The adverse effects range from the sad face of a 4-year-old to the extreme frustration, sense of failure, and resulting aggression in the "problem" child. In contrast, cooperative games are designed to create winners. Those effects range from the smiling faces of preschoolers to the therapeutic decreases in aggression and increases in prosocial behaviors. Children learn, behave, respond, and grow from within their play environments. Our thoughtfulness about games and play, and our understanding their effect and the power they hold, will help us to help our children have fun and learn to have fun with each other.

APPENDIX 10.1:
COOPERATIVE BOARD GAMES

Cooperative board games can be obtained through Animal Town Game Company, P.O. Box 485, Healdsburg, CA 95448; Past Times Publishing, Ontario, Canada; or Childswork/Childsplay, P.O. Box 1604, Secaucus, NJ 07096-1604; or, call 1-800-962-1141. Multiple examples of cooperative activities can be found in Orlick's *The Second Cooperative Sports and Games Book* (1982).

In the board game Max®, all children work together to save the animals of the forest from a cat, Max. Every time Max gets close to its prey, the players can call Max back to home point by using the group's reserve of Max's treats (e.g. milk, cheese). The object of the game is for all players to get around the board and save the forest animals from Max. Harvest Time® can have four to eight players, all working together to harvest each other's land before "Old Man Winter" comes. The players quickly learn that it is to their benefit to work together to harvest each other's land, not just their own. In the game Granny's House®, children work together to move through obstacles to get to Granny's house. To overcome various obstacles, the children must make group decisions using a limited supply of resources. All players either win by reaching Granny's house, or lose by running out of resources before reaching the end. Sleeping Grump® has children 4 to 7 year of age work together to climb the stalk to recover treasures before the sleeping Grump awakens. All players win if they reach the top of the ladder and all lose if the Grump wakes up before they finish.

APPENDIX 10.2:
AGGRESSIVE AND COOPERATIVE BEHAVIORS DEFINED

Aggressive behavior is defined as any behavior that involves a destructive or hurtful action toward a person or object, and includes both physical and verbal responses. Aggressive behaviors are scored when a child engages in any of the following responses: (a) hitting, kicking, biting, scratching, pulling, grabbing, jumping on, bumping, tripping, throwing an object at another person, or attempting to do so; (b) throwing materials or equipment, kicking doors, walls or furniture, overturning furniture, knocking materials off shelves, breaking or destroying toys or equipment; or (c) threatening physical assault, verbally resisting instructions, stating dislike or other negative feelings about another person, name calling or other derogatory remarks, threatening physically destructive actions, or verbal attempts to exclude another child from an activity.

Cooperative behavior is defined as behavior that is directed toward another child and that involves a shared, reciprocal, mutual, or helpful quality. Cooperative behavior includes (a) sharing, assisting, or executing a task with another child, working together toward a common goal, sharing material, or explicitly helping another child; (b) physically supporting another child (e.g., one child carries another child or helps a child off the ground or over a barrier) or engaging in physical contact of an affectionate nature; or (c) verbal behavior such as giving a child instruction on how to do something, verbally offering to help or to share, or agreeing to a request made by another child.

APPENDIX 10.3:
AGGRESSION DATA SHEET

Date: _____

Time: _____

Observer's Name: _____

Child's Name: _____

> Aggressive behavior = Any behavior that involved a destructive or hurtful action toward a person or object, including both physical and verbal responses.

Please mark a tally for each instance of aggressive behavior and where the aggressive behavior occurred.

Context/ Name of Game	Number of Aggressive Behaviors		Context/ Name of Game	Number of Aggressive Behaviors
Context/ Name of Game	Number of Aggressive Behaviors		Context/ Name of Game	Number of Aggressive Behaviors
Context/ Name of Game	Number of Aggressive Behaviors		Context/ Name of Game	Number of Aggressive Behaviors
Context/ Name of Game	Number of Aggressive Behaviors		Context/ Name of Game	Number of Aggressive Behaviors
Context/ Name of Game	Number of Aggressive Behaviors		Context/ Name of Game	Number of Aggressive Behaviors
Context/ Name of Game	Number of Aggressive Behaviors		Context/ Name of Game	Number of Aggressive Behaviors

REFERENCES

Bay-Hinitz, A. K., Peterson, R. F., & Quilitch, H. R. (1994). Cooperative games: A way to modify aggressive and cooperative behaviors in young children. *Journal of Applied Behavior Analysis, 27*, 435–446.

Boe, R. B. (1977). Economical procedures for the reduction of aggression in a residential setting. *Mental Retardation, 15*, 435–446.

Boot, H. (1928). Observation of play activities in a nursery school. *Genetic Psychology Monograph, 4*, 44–88.

DeVries, D. L., & Slavin, R. E. (1978). Teams–games–tournament (TGT): Review of ten classroom experiments. *Journal of Research and Development in Education, 12*, 28–38.

Doyle, P. H. (1976). The differential effects of multiple and single niche play activities on interpersonal relations among preschoolers. In D. F. Lancy & B. A. Tindall (Eds.), *The anthropological study of play* (pp. 189–197). New York: Leisure Press.

Finlinson, A. R., Austin, A. B., & Pfister, R. (2000). Cooperative games and children's positive behaviors. *Early Child Development, 164*, 29–40.

Green, G. (1989). Least restrictive use of reductive procedures: Guidelines and competencies. In A.C. Repp & N. N. Singh (Eds.), *Perspectives on the use of nonaversive and aversive interventions for persons with developmental disabilities* (pp. 479–493). Dekalb, IL: Sycamore Press.

Green, L. (1933). Friendship and quarrels among preschool children. *Child Development, 4*, 327–352.

Helmreich, R. L., Spence, J. T., Beane, W. E., Lucka, G. W., & Mathews, K. A. (1985). Making it in academic psychology: Demographic and personality correlates of attainment. *Journal of Personality and Social Psychology, 39*, 896–908.

Hoving, K. L., Wallace, J. R., & LaForme, G. L. (1979). Aggression during competition: Effects of age, sex, and amount and type of provocation. *Genetic Psychology Monographs, 99*(2), 251–289.

Johnson, D. W., & Johnson, R. T. (1975). *Learning together and alone: Cooperation, competition, and individualization.* New Jersey: Prentice-Hall.

Johnson, D. W., Johnson, R. T., & Scott, L. (1978). The effects of cooperative and individualized instruction in student attitudes and achievement. *Journal of Social Psychology, 104*, 207–216.

Johnson, D. W., Maruyama, G., Johnson, R. T., Nelson, D., & Skon, L. (1981). Effects of cooperative, competitive, individualistic goal structures on achievement: A meta-analysis. *Psychological Bulletin, 89*, 47–62.

Kernan, J. B. (1983). On the meaning of leisure: An investigation of some determinants of the subjective experience. *Journal of Consumer Research, 9*(4), 381–392.

Kohn, A. (1983). *No contest: The case against competition.* Boston: Houghton Mifflin.

Lejeune, C. W. (1995). The effects of participation in competitive and cooperative games on the free play behavior of preschoolers. *Dissertation Abstracts International: B. The Physical Sciences and Engineering, 55,* 4123.

Madden, N. A., & Slavin, R. E. (1983). Mainstreaming students with mild handicaps: Academic social outcomes. *Review of Educational Research, 53*(4), 519–569.

Murphy, H. A., Hutchinson, J. M., & Bailey, J. S. (1983). Behavioral school psychology goes outdoors: The effect of organized games on playground aggression. *Journal of Applied Behavior Analysis, 16,* 29–36.

Nelson, J. D., Gelfand, D. M., & Hartmann, D. P. (1969). Children's aggression following competitive exposure to an aggressive model. *Child Development, 40,* 1085–1097.

Orlick, T. (1981). Positive socialization via cooperative games. *Developmental Psychology, 17*(4), 426–429.

Orlick, T. (1982). *The second cooperative sports and games book.* New York: Pantheon Books.

Phillips, K. M. (1981). Aggression and productiveness in emotionally disturbed children in competitive and noncompetitive recreation. *Child Care Quarterly, 10*(2), 148–156.

Provost, P. (1981). *Immediate effects of film-mediated cooperative games on children's prosocial behavior.* Unpublished master's thesis, University of Ontario, Ottawa, Canada.

Quanty, M. B. (1976). Aggression catharsis: Experimental investigations and implications. In R. Green & E. O'Neal (Eds.), *Perspectives on aggression* (pp. 99–104). New York: Academic Press.

Quilitch, H. R., & Risley, T. R. (1973). The effects of play materials on social play. *Journal of Applied Behavior Analysis, 6*(4), 573–578.

Rocha, R., & Rogers, R. W. (1976). Ares and Babbitt in the classroom: Effects of competition and reward on children's aggression. *Journal of Personality and Social Psychology, 33*(5), 588–593.

Sheriff, M., Harvey, O. J., White, B. J., Hood, W. R., & Sherif, C. W. (1961). *Intergroup conflict and cooperation: The Robbers' Cave Experiment.* Norman, OK: University Book Exchange.

Shure, M. (1963). Psychological ecology of a nursery school. *Child Development, 34,* 979–992.

Smith, P. K. (1974). Aggression in a preschool playgroup. In J. DeWit & W. Hartup (Eds.), *Determinants and origins of aggressive behavior* (pp. 97–105). The Hague, Netherlands: Mouton.

Wolfe, V. V., Boyd, L. A., & Wolfe, D. A. (1983). Teaching cooperative play to behavior-problem preschool children. *Education and Treatment of Children, 6*(1), 1–9.

IV

EMPIRICALLY BASED PLAY INTERVENTIONS FOR DEVELOPMENTAL DISORDERS AND RELATED ISSUES

11

PLAY INTERVENTIONS FOR YOUNG CHILDREN WITH AUTISM SPECTRUM DISORDERS

SALLY J. ROGERS

In 1943, a renowned American psychiatrist, Dr. Leo Kanner, published the first scientific paper describing "Early Infantile Autism." Drawing on an entire career spent seeing children with developmental and psychiatric impairment, Kanner described a group of 13 children whose symptoms seemed similar to each other and unique from all other diagnostic groups of children he had seen. He focused on the major characteristics that set this group apart: their lack of reciprocal, affective social interactions with others, their unique communication impairments, and their repetitive, stereotypic, and ritualized play patterns (Kanner, 1943). A variety of empirical studies conducted over the past 50 years have delineated additional cognitive and affective differences in play in autism. Cognitive aspects of early play have been carefully examined, and the impact of autism on development of symbolic play is so profound that it is one of the defining features of the disorder in childhood (American Psychiatric Association, 1980). In fact, difficulties

Dr. Rogers received partial support for this work from The National Institute of Child Health and Human Development HD 35468, National Institute of Deafness and Communication Disorders, DC 05574, and the U.S. Department of Education and Rehabilitation G0081000247 and G008401921.

215

with play have been found to be a more prominent symptom in very young children than the classic symptoms involving insistence on sameness and repetitive routines that Kanner emphasized (e.g., Stone, Hoffman, Lewis, & Ousley, 1994; Stone, Lemanek, Fishel, Fernandez, & Altemeier, 1990). Such findings have helped the field move to an understanding of autism as a developmental disorder with changing symptom patterns across developmental periods (Rogers, 1999).

COGNITIVE ASPECTS OF PLAY IN AUTISM

The unique difficulty that children with autism have in symbolic play was highlighted in early work by Wing and colleagues (Wing, Gould, Yeates, & Brierley, 1977) and elaborated in a series of studies from Marian Sigman's laboratory at UCLA. Beginning in the 1980s, this group demonstrated that young children with autism were uniquely impaired in symbolic play (defined as use of symbolic substitutes and use of a doll as an independent agent), and in functional play (combining related objects, including dolls, in conventional ways). These children were found to engage in less diverse play and lower frequencies of doll-related play and symbolic play, even in adult-structured situations, than comparison groups (e.g., Mundy, Sigman, Ungerer, & Sherman, 1986; Sigman & Ungerer, 1984; Ungerer & Sigman, 1981). These play deficits were related to language comprehension and to general developmental levels in children with autism (and other groups as well), both concurrently and predictively (Sigman & Ruskin, 1999). Similar findings have been reported by many groups (Charman, Swettenham, Baron-Cohen, Cox, Baird, & Drew, 1997; Curcio, 1978; Wing et al., 1977) using standard measures of symbolic play in unstructured procedures that require children to generate their own symbolic play ideas. Virtually all studies of preschoolers with autism report symbolic play deficits, in both frequency and maturity, compared to both clinical and typical comparison groups (as reviewed below).

However, autism-specific effects on functional play have been reported less consistently across studies. Functional play as defined above is developmentally simpler play than symbolic play. Some groups, particularly those studying the youngest groups of children with autism, have reported no group differences on functional measures (Charman et al., 1997). Those studies that examine older preschoolers tend to report more group differences (Libby, Powell, Messer, & Jordan, 1998; Sigman & Ungerer, 1984; Williams, Reddy, & Costall, 2001).

The reason for the play deficits in autism is still an open question. Over the past decade, symbolic play difficulties in autism have been attributed to a cognitive difficulty with metarepresentation associated with development of theory of mind (Leslie, 1987). However, several findings have challenged the metarepresentational deficit theory (see Jarrold, 1997, for a detailed discussion of these views). One challenge involves the functional play difficulties in autism. Because functional play has no symbolic elements but instead involves handling toys in culturally defined ways (i.e., using a hairbrush to brush hair), it cannot be explained by the metarepresentational account, as functional play does not require representing another person's mental state (Williams et al., 2001).

Conflicting findings in the symbolic play area have also challenged the metarepresentational theory. Several groups have developed paradigms in which children with autism are presented with various objects and are requested to create, imitate, or identify specific symbolic transformations (e.g., Boucher & Lewis, 1989; Charman & Baron-Cohen, 1997; Kavanaugh & Harris, 1994; Libby, Powell, Messer, & Jordan, 1997; McDonough, Stahmer, Schreibman, & Thompson, 1997). In these studies, children with autism have performed at equivalent levels of symbolic ability as clinical comparison groups (though Libby et al.'s group reported autism-specific difficulties involving sequences). Furthermore, several studies have demonstrated the ability of older children with autism to carry out pantomime on request, both with and without objects (though their performance is not as precise as comparison children; Bartak, Rutter, & Cox, 1975; Rogers, Bennetto, McEvoy, & Pennington, 1996). Pantomimed sequences can be considered symbolic acts with imagined objects (Rogers et al., 1996).

These studies demonstrating preserved symbolic capacities in autism have a common element that differs from other studies of symbolic play in autism: The adult requests a particular symbolic enactment. The performances of children with autism in these situations suggests that they are cognitively capable of symbolic representations but appear to have difficulty in generating the pretend play acts spontaneously (Jarrold, 1997; McDonough et al., 1997). Generativity—the ability to create novel actions (like creativity)—is considered to be one of the executive functions, which are markedly impaired in older children with autism (e.g., Ozonoff & McEvoy, 1994; Ozonoff, Pennington, & Rogers, 1991; Ozonoff, Rogers, & Pennington, 1991) and contend for the status of primary psychological deficit in autism (Russell, 1997). A generativity explanation can also account for the functional play differences that are apparent in autism (Jarrold, 1997; Williams et al., 2001). Two groups have tried to test these two theories against each other, with inconclusive results (Craig & Baron-Cohen, 1999; Rutherford & Rogers, 2003).

AFFECTIVE ASPECTS OF PLAY IN AUTISM

Affective and interactive behaviors involved in play in autism have received far less attention. Unlike Kanner's (1943) descriptions of the aloofness and withdrawal of his patients, Sigman's group found that children with autism demonstrated positive responses to playful adult initiations, both from experimenters (Mundy et al., 1986), and from parents (Kasari, Sigman, & Yirmiya, 1993). In the Kasari et al. study, no social differences existed between children with autism and children with other developmental disorders in situations in which mothers were asked to play briefly with their child, without toys. However, children with autism do not initiate social interactions anywhere near the frequency of children with other disorders, or children with typical development (Kasari, Sigman, Baumgartner, & Stipek, 1993), and they do not "send" smiles and positive expressions to other people as frequently or as clearly as children with other diagnoses (Kasari et al., 1990; Yirmiya, Kasari, Sigman, & Mundy, 1989). This is not merely due to a lack of smiling in general, which has been shown to be equivalent to comparisons (Dawson, Hill, Spencer, Galpert, & Watson, 1990; Kasari, Sigman, Baumgartner, & Stipek, 1993). The difference is specifically in sharing affect with others (Kasari et al., 1990). This affective aspect of autism was the target of an early play-based intervention approach by Austin DesLauriers (1969). He described the use of affectively arousing physical play activities to create an optimized affective state for learning about others and stimulating development.

THE DENVER MODEL

The Denver model began in 1981 as a developmentally-based daily intervention program focused on play, relationships, and language development for young children with autism or other disorders of development, language, and behavior. The main features of the Denver model approach involve (a) focus on all developmental areas, with specific emphasis on interpersonal, constructive, and symbolic play skills; (b) development of affectively rich and reciprocal relationships with others, including development of imitation skills; (c) development of symbolic language, with particular focus on verbal language; (d) use of high quality teaching strategies, in both small groups and individual teaching sessions, delivered in carefully planned teaching episodes across the child's natural environments for 25 or more hours per week; and (e) positive behavior support approaches to unwanted behaviors. The underlying developmental model was described by Rogers and Pennington (1991) in a theoretical paper strongly influenced by Stern (1985). The theoretical orientation of the approach, goals, beliefs, and treatment approach have been described in detail in Rogers, Hall, Osaki, Reaven, and Herbison (2000).

Unlike behavioral treatment approaches, this approach was built on understanding autism as a developmental disorder. The use of a developmental approach to understanding atypical development has been elegantly described by Cicchetti as the discipline of developmental psychopathology (Cicchetti, 1989). The processes and products of typical development provide a framework for the study of a developmental disorder. Similarly, what is learned from a developmental disorder like autism gives us greater understanding of typical development as well.

Key Treatment Ingredients

In the Denver model, the use of play as a core of treatment of autism in very young children recognizes the two types of play that are affected by autism. One involves the social–communicative aspects of play, typically present in the first year of life as affective exchanges between infants and adults through infant social games. This type of ritualized social exchange was recognized by Bruner (1975), among others, as providing critical pragmatic foundations for the development of language. In the Denver model, emphasis on this aspect of play is considered to provide some of the building blocks needed for development of language and for social awareness of self and others as subjective beings, with mental states and minds that can interface.

Case Example: Affective Play

In the Denver model, affectively rich, dyadic play episodes are a crucial part of the therapy and they occur throughout the child's day. These are known as "sensory social routines," and they are used quite heavily, especially in the beginning of treatment, to establish a positive affective relationship between child and adult. Here is an example from a very first therapy hour.

Amy and her parents entered the therapy room for the first time, with a bag of snacks and drinks. Amy, completely nonverbal and very busy, was a darling blond with blue eyes and beautiful curls. She immediately started to fuss and pull on her parents to leave. Her new therapist had the parents sit down and asked them to become very boring for the next hour. Her therapist then pulled out a large rubber ball, so big that it came up to Amy's waist, and approached Amy with the ball, patting on it so it made a lively sound. Amy reached her hands out to touch the ball; the therapist picked Amy up and sat her on the ball, holding her securely at the waist, facing her, and bouncing her rhythmically up and down with fairly big movements. Amy smiled and laughed, and the therapist got excellent eye contact in these smiles. Then the therapist introduced a chant: "a bounce, a bounce, a bounce, a stop," and then stopped moving Amy. Amy jiggled her body to repeat the movement, and her therapist said, "Oh, you want more bounce. Okay, let's bounce." She began the routine again, bouncing and chanting with shared smiles and eye contact for just a few seconds, and then stopping and waiting for Amy to respond. For the next two repetitions, the therapist reactivated the routine when Amy moved her body to continue the game. The therapist then added a variation—Amy needed to make eye contact to continue the game. She simply waited during the pause; after Amy moved her body up and down with no response from the therapist, Amy looked at her, to which the therapist immediately responded, "You want to bounce," and bounced her.

Now eye contact was part of both bouncing and requesting; in just a few minutes the therapist had created a lovely, affectively rich, reciprocal routine in which both partners shared smiles, eye contact, and an enjoyable activity, with the child taking major initiative to begin and continue, using eye contact and gestures to do so. The parents commented on how social and responsive she appeared. This activity was quickly followed by several others, including sitting down to get her juice (at which her parents were amazed because she never sat to eat or drink at home) and doing several simple object tasks under the therapist's initiative. The two returned to the bouncing game several times during this first hour, at Amy's initiative, after a structured task.

The good feeling created by this first pleasurable activity may have helped Amy tolerate simple demands by the new therapist, such as sitting; the repeated bouncing kept the new demands from becoming too negative. The nice affective exchange marked the beginning of reciprocity, communication, and shared affect that was crucial for developing language and an interpersonal relationship. Amy was cooperative throughout the session and functioned under a level of structure that she had never tolerated before.

The second affected type of play is symbolic play. Vygotsky (2000) suggested that symbolic play provides the young child with early experiences in the power of the mind, in the ability to let thought prevail over the environment—a critical quality for development of abstract thought. Piaget (1962) highlighted the role of symbolic play as an opportunity to review and practice events in one's life, social roles, and rituals through repetition in play. Both of these qualities of symbolic play should be helpful for young children with autism, as they develop language and the ability to represent and think about past and future experiences, rather than being tied to the immediate moment and the world of objects and sensations. Symbolic play routines can be helpful in teaching verbal preschoolers with autism social language conventions and social role behaviors. Finally, symbolic play routines are a main source of play and an educational activity among typically developing children in preschool settings. Teaching verbal and nonverbal children with autism to play appropriately with thematic play materials provides an important vehicle for their interactive play with peers. Thus, in the Denver model, both the interpersonal and the cognitive aspects of play are considered integral aspects of the curriculum.

Case Example: Symbolic Play

Tyler was a bright and lively African American 4-year-old with autism, a sturdy and smiling child who spoke in phrases and had excellent sensorimotor play skills. He did not use objects to represent other things, however; thus, developing symbolic play skills was an immediate objective. Using dolls and a dollhouse to act out household events such as making dinner seemed uninteresting to him, though he understood the language and the acts involved. Symbolic play came alive for Tyler when we began to use the dolls to act out his daily life in preschool. His therapist named several child dolls for Tyler and his five classmates, and the adult doll was named for the teacher. The therapist set the dolls in a circle and began the "hello circle" routine that Tyler knew so well from class. Tyler responded with excitement and delight as he picked up two of the dolls and began to sing the special songs and have the dolls act out the special movements from the circle time routine. Tyler then initiated another group routine from class with the dolls, and prompted his therapist to take the teacher role: "Dr. Sally, you be Jean." Using pretend figures to act out his own life experiences became thoroughly enjoyable for Tyler, and his therapist found that this could be used to prepare him for new events, such as his first trip to the dentist and the arrival of a baby sibling.

Setting and Sessions

The model was originally developed for a daily, 12 month, therapeutic preschool. It was designed to be delivered in small groups of six children and three adults for several hours per day and to be accompanied by consistent parental interventions at home on targeted areas. The outcome studies described below result from this model.

In the past 10 years, the approach has been adapted for use in several different settings, including (a) use in inclusive preschools, where a child with autism attends along with typically developing children; (b) one-hour, weekly therapy sessions delivered by a professional trained as a generalist in the Denver model and accompanied by daily, one-hour, carefully structured home sessions delivered by a parent; and (c) intensive home intervention programs. These delivery methods are all meant to include a carefully structured half-day (inclusive) preschool experience as part of the overall treatment package. In all situations, the goal is to provide a minimum of 25 hours per week of carefully structured treatment across the various life settings of the young children with autism, accompanied by parentally delivered home interventions for maintenance and generalization, and to work on skills that only occur at home.

Resources

The Denver model is built to be delivered by an interdisciplinary team that includes parents as well as specialists in early childhood special education, occupational therapy, speech–language therapy, clinical child psychology, and assistants. In a preschool, the educational team provides most of the treatment, with the other disciplines providing consultation and some individual therapy. In the therapy and home based models, one of the disciplinary professionals heads the team while the other disciplines are in a consultative role to the main therapist or team leader. Assistants contribute greatly in the classroom-based and intensive home models. In all scenarios, parents are an integral part of the treatment team; parents attend weekly or bi-weekly progress meetings, focus the team on the most important areas of intervention, and provide daily structured interventions within natural home routines.

Treatment Delivery

Treatment is organized around a set of short-term developmental objectives that are developed by the lead therapist and parent with input from the entire interdisciplinary team. These objectives are based on the Denver model curriculum tool, which covers the full range of developmental areas: cognition, play, receptive and expressive language, social interactions, fine motor, gross motor, and self-care. Each child has approximately 16 written objectives that are to be accomplished in a 12-week period. A teaching plan and data system that are developed for each objective form the curriculum for the child's home and preschool programs. In preschool, the teaching plans are developed in relation to the group activities and are embedded in group and individual classroom instruction. In home programs, the teaching plans are delivered in individual teaching–play sessions and embedded into household routines.

The objectives, teaching plans, and data sheets are organized into a notebook for each child that accompanies the child from home to preschool to therapies and back again. Thus, the plan and notebook serve as a vehicle for organizing the many people that may be on a child's treatment team. This kind of tight organization and focus on a specific set of teaching skills is crucial for child progress.

Process and Flexibility of the Treatment Delivery

The process of delivering the Denver model is flexible. Although the basic tenets involve play, communication, positive affect, relationships, careful teaching in all areas of development, and a carefully structured environment, the amount and type of structured teaching can vary greatly from one child to the next, depending on the each child's specific needs. The style of the teaching can vary while the organization of the treatment, from assessment to objectives to teaching plans, delivery, and data collection, is invariant.

OUTCOME EVALUATION

Three outcome studies of the children involved in the Denver model classrooms were conducted from 1985 to 1990, using simple pre–post designs that were considered appropriate for educational studies at the time (Rogers, Herbison, Lewis, Pantone, & Reis, 1986; Rogers & Lewis, 1989; Rogers & DiLalla, 1991). The first two studies examined changes in developmental rates of children with autism spectrum disorders across the intervention period. The final study compared developmental changes for two groups of children: those with autism spectrum disorders, and those with other disorders involving communication and behavior.

Initial Study (1986)

The 1986 study involved 26 children, including 8 who met *DSM–III* (American Psychiatric Association, 1980) criteria for autism, 6 who met *DSM–III* criteria for another pervasive developmental disorder, and 10 who had other psychiatric diagnoses. The mean age of children with autism spectrum disorders was 48 months, and the children and families demonstrated considerable cultural and economic diversity. The mean nonverbal IQ of the children with autism was 72, based on standardized measures with a calculated language ratio quotient of 57. The interventions were delivered in a classroom setting for 2.75 hours per day, 4 days a week, by an early childhood special education teacher, two assistants, and consulting speech–language pathologist and child clinical psychologist. An assessment battery was administered before enrollment and after 6 months of daily intervention. This battery consisted of three instruments. (a) The Michigan Scales (Rogers et al., 1979) include six developmental subscales that assess receptive and expressive language, cognition, fine and gross motor development, social interactions, and self-care skills; these were administered every 6 months by the child's classroom teacher. (b) The Play Observation Scale (Rogers et al., 1986) assessed levels of sensorimotor play, symbolic play, and social communication skills from videotapes of a semistandard 20-minute play procedure carried out by a trained staff person and scored by raters blind to child diagnosis. (c) The Mother–Child Play Interaction Scale (Rogers & Puchalski, 1984) involved a 10-minute play interaction between child and mother to assess social engagement. Coders rated the videotaped interactions using a microanalytic rating system for both child and parental behaviors coded every 15 seconds, and assessed hedonic tone and social initiations and responses.

We examined the effects of the intervention on overall development with the Michigan scales. For each of the six developmental areas assessed, we created a change index that represented the difference between actual developmental outcomes after 6 months of Denver model intervention and the predicted outcomes had the Denver model not been introduced. We first calculated the estimated developmental levels by (a) calculating their developmental rate at the baseline measurement point (by dividing developmental age by chronological age for each subscale of the instrument); (b) multiplying this rate by the number of months between the two assessment points; and (c) adding this amount to the baseline developmental age on each subscale. We then calculated the group mean for each of these estimated subscale scores and compared them to the actual group means achieved after Denver model intervention.

Results

The first report focused on the first 18 children with complete data sets to receive the treatment. The children demonstrated considerable acceleration of *developmental rates* on the Michigan scales in four areas: cognition, language, social–emotional, and fine motor. The differences between actual and estimated scores were statistically significant for the first three areas, (p's ranged from .03 to .007) and approached significance for fine motor (p = .06). The children gained twice as many months of development in this 6 month period as was estimated by their baseline scores.

Symbolic play skills demonstrated significant gains in the initial 6 months of treatment. The children demonstrated statistically significant increases in complexity of their use of symbolic agents in play, of representing objects symbolically, and with the number of symbolic schemas combined in play. In terms of their *social–communicative development* with the experimenter, the children demonstrated statistically significant gains in continuing interactions, turn taking, and sharing play schemas.

In terms of *social interactions with parents*, children demonstrated statistically significant increases in positive affect and number of social initiations toward their mother and significant decreases in episodes of negative affect in response to mother's initiations. In addition, there was a significant increase in episodes of positive affect in response to maternal social initiations and a significant number of vocalizations. Maternal social behavior was also rated to determine whether changes in maternal behavior were correlated with changes in child behavior. Maternal behaviors were characterized by responsivity, social engagement, and positive affect at both times. Maternal behavior was quite stable over this 6-month time period, with no significant difference in any of the seven interactional variables rated. Thus, child differences appeared to reflect child change, rather than responses to parental change. The large majority of children in each of these analyses (75%) had the diagnosis of autism, so the gains demonstrated were not due to large changes in nonautistic children, but in fact, represent the effect of the model on children with autism spectrum disorders.

Finally, an examination of educational placements following Denver model intervention for 20 children revealed that 35% of the group were functioning in the normal range on all measures and went to nonspecialized settings (this was in the mid-1980s, before inclusion was a common educational practice); 30% were considered to have developmental difficulties but not significant social–emotional or autism-specific difficulties; and 35% continued to have difficulties focused in the social or emotional area, including autism.

This initial report indicated that the Denver model might have significant positive effects on children's development across many areas of development. However, many questions remained after this first examination of short-term outcomes in a small group of children with mixed diagnoses. Two studies followed that provided better definition of groups, larger numbers, and a longer period of treatment.

Replication Study (1989)

In 1989, Rogers and Lewis described the treatment response of 31 children with an autism spectrum disorder (a group that included children from the 1986 study). The group of 24 boys and 7 girls from diverse ethnic and economic backgrounds were carefully diagnosed using *DSM–III* criteria, the Childhood Autism Rating Scale (CARS) score in the autistic range (Schopler, Reichler, & Renner, 1988), and current clinical judgment. The mean age of the group was 45 months, mean nonverbal IQ was 69, and incoming language developmental level was 23.95 months. The children attended the 12-month per year, five days per week treatment program for 4.5 hours a day.

Autism Symptoms

We examined changes in symptoms of autism based on use of a standard 20-minute procedure used to rate the CARS (Schopler et al., 1988). Trained and reliable raters, who were independent of the data gathering, scored the CARS from videos. The number and severity of autism symptoms decreased significantly in 6.5 months of treatment, as demonstrated by a reduction in mean CARS scores from 35 (moderately autistic) to 29 (not autistic; $p = .001$). Of the 31 children, 30 demonstrated decreases in CARS scores from Time 1 to Time 2.

Developmental Changes

The index of change score was calculated as described above for each of the six subscales of the Michigan scales. After 6.5 months of treatment, the group demonstrated statistically significant increases in all areas of functioning (p's ranged from .001 to .009) except self-help (which approached significance $p = .09$). A procedure for examining the amount of change that appeared due to treatment, rather than maturation (described by Wolery,

1983), indicated that 53% of the change in language functioning was attributable to treatment effects, rather than general development. Similar effects were found for cognition (43%), social–emotional (42%), fine motor (41%), and gross motor (33%). At the time of intake, 47% of the entire group of children were nonverbal or had extremely minimal speech. At the end of this treatment period, 73% of children had useful, communicative, generative multiword utterances. Of the initially nonverbal children, 47% had acquired useful, multiword communicative speech by the end of the treatment period. As in the earlier paper, symbolic play abilities in agency, symbolic substitutions, and schema complexity demonstrated statistical significant gains, as did the social-communicative aspects of their play skills.

In addition, a subgroup of 15 children had been enrolled long enough to examine change over a 12-month period. Their developmental rates at the 6-month point was compared to their developmental rate at the 12-month point to determine whether the original developmental acceleration was a short-term phenomenon following the start of intervention. For two areas, social–emotional and self-help, developmental rates continued to increase significantly over earlier rates at the 12-month point. The other four areas demonstrated stable development at the new accelerated rate achieved at the 6-month evaluation point. Thus, the accelerated developmental rates were sustained over the treatment period.

Comparison of Children Diagnosed With Autistic Disorder and Those With Pervasive Developmental Disorder Not Otherwise Specified (PDD/NOS)

Finally, treatment responses of the children who met all criteria for autistic disorder were compared to those who were diagnosed with PDD/NOS, a diagnostic herding for children who show some of the core features of autism but do not meet all diagnostic criteria. At the start of treatment, the mean nonverbal IQs of these two groups did not differ, but the PDD/NOS group was older, had higher levels of functioning in all areas, and had lower CARS scales than the group with autism. The children with the autism diagnosis demonstrated greater actual gains from pre- to posttreatment than did the PDD/NOS group, who also demonstrated improvements in all areas. Both groups demonstrated marked decreases in their CARS scores. Although this may be partly due to regression to the mean for the more severely involved group, it also demonstrates that children with the most severe symptoms demonstrated significant acceleration in developmental rates in all areas, and that this developmental treatment approach was as effective for younger, more severely involved children as it was for somewhat older, more mildly involved preschoolers on the autism spectrum.

Comparative Study (Rogers & DiLalla, 1991)

The final outcome study focused on a comparison of children with an autism spectrum disorder and children without any evidence of an autism spectrum disorder but with other diagnoses involving behavioral and developmental symptoms (Rogers & DiLalla, 1991). The research question asked whether the programmatic emphasis on language, cognition, play, and relationship development would be more effective for children without the social and communicative impairments involved in autism than for children with autism. There were 49 children in the autism group and 27 in the other diagnosis group. Children in the other diagnosis group (mean age of 50 months) had significantly higher verbal and nonverbal scores and significantly lower CARS scores and SES ratings than the autism spectrum group (mean age of 46 months).

We predicted that although both groups would progress in the treatment program, the nonautistic group would make greater gains because of their more intact social and communicative skills. After six months of treatment, both groups made significantly greater progress than were predicted by their initial scores; the group with autism demonstrated greater accelerations in developmental rates posttreatment than the other diagnosis group.

To examine the second hypothesis, we created two subgroups from the original diagnostic groups who were matched on initial age and language abilities. When we compared their initial profiles, there were no significant differences between these two subgroups. After 6 months of treatment, the profiles of the two groups continued to be similar. Thus, the children with autism were demonstrating the same rate of progress as the children without autism. After this surprising finding, we examined language development more closely in these matched subgroups. The children with autism entered treatment with a learning rate index of .40 (4.8 months of language progress in a 12-month period). In the first 10 months of treatment, they achieved 10 months of progress, indicating a learning rate of 1.00. Examination of children who remained in the program a second year demonstrated continued language learning at essentially a normal learning rate, that is, one month of progress for each month of treatment. The children in the other diagnosis group also demonstrated acceleration of progress and sustained rate of progress at a normal learning rate; both groups made twice as much progress during treatment as would have been predicted from their initial learning rates.

REPLICATION AND TRANSPORTABILITY

Replication studies were carried out at several sites in Colorado (Rogers, Lewis, & Reis, 1987) to determine whether (a) other teams could learn the model and implement it with high levels of fidelity, and (b) children at other sites would demonstrate developmental accelerations in the targeted areas.

Sites

The four rural and one urban site in the studies involved publicly funded early childhood special education programs that served preschool children with a wide range of disabilities, including autism. The rural settings were typical of those in many western states, with agricultural and ranching communities containing a culturally diverse population. The urban site was located in a metropolitan area that extends along 100 miles of the eastern border of the Rocky Mountains, from Colorado Springs to Boulder and several small cities beyond.

Four of the five replication sites provided data reported here. The programs were generally well-equipped with materials but varied significantly in terms of space; provided direct service to the children, ranging from 12 to 26 hours weekly; were developmentally oriented; and included a special education teacher, a teaching assistant, a speech–language pathologist, and a social worker or family coordinator as key team members. All 16 team members received the full training package and several additional supportive personnel from three of the four sites also received training.

Each site was required to have at least one child with autism, to support all of the preschool team in attending 40 hours of training, to allow the consulting staff bi-monthly visits to each site to evaluate and train, and to gather and provide the necessary data at the required times. These four sites served 11 children with autism and 20 with other developmental disorders. Of the children with autism, 6 were boys, and 5 were girls; they ranged in age from 39 to 74 months, with a mean age of 56 months. In addition to autism, all had mental retardation that ranged from mild to profound levels of severity; their mean level of cognitive development on the Michigan scales was at 14.65 months.

Training

The Denver model involves specific approaches to (a) classroom management, (b) designing an individual educational program, and (c) interacting with the children. A variety of training procedures was used to teach the model to the adults; to measure the quality and frequency of their implementation of the key interventions; to teach the replication staff members to monitor and evaluate their use of the new procedures; and to measure the effects on children's behavior and development.

The training occurred in four stages. (a) A one-day workshop and one-day visit to each model site began the training, in which the basic principles, philosophy, and techniques of the Denver model were described. The target child was assessed and videotaped, classroom observations were made, and a meeting was held with administrators and staff members to discuss the requirements of the outreach activity and the expectations. At the end of this meeting, both parties signed a formal replication agreement. (b) The next step involved the entire replication site team receiving a full week of training on the model site in Denver. (c) After each replication team returned to their site, they implemented the model and videotaped their classroom at six week intervals for 24 weeks, according to a specific time sampling procedure. They sent the tapes to the investigators, who reviewed and scored them, and prepared a feedback document for each team. Finally, (d) a member of the Model suite team made two 2-day visits to each site at eight-week intervals after implementation began, to assess current strengths and to deliver needed training.

Measurement of Model Fidelity and Outcomes

The measurement approach involved four components: subjective perceived utility of the training; objective assessment of knowledge regarding child development, autism, and the Denver model; fidelity of implementation of each of the five Denver model components; and changes in the developmental rates of the target children. Trainees highly rated the usefulness, applicability, and consistency of the training.

Objective tests of knowledge demonstrated an increase of 50% following the training workshop, which is a significant change. In terms of treatment fidelity, a scale was developed that rated the presence and the quality of the five target features of the Denver model on a Likert based scale. The increase in fidelity scores in the 12 weeks following the training was marked (between two and three standard deviations of gain), and t tests revealed high levels of statistical significance (probabilities ranging from .04 to .007). Each of the four sites demonstrated gains in fidelity scores in each of the five components, suggesting that the Denver model could be learned to high levels of fidelity and sustained over several months.

To examine child effects, we created change index scores, as described above, that represented the difference between actual and predicted developmental outcomes after five months of Denver model intervention. The estimated developmental scores represented a gain of 1-month over a 4-month period. The group essentially tripled their developmental rates during this period, making between 2 to 7 months of gain in the same time period in each developmental area. These differences reached statistical significance in five of the six developmental areas, with the sixth area, self-care skills, approaching significance.

These replication studies thus demonstrated both first and second order effects of the approach used. The changes in knowledge base and actual educational practices of the teaching staff represented the first order of change. The dramatic effects on children's developmental performance represented second order effects. The children had been attending the preschools for a significant time period before this intervention began. Thus, the increase in performance was not a short-term response to beginning a structured intervention program. Furthermore, the children had severe developmental impairments in all areas of development, and at age 56 months, they were close to kindergarten age at the start of the intervention. No additional hours of intervention or staff members were added. The only change was in style of educational delivery, using principles of Denver model intervention, and the children responded with a rapid acceleration of developmental rates in all areas and enhanced performance on developmental batteries. The intervention effects were not limited to the children with autism. Both anecdotal reports and quantitative information from the staff indicated that the use of Denver model principles had been quite beneficial to the other children in the classroom as well. Thus, the replication studies demonstrated the transportability and teachability of the Denver model and its ability to stimulate significant developmental gains in children with severe autism and concomitant severe developmental delays.

Other Interventions That Focus on Symbolic Play

Given the effects of autism on development of play, it is not surprising that treatment approaches for autism have explored the therapeutic use of play. Play-based and relationship-based approaches dominated writings about autism treatment in the 1960s. Early clinical descriptions like Axline's (1964) *Dibs: In Search of Self* described efforts to use play as a vehicle for stimulating development of improved communication and social interaction, described in case studies in the clinical literature.

In addition to the Denver model publications, several other groups have published data demonstrating the effectiveness of specific intervention approaches to development of symbolic play. Work from Laura Schreibman's lab in San Diego has demonstrated the successful use of symbolic play intervention using pivotal response training. Papers by Stahmer (1995) and Thorp, Stahmer, and Schreibman (1995) report on interventions carried out in 1:1 treatment several times a week for several weeks. Freeman, Kasari, and Paparella (2002) reported that a short-term intervention that taught symbolic play to 42-month-olds with autism resulted in short-term decreases in nonfunctional play, nonsignificant increases in functional play, and significant increases in level of symbolic play. Goldstein, Wickstrom, Hoyson, Jamieson, and Odom (1988) described the successful use of a peer-mediated strategy to increase the frequency and complexity of thematic role-play and related communication with several children with autism. One important paper from Lifter, Sulzer-Azaroff, Anderson, Coyle, and Cowdery (1993) demonstrated the importance of assessing developmental skills prior to intervention and using developmental readiness to guide the choice of targets for intervention.

Interventions With a Social and Affective Focus

Emphasis on dyadic, affectively based, playful exchanges as a possible therapeutic approach to early autism has been described by several different groups in research-based journals over the past 20 years, starting with the work of DesLauriers (1969). The papers by this author and her colleagues, reviewed above, described positive affective outcomes from a play-based, affectively rich intervention model. Dawson and Galpert (1990) described an intervention in which mothers were taught to imitate their child's behavior in daily brief toy play episodes. After two weeks of treatment, lab measures indicated increases in positive eye contact and creative toy play. Similar work by Nadel et al. (2000) has replicated this finding of the enhancing effect of being imitated on social initiative in children with autism.

A well-known, current therapeutic approach to autism that emphasizes the affective component comes from Greenspan et al. (1997). These authors describe an intervention approach that combines professional interventions from several different disciplinary therapists with a daily extended interactive period called "floortime," a technique that shares many commonalities with the above interventions. Parents are taught the floortime intervention, which involves scaffolding positive dyadic exchanges with their children at home. A review of the clinical notes from medical records of 200 children with autism receiving this approach demonstrated that 58% developed conversational speech, pretend play abilities, use of gestures, and reciprocal engagement (Greenspan & Wieder, 1997). Twenty-five percent of the group improved in affect, reciprocity, and use of communicative gestures but continued to have great difficulty with language and play; 17% continued to have severe difficulties.

Other interventions have focused on social, rather than affective, aspects of play interventions. Coe, Matson, Fee, Manikam, and Linarello (1990) used a single subject, multiple baseline design to demonstrate successful teaching of two children with autism and one with Down syndrome to initiate and maintain a game of catch. A groundbreaking series of studies published by Strain, Odom, and Goldstein (Goldstein & Strain, 1988; Odom & Strain, 1986) studied peer play intervention techniques using peers as the agent of change. Schuler and her colleagues in San Francisco have described similar interventions using typical peers (Wolfberg & Schuler, 1993; Zercher, Hunt, Schuler, & Webster, 2001). As described in a wonderful review paper by Hwang and Hughes (2000), these peer-mediated interventions have demonstrated collateral effects via increases in appropriate use of imitation, eye contact, social and affective responses, and verbal and nonverbal communication after peer-mediated training, as well as cognitively more mature play.

RECOMMENDATION FOR OUTCOME EVALUATION IN CLINICAL PRACTICE

Four aspects of interventions focused on play development in children with autism stand out as guidelines for practitioners. First, providing play interventions is considered part of best educational practices for young children with autism (e.g., National Research Council, 2001; Hurth, Shaw, Izeman, Whaley, & Rogers, 1999). Given the importance of developing peer relations and a range of appropriate activities in early childhood, focus on play is part of virtually every comprehensive curriculum for children with autism in current use. Thus, interventions for young children with autism must include a focus on increasing play skills.

The second aspect involves the choice of play skills for intervention. Play has a strong developmental trajectory; the effectiveness of choosing play goals based on the child's current developmental level has been demonstrated in several outcome studies that have shown growth in skills targeted in this way, most definitively by the work of Lifter et al. (1993). Thus, there is empirical evidence that using a developmental framework to choose play goals for young children with autism appears to enhance progress in play development. In addition, using child interests to guide choice of toys and play activities has been demonstrated to increase motivation and cooperative, motivated responding to the teaching (Koegel, Koegel, & Surratt, 1992).

The third aspect involves the delivery of the intervention. Progress in play has been documented by several different types of teaching approaches: peer mediated strategies, developmental work in small group settings, inclusive preschool settings, and individual sessions. We do not have findings that indicate that one particular teaching approach is "best" for all children with autism. There are few comparative studies of different teaching approaches in the autism literature (but see Koegel et al., 1992 for one such study). However, the common element among all these approaches is structured, preplanned approaches to teaching in which the behavioral objective is clearly specified, the teaching is carried out systematically, and ongoing progress is monitored. The autism intervention literature is replete with examples of successful learning via the use of carefully defined and systematic teaching approaches. Using such intervention approaches does not constrain the settings in which play can be taught, but it requires that the adult use a planned, structured teaching approach.

The fourth aspect is the need to assess ongoing progress objectively. As in all other areas of teaching children with autism, it is not enough to provide rich and varied experiences with the assumption that children will learn and develop. It is crucial that ongoing assessment occurs to ensure that children are indeed progressing from the intervention and if they are not, the intervention is altered to ensure that learning occurs. The intervention reports in the literature commonly use a two-stage approach to evaluating progress, with the first targeted at examining day-to-day progress in the specific teaching objectives and the second focused on evidence of developmental increases in play using more generic tools.

The first level of assessment of progress involves constructing some type of data system that can reflect the individual teaching objectives. If the play objective is well-written and includes a stimulus, a measurable behavior, and a criterion for mastery, the construction of a data collection system should be relatively straightforward. Following is an example:

Objective: When presented with dolls and miniature toys involving self-care activities (e.g., props for mealtime, bathing, grooming) and a play partner who models doll-related acts with the materials, Michelle will respond by using one or more of the props to complete at least three different conventional acts with a doll in a 5-minute play period (see Exhibit 11.1 for the related data sheet).

A simple recording system, such as the data content sheet in Exhibit 11.1, allows the clinician to track the number of different acts exhibited for each set of toy props, the level of support the adult provided, the time elapsed, and the total number of play acts the child used in a particular play session. It provides all the data needed to record progress on the objective when examined over several weeks. Progress would be indicated by an increasing number of different play acts, increasing total play acts, increasing

EXHIBIT 11.1
Data Sheet Content

Skill:	Pretend Play
Codes:	S, M, V, P, F (Spontaneous, model, verbal instruction, partial physical, full physical)

Theme:	mealtime with dolls
Props:	cups, bottles, dishes, spoon, fork, bib, napkin, pitcher, miniature foods, pan, stove
Acts:	___ feeds ___ drinks ___ pours ___ stirs ___ uses napkins ___ other (list) _____

Start time: _____   Stop Time: _____

Theme:	grooming with dolls
Props:	little bathtub, miniature soap, washcloth, towel, comb, brush, toothbrush, glass
Acts:	___ combs ___ toothbrush ___ washes ___ bathes ___ undresses ___ dresses ___ other

Start time: _____   Stop time: _____

spontaneous acts, and decreasing levels of supports needed in the prompts. If such progress is not occurring, the teaching strategy needs to be altered.

The second level of evaluation would examine play skills at a more general level. For the clinician, using a play assessment instrument that evaluates a number of developmental variables and provides some kind of play maturity level would reflect generalized growth in play abilities over time. There are a variety of tools in the special education literature for assessing developmental aspects of constructive and symbolic play. Many early childhood educational curricula list cognitive aspects of play. These are available from publishers such as Pro-Ed and Brookes. Two such instruments with demonstrated psychometric strengths include: Rebecca Fewell's 1992 *Play Assessment Scale, 5th Revision*, and Vicky Lewis and Jill Boucher's 1997 *Test of Pretend Play*, The Psychological Corporation.

CONCLUSION

Several main points have been discussed in this chapter. First, autism impairs the development of several aspects of play: the rich affective exchange that occurs between play partners, the novelty and flexibility of object play, and the use of symbolic play to act out personal life events and to develop increasingly abstract thought. Thus, both social and cognitive aspects of play are affected. Second, play is considered to be so important to all children's emotional, cognitive, and social development that focusing on play development is considered fundamental to appropriate education and intervention for young children with autism. Each of the best known intervention approaches for young children with autism directly addresses play as part of the intervention curriculum. One model, the Denver model, which heavily emphasizes play, was described in depth, and the outcome data from this approach were reviewed.

Although play is quite affected by autism, children with autism have consistently demonstrated their ability to learn and grow in play skills through a variety of interventions. A number of intervention studies were presented that demonstrated successful learning of targeted play skills by preschoolers with autism at various levels of cognitive and language development, illustrating that this is an appropriate area to target for all young children with autism. However, developmental aspects of play learning are important, and it is crucial that interventionists assess children's play abilities and build objectives for play that begin with a child's current level of understanding. Play is a developmental skill; a developmental approach to choosing what aspects of play to teach has been demonstrated to be a powerful factor in the improvement seen in children with autism.

Finally, the chapter discussed what the critical teaching elements were likely to be in ensuring progress in play for young children with autism. As in other learning areas in autism, effective interventions for play occur via thoughtful planning, careful delineation of treatment objectives, careful and regular application of preplanned teaching procedures, ongoing evaluation of child learning to ensure that progress is occurring, and frequent opportunities for use of new skills across settings and people to promote generalization of skills. Teaching young children with autism to use their developing play skills with typical peers is a particularly important teaching objective.

In summary, autism presents a significant impediment to young children's development of cognitive, affective, and social–communicative aspects of play. Yet the impairment is not absolute, and the mechanisms by which autism impairs play development have not been elucidated. The empirical data demonstrate the capacity of young children with autism to improve play skills, regardless of functioning level. Thus, the key variable in promoting progress appears to be quality of intervention, not capacity of the child. However, no studies have demonstrated that focusing on play alone results in significant and comprehensive changes in the developmental patterns or rate of young children with autism. Play is part, but only one part, of a comprehensive intervention approach.

REFERENCES

American Psychiatric Association. (1980). *Diagnostic and statistical manual of mental disorders* (3rd. ed.). Washington, DC: Author.

Axline, V. (1964). *Dibs: In search of self.* New York: Ballantine Books.

Bartak, L., Rutter, M., & Cox, A. (1975). A comparative study of infantile autism and specific developmental receptive language disorder. *British Journal of Psychiatry, 126,* 127–145.

Boucher, J., & Lewis, V. (1989). Memory impairments and communication in relatively able autistic children. *Journal of Child Psychology and Psychiatry, 30,* 99–122.

Bruner, J. (1975). The ontogenesis of speech acts. *Journal of Child Language, 2,* 1–19.

Charman, T., & Baron-Cohen, S. (1997). Brief report: Prompted pretend play in autism. *Journal of Autism and Developmental Disorders, 27,* 321–328.

Charman, T., Swettenham, J., Baron-Cohen, S., Cox, A., Baird, G., & Drew, A. (1997). Infants with autism: An investigation of empathy, pretend play, joint attention, and imitation. *Developmental Psychology, 33,* 781–789.

Cicchetti, D. (1989). Developmental psychopathology: Some thoughts on its evolution. *Development and Psychopathology, 1,* 1–4.

Coe, D., Matson, J., Fee, V., Manikam, R., & Linarello, C. (1990). Training nonverbal and verbal play skills to mentally retarded and autistic children. *Journal of Autism and Developmental Disorders, 20,* 177–187.

Craig, J., & Baron-Cohen, S. (1999). Creativity and imagination in autism and asperger syndrome. *Journal of Autism and Developmental Disorders, 29,* 319–326.

Curcio, F. (1978). Sensorimotor functioning and communication in mute autistic children. *Journal of Autism and Childhood Schizophrenia, 3,* 281–292.

Dawson, G., & Galpert, L. (1990). Mothers' use of imitative play for facilitating social responsiveness and toy play in young autistic children. *Development and Psychopathology, 2,* 151–162.

Dawson, G., Hill, D., Spencer, A., Galpert, L., & Watson, L. (1990). Affective exchanges between young autistic children and their mothers. *Journal of Abnormal Child Psychology, 18,* 335–345.

DesLauriers, A. (1969). *Your child is asleep: Early infantile autism.* Homewood, IL: Dorsey Press.

Fewell, R. (1992). *Play Assessment Scale* (5th Rev.). (Available from author, University of Miami, Mailman Center, P.O. Box 014621, Miami, FL 33101.)

Freeman, S. F. N., Kasari, C., & Paparella, T. (2002). *Play intervention and the effect on play, language, and cognitive outcomes.* Paper presented at the Gatlinburg Conference, San Diego, CA.

Goldstein, H., & Strain, P. S. (1988). Peers as communication intervention agents: Some new strategies and research findings. *Topics in Language Disorders, 9,* 44–57.

Goldstein, H., Wickstrom, S., Hoyson, M., Jamieson, B., & Odom, S. L. (1988). Effects of sociodramatic play training on social and communicative interaction. *Education and Treatment of Children, 11,* 97–117.

Greenspan, S., & Wieder, S. (1997). Developmental patterns and outcomes in infants and children with disorders in relating and communicating: A chart review of 200 cases of children with autistic spectrum disorders. *Journal of Developmental and Learning Disorders, 1,* 87–141.

Greenspan, S. I., Kalmanson, B., Shahmoon-Shanok, R., Wieder, S., Gordon-Williamson, G., & Anzalone, M. (1997). *Assessing and treating infants and young children with severe difficulties in relating and communicating.* Washington, DC: Zero to Three.

Hurth, J., Shaw, E., Izeman, S. G., Whaley, K., & Rogers, S. (1999). Areas of agreement about effective practices among programs serving young children with autism spectrum disorders. *Infants and Young Children, 12,* 17–26.

Hwang, B., & Hughes, C. (2000). The effects of social interactive training on early social communicative skills of children with autism. *Journal of Autism and Developmental Disorders, 30,* 331–343.

Jarrold, C. (1997). Pretend play in autism: executive explanations. In J. Russell (Ed.), *Autism as an executive disorder* (pp. 101–140). Oxford, England: Oxford University Press.

Kanner, L. (1943). Autistic disturbances of affective contact. *Nervous Child, 2,* 217–250.

Kasari, C., Sigman, M., Mundy, P., & Yirmiya, N. (1990). Affective sharing in the context of joint attention interactions of normal, autistic, and mentally retarded children. *Journal of Autism and Developmental Disorders, 20,* 87–100.

Kasari, C., Sigman, M., & Yirmiya, N. (1993). Focused and social attention of autistic children in interactions with familiar and unfamiliar adults: A comparison of autistic, mentally retarded, and normal children. *Development and Psychopathology, 5*, 403–414.

Kasari, C., Sigman, M. D., Baumgartner, P., & Stipek, D. J. (1993). Pride and mastery in autism. *Journal of Child Psychology and Psychiatry, 34*, 353–362.

Kavanaugh, R. D., & Harris, P. L. (1994). Imagining the outcome of pretend transformations: Assessing the competence of normal children and children with autism. *Developmental Psychology, 30*(6), 847–854.

Koegel, R. L., Koegel, L. K., & Surratt, A. (1992). Language intervention and disruptive behavior in preschool children with autism. *Journal of Autism and Developmental Disorders, 22*, 141–153.

Leslie, A. (1987). Pretense and representation: the origins of "Theory of Mind." *Psychological Review, 94*, 412–426.

Lewis, V., & Boucher, S. (1997). *Test of pretend play.* London: Harcourt Brace.

Libby, S., Powell, S., Messer, D., & Jordan, R. (1997). Imitation of pretend play acts by children with autism and Down's syndrome. *Journal of Autism and Developmental Disorders, 27*(4), 365–383.

Libby, S., Powell, S., Messer, D., & Jordan, R. (1998). Spontaneous play in children with autism: A reappraisal. *Journal of Autism and Developmental Disorders, 28*, 487–497.

Lifter, K., Sulzer-Azaroff, B., Anderson, S. R., Coyle, J. T., & Cowdery, G. E. (1993). Teaching play activities to preschool children with disabilities: The importance of developmental considerations. *Journal of Early Intervention, 17*, 139–159.

McDonough, L., Stahmer, A., Schreibman, L., & Thompson, S. J. (1997). Deficits, delays, and distractions: An evaluation of symbolic play and memory in children with autism. *Development and Psychopathology, 9*, 17–41.

Mundy, P., Sigman, M., Ungerer, J., & Sherman, T. (1986). Defining the social deficits of autism: The contribution of nonverbal communication measures. *Journal of Child Psychology and Psychiatry, 27*, 657–669.

Nadel, J., Croue, S., Mattlinger, M., Canet, P., Hudelot, C., Lecuyer, C., et al. (2000). Do children with autism have expectancies about the social behavior of unfamiliar people? *Autism, 4*, 133–145.

National Research Council. (2001). *Educating children with autism.* Washington, DC: National Academy Press.

Odom, S. L., & Strain, P. S. (1986). A comparison of peer-initiation and teacher-antecedent interventions for promoting reciprocal social interaction of autistic preschoolers. *Journal of Applied Behavior Analysis, 19*, 59–71.

Ozonoff, S., & McEvoy, R. E. (1994). A longitudinal study of executive function and theory of mind development in autism. *Development and Psychopathology, 6*, 415–431.

Ozonoff, S., Pennington, B. F., & Rogers, S. J. (1991). Executive function deficits in high-functioning autistic children: Relationship to theory of mind. *Journal of Child Psychology and Psychiatry, 32*, 1081–1105.

Ozonoff, S., Rogers, S. J., & Pennington, B. F. (1991). Asperger's syndrome: Evidence of an empirical distinction from high-functioning autism. *Journal of Child Psychology and Psychiatry, 32*, 1107–1122.

Piaget, J. (1962). *Play, dreams, and imitation in childhood.* New York: Norton.

Rogers, S. J. (1999). Intervention for young children with autism: From research to practice. *Infants and Young Children, 12*, 1–16.

Rogers, S. J., Bennetto, L., McEvoy, R., & Pennington, B. F. (1996). Imitation and pantomime in high functioning adolescents with autism spectrum disorders. *Child Development, 67*, 2060–2073.

Rogers, S. J., & DiLalla, D. (1991). A comparative study of a developmentally-based preschool curriculum on young children with autism and young children with other disorders of behavior and development. *Topics in Early Childhood Special Education, 11*, 29–48.

Rogers, S. J., Donovan, C. M., D'Eugenio, D. B., Brown, S. L., Lynch, E. W., Moersch, M. S., et al. (1979). Early intervention developmental profile. In D. S. Schafer & M. S. Moersch (Eds.), *Developmental programming for infants and young children: Vol. 2.* Ann Arbor, MI: University of Michigan Press.

Rogers, S. J., Hall, T., Osaki, D., Reaven, J., & Herbison, J. (2000). A comprehensive, integrated, educational approach to young children with autism and their families. In S. L. Harris & J. S. Handleman (Eds.), *Preschool education programs for children with autism* (2nd ed., pp. 95–134). Austin, TX: Pro-Ed.

Rogers, S. J., Herbison, J., Lewis, H., Pantone, J., & Reis, K. (1986). An approach for enhancing the symbolic, communicative, and interpersonal functioning of young children with autism and severe emotional handicaps. *Journal of the Division of Early Childhood, 10*, 135–148.

Rogers, S. J., & Lewis, H. (1989). An effective day treatment model for young children with pervasive developmental disorders. *Journal of the American Academy of Child and Adolescent Psychiatry, 28*, 207–214.

Rogers, S. J., Lewis, H. C., & Reis, K. (1987). An effective procedure for training early special education teams to implement a model program. *Journal of the Division of Early Childhood, 11*, 180–188.

Rogers, S. J., & Pennington, B. F. (1991). A theoretical approach to the deficits in infantile autism. *Development and Psychopathology, 3*, 137–162.

Rogers, S. J., & Puchalski, C. (1984). Social characteristics of visually impaired infants' play. *Topics in Early Childhood Special Education, 3*, 52–57.

Russell, J. (1997). *Autism as an executive disorder.* Oxford, England: Oxford University Press.

Rutherford, M. D., & Rogers, S. J. (2003). The cognitive underpinnings of pretend play. *Journal of Autism and Developmental Disorders, 33*, 289–302.

Schopler, E., Reichler, R. J., & Renner, B. R. (1988). *The childhood autism rating scale.* Los Angeles: Western Psychological Services.

Sigman, M., & Ruskin, E. (1999). Continuity and change in the social competence of children with autism, Down's syndrome, and developmental delays. *Monographs of the Society for Research in Child Development, 64*, 1–113.

Sigman, M., & Ungerer, J. (1984). Cognitive and language skills in autistic, mentally retarded, and normal children. *Developmental Psychology, 20*, 293–302.

Stahmer, A. C. (1995). Teaching symbolic play skills to children with autism using pivotal response training. *Journal of Autism and Developmental Disorders, 25*(2), 123–142.

Stern, D. N. (1985). *The interpersonal world of the human infant.* New York: Basic Books.

Stone, W. L., Hoffman, E. L., Lewis, S. E., & Ousley, O. Y. (1994). Early recognition of autism: Parental reports versus clinical observation. *Archives of Pediatric and Adolescent Medicine, 148*, 174–179.

Stone, W. L., Lemanek, K. L., Fishel, P. T., Fernandez, M. C., & Altemeier, W. A. (1990). Play and imitation skills in the diagnosis of young autistic children. *Pediatrics, 86*, 267–272.

Thorp, D. M., Stahmer, A. C., & Schreibman, L. (1995). Effects of sociodramatic play training on children with autism. *Journal of Autism and Developmental Disorders, 25*, 265–282.

Ungerer, J., & Sigman, M. (1981). Symbolic play and language comprehension in autistic children. *Journal of the American Academy of Child Psychiatry, 20*, 318–337.

Vygotsky, L. S. (2000). Play and its role in the mental development of the child. In J. Bruner, A. Jolly, & S. Sylva (Eds.), *Play: Its role in development and evolution* (pp. 537–554). New York: Basic Books.

Williams, E., Reddy, V., & Costall, A. (2001). Taking a closer look at functional play in children with autism. *Journal of Autism and Developmental Disorders, 31*, 67–77.

Wing, L., Gould, J., Yeates, S., & Brierley, L. (1977). Symbolic play in severely mentally retarded and in autistic children. *Journal of Child Psychology and Psychiatry, 18*, 167–178.

Wolery, M. (1983). Proportional change index: An alternative for comparing child change data. *Exceptional Children, 50*, 167–170.

Wolfberg, P. J., & Schuler, A. L. (1993). Integrated play groups: A model for promoting the social and cognitive dimensions of play in children with autism. *Journal of Autism and Developmental Disorders, 23*, 467–490.

Yirmiya, N., Kasari, C., Sigman, M., & Mundy, P. (1989). Facial expressions of affect in autistic, mentally retarded, and normal children. *Journal of Child Psychology and Psychiatry, 30*, 725–735.

Zercher, C., Hunt, P., Schuler, A., & Webster, J. (2001). Increasing joint attention, play and language through peer supported play. *Autism, 5*, 374–398.

12

FILIAL THERAPY: A CRITICAL REVIEW

RISË VANFLEET, SCOTT D. RYAN, AND SHELLY K. SMITH

One of the primary developmental tasks of families is to help children feel safe, secure, and cared for in an unpredictable and often unsafe world. Secure attachments and healthy relationships between parents and children are linked to better psychosocial health (Belsky & Nezworski, 1988; Clark & Ladd, 2000; Ladd & Ladd, 1998; Youngblade & Belsky, 1992) and provide a buffer for the family when faced with life difficulties (Figley, 1989; La Greca, Silverman, Vernberg, & Roberts, 2002).

Filial therapy was conceived and developed by Bernard and Louise Guerney and beginning in the early 1960s, reported by them and their colleagues (Ginsberg, 1997, 2003; B. Guerney, 1964; B. Guerney, L. Guerney, & Andronico, 1966, 1969; L. Guerney, 1983, 1997; L. Guerney & B. Guerney, 1994; VanFleet, 1994; VanFleet & L. Guerney, 2003) as a means of strengthening parent–child relationships and alleviating a wide range of child and family problems. Filial therapy is a theoretically integrative model of intervention in which therapists engage parents as partners in the therapeutic process. An alternative to the medical model of mental health treatment, filial therapy is based on a psychoeducational framework (B. Guerney, Stollak, & L. Guerney, 1970, 1971). The therapist views mental health difficulties as often arising from lack of skill rather than from some inherent flaw or "illness."

Filial therapy is a relationship therapy in which the therapist uses the parents as the primary change agents for their own children. It is designed not only to resolve the child's problems but also to strengthen the parent–child bond, which in turn fosters the healthy psychosocial development of the child and family. The therapist trains parents to conduct special nondirective play sessions with their children. Initial play sessions are held under the therapist's direct supervision. After the parents become competent in conducting the play sessions, the therapist helps them transition to unsupervised play sessions at home. Parents typically notice significant progress by this time, and the therapist helps them generalize the skills and attitudes they have adopted during the play sessions to the broader home environment. The approach has wide applicability and has been used preventively as well as an intervention for multiproblem families with significant trauma and attachment difficulties.

This chapter describes the filial therapy approach, its uses with a wide range of child and family problems, a review of its empirical history, and a summary of several of the most rigorous outcome studies of filial therapy.

DESCRIPTION OF FILIAL THERAPY

It should be noted that filial therapy has been conducted and researched in a variety of formats that are described elsewhere, including the original group model (Ginsberg, Stutman, & Hummel, 1978; Guerney, 1964), with individual families (Ginsberg, 1997; VanFleet, 1994, 2000; VanFleet & Guerney, 2003), and in a 10-week group format (Landreth, 1991; VanFleet & Guerney, 2003). There is considerable agreement among these adaptations on the principles, goals, and basic methods of filial therapy, which are described below.

Principles of Intervention

Filial therapy is based on several unique ingredients: (a) the therapy is focused on the relationship that exists between parents and their children, rather than on the child or the parent as an individual; (b) parents are viewed as essential partners in the change process; (c) the therapist views the parents as capable of learning new skills and attitudes; and (d) there is a fundamental belief in the importance of parents in their children's lives. Filial therapists approach their task with humility and patience. They believe that even seriously impaired parents can become better parents if given the tools and support to do so.

Goals of Filial Therapy

Filial therapy is designed to strengthen family relationships. Stinnett and DeFrain (1985) studied 3000 strong families in the United States to determine their most salient characteristics. They described six characteristics that strong families shared: (a) members of strong families were *committed* to each other's growth as individuals and encouraged the pursuit of different interests; (b) they told each other frequently and specifically how much they *appreciated* them; (c) family members *communicated* frequently with each other using good communication skills, making it a priority to stay in touch with each other; (d) they made it a priority to *spend time together*, and some of that time was used for having fun together; (e) these families valued *spiritual wellness* and believed that spirituality helped them keep a perspective, especially when times were tough; and (f) when times were difficult and relationships stressed, the strong families used their *coping ability* to face and overcome the problems together in a supportive manner.

Filial therapy helps families develop or strengthen almost all of these characteristics. Emphasis is placed on parental understanding and acceptance of each child in the family, improving the empathy skills and attunement of parents, permitting the children to solve many of their own problems, placing a priority on parent–child special times, and improving parents' parenting skills. All of this happens in the context of the play sessions.

VanFleet (1999b) outlined treatment goals for the child, for the parent, and for the family as a whole. It is hoped that *children* involved in filial therapy will be able to (a) understand, express, and regulate their emotions; (b) develop problem solving skills; (c) reduce maladaptive behaviors; (d) feel more trust and security with their parents; (e) gain mastery while being responsible for their own actions; and (f) develop interpersonal skills. *Parents* in filial therapy are expected to be able to (a) increase their understanding of child development and set more realistic expectations for their children; (b) increase their understanding, warmth, trust, and acceptance of their children; (c) learn the importance and interplay of their children's play, emotions, and behaviors; (d) communicate more effectively with their children; (e) develop greater confidence as parents; and (f) reduce the frustrations experienced with their children and enjoy them more. Filial therapy aims to empower the *entire family* to (a) reduce or eliminate presenting problems and conflicts; (b) strengthen family relationships and bonds; (c) develop greater mutual trust and higher cohesion; (d) improve communication and coping skills; (e) have more enjoyable interactions with each other; (f) be more flexible and adaptive overall; and (g) develop relationship tools that will serve them now and in the future.

KEY TREATMENT INGREDIENTS

The sections that follow provide an overview of the filial therapy process and the training required to conduct it effectively.

The Filial Therapy Method

Because the focus of filial therapy is on the parent–child relationship and represents a form of family therapy, the parents hold special play sessions with each child in the family. Child-centered play sessions (Axline, 1947, 1969) are best suited to children between 3 and 12 years of age, when children use their imaginations most predominantly to explore and understand their world. Parents can certainly hold special play times with children under 3, but some adaptations are necessary to suit the child's developmental level. An empirically based dyadic infant-led play intervention, *Watch, Wait, & Wonder*, with similarities to filial therapy, shows promise in enhancing secure parent-child attachment (Cohen, Lojkasek, Muir, Muir, & Parker, 2002; Cohen et al., 1999; Muir, Lojkasek, & Cohen, 1999). Parents can also hold special parent–child fun times with adolescents, again with developmental adjustments that incorporate the child's cognitive, social, and physical development. A Parent–Adolescent Relationship Development program has grown out of the filial therapy model (Ginsberg, 1997).

Filial therapists ask parents to hold 30-minute dyadic play sessions with each of their children every week. The one-to-one play sessions help parents develop their own relationships with each of their children while strengthening their parenting and attunement abilities. Parents are encouraged to observe each other's play sessions to maximize vicarious learning opportunities when possible.

Filial therapy with individual families typically takes between 10 and 20 1-hour sessions, depending on the presenting problems, the family's ability to participate fully, and the specific model of filial therapy that is used. Group filial therapy sessions typically last 2 hours and require 10 to 20 sessions. As long as they remain true to the basic principles of the intervention, filial therapists have a great deal of flexibility in adapting the approach to specific client or group needs or circumstances.

In filial therapy, parents learn four primary skills. A *structuring skill* is used to set an open tone when entering the playroom and to help the child realize when there are just a few minutes left to the play session. Parents learn to use *empathic listening* to understand and convey greater acceptance to their child. When asked by the child to play a role, parents use *child-centered imaginary play* to enact the scene or interaction as the child directs them, which is actually another form of empathy and attunement when done well. Finally, parents *set limits* firmly and enforce them consistently when children endanger their parents, themselves, or become destructive during the play sessions. Filial therapists help parents develop a fifth "skill" once the play sessions begin—*understanding the meaning* or essential communication of the children's play themes. For example, the grandfather of a 5-year-old, oppositional boy eventually realized through the boy's play activities that his misbehavior was driven by anxieties relating to his abandonment by both parents, rather than from deliberate wishes to make life difficult for the grandfather.

The therapist trains the parents in the play session skills using a variety of methods (L. Guerney, 1983; VanFleet, 1994, 1999a, 2000). The therapist initially models the play session skills by holding child-centered play sessions with each child involved while the parents or caregivers observe. In a discussion afterward, the therapist invites parent reactions and highlights the way he or she used the skills during the sessions. Following a thorough explanation of the rationale and how-tos of each of the skills, the therapist helps parents master them through the use of skill-practice sessions in which the therapist enacts the child role, guiding and coaching the parent's use of the skills. Reinforcement and brief suggestions for improvement are used to help parents develop competence and confidence. After an average of three 1-hour practice sessions, parents begin to hold play sessions with their own children, one at a time, under the therapist's supervision. At the end of each play session, the child is excused to a play area (with childcare provided), while the therapist discusses the play session with the parents. Parents share their reactions, and the therapist provides specific feedback, focusing on the things the parents did well and suggesting just one or two areas for further improvement. Training follows a behavioral shaping approach in which the therapist encourages the parents in incremental steps until they have attained competency.

Therapists typically observe between four and six play sessions of each parent before preparing the parents to hold unsupervised home sessions. Parents continue to meet with the therapist without the child present to discuss the home play sessions, the child's daily behaviors, and to learn how to generalize the skills they have learned during the play sessions. Parents sometimes videotape their home play sessions and review portions of the tape with the therapist, similar to case consultations between professionals. They review significant portions of the home play sessions, discuss aspects that the parents feel they did well, discuss questions and problems that arose, and explore the meanings of possible play themes. It is during this final phase of therapy that the therapist helps the parents generalize the skills they have mastered during their special play sessions. Each week, some time is spent on the use of one of the skills in daily life situations and homework assignments to use the skill are given. Additional parenting skills are covered as well.

Termination occurs when therapeutic goals have been met and the parents are competent in the play session and parenting skills. A phased-out discharge is often used, with the frequency of meetings lessened to alternate weeks, then monthly, and so forth.

Training Required to Conduct Filial Therapy

Because filial therapy combines play therapy with family therapy, a background in each is important. Although filial therapy is a straightforward, structured intervention, it is a complex one, requiring the therapist to function as an educator, coach, and clinician. Much of the parent training approach is drawn from behaviorism and learning theory. The actual child intervention is conducted by the parent or caretaker, but the filial therapist must oversee the entire process to ensure the success of the intervention for the child and the parent. Filial therapists must be competent in both child-centered play therapy and filial therapy and extremely empathic to the family's needs and concerns. Their acceptance and humility are reflected in their core belief that parents have much to offer the therapeutic process and in the therapist's willingness to engage parents as true partners. Filial therapists must also be able to help parents understand their children's play themes as well as their own reactions to their children's play. Using a short-term approach, filial therapists help parents understand their children and themselves better through this process, and assist them in making meaningful changes in their lives. Responsible filial therapists undergo extensive training, followed by supervision or case consultation as they work with a number of families.

THE IMPACT OF FILIAL THERAPY

Filial therapy is designed to alleviate child psychosocial problems, enhance parents' child-rearing abilities, and strengthen family relationships. The change mechanisms of filial therapy are described below.

For the Child

Children's social, emotional, and behavioral problems seem to improve after filial therapy for several reasons. First, children are permitted to play largely as they choose, so they can express a full range of feelings and themes reflective of their "real-life" reactions, struggles, and developmental or clinical issues. Second, they benefit from the undivided attention, acceptance, and understanding of their parents. Third, they experience more consistent parenting by their parents. Fourth, they develop a closer, more secure relationship with their parents.

For the Parents

Parents' competence and confidence as parents seem to improve for several reasons as well. First, parents learn and practice specific skills. They receive individualized and ongoing feedback from the therapist to help them master these skills. Second, they learn to interpret more accurately their children's emotions, concerns, and communications as expressed through their play. Greater understanding seems to lead to greater patience and more realistic expectations. Third, they discuss their personal reactions to the play sessions with the therapist and often develop a greater degree of understanding about their own feelings and behaviors. Fourth, they learn how to become better problem-solvers of family difficulties and conflicts. Fifth, they seem to become more motivated to make changes in themselves. Sixth, they receive a significant amount of empathy, support, and guidance from the therapist, and this can help them turn their insights into long-lasting change for their child, themselves, and the family.

In addition to its extensive research history described in the sections that follow, filial therapy has increasingly grown in clinical use and popularity. Its robustness as a preventive and clinical intervention has been described with (a) *a variety of child or family problems:* oppositional defiant disorder, attention deficits, chronic medical illness, child or family trauma, adolescent parents, single parents, domestic violence, attachment disruptions, family reunification, kinship and foster care, and adoption; (b) *different settings:* independent practice, Head Start programs, school counseling programs with teachers, as part of a GED program, and with incarcerated fathers and mothers; and (c) *multicultural adaptations:* with inner-city families and with Native American, Chinese, and Korean families (VanFleet & Guerney, 2003).

EMPIRICAL HISTORY

Guerney (1964) first described the filial therapy concept in the *Journal of Consulting Psychology*. The initial response of the professional psychological community was less than enthusiastic. Questions were raised about its appropriateness, with concern focused on the presumed inability of parents to learn the psychological principles and skills involved and the potential misuse of them. This reaction stimulated a series of early studies on the approach. These studies (Andronico & Guerney, 1969; Stover & Guerney, 1967) tested the assumption that parents would be able to develop competence in conducting the play sessions. Therapists and parents trained in nondirective play sessions were observed by a group of blind raters. No significant differences were found in their skill levels, suggesting that parents were capable of learning and using the play session skills.

Guerney and Stover (1971) conducted a nationally funded research project that still stands as a landmark study of filial therapy and a significant contribution to the filial therapy research methodology. The study details the filial therapy intervention as initially conceived. The study is expansive, describing all relevant areas, such as sampling participants, characteristics of the parent and child sample, exact time frames for training mothers, specific toys that were included in toy sets, psychometric properties of instruments used for evaluation, as well as including a thorough discussion of the results in both statistical and narrative format.

Guerney and Stover (1971) were interested in obtaining empirical support for filial therapy with families. Other constructs examined included what types of families and children benefited most from the intervention. Although one limitation of the study is the use of an experimental group only with no control, Guerney and Stover explained that this study was a first look into the viability of filial therapy and a controlled experiment would be premature at that time. Outcome and process variables were studied. The study involved 51 mothers of children 3 to 10 years old with serious emotional disturbances who received filial therapy in a small group format over a period of 12 to 18 months. Using multiple indices including codings of over 60,000 actual play session behaviors, the results indicated that mothers were highly motivated by filial therapy; mothers improved on amount of empathy for their children; mothers decreased their dissatisfaction with their children; children's problematic behaviors decreased; and children's social adjustment increased, among other significant changes.

Guerney and Stover's (1971) study paved the way for further investigation, including a comparison study by Oxman (1972). Using the same 51 mothers of the Guerney and Stover study as her experimental group, Oxman established a general population no-treatment control group for comparison of the data. Control group subjects were 77 mothers of children who had not received filial therapy who had responded to an ad in a local paper. The control group matched the experimental filial therapy group on a number of key socioeconomic and demographic variables. Comparisons between the filial therapy experimental group and the control group indicated that filial therapy mothers reported significantly more improvement in their children's behavior and significantly more satisfaction with their children.

A follow-up study by Guerney (1975) demonstrated that the effects of filial therapy remained from 1 to 3 years after therapy termination. She administered a questionnaire to 42 of the 51 original mothers in the Guerney and Stover (1971) study and found that 86% reported that the gains had been maintained and 76% reported continued improvement in their children. Most mothers attributed the child improvements to their improved relationships and were positive about their involvement in filial therapy.

Sywulak (1978) studied filial therapy using 32 parents (19 mothers and 13 fathers of 19 children between 3 to 10 years of age) who served as their own controls. Variables were measured during a waiting period 4 months prior to treatment, immediately prior to the program, after 2 months of filial therapy, and after 4 months of treatment. A wide range of demographic variables and child problems was represented. Results indicated that parents were significantly more accepting of their children after 2 months of treatment, and the greatest gains were made during this period. Parents continued to demonstrate increasing acceptance after 4 months, but to a lesser degree. Significant improvements in overall adjustment and a variety of specific child problems were also found at the 2-month and 4-month measurement periods. Significant reductions were found in a wide range of aggression problems, withdrawn behaviors, and other types of problems. Analyses indicated that child adjustment gains started as early as 2 months after filial therapy began and continued after 4 months of treatment. Finally, parents reported high levels of satisfaction with the filial therapy program and said that it had many positive effects in their relationships with their children and in their feelings of competence as parents.

Sensue (1981) studied families who 3 years earlier had participated in the Sywulak (1978) filial therapy research program. She developed a comparison sample of 24 parents (15 mothers and 9 fathers) who were friends of the parents who had participated in filial therapy. The comparison families were similar to the treatment families on a number of key variables, with the exception that they had not sought psychological services for their children. Study results indicated that filial therapy parents demonstrated significant improvement in parental acceptance and in perceived child adjustment from the pretreatment phase at both a 6-month and a 3-year follow-up. At the 3-year follow-up, the 6-month behavior gains of the filial therapy children were maintained, and filial therapy parents scored higher on parental acceptance measures than parents in the normative sample. Prior to filial therapy, the treatment parents viewed their children as more problematic than the comparison group parents, but at the 6-month and 3-year follow-ups, treatment parents were similar to the no-treatment, normative, control group parents in their assessment of their children's problematic behaviors. Treatment group parents and children continued to view filial therapy as a mechanism of positive change in their families.

These early studies that used a variety of research methodologies helped establish the viability of filial therapy as an intervention and set the stage for the continuing research on filial therapy that has followed.

REVIEW OF OUTCOME STUDIES

This section examines findings from the growing body of filial therapy literature. The publications that are considered the most rigorous in the field have been selected for summarization on the basis of a given set of criteria:

(a) published within the last 15 years; (b) published in English; (c) a sample size of 20 or more; (d) the use of a control group; (e) at least two standardized outcome measures; and (f) results clearly described in statistical and narrative terms. This empirical summary highlights the major findings of each selected study and is not, per se, a critical review of the literature in terms of methodology, measurement properties, or statistical procedures used in each study. The summary of each selected study, however, addresses any serious limitations, as this is an important part of determining the effectiveness of the intervention. When "significance" or "statistical significance" is reported in the empirical history section above and in the section below, it refers to significance levels of $p < .05$ or better.

An extensive search of the literature was conducted to determine the total number of filial therapy publications. The search was broken down into two main categories: those that describe the intervention (such as articles, chapters, and other texts that discuss the theoretical framework of filial therapy or how to implement it); and those that measure the change in target variables through the use of an objective instrument, as well as discussing the intervention's results (i.e., outcomes). To that end, a search was conducted using PsycINFO and PsycLIT databases with the term "filial therapy" used as the search criteria, with all years accepted. Other searches included the meta-analysis compiled by Bratton, Ray, and Rhine as an ongoing project through the Association for Play Therapy (Ray, Bratton, Rhine, & Jones, 2001; Bratton, Ray, & Rhine, 2002), the bibliography from the National Institute of Relationship Enhancement on filial therapy (L. Guerney & B. Guerney, 2002), and The World of Play Therapy Literature (Landreth, Homeyer, Bratton, Kale, & Hilpl, 2000). The total number of publications reviewed was 102. Of these, there were 7 publications from the 1960s (with 2 meeting the selection criteria), 13 publications from the 1970s (with 4 meeting the criteria), 15 publications from the 1980s (4 meeting criteria), 52 publications from the 1990s (18 meeting criteria), and since 2000, 15 publications (7 meeting criteria). The number of filial therapy publications has clearly been increasing over the past four decades; this trend in empirical study is promising, as it continues to add to and support the knowledge base of filial therapy.

This body of literature consists of a mix of descriptive articles that discuss filial therapy theory, case studies, qualitative research, and quantitative research (single subject designs, quasi-experimental, and experimental studies). Each article serves as a unique contribution to the field of filial therapy and helps those working, teaching, and researching in the area of filial therapy to move closer to understanding human relationships, family interactions, child behavior, and many other aspects. Quantitative research methodology is helping to answer such questions as, "How do we know this intervention works?" "What types of families benefit from filial therapy?" and "What types of families have not responded positively to this intervention?"

Several of the studies that focus on the outcomes and ultimate effectiveness of filial therapy are summarized in this chapter and allow us to approach the question of how and what do we know about filial therapy?

Essentially, this ontological inquiry requires a systematic selection process to sort through the filial therapy literature. This process encompasses a breakdown of the types of literature found through the search. Articles that describe filial therapy, as well as case studies, are essential pieces in providing information to consumers, whether they are clinicians, parents, educators, or others. Because filial therapy is a hands-on intervention, the literature that clearly explains what the intervention is, how it is conducted, and describes different types of families that have used filial therapy is necessary and important to the field. Nevertheless, despite their inherent worth, these articles are not included in summarizations below. Instead, because of their potential generalizability and enhanced designs with improved reliability and validity of findings, only those studies meeting the criteria listed previously are included. Twelve publications that met these criteria are summarized below. The age range of the children included in most of these studies was 3 to 10 years of age.

Bratton and Landreth (1995): Filial Therapy With Single Parents

The researchers used filial therapy to assist single parents in accepting and understanding their children through increased empathic interaction within the play environment. It was hypothesized that changes in these factors would significantly reduce parental stress related to parenting. The sample of 22 parents in the treatment group and 21 in the no-treatment control group was comprised of 19 divorced or separated parents in each, with 3 treatment group parents and 2 control group parents who had never been married. The mean age of children in the treatment group was 4.45; their mean age in the control group was 4.85. The investigators randomly assigned participants to either the experimental treatment group or the no-treatment control group. The treatment followed the 10-week filial therapy protocol established by Landreth (1991), with pretests administered the week prior to the intervention and posttests completed the week after the intervention ceased.

The authors reported significant findings on each of the measures used. The parent members of the experimental group showed significant increases in empathic behavior within the play sessions, as indicated by the Measurement of Empathy in Adult–Child Interactions (MEACI; Stover, Guerney, & O'Connell, 1971). Parental acceptance of their children, as measured by the Porter Parental Acceptance Scale (PPAS; Porter, 1954), increased significantly for the parents in the treatment group. Significant decreases also occurred in parental stress as measured by the Parenting Stress Index (PSI; Abidin, 1983), and in the child's problematic behaviors. This study, despite some limits that reduce its generalizability, supports the value of filial therapy for use with single parents. It appears that the special filial play sessions helped parents learn new parenting skills and provided needed emotional supports.

Johnson-Clark (1996): The Effect of Filial Therapy on Child Conduct Behavior Problems

Conduct problems among children can inhibit appropriate psychological growth. Fifty-seven mothers were recruited for the study; however, only 52 completed all of the requirements. Children's ages ranged from 3 to 5 years old. All mothers were randomly assigned to one of three groups: filial therapy experimental group, attention-only condition, or no-treatment control. Mothers in the attention-only condition were instructed to have 30-minute weekly play sessions with their child, but received no specific instruction on play or interaction behaviors. All three groups reported decreases in child conduct problems as measured by a child behavior inventory. The filial therapy group, however, had a significantly steeper rate of change that continued at least until a 2-month follow-up. In addition, the majority of children in the attention-only condition or no-treatment control groups continued to meet the measurement cutoff score for behavior problems; however, most of the children in the filial therapy group did not. This is the best-designed empirical study of filial therapy to date. Because of its strong design, it is possible to demonstrate the efficacy of filial therapy in reducing child conduct behavior problems more than by mere attention. Thus the reduction of problem behaviors, as reported by the mothers, lends confidence to this intervention and its applicability to families experiencing child conduct difficulties.

Beckloff (1997): Filial Therapy With Children With Pervasive Developmental Disorders

Pervasive developmental disorders (PDD) are characterized by several developmental impairment factors of neurobiologic origin, resulting in severe social disability, impairments in communication, and restricted play and interpersonal activities. Parents with children diagnosed with PDD were recruited to participate in filial therapy to increase the parents' empathy toward their child and to reduce behavior problems, social difficulties, and parent–child stressors.

Twenty-eight parents initially participated in the study. Parents were randomly assigned, with 14 parents in the experimental group and 14 in the control group. Two parents in the experimental group and three parents in the control group were dropped. Children's ages ranged from 3 to 10 years old (in the treatment group, 59% were 3–5 years of age, 16% were 6–8, and 25% were 9–10; in the control group, 27% were 3–5 years of age, 36% were 6–8, and 37% were 9–10). Although there were no statistically significant differences between the experimental and control groups on any of the total scores for the measures used, the PPAS subscale, Recognition of the Child's Need for Autonomy and Independence, improved significantly. The author suggested that children with PDD and their parents may need longer than the 10-week, structured format used to experience significant changes. Although this study had low significance, it helps demonstrate filial therapy's wide applicability through its use with this challenging population. The significance of the subscale "Recognition of the Child's Need for Autonomy and Independence" is especially important for parents of children with PDD. These children, as stated by Beckloff, are highly susceptible to stressors and transitions, and parents often feel extremely protective. This may allow practitioners to use filial therapy with parents to assist in understanding their child's needs for autonomy and individuation.

Chau and Landreth (1997): Filial Therapy With Chinese Parents

The authors used filial therapy to alleviate the stress caused by the difficulties faced by parents of a nondominant culture in the United States; in this case, Chinese parents. This study was undertaken to determine if filial therapy would be useful in increasing Chinese parents' empathic acceptance and in reducing their parenting-related stress level. Thirty-six participants were assigned to either the experimental or control groups. Two control group members dropped out, leaving 18 in the experimental group and 16 in the control group. The mean age of children in the experimental group was 5.47, and was 4.8 for the control group. The instructor conducted sessions in Chinese. Significant findings were obtained on each of the measures used. Chinese parents in the experimental group significantly increased their empathic behavior toward their children, as indicated on the MEACI. According to the PPAS, they also increased their level of acceptance toward their children. Last, reductions in parenting-related stress were also recorded through the PSI. The use of filial therapy cross-culturally assists in its overall generalizability. As such, this intervention may be useful in assisting other minority parents in managing the stress associated with this parenting balance.

Harris and Landreth (1995): Filial Therapy With Incarcerated Mothers

Children of incarcerated mothers often experience increased behavior problems and have lower self-concepts and achievement scores. In addition, incarcerated mothers experience difficulties such as decreased self-esteem, loss of control, and emotional problems because of the separation. Filial therapy was therefore proposed as an intervention to be used with women inmates of a local county jail with 22 subjects in the final sample, resulting in a quasi-experimental design with 12 experimental and 10 control group participants. The mean age of the children was 5 years old. Participants jailed for at least 5 weeks completed the protocol that used an accelerated version of the Landreth (1991) model. The authors reported significant increases in the mothers' empathic behaviors and acceptance, as well as decreases in children's problem behaviors, as measured by the MEACI, PPAS, and Filial Problem List (FPL; Horner, 1974a, 1974b), respectively.

It is remarkable that change can occur between parents and children in a prison environment, but filial therapy appears to have been effective in assisting mothers and their children through this difficult time. The results are encouraging to practitioners who must work with parent–child dyads in less than perfect conditions, such as foster care visitations, homeless shelters, or substance abuse facilities.

Tew (1997): The Efficacy of Filial Therapy With Families of Chronically Ill Children

The author provides a compelling description of the difficulties faced by parents with a child who has a chronic illness. The challenges faced by parents may alter their lives and expectations, thus creating feelings of sadness, resentment, and stress. Filial therapy was used to increase parents' acceptance of their child and to decrease parental stress and problematic child behaviors. Twelve parents completed the filial therapy program, with an additional 11 parents in the control group. Statistically significant differences were found on the total score of all measures used. Through the use of filial therapy, the parents were able to experience healthier and more rewarding relationships with their children. Furthermore, the apparent improvement of parents and children further demonstrates the robustness of filial therapy's use.

Landreth and Lobaugh (1998): Filial Therapy With Incarcerated Fathers

The goals of the study were to increase the incarcerated fathers' acceptance of their children, improve the children's self-concept, and reduce fathers' stress levels and problematic family interactions. The intervention occurred in a medium-security federal prison, with 16 fathers assigned to each of the experimental and control groups. The mean age of children in the treatment group was 5.94; the mean age of control group children was 6.52. The treatment group fathers scored significantly higher on the PPAS, indicating increases in parental acceptance of their children. There were also significant increases in the children's self-concept, as measured by the Joseph Preschool and Primary Self-Concept Screening Test (JPPSST, Joseph, 1979). Reductions were noted in paternal stress levels and problematic familial interaction because of child behavior problems, as measured by the PSI and FPL, respectively. This study's differences from other filial therapy research has great relevance to practice, as the intervention in this case has been shown to be effective with fathers. Other samples are largely female; however, this study has shown that fathers can also benefit from this intervention.

Costas and Landreth (1999): Filial Therapy With Nonoffending Parents of Children Who Have Been Sexually Abused

The authors used filial therapy to increase nonoffending parents' levels of acceptance toward their sexually abused child, increase parents' empathic behaviors, and enhance the child's self-concept and emotional adjustment. In addition, reductions in the nonoffending parent's stress level, and the child's level of anxiety and problematic behaviors, were expected. Twenty-six families completed the intervention protocol. Group assignment was nonrandom, based on geographic location. There were 13 parents in the experimental group and 9 in the control group. Children's ages ranged from 4 to 10 years old. All of the parent measures were statistically significant. Parental acceptance of the sexually abused child increased significantly, as did their empathic interactions with their child. Parental stress levels also decreased. Filial therapy was shown to be helpful for parents of sexually abused children in creating an accepting, empathic environment for their children. This intervention may be useful for practitioners working with nonoffending-parent–child dyads who have experienced other forms of abuse or neglect to provide support and assistance through the healing process.

Kale and Landreth (1999): Filial Therapy With Children Experiencing Learning Difficulties

The authors explain that parenting a child with a learning disability can be very stressful, causing strain in the parent–child relationship. They suggested filial therapy to increase parental acceptance of a child with a learning difficulty, reduce parental stress, and decrease the child's social and behavioral problems. Twenty-two families completed the study protocol, 11 from the experimental group and 11 from the control group. Children's ages ranged from 3 to 10 years old. The intervention was conducted in the local school's library.

Four measures were used: the PPAS; the PSI; and the Child Behavior Checklist—Parent and Teacher versions (CBCL–P and CBCL-TRF,

Achenbach, 1991). Statistically significant results were reported for the PPAS and the PSI. Filial therapy appears to have assisted the parents in resolving some issues and in better accepting their child's strengths and needs. Filial therapy appears to have been a powerful intervention for parents with children experiencing learning difficulties.

Glover and Landreth (2000): Filial Therapy With Native Americans

The researchers support the potential use of filial therapy with this population based on the congruence between filial therapy and traditional Native American values such as deep respect for the individual. It was hypothesized that filial therapy would reduce parental stress and increase parent levels of empathy and acceptance toward their children. Twenty-one tribal parents completed the intervention protocol, with 11 experimental group parents and 10 control group parents. The mean age of children in the experimental group was 5.5, and the mean in the control group was 5.2. Although there were no significant increases in parental acceptance as measured by the PPAS, nor any significant decreases in parental stress as measured by the PSI, there was a significant increase in the parents' level of empathic interactions, as indicated by the MEACI. There was also a significant increase, as shown by parents' ratings of children's play behaviors, in the desirable play behaviors exhibited by experimental children with their parents. The overall results of this study support filial therapy as an effective method for working with Native American families, with parents exhibiting increased empathic behaviors, and children demonstrating increases in desirable play behaviors.

Jang (2000): Effectiveness of Filial Therapy With Korean Parents

This study tested the effectiveness of filial therapy with Korean parents. Jang believed that Korean parents tend to stress cognitive achievements and, oftentimes, the parent–child relationship is not nurtured in an empathic manner. Jang tested filial therapy as an intervention for mothers wishing to learn new ways of interacting and developing relationships with their children. The parent–child relationship was the construct of interest and was captured by the use of the PPAS, the PSI, and the FPL. Mothers completed these instruments before the training and again when the program had concluded. The intervention included two filial sessions per week for 4 weeks and was based on the Landreth (1991) model. Fourteen mothers were in the treatment group and 16 in the control group. The mean age of children in the experimental group was 6.0, and the mean age in the control group was 6.43. The study included a qualitative portion in which a therapist interviewed parents after completion of the program. Videotapes of mother–child play sessions were rated using the MEACI. Results indicated that there was a significant increase in empathic parent–child interactions, as directly observed in play sessions. Although no statistically significant difference in parental acceptance was found between experimental and control groups, the qualitative portion of the research showed that parents felt their acceptance of their children had indeed increased as a result of the filial therapy. Parent stress and children's problematic behaviors both decreased comparing treatment and control groups.

Smith (2000): Comparison of Filial Therapy and Other Treatments With Child Witnesses of Domestic Violence

This study using Landreth's (1991) model examined intensive filial therapy as an intervention for child witnesses of domestic violence from 22 families. Comparison groups from two previously conducted studies were used in which the interventions were intensive individual play therapy and intensive sibling group play therapy. Smith's (2000) study was conducted at two shelters at which mothers and their children sought safety from domestic violence. The daily trainings were provided on site at the shelters for the mothers. The mean age of children in the filial therapy group was 6.1 years, and the mean age of comparison group children was 5.9 years. Results indicated there were statistically significant changes on several variables of interest.

Substantiated results showed that (a) children in the intensive filial therapy improved their self-concepts; (b) child problem behaviors decreased significantly for the filial therapy group as measured by the CBCL; (c) mothers in the filial therapy group increased empathy; and (d) filial therapy mothers increased their ability to communicate acceptance and allow greater child self-direction. Results from this study indicate that intensive filial therapy is an intervention that is effective with the given population, as are intensive individual play therapy and intensive sibling group play therapy. Comparisons indicated that the filial therapy mothers were just as effective in reducing children's problematic behaviors as professional play therapists.

REPLICATION AND TRANSPORTABILITY

The many years of filial therapy research show its efficacy with a wide range of different child and family problems, its adaptability to a variety of settings, and its flexibility as conducted in several different formats. The significance of this intervention lies in the observed and reported changes in families after engaging in filial therapy. The articles summarized here point to the malleable nature of this intervention and the ease with which it can be adjusted to fit the needs of the family or the setting, while maintaining its demonstrated effectiveness. The research also attests to its value as a multi-culturally adaptable intervention.

Studies of the efficacy of filial therapy show quite similar promising results in spite of their focus on different populations, settings, and formats. Earlier studies have also suggested that the positive results of filial therapy last at least for several years, although it would be beneficial to collect follow-up data to determine the enduring impact of filial therapy with some of the populations and model adaptations reported recently. Meta-analytic results confirm these conclusions, showing child interventions to be significantly strengthened when parents become an integral part of the process in filial therapy. Ray et al. (2001) conducted a meta-analysis of 94 play therapy studies, including 28 filial therapy studies. They found the following effect sizes: For play therapy studies only, they found an effect size of .70. For combined play therapy and filial therapy studies, treatment groups performed at .80 standard deviations better than nontreatment groups. For the filial therapy studies only, treatment groups performed 1.06 standard deviations better than nontreatment groups. These results support the efficacy of filial therapy and suggest the importance of including parents more fully in play therapy and child treatment. It is important to continue this trend of evaluating filial therapy as it is applied to heterogeneous families and settings.

RECOMMENDATIONS FOR EVALUATION IN CLINICAL PRACTICE

A common problem for the helping professions is meshing research with practice. Much of the filial therapy literature consists of theoretical and application-type articles. These articles explicate treatment procedures and discuss implications for practice. For clinicians in the field, this literature is readable, understandable, and applicable to everyday practice. Nonetheless, descriptive articles lack a systematic way to determine if the intervention was effective with the given population. Although there is a growing body of controlled filial therapy research, much more could be done. Many clinicians are not affiliated with research institutions and do not have access to large sample sizes, thereby lacking the ability to form treatment and wait list control groups. In fact, the priority of many mental health service organizations is treatment, rather than evaluation. With this in mind, it is understandable why researchers and clinicians have had a difficult time merging thoughts and ideas. It is therefore feasible to urge clinicians to use single subject designs as a possible way to bridge the gap between practice and evaluation. Although sometimes considered weak by researchers, expanding the oft-used case study approach to a single subject design could help filial therapy researchers and clinicians strengthen knowledge in the field. Single subject designs differ from case studies in that baseline measurements are taken, and the client's progress is evaluated throughout and at the close of the intervention. Change can be quantitatively documented, usually in the form of questionnaires or standardized instruments. No random sample is needed for a single subject design. Instead, therapy with each family is considered a mini-study in which the intervention is evaluated.

Employing single subject designs in clinical practice does not interfere with treatment. Questions or observations can be unobtrusive and need not be time consuming. The following sample framework highlights how an evaluative piece can be added to filial therapy. A baseline is essential in obtaining information about a family prior to the intervention. Examples of baseline measures are direct observations, standardized instruments, and simple questionnaires. Standardized instruments common in the filial therapy literature include the CBCL (Achenbach, 1991), PPAS (Porter, 1954), PSI (Abidin, 1983), and FPL (Horner, 1974a, 1974b). Depending on the available time, more than one baseline measure can be made. One example is to ask parents to complete two different standardized instruments before the intervention. The goal would be to capture different constructs through these instruments, such as child behavior and parental stress. Direct observations of parent–child interaction during playtime prior to intervention could also be used, preferably at two different preintervention measurement points. Direct observations can be taken in the form of case notes by the clinician or through a more structured format, such as the MEACI (Stover et al., 1971). It is recommended that a combination of sources, such as direct observations and standardized surveys, be used to obtain information whenever possible.

The next step in a single subject design is to conduct the intervention while obtaining measurements through points in time. With filial therapy, it is recommended that both paper-and-pencil and coded therapist observations be taken frequently so that progress can be tracked. Completing a standardized instrument each time the family presents for therapy could become burdensome, however. It may be necessary to weigh the options and consider using briefer instruments or taking measurements a bit less frequently. For example, measurements could be taken on the third, sixth, and ninth week of a 12-week intervention. Finally, when the intervention has concluded, a posttest should be given to the family. The posttest is the same measurement package that was given prior to the intervention. This can also include direct observation of parent–child interaction during play. After the posttest has been completed, the results of the various measurement points can be compared.

Single subject designs are often criticized because of their inability to rule out measurement practice effects and factors other than the intervention that may have caused change in the client. In more rigorous research this is controlled for in experimental designs that have control groups, random selection, and random assignment. In the case of practice evaluation, this is usually impossible; hence, the need for an alternative. When examining the results of the measurement points taken throughout a single subject design, the data should be interpreted carefully and one should be cautious in making claims of significant change.

To summarize, single subject designs are a useful way for clinicians to incorporate filial therapy into practice while evaluating the results for their client family. Single subject designs can take many forms. At its simplest, one baseline measurement point is taken. A more sophisticated and informative single subject design would be one outlined above in which multiple measures are taken at many different points in time: before, during, and after the intervention.

Single subject designs have the advantage of practicality, but they need to be augmented by research using control and comparison groups, studies that continue to explore the long-term impact, and quantitative and qualitative explorations of the filial therapy process with various models and adaptations of the approach. Filial therapy research continues at a number of universities and organizations. As awareness of filial therapy has increased among mental health professionals and the public, there are likely to be many more opportunities to conduct outcome, process, and longitudinal research, ranging from single subject designs to rigorously controlled experimental studies.

CONCLUSION

Filial therapy was developed in the early 1960s by Drs. Bernard and Louise Guerney. It was conceptualized as a psychoeducational, theoretically integrative, family therapy approach in which therapists train parents to conduct special, nondirective play sessions with their own children. The therapist then supervises the play sessions, providing individualized feedback to parents as they gain competence and confidence. Eventually the parents conduct the play sessions independently at home. The parents learn to understand their children and themselves better through this process, improve their parenting skills, and most importantly, strengthen their family relationships. The didactic and dynamic aspects of filial therapy help parents, children, and families address a wide range of problems, and can also be useful in a preventive program.

This chapter has documented key features of filial therapy's extensive research history and controlled studies during the past 45 years. Results to date consistently demonstrate filial therapy's effectiveness with a wide range of problem areas in alleviating parental stress and child behavior problems, while improving parental empathy, skills, and child adjustment. Early studies have demonstrated its long-term effectiveness. With such a promising empirical base, practitioners are urged to incorporate simple, but stronger, research designs in their daily work with families. This can only enhance

Lestrade and the Hallowed House

Volume III in the Sholto Lestrade
Mystery Series

M.J. Trow

A Gateway Mystery

REGNERY
PUBLISHING, INC.
Since 1947 • An Eagle Publishing Company

Published in the United States by
Regnery Publishing, Inc.
An Eagle Publishing Company
One Massachusetts Avenue, NW
Washington, DC 20001

Distributed to the trade by
National Book Network
4720-A Boston Way
Lanham, MD 20706

Printed on acid-free paper.
Manufactured in the United States of America

10 9 8 7 6 5 4 3 2 1

Books are available in quantity for promotional or premium use. Write to Director of Special Sales, Regnery Publishing, Inc., One Massachusetts Avenue, NW, Washington, DC 20001, for information on discounts and terms or call (202) 216-0600.

International Standard Book Number:
0-89526-341-6

To the Bills

'Not a mouse
Shall disturb this hallow'd house:
I am sent with broom before,
To sweep the dust behind the door.'

A Midsummer Night's Dream Act V sci

Contents

A Scandal in Belgravia

The Great Queen was dead. All the years of tribulation – and the trials – over at last. The century had barely begun before the great heart had given up the ghost. And peace came. So much for Oscar Wilde.

Within three months, at Osborne in the Isle of Wight, Victoria, Queen Empress by the Grace of God, also shuffled off the mortal coil. Her passing went more noticed than Oscar's. After all, she had not outraged society during one of its periodic bouts of morality. Neither had she called the Marquis of Queensberry a libeller. And she remained strangely unmoved by errand boys. All in all, most people said, a very pointful life. Under her auspices, Britain had become truly great. And the Empire had been created on which the Sun Never Set. It was a gilded age of cliché and pomposity. But most people, while looking back with more than a hint of *fin de siècle*, looked forward too. A king again after sixty-four years! Only the feminist coterie around Mrs Pankhurst failed to stand and cheer for that. It was a brave new world, a new century. And if the tiresome Boers insisted on dragging their petty problems into that century, well, rest assured that Bobs and this new fellow – what was his name? – Kitchener? They would soon put that right.

Walter Dew stood in the changing room in the basement of Scotland Yard. He carefully macassared his hair for the second time that morning and admired again the metaphorical stripes on his sleeve. Not bad, he thought to himself. Fifteen years in the Force and a sergeant at last. He was just burnishing the new tiepin in the spotted green of the mirror when a face appeared over his shoulder.

'Very nice, Dew. Very nice.'

'Oh, good morning sir.' Dew snapped to attention as the Donegal and bowler hat hit him in the chest.

'Vanity,' the newcomer clicked his tongue, 'all is vanity.'

'Well sir, it's just . . . my new position sir.'

The newcomer wondered if it was the translation of that naughty Indian book by Sir Richard Burton which was currently doing the rounds at the Yard that prompted the new sergeant's remark, but he dismissed it. Dew didn't have the intellect.

'Tell me, Sergeant, between polishing your stripes and your hair, have you had a chance to read the Orders of the Day?'

Dew racked his newly promoted brain. 'Quantity of ping-pong balls stolen, sir. And the Egyptian Ambassador has reported people calling him a damned fuzzy-wuzzy again.'

'Forgive me, Dew,' the newcomer checked his half-hunter, 'I was under the impression this was H Division. I'm sure Superintendent Abberline can handle serious crime of the ping-pong variety. As for the Egyptian gentleman, I don't think we need trouble Special Branch, do you? Especially since the last person I heard refer to His Potentateness as that was the Commissioner of the Metropolitan Police!' He tried again, 'Anything for me?'

'Ah, yes sir. His Nims would like to see you, sir. Matter of the utmost urgency, he said.'

The newcomer nodded with a tired look on the narrow, parchment-coloured face. He checked his moustaches in the mirror momentarily, careful not to let the sergeant see, and made for the stairs. Dew reached for the telephone on the wall. It clicked and vibrated and a whistle answered.

'Mr Frost sir, this is Sergeant Dew.'

A silence ensued.

'Sergeant Walter Dew, sir. H Division.'

'Well?' an unreasoning crackle snapped back at him.

'Inspector Lestrade is on his way up, sir.'

'Well, you'd better hang up his hat and coat, hadn't you?' And the whistle sounded in his ear. He was still standing there, open-mouthed, wondering how Nimrod Frost knew he was holding Lestrade's accoutrements, when the inspector reached the lift.

He missed old Dixon on the front desk. There was a blue-eyed boy there now – whose, he wasn't sure. But certainly it was true what they said. When policemen started looking younger than you, it was time to hang up your truncheon.

'Come!' the voice bellowed through the ornate glass-fronted door. Why was it, Lestrade wondered, that Heads of the Criminal Investigation Department never said 'in' at the end of that sentence?

'Good morning, sir.' The inspector beamed.

'Lestrade, you look terrible. Have a cigar.' Frost shoved a cheroot into the inspector's lips. He rang a bell, which summoned a demure, middle-aged lady with iron-grey locks and a face to match.

'Miss Featherstonehaugh, tea, please.'

'Lemon?' she asked.

'No. Cream and sugar.'

'It's not good for you, Mr Frost. Your arteries.'

'My arteries,' Frost heaved himself upright to his full five foot six and his complete nineteen stone, 'are the least of my problems this morning. Inspector Lestrade always looks worse than I do.'

Miss Featherstonehaugh smiled coyly at the inspector, then reached up and tweaked his cheek, chuckling as she did so. 'Never,' she sighed, her matronly bosom heaving with lust or the discomfort of her stays, 'you gorgeous boy,' and she swept from the room. Lestrade wished again that the ground had opened up for him.

'She'll have to go,' grunted Frost, accepting Lestrade's

proffered Lucifer. 'You wouldn't think a woman of her age and marital status would harbour such indecent thoughts, would you?'

'I prefer not to think about it, sir. I'm a funny age myself.'

'How old now, Lestrade? Not long to retirement, eh?' The Head of the Criminal Investigation Department blew smoke rings to the ceiling.

'Forty-eight, sir. I have given it some thought.'

Frost grinned. 'I can't see you growing petunias in Peckham, Lestrade. Not for a while yet at least. Which is just as well.' His face darkened. To business thought Lestrade. 'What do you know about Ralph Childers?'

'Nothing, sir.'

Frost was checked, momentarily. 'Come, come, Lestrade. You are a man of affairs . . .'

For a second, Lestrade's heart skipped a beat. Who had been talking?

'I happen to know you read the *Sun*. News, man. Parliament. You know, that collection of misfits and pederasts who presume to run the country.'

A little strong, Lestrade thought, for the Head of the Criminal Investigation Department, but it wasn't his place to say so.

'Ah,' he volunteered, 'Ralph Childers the MP.'

'Ex-MP.' Frost corrected him.

'XMP, sir?' Clearly the *Sun* had let Lestrade down. He hadn't met those initials before.

'His body was found early this morning, Lestrade. At his home in Belgravia.'

'And you suspect—'

'Everyone.' Frost nodded.

Miss Featherstonehaugh scuttled in, fussing round Lestrade with the cream and sugar and leaving Frost to help himself.

'When you've finished,' bellowed Frost, more loudly than he intended, 'helping the inspector, Miss Featherstonehaugh,' mellower now, 'perhaps you could leave us?'

She snorted indignantly and drew up her skirts, sweeping

noiselessly from the room.

'You'll find the local boys on hand of course,' Frost went on, applying his blubbery lips to the porcelain. Lestrade enjoyed the luxury of a cup with a handle. So superior to the mugs in his own office on the floor below. Frost leaned forward. 'But this is a delicate one, Lestrade. There are rumours . . .'

'Rumours, sir?'

Frost looked around him, checking particularly that the horizon was free of Featherstonehaughs.

'Let's just say,' he whispered, 'that the late Mr Childers' favourite reading, apart from Private Members' Bills, was the Marquis de Sade.'

Lestrade was sure there was a joke there somewhere about the bills of private members, but he let it go. What did Frost mean? Was there a French connection?

'Any leads, sir?'

Frost slurped his second cup, having doled in his usual three sugars.

'None. Apparently, the body hasn't been moved. The coroner will take over when you've finished.'

Frost looked up. Lestrade knew the interview was at an end. He left what remained of his tea and took his leave. 'Oh, and Lestrade,' Frost stopped him, 'let's be careful, shall we? It's a jungle out there.'

Lestrade collected his accoutrements from his sergeant. For a moment, he toyed with taking Dew with him. He could see the mental anguish on the man's face as he screwed his courage to the sticking place and sharpened a pencil prior to tackling the morning's paperwork. But no, Frost had implied the matter was delicate. And Dew would be no use in this case. He could barely read English, let alone French. The inspector caught a hansom and hurried west.

He alighted within the hour – the new Underground *would* have been quicker, he now realised – and looked up at the Corinthian columns of 102 Eaton Square, an imposing edifice, Georgian and opulent. Lestrade didn't like it. Wealth on this scale both annoyed and unnerved him. Two burly constables saluted as he leapt up the steps between them and turned not a hair as the inspector somersaulted gracefully over the top step and caught himself a sharp one on the brass jaws of the lion knocker. Another constable opened the door, by which time Lestrade had recovered his composure and wiped the tears from his eyes.

'Who are you?' a voice from the aspidistra grove in the far corner demanded.

'Inspector Lestrade, Scotland Yard,' he answered.

'Oh, I'm Smellie.' A man appeared from the foliage.

Probably, thought Lestrade.

'Pimlico.'

'Inspector?' asked Lestrade.

'Nine years tomorrow.'

'Doesn't time fly?'

Lestrade had worked with bobbies outside the Yard before. To a man they resented him. The Yard. The very Force itself. No point in being polite to them. As you walked away, you felt the knife between your shoulder blades.

'He's in here.' The uniformed inspector led the way into a vast library, wall to wall in red leather. Chairs, lamps, books by the hundred. It was a veritable British Museum. But there was no body. In answer to Lestrade's silent enquiry, Smellie pressed the spine of a rather out of place Mrs Beeton and the entire wall swung away to reveal a passage, dark and bare.

'After you, Inspector.'

And although that sounded uncomfortably like a sentiment of Miss Featherstonehaugh's, Lestrade complied.

For a man with Lestrade's problem, to lead the way in a darkened space, especially a confined one, was not the safest of moves. Still, he wasn't about to embarrass himself in the presence of this lesser mortal from the Metropolitan Police. Lestrade had his pride. It was the Smellies of this world who brought it out. Even so, he was grateful for the glow of light as he turned the corner.

'We're going west under the servants' quarters, now,' Smellie informed him. Lestrade turned in the gloom to look for the compass. There wasn't one. Perhaps Inspector Smellie had a naval background.

The glow was coming from a single oil lamp which threw long shadows on the red walls of another room, smaller than the one upstairs and almost directly under it. The passage must have wound back on itself in a tight angle. But there were no books. Lestrade saw a second lamp, a third, a fourth, until he realised he was surrounded by mirrors and it was the same lamp. Even on the ceiling, though the ascending smoke there had darkened the glass and spoiled the effect. The blood red around the mirrors burned back from every side, plush and sickening.

A study in scarlet, mused Lestrade until something more prosaic caught his attention. Smellie moved to turn up the lamp.

'Gloves, man.' Lestrade checked him.

Smellie complied, cursing himself that the Yard man had caught him out in an elementary slip.

The full light rose on the late Mr Ralph Childers. Or what was left of him. He was hanging upside down from a chain pulled taut from the centre of the ceiling. He was naked, his hands manacled together and wrenched behind his back. From them the chain ran back to his ankles and joined the single links from the beams. His back and buttocks were scarred. Old ones, new ones. Some still sticky with blood. Others livid white in the flickering lamplight. Lestrade pulled Smellie's arm closer. There was no sound but the quiet click of the chains as the former Member of Parliament swung gently in the draught. The odour in the room was sweet – a sickly combination of sandalwood and cedarwood – and lurking there, in the experienced nostrils of Lestrade, the familiar smell of death.

As Lestrade urged Smellie's arm lower, the local man paused, 'It's not a pretty sight down . . . there.'

Lestrade glanced at the deceased's private parts. Not the prettiest he'd seen, but he felt Smellie was over-reacting. Then he realised it was the head to which his colleague referred. The hair swept the ground. It had been grey; now it was matted with blood and the head above it was split open, like the water melons Lestrade had seen at the Albert Dock when he'd been a Bluebottle in the days of his youth, catching villains at Wapping and wading up to his armpits in cold, brackish water at Shadwell Stair. One bulging eye, sightless and dull, gleamed white as the body twirled. Carefully, Lestrade parted the unkempt beard to reveal the iron collar with its spike driven deep into the throat.

'Is he dead?' Smellie asked.

Lestrade straightened. 'I thought you'd checked all this,' he said.

'No, I only just came on duty. My constables told me it was a messy one. I've never seen anything like this.'

Lestrade noticed how the colour had drained from Smellie's face. 'Come on,' he said, 'let's get some fresh air. Then I want more light down here. And no one,' he paused and took Smellie's sleeve, 'no one gets in here until I say so.'

'There is a coroner upstairs.'

'Let him wait. The last thing we want is his great feet sloshing about down here. Who found the body?'

The policemen reached ground level. 'Beales. His man.'

'How many other servants?'

'Eight. The others are at the weekend retreat in Berkshire. A house called "Draughts".'

Lestrade gave explicit instructions to Smellie, who vanished with his constables to carry them out. At least, thought Lestrade, the man isn't going to be obstructive. Whatever private thoughts he harbours about the arrogance of the Yard, he's keeping them to himself.

It was nearly lunchtime before the inspector sat down at Mr Childers' magnificent desk in the library. He had gone back to the weirdly scented little room below. This time he had gone alone. Years of 'the sights' had taught Lestrade that he operated best on his own. He was surer of his emotions – and his stomach – that way. He flicked open the notepad to make sure he hadn't overlooked anything. Cause of death? A blunt instrument to the back and top of the head, he would guess. Or perhaps the collar had been snapped shut first so that the iron spike had penetrated windpipe and spinal cord. So was he dead when he was hauled upside down so cruelly near the floor? And what about the whipmarks on the body? Or was 'whipmark' too much of an assumption? Lestrade had learned a long time ago to keep an open mind, almost as open, he mused in one of his more grisly moments, as that of the late lamented who had been twirling below stairs. Childers had been taken away through the tradesmens' entrance, of course, but even there a crowd of fascinated sightseers had slowed his undignified journey to the waiting Maria. Lestrade had watched from an upstairs window. Errand boys and shop lads nattering like fishwives over the handlebars of their Raleighs; the servants of neighbours who 'happened-to-be-passing', and as Lestrade's eyes shot up to the nearest windows on his own level, the neighbours themselves, curious behind the shivering nets. Smellie's constables elbowed the gathering crowd aside and Lestrade heard the familiar cry, 'Move along there, move along.' He noticed one or two young men scrabble nearer than the rest, prying under the grey, regulation blankets and then break away, scattering in different directions, ahead of the more idly curious. He recognised the gait and the lean and hungry look – newshounds from Fleet Street. So much for Nimrod Frost's 'delicate one'. It would be all over London by nightfall – the *Standard* would see to that.

'You found the body?' Lestrade looked up from his notepad.

Beales, the gentleman's gentleman, nodded. Lestrade looked at him hard. Every gesture, every move was ordered and precise. He mentally crossed the man off his list of suspects. Here was a man who did not like to soil his hands or spoil his routine. A little Goddards for the silver cleaning, the odd funeral of a maiden aunt in Cheltenham, but not a waistcoat drenched in his master's blood and not the appalling physical and emotional wrench of smashing in a skull. Where was the economy of word and manner in that? But Lestrade was leaping howitzers. He had already envisaged a frenzied attack – the work of a deranged maniac. As for the bloodsoaked waistcoat, the murderer had been as naked as his victim . . . But all this was surmise. Facts, he told himself. What of the facts? And this careful, calm, studied man before him. He at least knew something of his former master's habits. Lestrade slowly produced a cigar and it shook him a little as Beales leapt upright to light for him. The gentleman's gentleman's nostrils quivered disapprovingly as he inhaled the smoke. He found himself looking Lestrade up and down. A man of middle years – forty-five, forty-six. Five foot nine or ten. Appalling dress sense. No one wore Donegals any more. He looked like a coachman.

'You found the body?' Lestrade's question ended the valet's rambling assessment of his interrogator.

'Yes sir.' Beales thought perhaps a vocal answer would satisfy the man. A nod clearly hadn't worked.

'Tell me about it.' Lestrade began to circle the room, glancing occasionally at Beales, occasionally fingering a book on a shelf. To Beales' domestic brain, it appeared as though the inspector was looking for dust.

'It was six thir—' Beales was unnerved by the whirling policeman. He turned one way, then the other, trying to fix him with his eyes. All his training had taught him to look a man in the eyes, except of course when receiving a gratuity or when one's master, believing himself to be alone, began to pick his nose.

'You are very precise,' Lestrade cut in.

'I am a gentleman's gentleman, sir. Precision is my trade.'

Lestrade stopped. 'Go on.'

'My late master was also a creature of habit. I had strict instructions to wake him at six thirty each morning. He invariably bathed and took a ride along the Row before lunching at his club or going to the House.'

'His club?'

'The Diogenes.'

'The House?'

Beales looked up, his look of amazement turning to contempt. 'Of Commons, sir,' he said acidly.

'Just checking,' said Lestrade. 'Go on.'

'Mr Childers was not in his room. I brought the tea here, thinking he might be working on some papers. He was not.'

'So you went downstairs?'

'Not immediately. I checked the dining room and the breakfast room, although I knew his breakfast was only then being prepared. I was about to try the stables in the mews. Sometimes Mr Childers could not sleep and had been known to saddle his horse himself.'

God, thought Lestrade, the versatility of the landed classes.

'I don't know what made me go to the Cell.'

'The Cell?' repeated Lestrade.

'The room in the basement, Inspector. Where your constables found the . . . Mr Childers.'

'You said Cell. Do you mean cellar?'

'No sir . . . Perhaps I had better explain. After all,' Beales began to twitch his fingers a little, the first sign of a slipping composure, 'I am anxious to help all I can. It's just that a gentleman's gentleman must be loyal. And discreet.'

Lestrade played the moment as it came. He supposed, at that moment, that Beales was everything he appeared to be. The inspector placed an avuncular hand on his shoulder. 'It's a little bit late to be loyal, Mr Beales. And discretion isn't going to help me catch his murderer, now, is it?'

Beales breathed in tortuously and nodded. 'Have you heard of the Hell Fire Club, Inspector?'

'Is that the little one in Cleveland Street?'

Again, amazement swept briefly over Beales' face. This time it was not followed by contempt.

'No sir. It was organised by Sir Francis Dashwood a hundred and fifty years ago. It was composed of gentlemen – bloods or rakes I suppose they would have been called – who were known as the Monks of Medmenham. They practised every vice known to man. Not to mention woman.'

'Women?'

'Please,' Beales started in the seat, 'I asked you not to mention women. Mr Childers was a bachelor, sir. He never officially entertained ladies. Nor was he seen in their company. Without wishing to be unkind to my staff, he chose the plainest of females for his household. His misogyny was well known.'

Lestrade had no answer to that, but his straying hand came fortuitously across a dictionary and he riffled through its pages. After what seemed to both men an eternity, Lestrade snapped shut the book triumphantly.

'So he didn't like women?'

'No, sir.' Contempt had returned to the gentleman's gentleman. 'However, when the fit was on him, sir, he . . .' Beales was uncomfortable, 'he occasionally gave way to . . . excesses.'

'You interest me strangely,' said Lestrade, stubbing the cigar on an ashtray as he alighted again in Childers' chair.

'He would put rough clothes on and slip out at night.'

'And?'

'He would find an unfortunate, a lady of the streets, and bring her back here. There is a door your men will not have found, Inspector. It leads directly to the Cell. There, Mr Childers would don his monk's robes and indulge in . . .'

Lestrade remembered the whips and thongs that lined the scarlet walls below. And the iron shackles. And the chains. And the mirrors for a better view.

'Hunnish practices?' he asked.

'The English Vice,' nodded Beales, as though it were a loyal toast.

'Tell me, was Mr Childers the only member of this reincarnated club?'

'No sir. On high days, the Cell was a hive of activity.'

'Beales,' Lestrade was perambulating again, 'I pride myself on being abreast of current affairs.' He hoped Frost couldn't hear him. 'How is it that I have never heard a whisper in what Fleet Street have been known to call their "newspapers" of Mr Childers' habits?'

'I clean them myself sir. Oh . . .' And for once it was the

gentleman's gentleman's turn to misunderstand. 'There are laws of libel as I am sure you are aware, Inspector Lestrade. In any case, Mr Childers was the soul of discretion. The Cell is carefully padded so that no sound escapes. That is why I would have heard nothing of this dreadful deed in the night. Only I – until today – knew of the room's existence. No one else – not the staff, not the master's colleagues – knew that he ... er ... entertained. He used to say . . .' Beales stopped.

'Yes?' Lestrade chipped in.

'He used to say that when his back and buttocks hurt him after a debauch, he would find the seats in the House very uncomfortable. And at those moments, he swore that the Grand Old Man was watching him.'

'You mean Gladstone?' Lestrade asked.

'When the old gentleman was alive.' Beales assented.

'Didn't the late Prime Minister have similar habits?' the inspector ventured.

'I'm sure I don't know, sir. But you must remember, Mr Gladstone was a Liberal.' To Beales that explained it all.

'When you said earlier,' Lestrade flicked aside the nets to look at the mews in the watery afternoon sun, 'that no one but you knew of the Cell, you were not, of course, including the other members.'

'Members?'

'Of the Hell Fire Club, man,' beamed Lestrade. 'Those latter-day bloods and rakes who joined your dear departed master in his interesting habits.'

'They of course knew of the room, sir.'

'Tell me, was 102 Eaton Square the headquarters of the club?'

'As far as I am aware, sir.'

Lestrade dropped the joviality. 'I want their names.'

Beales leapt to his feet. 'Sir, I am a gentleman's gentleman. Loyalty and discretion are my watchwords. Nothing will drag that information from me.'

'Beales,' Lestrade leaned towards him, 'I am an Inspector of the Metropolitan Police. I don't have any watchwords at all.

And I can get you fifteen years for obstructing a police officer in the pursuance of his duty. I think Pentonville will drag any information out of you.'

For a moment, the two men looked at each other. Then Beales summoned what dignity he could. 'If you go to Mr Childers' country house in Berkshire,' he said, 'you will find a red leather box in the centre drawer of his study desk. This,' he produced it deftly from his pocket, 'is the key to that box. I think its contents will give you the answers you need.'

'And why should you have a key to such a Pandora's delight?' It was the only bit of mythology that had stayed with Lestrade since Blackheath crammer days.

'I was to destroy the box, sir. In the event of Mr Childers losing an election. But now that he has lost his life . . .'

Lestrade took the key. 'What will you do now, Beales?' he asked.

The gentleman's gentleman shook himself from the new realisation of his master's death. 'Mr Joseph Chamberlain has often hinted to me that I would be most welcome in his service, sir.'

'Well, then.' Lestrade patted the valet's shoulder.

'Oh, no, sir,' Beales looked horrified, 'Mr Chamberlain *was* a Liberal!'

And that again seemed to say it all.

On his way through the hall, Lestrade met Smellie.

'I'll leave the other servants to you,' he said, 'they may be able to add something. Send your report to the Yard, will you? Oh, and Smellie . . .'

The inspector looked up.

'With your compass-like sense of geography, where is Berkshire?'

Smellie thought hard. 'On the map, it's the bit on the left-hand side. Turn right out of the door.'

Lestrade took the train to Hungerford and a carrier's cart to Ogbourne Maizey. Smellie's geography may not have been what it once was, but he had elicited the name of the village of which the great house of 'Draughts' was the manor. It was sunset when the cart crunched on the gravel outside the mellow, yellow entrance porch. The dying sun threw long shadows of the twisted chimneys across the lawns. Lestrade tipped the carrier, making a mental note to charge it to expenses and pulled the doorbell. He heard the answering ring down the hall and waited as the bolts slid back. A sour-faced housekeeper appeared. She had heard the news from Mr Beales via the telephone. Yes, the house had all the modern conveniences. There was a shower, if the gentleman cared to use it. Lestrade wondered if his armpits had betrayed him; but he stoically declined the offer and was shown into the study.

It was scarlet again, a copy, if the inspector's memory served him aright, of the one in Eaton Square. Around the walls hung a number of framed Spy cartoons, characters of today and yesterday, colleagues of the former back-bencher. There was even one of Nimrod Frost, looking stones lighter than he actually was. Was one of them, Lestrade wondered, the murderer of Ralph Childers? He'd always thought the Archbishop of Canterbury looked a bit shifty, but the man was eighty if he was a day. How many octogenarians were capable of hoisting a dead weight of twelve or thirteen stone off the floor with chains? No, Cantuar could sleep easy in his bed. Lestrade unlocked the drawer and placed the walnut burred box on the desk. It was inlaid with the initials of the late lamented, and a series of incomprehensible hieroglyphics. The inspector inserted the key and the lid flipped open. Nothing. The box was perfectly empty. So Beales had sent him here on a wild goose chase. Lestrade fumed at the waste of his time. He fumed still further at being taken for such an idiot. In an uncharacteristic gesture he slammed the box down hard on the red leather of the desk only to see a drawer at its base slide open. 'Ah,' he smiled, 'the old secret-drawer ploy.'

In it lay a book, in plain black leather and its pages were filled with notes in Childers' handwriting. Lestrade had seen examples of it at Eaton Square. The book appeared to be a diary and the inspector read until darkness drew over the house. The sour-faced housekeeper solemnly lit the lamps around Lestrade.

'Mrs . . . er . . .' The inspector stopped her.

'Smith,' said the housekeeper.

A likely story, thought Lestrade. 'Tell me, does – did – Mr Childers entertain?'

'Now and again, sir. But he didn't come here often. Most of his friends were Members of Parliament, sir, like himself. He didn't bring many of them here.'

'And has he had any condolences?'

'The vicar, sir. Nobody else. His colleagues would use his London address.'

'Mrs Smith, is there lodging in the village?'

'There's an inn, sir, but it's not the best. I had instructions from Mr Beales to accommodate you here. There's plenty of room now the master's gone.'

And so it was that Lestrade spent the night at 'Draughts'. He couldn't sleep. It was probably the pork and pickles of the melancholy Mrs Smith. Or the changeable weather of the early spring. He'd seen no other servants, only a couple of gardeners pruning the privet, glimpsed from the study window. There was no life in this house. It was obvious that Childers used it infrequently. Everywhere druggets were pulled over the furniture, giving each room a ghostly appearance in the gloom of the April evening.

A little before midnight, showers beat on the leaded panes of Lestrade's window. He disliked four posters. They made him feel claustrophobic. And he'd never really recovered from being seduced in one. So he sat in the deep recess below the window, and ploughed on through the diary he had found. What was it Beales had said? The contents of the box would give him the answers he needed. But most of it was cryptic nonsense. A series of jumbled letters, spaces and dots. Perhaps the cypher department at the Yard could make something of it. Certainly Lestrade could not.

The inspector wandered with his oil lamp through the upper reaches of the house. The modern conveniences of which Mrs Smith had spoken did not extend to electricity and by the morning Lestrade had hammer toes to prove it, where he had tripped over the wainscotting in the long, dark shadows.

Breakfast was as unadventurous as his supper of the night before and he was glad to be aboard the Western Region again, rattling towards the City, with his book and his problem. He turned to his own face in the window. Who would kill a Member of Parliament? Six hundred odd other Members of Parliament? But no, this was not political. It was sexual. Whatever torrid events went on in the Cell at Eaton Square, there was one person who was sure to know. And it was on her door that Lestrade was knocking by mid-morning.

The grille in the little door in Greek Street slid back. A heavy black face shone through. 'Yes?' it asked. Lestrade fanned the air with a roll in the time-honoured manner.

'Miss Labedoyere.' He made a brave stab at the French.

The shining pink eyes in the shining black face didn't blink. 'Who sent you?'

Lestrade gambled on the inhabitants of Greek Street bordellos not reading newspapers. 'Ralph Childers,' he answered.

The grille slammed shut. Had he said the wrong thing? Given the wrong password? Perhaps if he'd said, 'The boy I love sits up in the gallery'? Still, it was too late now. He heard the bolts jar and clank. The way was opened by a huge negro, in loud check suit and silk shirt. The black man snatched Lestrade's money and locked the door behind him.

'Miss Labedoyere don't really receive guests at this hour.'

Lestrade tried to place the accent. Caribbean with a hint of Seven Dials.

'I'm sure in my case she'll make an exception.'

'Wait here.'

Lestrade was shown into an anteroom, hung with plush velvet and heavy flock wallpaper. Everywhere was the smell of cedarwood and sandalwood. It was the Cell at Eaton Square. He sensed he was on the right track. The beaded curtain swished and rattled behind him and a powerful woman strode into the room wearing a basque bodice bedecked with bows, and a vast plume of ostrich feathers in her hair.

'Mr . . . er . . . ?'

'Lister.' Lestrade used his favourite alias.

'I am Fifi Labedoyere.'

No, mused Lestrade.

'What can I do for you, for' – she riffled the notes in her hand – 'five pounds?' She swirled around Lestrade, studying him carefully. 'A bit of brown?' She laughed. 'No, silly of me. A handsome, full-blooded man like you,' she swept off his bowler hat, 'will want a bit of red.' She pushed him back onto a *chaise-longue* with a tap which could break a swan's wing. 'Now . . .' She tickled his moustache with her tapering, pointed finger nails.

You're a man of the world, Lestrade told himself. Don't sneeze.

'There is Charlotte. Fresh from the country. A virgin, Mr Lister. Only fourteen years old.'

Yes, Lestrade could imagine. A raddled bag of forty done up in ringlets and rouge.

'Ah, but no. I have Celeste. A nymph of the Orient. With skin like a ripe peach. She has ways of driving a man mad.'

Some dragon from Chinatown, without a tooth in her head, Lestrade imagined.

'I . . . er . . . was hoping for something a little . . . stricter,' he ventured.

'Ah,' Fifi's eyes lit up, 'you require Tamara. She is Bavarian. I have seen her reduce men to putty under her tawse.'

'Miss Labedoyere, forgive me,' smiled Lestrade, 'but I was hoping for your own exquisite services.'

Fifi laughed so that her bosoms, threatening and wide, wobbled above their whale-bone cages. 'For five pounds, dearie? I'm not that good natured.'

'A pity,' Lestrade was trying to keep the madam's fingers

away from his groin. 'Ralph Childers highly recommended you. What was it he said? "The iron of a gauntlet and the velvet of a glove."' Lestrade flattered himself on that one. Look to your laurels, Alfred Austin!

'And how is dear Ralph?' Fifi had expertly undone three of Lestrade's buttons and was whisking aside his shirt flaps.

'Dead.' Lestrade stood up, hastily adjusting his dress.

Fifi was alongside him. 'Dead?' she repeated. And realisation dawned. 'I smell copper.' The soft French had become harsh Bermondsey.

'Very astute, ma'am,' answered Lestrade.

'Bert!' the madam bawled and the Caribbean gentleman blocked the doorway. 'It's the Bill,' she snarled in a confusion of Christian names, 'he's leaving.'

Lestrade had to think fast. The bouncer was four or five stone heavier than he was and if the inspector had stood behind him, he wouldn't have been visible at all. And he appeared to have muscles like a steam hammer. Lestrade fumbled in his pocket for the brass knuckles he kept there but when he pulled his hand free, he was only holding a pair of spectacles. They helped with the mild disguise. Men called Lister always wore glasses. The negro paused momentarily, one hand on Lestrade's lapel, the other in mid-air, lining up the copper's jaw with all the science of an ex-prize fighter.

'You wouldn't hit a man with glasses?' Lestrade whined, gripping the useless rims in both hands.

'No, I'd use my bloody fist,' the negro snarled.

But Lestrade was faster. For years, the bouncer had been used to cringing middle-aged men and had learned to take his time. This time, the pause was nearly fatal. Lestrade jabbed upwards with both hands, the spectacle arms ramming painfully into the bigger man's nostrils. As the black buckled, clutching a bleeding nose, Lestrade's knee came up. Simultaneously he found the knuckles in his other pocket and brought them down with both hands on the bouncer's skull. There was a dull thud and a gurgle and the building shook as he hit the floor.

'Now then, Miss Labedoyere.' Lestrade turned to the madam. Fifi spat contemptuously, although she was a little nonplussed at seeing the unstoppable Bert lying in such an ungainly heap. She backed away, uncoiling a whip which Lestrade had not noticed dangling from her wrist.

'Nice of you to offer,' said Lestrade, 'but I'm afraid I told you a teensy fib. Mr Childers did not recommend you. His tastes and mine scarcely coincide at all.'

'You flatfoot bastard!' Fifi shrieked, her breasts slapping from side to side as she let fly with the rawhide thong. It ripped across Lestrade's nose and cheeks, drawing a crimson line the width of his face. He spun round, bouncing off the wall and stumbling over the prostrate Bert. Can't win them all, he mused as his tear-filled eyes attempted to focus on Miss Labedoyere. The lady in question was snaking back her arm for another lash, when Lestrade rolled backwards, tugging hard on the beaded curtain. It ripped away from the wall, a shower of beads clattering and bouncing on the floor. Lestrade was already down and within seconds, Miss Labedoyere had joined him, floored by the rolling beads. She cursed and swore until Lestrade wrapped the whip around her neck and sat back against the wall with the quivering heap trussed in his lap.

'Here's a new position for you, Gertie,' he hissed, trying to catch his breath. A man on the brink of his fifties shouldn't be doing this. Time to leave it to the younger coppers.

'Who?' Fifi snapped.

'Gertie Clinker,' said Lestrade, 'late of Wapping and all points east. You know, you and I are getting a bit old for this sort of game, aren't we?'

'You speak for yourself, copper!' she bellowed.

'Shame on you, Gertie. You didn't know me, did you? And me the only boy in blue who ever gave you the time of day.'

'Blimey,' she muttered, 'Sergeant Lestrade!'

'Well, that dates you, dearie,' Lestrade said. 'I've been an inspector for sixteen years.'

Gertie giggled, despite the ligature around her neck, 'Course you 'ad a nose then. Where d'you get all them cuts?'

'Well, at least one of them I got from a madam of a bordello in Greek Street.'

Gertie giggled again, 'Sorry, lover. Me eyes ain't what they used to be.'

'Are you sitting comfortably? Or shall I go on talking to the back of your head?'

'I won't give you no more trouble, Mr Lestrade. Onest. I'll come quiet. Make a change for me.' And she giggled again. Lestrade uncrossed his hands. He was glad because Gertie was a big girl and his knuckles had long ago turned white.

'Without wishing to offend, Gertie,' he said, uncrumpling his Donegal and skating warily to the corridor, 'it's not you I'm after.' He mechanically checked the bouncer. Broken jaw, he guessed. 'You will, however, need a new fancy man.'

'Well, after today's performance, I should think I do,' agreed Gertie.

'Ralph Childers,' Lestrade came back to the point.

'Oh yeah, you said.' Gertie poured them both a sizeable slug of gin. 'Here's mud in your eye, Mr Lestrade.' And she downed hers in one.

'You know I can't drink on duty.' The inspector toasted the madam and sipped the clear liquid. It affected his focus again.

'Come on dearie. Let me put something on that face.' And she ferreted in a cupboard and began dabbing away the blood. Between Lestrade's jerking and inward gasps, Miss Clinker took up his line of enquiry.

'Did I hear you say Mr Childers was dead?'

'As a doornail, Gertie.'

'Well, I'm not surprised. Did 'e overdo it a bit?'

'It?'

'E took and gave, 'e did. A right one. My arm would ache for days after one of his visits.'

'Could he have overdone to death, Gertie?'

She looked at him, pausing from her ministrations. 'In all my years in the business, Mr Lestrade, I've never known it.

Everybody has a point when enough is enough. Course if 'is ticker was dicky—

'I don't think it was his heart that took the punishment, Gertie. When did you see him last?'

'Oohh, three, maybe four months ago. 'Ere, you ain't suggestin . . . ?'

'Did you ever pay Mr Childers a house call?'

'I don't do house calls, Mr Lestrade. Mr Childers may have had floozies at his place, but for a professional service, 'e always came here.'

'Did he have any friends with him on any occasion? Or was anyone introduced to you by him? Someone with similar tastes, perhaps?'

Gertie racked what passed for a brain.

'There was one bloke. In politics 'e was, like Mr Childers. Name of . . . cor, luv a duck. What was it now? Cor, brain like a sieve, Mr Lestrade, I always 'ad.'

Lestrade reached wearily into his pocket and produced another handful of notes. 'This is the second roll, Gertie, and the last.' He placed it in her hand. She smiled triumphantly, squeezing the money into the infinitesimal space that formed the edge of one breast and the beginning of another.

'Holmes,' she said. 'Tall bloke. Thin face. Smoked a pipe.'

Lestrade was halfway down the corridor before the bewildered Gertie called him.

'One roll deserves another, dearie,' she said, standing with legs apart and hands on hips, 'for old times' sake.'

Lestrade glanced back as he reached the door.

'Gertie, I couldn't afford you,' he said.

The Blue Carb Uncle

They had found him in the morning, when the grass was still wet from the night and the woods were dripping in their dampness. He lay on his back, legs outstretched, hands gripping with all the iron of rigor mortis the shaft of the bamboo lance jutting upright from his chest.

His friends and his beaters had carried him back on a barn door and they had laid him out on his bed. The woman of the estate, who knew about these things, had stripped off the bloodied hunting pinks and had washed him. The lance was removed and wiped clean. They had to break his arms to relax his grip. And it was over sixteen hours before the local constabulary were contacted. The Chief Constable was a thinking man. He had the sense to call in the Yard. And no faith in his own clodhoppers. Lestrade had just finished typing up his reports – in triplicate, of course – when the urgent summons came. 'Major Deering dead. Stop. Suspect foul play. Stop. Send your best man. Stop. Or failing that, Lestrade. Stop.'

Immune to the insult, eyes bleary with the concentration of typing and the bruising of Gertie's whiplash, the inspector dug out his faded Gladstone, threw in a shirt, a spare collar and his cut-throat and made for King's Cross. He had had no time to check the coroner's report on the late Childers. No time to deposit the diary with the Yard's code breakers. No time to brief the two new men that Frost had sent him. They, like all else on the first floor, would have to wait.

They met him at the station in a landau draped in black.

Introductions were made briefly, sombrely, in the twilight and
the vehicle rattled through the gathering dark.

'So you are the deceased's brother?' Lestrade asked the man
facing him under the silk of a top hat.

'I am,' he asserted.

'I have no information, sir. Could you tell me what
happened?'

'We have no idea, Inspector. There was a hunt yesterday. The
Hall was packed. Loving cups and hounds all over the place.
Uncle was in fine fettle in the morning, eager for the fray, as
always.'

Lestrade turned to the older man on George Deering's left.
'You would be the deceased's uncle, Mr Sheraton?'

Mr Sheraton looked a little surprised as his monocle slipped
from his eye.

'No, sir. I was a brother officer.' And both men looked to an
imagined altar in the middle distance.

'Forgive me,' said Lestrade, sensing he was about to be
crushed by the falling branches of the family tree, 'then who is
your uncle?'

'John,' they both chorused.

Lestrade looked uncomprehending.

'Major Deering,' Sheraton went on, as Lestrade saw the lights
of Deering Hall shining through the evergreens, 'was known as
"Uncle" to all the officers of the regiment.'

'Regiment.' Lestrade was blankly registering the deceased's
rank.

'The Carabiniers, man,' Deering explained a little testily, 'the
Sixth Dragoon Guards. We are all – were all – officers of that
great and distinguished company.'

It had been some time since Lestrade had been in the company
of army men. He had forgotten their lack of chin, their narrow
vision, the extent of their snobbery and the flash of the spoons
they carried with such hauteur in their mouths.

The landau jolted to a halt and Lestrade was shown into
Deering Hall. He felt as though he was being frogmarched to his

.

own execution, the riding boots of his fellows clanking on the polished wood and marble of the floors. He was shown into a room lit with candles. The walls were hung with banners and portraits of flinty-eyed colonels, proud in their scarlet and gold. On a gun-limber in the middle of the room lay Major John Deering, late of His Majesty's Sixth Dragoon Guards. Lestrade looked at the corpse. Peaceful. Content. He lay with his arms crossed over his chest, resplendent in the dark blue and white of the Carbs, the candlelight flashing on the gold lace at his throat and his cuffs. They had buckled his sword around him and on the velvet cushion by his head lay his gauntlets, his spurs and the tall, white-plumed helmet. It reminded Lestrade of the tomb of the Black Prince he had seen at Canterbury. Even the major's sweeping moustaches were reminiscent.

'Who certified the death?' he asked.

'I did,' said Sheraton. 'I am the regimental surgeon.'

'We don't hold that against him,' the younger Deering proffered as a matter of fact rather than an attempt at humour.

'And?' the inspector was waiting.

'The aorta was severed by the head of a cavalry lance.'

'A cavalry lance?' Lestrade looked up incredulously.

Deering crossed to a corner and returned with the weapon, handing it to Lestrade, who hesitated, then with a certain resignation, took it. 'It's been wiped, I suppose?'

'Of course,' said Deering. 'People have been coming all day to pay their respects to Uncle. There'll be more in the morning. One couldn't just leave that lying around covered in Uncle's blood, could one?'

'The wound, doctor?' Lestrade turned to Sheraton.

'Captain,' insisted the doctor.

'How was it made?'

'A single thrust, I would say, from the front, probably when Uncle was on the ground.'

'Is it customary to hunt foxes with lances?' Lestrade put the point to his not-so-genial hosts.

'We are a heavy cavalry regiment, Lestrade,' snapped

Deering, we don't use lances at all. I believe the Scots Greys employ the lance for their front ranks, but . . . well, the Greys . . .' He and Sheraton snorted in joint contempt.

'Then whose is this?' Lestrade asked.

'I've no idea,' said Deering. 'It doesn't belong in the house. It has to be the murderer's.'

Lestrade held the weapon horizontally for a moment, then swung it upright.

'Show me how it was done, Captain,' he said to Sheraton, 'in your opinion.'

The good captain took the shaft, curled the leather thong around his wrist and tucked it under his right arm.

'A lancer would use it like this. Elandslaagte, Omdurman, all lancer actions involve the weapon this way. I would say for the depth of the wound, it was used thus,' he gripped the lance in two hands, like a spear, 'and delivered from a standing position.'

'There were no other wounds on the body?'

'None.'

'I suppose it would be superfluous of me to ask whether the major was a good horseman?'

Sheraton looked at Deering.

'The best,' George Deering affirmed.

'Gentlemen, I was unable to bring a constable with me. Perhaps I might use your telephone, Mr Deering?'

'Captain,' insisted Deering.

'To ring the local constabulary?'

'Can't you manage by yourself, Inspector? After all, we don't really want the local bobbies trampling all over the place. Our Chief Constable expressly asked for you, I understand?'

'In a way,' mused Lestrade. 'Cheer up, gentlemen,' he said, making for the door. 'We at least know that Major Deering's murderer is unlikely to be a lancer. Such a one would surely have killed from the saddle. And he would not have left his weapon behind. That must eliminate two or three thousand men.'

Lestrade's cheery optimism was not shared by his hosts. For

the remaining hours before the clock in the hallway struck twelve, they continued their story of the previous day. The hunt had got off to a flying start and they expected a good day's sport. Uncle was mounted on a new gelding, a bay, and was soon ahead of the field. There had been some confusion at the water and the pack had separated, Sheraton and George Deering taking the high ground towards the moor. Uncle and a few others had cut through the gorse bushes after the other hounds, trusting to luck in the tangle of undergrowth. When the two groups met up again, there was a terrible to-do because Lady Brandling's horse had thrown her and there was some suggestion on her part that as she lay dazed in the Lower Moorgate, she had been interfered with. Certainly, she said, she had felt a man's hand on her knee. Anyway, it was some time before it was realised that Uncle was not among those solicitous for her full recovery. But he was a good horseman, George Deering was at pains to remind Lestrade, and he knew the estate and the neighbouring woods like the back of his hand. He would return in his own good time and with a brush to boot. But evening had come and the bay had been found in the gorse, wandering alone, its saddle ominously empty. Deering, Sheraton, the others and the beaters had gone out again to look for him. Perhaps he had hit a tree. The bay was relatively untried. Who knew what might have happened. Perhaps he had seen the bounder who had accosted Lady Brandling and had taken off after him. But the beaters found nothing and he did not answer the calling of his name. At nightfall, they called off the search, to resume again at first light. And it was then that one of the gamekeepers on the estate found him.

'Why a lance?' Lestrade was talking to himself really.

'India,' mused Sheraton, fitting his monocle as he poured himself another brandy.

Lestrade looked at the reflection of the flames in the monocle.

'India?' he repeated.

'When I first joined the regiment,' Sheraton explained, 'we were stationed in India. Meerut. Our favourite sports there were horse-racing and pig-sticking.'

'Pig-sticking?'

'Boar hunting, to be precise,' Deering explained. 'Tricky beggar, your boar. Nasty. Turns on you in a tight corner. And those tusks are no joke.'

Sheraton concurred.

'So our man may be someone who knew Major Deering in India? Did he have enemies?' asked Lestrade.

'What man doesn't have enemies?' Deering replied. 'John was an enormously popular man, Inspector. Everyone in the mess called him "Uncle". But couldn't that very popularity have made him the envy of one?'

'Any one in particular?' Lestrade asked.

Deering shrugged. Time for Lestrade to try a bit of pig-sticking of his own.

'One who stood to inherit his elder brother's estate, perhaps?'

George Deering leapt to his feet. 'That's a foul and offensive remark, Lestrade. You will withdraw it immediately.'

Lestrade looked at Sheraton, also on his feet by now. 'One who, as a surgeon in a fashionable cavalry regiment, is regarded as the lowest of the low, and who was insanely jealous of the most popular officer in that regiment?'

'Lestrade, you go beyond the bounds of decency!' roared Sheraton.

'Frequently,' said Lestrade, rising now to their level, 'but only because murder takes me there. Sit down gentlemen. If I have given offence, I am sorry. But I need to start eliminating suspects. I have just eliminated two.'

'How so?' Deering demanded.

'Captains, I have been in the murder game for a long time,' he stared wistfully into the crackling fire, 'a very long time, I sometimes think. And I get to know a lie when I hear it. And a murderer when I see him. Oh, not every time, of course. But there is usually something. And in your case, I can't see it. And I can't hear it.'

'As well as the fact of course,' Deering went on, 'that we have witnesses who will swear we were with them all day.'

'You give me ten men who all see the same thing at the same instant and I'll give you ten different versions of that thing,' said Lestrade. 'Your friends will swear you were there because they are your friends. Because they would have expected you to be there. Because they saw a horse similar to yours. Because someone mentioned they had seen you. Even so,' Lestrade quaffed the last of his brandy, 'I would like a list of those who rode with you and especially those you remember riding with Major Deering when the pack parted. If you'll excuse me, gentlemen, I'll to my bed. I will have to intrude on the solemnities tomorrow in order to ask your mourners a few questions.'

And he left.

George Deering blew out the lamp and turned to Sheraton still standing by the fire.

'I think our flatfoot friend has presumed too far, Arthur, don't you?'

'Suggestions, George?'

'If our dear Chief Constable has the measure of this man,' Deering was making for the door, 'he's the no-stone-unturned type. When he's finished annoying our friends with his ghastly bourgeois questions, he'll probably go to Brighton.'

'To the regiment?' Sheraton was aghast. 'The disgusting boundah!'

'Quite. I think we can manage something for him there, don't you?'

They came and went all the next day, depositing their cards in the morning, returning in the afternoon. The drive looked like Hyde Park on a sunny Sunday, choked with carriages and cabriolets. Lestrade ensconced himself, with Captain Deering's grudging permission, in the late major's study. He had got his reinforcements after all – a sergeant and three constables to take notes and otherwise do the bidding of the man from the Yard. Deering and Sheraton kept out of his way, but could not fail to notice the sour looks of those whom Lestrade had questioned. Of those who had ridden to hounds two days earlier and whose names appeared on Deering's list as having ridden with the deceased when the pack broke up, Lestrade interviewed eight. Their stories were substantially the same and of little help. They had all lost sight of the major at the watercourse. One of them said he seemed to be having trouble with the bay. Another mentioned a figure on a grey horse he did not know, riding near to Deering and a little to his right, but there were several faces in the hunt he did not know and he could not place much significance in that particular one.

Then, Lestrade interviewed Lady Brandling. She was a large woman, probably the wrong side of forty, but then, who wasn't these days? She wore purple as a token of mourning and her golden hair hung in tresses – a style a trifle passé – over her shoulders. Her eyes sparkled with a sapphire intensity however and she insisted Lestrade walk with her in the garden and without the constable in attendance if the inspector didn't mind, as the matter they were to discuss was a delicate one.

'You are here about . . . the incident?' Lady Brandling asked him as they passed beneath the apple blossom.

'Indeed, ma'am,' he replied.

'There is little I can tell you.' She sighed.

Lestrade had heard all this before.

'Whatever crumb you may have, ma'am, is of the utmost importance.'

She looked at him. 'Of course,' she said, 'I had been riding for nearly an hour. There had been no sign of a fox in that time, but the hounds clearly had a scent. I had just heard the "View Halloo" when I realised I had ridden too high into the woods. I was alone, although I saw various people below me, through the trees. I must have hit a branch, because when I awoke, I was lying on the ground, and my head hurt.'

Lestrade noted the small bruise.

'There was . . . a man . . . bending over me. He . . . had his hand on my knee and was pushing up my riding gown. Then he tried . . . to kiss me . . . Inspector, is all this necessary?'

'No, ma'am, it is not. I am making enquiries into the death of Major John Deering. I fear you and I are talking at cross purposes, Lady Brandling.'

She broke away with a start, then turned back to him. 'No, Inspector, I do not believe we are. You see the man in question *was* Major John Deering.'

Lestrade narrowed his eyes and took the lady's elbow gently. 'Are you saying the deceased attempted to rape you?'

Lady Brandling blushed. 'He had been . . . amorous, shall we say, for some time. Making advances . . . suggestions.' She heaved her more than adequate bosom. 'I of course resisted.'

'Of course.' Lestrade was solicitous.

'He was a fine horseman, Inspector Lestrade. He would never have allowed an animal to throw him. He had obviously been following me. Waiting for his chance.'

'What happened then?'

'As soon as I realised what was going on, I fought him off.'

Highly probable, thought Lestrade, having sensed Lady Brandling's biceps beneath the velvet.

'He must have felt ashamed, because he helped me up and rode away. That was the last time I saw him until . . . this afternoon.'

'Who else knows of this?' Lestrade asked.

'No one. And that is how I would like it to stay. Uncle was a fine man in many ways. The regiment loved him. The county loved him. Here and there you might find a lady – or a downstairs maid – who did not choose to love him. He had this fatal weakness you see. A weakness for women.'

'Fatal, indeed, ma'am,' echoed Lestrade. 'Tell me, my lady, do you yourself come of a military family?'

'Why yes, Inspector. My father was a colonel in the Dorsetshires and my grandfather fought in the Crimea, in the Royal Horse Artillery.'

'So your home . . . er . . . forgive me . . .'

'Brandling Hall.'

'Brandling Hall, is hung with trophies of a military kind?'

'Why, yes.'

'Cavalry lances?'

'Yes, I believe ...' Lady Brandling was suddenly on her guard. 'Inspector, what are you implying?'

'You are a woman outraged, Lady Brandling,' Lestrade reminded her. 'What is more natural than that you should want revenge?'

'And how was I to achieve this revenge?' her ladyship asked. 'Did I secrete a lance in my skirts with which to skewer Uncle Deering? Or did I ostentatiously carry it as lancers do, in a lance shoe fitted to my stirrup? No, wait. Perhaps I hid it privily in the woods, persuaded the fox to run that way and waited there until Uncle pounced on me. Then I ran him through with it.'

Lestrade burst out laughing in spite of himself. And after a moment or two, Lady Brandling joined in.

'Forgive me, my lady. My job is to leave no stone unturned. You have reminded me of the little matter of logic, however. And you have admirably acquitted yourself in the process.'

'Inspector,' she said, when the laughter had subsided, 'it is not proper that we should be so merry on a day like this. I trust that the incident to which I referred earlier will go no further?'

Lestrade looked gravely at her. 'I see no reason, ma'am,' he said, 'why it should. One last thing,' he led her towards the house, huge and impressive in its Palladian red brick, 'did you see a rider on a grey horse?'

'Three or four, Inspector. Is it important?'

'Probably not.' And they went indoors.

Lestrade had not visited this part of Norman Shaw's noble pile in eight years. Not since he'd been working on the Baskett case and that was in very different circumstances. It was somewhere in the bowels of the earth. In fact, he fancied if you kept very still you could hear Old Father Thames, gurgling and growling only feet away.

'Not much headway yet, Inspector,' the boffin said, scrutinising Lestrade over his pince-nez. 'It does appear to be a diary, but the system is a complex one. Do you know anything about codes?'

'Not much.' Lestrade shrugged.

'Well, there are numerical and alphabetical, syllable and word, stencil and blackline. On the other hand, there is the miscellaneous range – angle writing, thread writing, the puncture system, the foot rule cypher and so on.'

'Which is this one?'

'I don't know. But I think I've ruled out puncture, stencil and foot rule.' He riffled through a forest of papers, 'That's progress. The simplest of all is the five element code – Francis Bacon's – for example "fly" is written "aabab". But it could be written "ababa" or even "babba" – do you see?'

'No,' said Lestrade. It was no more than the truth. Give him a corpse, a bloodstain, a fingerprint even and he was on firm ground. But this man was talking nonsense.

'The Paris International Telegraph Conference issued an Official Vocabulary of some two hundred thousand words in eighteen ninety. That was for commercial codes really, but it has its application in other spheres of course.'

'Of course,' concurred the bewildered Lestrade.

'The New Official Vocabulary has extended this to one million words. That was supposed to reduce the risk of faulty transmission, but I don't personally think it's very successful.'

'Er . . . no, I suppose not,' Lestrade observed.

'Of course, if this diary – if that's what it is – uses artificial words, then we're sunk.'

'Without trace.' The inspector was forced to agree.

'I've even tried tilting the book through three hundred and sixty degrees, to find a cryptographic disc. No luck. What I'm working on now is . . .' But he was talking to himself. Lestrade had gone to the upper reaches of the Yard, where men spoke a language he understood.

Three such men stood before his desk in the office on the first floor. One of them was Walter Dew, newly promoted sergeant

of H Division, Scotland Yard. The other two were recruits –
Constables Dickens and Jones – bright eyed and bushy tailed in
their Cheapside suits.

'Dickens,' said Lestrade, surveying the paperwork before
him. 'Christian names Charles Boothby.' He looked up as the
young man advanced. 'Charles Dickens?' Lestrade scowled.
'Any relation?'

'To whom, sir?' the constable asked intently.

'No relation,' sighed Lestrade. 'How many years in the
Force?'

'Three, sir – next September.'

'Two and a half,' Lestrade observed mechanically. He scanned
the papers again and his attention fixed on something. 'You
were the arresting officer in the Terris case?'

'Yes, sir. It was my first night on the beat. On my own that
is.'

'It took some bottle to face that maniac, Constable.' Lestrade
was not a man easily impressed.

'No, sir, I didn't use a bottle. I relied on my truncheon.'

Thank God, thought Lestrade to himself, you didn't use your
brain. 'Why did you put in for the Yard, Dickens?' he contented
himself with asking.

'Scotland Yard are the finest body of detectives in the world,
sir. I wanted to be part of that body.'

Lestrade refrained from mentioning which part of the body he
felt Dickens was most likely to resemble and turned to the
second constable.

'Jones,' he said. The aforementioned stepped up smartly and
saluted. 'No,' said Lestrade dejectedly, 'we don't do that in
plainclothes. It sort of gives the game away, you know. There
you are, working undercover in a gin palace, about to break a
ring of opium smugglers or white slavers. I walk in, looking for
all the world like a punter and you salute! So you see, thanks,
but no thanks.'

Now it was Jones' turn to look dejected.

'Christian names, John Thomas . . .' Lestrade looked at him

and saw the smirk vanish from the faces of Dew and Dickens. He checked the record sheet, 'So you're Athelney Jones' little boy?' he clicked his tongue.

'Not so little, sir. I shall be nineteen next month. One year in the Force.'

'How's your old Dad? Enjoying his retirement?'

'Thank you, sir. He sends his regards.'

'Bearing in mind he and I barely exchanged the time of day, Constable, that must represent quite an effort on his part. So you've spent most of the last year walking up and down the Mile End Road. Any action?'

'A few trassenos . . . er . . . villains, sir.'

'Good. A man who can patter East End. That's useful. Why the Yard? Daddy's footsteps?'

'Yes, sir.' Jones was making no apology for the fact.

'Fair enough.' Lestrade lolled back in his chair. They stood before him like peas in a pod, like Tweedledee and Tweedledum. What a trio – Dee, Dum and Dew. Why did he always seem to get the rookies? And simple rookies at that? It didn't seem all that long since he had sat in this chair and looked at the granite bulk of young Harry Bandicoot. But Harry, with all his faults and his Old Etonian sense of honour and fair play, had been a useful man to have at your back. Lestrade could always rely on Dew. But what of these two? What if Tweedledee and Tweedledum should happen on a battle? And what, if any, routines of police procedure could he expect them to follow? They had less – appreciably less – than four years' experience between them. Anyway, no time like the present.

'Dickens.'

'Sir?'

'What do you know of the Sixth Dragoon Guards?'

Dickens looked blank for a moment then launched himself.

'The Sixth Dragoon Guards. His Majesty's Sixth Regiment of Heavy Cavalry of the Line. Raised in sixteen eighty-five. Originally called "The Queen Dowager's". Later "The Carabiniers" because of the short musket they carried into action. Due to be converted to Light Cavalry in India forty years ago. They were ordered to change their uniform from blue to scarlet. The conversion never took place, and they are now the only Heavy Cavalry Regiment to wear blue tunics. Battle honours include—'

'Thank you, Constable!' Lestrade's amazement had been growing for a while. 'You know all this and you don't know anything of your namesake?'

'Who might that be, Inspector?'

'Never mind.' Lestrade managed, when he found the ability to close his mouth. 'Where are the Carbs stationed now?'

'Carbs, sir?'

'Carabiniers, man. The regiment we – you – have just been talking about.'

'Oh, Brighton, sir.'

'All right.' The inspector reached with trembling fingers for a cigar. Dickens' Lucifer was waiting for him before it reached his lips. Lestrade blew smoke through his nose, living up to the grim picture which Dew had enjoyed painting of him for the new lads.

'Jones.' Lestrade turned his guns on Tweedledum.

'Sir?'

'What do you know about cavalry lances?'

'Cavalry lances, sir?' Jones checked that he had heard right.

Lestrade nodded, waiting for the 'Nothing' or the silence. Instead he got a lecture.

'The lance as a weapon of war disappeared from the battlefield during the seventeenth century as it was found to be unwieldy and no match for firearms. It returned into the British service in eighteen sixteen as a result of the impressive use of the said weapon by Napoleon's Polish levies, especially the Lancers of the Vistula, under Marshal Poniatowski. British lance regiments at first carried a sixteen-foot shaft weighing four pounds and made of ash wood but recent experience in India has led to the development of a shorter weapon, made of bamboo and weighing—'

'Thank you, Constable.' Lestrade had let his cigar go out in amazement at the display of erudition. 'Sergeant Dew,' he said, 'I'll wager you still make a better cup of tea than either of these walking encyclopedias. Hot, and lots of it. I'm not feeling well.'

Lestrade could have sent Walter Dew. He could not yet trust Dickens or Jones. But he had a grudging respect for them in an odd sort of way. Though how two men from such humdrum backgrounds – and one of them the son of the biggest idiot ever to put on a Metropolitan uniform – could possess such knowledge, Lestrade was at a loss to explain. No wonder Nimrod Frost had said he thought Lestrade would like these two. But he had liked constables before. Two had been killed serving under him. One had been crippled. One had resigned to marry a rich widow. Constables had a habit of not staying around. Except Dew, but even he was a sergeant now. Best not to get too fond of them. Lestrade caught the noon train to Brighton by himself.

He knew the town vaguely. In the short time he and Sarah had had together, they had occasionally come down, by this very train, if he remembered rightly. Still this was no time to be maudlin. He'd promised her he wouldn't be. And he had a murderer to catch.

Lieutenant-Colonel Gilmartin, officer commanding His Majesty's Sixth Dragoon Guards, the Carabiniers, was a martyr to gout. Lestrade found him growling behind a pair of huge white dundrearies at least forty years out of date, lying on a *chaise-longue* in his quarters at the camp. A subaltern taking down the colonel's memoirs in longhand was ushered out of the room and Lestrade took his place on the stool.

'Pour me a brandy,' grunted Gilmartin, 'before my good lady wife returns from her blasted temperance meeting. Are you married, Inspector?'

'A widower, sir.'

'Oh,' the colonel grunted. 'Don't mean to be offensive, old boy, but you're a lucky man.'

Lestrade smiled.

'Now ... agghh,' and he grimaced as he tried to settle his heavily bandaged foot on the cushion, 'how can I help you on poor old Uncle?'

'What kind of man was he?' asked Lestrade.

'Marvellous fellow. Marvellous. Competent soldier. Thoroughly good egg of course. A demon at baccarat ... er ... have they legalised that yet?'

'I'm looking for a murderer, Colonel Gilmartin, not a card-sharp.'

'Quite, quite.' The colonel swept his moustaches into the brandy. 'Something of a ladies' man, I understand.'

'I understand that too,' said Lestrade. 'Did he leave a string of loves scorned? Jealous husbands?'

'God knows. I had the misfortune to marry the only filly I ever paid my devoirs to. Completely misunderstood the term filly. By the time I realised, it was too late. I don't see what men see in women. Give me a horse and a brandy any time.'

Each to his own, thought Lestrade, that must be what gout does to a man.

'He was popular in the regiment?'

'God, yes. People here in Brighton call us Uncle's Own, y'know. Good for morale, was old Uncle. We'll miss him. Here's to you, Uncle Deering, wherever you are!' And he downed the brandy and hurled the glass at the grate. Lestrade drank the toast, but refrained from following suit. The cut glass would cost him two months' salary.

'I don't know what I can tell you, Inspector.' The colonel was rearranging his feet as painlessly as possible. 'Uncle had been with us for nearly twelve years. His father was with the regiment, and his father before him. But we'd have missed Uncle anyway.'

'I don't think I follow, sir,' said Lestrade.

'He was leaving us, Inspector. Didn't his brother tell you? Perhaps George didn't know. How odd. Yes, he was going to resign his commission. Going into politics, I believe. Now, there's a rum life for a man. Can't abide it myself. Not done in the mess, y'understand? No religion. No politics. Yes, we'd have missed him.'

'Politics,' repeated Lestrade, and faint warning bells began to ring in his head. The itch he couldn't scratch was starting up. He thanked the colonel for his time and his brandy and an orderly showed him out. On the way, he tipped his bowler to a lady he presumed to be the colonel's good lady wife. He knew her by her resemblance to a filly, swathed in the ribbons of the Rechabites, piety and starchiness etched into every line of her face.

He found himself in a lane, cobbled and twisting, with high brick walls. This was not the way he had come and he was temporarily lost. As he rounded a corner, he was faced by two burly troopers of the Carbs, the afternoon sun shining behind them, silhouetting their stable dress and forage caps. There was something in their walk, something in the clubs they carried that told Lestrade they were not out for a stroll. Discretion, ever a policeman's ally on these occasions, came to the rescue of valour and Lestrade turned back the way he had come. There stood two more Carbs, bigger and uglier than the first. They advanced at a measured tread, cradling their wooden sticks in their arms. Lestrade knew the damage those things could do. They looked uncomfortably like the batons of the Mounted Police. He had swung one himself in his time. He felt for his brass knuckles, raising his other hand in a token of surrender. He saw for the first time the black arm bands above their left elbows. Mourning for their Uncle. He twisted round, this way and that, watching for the first blow. What he said was pointless, but he said it anyway.

'I am Inspector Lestrade of Scotland Yard. Striking a police officer is a serious—' And the first cudgel hissed towards him before he'd finished the sentence. He caught it expertly and wrenched its wielder forward, slamming him into his second attacker. The second club was faster, or Lestrade slower and it caught him square in the back. He hit the wall, the rough bricks grazing his already scarred face. He swung round, crouching low, and heard two more clubs crunch uselessly against the wall. His boot jabbed into the knee of one of the four and the man stumbled. Lestrade's brass fist came up for the first time and bloodied the man's nose. For a second he heard the cursing and grunting of the others, then dull aches on both arms, a sickening crack on his head and the cobbles hurtled up to meet him. The rest was silence.

Boscombe's Odd Place

Lestrade awoke to a resplendent evening, more typical of July than April. There wasn't a cloud in the sky and the sun dazzled through the boughs of the elm towering over him. At first, his head felt detached from his body, as though when he struggled upright, anything above his neck was still lying on the grass beside him. Only slowly did his vision focus on the clump of bushes to his right and the sweep of the downs beyond. He felt the rough bark of the trunk at his back and was about to attempt to rise when a shattering scream ricocheted around the empty echoing space which had been his head. For an instant his eyes took in a bevy of young ladies in frothy blouses and straw boaters. He registered that it was they who screamed. He knelt up with difficulty and reached out as though to calm them, when he realised the full horror of his situation. Beneath the voluminous Donegal, he was stark naked.

He leapt for the shelter of the nearest bush, but landed badly and found out the hard way, as most non-countrymen do, that it was gorse. As decorously as possible, he wrapped the coat around the portion he assumed had given offence, but by that time the bevy of ladies were scurrying out of the little hollow and making for high ground.

Lestrade had little time to consider his situation further, for as he emerged, battered but unbowed from the tangle of the bush, he caught the full impact of a hockey stick across his nose. Eyes swimming with tears, he ducked and stumbled backwards, so that the coat flapped open again to reveal his all.

'You disgusting beast!' his assailant roared in a falsetto shriek, covering her face with her left hand, while holding back with the hockey stick in her right the hastily returning bevy of young ladies. 'Don't look, girls!' she bellowed. 'Keep behind me!' And she swung to the attack again, brandishing her stick with all the zeal of a whirling dervish. Even her hairstyle bore similarities.

'Madam, I—' But Lestrade had to duck before he finished his sentence and thought it best to take to his heels. He found himself in a broad field, angling down to the sea and heard, rather than dared look at, the pack of furious females at his back. The air was alive with the hissing of a hockey stick and he actually heard at least one 'View Halloo' before he leapt the barbed wire fence and rolled headlong through the long yellow grass into a steep ravine.

It may have been muddy, wet and rank at the bottom, but it was preferable to the harpies who had driven him to its brink. He crouched in the sheltering bushes until the pack gave up the chase at the boundary fence and went away.

Now, the problem was to get back to the road. This time he buttoned his Donegal and picked his way gingerly through the ravine into which he had fallen. The sea sparkled away to his right and the winds from it began to rise as the purple shadows lengthened. He had just picked his way over the agonies of ling, unable to decide whether it was his head or his feet which bothered him most, when he heard a distant voice shout, 'Fire!' Turning to find the pall of black smoke that cry had led him to expect, his eyes caught instead a lone figure silhouetted on a curve of the downs. In an instant, he realised that the figure was not alone, but that a row of heads bobbed up along a ridge to his left. The shout was followed by a noise he had heard before, though not often and a sharp whipping wind which came from nowhere and ripped the flap of his Donegal. Instinctively, he followed the path of the wind and saw a hole appear in a black and white painted post between him and the sea.

'Good God!' he heard the watcher cry. 'Cease fire!'

It was only then that Lestrade understood the ambiguity of the word and flung himself headlong on the grass. He was lying, he now realised, on a rifle range and was inches from the targets. He saw the heads emerge as men, running towards him through the gathering dusk.

'I told you we should have finished before this, Gigger!' he heard one say. 'You can't see a damned thing in this light.'

'I can't see much, anyway,' Gigger replied and then to Lestrade, 'My dear chap, let me help you up.'

Two or three of the men began to brush Lestrade down until they noticed his bare legs below the Donegal, and one by one they drew back, looking with varying degrees of puzzlement and distaste according to their predilections and their view of the world.

'Didn't you see the sign?' one of them snapped. 'It says quite clearly "Keep out".'

'No,' said Lestrade, 'as a matter of fact I was being pursued by a rather irate group of young ladies.'

'I'm not surprised,' said another, 'dressed like that.'

'Obviously a pervert, Gigger. What'll we do?'

'Call the police,' another offered. 'This is private property. I don't care what a man does in his spare time, but this is the Rottingdean Rifle Club. He can't do it here.'

'No, no, wait a minute,' Gigger answered. 'I'm sure there's a reasonable explanation, Mr ... er ...?'

'Lestrade, Inspector Lestrade – of Scotland Yard.'

'Good God,' murmured Gigger, 'undercover work, eh?'

'You might say so,' Lestrade replied.

'Come on,' said Gigger, grinning through his pebble glasses, 'you look as though you could do with a pair of trousers. I've a Lanchester at the club house.'

Lestrade had not heard of that make of nether garment before, but if it kept the downs winds from racing up his Donegal, he was all for it. Amid mutters of abuse from the rest, Lestrade and his shooting companion strode for the club house.

'I fear I have upset your friends,' said Lestrade.

'Ah, flannelled fools at the wicket,' grunted Gigger. 'Besides, it's too dark for any more practice tonight. I'm Rudyard Kipling.' And he heartily shook Lestrade's hand.

The Lanchester to which Kipling referred was not a pair of trousers at all but a horseless carriage. It didn't help Lestrade that his new-found acquaintance kept referring to the machine as Amelia. At least, Lestrade assumed that, as he couldn't believe that Kipling would be so tasteless as to imply that a lady known to him was a bitch to start of a frosty morning. On second thoughts, Lestrade had known women like that.

They drove through the dusk of the April countryside, Lestrade cold and dispirited, aching and annoyed, while Gigger was roaring above the rattle and growl of Amelia sonorous comments on Sussex by the sea which Lestrade supposed must be poetry. It was not the inspector's first ride in such a contraption, but by the time they reached the looming granite of Kipling's house, he was heartily hoping it would be his last.

'So how did you come to be trouserless on the downs, Lestrade?' asked Kipling over an especially cheering glass of port.

'I'm afraid I am not at liberty to divulge . . .' began Lestrade in the jargon which constabularies the country over had made their own, but Kipling was persistent.

'Come on, man. Here you are drinking my port, warming yourself by my fire. You've ridden in my Lanchester and now you're wearing my clothes. Don't you think I deserve a little confidence?'

Lestrade looked at the man. He was the colour of mahogany, his Indian complexion tanned further by the sun of the veld. A firm imperial chin jutted below a walrus moustache of total blackness and over the spectacles which gave him the nickname of Gigger – 'Giglamps' – the eyebrows met with a fierce friendship. Lestrade's old granny used to say that those whose eyebrows did that were destined to hang. He told the poet the gist of his clash with the Carbs, but was at a loss to explain his arrival on the downs near Rottingdean wearing only his overcoat.

'Well, one thing's for sure,' Kipling mused, 'the Misses Lawrence will be out for your blood.'

'Misses Lawrence?' Lestrade repeated.

'Almost certainly the matron who set about you with her hockey stick was a Miss Lawrence. Oh, she's a formidable dragon. And you exposing yourself to her young ladies, well . . .'

'It was a girls' school then?'

'Roedean. Founded some years ago by three dreadful sisters. The eldest of them was called Medusa . . .'

The classical quip was lost on Lestrade, whose antiquarian knowledge all began and ended with Pandora. But Kipling had moved from the fire now and he picked up a framed photograph of a little girl. His mood suddenly changed. 'I might have sent her there,' he murmured.

'Mr Kipling?'

'Have you ever lost anyone dear to you, Lestrade?' His eyes were sad in the firelight.

'I have,' the inspector answered.

Kipling nodded, then he blew his nose with a deafening report and poured them both another drink.

'What will you do about those chappies in the Carbs?' he asked. 'If I may retain your clothes, sir, until I can get to the nearest tailors—'

'My dear fellow, the nearest tailor is an ass. I saw better stitching in Zulu Kraals when I was in South Africa. Besides, my time is my own for a while. I'm not on semaphore duty at the club again for a week. And I'm intrigued by you police chappies. The lure of the bizarre, I suppose. I saw some of it in India. Oh, inferior, I'm sure, to your *métier*.'

Lestrade was equally sure, although he didn't know what that was.

'I could be your driver,' Gigger volunteered.

Lestrade hesitated. 'Well—'

'Good!' shouted Kipling. 'So it's agreed. Now, let's eat. Mrs Kipling makes exceedingly good cakes.'

*   *   *

Lestrade had a memory for faces, especially those belonging to men who had beaten him up. While Kipling adopted curious poses on the road, his head and body hidden under Amelia, in the nicest possible way, the inspector in poet's clothing waited near the barracks gate. Shortly after eleven, his target emerged, in walking-out dress, and began the journey into town. He caught an omnibus on the corner and alighted near the shore where the old Daddy Longlegs used to run (when it did run, so prone was it to break down). He was crossing the sands already strewn with early holiday-makers with their parasols and deckchairs in the warm April winds when Lestrade caught up with him.

'A word in your ear,' hissed the inspector, spinning his man round and pushing him backwards so that his head jarred against a great girder of the palace pier. The trooper cried out, but Lestrade was faster and slapped him round the cheeks a few times.

'You bastard,' the soldier roared and lunged at Lestrade. He was younger and bigger than his opponent, but it had to be said that he had not Lestrade's experience in tight corners. The inspector merely stepped aside and with the grace of a music-hall turn, caught the man's ankle with his own and sent him sprawling in the sand. He landed with a crunch on the sandcastle of an indignant infant who bawled with such vigour that his mamma hurried over to accost the men.

'Disgusting!' she snorted, snatching the wailing child away. 'Drunken brawls in broad daylight,' and she turned to see Kipling dashing towards the group. 'You there! Call the police!'

'Inspector!' obliged Kipling.

'Yes, sir,' Lestrade played along for the lady's benefit, 'what seems to be the trouble?'

'Disgusting!' the woman said again, 'I'm going to call a *real* policeman!' and she hastened away in a flurry of sand, dragging the sobbing urchin in her wake.

Lestrade had not time to ruminate on the philosophy of her

remark – whether or not he was a *real* policeman – because he was too busy sitting on the recumbent Carabinier.

'Blast. I missed all the fun,' moaned Kipling. 'That crank shaft of Amelia's has got to go.'

'There may be more fun yet,' said Lestrade, tugging up the trooper's head by his hair, 'if our friend here is going to be uncooperative. I am Inspector Lestrade of Scotland Yard. Who are you?'

'Williams, Ezekiah, Private three-four-one-eight-two, Sixth Dragoon Guards.' The reply was to the point and, as far as Lestrade could judge, honest. He was after all half throttling the man by virtue of the angle at which he held his head.

'Why did you and your messmates set about me the other day?'

'Orders.'

'Whose?'

A hesitation. Until Lestrade reminded the soldier of the vulnerability of his windpipe.

'Captain Deering's.'

'Would you care to elaborate?'

Kipling sat cross-legged in the sand, evidently enjoying Lestrade's bedside manner.

'He just told us to – rough you up a bit, that's all. He didn't say why.'

'What did he pay you?'

'Five shillings,' the trooper rasped.

Lestrade stepped off him and pulled the man up by his hair.

'Think yourself lucky, Williams, that I've got bigger fish to fry. Or you'd be serving of His Majesty the King behind prison bars by tonight. And they haven't banned flogging in military prisons yet, have they?'

Williams shook himself and stumbled off up the beach, cursing under his breath.

'You let that bounder get off lightly,' observed Kipling. 'Fancy a crack at the rifles on the pier? I'll buy you a hot potato.'

And that was an offer Lestrade could not refuse.

* * *

By evening, the inspector was back in his native city again, where he felt at home. And back too in his own suit. He was still shaking from his ride to Brighton station in Kipling's Lanchester and he reminded himself that he must return the poet's clothes by the morning post. As it was, he took advantage of a break in duty and caught a hansom to the Yard. It was raining as he crossed the courtyard, shining in the lamplight that flickered with the rustling trees. Strange how chill it was after the glory of the downs and the baked potatoes with Kipling on Palace Pier.

He had not reached the side door which led to his office when the bright young face of Jones appeared in the half-light.

'Ah, I was on my way to your chambers, sir.'

'Chambers?' Lestrade didn't live in the Inner Temple.

'Telegram, sir. Just arrived.'

Lestrade pushed the constable back into the doorway. He scanned the telegram's contents. 'Where's Dickens?' he asked.

'Off duty, sir – an hour ago.'

'Dew?'

'I believe he's looking for that stolen cache of ping-pong balls, sir.'

'Where? Chinatown?'

'Sir?'

Lestrade looked at Jones. As he thought, the same lack of humour his old man had.

'Can you drive a Maria, Jones?'

'Yes, sir.'

'Then what are we standing here for, like the weather man and woman? Get one. I'll handle the paperwork later.'

The telegram was from one John Watson MD and it spoke of dark doings at the Diogenes Club.

'Diogenes, Jones,' said Lestrade as he gripped the seat rail on top of the Maria lurching towards the Mall. 'What can you tell me?'

'Would that be Diogenes of Apollonia, Diogenes of Babylon,

Diogenes Laertius or Diogenes the Cynic, sir?'

'If there are four of them, Jones, I haven't got time to listen to the answer. Did any of them have a club?'

'Not as far as I am aware, sir.'

'All right. Just drive.'

They rattled through the advancing night, Lestrade increasingly aware that Jones was an infinitely worse driver than Kipling. At least the lurches of the Maria were comfortable ones, however, and the horse did not growl and cough like a tuberculous tin can. They found a uniformed man on the door of the Diogenes and a number of faces peering through the upper windows of the Carlton down the road. The bobby saluted Lestrade who took one look at the clubland portico and ordered Jones to stay outside.

In the entrance hall, with its double stairway and its marble pillars, a crimson-faced gentleman, the years catching up with him, hurried across to Lestrade. For a silly moment, the inspector stood rooted to the spot, his hand extended inches from that of the gentleman, until he realised his coat tails were caught in the door. Why did he always have trouble with his entrances?

'Lestrade. Thank you for coming so promptly.'

'Sssshhhh!' The sibilance echoed down the corridor although there was no one about.

'He's in here,' he went on in a whisper.

'Are you a member of this club, Doctor Watson?' Lestrade said.

'Be quiet!' a disembodied voice snapped. Lestrade could still see no one.

Watson led him down a short flight of carpeted stairs to a niche, heavy with flock wallpaper and lit by a small lamp. A member of the Diogenes lay dozing in his chair, *The Times* folded over his face. Watson pulled away the paper and Lestrade saw that the member was not dozing. He was dead.

Mechanically, the inspector checked the pulse, placed his ear against the immobile chest.

'Your story, Doctor?' Lestrade had dropped his voice to a whisper now.

'We can't talk here, Lestrade,' Watson's eyes swivelled nervously from side to side. 'This club is not like the others.'

A black-velveted flunkey appeared from nowhere, carrying a silver tray with brandies. He began to place one at the dead man's table.

'I don't think he'll need that,' said Lestrade.

'Sir?'

'The gentleman is dead,' the inspector informed him.

'Oh dear,' said the flunkey and stood with his head bowed for a moment.

'Who is in charge here?' Lestrade asked.

'Well, Mr Mycroft Holmes is a founder member – I believe he is the only such present this evening.'

'Where will I find him?'

The flunkey bowed and vanished through a forest of aspidistrae.

'One moment,' Lestrade raised his voice.

'Bad show!' someone grunted.

'Resign,' growled someone else.

'No, no, Lestrade. It's a club rule in here. No one, not even the staff, may speak more than three times or they are dismissed or black balled,' Watson told him.

Lestrade looked nonplussed.

'Diogenes,' said Watson, by way of explanation.

Lestrade looked blanker than ever.

'Diogenes the Cynic,' went on Watson, 'one of the most anti-social men in classical antiquity. This is a club for the anti-social.'

'Shut up!' a voice bellowed.

'Get out!' roared another.

Lestrade strode for the door.

'Constable,' to the man on the steps, 'has anyone left by this way since you arrived?'

'No, sir.'

'How long have you been here?'

'Since that gentleman,' pointing to Watson, 'hailed me in the street over an hour ago.'

'Is there another way out?' Lestrade asked Watson.

'Yes, a back way, I believe,' the good doctor answered.

'Damn! Jones, find it and stay there until relieved.' The young constable sprang down from the Maria's high seat. 'And, by the way, it's Diogenes the Cynic.'

'Ah,' said Jones, scurrying off in search of the back door, 'Diogenes the Cynic. Circa four hundred to three hundred and twenty-five BC. Born at Sinope on the Euxine. Pupil of Antisthenes . . .' But Lestrade had gone, urging on the other constable the need to let no one pass.

'There must be somewhere in this mausoleum where we can talk at more than a whisper, Doctor Watson.'

'Yes, the visitors' room. This way.'

As the door of that room closed, Watson raised his voice to its usual level.

'My dear Lestrade. How are you? It's been a little while.'

'It has indeed, Doctor, but I fear we must dispense with the pleasantries. A man has been murdered.'

'How do you know it was murder, Lestrade?'

'Come now, Doctor Watson. I'm not playing one of your detective games. I've still got blood on my ear from the hole in the deceased's chest. And a hole in the chest is not a natural cause. Not in my book. Why else did you send for me?'

'Talking of books, I've nearly finished my latest – *The Hound of the Baskervilles*. Like the sound of it?'

Lestrade raised the Eyebrow of Exasperation.

'Well, er . . . where shall I start, Inspector?'

'A good story writer like you should know the answer to that one, Doctor – I'm sure Conan Doyle would. At the beginning of course.'

And he did.

But he hadn't finished when the door was opened by the monosyllabic flunkey, who ushered in a large man in evening suit. He was not unlike Nimrod Frost viewed in a funny fairground mirror and he shook hands as though with the flipper of a circus seal. There was something else in the steel grey of the eyes that was vaguely familiar and when Watson introduced him, Lestrade knew what it was.

'May I present Mr Mycroft Holmes, founder of the Diogenes Club. This is—'

'No!' Holmes held up his flipper, 'Let me guess. You are a policeman, sir, a detective of Scotland Yard. With the rank of . . . let me see . . . inspector?'

Holmes began to perambulate around Lestrade. 'You lost the tip of your nose in a duel with swords and have recently been on the receiving end of several blunt instruments – wooden clubs, I would deduce. You are married . . . no, a widower. Without children.' Holmes beamed. 'How am I doing so far, Inspector Lestrade?'

'Better than your late brother, Mr Holmes,' the inspector answered.

'Have a care, Lestrade,' the loyal Watson felt bound to interject.

'Yes, Sherlock always said I was,' grinned Holmes. 'Actually I cheated. I've seen you before – in the *Police Gazette* wasn't it? Weren't you wanted for attempting to murder the Kaiser?'

'You have a remarkable memory, Mr Holmes,' smiled Lestrade. 'All that was, of course, a misunderstanding.'

'Of course,' Holmes smiled in return. 'Boscombe,' he turned to the flunkey, 'brandies. Large ones. And would you ask Mr Aumerle Holmes to join us?'

The flunkey vanished.

'Should have succeeded – the bounder!' growled Watson.

'Aumerle?' Holmes challenged him.

'No – the Kaiser. Lestrade should have succeeded in killing him. Damned upstart. I've never forgiven him for the Kruger telegram, you know.'

'Gentlemen,' Lestrade broke in, 'as much as I would like to reminisce on assassination attempts past, I fear we have one which is with us in the present and was very much successful. Mr Holmes, I wonder if you'd mind accounting for your movements since . . . say . . . five o'clock this evening.'

'I'll make myself scarce, Mycroft—' Watson began.

'I'd like you to stay, Doctor,' Lestrade stopped him.

'Oh, very well.' And the good doctor sat down.

'I was in my office in Whitehall at five, Inspector.' Holmes made himself comfortable. 'It had been a devil of a long day – I'd been there since three—'

'Your office, sir?' Lestrade checked him.

'The Foreign Office, Inspector.'

'What is the nature of your work there, sir?'

'My dear fellow, I am not at liberty to divulge that. National security, you know.'

All this reminded Lestrade of his deranged colleagues in the Special Branch, but he dismissed the idea and Holmes went on, 'At six precisely, I crossed to my rooms, washed and changed and came here to the club.'

'What time did you arrive?'

'Oh, it must have been nearly seven. For once, I broke my habit.'

'Habit?' Lestrade wondered what nauseating little confession was to follow.

'I invariably arrive at a quarter to five and leave promptly at twenty to eight. As I said, it had been a devil of a day and of course I would have left almost an hour ago had it not been for poor old Waldo.'

'How well did you know the deceased?'

'Know him? Watson, have you told the inspector nothing? This is the Diogenes Club, Mr Lestrade, and I am a founder member. We are the most anti-social and unclubbable men in London. We don't *know* each other. We merely come here for the certainty of peace and quiet. Many of us lead very exacting lives. It is a rule of the club that we ignore each other as far as possible.'

'Even to the point of murder, Mr Holmes?'

'Ah, yes, unfortunate. But if I may shift your meaning, my dear Lestrade,' Holmes patronised very well, 'there is in my experience always a point to murder.'

'And in this case? You've seen the body?' Lestrade too was capable of semantics when pressed.

'Ah yes. 'The "point" in this case, I would say, was that of a stiletto. Clean, precise. Straight through the heart.'

'You disturbed the body?'

'Dear me no, Inspector. I leave that sort of bungling to the police – excepting present company, of course.'

'You are more than kind,' Lestrade bowed in his chair. 'What happened when you arrived at the club?' he asked.

'Let me see. I had a sherry wine and ordered dinner. Doctor Watson joined me as my guest a little after seven. He wished to discuss his latest masterpiece with me.'

'Masterpiece?' Lestrade was glad to see that Holmes was finding it difficult to stifle a guffaw, too.

'What's it called, Watson? *The Dog of the Barsetshires?*'

'*The Hound of the Baskervilles*, as well you know, Holmes.' Watson bristled and he attempted to shift the blame, 'Actually it was Lestrade who gave me the idea.'

'Oh?' Lestrade raised an eyebrow.

'That thing you caught in Cornwall a few years back.'

'Food poisoning?' Holmes asked in all innocence.

'A Tasmanian wolf.' Lestrade put him right.

'Yes, that's the chappie. Well, I talked to Conan Doyle about it and that's what we came up with. I think it's pretty good. I think Sherlock would have approved.'

'Anyway, we'd just sat down for a chat and Boscombe told me Aumerle had arrived.'

'O'Merle?'

'My cousin, Inspector. Aumerle Holmes. He joined us here in the Strangers' Room – it's the only place where conversation is allowed.'

'And then?'

'Then we ate a hearty dinner. Capital pig, Watson.'

'I beg your pardon?' The doctor flushed behind his off-white whiskers. 'Oh, I see. Yes, it was. Capital.'

'And after the meal?'

'Boscombe came over to me and told me that Waldo didn't look well. I left my guests and went to his alcove. He was dead. Recently, I'd say. Perhaps half an hour. There was no sign of rigor mortis.'

'He's as stiff as a board, now,' Watson informed them, almost gleefully.

'What happened then?' Lestrade continued to press his man.

'Watson here suggested we contact you. So you see, my deductive reasoning when we met was not so impressive.'

'Impressive enough,' grunted Watson. 'Er . . . mind telling me how you did it, Holmes?'

'May I indulge him, Inspector?'

Lestrade nodded.

'Without wishing to be unkind to Mr Lestrade, no one but a policeman wears a Donegal these days. Or a coachman. And his hands weren't rough enough. I'd just shaken one of them.'

'What about the rank?'

'Yes, I cheated there. Remember the *Police Gazette*?'

'The nose?' Watson pursued, mentally making notes for his next outpouring with Conan Doyle.

'Straight cut. Clean. The blow must have been delivered by a single-edged weapon and with some force. It was either a sword or a meat cleaver. I opted for the former. Call it a lucky guess. The widower is easy. The inspector wears a wedding ring on the relevant finger, but his clothes and general air are of a man without the fussing attention of a woman. An inspector cannot afford divorce. So I surmised that Mrs Lestrade must be deceased. My condolences, Lestrade.'

The inspector smiled fleetingly.

'Which reminds me, Watson. How is Mrs Hudson these days?'

'Anything you may have heard . . .' Watson blustered, and then relented, 'oh . . . well, well.'

'Unlike the deceased in his alcove.' Lestrade brought them back.

'Ah, yes . . .'

The door opened and a tall young man came in. He was stones lighter than Mycroft and he carried a white stick.

'Ah, Aumerle.' Mycroft led the man to the inspector.

O'Merle? mused Lestrade. Was this the Irish branch of the family?

'I'd like you to meet Inspector Lestrade of Scotland Yard. My cousin, Aumerle.'

'Not *the* Inspector Lestrade?' Aumerle clumsily transferred his stick and grasped for the policeman's hand.

'None other,' grunted Watson.

'When cousin Sherlock was alive he spoke highly of you.'

'Highly?' Lestrade repeated quizzically, staring at the sightless eyes gazing at the ceiling.

Aumerle broke into a short, brittle laugh. 'All right then, not so highly. But Watson has been kinder.'

'Gentlemen.' Lestrade aided Aumerle Holmes to his seat and turned to the others. Boscombe brought the brandies and left with Holmes and Watson as Lestrade's gesture had indicated he should.

'Why did you do that, Mr Lestrade?' Aumerle asked.

'What, Mr Holmes?'

'You have cleared the room, have you not?'

'You are very perceptive, Mr Holmes. May I ask, how long . . . er—'

'How long have I been blind? For nearly two years, Inspector. An unfortunate accident, but I am learning to cope. These things take time. For instance . . .' And his hand snaked out to the brandy balloon on the table. He took it unerringly to his lips. 'My sense of smell has come on apace.'

And he laughed with Lestrade.

'What happened this evening?' the inspector asked.

'Let me see. Ah,' he smiled, 'strange how these meaningless phrases come to mean so much. I took a hansom to the

Diogenes. My rooms are in Jermyn Street – one day I'll walk it. The clock was striking the half hour in the lobby. That must have been half past seven, I suppose. Mycroft met me and escorted me here. Watson had already arrived. We went into dinner. Excellent fare. And then Mycroft was called away. One of the club members taken ill. I remember hoping it wasn't the pork.' He chuckled. 'When Mycroft returned, he told us the man was dead. He couldn't say more in the dining room. He'd used up his three conversations to us in passing the cruet. Watson took me into the Snug. The poor man gave me a copy of *The Times*. In the excitement, he'd forgotten I couldn't read it. The dear man was quite upset, but I told him not to trouble himself. He'll get his reward in heaven.'

'Won't we all,' murmured Lestrade.

'That's all I know. Until Boscombe fetched me, I'd heard nothing. What has happened, Inspector?'

'A man has been murdered, Mr Holmes. You chose a bad night to dine out.'

Lestrade left the blind man where he was, making successful inroads into the brandy and rejoined the corpse in the alcove. 'Poor old Waldo' was a man in his early sixties, he surmised; thinning grey hair, a monocle dangling now on his bloodied chest. Lestrade checked the position of the body. Never leave to a coroner what you can do better yourself. It lay back on the velvet, hard now with dried blood. The newspaper lay in a discarded heap on the table, together with an empty glass. Lestrade fished out his Apache knife cum knuckle duster and scooped the glass up on the blade. He sniffed. Port. He wasn't gentleman enough to tell how good, bad or indifferent it was. A club member walked past, studiously avoiding the sniffing policeman and the stiffened corpse. What did it take, Lestrade wondered, for anyone to take notice in the place? He checked the carpet under the deceased's feet. Unmarked. No sign of a struggle. He looked with the aid of an oil lamp at the wound itself. Mycroft Holmes had been right – a slim, narrow blade through the centre of the heart. Lestrade felt gingerly along the shoulder blade and realised Holmes had been wrong. No stiletto could have gone straight through. The blade had been longer – a rapier, perhaps. And of course everybody carried rapiers in twentieth-century London.

'Well, that's it then,' a voice behind him whispered. Lestrade straightened. 'That's another damned by-election.'

It was Mycroft.

'By-election?' Lestrade echoed.

'Of course. I may not have known Hamilcar Waldo, Inspector, but I do know what he did for a living. He was a Member of Parliament.'

The Adventure of Roedean School

'Right, gentlemen!' Sergeant Walter Dew of the Criminal Investigation Department was getting into his stride nicely. He had held this august position for nearly three months by now and not a day had gone by without a reminder of the fact. Even Mrs Dew and the eight little Dews had to call him 'Sergeant'.

Tweedledum and Tweedledee, alias Constables Dickens and Jones, newly assigned to H Division, stood staring at the blackboard, on which were scrawled in the joined-up writing at which Dew was improving all the time, the facts of the case of Major Deering, late Carabiniers.

'Mr Lestrade has much to occupy his time. Two other murders on his desk. So he has given me the honour of solving this one. And while other officers are out ... er ... following leads – that's the phrase we use here, you know – I intend to teach you lads a bit about policing. So, Jones. What have we got?'

'Sergeant?'

'What are the facts as presented in this case?' Dew was being as patient as he knew how.

'Well, Sarge—'

'Sergeant.'

'Well, Sergeant. We have a corpse. Major John Deering, age forty-one. Late Sixth Dragoon Guards.'

'Modus of opera?'

Constable Jones looked oddly at him.

'Death was due to shock as a result of being skewered by a cavalry lance.'

'And how do we know that?' Dew paced the floor, his hands locked behind him, contorting his lips much after the manner of a ruminating cow.

'The coroner's report, sir.'

'And what do we know about coroner's reports, lad?'

'Sergeant?'

'You remember the old rhyme, surely – "Five per cent wit, ninety per cent shit" – all right?'

'Sergeant?' Dickens interrupted.

'What is it, lad?' Dew was polishing the frosted glass of Lestrade's door.

'What happened to the other five per cent?'

'What?'

But Dew was saved any mathematical embarrassment by a knock at the door he was polishing. Indeed, the knocker's knuckles bounced dangerously near his nose.

'Yes?' he opened it to reveal the desk sergeant. 'Hello, Tom. How's the missus?'

'Same as ever,' grunted the other, 'suicidal. You owe me two bob from last Friday. That horse had three legs—'

'Thank you, Sergeant.' Dew stiffened as the Donegal and bowler swept along the corridor. 'I'll be sure to give Inspector Lestrade the telegram. Ah, there you are, sir.'

Lestrade snatched the missive the sergeant had brought with the air of a man in a hurry. 'Dickens, tea,' he ordered, and threw himself into the worn old chair. The blackboard caught his eye, but it only caused minor bruising. And when he'd recovered, he read Dew's jottings.

'I see you've been playing at being a policeman again, Walter.'

The sergeant blushed a little, needled by the attitude of his superior officer in front of the constables.

'No, seriously, Sergeant. You can forget all that. I have a sneaky feeling that we are not talking about three murderers but one. Gentlemen, what do Ralph Childers, John Deering and Hamilcar Waldo have in common?'

'They're dead, sir,' Jones announced proudly.

Lestrade's look would have calcified a brighter man.

'Think again,' he said.

There was silence.

'Were they all single, sir?'

'No, Dickens. Waldo was married, though not closely. Do your homework.'

'Wasn't there mention of a certain club, sir?' Dew hazarded.

'The Hell Fire, yes. But as far as I know so far, only Childers was a member of that. Unless there's more to the Diogenes than meets the eye. Childers was a member of that, too. You're getting warm, Dew.'

'Give up, sir,' said Jones cheerily.

'Well, that runs in the family,' Lestrade observed. 'Politics, gentlemen. Ralph Childers and Hamilcar Waldo were both Members of Parliament. John Deering had intended to resign his commission and go into politics. No one but his commanding officer seems to have known that, probably because politics isn't discussed in cavalry messes.'

'So it's a job for Special Branch?' Dew was excelling himself.

'You're excelling yourself, Dew.' Lestrade had noticed too. 'But I'll rot in Hell before I hand this one over to that bunch of maniacs.'

'Would that be Inspector Bradstreet, sir?' Dickens asked.

'It would. When I knew him he was a sergeant. Amazing how promotion goes to people's heads.' For an unkind second, Lestrade flashed a glance at Dew. 'He's not a bad copper. But for the moment, we'll keep it to ourselves. Ah,' he took the steaming mug, 'the cup that cheers.'

As he sipped, contemplating Dew's puerile scribblings on the board, he opened the telegram. His face darkened as he read it. He snatched up the battered Gladstone.

'Dickens. Jones. How would you like some sea air?'

'Sir?' they chorused.

'Get your things. We're off to Rottingdean.'

'Rottingdean?' Dew repeated.

'Rottingdean,' Dickens answered. 'A small resort on the

south east coast between Brighton and Newhaven. The beach is rocky and the houses are built of the same flinty—'

'Thank you, Constable,' Lestrade swigged the last of his tea.

'Sergeant, tell His Nims where we've gone. Attempted murder of a celebrity, national figure etc. He'll like that. We'll be back Thursday.'

'Right, sir.' Dew made for the door, bellowing for a constable as he reached it, 'Macnee! Get in here!'

'Walter,' Lestrade extended an avuncular arm around his sergeant's shoulders, 'you want to get on, don't you? Be somebody in the CID?'

'Oh, yes, sir.' Dew squared his shoulders.

'Well then, remember,' Lestrade was whispering, 'a sergeant may shout, but an inspector calls.'

Carrie Kipling hadn't expected three officers of Scotland Yard by the afternoon train, but three they were, Donegalled and bowlered despite the mellow warmth of May.

'He isn't here, Inspector. Rudyard is at the school, helping the police with their enquiries.'

'The school, ma'am?'

'Roedean, Inspector. Where it all happened.'

'You'd better tell me the full story, Mrs Kipling. Jones, your pad.'

At Mrs Kipling's behest, the policemen sat in the drawing room and listened to the extent of the problem.

'It all began over a year ago, at least, that's when Rudyard first told me about it. He didn't think much of it at first. A horseless carriage backfiring. A narrow miss with a tram. A stampeding herd of cattle – we were in Calgary at the time,' she offered by way of explanation when she saw Lestrade's incomprehension. 'Rudyard put it all down to coincidence, accident. But yesterday. There could be no mistaking yesterday. I rang the police at once. He hesitated and then sent you a telegram.'

'What happened yesterday, Mrs Kipling?'

'I am still reeling from the shock, Inspector.' Carrie Kipling looked remarkably solid to Lestrade.

'Excuse me, sir,' Jones butted in, 'how do you spell Calgary, Mrs Kipling?'

Lestrade flashed an inspectorial glance in the constable's direction and he withered on the spot.

'Please go on,' he said.

'Well, Rudyard was invited to a Founders' Day celebration at Roedean. He's such a silly when it comes to girls. I think it's because we lost our favourite, you see.' She smiled and Lestrade noticed her eyes shining at the portrait Mr Kipling had been holding when he was last there. 'There were several dignitaries – oh, no one quite of dear Rudyard's stature, of course—'

'Your husband is a big man, Mrs Kipling?' Dickens interjected.

'I'll ask the questions, thank you, Constable,' said Lestrade, 'you stand by with your trusty penknife should Jones' pencil give out.' Dickens folded in on himself like a pack of cards.

'Rudyard had just risen to make his speech. He'd read it to me the night before. It was marvellous. When, suddenly, while the applause was still ringing out, a maniac stepped forward and fired at my husband . . .'

A superbly timed handkerchief fluttered into view and Carrie Kipling blew her nose with a resonance not quite becoming the wife of a possible future Poet Laureate. They waited for her to recover.

'The bullet was wide of the mark, thank the Lord, but the assassin escaped in the confusion.'

'Did Mr Kipling – did anyone – get a good look at this man?'

'I fear not, Inspector. My husband's eyesight is not of the best. At school, they called him Giglamps, you know, because of his spectacles.'

'Indeed so, ma'am.'

Mrs Kipling could help them no further. With various reassurances they left her, although Lestrade left Dickens at the front door in case some maniac should try again, assuming the master of the house to be at home. The inspector and his remaining constable caught a cab to the school.

Roedean School for Ladies of Good Family was a new building on the broad sweep of the downs above the sea where Lestrade had stumbled, naked but for his trusty Donegal weeks earlier. Now, despite the fact that the young ladies of those good families lived in, the playing fields were deserted and the place had a general air of fear and stealth. Two police vehicles, stamped with the crest of the Sussex Constabulary, tried to look inconspicuous under a clump of elms. Here and there, pairs of policemen patrolled, in the time-honoured tradition, bull's-eyes and truncheons swinging at their waists.

Lestrade announced his presence to the constable on the door and entered the main hall. Why was it, he wondered, that all schools, even this one for young ladies, smelt like that? Only the liniment and linseed oil for the cane was missing from this one. It had not been from his own. The officers from Scotland Yard entered a large hall, with high oriel windows and a platform at the far end. Lestrade took in the neat rows of wooden chairs, the music stands now derelict and behind him as he turned a minstrels' gallery with winding stairs.

'That's him!' a voice shrieked from nowhere. 'That nasty little man in the Donegal. I'd know that ferret face anywhere.'

The hall was suddenly alive with uniformed men, who variously laid hands on Lestrade. Jones too was leapt upon, his head forced to the ground and a knee jammed into the small of his back while his hands were wrenched behind him and the cuffs put on.

'Are you sure, ma'am?' A burly grey-haired figure led the way, but he was dwarfed by a giant apparition in frothy blouse who lurched forward to identify the culprit.

'I am positive, Inspector. Arrest him at once!'

Lestrade was prevented from commenting on any of this by the firmness with which a constable's hand covered his mouth.

'I arrest you in the name of the law. You are charged with the attempted murder of Mr Rudyard Kipling on the—'

'Imbecile!' roared the iron matron. 'This is not the man. He's a foot too short!'

The local inspector looked perplexed.

'Then why—'

'This is the sickening monster who exposed himself to me and my girls last month. Lurking in the bushes, he was, and unless I am mistaken, wearing that same Donegal.' She bridled. 'He was certainly wearing the same leer.'

Lestrade attempted a defence, but a gurgle was all he managed.

'I've heard that criminals always return to the scene of their crimes. You bestial swine!' And she walloped Lestrade around the head with a sheaf of papers.

'Lestrade!' a voice called from overhead. Everybody looked up to where Gigger Kipling was peering myopically over the gallery rail. 'You've got the wrong man!'

He scuttled down the stairs to the tableau in the hall.

'Inspector, you are about to arrest a fellow officer.'

'What?' the iron matron roared. 'This Peeping Tom is a policeman? Disgusting!'

The constables relaxed their grip on Lestrade and Jones.

'It's what I've come to expect now that the old Queen has gone. It's a world gone mad,' she went on.

'Who are you?' the inspector asked the inspector.

'I might ask you the same thing,' Lestrade retorted.

'I asked first.' The conversation was already degenerating.

'Inspector Sholto Lestrade, Scotland Yard.'

'Oh.' The local man's face fell and his constables stood sheepishly by, vaguely wishing the ground would swallow them. 'Inspector Daniel Clutterbuck, Sussex Constabulary. Er ... I'm sorry, Mr Lestrade. I appear to have been a little over-zealous.'

Lestrade brushed himself down, 'No real harm done, Mr Clutterbuck. Jones?'

'I'm all right, sir.' The constable was trying to bend his neck back into position.

'When you have finished being polite to each other,' the grey lady stormed. 'This man, from Scotland Yard or not, is a pervert, Inspector. I demand that you take some action.'

Clutterbuck looked agonised. God knew, he wasn't fond of the Yard, but to arrest his equal, nay, his superior, on the insistence of a madwoman was risking all. In the event, it was Lestrade who took charge.

'Who might you be, madam?'

'I might be Lord Salisbury!' she replied.

No, thought Lestrade, the beard isn't full enough.

'In point of fact, I am Miss Lawrence, Headmistress of Roedean School.'

'Then, Miss Lawrence, I would like to talk to you in your study. Clutterbuck, whatever you've done so far, I want a detailed account of it. And post some constables at Mr Kipling's house in Rottingdean. You'll find one of my men there. Constable Jones here will take notes. He's getting quite good at it.'

'I will not be alone with this man.' Miss Lawrence was obdurate.

'May I act as chaperone, Miss Lawrence?' Kipling suggested.

She reflected for a moment. A man who wrote such stirring poetry and such beautiful stories for children was surely a man to trust. 'Very well,' she assented.

Kipling winked at Lestrade and they followed her through cheerless corridors to a panelled door. Here a willowy child in school uniform stood, curtseying as the headmistress approached.

'Oh, not again, Annabelle. I've told you before about those second helpings of mince, have I not? Go and find Nurse – and quickly!' The pale child vanished. Miss Lawrence suddenly lunged sideways and crashed through another door.

'Remember the ablative absolute!' she bellowed.

'Yes, Miss Lawrence,' a dozen voices trilled.

Lestrade and Kipling looked at each other, each according to his level of understanding and his upbringing, rather surprised by the meaninglessness of the remark.

'Gentleman,' Miss Lawrence ushered them into her study, 'and Inspector Lestrade.'

'May we clear up one thing?' Lestrade ventured.

Miss Lawrence raised a matriarchal eyebrow.

'I am entirely innocent of the crime of which you accuse me. The truth is I was set upon by paid ruffians in Brighton and deposited senseless in your playing fields. My clothes, with the exception of the Donegal, had been stolen.'

The headmistress looked unsure.

'It's true, Miss Lawrence,' Gigger confirmed. Thank God, thought Lestrade, for one sane voice in all this.

'If you say so, Mr Kipling, then it must, perforce, be so.' She gave him a saccharine smile which sent Lestrade's scalp crawling with unease. He preferred the Medusa scowl any day. 'But,' and it duly appeared, 'on no account will you interview any of my young ladies unless I am present throughout. Is that understood? It's high time there were women on constabulary forces, revolting though I find the idea.'

If they were all like you, Lestrade mused, the rest of us could go home.

'Now, madam, to the events of yesterday.'

But the redoubtable Miss Lawrence had barely embarked on her tale when the door opened and two ladies, larger and more terrible than she, swept in.

'Violet, my dear. We came as quickly as we could,' said the first, hugging and patting the headmistress.

'Petronella, how kind. Agatha, my dearest.' And the claspings to matronly bosoms were only disturbed by a discreet clearing of the throat from Lestrade.

'Oh.' The headmistress remembered the presence of the men. 'These gentlemen are involved in their differing ways in the horrors of yesterday. Oh, I don't know what the bishop must have thought. This is Mr Kipling, the poet and author. My sisters, founders with me of this school – Petronella and Agatha.'

'Charmed, ladies,' Kipling bowed ceremoniously.

'Ah, Mr Kipling. I particularly liked your Departmental Ditties. May I ask what you are working on now?'

'A tale of the Raj has just been published, ma'am. It is called *Kim*.'

'How marvellous!' Petronella clapped her hands excitedly.

'Ladies, may we return to the matter in hand?'

The withering look of all three Miss Lawrences was directed at Lestrade.

'This is a policeman,' the headmistress informed her sisters.

'From Scotland Yard.' Lestrade felt he ought to establish some sort of level. 'Ladies, may I ask you to retire until I have spoken with your sister?'

'We *have* retired, young man,' Petronella informed him.

'Anything Violet has to say concerning this school concerns us.' Agatha was defiant.

'Very well,' Lestrade bowed to the inevitable, 'but first, would you tell me why two out of the three founders of Roedean were not present on Founders' Day?'

Agatha blushed the colour of her sister's curtains.

Petronella blustered, 'Personal reasons. Absolutely nothing to do with you. Violet sent us a telegram last evening. We came as quickly as we could. Poor dear.' And the sisters began again the handkerchief-waving routine they had just finished.

'Miss Lawrence.' Lestrade's patience was wearing a little thin.

'Yes,' they all chorused.

'Your story, ma'am.' He tried to be gentler.

'Well, Inspector, the day was progressing well. There had been that nasty moment when the Bishop of Bath and Wells had fallen down the stairs, but I am a great believer in splints. Mr Kipling was about to speak – *such* a speaker –' she gushed in Gigger's direction, 'when suddenly, there was a scuffle at the back of the hall, under the minstrels' gallery. I thought at once it was Angelique—'

Again the Lawrence sisters chorused in assent.

'Angelique?' Lestrade repeated.

'Angelique D'Umfraville. Our French girl. Not quite the

ticket. Given to odd bursts of nervous energy.'

'She is deranged, young man.' Petronella was more direct.

'A trifle strong, Petra, old thing. A trifle strong—'

'It was not Angelique,' Lestrade broke in. Anything, he thought, to prevent them from going off at a tandem.

'Indeed no. The cut of the deerstalker was all wrong for her.'

'Deerstalker?' said Lestrade.

'That is what I said, Inspector. One of those shooting caps that disgusting man Keir Hardie wears. This man stepped forward, as though dressed for a coach journey and aimed a gun at Mr Kipling.'

Miss Lawrence wavered, but was saved from total collapse by a bottle of smelling salts thrust under her nose by Agatha.

'And then?' Lestrade pressed, once Violet's eyeballs had ceased to swivel.

'We all just stood there, rooted to the spot. There was a report—'

'The chairman of the governors' report, dear?' Petronella asked for clarification.

'A gunshot, dear lady.' It was Kipling who translated for her.

'I don't remember much else. The bishop fell over again, I do remember that, because the poor man broke his other arm.'

'He must look rather like a windmill,' Agatha ruminated.

'There was screaming and panic. But, I must say, the gels behaved admirably. Two or three of them took after the fiend, I understand, with hockey sticks.'

'Did you recognise the man?' Lestrade asked.

'No. He was tall.'

'I thought of medium height,' said Kipling.

'Would you know him again?'

'Most assuredly,' asserted the headmistress.

'Possibly,' hedged the poet.

'Mr Kipling, may I talk with you? Misses Lawrence, thank you for your patience. I shall need to talk with all those who were present yesterday, especially those at the back of the hall.'

'My gels have been subjected to enough, Inspector.' Violet

was on her feet, lowering down at Lestrade. 'Shot at, bullied by policemen from Sussex, and now threatened again by policemen from London. The Lord knows what the newspapers will do with all this. I shan't have a gel left. Roedean must close.'

Petronella and Agatha supported the wilting Violet as Lestrade bowed three times and took his exit with Gigger.

'What do you make of the weird sisters?' Kipling asked Lestrade as they reached the gravel drive.

'I don't know what our education system is coming to,' observed Lestrade. 'Tell me, this man who is trying to kill you. Why didn't you mention him when we last met?'

'The whole thing wasn't apparent – until yesterday. You must understand, dear Lestrade, that a man in my position makes enemies. If you support the things I do, you must expect to encounter opposition. True, that opposition usually appears in the form of literary critiques or angry letters to *The Times*. But after yesterday, any vague sense of unease has now crystallised. What I took to be a series of unrelated incidents are now obviously attempts at murder – mine.'

'And yesterday? The man with the deerstalker?'

'I was probably the last to see him. These poor old eyes of mine,' he rubbed them behind the thick lenses, 'years of close work by candlelight. By the time I'd focused he was firing.'

'Did you see the gun?'

'I think it was a carbine. Too short for a Lee-Metford, though. Perhaps a Martini-Henry.'

'Your poor old eyes couldn't make out the man, but you could tell the make of a gun, whose narrow end was towards you, what,' Lestrade glanced back at the hall behind them, 'sixty, seventy feet away.'

'Ah, but I know my guns, Inspector. I did establish a rifle club down the road.'

'Am I right in assuming that a carbine is a weapon used by cavalry?'

'And mounted infantry.' Kipling had recently returned from the theatre of war.

'A pity we couldn't make some headway there,' Lestrade mused.

'But we can, Inspector. Don't you have coroner chappies who dig bullets out of people?'

'Er . . . yes,' said Lestrade, not following Kipling's drift.

'Well, then. Have a rummage around in poor old Arthur L'Estrange. You must come up with something. Isn't it called ballistics?'

'Arthur L'Estrange?' Lestrade had stopped walking.

'Yes.' Kipling began to realise something was amiss. 'My dear fellow, has no one told you? The bullet that was meant for me went wide as Miss Lawrence told you, but it hit another guest of Founders' Day, standing feet from me. When I think how close I came—'

'Where is he now?'

'L'Estrange? In the morgue, I suppose. Isn't that where you chappies put people? Better ask Clutterbuck.'

'I will. Now, to your description of the man under the deerstalker . . .'

The poet and the policeman strolled along the downs for an hour or more, Lestrade learning all he could of the various attempted murders. In the end, for all the informant's powers of observation as a storyteller of distinction, it was vague and inconclusive. A man of medium height, middle build, clean shaven, though possibly with a moustache; hair – so-so; eyes – indeterminate; no other distinguishing features. Only the deerstalker and the Ulster and a short gun. The last at least made sense. The gun would need to be short to fit under the Ulster and not attract attention. People didn't go to speech days armed openly with Martini-Henrys. Not even at Roedean.

For a day and a half, Lestrade, Jones and Dickens went over the ground traversed with enormous feet by the Sussex Constabulary. Dickens got the gels – forty-three of them who all swore they were standing right next to the assassin. It was interesting that when Inspector Clutterbuck had asked for such eyewitnesses, he had got one, an odd, manic young lady named

Angelique something or other. When young, blue-eyed Dickens asked, the queue went round the chapel. Jones got the staff, except the redoubtable Miss Lawrence, who now refused to speak to any policeman below the rank of Chief Superintendent. Lestrade telegraphed Nimrod Frost whose answer was to the point, monosyllabic and rather Anglo-Saxon. Lestrade himself interviewed the guests – septuagenarian governors and Friends of the School, variously cobwebbed and mildewed – all screaming to the best of their abilities that the country was going to the dogs and why weren't the Labour Party behind bars? Lestrade coped as best he could and spent the day he had promised to return to London knee deep in depositions in Clutterbuck's office, drabber and more tawdry than his own, in the less salubrious part of Brighton. The only thing which kept him going, apart from endless cups of tea, was the fact that Jones had unearthed a carrier, delivering to the school on that day, who had come from Goodwood. Said carrier knew the Lawrence sisters well and had seen them that morning. Lestrade now knew that the personal reason intimated by Petronella Lawrence to explain their absence from Founders' Day, was that Diamond Jubilee was running in the two-thirty and they were having a flutter.

The corpse of Arthur L'Estrange told him one thing only – and that he knew already – namely that the man had been shot. After interminable queries as to whether the inspector and the deceased were related on account of the similarity of their names, the coroner showed Lestrade the entry wound, high above the heart. The bullet must have hit the shoulder blade and deflected to smash the aorta. Death occurred within minutes. The bullet? The coroner showed it to Lestrade. It had probably come from a Martini-Henry. That narrowed the field down to a few thousand.

Lestrade was dozing by the oil lamp in Clutterbuck's back room late that night, when his eyes fell fleetingly on a folded copy of the Brighton *Argus*. The banner headlines read, 'Brighton Mourns MP'. Lestrade's stupor gave way to amazement as he read the rest. A lavish funeral was planned for the following Wednesday. No expense was to be spared. It was hoped the Bishop of Bath and Wells could be winched in to conduct the service. A glowing obituary followed. Yes, Brighton would miss the man who had served it faithfully and well for nigh on seven years. It would miss the Right Honourable Arthur L'Estrange.

It was with a mixture of emotions that Lestrade broke the news to Rudyard Kipling the following morning. In Lestrade's view, and it was still a guess, though one borne of years of experience, the maniac in the deerstalker had not been an erratic shot. The fatal bullet was not at all wide of the mark. On the contrary, it had found its home.

The Fine Oloroso Problem

That was the summer that Nimrod Frost died. Rumour had it that he had been ill for years, a shadow of his former self. Those in the know claimed it was the strain of the job that killed him. No one in the City Force was in the least surprised. Faced with a rabble like the Metropolitan Police, the man had obviously found it all too much and had taken his own life. Miss Featherstonehaugh knew better. It was the endless sugar and cream that finally got him, that and the exertion of pressing the button in the lift each morning. She had warned him and reminded everyone of the fact at every conceivable opportunity. A man couldn't go on carrying that weight around indefinitely. There were those, of course, and at times Lestrade was one of them, who reasoned that Frost's arteries had hardened in order to escape further contact with Miss Featherstonehaugh – but perhaps that was unkind.

It was an impressive funeral for a grocer's son from Grantham. The commissioner was there, of course. Sir Frederick Ponsonby represented the King. Chief Superintendent Abberline was chief mourner and most of the other superintendents came. Because of the deceased's nineteen stone, it took six bobbies rather than the customary four, to carry the coffin, draped in purple velvet and surmounted by Frost's cap and ceremonial sword. The stream of policemen, uniformed and plainclothes, stretched for nearly a mile. Frost would have liked that. Even a few of the underworld came to pay their grudging respects, standing like shadows along High Holborn, their caps in their hands. Frost would have liked that even more.

It was a curious choice of cemetery, the graveyard of St Sepulchre's. Mrs Frost, erect and dignified throughout, explained through the vicar that dear Nimrod had expressed a wish to be buried near to Newgate, to keep an eye as it were, on the reprobates he and his men had put there. She had not, apparently, realised that they had pulled Newgate down and as the procession reached the church, the workmen on the roof of the criminal court in the Bailey tugged off their caps.

Lestrade looked up at the gilded figure they were winching into position. Justice, sworded and balanced. He mused again, as he had countless times before, on the ambiguities of her blindness. He read the inscription on the great bronze bell: 'And when St Sepulchre's bell in the morning tolls, the Lord have mercy on your souls.' But it tolled for executions no longer. As he took his seat, with Bradstreet and the other inspectors of the Yard, he noticed the fresh cement at the entrance to the tunnel which had led to Newgate's condemned cell. It was a tunnel he knew all too well. More than once, he'd walked that way himself, with men bound for the gallows. Now, they were even considering the removal of the black flag to show the crowd that justice had been done. What was the world coming to? The smugness of Miss Featherstonehaugh at last gave way and she sobbed quietly into Dew's handkerchief as the Scotland Yard Glee Club broke into 'Nearer My God to Thee'.

It was nearly three weeks before Nimrod Frost was replaced. In that time, Lestrade absented himself again and with Sergeant Dew at his elbow, returned once more to Brighton. At the height of June, this was clearly a mistake. The sun burned fiercely through the serge which a sergeant's pay allowed him to buy. Had Dew's spelling been better, he might have made a whimsical connection between his rank and the material of his suit. As it was, he contented himself with sweating. And envying the cooler attire of his guv'nor, nattily turned out in white waistcoat and boater. There were children everywhere, scampering between the two men as they strolled the promenade. More than once, Dew 'accidentally' tripped a sailor-suited darling and offered the most hollow of apologies to it and its adjacent parents.

Lestrade waded through the dollops of dropped ice-cream and made for the Grand Hotel, magnificent in the ivory of its classical lines. He flicked open the register, despite the protestations of the clerk and found what he wanted, staying in room 15. The officers of the Yard took the stairs and waited for the occupant to answer the knock.

'Good morning, Captain Deering. So glad I found you.'

'Who the devil are you?'

'Tut, tut.' Lestrade pushed past the good captain, still in smoking jacket and carpet slippers, 'Lestrade of the Yard. This is Sergeant Dew. And you have a very short memory.'

'Oh, yes,' Deering was calmer. 'Well, what do you want? I haven't finished my breakfast.'

'I am continuing my enquiries into your brother's death, sir.' Lestrade trailed round the room, observing in a desultory way, calculated to irritate the officer of Carabiniers. Dew stood like a door stop to prevent any escape. Lestrade had not discussed tactics with him, but he knew his guv'nor too well not to be ready for any eventuality. He stood with one hand poised over his notebook and the other near his cuffs, ready to leap into action with either or both.

'I believe your brother's murder to be one of a number.' Lestrade looked levelly at Deering. 'The common factor in all of them is politics.'

'Politics?' Deering looked blank.

'Your brother was about to leave the regiment. To resign his commission and enter politics.'

Deering stood with his mouth open, the buttered toast drooping limply in his hand.

'Rubbish. Preposterous nonsense!' he finally managed.

'I must ask you, sir, as perhaps the man closest to your brother. What party was he about to join?'

'Damn your impudence, Lestrade!' Deering slammed down the wilted toast. 'A man's politics is his own business. We do have the ballot, you know! I mightn't agree with it totally, but I'll be damned if I discuss my brother's convictions with a common policeman.'

Dew shifted uncomfortably. He'd never really thought of the inspector as a common policeman, but then he hadn't realised the late John Deering had any convictions, either. He wondered momentarily what they were for.

'Ezekiah Williams,' Lestrade said quietly.

'Who?'

'One of your troop, isn't he?'

'Williams, you say?'

'You are trying my patience, Captain Deering!' Lestrade stepped forward. 'Shall we pay a call on Colonel Gilmartin this morning?'

Deering's composure temporarily failed him. 'All right, Lestrade. What do you want?

'We'll overlook the fact that you or Captain Sheraton or both hired four regimental thugs to beat the living daylights out of me. If I chose to push matters, you'd go to jail for four years for that.'

Lestrade perambulated again. 'We'll also overlook the Army Remount business—'

Deering was back on the attack again, 'You haven't a shred of proof. I . . .' and he fell silent.

Well, thought Lestrade smugly, amazing what targets shots in the dark can find.

'As far as I am aware, Inspector, my brother always voted for the Conservative and Unionist Party. But as God is my judge, I had no inkling he planned to leave the regiment. Er . . . about the . . . other business . . .'

'All I lost was my consciousness and a bit of pride, Captain,' Lestrade answered, 'but take care our paths don't cross again, or I'll call it attempted murder.'

The policemen made for the sunlight.

'Army Remount Service, sir?' Dew was the first to break silence.

'You read about it, surely, Dew? The papers were full of it. I was fishing.'

'And what did you catch, sir?' Dew was proud of himself for taking up the metaphor.

'The quarter past twelve train to Victoria, Dew. If we hurry.'

Mr Edward Henry was the umpteenth occupant of the Assistant Commissioner's office on the first floor of Scotland Yard. Rowbottom, Anderson, McNaghten, Frost, they had come and gone. And now Lestrade stood on the timeworn carpet, the one Rowbottom had brought from Egypt, facing the Coming Man. Rumours had been flying around the Yard for weeks. He was from India, some said. A Jat. Others claimed he was from South Africa. Black as your hat. Still others reckoned he was a Boer spy. Inspector Bradstreet of the Special Branch would have to watch him.

'What's this?' the small, balding, dark-skinned little man said to Lestrade.

'It's your finger, sir.' Lestrade was convinced this was some sort of initiative test.

'No, no, man, on the end of my finger.'

'A nail, sir?' Lestrade was doing his best.

'Are you deliberately being obtuse, Inspector?'

Lestrade cleared his throat. In effect, he refused to answer on the grounds that it might incriminate him.

'We've met before, you know,' Henry went on, 'the Belper Committee, in 'ninety-nine.'

Realisation dawned. 'Forgive me, sir. Of course. Finger-prints.'

'Fingerprints,' beamed Henry, 'you've read my book?'

'Er . . . no, sir.'

Henry's face fell, the walrus moustache obscuring his chin completely.

'But I have been taking fingerprints from known criminals for about six years, sir.'

'Yes, I remember your testimony before the Belper people. I was impressed, Lestrade. Now, I want your help. I want to set up a Fingerprint Department, here at the Yard. Chief Superintendent Abberline suggests a sergeant named Collins. Your views?'

'Stockley Collins is a good man,' Lestrade concurred, though it stuck in his throat to have to agree with anything Abberline suggested.

'What would the chaps think of such a venture, Lestrade? You must have your ear pretty close to the ground. How would they view it?'

'Would you like the political answer, sir? Or the truth?'

'When you come to know me better, Lestrade, you'll know that I will settle for nothing but the truth.'

So help me, God, mused Lestrade to himself. 'Most of my brother officers are still taking the inside leg measurement of known criminals, sir. Some of them wouldn't know a fingerprint if it upped and bit them.'

'That's what Abberline said.' Henry nodded.

Damn, thought Lestrade, twice in one day.

'Now, to your caseload, Lestrade. You'd better sit down.'

God, thought Lestrade, is it as large as that?

'You smell conspiracy?'

'The coincidence seems extraordinary if not, sir.'

'Coincidence?' Henry pursued his man with the ferocity of a miffed ferret.

'The fact that all the deceased had a parliamentary connection.'

'So do I, Lestrade. My cab passes Parliament Square every morning. So, I imagine, does yours.'

'I walk in the summer, sir.'

'What about this one?' Henry consulted the typed papers on his desk. 'John Deering. He was a soldier.'

'But one with political leanings, sir. As the report says—'

'I've read the report, Lestrade. And up to this point, I buy your story. But either Major Deering is a different case altogether, or your whole theory falls flat. Consider the methods of murder. What do we have? One man tortured to death, another impaled on a lance, a third shot. What sort of murderer employs that range of methods?'

'Are you familiar with the Struwwelpeter case, sir?'

'I've read those reports too, Lestrade. But you didn't catch your man there, did you?'

Lestrade was stung by the rebuke. It was untrue. He had caught his man, but for old reasons, for personal reasons, he had not committed the fact to paper.

'Are you saying this is the work of the Struwwelpeter maniac?'

'No, sir.'

'So positive?'

Lestrade smiled. 'Let's just say I have a sixth sense.'

'I'm not sure how much sense you have, Lestrade. It will take me time to learn that. In the meantime,' Henry rang a little silver bell on the desk, 'I think we'll play it my way.'

There was a knock and two men entered, both known to Lestrade and both calculated to get right under his skin.

'Lestrade, you know Inspectors Gregory and Bradstreet?'

'Intimately, sir.'

'Let's assume for a moment that your conspiracy theory is correct – that someone is killing off Members of Parliament. If that is a fair assumption, it is a job for the Special Branch. The Commissioner has graciously allowed us the time and talents of Bradstreet, here.'

'Sholto.' The aforementioned grinned icily.

'Edgar,' Lestrade replied with the affability of a corpse.

'Bradstreet, your views,' Henry gestured to the newcomer to sit.

'Well, sir, at first sight it looks like the Irish.'

Lestrade's eyebrows disappeared under his hairline, which gave them a fair distance to travel. How often had he heard this rubbish? From a man of Bradstreet's intelligence, he'd hoped for better.

'Why?' Henry badgered him.

'Ralph Childers, Arthur L'Estrange and Hamilcar Waldo were all Conservatives – and Unionists. Natural targets of the Fenians.'

'We haven't seen a Fenian in the last twelve years,' Lestrade replied.

'Allow me to correct you—' Bradstreet began.

'Gentlemen, gentlemen,' Henry refereed, 'it seems to me there is room in this enquiry for Inspector Bradstreet to pursue the Irish track and for Inspector Gregory to follow other lines.'

'Gregory?' Lestrade was unaware of the man's involvement in the case.

'Gregory will be working with Dew and your men during your leave, Lestrade.'

'My leave?' Lestrade was on his feet.

'Yes. I intend to give all my officers a period of leave as soon as possible. It will have to be staggered, of course. I'm giving you a week – next week to be precise. I know what overwork can do. It makes you stale, careless.'

'With respect, Mr Henry, I don't—'

'I'll brook no arguments, Lestrade. You will take your leave. Gregory will keep you posted on your return. Well, gentlemen, I think that must suffice for now. I have a meeting with His Majesty.'

The inspectors filed out, Lestrade smarting from this first encounter more than somewhat.

'Sorry, Sholto,' said Bradstreet, 'it really wasn't my idea.'

'When we worked together last, Edgar, you were a sergeant. As far as seniority goes, I still outrank you.' It was beneath Lestrade's dignity, unworthy of him, perhaps. But he was miffed. He turned to Gregory, acknowledged by all and sundry as the Most Boring Man at the Yard, a title he had held, behind his back, for four consecutive years.

'Tom, don't tread on my feet, there's an old love.' Lestrade patted his shoulder.

'Do my best, old chap. I say, have you fellows heard the one about the bishop and the chorus-girl?'

'Yes,' echoed Lestrade and Bradstreet in unison and left their colleague telling the tale to a hat stand before he realised they had gone. At the end of the corridor, the inspectors went their separate ways.

It had been three years since Lestrade had seen her. Three long years of aching feet, of clicking typewriters, of stewed, cold tea and wet socks. He kept telling himself, give it up man, give it up. Put in for retirement. But what would he do? The pension went nowhere. He had no yen, like Dew the Semi-Literate, to write his memoirs. He didn't like petunias and the thought of growing them for the rest of his life filled him with foreboding. What, then? Nightwatchman? Jailer? Tinker? Tailor? Soldier? He was too old, too stubborn, too proud and too ham-fisted for any of these. Harry Bandicoot of course, years before, had found himself a rich widow ... There was still, perhaps, even now, that possibility. And it was to Harry's he caught the train. To see her again. Three years. How had she changed? Would she know him now? What would he say to her?

These thoughts and a jumble of others rolled around the grey area he called a brain. Even as he reached the door and rang the bell, nothing was resolved. He renewed his acquaintance with the butler and was shown into the grounds, where the family were taking tea.

'Sholto.' It was Harry who saw him first. Three years hadn't changed him. He must be in his late thirties by now, but apart from the air of affluence and tranquillity, he hadn't changed a jot since Lestrade first knew him, a young copper, lettuce-green. The huge, amiable Old Etonian heartily shook the hand of the raddled old Yard man. Bandicoot saw an older man before him, rather more perhaps of the ferret face attributed to him by the dubious Dr Watson and the collaborating Conan Doyle.

'Sholto, what a surprise.' Harry's wife, Letitia, ravishing as ever in the frothy lace of the first Edwardian summer, crushed him to her ample bosom.

'I should have written,' he said.

'Nonsense,' Letitia kissed his cheek, 'you're always welcome. You know that. Children!' she called down the lawn.

From the twisted old trees of the orchard, three baby Bandicoots scampered, laughing and tumbling. 'Say hello to Uncle Sholto,' Letitia said. The two boys hit him first, the time apart forgotten in a second as they climbed onto his lap.

'Rupert. Ivo. Don't hurt your Uncle,' Letitia scolded them.

'Now then, now then,' Lestrade did the bobby-on-the-beat impression he had done since the boys were in their cradles, seven years ago, 'you'd better come along with me, if you please,' and he buried a hand in a battered Gladstone. The boys fell silent and tried to peer into his bag, their eyes shining with excitement. Lestrade made a great play of lifting something heavy and then, in a move which astonished all present, handcuffed the boys together. They laughed and cackled, falling over each other on the floor in their attempt to get free.

'The cuffs are a present for you,' Lestrade said to them. 'And the key,' he handed it to Letitia, 'a present for your mother.' They all laughed.

Emma was slower, shyer than the boys. She came forward, nestling a little against Harry's legs. She wore a cream dress like Letitia's but it was not Letitia's eyes that looked up at her Uncle Sholto from beneath the bonnet. It was Sarah Lestrade's. Lestrade pulled from his Gladstone a doll, with a pale, smiling, china face. The little girl held out her hands and hugged Lestrade and the doll. The Inspector of Police pressed her gently to him, suddenly aware of his rough hands and the coarseness of his waistcoat. Little Emma pulled back and looked up at his face, drawing her fingers over the scars that crossed it, wondering in her own childish way where the top of his nose had gone. Sholto Lestrade had come home.

He stayed for three days, though he had intended not to stay at all. It was like another world, the Bandicoots' summer retreat. Warm and sunlit, noisy with the rough and tumble of the children and hot with the breath of dogs. That was the only thing that jarred a little. Lestrade had never been able to bring himself to like dogs. But Squires, Harry's gamekeeper, had them well trained and only the St Bernard, its nose constantly nudging Lestrade's groin, caused him any real worries.

On his last evening, Letitia had retired after a magnificent dinner, leaving Harry and Lestrade to their brandy and cigars. They discussed Kruger and the de Dion Harry had his eye on, Lestrade expressing his doubts whether the horse would ever be replaced by a lump of iron you had to pump up each morning. As a small boy, of course, he remembered the red flag.

'About Emma, Sholto.' Bandicoot suddenly changed tack.

'What about her?' Lestrade asked.

Bandicoot poured him another brandy. 'Letitia and I have been talking,' he said. 'We were wondering—'

'Is she a burden?' Lestrade asked.

'My dear fellow, absolutely not. When you asked us to take her in after . . . after Sarah died, we were delighted to be able to help. And we'll go on helping. For as long as you need us to. But . . .'

'But?' Lestrade blew smoke rings to the ceiling – the one thing he and Conan Doyle shared, a love of good shag.

'Damn it, Sholto, she is your daughter. You've seen her these past few days. She's a lovely girl. She ought to be with her father.'

'You haven't told her—' Lestrade sat upright.

'No, of course not. As far as Emma is concerned, Letitia and I are her parents and Rupert and Ivo are her brothers.'

'And that's how it must stay, Harry. For her sake.' Lestrade strolled to the window where the last glimmer of day was disappearing. 'Seven years ago, when Emma was born and Sarah died, I couldn't provide a home, not a real home for a little girl. I still can't, Harry. The only difference is that I'm older. Slower. I'm still living in rooms – and I don't exactly mean the Grand, either. Most of my life is in that Gladstone bag upstairs. Some nights, I don't go home. And one day, one night, who knows? Perhaps I won't come home again.'

He caught Bandicoot's look in the oil lamp's flicker. 'That sounds like self-pity, doesn't it? It isn't meant to. I've made my bed and I'm quite content to lie in it. But it's a single bed, Harry, and I can't take Emma back to it.'

He stubbed out the cigar. 'Better for her to know me as Uncle Sholto, and to see me now and then, if that's all right with you.'

'My dear fellow.' Bandicoot rose and placed a hand on his shoulder.

'It's late,' said Lestrade.

'It is,' Bandicoot agreed. 'And tomorrow you're going?'

Lestrade nodded.

'Yard can't do without you, eh?'

'It never could, Banders old thing. Only it hasn't realised that yet.'

'When does your leave end?'

'Wednesday.'

'Good. Then, tomorrow, you and I are going to an auction.'

'An auction?' Lestrade echoed.

'You've drunk me out of house and home the past three days,' Bandicoot was mock-indignant, 'I've got to replenish my stock of sherry!'

Lestrade read the catalogue again. 'For sale by auction, by Messrs Christie, Manson & Woods, at their Great Rooms, 8 King Street, 5000 dozen bottles of fine old sherry, all laid down before 1890 and conveyed from a number of Royal estates. Proceeds to the Prince of Wales' Hospital Fund.'

'Five thousand dozen,' Lestrade repeated as they entered the building.

'Defies belief, doesn't it?' Bandicoot agreed, 'and that's just surplus to requirements, you realise. I didn't know the old Queen was such a tippler.'

'Tsk, tsk,' scolded Lestrade, 'and you an Old Etonian.'

Bandicoot flustered. 'Oh, I meant no disrespect, Sholto, I assure you.'

Lestrade laughed. Fatherhood had not altered Harry Bandicoot one jot. He was still an idiot.

'Now there's someone who *is* a tippler. I thought he'd be here.' Bandicoot motioned to a corner of the crowded room. From his vantage point several inches lower, all Lestrade could see was a jostle of top hats. In his bowler, he felt decidedly out of place.

'Who's that?' he felt it polite to ask.

'Christian Barrett, the MP for my constituency. Drinks like a fish. Sherry?'

The policeman and the ex-policeman, retired, now of private means, each took a glass from the lackey's silvered tray. As they did so, a fanfare threatened to smash all the glassware in the place.

'That'll be His Majesty,' said Bandicoot, 'we'd better get upstairs. I hope the speeches won't be too interminable. Ah, Mr Barrett, how are we?'

The Member of Parliament for Bandicoot's constituency swung round, vaguely in the right direction.

'Ah, Mr . . . ah . . . er . . .'

'Lovely to see you. May I present Inspector Lestrade, an old friend.'

'Charmed, Mr . . . er . . . Charmed. Er . . .' and he pointed approximately to the stairs, 'the King.'

Lestrade wondered how long Barrett had been in the cellars, sampling the olorosos. From the look of him, at least a week. They headed for the stairs, the fanfares still resounding in the chandelier-lit rooms above. The good-natured banter turned to something more alarming as a commotion occurred on the top flight of the stairs. Someone had stumbled, someone else went over him and a third plummeted over the rail to crash into a cask of amontillado.

'Not the best of years,' commented Lestrade drily.

'Look out there,' someone shouted.

'Have a care. That's my eye,' sobbed another.

It was a miracle Lestrade escaped with all his limbs intact, but then he wasn't going to admit to the fact that he'd already caught his teeth a sharp one on his sherry glass.

'Good god,' a voice rose above the hubbub, 'I think he's dead.'

'Dead drunk,' said another in one of those silences which always descend as someone puts his foot squarely in it. True to form, that someone was Harry Bandicoot. 'Make way. Mind your backs. I'm a doctor.' And another tippler fought his way to the stairs. The crowd surged back, clearing the area so that Christian Barrett lay alone on the steps, his head dangling over the edge. The doctor fussed around him and stepped back. Hats were removed as realisation dawned. Lestrade took charge, as he tended to in these situations. Of all the men in that fume-laden room, he was the one most accustomed to sudden death. He called up the stairs, 'Mr Christie!'

A frail white-haired gentleman appeared. 'Would you inform His Majesty there has been a tragic accident here. I fear the auction will be postponed ...' He stopped in his tracks as he reached the corpse. He dropped to one knee, sniffing the nose and mouth as he did so.

'Good God,' someone said, 'what's he doing?'

'Gentlemen,' Lestrade straightened, straddling the stairs, 'I'm afraid the auction will be postponed indefinitely. Harry,' he summoned Bandicoot to him and whispered in his ear, 'get the keys from Christie and lock the doors. Then call the Yard. Ask for Gregory – he's marginally the better of two evils. He'll need constables. Lots of them.'

'Just like the old days, eh?' Bandicoot grinned.

I hope you've got brighter since then, thought Lestrade, though he would not have said so for the world.

'What's going on?' someone asked as Bandicoot made his exit. 'Who the hell are you?'

'I am Inspector Lestrade of Scotland Yard,' he answered, 'and as of now, you gentlemen are all suspects in a murder enquiry.'

The Heckled Band

Messrs Christie, Manson, & Woods made one of their great rooms available for Scotland Yard. Bandicoot barred the main doors with his Etonian bulk, but he was having trouble with one gentleman who refused to accept the temporary imprisonment. Lestrade came to the rescue, having ensured the cellar was emptied and the doors to it locked.

'Is there a problem, Harry?' he asked.

'I want to know by what authority we are being kept here,' the gentleman snapped.

'By mine, as an officer of the Criminal Investigation Department, Metropolitan Police.'

'Well, my authority outweighs yours. I am Sir Frederick Ponsonby, Equerry to His Majesty. We cannot have His Majesty compromised by this matter.' He became more confidential, 'Did I hear you say a murder had been committed?'

'It has.'

'Good God, man. Don't you realise the implications of this? His Majesty's life may be at stake.'

'Now then, Freddie. What's going on?'

The knot of remonstrators at the door turned to face the stolid figure of the King, wreathed in smoke from his giant Havana. They bowed.

'This ... gentleman, sir, is refusing to let Your Majesty's party leave.'

'Quite right. Do you know who this man is, Freddie? Inspector Lestrade – Lestrade of the Yard, in fact. I have every confidence in him. How have you been, Lestrade?'

'Well, Your Majesty, thank you.' He was amazed the King should remember.

'Let me see, when was it – 'ninety-four at Ladybower. Old Harnett's place.'

'I believe it was 'ninety-three, sir.'

The nerve of the man, fumed Ponsonby, correcting the King.

'You're right. It was. Well, well, where have the years gone, eh?'

'May I congratulate you, sir, on your accession?' Lestrade found it hard to grovel, but he could manage it from time to time. 'And may I crave Your Majesty's indulgence? The murderer may still be on the premises.'

How crass, observed Ponsonby to himself.

'If I may begin with you, sir,' Lestrade ventured, 'I won't keep you longer than I need.'

'Lestrade!' roared Ponsonby. 'Have you lost your mind? You are addressing the King of England!'

'Now, Freddie, watch your blood pressure.' The King patted his man on the arm. 'I've been through baccarat scandals and divorce trials. A few questions about a little murder aren't going to do any harm.'

'Thank you, Your Majesty. This way, please.'

But before Lestrade could begin his enquiries, there was a thunderous knocking at the front door.

'The Yard,' said Lestrade, 'they're improving. Harry, let them in.'

Uniformed constables swarmed into the main concourse, the auctioneers attempting to restore order to the scene with the odd judicious tap of their hammers, utterly drowned, of course, by the hullabaloo. Unfortunately for all present, or fortunately if they had something to hide, Edward Henry, not Tom Gregory, led the invasion, and promptly took over from Lestrade as the most senior officer present. Having bowed almost double before the King, he acceded immediately to Frederick Ponsonby's request and allowed the royal party to leave. He continued to grant such concessions, his constables furiously taking notes of names and addresses, until the only people left in the establishment were the auctioneers, their staff and a huge crowd of policemen with nothing to do. Rather than risk losing his temper and breaking Edward Henry's nose, Lestrade retired to the cellar for a further look at the corpse. Bandicoot went with him.

'What makes you so sure it's murder, Sholto?' the younger man asked.

'Smell,' said Lestrade.

Bandicoot did.

'Sherry,' he said.

'And?'

'Other drinks?' Bandicoot guessed.

'Probably. But there's something else.'

Bandicoot shook his head.

'Bitter almonds. Cyanide.'

'Good God. I can't smell a thing.'

'Many people can't. That's why it's so useful. Actually, it's not a common poison, though I came across it in the Brigade case, in 'ninety-three. Look here,' Lestrade lifted the deceased's head, 'notice that froth on the lips? Classic symptom.'

'But how ... the sherry!' Bandicoot expounded suddenly, with the triumph of a man who has found the lost chord.

'Yes, the sherry. But there are problems there. I can't see our new Lord and Master allowing us to test all five thousand dozen bottles. Not if his performance in the last few minutes is anything to go by. You know, Bandicoot, I still can't believe it. He almost certainly let the murderer walk out.'

'A man who plays things by the book. But isn't it likely that the murderer wasn't here at all? And why bother to kill old Barrett? He was harmless enough.'

'When I can answer your last question, Harry, I'll have my man. This is one of a pattern. Christian Barrett is the fourth Member of Parliament to die in mysterious circumstances in as many months.'

'Good Lord. Really?'

'In answer to your first question, the murderer had to be here. Barrett wasn't an accident. The man I'm looking for is careful and clever – very clever. He takes chances only when he has to. How could he be sure Barrett would get the poisoned bottle among all these thousands of bottles?' He began to sniff glasses lying where they had been left in the confusion. 'How could he be sure that only Barrett would drink the cyanide?'

'I give up,' said Bandicoot, uncomprehendingly.

'Answer,' Lestrade beamed triumphantly, 'because it wasn't in a bottle. That'll please Edward Henry. We don't have to confiscate the King's sherry and I've got a set of fingerprints for him.'

'Fingerprints?' Bandicoot was as lost as ever.

'Never mind, Harry, it's too long a story. But *this*,' he held it up to the light, 'is the poisoned glass. Barrett's glass.' He sniffed at it again. 'Bitter almonds.'

Lestrade came back on duty a day early. In fact, he travelled with his new chief in his very own cab, past the Houses of Parliament and on to the Yard. For the rest of the day, the two men were incarcerated with the scientific Sergeant Collins in the bowels of the building. Dew, Dickens and Jones were buried somewhere above in Hansard's volumes, trying to trace speeches by any of the deceased. It would not make light reading. With his test tubes, his Bunsen burners, his powders and his brushes, it was evening before Collins had finished.

'There,' Henry beamed, 'are the fingerprints of your man, Lestrade. Let the others scoff now. We've got him.'

'Who is he, sir?'

'Well, I don't know. We'll have to fingerprint all those who attended the auction.'

'How many were there?'

'Two hundred. Three hundred. Can't remember.'

'Can we insist on that, sir?'

'Insist? Lestrade, some of the richest men in England were

there today. Not to mention ladies. You were all for interrogating the King this morning. You really must learn some discretion, you know.'

Collins stifled a chuckle.

'May I make a telephone call, sir?' Lestrade asked.

'Of course. What for?'

'Just an idea, sir.' And he left.

It was not a good line, the one between the Yard and Christie's auction rooms, but Lestrade got the answer he wanted. Or rather, didn't want.

'Collins, have you taken Christian Barrett's prints?'

'Er . . . no,' the sergeant admitted.

'You'll find him in the morgue. Jump to it.'

'Just a minute, Lestrade. What's your point?' Henry asked.

'I've just spoken to Mr Christie of Christie, Manson, & Woods.'

'And?'

'And, as I suspected, their staff wear gloves when handling items for sale.'

'I don't follow.'

'Bear with me, sir. The cyanide was placed in a glass. Correct?'

Henry nodded.

'That glass was handed to Christian Barrett.'

He nodded again.

'He drank from it. And was dead in five minutes.'

'So?'

'So the murderer evidently did not have time to wipe the glass, since there are prints still on it. I'll wager my next month's pay that Collins will find that all these prints are Barrett's.'

'Well of course some of them are.'

'*All* of them.' Lestrade was emphatic.

'How do you know?'

'Because the auction-room staff wear gloves when handling exhibits for sale.'

'Are you trying to tell me—'

'That our murderer was one of the auction staff? I

suspect he was temporary, sir. I'll check, of course, but I think we'll find not a trace of the man by now. Of course, if I'd been able to question everyone this morning—'

'Impossible, Lestrade.' Henry was quick to defend himself. 'Anyway,' a vindicating thought occurred, 'you were probably served sherry by the same man. He was right under what's left of your nose, Lestrade, and you let him go.'

'Well,' Lestrade curbed his rising annoyance, 'we must see that it doesn't happen again, mustn't we?'

'It's a pity,' Henry turned back to the murderous glass, 'I'd just begun to work out from the patterns of the whorls that our man was a left-handed Irishman who suffered from gout. Ah well, back to the drawing board.'

Summer died. And it was autumn, raw and cold before any further headway was made in Lestrade's case. He and Bradstreet and Gregory gave each other wide berths, nodding in the corridor, exchanging bitcheries in the ghastly monthly inspectors' meetings which Edward Henry continued from his predecessor, who had continued them from his predecessor. It was December by now, skies dark with threatening snow and little cheer for the Christmas season. Enquiries at Christie's had come up with a name – a name that rang bells in Lestrade's head each time he re-examined it. But he couldn't place it. Messrs Christie, Manson, & Woods had taken on, the previous Friday, a man named Henry Baskerville. His credentials had been excellent, but he had vanished without trace on the day of the unfortunate incident, the day that Christian Barrett died. Surprise, surprise.

As for the other murders, little new was forthcoming. Lestrade interviewed Beales again, but he was able to offer nothing else on the brutal killing of his former master, Ralph Childers. Besides, now he was in the employ of Lord Rosebery and had strict instructions not to talk to the police more than he had to. Lestrade had met Rosebery before and knew him to be a man cautious to the point of hysteria. There was no fathoming

Knights of the Garter. The friends and colleagues of John Deering clammed up. Just what the remaining Deering's involvement in the Army Remount scandal was or how much he wished to save family and regimental honour, Lestrade was not able to say. For a while, he had Dickens observe, from a safe distance, the rather attractive Lady Brandling, since Lestrade could not be sure, despite her logical protestations of the problematical murder weapon, that her story was quite straight. He had to admit that he was clutching at straws. Then another man died. The news was brought, curiously enough, by that doyen of Yard detectives, the man who handled, entirely to his own satisfaction, but to no one else's, the Ripper case, Chief Superintendent Abberline.

'Chief Superintendent Abberline to see you, sir,' Jones announced him.

'Don't I know you, Constable?' The large man with the large gardenia paused in the doorway.

'No, sir. You knew my father, Athelney Jones.'

'Ah, yes. I never liked him.'

'Chief Superintendent,' Lestrade hailed him. 'Dew, where's that red carpet?'

'Talking of people I don't like, morning, Lestrade.'

'Chief Superintendent.' The inspector snapped his fingers for Dickens to make the tea. He was coming on well. One day he might be as good at it as Dew.

'I've got a case for you, Lestrade.'

'Oh?'

'You may know I've been looking for a gang of ruthless cut throats who stole a quantity of ping-pong balls.'

'I knew you were assigned to Serious Crimes, sir. I had no idea just how serious.'

Dew just managed to change his snorting laugh into a sneeze in time.

'I don't care for your attitude, Lestrade. Here I am, giving you a lead—'

'I'm sorry, sir. Please go on.'

'My enquiries led me to Sir Geoffrey Manners, Bart.'

'Would that be the Yorkshire Manners-Barts, sir?' Dew chipped in.

'Ignore him, Mr Abberline. He's been trying to better himself by reading Debrett. Geoffrey Manners, MP?'

'Well, I'm glad to see someone's awake in H Division.' He threw an accusatory scowl at Dew. 'He's dead.'

Lestrade's air of levity vanished. Dickens stopped with the steaming mugs in mid-air. 'Put them down, Constable, before you pour that tea all over the Chief Superintendent. When?'

'Yesterday, my inspector thinks. His men found the body this morning.'

'How?'

'He didn't know. My men aren't used to murder, Lestrade. That's your department.'

'Have you told Mr Henry?'

'I didn't think there was any hurry—'

'Chief Superintendent, you have risen in my estimation. Stay and finish your tea. What's the address?'

'Oh, no, Lestrade. I'm not passing it over to you entirely. I remember how you wormed your way into the Ripper case.'

Dew's tea trembled slightly in his hand. Lestrade leaned forward confidentially to Abberline. 'He was on Mary Kelly's beat that October. He was first on the scene. Never been the same.'

'Well, this isn't a pretty one, either. Shall we?'

'Dickens, you've had your tea break. Get back to those Hansards. Remember you're looking for a pattern.'

The officers of the Yard took a cab to Jermyn Street, the shady side, and were shown in by a stalwart constable of Abberline's division.

'He's in the Games Room, sir.'

They were shown by a uniformed inspector whom Lestrade knew vaguely to a large room at the back of the house, in the basement. In the centre, under the swinging electric light, was a large table, painted green, across which was slung a net.

'What's this?' Lestrade asked the inspector.

'It's a table,' the other answered.

'Obviously, man. The inspector wants to know what it's for,' Abberline rounded on him.

'For ping-pong, sir.' The inspector looked suitably chastened.

'I am not familiar with the game,' Lestrade said.

'It's all the rage, man,' Abberline told him. 'Two people play it. It's like tennis, but played indoors, with the table as the court.,

'Tennis for midgets?'

Abberline ignored him. 'Sir Geoffrey was a devotee of the sport. Ruxton here was making a routine enquiry concerning the loss of his balls when the deceased's man came hurtling out of the house screaming there was a murder. Here he is.'

'The man?'

'The deceased.'

Lying slumped in the far corner was Sir Geoffrey Manners, Bart. He was wearing a dressing gown, thrown open to reveal an expensive nightshirt and his face was covered in lurid pink patches. The mouth was distorted and the eyes rolled upwards. Oddly, one of his arms was resting on an upturned chair, his index finger pointing towards his face. The other hand still clutched his throat.

'Fingerprints?' asked Lestrade.

Abberline took him aside. 'Look, Lestrade, it's not for us to criticise our superiors, but this nonsense of Henry's, well, I mean . . . Let's get down to some serious policework, shall we? You can borrow my craniograph.'

'Your what?'

'Really, Lestrade, I always thought you were abreast of scientific developments. A craniograph measures the skulls of murderers. It helps in the identification of criminal types.'

'Haven't we got to catch him first?'

Abberline apparently hadn't thought of that.

Lestrade lifted the bat. 'Do they always break like that?'

'They can,' the inspector told him. 'It's the vellum, you see.'

Lestrade sniffed it. Bitter almonds. 'Where are these things made?' he asked.

'This one,' Ruxton found the other bat, 'seems to have been bought from Hamleys of Regent Street.'

'Can I borrow the inspector, Chief Superintendent?'

'All right.' Abberline was not keen. He had been helpful once already today. Twice was painful for him.

'Ruxton, be a good fellow and get over to Hamleys, will you? Talk to Hamley himself. Find out how these things are made. I'll meet you at the Yard later. My office.'

'Any ideas, Lestrade?'

'Do you want a guess?'

'Why not? Of academic interest only, you understand.'

'First, sir, whose case is it? Yours or mine?'

Abberline pursed his lips. 'All right, Lestrade. It's yours.'

'Cyanide gas. I've read about it. Never seen it. It could be carbon monoxide, that leaves this pink discoloration too.'

'I take back what I said, Lestrade. Quite the budding coroner, aren't you? But how was it administered? No one detected a smell in the room. Wouldn't a gas affect anyone and everyone in the room? I assume Sir Geoffrey wasn't playing with himself.'

'It's not his solitary vices I'm interested in, sir. Not at the moment. Let me try another guess on you. I don't think Ruxton will have much luck at Hamleys. I think our man bought these bats and pulled away the outer cover of leather. Then he inserted a capsule of cyanide between the layers of vellum. If, as Ruxton says, the vellum is always breaking, it would only be a matter of time before it broke. A sudden rush of air may cause an explosion, which would account for the shattered bat and the look of horror on Manners' face. It's only a guess, but I doubt if we'll find much better. The murderer would have time, if he was quick, to leave the room. May I talk to the servants?'

Lestrade did just that. For the rest of the day he examined and cross-examined. And for the first time in a long time he felt he was getting somewhere. Twenty-four Jermyn Street was the town house of Sir Geoffrey Manners, his quiet retreat from the hurly-burly of the House. His family seat was not, as Dew had surmised, Yorkshire, but Devon, near Okehampton. Consequently, his staff were few. He had a man, and two maids. He had no cook, for he usually ate at the House or his club, and much of his time was spent riding in the Row or rowing on the river. He was known as a keen sportsman and excelled as a shot, billiards player, cricketer and oarsman. His study, Lestrade noted, was festooned with trophies going back to his schooldays.

His man, who had discovered the body, had understood that a gentleman was due to call the previous evening, to engage Sir Geoffrey in a duel of ping-pong. The gentleman's name was, apparently, Sherrinford Holmes?

Lestrade rocked back in his chair.

'Did you say Sherrinford Holmes?'

'Indeed, sir, I believe that was the name Sir Geoffrey mentioned. I *could* have misheard.'

'Did Sir Geoffrey ever mention this name to you before?'

'No, sir, I don't believe so. But Sir Geoffrey had a host of friends and acquaintances, sir. I couldn't hope to keep track of them all.'

'Who let Holmes in?' Lestrade asked.

'It must have been Sir Geoffrey himself, sir. I was on an errand in the City and on returning went to my bed. I had a feverish cold.' Indeed, to be fair, the man still had.

'And the maids?'

'Annie is deaf. She would have heard nothing. Mrs Elkins was visiting her sister in Deptford.'

'Not very sensible, employing a deaf girl,' Lestrade commented.

'Sir Geoffrey used to say he liked the exercise of answering the doorbell himself, sir. Even when we were all in the house, he would race us to the door. He usually cheated by sliding down the banisters. He was very vigorous.' The man blew his nose and sat there, a martyr to catarrh.

'Lady friends?' Lestrade thought he'd better explore every avenue.

'Oh, yes, sir. Many. It's funny . . .' Lestrade thought he saw the beginnings of a chuckle, but it was only a trick of the light.

'What is?'

'Sir Geoffrey was very fond of the ladies, sir. But he was so outspoken against them in the House. He and Mr Churchill.'

'Churchill? Winston Churchill?'

'Yes, sir. Do you know him?'

'As a matter of fact, I do – when he was a cadet at Sandhurst.'

'Ah, he's come a long way since then, sir. His exploits in the war. We followed it avidly.'

'And now?'

'Why, he's Member for Oldham now, sir. Eleven con-stituencies asked him to stand, but he chose Oldham.'

'Yes, well, there's no accounting for taste,' said Lestrade. 'So it looks as though he will be Home Secretary after all.'

'Sir?'

'Nothing,' Lestrade broke out of his temporary reverie and made his farewells. He sent a message via a constable for Inspector Ruxton to present his findings at Hamleys to Sergeant Dew and he took the Underground train to Baker Street.

Lestrade had always promised himself he would never return to Number 221B. It had too many sour memories. But here he was, ringing the bell again and here was Mrs Hudson opening the door, as though there had been no lapse of time at all. She was rounder, shorter than Lestrade remembered. He was thinner, taller than she remembered. She showed him up the stairs to the study which had been that of Sherlock Holmes.

'Doctor Watson, it's Inspector Lestrade to see you.'

'Lestrade. My God, this is a surprise,' Watson shook his hand heartily, 'I was just putting a few finishing touches to my . . . er . . . our latest novel. Conan Doyle is so careless with his punctuation.'

Lestrade glanced at the papers lying on the cluttered desk. Mrs

Hudson had scurried away in the time-honoured tradition to fetch a sherry. 'No thank you, Mrs Hudson,' said Lestrade on her return, 'I am less fond of sherry than I was.'

'You'll stay for supper, Lestrade?' Watson asked.

'Thank you, no.'

'Not a social call, then?'

'That name,' he pointed to the papers, '*The Hound of the Baskervilles* – your latest novel.'

'What about it?'

'How did you come by it?'

'Well, don't you remember? It was your idea. That hyena thing you caught in Cornwall. It gave me the idea of a monstrous beast that slaughtered men on the moors. Really, Lestrade, we had this conversation at the Diogenes Club the night old Hamilcar Waldo died.'

'Indeed we did,' said Lestrade, 'I knew I'd heard the name, now I know where.'

'What name? Look, Lestrade, you can't be suggesting plagiarism. I mean, I know Conan Doyle and I . . . well, Conan Doyle has been a little harsh on you, but . . . well, nobody reads the *Strand* magazine, anyway.'

'Tell me, Doctor, is there a Henry Baskerville in your book?'

'Why, yes, he's the central character. Apart from Holmes and myself, of course.'

'Who has read this book?'

'Who? Well, I . . . er . . . myself, of course. Conan Doyle. My publisher, some proof readers . . .'

'I shall need their names, Doctor. And the address of Mr Conan Doyle.'

'I believe he's still with his field hospital in South Africa. Rumour has it he's to be knighted, you know.'

'Bully,' said Lestrade, 'but it doesn't exempt him from a murder enquiry.'

'Murder? What has dear Arthur to do with Hamilcar Waldo?'

'Ah, my dear doctor, I am not, in this instance, talking about Hamilcar Waldo.'

'Not?' Watson now turned from his sherry to his brandy.

'Tell me something else. Did your erstwhile colleague ever use the name Sherrinford?'

'Conan Doyle? Never.'

'I was referring to Sherlock Holmes.'

'Oh, I see,' Watson swigged heartily, 'er . . . yes, I believe he did. As you know, Inspector, he was a man of many parts.'

'Indeed, although I seem to remember not all of them were working?'

'Have a care, Inspector. You are talking of a man who was closer to me than a brother. And a genius, to boot.'

Lestrade leaned one arm on the desk, so that their eyes drew level. 'I am talking of a man who was so deranged through the misuse of narcotic substances that he tried to kill you, Doctor Watson. And he was a detective of very limited ability.'

Watson poured himself another glass, infinitely larger than the first.

'Why are you using the past tense, Lestrade?' he asked nervously.

The inspector straightened. 'Doctor, I know it is your pious hope to keep Holmes' memory alive. And in view of your former friendship, I understand that.'

'His memory, Lestrade? Who's talking about his memory? I'm talking about the man himself. I've seen him!'

Lestrade narrowed his eyes and glanced at the decanter from which Watson poured another brandy.

'No, Inspector. It isn't the brandy. Mrs Hudson has seen him too.'

'Perhaps you'd better tell me about it,' said Lestrade.

'I've seen him four or five times now. Always at evening, out there in the street.'

The two men went to the window. 'Down there.' Watson pointed. 'He always crosses from right to left, pauses below the window and glances at the door. On two occasions he has lit his meerschaum.'

'What was he wearing?'

'The ensemble Paget usually drew him in – an Ulster and a deerstalker. It's funny, really,' though Watson clearly wasn't amused, 'Holmes very rarely wore that hat.' And he drained his glass again.

'Doctor Watson, you can't imagine that the figure you've seen *is* Sherlock Holmes?'

'Why not, Lestrade? Conan Doyle is a spiritualist, you know.' Lestrade knew.

'He accepts it perfectly well. A phantasm, he calls it.'

'Doctor, you and I are men of the world. So was Holmes.'

'There are more things in heaven and earth, Lestrade . . .'

Lestrade nodded. His old boss, Melville McNaghten, had said that to him once. *He* was a believer, too.

'But he was killed. His body was found at the foot of the Reichenbach Falls. You were at the funeral, man,' Lestrade persisted.

'Yes, I was at the funeral. And I saw what everyone else saw. A mahogany coffin complete with brass fittings. How do I know what was in it?'

That indeed was food for thought. 'All right,' said Lestrade, 'let's assume Holmes was not in that coffin – is not dead. Why should he fake his own death?'

'Who knows? International espionage, foreign intrigue.'

'Hogwash, Doctor – with respect. I want facts, not fiction.'

'All right, Lestrade. But my contention is the same. Holmes was neurotic – he always had been. And towards the end, the cocaine finally got him. But did it? You'd better look at this.'

Watson unlocked a drawer in the desk and handed a letter to Lestrade. 'I received that a month ago. It's postmarked from Switzerland.'

Lestrade read the contents, 'Watson, old friend, will be home sooner than you think. S.'

'Are you telling me this is genuine?'

'It's his hand, Lestrade. I virtually lived with this man for ten years, I ought to know his handwriting.'

'Wait a minute,' Lestrade checked the postmark, 'the letter

itself is undated – and the stamp a blur. What if this were sent before Holmes' death?'

'Ten years ago? Good God, Lestrade, I know foreign postal systems aren't a patch on our own, but even so . . .'

Lestrade returned to the window. Dusk was settling fast on the hurrying crowds, the evening newspaper sellers calling raucously to each other in the raw cold of another winter's evening.

'Let's assume all this is correct,' he said. 'Let's assume that Holmes for reasons of his own engineered his own death, engineered his own funeral and remained abroad. Let's assume he wrote to you, from Switzerland a month ago, telling you he would be home soon—'

'"Sooner than you think" are his words, Lestrade.'

'Quite. Let's also assume that he is now in London and that on a few occasions he has appeared in his familiar – though apparently not too familiar – garb beneath your window and has lit his meerschaum. I have one question for you, Doctor – why?'

Watson shrugged. 'And I have one question for you, Lestrade. Why did you come here tonight, asking about Holmes?'

Lestrade's eye caught the bullet holes in the wall near the door – the holes made by Holmes in some of his more half-hearted murder attempts on Watson.

'What if I told you,' the inspector said, 'that I am looking for a murderer who is a crack shot, who wears an Ulster and a deerstalker and gives his name as Sherrinford Holmes?'

Watson's glass shattered on the hearth, causing a minor explosion as its contents hit the flames. 'Then you believe it too. That Holmes is alive?'

'No, Doctor. I believe that someone is trying very hard to make us *think* he's alive.' He made for the door. 'Even so, I'll check with the Swiss authorities. If you receive any more letters – or have any more sightings – you'll let me know?'

Watson nodded. He was a frightened man.

As Lestrade had suspected, Gregory had drawn a blank at

Hamleys with the ping-pong bat. It was inconceivable that a cyanide capsule could have been placed into the thing during its manufacture – unless the murderer was of course a manufacturer of ping-pong bats, which was not beyond the realms of possibility. One curious little footnote to the episode was that Mr Hamley had written personally to Edward Henry complaining of the fact that Inspector Gregory had insisted on telling the said Mr Hamley a number of excruciatingly boring jokes, all of which Mr Hamley had heard before and did not wish to hear again. This was, of course, a confidential matter between Assistant Commissioner Henry and Inspector Gregory. Or it would have been, had not Sergeant Dew been waiting outside Mr Henry's office and accidentally dropped his half-hunter on the carpet, so that in picking it up – an oddly lengthy process – his ear chanced to be very near the keyhole.

Dickens and Jones however had come up with something – they had verified from Hansard a chance remark by Geoffrey Manners' man, namely that the same Sir Geoffrey was highly outspoken of ladies in society and seemed to work every speech he made round to the subject. Lestrade decided to renew an old acquaintance.

'Well, Lestrade,' said the Member for Oldham, 'how long has it been?'

'More years than I care to remember, Mr Churchill. So you decided on politics after all?'

'I suppose my father's death ensured that. Anyway, too much blockage in the army, Lestrade – especially in the cavalry. It's full of chinless wonders and people called Nigel these days. No hope there.'

'And in politics?'

'Ah, in the House, Lestrade, you make your own mark. Another muffin?'

Lestrade declined.

'If it wasn't for this infernal rain, we could have taken tea on the terrace. I've got a soft spot for Old Father Thames, you know.'

Lestrade had noticed Winston Churchill's soft spot. There was certainly more of him than when they met last. Churchill had been a slim young man then, a cadet awaiting placement with a regiment. The Fourth Hussars, the Malakand Field Force and countless clashes with fuzzy-wuzzies and Boers had certainly left their mark. He was now a national hero, a respected back-bencher and nearly three stone heavier.

'But, confess it, Lestrade,' Churchill lit the inspector's Havana, 'you didn't catch me before the Christmas recess just to relive old times.'

Lestrade smiled. Yes, the man would be Home Secretary one day.

'It's these murders, isn't it? I've noticed an increasing – what do you fellows call it – police presence in the House recently.'

Bradstreet, thought Lestrade. 'Sir Geoffrey Manners,' he said.

'Ah, yes, poor Geoffrey. A damned nice fellow. It's the Irish, I suppose?'

'Why do you suppose that, Mr Churchill?'

'Well, naturally I . . . Matters are coming to a head, Lestrade. You mark my words. There'll be a bloodbath.'

'And you think these murders are the start of it?'

'Stands to reason, surely? I don't mind telling you, everyone's a bit on edge. Do you know we're all searched, morning, noon and night. Policemen in the Yard – that's Westminster, not Scotland – policemen in the Chamber, I'm not sure that's legal. Even in the committee rooms. Only here in the dining room do we get privacy. Couldn't bear some flatfoot – oh, sorry, Lestrade – watching me eat me buns!'

Lestrade glanced round. Most of the diners had the air of rather worried Members of Parliament. But the man nearest the door, in ill-fitting topper and tails, carried all the hallmarks of an utterly bored copper.

'I don't think it's the Irish,' said Lestrade.

'Oh? Who then?'

'I gather that Sir Geoffrey was an outspoken critic of the ladies?'

'Well, yes, but who isn't?'

'Sir?'

'Well, Lestrade, if you must know, there's a little band of us who rather enjoy needling the female suffragists. Manners, myself, even old Lloyd George and Asquith aren't averse to the odd dig.'

'Does no one object?'

'Good God, Lestrade, you aren't a feminist, are you? I took you to be made of sterner stuff. Well, to be candid, we do occasionally have rather a rough time of it in the House, when Emily Greenbush or the Pankhursts are in.'

'Emily Greenbush?'

'Yes, a militant feminist. I'm glad there's only one of her.'

Realisation dawned.

'Lestrade, if I follow your devious mind aright, you're not suggesting that Emily Greenbush killed Geoffrey? No, it's too preposterous.'

'It's too preposterous that a handful of Dutch farmers should have taken on the British Empire, Mr Churchill, but until a few months ago, I wouldn't have taken any bets on the outcome of that one.'

Churchill looked suitably abashed. 'Point taken,' he said.

'Do you happen to know where Emily Greenbush lives?' Lestrade asked.

'As a matter of fact, I do. It's splashed all over the noxious handbills which she throws at Members as they arrive for a debate. It's Thirty One, Curzon Street. You know, I'm glad you're going to pay her a visit, Lestrade. It'll do her good to have her collar felt. She's a dangerous woman.'

Lestrade thanked his host for the tea and made his farewells. As he passed the all too cognito policeman near the door, he called cheerily under his breath, 'Give my regards to Bradstreet!'

At Curzon Street, Lestrade met his Waterloo – or very nearly. But first he met Emily Greenbush. From Churchill's description, he expected a fire-breathing dragon at the very least. Instead, it was a sylph-like creature who showed him into the drawing room as the lamps were lit. The room of candles sparkled in her eyes and shone on her long hair, the colour of fine-spun copper. She wore a long dress of claret velvet laced with threads of silver and her eyes were clear and blue.

'I've been expecting you,' she said, and held out her wrists as though for cuffs.

'Indeed, ma'am?' Lestrade was uncomfortable in the company of intelligent women. And beautiful ones. Emily Greenbush was both.

'Tell me, who is it who sent you? Winston Churchill? Asquith? Not that old goat Lloyd George – who before you ask, did not know my father.'

'As a matter of fact, Mr Churchill—'

'I knew it. Well, take me, Inspector . . . er . . .'

'Lestrade.'

'Lestrade. Weren't you on the Hyde Park case?'

'Indeed, ma'am. Why do you ask?'

'It's as well to know your enemy, Inspector. What is the charge? Heckling in a public place? Loitering with intent to pester a politician? Come on, my arms are beginning to ache.'

'I am here on a more serious matter, ma'am. The murder of a number of Members of Parliament, most recently Sir Geoffrey Manners, Bart.'

'Ah, yes,' Emily let her hands fall. 'Can I offer you a Scotch?'

'Not when I'm on duty, Miss Greenbush.' He checked his half-hunter. 'Ask me again in half an hour.'

To Lestrade's surprise, she poured herself a large one and swigged it back, pouring another immediately. Catching the look on his face, she offered by way of explanation, 'In a man's world, we women must learn to do what men can. Would you care to wrestle?'

'Thank you, no, ma'am. It's Thursday. I never wrestle with ladies on Thursdays.'

'Cigarette, then?' She produced a silver case.

'I prefer my own.' Lestrade produced a Havana, but Emily promptly lit it for him. Despite all Lestrade's prejudices, the cigarette looked particularly becoming between her delicate fingers.

'My dear!' The door suddenly crashed open to reveal three ladies of the Miss Lawrence school, not Roedean perhaps, but mannish lasses all. 'Rawlins tells me *this*,' the leading lady pointed with evident distaste at Lestrade, 'is a policeman.'

'Yes, Emmeline, he is.'

'Rotter!' And Emmeline fetched Lestrade a sharp one with her umbrella.

The inspector sprang more nimbly than he thought possible behind the sofa, keeping the horsehair beast between him and them.

Emily was giggling helplessly. 'May I introduce you. Inspector Lestrade, of Scotland Yard, this is Emmeline Pankhurst and her daughters Christabel and Sylvia.'

'Chauvinist lackey!' Christabel hissed.

'Despoiler of women!' Sylvia accused.

Emmeline threw herself bodily across Emily Greenbush. 'What are you accusing her of?' she demanded. 'What are the charges?'

'With respect, ma'am, we've just been through this. I am making enquiries into a murder—'

'Murder? Isn't that just what it's been for womankind for centuries? You see these?' Emmeline shook her fists at Lestrade.

'They're fists, ma'am.'

'No, they're not. They're chains, Inspector. Chains. Oh, invisible, I'll grant you, but chains nevertheless. Who put them there?'

'Er . . . your husband, ma'am?' Lestrade was beginning to see this madwoman's method.

'Mr Pankhurst, God rest his soul, was a sainted man. The *only one* of his sex to realise the injustice of the situation. Until all others are like him, we ladies of the Women's Franchise League will fight – *fight*, Inspector, to obtain our God-given rights.

Christabel, Sylvia, with me.' And the trio advanced on the Chauvinist Lackey Who Despoiled Women.

'Ladies!' It was Emily who halted the advance. 'I think you can leave me to handle the inspector. Really, I am in no danger.'

Slowly, the assault dwindled. There was much whispering and flashed glances and scowls. Eventually, the feminist trio were womanhandled out of the door. Emily leaned her full weight against the door and roared with laughter. To his surprise – and annoyance – Lestrade found himself laughing too.

Emily patted the sofa and the inspector sat beside her. Her mood changed. 'Geoffrey Manners,' she said quietly, 'I was as shocked as the next man to hear of his death. Oh, we had our disagreements, Inspector. I may have shouted some unpleasant things – all quite richly deserved at the time – from the Ladies Gallery ... Now, there's a *non sequitur,* Mr Lestrade.' He found himself looking on the carpet for it. 'A Ladies Gallery in the House of Commons. We should be down there on the floor.'

Lestrade looked again. Or perhaps this was an offer he would be hard put to refuse.

'Do you know what Edward I said?'

'Er ... about what, ma'am?'

'About Parliament, Inspector. He said, "Quid omnes tangit, ab omnibus approbetur." Don't you think he was right?'

'Well, I—' Lestrade began to waffle.

'Oh, forgive me, Inspector. I spend so much of my time putting men in their place in public I find it difficult to desist in private. It's the legacy of a classical education. You see, the late Mr Pankhurst wasn't *quite* the only defender of the cause. My father too saw the injustice of the world, and saw to it that I received as good an education as any man, in the confines of my own home. Edward I said, concerning Parliament, "That which touches all, must be decided by all." I like to think that makes him the first advocate of female suffrage.'

'And Geoffrey Manners?'

'Ah yes,' Emily poured Lestrade his Scotch, the half hour

being up, and blew smoke-rings to match his own, 'I really am sorry. Any theories?'

'Do you by any chance own a Martini-Henry rifle, carbine variety?' Lestrade asked. Nothing about Miss Greenbush would surprise him.

'No,' she answered, unruffled, 'but I have a Webley Mark IV, an old navy cutlass and a couple of cavalry lances.' The smile vanished from her face as she saw the darkness spread over Lestrade's.

'Forgive the question, ma'am, but do you, in your quest to equal men, to drink their Scotch and smoke their cigarettes, ever wear men's clothes? A deerstalker, perhaps? Or an Ulster?'

Emily laughed. 'No, Inspector. I'm sorry to disappoint you. I don't take things that far. You'll stay to dinner?'

'Ma'am, I—'

'You won't compromise me, Inspector, if that's what's worrying you. You see, I've had dinner with men before.'

For the rest of his life, Lestrade never knew how he ended up in Emily Greenbush's bed later that night. Was it the Scotch? The exhaustion of a maddening and fruitless case? Long years without a woman's touch? He could never say. Certainly, it was unprofessional. If Edward Henry ever found out, he'd have a fit – of morality, probably. She rolled on top of him, her breasts jutting defiantly from the fragrance of her long, auburn hair. She began to rise and fall on him, stroking and teasing his chest with those long, slender fingers, her powerful thighs bringing him to a sudden and shattering climax. She stretched out beside him, her arm across him, her face buried in the pillow. After a while, when he'd come to, he noticed that she was crying. He lifted her face and kissed her softly on the lips.

'What's the matter?' he asked. 'I haven't upset you?'

She smiled through her tears, shaking her head. 'No, Sholto,' she said, 'some of us have feminism thrust upon us. From the time I was so high, it's all I heard.' She choked back the tears, 'For twenty years I've been sharpening the argument, honing the wit, learning to give as good as I got. "Never let a moment pass, Emily." "You're as good as they are, Emily." Didn't they know? Didn't they realise all I wanted to be was myself? A little girl who was not a little girl. A woman who is not a woman.'

Lestrade closed her lips with another kiss. 'You *are* a woman,' he whispered, 'a lovely one.'

She looked at him in the lamplight. 'Tomorrow,' she said, 'I will deny that this ever happened. I shall be Emily Greenbush, man-hater again. But for tonight, can I drop the mask with you?' And she folded into his arms.

The Irish Interpreter

It was the night before Christmas and all through the House not a creature was stirring, except for Edgar Bradstreet and Sholto Lestrade, officers of the Yard.

'Irishmen,' said Lestrade again.

'Absolutely,' Bradstreet was emphatic, 'or women.'

'Women?'

'You met Miss Greenbush?'

For an instant Lestrade's sang-froid slipped. 'In a manner of speaking,' he said.

'What did you think?'

'An interesting lady.'

Bradstreet stopped. 'Sholto, she is a member of the Women's Franchise League. Not to mention the Independent Labour Party.'

'And that makes her a murderess?'

'Perhaps not, but there are others. Millicent Fawcett, for instance.'

'Oh?'

'She's militant, Lestrade. Rabid, in fact. Good God, man, you and I are rational, liberal human beings. We're prepared for change. But these women are lethal. I fear what is to come. Just imagine,' Bradstreet became confidential, 'just imagine being examined by one.'

'In court, you mean?'

'No, Lestrade. I don't. Imagine the inner sanctum of a doctor's surgery. You go along ready to bare your . . . soul, and a *female* doctor asks you to cough. It defies credulity.'

'I understand there are a dozen or so of them already,' Lestrade said – a snippet he'd picked up, no doubt, in the *Sun*.

'Well, there you are. It's not natural. You wouldn't want a son of yours to marry one, would you?'

'I haven't got a son, Bradstreet. But what I have got is a hot rum waiting for me at the Yard. And walking round this cheerless mausoleum, I could do with it. Why did you ask me down here?'

They took the stone steps into the stark medieval grandeur of Westminster Hall.

'Padraig O'Leary,' said Bradstreet.

'Who?'

'He's a Fenian leader, Lestrade. I've been after him for years. If it is the Irish, he's the one mixed up in it.'

'What's it got to do with me?'

'Well, I'll be frank. I've had him in the Special Wing at the Yard for a fortnight. I can't get through to him. He does his stage Oirish and that's all. It's not much better than name, rank and serial number. I can't hold him for much longer. If the Press find out, they'll have a field day.'

'So?'

'So I wondered whether you would have a chat with him, Sholto? I've tried all I know. The commander's been through his paces too. Even Gregory's tried.'

'Without success, I take it?'

'Totally. Gregory tried to wear him down by telling him endless Irish jokes.'

'And?'

'O'Leary didn't understand them.'

Lestrade sighed and looked at his watch. 'All right,' he said, 'I'll have a word in his ear, but I can't promise anything. And anyway, you're barking up the wrong tree. You know something, Edgar?' Lestrade threw it out across the hall. 'Don't take this personally, but I preferred you when you were a sergeant.' And he turned into the cold.

The caped constable on the door saluted him. The night was

studded with stars, the river a slow-moving gleam of chiselled silver. Lestrade's breath curled back on him as he buttoned up the collar of his Donegal and buried his hands as deeply as he could in his pockets. What happened next was completely his fault. He was gazing idly at the statue of the Lionheart, head thrown back, sword in fist. His mind had left the chill of the House and the silent policemen who guarded it. It turned now to Christmas Eve and to little Emma, sleeping soundly, he knew, at the Bandicoots'. It would be dawn in a few hours. She would leap from her bed, bright eyed and morning fresh and scamper to open her stocking with the boys. She would find the present from Uncle Sholto. He hoped she would like it. He was still hoping that when he collided with someone walking in the opposite direction. The figure went sprawling across the pavement, to land heavily at the base of the Lionheart statue. It was only then that Lestrade saw the white stick. And only then that he saw that he knew the man.

'Mr Holmes?'

'Who is it?' the blind man asked, still recovering from the shock.

'Inspector Lestrade. We met at the Diogenes Club.'

'Ah, of course, Inspector. I never forget a voice. How are you?'

'Damnably sorry,' said Lestrade, helping him up, 'I wasn't looking where I was going.'

'Neither was I,' said Holmes.

Lestrade chuckled uneasily. 'Are you all right?'

'I'm fine. Fine. What brings you out on a raw night like this? Spreading Christmas cheer?'

'Duty, sir, I'm afraid. We never sleep, you know.'

'Ah, indeed not.'

'And you, sir? On Christmas Eve and alone?'

'Oh, night and day are one to me, Inspector. I often stroll late – fewer people,' he laughed brittlely, 'less chance of accidents.'

'May I get you a cab, Mr Holmes? You're a long way from Jermyn Street.'

'Thank you, Lestrade. By the way, my bumping into you like this is very fortuitous. I remembered something about the night Hamilcar Waldo died at the Diogenes.'

'Oh?'

'It's probably nothing, but when I arrived at the club and cousin Mycroft met me . . .'

'Yes?'

'We were crossing the lobby and I heard someone asking for Waldo.'

'Asking for him?' Lestrade hailed a hansom.

'Yes, whether he was there and if so, which was his table.'

'And that was all?'

'I'm afraid so. Probably of no importance.'

'On the contrary, Mr Holmes. It might be of the greatest importance. To whom was this addressed?'

'Ah, there you have me, Inspector. One of the questions a blind man cannot answer. I wonder Mycroft didn't mention it.'

The cab lurched to a halt by the kerb.

'Isn't it so,' Lestrade asked, 'that when a sense is lost, others are improved?'

'To an extent, yes,' said Holmes, 'as I think I told you at the Diogenes, my sense of smell has vastly improved.'

'What about your sense of hearing?'

'Eh?'

Oh, God, thought Lestrade, that doesn't bode well. 'I said—' he began.

'No,' Holmes laughed, 'I heard you, Lestrade. I simply don't follow you.'

'You said a moment ago you never forget a voice. What about that one? The voice you heard asking for Hamilcar Waldo.'

'Well,' Holmes frowned with the effort of remembering, 'it had a slight lisp. No, not a lisp, exactly, but some sort of impediment. And it was Irish, of course.'

'What?'

'I said—'

'Yes, I know what you said.'

'Look, guv'nor,' the cabbie leaned over from his perch, 'it's Christmas. I've got a family at 'ome.'

'Right, Santa,' said Lestrade, 'Mr Holmes, would you like to accompany me to the Yard?'

'Are you arresting me for walking without lights, Inspector?'

'No, I'm going to break the habit of a lifetime. And a few rules as well. I think you can help me.'

'A hot toddy, Mr Lestrade?' The desk sergeant raised a glass to him.

'Tut, tut, Dalgleish. Drinking again?' Lestrade took it and quaffed its contents. 'And one for my friend here.'

Holmes quietly collided with a column. Dalgleish, who had not seen the white stick nor the upturned, sightless eyes, motioned Lestrade to him. 'He's blind drunk already, sir.'

'It's all right, Sergeant,' Lestrade assured him, 'he's not driving.'

He gave Holmes the rum punch and led him through the labyrinthine corridors of the Yard. It was Christmas Day before they reached the relevant door in the seldom-seen wing of the building set aside for the Special Branch. Lestrade noticed the bunch of mistletoe blowing in the draught over the door. Singularly inappropriate he thought. A knock brought a constable.

'Inspector Lestrade,' the visitor announced, 'with Inspector Bradstreet's permission to talk to the prisoner.'

'Which one?' the constable asked with all the cheer and festive spirit of a man who drew the short straw to work over Christmas.

'Padraig O'Leary.'

'Oh, him. I'll have to search you, sir.' The constable proceeded to do just that, producing keys, knuckle duster, handcuffs, cigars and handkerchiefs from Lestrade's pockets like rabbits from a conjurer's hat. Lestrade winced a little as the constable measured his inside leg with his forearm.

'Sorry, sir. You'd be amazed what some of them hide up there.'

'I'm sure I would,' Lestrade agreed.

'Who's this?' the surly constable asked.

'Mr O'Merle Holmes,' Lestrade told him. 'He's all right. He's with me.'

The constable took Lestrade aside. 'Did you say O'Merle, sir?'

'No, he's not a Fenian, Constable.' Lestrade was at his most benign, as it was Christmas.

Even so, the constable duly searched Holmes too, although the contents of his pockets were rather less interesting. And there was less fluff.

'Mr Holmes, I'd like you to wait in the next room. The constable will show you a grille in the wall. Through it you'll be able to hear my conversation with O'Leary. Listen carefully to his voice. I want to know if you've heard it before. Constable, look after Mr Holmes, will you? We'll have you home before Santa arrives, Mr Holmes.'

Padraig O'Leary was a jaunty leprechaun of a man, sitting cross-legged on the bare iron bedstead in one corner of his grey, spartan room.

'Padraig O'Leary?' Lestrade had a knack of striking up conversations.

'Top o' the mornin' to yuz,' the Irishman replied.

God, thought Lestrade, it's worse than Bradstreet was letting on.

'You've led us all a merry chase, haven't you?'

'Ah, I have that, sor. I have that.'

'Why did you do it?'

'What would that be, sor?'

'Come off it, O'Leary. You've murdered five Members of Parliament and an officer of His Majesty's cavalry. I want to know why.'

'Ah, I refuse to answer that on the grounds of replenished responsibility.'

'What?'

'I didn't touch them, sor. As God is my witness.'

'With respect to the Almighty, O'Leary, you'll need a better witness than that.'

'Holy Mother of God, may yez be struck down for that, yer terrible blaspheming Englishman!'

'Don't give me that papist claptrap, O'Leary. I want answers.'

The Irishman twinkled and leaned forward. 'May I be knowin' who yer are, darlin'?' he said.

'I'm not your darling, O'Leary. I'm Inspector Lestrade.'

'Be Jabez, not the Lestrades of Kilkenny?' The Irishman sprang up with delight.

'No, the Lestrades of Spitalfields, Pimlico and Norwood.' A pause. 'Do you mean I've got relatives in Ireland?' He glanced at the picture of the Last Supper behind which he knew the grille to be. He'd have some explaining to do to Bradstreet because of this.

'Tell me how you poisoned Ralph Childers.' Lestrade sat on the only chair in the room, his legs astride it and leaning on its back.

'Ah, that would be with the terrible afflictin' stuff yuz English call beer,' O'Leary answered chirpily.

'And what about the blunt instrument you used on John Deering?'

'A policeman's wit,' the Irishman replied.

'Careful,' warned Lestrade, smiling now, 'you almost gave the game away there.'

'Did I now, sor?' The stage Oirish persisted.

Lestrade looked at his man. The Commander of the Special Irish Branch and his minions like Edgar Bradstreet had had this man inside for days. They'd got no further than this. Judging by the bruising around O'Leary's eyes and nose, they'd tried other methods too. Lestrade knew the jargon: 'Injury inflicted while resisting arrest.' What it really meant was 'Irish reprobate looked at me funny, so I hit him with my truncheon. Several times.'

'All right, O'Leary,' Lestrade got up, 'that's it. I was your last hope. Constable!' he shouted. The door unbolted and clanked open. 'A pity they've pulled Newgate down,' said Lestrade, 'but the prison yard at the Scrubs is as good a place as any for a hanging. And the shame of it is I know you didn't do it. What a waste.' And he made for the door, shaking his head.

'Wait a minute!' The leprechaun stood up. The stage Oirish had gone. Lestrade stopped. 'All right, Lestrade. May we talk alone?'

Lestrade motioned the laughing policeman outside.

'What do you want to know?' O'Leary asked.

'Why the change of heart?' Lestrade sat back on his chair. 'Collaborating with the enemy? Isn't that what some of your Fenian friends will say?'

'Probably. But I'm not made of the stuff of martyrs, Lestrade. I fear there are some coming up now, oh, mere lads as yet, but they'll lead you a merry dance, Lestrade. And they are the martyr kind. It'll be Phoenix Park all over again.'

'I'm not here to argue Home Rule with you, O'Leary. You're in no position to bargain. But I need answers. I need to eliminate you and your so-called cause from my enquiries.'

'You're not Special Branch, then?'

Lestrade shook his head.

'I thought the name wasn't familiar.'

'What about the Lestrades of Kilkenny?'

'All part of the act, Inspector, darlin'. But tell me, apart from avoiding the drop – and personally I don't think you'd have enough evidence anyway – why should I help you?'

'That's what this is all about, isn't it? Cause the maximum of bother. Be as difficult as possible. Well, I'll tell you why you should help me, O'Leary. Because there's a maniac going around killing MPs. And it's got nothing to do with Ireland. For all I know, an Irish MP might be next. Or perhaps that's what you want too? Perhaps that will further your cause?'

O'Leary shook his head. 'I've got alibis for the times those men died, Lestrade. All of them.'

'That's very pat,' said Lestrade, immediately wishing he hadn't.

'And that's an old trick, by the way – you feeding me the wrong cause of death a moment ago. Ralph Childers was beaten to death with your proverbial blunt instrument – and no, it wasn't a shillelagh. And John Deering was skewered with a lance. Your colleagues of the Special Branch have been over and over all this. And even before I was arrested, I read the newspapers avidly. Rather free with the details, weren't they? I'm surprised you haven't had people queueing up to confess.'

'Oh, we have. Two men who claimed to be King Charles I wreaking vengeance and another who swore on oath that he was Guy Fawkes and would get the bastards this time. I passed them on to another colleague of mine. I think you've met Inspector Gregory?'

O'Leary yawned.

'Yes, quite,' Lestrade concurred. 'Tell me, do you know the Diogenes Club?'

O'Leary shook his head.

'One last thing,' Lestrade rose to go, 'before you make a statement that makes sense and we let you go, would you say something for me?'

'Is it my brogue yuz likes, Inspector, darlin'?' O'Leary reverted.

'Would you say "Is Hamilcar Waldo here tonight?"?'

O'Leary shrugged and said it.

'Thank you, Mr O'Leary, and a Merry Christmas to you.'

In the adjacent room, Aumerle Holmes roused himself at Lestrade's entrance.

'I'm sorry, Inspector. It's difficult to tell. It was similar . . . but after all these weeks . . . I couldn't answer to it in a court of law. I'm sorry.'

'Not at all, Mr Holmes. Thank you for being so patient. Constable, get a Maria for Mr Holmes and see that he gets home, will you? I appreciate your help, Mr Holmes.' He took the man's hand and shook it. 'We'll be seeing each other soon, I hope.'

Again the brittle laugh at the badly chosen phrase. 'You can count on it, Inspector.'

By the day after Boxing Day, the Christmas spirit had left

Lestrade, particularly when Sergeant Dew gave him the news. Padraig O'Leary had been released. Well, that was right and proper. Whatever the man was involved in in the cause of Home Rule, he was not guilty of these murders. What annoyed Lestrade was that Bradstreet had changed his tack. Unable to pin anything on the Irishman, not even a bunch of shamrock, he had turned his attention to the fairer sex. He had arrested Emily Greenbush.

'Why?' Lestrade had asked him in Bradstreet's office, a murky corner high in the Yard's eaves.

'Look, Lestrade, I'm grateful in a way – but only in a way, mind you – for sorting out the O'Leary business. I still think the bastard's free to kill and maim again.'

'So that's it. It's an eye for an eye, is it? I let one of your suspects go, so you grab one of mine?'

'You're taking this very personally, Lestrade,' Bradstreet observed.

Lestrade checked himself. Bradstreet was no fool. Play it gently. He began to do that by sitting down. 'All right,' he said, 'what have you got?'

'One,' Bradstreet resorted to the policeman's finger exercise, 'Geoffrey Manners was a raving anti-feminist.'

'Five other men are dead, Bradstreet. Were they all anti-feminist too?'

'From your report I'd say Ralph Childers and John Deering certainly were. They used women as sexual objects, Lestrade. You'll notice there are no females among the victims.'

'Yet.'

'There'll be no more killings, Lestrade. I've got my woman.'

'All you've got is a damned thin motive. It'll never get to court.'

'Two,' Bradstreet's second finger came into play, 'Miss Greenbush is an outspoken critic of the Government, and with the exception of John Deering, all the victims were members of the governing party.'

'But not the Government itself, Bradstreet. Not the Cabinet.

If these are really political crimes, why hasn't the murderer had a go at Salisbury or Balfour? And John Deering is a pretty important exception, isn't he? He doesn't fit at all.'

'I'll grant you that,' Bradstreet concurred, 'and it's possible the Deering murder has nothing to do with this case at all. On the other hand, three,' but he was still using the same hand, 'Miss Greenbush owns a cavalry lance – a pair, in fact. Of the type used on Major Deering.'

'Motive?'

'Who knows? A personal thing perhaps. There may be a link between Greenbush and Lady Brandling. I'll find it.'

'You won't.'

'Four, Miss Greenbush by her own admission is a pretty fair shot. She could have killed Arthur L'Estrange with a Martini-Henry without too much difficulty.'

'So could a blind man on a galloping horse. It was close range in broad daylight – a standing duck.'

'Five, and this is the trump card, Lestrade. Two of them in fact—'

'You'd better call it five-a, you're running out of fingers,' said Lestrade.

'The late Horatio Greenbush, Emily's father, was a chemist.'

'So?' Lestrade chose to remain obtuse.

'So she may well have had a working knowledge of poisons.'

Lestrade laughed.

'*And*,' Bradstreet was undeterred, 'she bought a quantity of cyanide not six months ago. I have the chemist's log.'

'What was it for?'

'To kill wasps, she said.'

'Well, there you are.'

'Come on, that's what they all say.'

'I see,' said Lestrade, 'so she walked into a chemist's, gave her own name and address to obtain cyanide, made a compound, disguised herself as an auction-room attendant and poisoned Christian Barrett. Then she broke into Geoffrey Manners' house, doctored his ping-pong bat with the same stuff and challenged him to a game, knowing it would blow up in his face?'

'Precisely!'

Lestrade lolled back in his chair.

'All right, I know it's bizarre,' said Bradstreet, 'but murder is a bizarre business, Lestrade. Look at the Ripper killings, the Struwwelpeter case, that thing in Hanover Square—'

'All right, spare me the museum inventory. Let me pose one question. Ralph Childers. Where it all began. Where does Emily Greenbush figure there?'

'She knew his . . . inclinations . . .'

'And was a member of the reincarnated Hell Fire Club?'

'Ah, I've done research there. Did you know that the original Hell Fire Club had one female member? The so-called Chevalier d'Aeon – a woman in man's attire.'

'Have you read the coroner's report on Childers? And mine?'

'I have.' Bradstreet was triumphant.

'What would you say Emily Greenbush weighs? Eight stone, perhaps? Are you seriously implying she could have inflicted those injuries?'

'Yes, if Childers was manacled at the time and unable – or unwilling – to fight back until it was too late. Don't forget Lizzie Borden. She was little, but she still hacked her parents to death.'

'That was never proven, Bradstreet. Do your homework. Anyway, she was American.'

The two men looked at each other, all logic tried.

'Are you arresting her or her entire movement?' Lestrade asked.

'I'll get the Pankhursts later,' Bradstreet answered. 'For now, I'll stick to Emily Greenbush.'

The conversation was ended there by a furious pounding on the door.

'What is it?' Bradstreet asked.

It was Walter Dew who stumbled in. 'Mr Lestrade, sir, there's a telephone call for you. A man with an Irish accent. Says he knows who's been killing all these MPs.'

'Where?' Lestrade grabbed his hat.

'Mr Henry's office.'

'Wait for me.' Bradstreet snatched up scarf and Ulster and followed Lestrade along the maze of corridors to where a weak and pale Miss Featherstonehaugh stood holding a telephone receiver in a weak, pale hand.

'It's him,' she whispered hoarsely, covering the wrong part of the apparatus with the other hand.

'Yes?' Lestrade snatched it unceremoniously from her.

'Inspector Lestrade?' The Irish brogue crackled in his ear.

'Speaking.'

Bradstreet and Dew crouched as close as they could. In the silence a pin dropped from Miss Featherstonehaugh's mouth. Bradstreet looked at her. 'I travel home via the Strood tunnel,' she whispered by way of explanation. 'I might be kissed by a man.'

Fat chance of that, thought Dew, though now was not the time to say so.

'Go to the Houses of Parliament,' the telephone voice hissed, 'to the base of the clock tower. There's a surprise waiting for you. Is that imbecile Bradstreet there?'

'He is.' Lestrade passed the receiver across.

'Yes?' Bradstreet took it.

'I've got a surprise for you. Go to the foot of Victoria Tower.'

And the line went dead with a click.

'Hello, hello.' Bradstreet rattled the receiver. Nothing. 'Nothing,' he said.

Miss Featherstonehaugh fainted quietly behind them. No one noticed.

'"A surprise", he said,' Lestrade repeated.

'Yes,' said Bradstreet, 'at the foot of Victoria Tower.'

'Mine is at the foot of the clock tower.'

'It's a trap, of course.' Bradstreet rested against Henry's desk.

'Of course,' Lestrade did the same, 'perhaps it was Emily Greenbush throwing her voice over the telephone wires. Miss Feathers . . .' Lestrade noticed the grey lady down on the floor.

'Dew, get some water for Mr Henry's secretary will you? And find out all you can from her when she wakes up. I want to know *exactly* what the caller said. Get Dickens and Jones first. Bradstreet and I will meet them at the House.'

'You see, Lestrade,' Bradstreet chortled, 'an *Irish* voice. I told you, didn't I? I told you it was the Fenians.'

'So you'll be releasing Miss Greenbush?'

The inspectors made for the lift.

'If we survive tonight, Lestrade, yes. Otherwise—'

'Otherwise, I'll release her myself.'

Dew gave the orders to his constables and returned to pour water, none too gently, over Miss Featherstonehaugh. 'I wonder what made her faint?' he asked himself. 'Must have been the anticipation of the Strood tunnel.'

The Maria screeched and jerked to a halt outside the Houses of Parliament. It was dark now, another sharp, clear night made magic by the sparkling frost.

'You're the expert, Bradstreet, though it catches in my throat to say it. What do you think?'

'I think it's an explosive device, Lestrade.'

Dickens and Jones looked at one another.

'That's a bomb to you, gentlemen,' he said.

'Ever tackled one, Lestrade?'

The inspector shook his head. 'You?'

The inspector shook his head too. 'But I'm getting my men out. If this place is going to blow up, there's no point in half Special Branch going with it.'

'Dickens, Jones. Get round the building. Clear every copper out – Inspector Bradstreet's orders. Double up.'

The constables scattered.

The inspectors walked away from the Maria. Bradstreet checked his watch. Nearly half past seven.

'Of course, if I'm wrong—' he said.

'You?' mocked Lestrade. 'Surely not!'

'If I'm wrong and this isn't a bomb, but there are Fenians in there – we're playing right into their hands. Are you armed, Lestrade?'

'Only in the line of duty.' Lestrade slid out the brass knuckles and flicked the deadly blade upright.

'Likewise.' Bradstreet tugged free a Webley Mark IV.

'All regulation, of course. And above board,' Lestrade commented.

'Absolutely,' agreed Bradstreet.

They were gabbling aimlessly, somehow reassured by each other's voice. 'Damn, it's cold,' hissed Lestrade, burying his ears in the collar of his Donegal. As they reached the clock tower, they heard a constable call into the darkness of the public convenience nearby, 'Come along now, Mr Strachey, there's a good gentleman. Put that away and go home, will you?'

'Right, Lestrade. Here's your end. I'll get to mine.'

'Bradstreet, we'll try and work through this together. Whichever of us finds it first, if it is a bomb, that is, waits until the other has found his. Then we'll relay messages.'

'How?'

'Runners. I'll keep Dickens with me and send Jones to you. They can act as go-betweens. All right?'

Bradstreet nodded.

'Lestrade,' he called as the inspector entered at the side door, 'mind how you go.'

'I love you too,' grinned Lestrade and was gone. He'd lifted a bull's-eye from a passing constable and proceeded to flash it in every corner he came to, hoping that Mr Strachey had indeed taken the constable's advice and gone home. Security or not, His Majesty's Government had insisted on strict economy and the whole tower was bathed in the dimmest of lights. Lestrade's lantern threw eerie shadows on the Gothic walls, sharply faceted with corbel and ogee arch. But the niceties of Pugin's architecture passed Lestrade by. He walked as though on eggs, one hand gripping the lantern, the other cradling his switch-blade. There was no sound but for his footfalls, soft and steady like the snow that began to flurry outside. At first, he wasn't sure he'd heard it, but it got stronger. Footsteps. Behind him. He slid noiselessly round a pillar, extinguishing the bull's-eye as he did so and waited for the step to get nearer. Two of them, he'd say. He pressed himself back further into the darkness. Then his foot jerked out and his fist came down. The first caught the shin and the second the head of Sergeant Dew, who crumpled as one pole-axed.

A shriek from behind caused Lestrade to spin to face the second intruder. Constable Dickens stood staring with open mouth at the speed of the attack. He wouldn't have said the old man had it in him.

'Dew, Dew,' Lestrade was kneeling over the fallen sergeant, 'are you all right?'

'Yes, Guv'nor,' Dew struggled upright, 'just a bit of a headache, that's all.'

'Dickens, where's Jones?'

'Gone with Inspector Bradstreet, sir, as per your instructions. He met us outside the building.'

'Is the place cleared?'

'Yes, sir.'

'Right. Dew. Go home.'

'Sir?'

Lestrade looked at him in the rekindled light of his lantern. 'You're a family man, Walter. What are all the little Dews going to do if they haven't got a daddy by morning? Go home. And that's an order. Give my regards to Mrs Dew.'

The sergeant hesitated, 'I'll wait outside with the Maria, sir. See if I can't get you some tea for when you come out.'

Lestrade slapped his arm in appreciation and the sergeant vanished.

'Right, Dickens. Inspector Bradstreet believes there's either a bomb or a gang of roughneck Irishmen in here somewhere. It's my job to find out which. I could use your help, but I'm not ordering it. If you want to follow the sergeant now, there'll be no hard feelings.'

'What are we looking for, sir, exactly?'

Lestrade smiled. Nimrod Frost had been right. He *did* like this man.

'What do you know about the Houses of Parliament, Dickens?' the inspector asked.

'The present edifice was built in the reign of Queen Anne, of Yorkshire sandstone. A serious fire in eighteen thirty-four led to an extensive renovation under Sir Charles Barry and Augustus Welby Pugin—'

'Yes, yes. Never mind the history lesson. How big is the place?'

'It covers eight acres, sir, has eleven courts, one hundred stairways and eleven hundred apartments.'

'What about this?'

'The clock tower is at the north end.' Dickens looked up into the darkness above. 'Three hundred and eighteen feet. The bell above us, colloquially called Big Ben, although in fact many people believe this refers to the clock itself, was hung in eighteen fifty-eight—'

'Well hung, I hope,' observed Lestrade.

'It weighs thirteen and a half tons.'

Lestrade felt his throat tighten a little. Thirteen and a half tons plus a few floor levels and the roof cascading down on him should the thing blow up. Not to mention the clock. Time would indeed weigh heavily on his hands.

'All right, Constable,' Lestrade took command of his nerves again, 'you proceed in a clockwise direction,' he regretted the phrase, 'and I'll go the other way. Is that your watch ticking?'

'I don't have a watch, sir.'

The inspector and the constable looked at each other. They glanced to the floor. Dickens' bull's-eye shone on a small, rectangular box in the corner. Dew had missed it by inches when he fell.

'Dickens,' Lestrade whispered, 'I want you to take off your boots and walk to the other end of the building. Tell Inspector Bradstreet it's a bomb. And it's ticking.'

'Very good, sir.' And the constable gingerly unlaced his

footwear and padded into the vast halls and chambers where their Lordships, their Graces and countless Right Honourables were due to be sitting in a few weeks' time. Lestrade sat cross-legged on the floor, alone with the ticking and the dark.

It seemed hours before Dickens got back. He crouched by Lestrade. 'I found Jones, sir. It's quite straightforward really. I worked out a short-cut through the Lords' chamber.'

'Has Bradstreet found his bomb?' Lestrade whispered back.

'Yes, sir. From Jones' description, it's identical to yours.'

'What's he doing about it?'

'Jones said he said, and I quote, "Lestrade is the senior man, so it's up to him, but it sounds like a time bomb."'

'Brilliant!' hissed Lestrade. 'All right, Dickens. Tell Jones to tell Bradstreet I'm going to open my box. There are . . .' he adjusted his bull's-eye, 'four screws. I'm going to loosen them one at a time, top right, top left, bottom right, bottom left. Can you remember that?'

'*Please,* sir.' Dickens groaned exasperatedly. It was like asking a man with a photographic memory if his plate was clean. Lestrade put the rather offhand reply down to nerves. He didn't tolerate uppity young constables ordinarily, but tonight he'd make an exception. He switched the blade clear on his brass knuckles as Dickens exited left. He felt the sweat form on his forehead and more trickle down behind his ears. He took off the bowler and the Donegal before tackling the other screws. The first and second were fine. But the third jammed. Cross-threaded, he guessed. Why was there always one? He leaned his full weight on it, unable to tell now whether it was the bomb or his heart that beat louder. It gave way and he was able to turn the blade. Number four followed easily. He sat back on his heels. His wrists felt like lead.

Dickens padded back, breathing hard now with the exertion of his run. 'Right sir. Inspector Bradstreet had difficulty with the first screw apparently, but by now he should have managed it.'

'Right. How long does it take you to get to Jones?'

'About four minutes, sir.'

'And about the same for Jones to reach Bradstreet?'

'I would say so, sir. We meet under the central tower.'

'All right. It's . . .' he checked his half-hunter in the lantern beam, 'sixteen minutes past eight, now. At twenty-four minutes past eight, I'll take off the lid. You wait with Jones. If you don't hear an explosion, tell him to tell Bradstreet to do the same.'

'Yes, sir,' and Dickens was gone again.

While he sat there, trying to stay calm, Lestrade thought of all the places he'd rather be. He thought of little Emma with her shy morning face. Of Harry and Letitia Bandicoot. Of Sarah, his wife. Dear, dead Sarah. Then it was time. He worked quickly, his face contorted in a manic frown. One, two, three, four, the screws worked loose. He wiped his sweaty hands on his trousers and prayed as he'd never prayed before. He teased free the lid and it came away cleanly. He looked at the contents of the box. A clock. Set for eight-thirty. No wires. No gelignite. No bomb. He found himself giggling hysterically, kneeling in a rumpled heap on the floor when Dickens arrived.

'Tell Bradstreet it's all right,' laughed Lestrade. 'It's a hoax. A bloody hoax . . .' But no sooner had he finished than there was a dull roar from some distance away, echoing and re-echoing through the empty halls. 'My God,' murmured Lestrade and he and Dickens raced each other for the Victoria Tower. Through the darkness they hurtled, the bull's-eye's beams darting and flashing in every direction. Through polished corridors, past silent statues they ran, Dickens still in his stockinged feet sliding and slipping in Lestrade's wake. The smoke and flames beat them back as they reached the base of the furthermost tower. What was left of Inspector Edgar Bradstreet lay against the far wall. Lestrade and Dickens grabbed the badly injured Jones and hauled him free of the burning building, out into the raw night.

'It went up, sir. Right in front of us.' Jones mumbled, shivering with shock and pain, 'Inspector Bradstreet . . .'

'All right, lad.' Lestrade mopped the blood from the boy's head. 'It's all right. Dew!' Lestrade turned wildly to the milling mass of policemen, 'Get this man to hospital on the double. You there, get the fire brigade. The rest of you – there's a bloody river over there. Get some water and put this thing out.'

And the snow flurried in through the open door, spitting and crackling on the flames. Lestrade spent the rest of the night at Jones' bedside, hoping he would recover. Hoping he would regain consciousness. No one else slept.

The Second Stein

'So it's finally turned nasty.' Edward Henry tapped his fingers violently on desk, lamp and ephemera. 'How's the Jones boy?'

'The hospital were cagey, sir,' Lestrade told him. 'As well as can be expected, I think is the phrase.'

'It wasn't a very big bomb, then?'

'Big enough to kill one man and very nearly a second. No doubt the country will be delighted to know no damage was done to the fabric of the House.'

Henry was staring across the river where the last skies of the old year were full of unshed snow. He turned back to Lestrade and motioned him to sit.

'Your views, then,' he said, 'as one copper to another.'

'It's not only turned nasty, sir. It's turned personal. That phone call proves it. Whoever was on the other end of that line knows I'm on the case – and he knew Bradstreet was too.'

'Does that help pin it down?'

'No. The papers have had a field day with this one. My name, Bradstreet's, Gregory's. It's in all the dailies.'

'It certainly is.' Henry waved a bundle of that morning's at Lestrade. 'I insisted on total secrecy when I took over this job,' he said, 'and the gentlemen of Fleet Street have chosen to ignore me. Well, this afternoon I'm calling a meeting of City Editors. I'd like you and Gregory to be there. Before that, the commissioner wants to see us all. Best bib and tucker.'

Lestrade returned to the House later that morning. The whole area was heaving with coppers, uniformed and plainclothed. There was a strange air of tension about the place; Lestrade had remembered a similar atmosphere before the Mafeking news had broken.

'We've got her sealed as tight as a drum now, Lestrade,' the Commander of Special Branch had told him. Yes, now, thought Lestrade, now a man is dead. He walked back along the smoky river to the Yard. The wind was biting as he crossed the square. Miss Featherstonehaugh had been no help. The man who phoned had an Irish accent. He had asked – no, demanded – to speak to Inspector Lestrade. He had been insistent. He sounded nearby. The local exchange had been less help still. Now it had become a personal duel, and Lestrade was pretty well where he had been at the start of it all, back with Ralph Childers in the spring. He barely acknowledged Dalgleish's salute as he entered the Yard and when the new swing doors hit him on the back of the head, he only gave a grunt, not at all his usual rejoinder when life's little foibles turned against him. He was mulling over how the pattern had changed. So far, it had been a careful, calculated series of assassinations. Whoever the madman was, there was an obvious method in his work. And all the targets, save one, had been Members of Parliament. Even that one had had political leanings. So why now had the pattern changed? Why had the chain been broken? Why should the two men in charge of the case be lured to what Lestrade felt sure Emily Greenbush would call the scene of innumerable crimes? And why was there death waiting for only one of them? And why should that one be Bradstreet, and not Lestrade? They were each directed to a specific tower, one loaded, the other not. Bradstreet had drawn the short straw. Why? Was it because the late departed Edgar had been on the right track? After all, the man on the telephone *did* have an Irish accent. And, after all, Emily Greenbush *was* still in custody. Well, it was Lestrade's case now. He knew the commander wouldn't waste another man on it. He'd be content to leave it to Lestrade. Now, Lestrade would keep his mind open. Deep down, his sense that this was not a political case was wavering. It wasn't easy for him to admit he was wrong. But having come this far . . .

'Miss Greenbush, you are free to go.'

Emily rose in the cell doorway. The po-faced wardress who was with her scowled her disapproval. 'Her late Majesty,' she said, with an imperiousness above her station, 'was of the opinion these suffragists should be horsewhipped. I am of the same opinion.'

'Good for you,' said Lestrade and escorted the offending article up the steps to the daylight.

'What does this mean?' she asked him in the yard at the back of the Yard.

'That you are free to go,' he said again.

'Yesterday I was an accessory to murder,' she pointed out.

'That was yesterday,' Lestrade told her.

She looked at him with her pale, clear eyes. 'Sholto, what has happened?'

'A man is dead,' said Lestrade, 'a policeman.'

'I'm sorry,' she said.

'Are you?' His response was quicker, sharper than he had intended.

'Yes,' she said, facing him squarely, 'yes, I am.'

He smiled. 'Now it's my turn to be sorry,' he said. 'You'll know by the evening papers, anyway. It's Edgar Bradstreet. He was killed by a bomb last night.'

'My God,' Emily touched his arm, 'who?'

'About now I'd give my pension to answer that one,' he said.

'You look tired, Sholto.'

It wasn't something he had had time to think about.

'Come home with me,' she said.

He looked at her hard. Here was a would-be felon, whom only yesterday Bradstreet had sewn up for murder, inviting an inspector of the Metropolitan Police back to her house – and within the portals of Scotland Yard. On the other hand, it was nearly 1902; the world was changing. And Lestrade knew the charms of Emily Greenbush. Besides, she might yet provide him with some answers.

'Not yet,' he said, 'I've got to go to St Thomas's. One of my constables was hurt by the same bomb that killed Bradstreet. Besides, I've got more meetings today than Mrs Pankhurst has causes. Begging your pardon, of course.'

She laughed. The musical sound Lestrade had not heard from a beautiful woman in a long time. 'Later then?' she said.

'It might be very late,' he warned her.

'Later.' And she held his hand.

The commissioner was terse. Never a happy man, he was, that afternoon, decidedly morose. The new electric light in the Yard's Assembly Hall dazzled on the wealth of silver braid and the draughts caught the gusting plumes of a veritable millinery of cocked hat. The hard-bitten detectives of the first floor and the second, together with the macassared sergeants of the third floor back, sat like drab damson jam in the middle of a plate of gleaming tapioca. At least it seemed so to Walter Dew, now with his recent promotion that much nearer his goal – his biographical memoirs. Edward Henry exhorted, cajoled, threatened. The eyes of the country, no, the world itself were on the Yard at that moment. There was to be an all-out effort. No stone unturned. All leave cancelled. And any officer found revelling in the fountains in Trafalgar Square at New Year was to be dismissed without benefit of pension. A tough line indeed.

Later that day, in the offices of the *Daily Mail* newspaper, Edward Henry made history. He held what was henceforth to be called a Press Conference. The gentlemen of the Press, wreathed in cigar smoke, sat in the said offices, clutching pads and pencils.

'Are we to understand, Mr Henry,' said one, 'that you would have us publish nothing on this case at all?'

'Correct.'

There were rumbles and guffaws in the room. Lestrade looked at Gregory. Gregory looked at Lestrade.

'Er ...' another rose to his feet, 'T A Liesinsdad,' he

announced with the voice of a circular saw, '*Daily Mail*. Are you trying to muzzle the Press, Mr Henry?'

'I am trying to save lives, Mr Liesinsdad. And to catch a murderer to boot. I can't do that without your help.'

'How can we help if we aren't able to publish our stories?' Liesinsdad persisted.

'That's exactly it,' Henry repeated, 'we're not interested in stories, sir. We are in the fact business.'

Roars and shouts drowned him out.

'You are scaremongers, gentlemen!' Henry accused them.

Lestrade and Gregory were suitably impressed. Even though the audience appeared rapidly to be turning into a lynch mob.

'Is it the Boers?' someone demanded.

'No comment,' said Henry.

'The Germans, then. Could it be the Kaiser?'

'Nonsense, it's the French,' somebody else chipped in.

'The whole thing has the smell of gelignite,' said Liesinsdad. 'It's the Irish.'

'No comment,' said Mr Henry.

'What about the Labour Party?' another voice bawled above the din.

'Or the Liberals?' And the whole meeting collapsed in uproar.

'We haven't heard,' said a stately voice from the back, 'from these gentlemen here.' He pointed to Lestrade and Gregory.

'Mr Harmsworth, isn't it?'

'Yes, the *Daily Mail*,' Harmsworth replied, 'I am right in assuming that Inspectors Lestrade and Gregory are in actual charge of the case?'

'Well, if I may say so—' Gregory began.

'I was hoping to hear from Inspector Lestrade,' said Harmsworth.

Lestrade untangled his fingers from the cradle he had formed over his nose.

'I'll offer you a deal, gentlemen,' he said.

'Lestrade!' Henry snapped.

'If you will stop printing rumour and speculation, I will give you your murderer on a plate within a month of the New Year.'

'That's no sort of deal,' Liesinsdad retorted. 'What'll you do? Give us *all* an exclusive?' And mocking laughter filled the room again.

'Unless you can give us facts, Mr Lestrade, we will have to publish what we can,' Harmsworth said.

Lestrade stood up. 'And unless you stop the fiction, Mr Harmsworth, Fleet Street will have successfully spread a screen of smoke so thick across this case, we won't be able to see our hands in front of us. Mr Henry, with your permission, I have a job to do.' And he swept from the room amid cackles and screams for resignations.

Athelney Jones, Inspector, retired, of Scotland Yard, stood bareheaded in the corridor of St Thomas' hospital. He nodded to Lestrade, as he arrived, breathing heavily.

'Tell me one thing,' he said, 'did my boy volunteer?'

Lestrade nodded, 'Bradstreet I'm sure would have given him the option,' he said, 'and, knowing your boy, he chose to stay. Is there any news?'

Jones shook his head.

Lestrade patted his shoulder, something he would have said once he would never have done. Then he took a tram to Curzon Street.

'Is it done, Sholto,' whispered Emily, 'for officers of Scotland Yard to sleep with murderesses?'

'Murderesses?' Lestrade turned to her.

'Isn't that what Bradstreet thought I was?'

'He had no evidence.'

'And that's why you let me go?'

Lestrade nodded.

'Are you married, Sholto Lestrade?' she suddenly asked.

He looked at her in the candlelight, 'Not any more,' he said. 'She died.'

'I'm sorry.'

'Yes, so am I.'

'What was her name?'

'Sarah,' he told her. 'She died seven years ago.'

'And you've passed your apprenticeship without her.'

He smiled, 'Yes, I suppose I have.'

'Children?' she asked.

'A girl,' he nodded, 'Emma. She lives with friends. She doesn't know about me.'

'Doesn't know about you?' she repeated, lifting up on one elbow. 'Why not?'

'Bradstreet wasn't married,' he said, 'and he ended up in pieces all over Victoria Tower. That's bad enough, but how much worse if he'd been a father. What would I have said to his kids? I don't want somebody coming to tell my kid, one day. She's better off where she is.'

'Isn't that her decision, Sholto?' Emily asked.

Lestrade laughed, 'You feminists,' and he planted a gentle punch on her chin. 'Emma is seven years old. Would you have her voting?'

Emily laughed too. Then, as was her wont, she fell silent.

'Sholto. This case of yours. It's serious, isn't it?'

He nodded.

'Parliament reconvenes in five days' time. Let me help you. If your man is on the inside – if he's an Irishman, or a Frenchman or a Boer, I can help. I know more about that collection of misfits at Westminster than they do about themselves.'

'Really? I can believe that. But . . .' he took her hand and kissed it, 'I thought I was the enemy. Why the change of heart? Have you deserted the cause?'

She slowly shook her head. 'Never,' she said. She broke away from him, walking gracefully in the candlelight, her long copper hair swaying round her naked waist. She pulled on the frothy nightgown and looked out on sleeping Curzon Street. 'Oh, Sholto, haven't you guessed it yet?' She turned to him. 'I'm doing this for you because . . . because you need help, and I'm not the harpy the world thinks I am. But I'm also doing it for Geoffrey Manners.'

'Manners?' Lestrade sat upright.

She turned to the window, 'He and I were . . . lovers,' she said. 'Oh, we opposed each other in the House. As I would oppose you, if it came to it, in the street. But here, behind these doors . . .' And she hung her head. He crossed to her, holding her shoulders gently and pulling her back against his chest.

'Well, then,' he whispered, 'we each have our memories. And we each have our cause. Let that be enough.'

Lestrade began his assault as soon as Parliament reassembled. They were not due to sit again until February, but affairs of state brought them back earlier than usual. Back from their country mansions, back from their elegant town houses. Back to the business of Empire. There was a war to finish and a king to be crowned and a whole host of lesser fry. Security in Westminster had never been tighter. Members and their guests were scrutinised as they arrived and as they left. There was a special squad of men who spent most of their shift lying on their backs under carriages, checking for explosive devices. These men claimed to be able to grow marvellous roses in their tunics.

It was to the Irish question that Lestrade first addressed himself.

'And is that all, Mr Redmond, you have to tell me?'

The leader of the Irish bloc in the commons looked at the inspector from Scotland Yard. 'Do you see this?' he asked.

'It's a flag.' The years had not blunted the acuteness of Lestrade's mind.

'This particular part of it, Mr Lestrade, is the Harp of Erin. Did you know that the ladies of the Royal School of Needlework have refused to embroider it for His Majesty's coronation?'

'Indeed?' Lestrade clicked his tongue in mock disbelief.

'They claim, of course, that it's the nakedness of the human form they object to depicting, but I know – and my members know – that it's a deliberate snub to the Irish nation.'

'And that has driven one of your members to murder, Mr Redmond?'

'I have told you, Inspector,' Redmond was a man of infinite patience, 'we are pledged to reform by constitutional means. You have my word on that as an Irish gentleman. I cannot of course speak for the likes of Padraig O'Leary . . .'

'And none of your parliamentary people would stoop to planting bombs in the House of Commons and to murdering policemen in cold blood?'

'Never. But . . .' and Lestrade stopped as he made for the door, 'do you have any Gaelic, Lestrade?'

'I'm not partial to foreign food, sir.'

Redmond looked at him oddly. 'Sinn Fein, Mr Lestrade. It means "Ourselves Alone". That's what we intend to be, Inspector. The day will come. And when it does, I fear there will be blood.'

'Will it be on your conscience, Mr Redmond?'

The leader of the Irish party pulled himself up to his full height. 'No, sir, it will not.'

Most of Redmond's people agreed to having their voices recorded on the phonograph, each one of them asking the question which Aumerle Holmes had overheard at the Diogenes Club. 'Is Hamilcar Waldo here tonight?' Somehow, Lestrade was sure this was the clue to his man. But John Redmond finally complained to Edward Henry about undue police harassment, Lestrade had his knuckles rapped and the recordings stopped. When Aumerle Holmes heard them, he could not be sure. Two or three sounded right, but the phonograph crackled and spluttered and memory had by now well and truly gilded the lily. For all he knew, the Irishman at the Diogenes that night might well have been Miss Langtry. Sergeant Dew followed in his governor's footsteps and quizzed the Diogenes staff. It was slow going, what with their being able to give only three responses and Dew writing it all down in his less than immaculate copper plate. But it was all to no avail. No one remembered an Irishman asking for Mr Waldo and the only Irishman living considered intelligent enough for membership of the club was Mr Bernard Shaw – and he talked far too much.

From there, Lestrade ventured into the camp of the Labour Party, whose room was tucked away from the opulence of the rest and near enough to the river to give the whole place an air of mildew. At least here, the field was small. Two members who represented the labouring classes had been returned at the last election. One was a non-event named Richard Bell. Emily Greenbush had demolished him in a recent much publicised slanging match in the lobby of the Commons. Now he went in mortal fear of her. The other, Lestrade was intrigued to remember when he saw an election poster, habitually wore a deerstalker.

'You habitually wear a deerstalker, Mr Hardie?'

'I do, sir,' Keir Hardie answered in his soft-spoken Scots accent. 'Is that a crime?'

'Not yet,' said Lestrade.

'Let's get down to brass tacks, Inspector,' Keir Hardie closed the book on his desk, 'I happen to represent the people of this country. Not the gentlemen in their fine houses with their bank accounts and their carriages, but the people, Lestrade, ordinary men – and women too – people like you, in fact.'

'What is your point, Mr Hardie?'

'My point is that I haven't got the time to rush around the country killing members of my own Parliament. Good God, man, even laying aside the moral question, I've got an enormous opposition here. I'm forty-five years of age. I haven't got enough years left to finish them all off. There's still six hundred and fourteen to go! No, Mr Lestrade, you look to someone among the Conservatives' own ranks for this. That's where you'll find your maniac. Man, there are scores of them.'

Keir Hardie could not vouch, any more than John Redmond could, for his followers outside those hallowed walls. But something told Lestrade his man was not of the working class. The ease with which he passed unnoticed at exclusive gentlemen's clubs, at private school functions, in the mother of parliaments itself. No, his man was cultured, subtle, clever. And whereas such men, Lestrade knew, were to be found among the denizens of the proletariat (he'd read that phrase in the *Sun* only yesterday), he sensed that such a one was not guilty of the crimes in hand. He would have to look elsewhere.

'Still too cold for tea on the terrace, Inspector Lestrade.' It was Winston Churchill, the Member for Oldham, who hailed him. 'No matter, do join me here. Best fire in the whole damned place. Oh,' Churchill turned to a colleague, 'this is Mr . . . er . . .'

'Bonar Law,' said the colleague, 'Member for Glasgow, Blackfriars Division.'

Lestrade shook his hand before accepting Churchill's armchair and the tea and scones on the Commons china.

'I hear you've been bearding the bore in his lair.'

'Sir?'

'Keir Hardie, the redoubtable Member for Merthyr. Got enough to hang him?'

'I don't think we should make light—' said Bonar Law, but Churchill brushed him aside.

'Seriously Lestrade. What progress?'

'Do you want the political answer or the truth?' Lestrade tried the same line on the young Member that he had tried on his new boss at their first meeting. It was a useful yardstick, he found, in sorting men from boys and indeed, in more pastoral moments, sheep from goats.

'Well, they're never the same thing, are they?' mused Churchill ruefully. 'But there's an hour or so before the House reassembles. It'll make a change to hear the truth.'

'None.'

'But surely—' began Bonar Law.

'The trouble is,' Lestrade went on, 'it's rather like looking for a needle in a haystack.'

'Do you believe the murderer is one of us?' Bonar Law looked appalled.

'Do you mean one of you two, Mr . . . er?' Lestrade checked.

'Bonar Law. No, not precisely. I mean a Member of the Commons.'

'It had crossed my mind, sir.'

Bonar Law fell back in his chair with shock and with horror.

'Oh, come now . . . er . . .' said Churchill, 'logically speaking, it's quite likely. Who knows the moves of an MP better than an MP. Right, Lestrade?'

'I look forward to working under you as Home Secretary, sir.' Lestrade saluted Churchill with his tea cup, enjoying the luxury of a handle.

'Have a care, Lestrade,' Churchill leaned forward, 'walls have ears, you know.'

'Of course,' Bonar Law was summoning up all his powers to be profound, 'it could be someone in . . . the Other Place.'

Both men looked at him. 'The Other Place?' they chorused.

Bonar Law looked anxiously around, 'Don't forget the ears, Winston.'

'I'll try not to,' said Churchill and caught Lestrade's look of utter mystification. 'What Mr . . . er . . .'

'Bonar Law,' said Bonar Law.

'Yes, quite. What he means is the House of Lords.'

'I'll get to them eventually,' said Lestrade.

'Better hurry,' chuckled Churchill, 'some of them haven't got much time!'

And the silence fell as he realised the singular bad taste of the remark.

'Anyway,' Churchill sought to fill the embarrassed space, 'this thing has set us all on edge, Lestrade, I can tell you. I don't mind admitting my service revolver is never very far away nowadays. You know, just in case.'

Yes, Lestrade knew. He patted the brass knuckles in his pocket for his own reassurance before leaving the members to their tea. Then he bade farewell to Churchill and . . . the other one.

The shapely young lady bounced off the Honourable Member's knee, frantically buttoning up her blouse as she did so.

'Mr Lloyd George?' asked Lestrade. 'I hope I'm not interrupting anything?'

'No, no,' the Welshman beamed, 'nothing unusual anyway.' He casually flipped a photograph on his desk. The face of the young lady formerly ensconced on his lap disappeared to reveal that of his wife. 'So you are Lestrade of the Yard?'

'It's a little grandiose,' said Lestrade (another word he'd picked up in the *Sun* that week), 'but it's accurate.'

'And you want to know why I'm going around murdering my colleagues, is that it?'

Lestrade was still for a moment. But this was the Welsh Wizard. Emily had warned him about this one.

'I'm glad you can joke at a time like this, sir,' he said.

'Joke?' roared Lloyd George. 'Joke? My dear fellow, I am without doubt,' he slapped the ample rump of the secretary now returned demurely to continue some filing, 'the most detested man in England at the moment. The King dislikes me more than his mistresses' husbands. People like Kipling can wave their little Union Jacks, Inspector, but I happen to believe the Boers are right. My anti-war meetings have been broken up more times than you've had hot dinners. Tell me, what the bloody hell is there to joke about?'

'I'm not interested in the Boers at the moment, sir. I am trying to conduct a murder enquiry.'

'Aye, and not getting very far either, from what I have heard. Look, I'm not a Limp like Campbell-Bannerman.'

'A limp, sir?' Was this a gammy leg or a sexual complaint, Lestrade wondered.

'A Liberal Imperialist, Inspector.' Lloyd George was the model of patience. He crossed to his secretary and squeezed one of her breasts as she wriggled either with excitement or perhaps with embarrassment at the inspector's presence.

'But,' he wiped his hand down his waistcoat, 'I have been following these murders. Here,' he produced a sheet of paper from a desk drawer, 'is a list of the dates on which the murders took place. And alongside each one, where I was and who I was with in each case.'

'You've been very thorough, sir,' Lestrade remarked.

'The Most Unpopular Man In England has to be, Inspector. I knew you'd get to me sooner or later. After all, I am a Liberal and probably the most outspoken critic of the Government you will find in this House. And outside it. Sooner or later someone was bound to point the finger.'

Lestrade perused the list. 'I see,' he said, 'that Mrs Lloyd George's name occurs only once in this document. These other ladies—'

Lloyd George rushed to him, loudly drowning his sentence with fluster. 'Er . . . various er . . . members of my constituency er . . . friends of the Party and so on . . .' And he edged Lestrade to the door. 'Look,' he whispered, when the secretary was out of earshot, 'a little discretion, dear boy, there's a good fellow. I'm not yet in a position to pull any strings for you of course, but who knows, one day . . .' And he patted Lestrade's arm confidentially. 'In the meantime,' he reached behind the door and produced a cape and helmet of the Birmingham Constabulary, 'when I was at a meeting in Birmingham last year I was damned nearly killed myself. Had to escape dressed up as a bobby. You couldn't return this to them, could you, with my compliments?'

'No, sir,' said Lestrade at his frostiest, 'I think the Lost Property Department is at Paddington Green.' And he left.

It was the middle of the night when the constable hammered on Lestrade's door. In retrospect the inspector was grateful he wasn't in Curzon Street. A constable, all boots and bull's-eye, would not have understood the relationship the inspector had developed with the lady. In fact, Lestrade was not sure he understood it himself.

'You're one of Gregory's men, aren't you?' Lestrade pulled the Donegal over his pyjamas and stuffed his feet into the wrong shoes.

'Yes, sir. The inspector's compliments, sir. 'E says will you come double quick 'cos there's been another one.'

With a summons so gracious and precise, how could Lestrade

refuse? The Maria hurtled through sleeping Pimlico and on into the West End, finally rattling to a halt on the cobbles outside the Metropole. Lestrade followed the constable in, was extra careful to avoid the polished brass of the top step and jammed his hand in the letter box on his left. He only lost one nail in his eagerness to reach the lift and not knowing the constable too well thought it best not to alarm him unduly by screaming. One death in the hotel that night was probably enough.

On the fourth floor, a pale and worried Inspector Gregory met them.

'Hello, Tom. This had better be important,' said Lestrade.

'It is, Sholto.' And he led them to the door of room 83. A trickle of blood, dark and congealed, ran from a point below the brass numbers to the floor where it formed a brown pool on the carpet. At the top of the trickle, a steel point projected. 'That's only the tip of the iceberg,' quipped Gregory, as always grotesquely inappropriately and he forced open the door as far as it would go.

Lestrade saw what was blocking it when he went inside. The body of a man in smoking jacket and pyjamas was pinned to the door by an ugly sword, razor sharp and slightly curved. It had been rammed through his throat with such force that the epiglottis was shattered and the blade must have penetrated the spine and the two inches of oak behind his head. A similar trail of blood had run down his chest to form another stain on the carpet inside.

'He's dead, Sholto.' Tom Gregory, ever the incisive policeman, had done it again.

'Who is he?' asked Lestrade.

'Reginald Cobham, MP for Kettering.'

'Where?'

'Kettering? It's—'

'All right, Tom. Never mind the geography lesson.'

'I called you right away, Sholto. Quite frankly, and I'm not too proud to admit it, you're better at this sort of thing than I am. What do you think?'

Lestrade surveyed the body, carefully peeling back the pyjamas. No other wounds. No sign of bruising or abrasions. He checked the fingernails. No signs of skin or other tissue under them. The room bore marks of a scuffle of some kind. A coffee-table had been overturned. So had a chair. All the lamps were still burning. On the floor lay two beer steins of the type Lestrade knew the Germans favoured – ornately carved cups with hinged metal lids. They were both empty.

'Has anything been touched in this room?' Lestrade asked. Gregory turned to another constable, who shook his head.

'No, Sholto. Bearing in mind how the brass is about fingerprints. Nothing at all.'

'Who found the body?' Lestrade asked.

'I did, sir,' the constable admitted, 'when I came on duty at one o'clock.'

'Who was on before you?'

'Constable Mason.'

'Why did he notice nothing?'

'Well, sir, Mr Cobham wasn't the easiest man to protect, sir. He said he refused to have ... flatfeet ... outside his room. Made us stay in the lobby, downstairs.'

'The lobby?' Lestrade was appalled. 'So anyone could have entered by a side street, the back way or for that matter through a skylight in the roof.'

'Don't be hard on these lads, Sholto. You know we're strained to the limit. Cobham was lucky to have protection at all.'

'Yes,' said Lestrade, viewing the corpse before him, 'he was very lucky, wasn't he?'

He checked the window. No sign of forced entry. 'Constable,' he called the man to him, 'get back to the Yard. Find out if Sergeant Collins is on duty. If he is, tell him to bring his bag of tricks here. If not, find out where he lives and knock him up.'

'Very good, sir.'

'What do you make of the sword, Tom?'

'I've been puzzling over that one. Chinese, isn't it?'

'The Tong?'

'Chinatown isn't my beat, Sholto.'

Lestrade found it. The lamplight glinted on it as he crossed to the door again. Gingerly, he picked it up. A glass phial with a needle at one end.

'What's that?' asked Gregory.

'I'm not sure, Tom. But I think I know someone who is. Finish up here, will you? When Collins is finished, get the body to the morgue. And leave that sword with Sergeant Dew. You might make the point to him that it's sharp.'

Gregory chuckled.

'The question is, Tom, who drank from the second stein?' And he disappeared down the corridor.

Pausing only to have his finger bandaged at the infirmary at Charing Cross, Lestrade made for Baker Street. He was only marginally better dressed than Watson at that hour of the morning and it took a while for the good doctor's eyes to focus on the glass object in Lestrade's hand.

'It's a syringe,' he told him.

'I thought so. What did it contain?'

Watson adjusted his pince-nez and turned up the lamp. He sniffed it, tapped it, removed the needle and licked the base.

'I'd say it was . . . cocaine, Lestrade. Where did you get it?'

'Wasn't that Sherlock Holmes' little vice, Doctor?'

Watson stared at him, 'I think you and I could both do with a drink, Lestrade.'

He poured quadruple brandies.

'Have you seen him again?' Lestrade asked.

Watson nodded, swigging back the brandy. 'Yes, three times. So now you believe it too. You *know* Holmes is alive, Lestrade, don't you?'

'The Swiss authorities were beautifully vague, Doctor. All they could tell me were the official facts as they know them.'

'There's one way,' mused Watson, 'we could check his grave.'

'Body snatching now, Doctor? Isn't that a little before your time?'

'I'm serious, Lestrade. If Holmes is not in that coffin, we'll know he's back. And that he means to kill me.'

Lestrade finished his drink.

'If Holmes is not in his coffin,' he said, 'it's not you he's after, Doctor. Shall we go?'

The Copper's Speeches

'Well, Dew? What do you make of it?' Lestrade munched his bacon sandwich, the doorstep that passed for breakfast at the culinary hands of the sergeant.

'It's definitely a sword, sir.'

And that had taken all Dew's powers of deduction.

'Remind me to commend you to the Assistant Commissioner, Sergeant,' yawned Lestrade. It had been a long night. The Home Secretary was not available in the early hours and an inspector of Scotland Yard ought to know that and ought not to ask. Application for exhumation of a body could be made to the local magistrate. Lestrade and Watson were told to pester him. They did. And were told by an extremely irate gentleman that such procedures took time. It was the early hours of Saturday morning and if the King himself asked, nothing could be done until Monday. Lestrade had filled in the necessary forms and there, along with the bones of Sherlock Holmes, the matter rested.

'That's a nice looking tachi,' was Constable Dickens' comment as he hung up his bowler.

'What?' Lestrade and Dew chorused.

'The sword, sir. It's a tachi.'

Lestrade and Dew looked at each other.

'Of course, Walter. I should have realised. Simply unlock our walking encyclopedia here and we've solved the case.'

'Would that be a tachi case, sir, bearing in mind the parliamentary nature of our enquiries . . .' Dew's voice tailed off into silence as he caught the excruciated look on his guv'nor's face.

'A tachi, sir, is the shorter of the two swords carried by the Samurai or warrior class of Japan. They are made by a process of tempering steel—'

Lestrade grabbed the morning paper and scanned the headlines. 'Dickens, I want a report – in triplicate. Everything you know and don't know about that sword. Come on, Dew, this is where you learn Japanese.' And the inspector snatched his Donegal and bounded from the room.

'It's the blow to his finger,' said Dew to the astonished Dickens and scurried after him for the lift.

What Sergeant Dew was about to discover and what Constable Dickens realised as he read the Graphic's front page, was that there was a Japanese embassy in town. A whole host of grand-sounding Eastern potentates were in London on official high-level business of the first importance. But as the Graphic was furious to have to report, it was all very hush-hush. So was Lestrade as he tiptoed along the carpeted corridor of the Strand Palace Hotel. One thing the Graphic's foot-weary hack had been able to discover and had printed without a qualm, was that the embassy was staying at that hotel. The words 'Scotland Yard' muttered in the ear of the officious desk clerk had, as usual, opened doors. In this particular case, half the fourth floor was given over to Their Excellencies.

Lestrade tapped the nearest door. It opened to reveal a wizened little man in saffron coloured robes who bowed almost double to Lestrade.

'I am from Scotland Yard,' said the inspector.

The little old man bowed again. Lestrade looked at Dew, who was clearly going to be no help at all.

'Scotland Yard,' Lestrade repeated, 'police.'

The little old man bowed a third time. This was becoming monotonous.

'Allow me, sir.' Sergeant Dew prided himself on Orientals. Had he not, as a young constable, walked his beat in

Chinatown? And were not his shirts, even now, laundered by Mr Foo of the Mile End Road? It mattered not one jot that Mr Foo came from Peking, whereas the saffron-coloured gentleman was from an entirely different country. The niceties of the East were lost on Dew.

'Lookee,' Dew began, 'policee. Scotland Yard. You callee boss.' And with that brilliant entrée, he pushed the old man back gently into the room. No sooner was Dew inside than he found himself sprawling. From nowhere two men in armour had rushed the length of the room to the little old man's rescue. When Lestrade looked down, Dew was kneeling in a tight ball, the foot of one of the men firmly planted on his neck, and the tip of a sword in the middle of his back. The second man, with a series of snarls, advanced on Lestrade, his short, curved sword inches from the inspector's moustache. Lestrade found himself wondering how his four-inch bladed Apache knife was going to cope against that. He tried reasoned English, only louder than before, for one last time.

'Inspector Lestrade, Scotland Yard,' he said.

'Ishiro Yamomoto, Charterhouse and Sandhurst,' an impeccably English voice behind him replied.

Lestrade turned to see a young Japanese officer, with gold lace from cuff to shoulder and a chest full of medals. He growled something incomprehensible and both swordsmen sheathed their weapons with a frightening blur of speed and stood back from the crouching figure of Dew.

'You can tell your man to get up now,' said Ishiro. 'Ordinarily my man would have urinated on his back, but . . .'

He caught the look on Lestrade's face and chuckled.

'Yes, perfectly bestial, isn't it? I fear my country has a long way to go before we can hope to reach the sophistication of yours. Cock fighting and foxhunting and so on. Besides,' he returned to his former topic, 'it ruins the carpets.'

'Forgive me, Mr Yamomoto,' said Lestrade, 'may I ask your position here?'

Dew slowly unfolded himself as he realised that the hardware had been safely put away.

'Actually, it's Mr Ishiro,' the officer explained. 'In Japan we reverse the order of names. Another archaic practice. And actually, it's colonel. I am Military Attaché to His Excellency the Japanese Ambassador.'

'I told you, sir,' Dew whispered from the corner of his mouth, 'tachi. This bloke's involved up to his neck.'

'Tea, gentlemen?' Ishiro clapped his hands and led the policemen into a second suite of rooms. The only furniture here was a series of wooden blocks on the floor and the carpets were missing. He sat cross-legged on the polished boards and invited Lestrade and Dew to do the same.

'I'm sorry about this, gentlemen. Personally, I should have thought "when in London . . ." but the wheels of progress grind slow.'

A white-faced lady appeared in a plethora of silk robes, wearing long pins in her jet black hair. She knelt before Ishiro and placed the tray before him. 'Saki or Darjeeling?' he asked. Since Darjeeling was the one he'd heard of, Lestrade chose the latter. Ishiro grunted something to the girl, who poured the tea into the tiny, handleless porcelain cups. Both Dew and Lestrade were at home here. The mugs at the Yard hadn't got handles, either. The girl remained kneeling, her chin on her breast, glancing up shyly at Lestrade from time to time.

Ishiro caught her glance. 'Oh, dear me, I'm forgetting my manners. When our business is concluded, Inspector Lestrade, would you like to have this girl?'

'Have . . . ?' Lestrade nearly dropped his cup. He glanced at Dew, whose smile vanished at once.

'She is a geisha, Inspector. A lady of pleasure. It is her sole purpose in life to please honoured guests.'

'Would I be offending anybody if I declined?' Lestrade asked.

'In the days of the Shogunate you'd probably have lost your testicles or at least had your tongue split. But now we are a *little* more civilised. Despite the wooden pillows, we have come on no end in the last few years.'

Lestrade looked relieved.

'Of course,' Ishiro went on, 'it will mean that your subordinate will have to accept her favours.'

'Me, sir?' Dew nearly choked on his Darjeeling. 'I'm a married man, sir! What would Mrs Dew say?'

'The world is full of married men, Sergeant,' Lestrade observed, 'it's hardly the most onerous of duties. Besides, you'll be able to test the rumour for yourself.'

'Rumour, sir?' Dew looked aghast.

'You know the one.' Lestrade nudged him.

Dew looked at Ishiro. 'My dear fellow,' the attaché said, 'I wouldn't dream of denying you the pleasure of that particular voyage of discovery. But first,' he clapped his hands and the girl scuttled away, 'your business?'

'I am conducting a murder enquiry,' said Lestrade.

'Indeed?' Ishiro finished his tea. 'How can I help?'

'The victim was killed with what I understand you call a tachi – a warrior's sword.'

'Indeed?' said Ishiro again. He clapped his hands and the two swordsmen appeared again. Dew braced himself, wondering how, from a sitting position, he could possibly avoid being peed on this time.

'These gentlemen are *samurai*,' said Ishiro, 'knights I suppose would be your English equivalent of the term. They have less power of course in today's Japan and, to be quite candid, we don't let them wear their swords in public. Well, they're such a nuisance getting on and off the bus.'

'But you let them wear them in London, Colonel Ishiro,' Lestrade commented.

'Oh, the natives love it. No offence, Lestrade.'

The inspector waved it aside. He sensed that being offended by this man might lead to the loss of more than his dignity.

'This one,' he pointed to the longer of the two swords thrust through each man's waist sash, 'is the katana. The other, I fancy, is the one you're interested in, the tachi.'

He barked an order and the *samurai* sprang apart. Walter Dew nearly dropped his cup with surprise. With an astonishing flick of their wrists, both men drew the tachi and stood poised like marionettes on wires, waiting for the next command.

'They are the bodyguards of His Excellency the Ambassador,' Ishiro explained. 'One word from me now and they would kill each other or themselves.'

'Themselves?' said Lestrade.

'Yes. It is done by disembowelling. Using one of these.' Ishiro whipped a dagger from nowhere, a shorter replica of the swords now gleaming like arcs of light in the hands of the *samurai*. 'Shall I demonstrate?'

Lestrade noticed that Dew was beginning to look as yellow as their host.

'I'd rather see how the tachi is used, sir. Not for real, you understand.'

'Of course. Just as well, perhaps. Suicide – *hara-Kiri*, we call it – is usually a token of failure anyway.'

Ishiro got to his feet in a single movement and took the sword from one of the *samurai*. I'm a little out of practice, of course,' he apologised. 'Give me a Maxim, any day.' And he brought the sword up in both hands before letting it fall with an oath on one of the blocks of wood. The thing shattered on impact and Ishiro bowed before returning the sword to its owner. Lestrade picked up the pieces of wood, cut as though with a razor and handed them to Dew.

'This block must be four, five inches thick,' Dew muttered, feeling even more queasy than before when he remembered having one of them in his back a few moments ago.

'What you have there is a pillow,' Ishiro explained. 'You probably lose yours in the Chinese laundry. We slice some of ours for sword practice. Well, each country has its own little foibles. More tea, gentlemen?' He resumed his seat.

'No, thank you sir.' Lestrade spoke for both of them. 'Is the point of the sword ever used?' he asked.

'By a *samurai*, never. You see, we Japanese don't have the problem you English have; this extraordinary inability among

your cavalry officers to decide whether the edge or the point of a
sword is more effective. I suppose,' he scanned the middle
distance while draining his second cup, 'I suppose it *could* be used
that way, but if that was how your murderer struck, Inspector,
he is not from Japan.'

'Thank you, sir,' Lestrade stood up, 'that was all I wanted to
know. You have been most kind,' and he bowed low.

'My dear fellow, how admirably quaint, but do let me shake
your hand. I've been bowing all morning.' And he did so.

As they reached the outer door, the man in saffron robes
appeared again and motioned Dew aside, pointing to an open
door through which the sergeant and the inspector saw the
geisha, naked now and sitting demurely beside a bath of hot
fragrance. Lestrade pushed his sergeant towards her. 'Come
along now, Dew. You wouldn't want to offend these kind
people, would you?'

'But sir, I can't—'

'Nonsense,' Lestrade slapped his shoulder, 'lie back and think
of England. And don't worry. We don't make you stick a knife
into yourself at the Yard.'

He stopped at the door.

'Not for that, anyway!'

Despite the massed resources of Mr Edward Henry, Head of the
Criminal Investigation Department, and of Sergeant Stockley
Collins of the Fingerprint Room, nothing from the scene of
Reginald Cobham's demise produced much of interest. Both
beer steins had contained beer. 'Three cheers for modern
science,' applauded Lestrade mentally. There were no fingerprints on the sword hilt, the second stein or any of the furniture.
The door had not been forced and according to Gregory's
report, no untoward sounds had been heard either by staff or
guests. In short, it was a typical brick wall. Except that Lestrade
now knew his murderer was not Japanese (well, he now only
had all the other countries in the world to eliminate) and either
the murderer or his victim or both used, or at least carried,

cocaine. Not content, as a good policeman never should be, with one man's verdict, Lestrade had the laboratory at the Yard, that curious little room that doubled as the Police Museum, check the contents of the syringe. Even though it was Sunday, he used his considerable charm in the form of a mildly administered hammerlock to persuade the boffin to carry out the necessary tests. Yes, the good Dr Watson had been right. It had contained cocaine and search though he might the cold dead arms of the late Reginald Cobham in his refridgerated drawer at the morgue, he could find no signs of needle marks. That indeed began to limit the field. A deerstalker, an Ulster, a tall man who used cocaine . . . But he was running before he could walk.

And before he could do anything, there was an urgent summons from the Foreign Office. It was signed by Lord Lansdowne himself. The lights were burning that evening in mid-January as the inspector entered through the side door in the building in St James's Square. The constable of the watch recognised him and he went unchallenged to the top floor as requested. He knocked on the oak-panelled door. 'Inspector Lestrade,' he tucked the bowler under his arm, 'CID.'

It was Mycroft Holmes who met his gaze first, but that gentleman moved aside to close the door and to reveal the seated figure of Henry FitzMaurice, the Fifth Marquess of Lansdowne. His fierce eyes smouldered in the firelight and the heavy, grey moustache twitched with irritation.

'What do you know about CID?' he barked, pointing an accusatory finger at Lestrade. 'That's top secret information. Holmes, do we have a leak?' His voice cracked in panic for a moment.

Mycroft was his usual laconic self. 'I believe Inspector Lestrade is referring to the Criminal Investigation Department of Scotland Yard, sir, not er . . . the other thing.'

Lansdowne gasped and flicked his fingers. Holmes poured his lord and master a stiff brandy, which Lansdowne clutched convulsively. 'Thank God,' he muttered several times, 'thank God.'

'Sit down, Lestrade.' Holmes was without the comparative bonhomie he had displayed at their last meeting at the Diogenes Club.

'Would you mind telling me,' Lansdowne had recovered, both his composure and his seat, 'why an Inspector of Police should call on a Japanese military attaché at an accommodation which was kept secret?'

God, thought Lestrade, Dew's performance couldn't have been that bad, could it? In fact, he rather thought the sergeant looked a little pleased with himself on his return to the Yard, but men like Walter Dew were pleased if they got out of bed the right side of a morning.

'In the first place, sir,' he began, 'the accommodation was far from secret. I read it in yesterday's *Graphic*.'

'*Graphic*?' Lansdowne quailed. 'Holmes, check the Editor. The man's in the pay of China, or I'm the Queen of Sheba.'

'Very good, Your Majesty,' Holmes answered him po-facedly. Lansdowne glared at him.

'As for my reason for being there, I was conducting my enquiries. The late Mr Reginald Cobham was murdered with a Japanese sword.'

Lansdowne took another gulp at his brandy. 'Yes, yes. Reggie. I know. Shocking. Shocking.' He paused. 'You can't seriously think a member of His Excellency's staff—'

'I can safely say that the Japanese are not involved, sir.'

Lansdowne and Holmes breathed a sigh of relief.

'But it looks as though someone went out of their way to make it look as though they were.'

'What do you mean?' Lansdowne asked.

'I thought you might be able to tell me,' said Lestrade.

'Us?' queried Holmes.

'Lestrade,' Lansdowne persisted, 'whatever your motives in this matter, you had no right to go trampling on Japanese sensibilities. They are a strange people, you know, fierce, proud. And they are here on a matter of extreme importance. I cannot, of course, divulge too much, but our entire position in the Far East depends on the outcome of their visit. One breath of scandal—'.

'Is that why someone killed Cobham with a Japanese sword? To make it appear as though the Japanese were responsible?'

Lansdowne and Holmes looked at each other.

'Reggie Cobham was ... instrumental shall we say in working with the Ambassador's party,' Lansdowne said and, turning to Holmes, '*could* it be the Chinese, Holmes?'

'It could always be the Chinese, my Lord,' Holmes nodded, 'they've never forgiven us for the Boxer business, Lestrade—'

'That's enough, Holmes!' snapped Lansdowne. 'Walls have ears, you know.'

Obviously, Lestrade realised, Lansdowne was in touch with Winston Churchill. Perhaps even with the other one, whose name was on the tip of no one's tongue.

'Well, Lestrade,' Lansdowne steadied himself for the admonition, 'we'll say no more about it this time. But if I find you meddling in Foreign Affairs again, I'll have you out of the Yard so fast your feet won't touch the ground. Do you understand me?'

'Perfectly, sir,' said Lestrade.

'I'll see you out,' said Holmes, and they left Lansdowne with eyes and fingers whirling wildly.

'You must excuse Lord Lansdowne, Lestrade. He has a lot on his mind. What with the Japanese alliance ... Oh, God, what a giveaway!'

Lestrade stopped in the corridor. 'Mr Holmes, I could use a little help round about now.'

Mycroft looked at him, 'I appreciate that, Lestrade. But I don't see—'

'This doesn't come easy for me, Mr Holmes. I understand, however, that you, as well as your late brother, have an interest and ability in solving crimes.'

Holmes chuckled. 'This is rather more than a three-pipe problem though, isn't it?'

'Let's start with the basic question. Who is killing our MPs?'

'You see that, Lestrade,' Holmes pointed to a map of the world, 'that little red bit is us. Great Britain. The other little red bits are our Empire. It's because of them nobody likes us, Lestrade. They're green, you see – with jealousy rather than the colour in the atlas. Was it not our great Prime Minister himself who coined the phrase "splendid isolation"? Well, take it from me, Lestrade, it's getting less splendid by the minute. You want to know who's killing our MPs? My guess, as a senior civil servant in the Foreign Office, would be the Boers – they're losing the war, you know. It will all be over in a few months, mark my words.'

Lestrade turned to go.

'Or,' Holmes stopped him, 'it could be the Germans. Yes, I know the Kaiser is His Majesty's nephew, but blood is not thicker than water, Lestrade, especially when most of the world's water is ruled by the Royal Navy. It's that that sticks in His Imperial Majesty's stiff-necked craw. There again, there's always the French. You remember Fashoda in 'ninety-eight.'

Lestrade didn't.

'Well, it was an obscure village on the Nile then, but tomorrow, who knows? They've never really forgiven us for Waterloo, you see. Or for buying up the Suez Canal. Then, of course, it could be the Americans. Tricky lot, the Americans. Lansdowne thinks it's the Chinese—'

'With respect, Mr Holmes, this isn't narrowing my field down very much.'

'Well, that's Africa, as they say, Mr Lestrade. Now, there's a thought. The Watusi. Your man isn't a seven-foot negro, is he?'

'Not unless he's a master of disguise, Mr Holmes. Which brings me to another point. Are you aware that Doctor Watson thinks your late brother is still alive?'

Holmes' demeanour visibly changed.

'Watson is a very sick man, Lestrade. Very sick. I've said too much already. Your way out is down the corridor and second left for the stairs. Thank you for coming.'

'But—'

'Good night, Mr Lestrade.' And Mycroft Holmes vanished behind double doors, disappearing into the corridors of power.

It was raining as they exhumed Sherlock Holmes on that Monday morning. Dr John Watson of 221B Baker Street stood bareheaded beside the grave, irrespective of the weather. Inspector Sholto Lestrade, of H Division, Scotland Yard, stood with him, but his deference to the rain was greater than his deference to the late Great Detective and he kept his bowler on. Constable Dickens did likewise and the long-suffering grave-diggers toiled in oilskins. No one spoke. Exhumations were melancholy affairs. There were more jolly ways of spending a January morning.

'I'm surprised he wasn't buried in the family vault,' Lestrade observed.

'I didn't think it proper,' Watson was not his usual self, 'bearing in mind the circumstances of his death.'

The coffin was dragged to the surface by the grunting, cursing gravediggers.

'Open it,' said Lestrade.

They set to with crowbars and levers. It had been ten years. The screws had rusted fast. Watson braced himself. Dickens was wondering what state of preservation was possible after ten years in the London clay.

'Stop! I forbid it!' a voice roared across the silence of the cemetery. A tall figure, displaying less dignity than usual, was bounding over the graves towards them.

'It's Spring-Heeled Jack,' mused Lestrade, suddenly reminded of the tales of terror his father told him. And his father was one of those coppers who had seen the terror face to face.

'God, it's Mycroft!' growled Watson, wishing he was currently under any of the nearby stones.

'I didn't know he could move that fast,' Lestrade observed.

'This is an outrage, Lestrade, what is the meaning of this?' Mycroft fumed.

Lestrade handed Holmes the magistrate's papers.

'This is invalid,' Holmes shouted. '*I* am the next of kin. No exhumation can take place without my signature. Whose idea was this?'

'It was mine,' muttered Watson.

'Yours?' Holmes was speechless.

'If I may correct you,' said Lestrade, 'those papers are perfectly valid. They have been signed by Mr Edward Henry, Head of the Criminal Investigation Department.'

'On what grounds?' Holmes demanded.

'On the grounds that there is suspicion of a crime.'

'What crime?'

'Open it,' said Lestrade to the gravediggers, 'and we shall see.'

'No!' Holmes brought his cane crashing down on the hand of the nearest man, forcing him to drop his crowbar. He raised it again, but Lestrade caught it on his switchblade and wrenched Holmes' arm aside.

'That constitutes common assault, Mr Holmes. And I would urge you to refrain from using your cane as a weapon against me or it will constitute striking a police officer. It might also constitute a broken arm.'

Holmes was purple with rage, but he lowered the cane and glowered at Lestrade. The inspector slipped the knife back into his pocket and motioned the gravediggers to continue. With a jar and a squeal of timbers, the lid came loose. Watson was the first to peer in.

'Good God,' and he stepped back as though bitten by a snake.

Lestrade crouched by the coffin. It was full of rocks. If there had ever been a body in it, it was not there now.

'Can you explain this, Mr Holmes?' Lestrade asked.

Holmes was visibly shaken, but not for nothing was he the brother of the Great Detective, so the Great Civil Servant pulled himself up to his full height and said, 'No sir, I cannot.'

'Then I don't think we need to detain you, sir,' said Lestrade.

Holmes whirled away from the graveside.

'One thing more.' Lestrade stopped him. He turned to the injured person, 'Do you want to press charges against this man?'

The gravedigger looked at Holmes in his astrakhan collar and his gold watch chain and thought better of the whole thing. He shook his head.

Holmes stabbed the air with his cane. 'By the time I've finished with you, Watson, you'll be curing lepers in Tanganyika. And as for you, Lestrade, you won't just be policing the river, you'll be under it!' And he crunched away on the gravel to his waiting carriage.

'How do you suppose he found out, sir?' Dickens spoke for the first time.

'He's a member of His Majesty's Foreign Office, Constable. He only has to knock on the right door and he knows when any of us sneezes. Are you all right, Doctor?' He turned to the ashen Watson.

'I hadn't really imagined—' Watson began.

'Did you see Sherlock Holmes in this coffin ten years ago?'

'No. It came by train and steam packet from Switzerland, all sealed and signed for. I never dreamed—'

'But you asked for the exhumation,' said Lestrade.

'Because I'd seen the figure that resembled Holmes in Baker Street. I'm a man of science, Lestrade. Like you I kept telling myself it's not him. It's someone dressed as him. But now . . .' And he took a hearty swig from his hip flask.

'Constable,' he turned to Dickens, 'see the doctor home. I shall need a list of all those you can remember who were present at Sherlock Holmes' funeral, Doctor. The constable will take it down.'

Dickens led Watson away, but hung back with Lestrade for a moment.

'Is it Tanganyika that's bothering him, sir?'

Lestrade looked at him. 'Something like that, Constable,' he said.

It was towards the end of the month that Constable Jones returned from death's door and hobbled into the Yard for duty. Bradstreet had caught the full impact of the blast and Jones had been lucky. No one breathed a heartier sigh of relief than Inspector Lestrade. After all, as he explained to Dew, if Jones had died, he would have the palaver of training another constable. That would constitute inconvenience.

'So, gentlemen, we are looking for a man who, for reasons of his own, is impersonating the late Sherlock Holmes of 221B Baker Street.'

'The Great Detective?' Jones asked. He received an icy stare from the others.

'He hasn't been well,' Lestrade excused him by saying.

'Forgive me, sir,' Dickens was clearly puzzled. Anxiety furrowed his forehead, 'But if the coffin of the late Sherlock Holmes was full of rocks, aren't we looking for Holmes himself?'

'There is that possibility,' Lestrade agreed, 'but there are things about that that I'm not happy with. First,' he checked himself just in time from counting on his fingers in the Bradstreet manner, 'there is the time lapse. Holmes went over the Reichenbach Falls ten – no, eleven – years ago now. Why has he been silent all this time? Why does he wait until now to appear to Watson?'

Dew was excelling himself. 'But perhaps he was in hospital, sir. Some sort of foreign clinic. I believe he smoked cocaine.'

'He didn't smoke it, Sergeant, he injected himself with it.'

'Hence the syringe in the hotel room where Reginald Cobham died.' Jones *had* been ill.

'Quite so, Jones,' said Lestrade. 'And, yes, Dew, your clinic idea is a possibility. Without the full co-operation of the Swiss, I doubt if we'll ever find that out. I've been saying for years there ought to be an international police organisation, but nobody listens.'

'Why else do you think it's not Sherlock Holmes, sir?' Dickens asked.

Lestrade bit the end off a cigar. 'Second,' he said, 'I can see a motive for Holmes sending shivers up Doctor Watson's spine. He hated him. But why kill Members of Parliament? From what I remember of the man, he had no particular political leanings.'

'How er . . . reliable is Doctor Watson, sir?' Dew asked.

'He's hitting the hip flask a bit,' Dickens observed.

'Do you think he *really* saw Sherlock Holmes?' Jones enquired.

'If you're implying he's more likely to see little green caterpillars all over his wallpaper, I don't think so. Besides, his housekeeper, Mrs Hudson, saw him too.'

'Ah,' said Jones, 'housekeeper. Can we rely on her to be impartial, sir? Could there be something between them?'

Lestrade blew rings into the air. 'Spoken like a true detective, Constable,' he said. 'You know, you're a lot brighter than your old man.'

'Thank you, sir.'

'Not difficult,' Walter Dew was heard to mutter under his breath, but he changed it at the last moment to a cough.

'There is one possibility, sir.' Dickens had woken up. 'From what you've told us, and from the stories of Doctors Watson and Conan Doyle, Sherlock Holmes had little time for the Yard.'

'For policemen in general,' Lestrade agreed.

'Isn't it the perfect motive for him then, sir? For him to use what he considers his gigantic brain to outwit us? To sprinkle false trails left, right and centre – and still to leave deliberate calling cards like the deerstalker, the Ulster and the syringe – just to bolster his ego?'

'Better and better,' said Lestrade, a man rarely impressed.

'I want to know where Mr Mycroft Holmes fits in to all this,' said Dew.

'Yes, Walter,' Lestrade pointed at him with his cigar, 'so do I.'

In accordance with Lestrade's orders, gentlemen wearing deerstalkers and Ulsters were questioned by policemen, plain-clothed and uniformed. Mr Keir Hardie appeared three times in as many weeks at Cannon Street and Clapham, and each time there were apologies all round and a certain amount of egg on Metropolitan and City faces. It was interesting, however, how the two London police forces were working together. Only four punch-ups had been recorded between officers. Not even the dark days of the Ripper had produced such camaraderie.

So at first, when Lestrade looked at *another* man who 'fitted the description etc.' he was cool. Another over-zealous constable looking for a stripe had grabbed an innocent passerby. But then, he looked more closely. The man below the deerstalker bore an extraordinary resemblance to the Great Detective – the piercing, intense stare, the hawk's nose, the gaunt features.

'You are?' Lestrade asked.

'Mr William Gillette,' the other replied. 'Why have I been brought here?'

'Routine enquiry,' said Lestrade and waved his fingers at the still desk-bound Jones to dig out his notebook and put pen to paper. 'Please sit down, Mr Gillette. May I ask your profession?'

'I am an actor.' And he said it in such a stentorian way that no one could argue.

'Indeed.' It was not one of those professions with which Lestrade felt immediately at home. 'May I know something of your background, Mr Gillette – home, family . . . ?'

'No, sir, you may not.' Gillette produced a small glass bottle such as ladies use for scent and proceeded to squirt its contents down his throat. The policemen looked at each other. Lestrade gambled with his constable's encyclopedic memory.

'Jones?' he said.

'William Gillette,' the constable began, 'born twenty-fourth July eighteen fifty-five in Hartford, Connecticut, United States of America, the son of former senator Francis Gillette and Elizabeth Daggett. Educated at Harvard and Yale—'

'And the Massachusetts Institute of Fine Arts.' Gillette stood up, clearly peeved. 'Am I under arrest?'

'No sir,' said Lestrade quietly, 'you are merely helping us with our enquiries.' He paused. 'You *are* helping us, sir, aren't you?'

'Who are you?' Gillette asked him.

'Inspector Lestrade. This is Constable Jones.'

Gillette burst into a fit of laughter and sat down again. 'Well, that's all right then!' he managed, between hysterics.

'What is it?' Lestrade was prepared to be amused.

'Perhaps I'd better explain. I am playing against you every night at the moment. In *Sherlock Holmes* at the Lyceum. I never thought I'd meet you in the flesh.'

Apart from Gillette's chuckling, one could have heard a pen drop in Lestrade's office. It fell from the astonished hand of Constable Jones.

'Do I understand you correctly?' Lestrade was first to recover. 'You are acting in a play called *Sherlock Holmes*?'

'Acting?' exclaimed Gillette. 'My dear fellow, starring would be a better word. I *am* Sherlock Holmes.'

Another silence.

'And the garb you are wearing?' asked Lestrade.

'Ah, a little conceit of mine. I must confess . . .' Lestrade and Dew both stiffened, 'I wear it as a little extra publicity. It does no harm, you know.'

'Are you ever in the vicinity of Baker Street?' Lestrade asked.

'221B, you mean? No, in fact, I've never met John Watson. Although of course I know Conan Doyle very well.'

'You do?'

'Why, yes, we wrote the play together. I wrote to Watson asking him to join us, but I don't recall receiving a reply. Look Lestrade . . .' Gillette became confidential, 'you haven't taken umbrage, have you?'

Lestrade wasn't sure what that was, but he knew he had not knowingly taken it.

'I mean,' Gillette went on, 'I had no intention of causing you embarrassment. That piece in Act Three doesn't make you look a *complete* buffoon, does it?'

Lestrade raised an eyebrow.

'Damn it, man, I got the characterisation from Conan Doyle.'

'Who in turn got it from Doctor Watson. Yes, I know. Your

interpretation of my character is not my concern, Mr Gillette –
at the moment. What does concern me is that there is a maniac
going around London wearing the clothes of the late Sherlock
Holmes.'

'I beg your pardon?' said Gillette.

'And before you ask, impersonating idiots is not an offence
under British Law. But this particular maniac kills people.'

Gillette visibly subsided.

'Now do you understand why you have been brought here?'

'God, yes, I do,' said Gillette. 'Inspector,' suddenly the arch
actor lost his stage presence, 'I can assure you I had nothing
whatever to do with this. I—'

'That remains to be seen,' Lestrade cut him short. 'In the
meantime, my officers and I will wish to take statements from
you and everyone in your cast.'

'Oh, of course, of course,' offered Gillette. 'I shall see to it that
you gentlemen receive free tickets.'

'That will not be necessary, sir,' replied Lestrade, 'but could I
ask you not to impersonate Mr Holmes anywhere else but on the
stage in future?'

'Certainly, my dear fellow, certainly.' And he made gratefully
for the door.

'Rather a close shave, eh, Mr Gillette?' said Jones as the actor
exited left. 'Do you think he's got something to hide, sir?' to
Lestrade.

The inspector took the unprecedented step of pouring his own
tea. 'Probably only wrinkles and a few grey hairs,' he said, 'but
we'll have to delve further.'

Dew and Dickens thoroughly enjoyed the show at the Lyceum
and found themselves giggling helplessly as, on stage, Lestrade
tripped over the furniture, collided with the hat stand and
generally made a *complete* buffoon of himself. Lestrade remained
expressionless throughout, watching Gillette intently. Every
gesture, every word was so right. It was as though Sherlock
Holmes had risen from his grave.

Backstage, instead of the usual adulation, all was very subdued and tense as the three policemen interrogated cast and crew. Dew wasn't altogether happy with W L Abingdon who played the fiendish Professor Moriarty. Anyone who played a villain so convincingly must have something to hide. But he could pin nothing on him and had to let it go. All in all, it was a fruitless evening.

'Have you read this, sir?' Dickens bounded in some days later, a paper in his hand and the doorknob in Lestrade's ear. The inspector had been bending over to tie his shoelace at precisely the wrong moment. 'Oh, sorry, sir.'

'That's all right, Constable,' Lestrade said through clenched teeth. 'What is it?'

'The latest edition of *Punch,* sir.'

'Don't tell me,' said Lestrade, 'they're getting at the Yard again.'

'No, sir, not this time. Look.'

Lestrade read the relevant paragraph. 'Arthur Conan Doyle, forty-two, surgeon, and William Gillette, forty-four, actor, two able-bodied men, were flung into the dock charged with the exhumation of Sherlock Holmes for purposes of gain ... Professor Moriarty stated that Sherlock Holmes was never really dead, but merely in a comatose condition ...'

Lestrade flopped back in his chair. Then realisation dawned.

'It's what they call a review, Dickens. They are referring to the play at the Lyceum.'

'But the exhumation—' Dickens began.

'A figure of speech,' explained Lestrade, reading on. 'Mind you, here's a sentiment I can't fault: "The magistrates dropped the case, saying that if Sherlock Holmes was not dead, he ought to be"!'

It was some days later that a cryptic note addressed to Lestrade arrived. It was from William Gillette. And its contents sent the inspector post-haste to Mr Henry's office.

'Let me see if I understand you correctly, Lestrade. You want to go undercover as an actor. Why?'

'Because there's *another* play about Sherlock Holmes afoot – at Terry's theatre. They're auditioning now.'

'And you think—'

'You know my opinion, sir. Our man is using the Holmes disguise. It's perfect. People see – if they see anything at all – the deerstalker and the Ulster. They don't see the man inside them.'

'And one of the cast of this new play—'

'It's a stone I can't leave unturned, sir.'

Henry looked at the inspector from H Division. 'I don't like undercover work, Lestrade. It smacks of melodrama.'

'But that's exactly what this is, sir.'

'Are you any good?'

'Well, sir, I was persuaded to take part in the police revue two years ago.'

'And?'

'Modesty forbids, sir, but my Sarah Bernhardt was legendary.'

Henry humphed several times, then reached for his pipe.

'Very well, Lestrade. But be careful. I've lost an inspector on this damned case already. And keep in touch with someone – your sergeant, what's his name?'

'Dew, sir.'

'Yes.' He plugged the tobacco in the bowl and caught Lestrade's look. 'Yes, it *is* a meerschaum, Lestrade. And no, I have not been going round murdering MPs dressed up as Sherlock Holmes. If you'd care to check my alibis?'

'Nothing could be further from my thoughts, sir.'

Early February and empty theatres did not go together. Lestrade tried to look as Bohemian as possible. Despite his legendary Sarah Bernhardt, he really didn't have a great deal going for him on the boards.

'Next!' a stentorian voice roared from the darkness of the auditorium.

'That's you,' someone hissed behind him.

He shuffled self-consciously into the limelight.

'Name?' the voice roared.

'Lister,' he replied, using the time-worn alias, and then to make it a little more theatrical, 'Roderick.'

'What have you done?' the disembodied voice said. It was a little lighter, more effeminate now. He glanced down wondering if he'd trodden in anything.

'I beg your pardon?' he said.

'Oh, never mind. What part are you trying for?'

'Er . . . Doctor Watson,' said Lestrade.

'Oh, God,' he heard the voice mutter, 'not another one. Look,' it resumed its theatrical level, 'you're about a foot too tall and three stone too light. Still, I suppose this is supposed to be a comedy. All right, Clarence.'

Silence.

'Clarence, dear, where are you this time?'

A tall, rather limp character drifted on stage and looked Lestrade up and down.

'Ah, Clarence, there you are. From the top, sweet. Page four.'

Clarence stood with one arm locked behind his back, and furrowed his brows. 'Well, Watson,' he had the enunciation of a razor blade and it positively ripped Lestrade's ears, 'what do you make of it?'

Silence.

'Roderick,' wailed the voice in the darkness, exasperated now, 'that's you. You're on, dear.'

'Oh,' mumbled Lestrade. 'Sorry.'

'Clarence! Give it to him again, heart, will you?'

'Well, Watson,' Clarence declaimed, 'what do you make of it?'

Lestrade cleared his throat. It wasn't easy to see the script in this light, but he did have the advantage of knowing what the real Watson sounded like.

'I didn't care for the man's tone, Holmes,' he said. 'In fact, I—'

'Thank you. Next,' said the floating voice.

'I beg your pardon?' said Lestrade. Clarence wandered off again.

'Look, Roderick,' the voice appeared before the footlights now, an overweight gentleman with a wig which looked as though it once belonged to Oscar Wilde, 'it's nothing personal dear. It's just not Watson. I'm sorry.'

'Another part then,' Lestrade suggested. 'What about the policeman?'

'The policeman? Oh, you mean Lestrade? Oh, no, you're all wrong.'

The voice caught the look in Lestrade's eyes.

'Oh, very well. We'll try. Page two hundred and twenty-one. Clarence!'

Clarence swanned back on and assumed the same stance as before, the brows beetling as though crumbling under the weight of the gigantic brain.

'Well, Lestrade, what do you make of it?' he read. It all sounded depressingly familiar.

'I haven't a clue, Mr Holmes. There is no one at the Yard who can hold a candle to you, sir.'

'No! No!' the voice fumed, slapping his thighs with the script, 'Roderick, darling. Lestrade is as common as muck. He lacks any finesse whatever. You make him sound too ... well, too human. Do it again, Clarence, from the top.'

They repeated it. And although Lestrade nearly choked on the words, the voice seemed to like it.

'It'll have to do. We're running desperately late as it is. All right, Roderick. You've got the part, dear. Leave your address at the stage door, will you? I'll be in touch.'

'Thank you,' said Lestrade. 'Er ...'

'Yes?'

'How big a part is it?'

'Well, you just read it, dear. Decide for yourself.' And the voice bustled off into the darkness, muttering something about prima donnas.

* * *

Lestrade walked back home that night. It was crisp and clear and he needed air. Time to think. He was on the right track. He was sure. The slowest yet surest method there was: eliminate all the possibles, work on the probables and you have your answer. But would the answer be there before anyone else died? He wrestled with it, worried it, turned it this way and that in his mind. Then he turned right instead of left, towards Curzon Street.

The Tintagel Squires

Lestrade had been at the Yard all night. He was tired, very tired. Tired of staring at the board with its maze of chalked victims, places, times. He had known murderers before who broke the pattern, who killed by a variety of means, never allowing themselves to be pinned down to one method. But the difference with this one – and it was this which rattled Lestrade the most – was the man's coolness and his total disregard, and contempt, for the police.

'You and I have known cases,' Dew had said to him in an unusually patronising moment (the stripes having gone to his head), 'where the murderer was a woman posing as a man. Is that it now, I wonder?'

Lestrade was used to Walter Dew trying to better himself by ruminating aloud. Thought was such a strain for the man that he couldn't do it silently. Most of it was nonsense, but just occasionally there was a flash of something that approached reason. A woman. A woman? Bradstreet would have said that the obvious choice was Emily Greenbush. And even though Lestrade shared her bed and her innermost thoughts from time to time, he was too much of a policeman to let that cloud his judgement. All the same, it was a dangerous liaison. One that he would have to end – one day.

He was still wrapped in thought – cyanide gas, ping-pong bats, tainted wine glasses, Martini-Henrys – when Constable Jones hobbled in.

'Have you seen the morning papers, sir?'

Lestrade's eyes looked and felt like roast chestnuts on that February morning.

'Morning?' he grunted.

'Oh, sorry sir. Good morning.' Jones had forgotten his manners.

'Do you mean to tell me it's morning?' Lestrade unwrapped his feet from the desk top.

'Cup of tea, sir?'

'Music to my ears, Jones,' said Lestrade. 'It's your turn for the Bath Olivers.'

'Got 'em, sir.' Jones produced the biscuits.

'Good God!' Lestrade saw the headlines: 'Is Sherlock Holmes Alive?' He read the article. Speculation that Holmes had engineered his own demise, that he had been in hiding in Venezuela, that he was in the pay of the Boers, that his mind had gone. Well, certainly the last supposition made some sense to Lestrade. 'And where,' the article went on, 'does Professor Moriarty fit into this?'

'Moriarty,' snarled Lestrade, hurling the paper from him, 'is a figment of Doctor Watson's dubious imagination. When will these people in Fleet Street learn to sort fact from fiction?'

'There's a crowd of newspapermen outside,' said Sergeant Dew, brushing the snow from his Donegal. 'Filthy morning, sir.'

'Same to you,' grunted Lestrade. Dew and Jones exchanged glances.

'Bath Oliver?' Jones offered them to Dew.

'No thanks. I had one only last week. And don't call me Oliver. Ha. Ha.'

No one else laughed.

'What do they want?'

'Usual thing, sir. A comment from you. I told 'em you wouldn't be in until twelve. It didn't work.'

'It never does. What's Dalgleish doing about it?'

'Keeping them back, sir, as best he can. It's like Horatius and the bridge down there.'

'Horatius and the bridge?' Lestrade was frankly astonished by his sergeant's new-found culture.

'He features in *The Lays of Ancient Rome* by Lord Macaulay, sir,' said Jones. '"Lars Porsinna of Clusium—"'

'Thank you for that, Constable.' Lestrade cut him short. 'Dew, get down to Dalgleish and tell him to allow one – *one*, mark you – of the gentlemen of the Press to come up.'

'With respect, sir, that will cause a riot,' said Dew.

'Good,' said Lestrade, 'that'll give us a chance to arrest the lot of them. On your way.'

Dew and Dickens collided in the doorway. 'Sorry, Sergeant. Filthy morning, sir,' Dickens said to Lestrade.

'Don't tell me there's a crowd of newspapermen outside, Dickens,' said Lestrade.

'Well, yes, sir, how did you know?'

'Never mind. How far have you got with that list?'

'List, sir?' Dickens dived gratefully for the mug of tea Jones had poured for him.

'The mourners at Holmes' funeral.'

'Nothing of note, sir.' Dickens dug out his notepad. 'Two of them are dead. Or at least, everybody claims they are.'

'Well we can't go round exhuming all and sundry,' said Lestrade, 'even cynics like us must assume some people tell the truth. What about the living?'

'Eight have alibis for most of the murders, sir. One is inside.'

'Oh?'

'Defacing Westminster Bridge.'

'That hasn't been a crime since Robert Peel was Home Secretary – eighty years ago.'

'Ah, but he was trying to deface it with three pounds of gelignite, sir. Had a grudge against the Metropolitan Omnibus Company and wanted to make his point somewhere along their route.'

'Anything else?'

'Nothing untoward, sir. No one could shed any light on Holmes' death at all. Most of them seemed to be fond of him.

They didn't have much time for Watson, though. I've got three more to see.'

He handed the list to Lestrade. 'All right,' said the inspector, 'I'll deal with these.'

'Mr . . . er . . . Lise . . . Lis—' Dew stumbled at the doorway.

'Liesinsdad,' said the reporter, '*Daily Mail*. Inspector Lestrade, it's good of you to see me at—'

'Let's get down to brass tacks, Mr Liesinsdad. Is this your article?' He waved the paper under the man's nose.

'It is,' he answered.

'How did you come by it?'

'Oh, come now, Inspector,' Liesinsdad crowed with that nasal problem so common among the mid-Welsh, 'you can't seriously expect me to reveal my sources.'

'How would you like to spend a term in Pentonville for obstructing the police in the course of their enquiries?'

'Well,' the icy smile did not vanish from Liesinsdad's face, 'this is brass-tacks stuff, indeed.'

'And it's not an idle threat,' Lestrade went on. 'How did you know about the exhumation?'

'So it's true, then?'

Lestrade was not at his sweetest at this time of the morning. He leaned across to the reporter and jerked the end of his scarf, so their noses were on a level.

'I learned a new word the other day, Mr Liesinsdad,' Lestrade said through clenched teeth, 'defenestration. Do you know what that means?'

'Er . . . yes . . .' blustered the Welshman, 'it means to be pushed from a window.'

'Quite so,' said Lestrade, glancing ostentatiously across at the sash. 'It's such a quick way down,' he said, 'saves all that fuss of catching a lift, don't you think?'

'You wouldn't dare,' said Liesinsdad, but there was an air of uncertainty in his voice. 'I am a member of the Press.'

'And I am trying to catch a maniac,' Lestrade released the scarf, 'and by printing this sort of thing, Mr Liesinsdad, you aren't helping us at all. Now once again, can we work together for a change? Who was your source?'

'Very well.' Liesinsdad sat down. 'I received a telephone call at the *Mail* offices. A man with an Irish accent. He told me all about the exhumation and said that Sherlock Holmes was bent on revenge . . .'

'Revenge?' Lestrade repeated.

'Yes,' said Liesinsdad. 'Another new word you've learnt, Inspector?'

Lestrade blew the smoke from his newly lit cigar into the reporter's face. 'Anything else?' he asked.

'No. The accent sounded genuine, but it might not have been.'

'Why do you say that?'

'We Celts have an ear for these things, you know.'

'I see. Thank you, Mr Liesinsdad, that will be all.'

'All?' said Liesinsdad.

'Yes. A new word for you, Mr Liesinsdad?'

The reporter stood up, '*Is* Sherlock Holmes alive, Lestrade?' he asked.

'When I catch him, I'll ask him,' said Lestrade. It was all Liesinsdad was going to get.

Mrs Hudson answered the door as usual.

'Inspector Lestrade,' she said, 'I'm afraid Doctor Watson isn't in.'

'I know, Mrs Hudson,' said Lestrade. 'It was you I came to see.'

'Me, sir?'

She showed him up to what had been the consulting rooms of Sherlock Holmes.

'I'd like you to cast your mind back, Mrs Hudson,' said Lestrade, 'to the time of the late Mr Holmes' death. You went to the funeral?'

'Yes, sir.'

'Do you remember anything . . . odd about it?'

'Odd sir? In what way?'

'In any way, Mrs Hudson. Did anything strike you as peculiar?'

'It was a funeral, sir, like any other. There was a huge crowd in the streets I remember, but the funeral itself was a very private affair. I provided the baked meats.'

'Of course. Was there anyone among the immediate mourners who spoke in bitter terms? Did you hear anyone talk of revenge?'

'Sir, it was over ten years ago . . .'

Lestrade sighed, 'Thank you, Mrs Hudson. Oh, by the way, have you seen the figure Doctor Watson believes to be Sherlock Holmes?'

The housekeeper's face darkened. 'I have, sir.'

Lestrade leaned closer to her and stooped to look her in the eye. 'And it *is* Mr Holmes, Mrs Hudson?'

She returned his steady gaze and nodded. 'As God is my judge, sir. And I've heard his violin.'

'His violin?'

'The Stradivarius he played. I've heard it in this very room sometimes, after dark.'

Lestrade checked the locks of door and windows. No sign of a forced entry. 'Have you kept the effects of Mr Holmes?' he asked.

'Why, yes, sir. Exactly as Doctor Watson instructed.'

'May I see them?'

Mrs Hudson stood on her dignity for a moment; never, in Lestrade's experience, a less than painful process.

'If I may say so, sir, when Mr Holmes was alive, you were not exactly a welcome visitor here. Whatever he is up to, he has his reasons. You tell me why I should show you his things.'

Lestrade caught the tremble in the voice, the tear in the eye. He took Mrs Hudson by the hand. 'I do not believe,' he said, 'that Sherlock Holmes is still alive—'

'But the stones in the coffin . . .' Mrs Hudson interrupted.

'Someone wants us to think he's still alive, Mrs Hudson. Is

that what you want? The Great Detective,' and he nearly choked on the words, 'to be branded a deranged murderer? A madman?'

Mrs Hudson turned to the window, then produced a large handkerchief, blew her nose with the force of a dreadnought and said, decidedly, 'No, Mr Lestrade. Please come with me.'

She led him into a darkened room, where the heavy velvet curtains had not been undrawn for years. The room was dry with cobwebs like a tomb, still and dead. Mrs Hudson caught Lestrade's arm. Had she suddenly realised how forgetful she had been? Or was this the usual level of her housekeeping?

'It's gone,' she whispered.

'What has?' Lestrade peered into the gloom.

'Mr Holmes' violin. It was here, on this cabinet.'

Lestrade threw back the curtains and the dust flew every-where. Mrs Hudson recoiled from the light with a gasp. 'Is anything else missing?' he asked.

She checked surfaces, a wardrobe and drawers.

'His favourite meerschaum, his deerstalker and his Ulster.'

'Surprise, surprise,' mused Lestrade.

'He's been back for them,' Mrs Hudson clutched her handkerchief, 'here, in this very room.'

'This door is kept locked?' Lestrade asked.

'Yes. You saw me open it now with my key.'

'And where is the key kept?'

'Here, on my chatelaine.'

'Is there another?'

'Doctor Watson has one.'

'Anyone else?'

A pause. Then, 'Mr Holmes, of course.'

'Of course,' echoed Lestrade. 'Mrs Hudson, what you do with this mausoleum is up to you. If I can spare a man, I'll put him out there in Baker Street at about the time this Sherlock Holmes has been appearing. If I can't spare a man, or if my man should miss him and you see the figure again, I would be grateful if you would contact the Yard immediately. Will you do that?'

'Yes, sir,' said Mrs Hudson.

Lestrade found his own way out. He was making for the nearest tram when he suddenly became aware of someone following him. A youngish man, perhaps mid-twenties, shabbily dressed with the appearance of a coster. As Lestrade boarded his tram, the coster vanished, but the inspector became aware of a second follower, another young man who had caught the tram with him. He continued about his business and walked around the corner into Jermyn Street. The young man walked on as Lestrade rang the bell at the door of Mr Aumerle Holmes, the last but two on his list of mourners at his cousin's funeral. His man Blenkinsop ushered Lestrade into a study.

'What do you think of it, Lestrade?' Holmes arrived after a few moments.

'A delightful room, sir,' said the inspector.

'No, no, man, not the décor. The tapes. They've gone.'

'Tapes, sir?'

'Oh, my dear fellow, how silly of me. In my excitement, I'd quite forgotten you haven't been here before. Until yesterday I had cotton tapes all over the house, from doorknob to doorknob to enable me to get about. At last I don't need them. Brandy?'

'I shouldn't, sir—'

'Now, now, Lestrade. Don't make life easy for me. Let me show you how clever I am.'

He crossed with ease to the tantalus, unlocked it and rattled around until he found a glass. Lestrade stared fascinated at the sightless eyes. He had to knock his own hand down to prevent himself from helping the blind man.

'Two fingers, Lestrade?'

No need to be offensive, thought the inspector, the offer of help was kindly meant.

'Ah, I see,' he realised it was a means for the blind to measure the level of liquid in a glass, 'that will do nicely.'

Holmes brought it to him.

'Now, Inspector, delighted as I am to renew our acquaintance, I fear this call is not a social one.'

'I'm afraid not, sir.'

'Well, then, how can I help? Is it still those terrible murders of MPs? Blenkinsop reads me the papers every day.'

'Yes, sir, it is.'

'You want to know if my cousin is still alive.'

'Ah, you take the *Daily Mail*, Mr Holmes?'

'And *The Times* and the *London News*, Mr Lestrade. Just because I am blind does not mean I cannot keep abreast of current affairs.'

'I understand you were at Sherlock Holmes' funeral.'

'I was.'

'Do you remember anything unusual about it?'

'Unusual?' Holmes poured himself a brandy and edged his way into an armchair. 'Forgive me, Inspector. Blindness can cause inhospitality, quite unintentional, I assure you. Please, sit down.'

Lestrade did.

'Let me see. I had just finished at Harrow when news of dear Sherlock's death arrived. Doctor Watson informed us.'

'And what did he say?'

'I can't remember the exact words, Inspector, but the gist was that Sherlock had pursued an arch criminal to Switzerland and that they had both perished in a duel near a waterfall. Quite tragic. Sherlock was nearly the most brilliant man I have ever met.'

'Indeed?' said Lestrade. 'May I ask who was the most brilliant?'

'His brother, Mycroft, of course. It's no secret, Lestrade, that Sherlock would take his more baffling cases to him.'

'Would you say that Mycroft felt a sense of bitterness towards society?'

'Society? You mean the *haut monde*?'

Lestrade assumed that was a French breakfast, but stuck to his guns. 'I mean people in general.' It seemed to make sense.

'Why should he, Inspector?'

'Why should someone fill Sherlock's coffin with stones?'

'Yes, that was bizarre, wasn't it? Do I understand that you are asking questions of all those who attended the funeral?'

'Yes, sir, I am. I want to leave no stone unturned,' said Lestrade, and immediately regretted it.

'They were better days, Lestrade,' Holmes suddenly became wistful, 'lighter days. "When I consider how my light is spent . . ."'

'Sir?'

Holmes laughed. 'Did you know I once toyed with politics, Lestrade? I intended to do what this chappie Churchill has done. When I left the army, I—'

'You were in the army, sir?'

'Yes, didn't I tell you that?'

'I haven't asked before, sir.'

'No, of course not. Why should you? Yes, I served in South Africa. I joined Lumsden's Horse at the outbreak of hostilities. It was there I lost my sight.'

Lestrade looked up, 'Forgive me, Mr Holmes. I believe you once told me that you lost your sight as a result of a prank.'

Holmes laughed. 'What a memory you have, Inspector. You are quite correct. There was some tomfoolery with a Hotchkiss machine-gun. I was standing too close to the thing when it went off. You see these?' he pointed to the pale brown scars on his cheeks. 'Scorch marks, Inspector. Oh, they healed all right. But the doctors tell me my optic nerves are gone. I shan't be following Mr Churchill's success. Still,' he drained his glass, 'the way things are at the moment, it's probably healthier to stay out of politics, wouldn't you say?'

Lestrade would and did. He bade farewell to Holmes and was shown out by Blenkinsop.

'Blenkinsop.' Lestrade stopped in the hall.

'Sir?'

'Here is something for you,' he pressed a coin into his hand. Blenkinsop looked disparagingly at it. He hadn't seen so small a coin in years. 'I will walk to the end of the street. I want you to watch and see if I am followed by anyone. I will bend down to tie up my shoelace, that should make it easier for you. If you notice someone waiting, hanging back while I do it, when I get to the end of the street, I want you to pull down that blind. If you see no one behaving suspiciously, don't touch it. Understand?'

'Very good, sir.'

Lestrade buttoned his Donegal against the chill of the late February day. He noted the silent shuttered house that had belonged to Sir Geoffrey Manners, Bart, and he stopped to retie his laces. When he reached the end of the street he looked back to see Blenkinsop lower the blind. But by now, the street was empty save for a chestnut seller Lestrade had already noticed and who had not moved. But now he was certain he was being watched. The game, whatever it was and whoever was playing it, was afoot.

Mycroft Holmes was unaccountably unavailable to Lestrade. Or any other officer of Scotland Yard. He was away on business of the gravest international concern and was not expected back for some time. Further than that the Foreign Office were not prepared to say. This left Lestrade with only one remaining witness at the funeral of Sherlock Holmes: Dr John Watson. Deliberately, Lestrade had left the good doctor until last. The wheel had come full circle. It was from Watson that Dickens had obtained the list of mourners in the first place and it was to Watson that Lestrade now returned. After all, he said to himself on the Underground train to Baker Street that last day of March, wasn't it Watson who had seen *Sherlock Holmes*? Wasn't it Watson who paid Mrs Hudson, the only other eyewitness to the visitations? Wasn't it Watson who had a key to Holmes' personal effects? And wasn't it Watson who had demanded the exhumation, which seemed to suggest that the man was not dead after all? And who, apart from Conan Doyle, had a motive for keeping 'Holmes' alive? John Watson, MD. Lestrade had suspected Watson before. He had a knack of turning up at the right place at the right time, of being involved in cases where, by all reason, he had no right to be.

But for the moment, Lestrade was thwarted. Watson had gone to Tintagel, to the pageant. The man he had left in Baker Street had seen three men wearing deerstalkers. One, it transpired, was a retired bishop from the colonies. Another, a stockbroker's clerk who was obsessed with the idea that people found his ears funny and so wore the deerstalker, even in bed. The third was Mr Edward Henry, Head of the Criminal Investigation Department and what idiot had told the constable to accost innocent passersby with the asinine question 'Excuse me, sir, where did you get that 'at?' On being told the order came from Inspector Lestrade, that seemed to Mr Henry to say it all. None of them was smoking a meerschaum. None of them was carrying a violin. The constable looked utterly wet and dispirited.

'Never mind, Braden,' said Lestrade, 'you stay on the beat.'

It was to be the first and most spectacular pageant of the season, a little ahead of schedule, perhaps. Several had been planned for what was to be a Royal Summer, culminating in the festivities of the coronation itself, fixed for 26 June. Lestrade took Dew, who needed some fresh air, and boarded the Great Western's morning train for Cornwall. The first-class carriages were packed with Aumerle Holmes' *haut monde* bound for exactly the same destination as the officers of the Yard, although their motives may have differed.

Dew had never been further west than Wimbledon and the experience clearly unnerved him. By the time they reached Swindon, he was most homesick and consoled himself with the sandwiches Mrs Dew had made him. Lestrade liked tripe and onions too, but not between slices of bread.

'There are more coppers here than members of the public,' Dew observed as they walked over the springy grass towards the village of Tintagel.

'Protection,' explained Lestrade. 'There are four MPs here today in various capacities. You'd think they'd use their sense and stay home.'

They were directed to the officer in charge, the chief constable of the county, no less, hoping that the plumes and lace of officialdom would scare away an assassin.

'We're honoured, of course,' said the chief constable through the gritted teeth of barely concealed resentment.

'Don't worry, sir,' said Lestrade, 'we're not here to tread on toes. We are anxious to ask a few questions of a guest, Doctor John Watson, of London.'

The chief constable conferred with one of his officers. 'He's probably over there.' He pointed to a brightly painted pavilion beyond a broad, grassy concourse. 'He's on our guest list. Ticket holders are in those tents.'

Lestrade thanked him and the Yard men began to weave their way through the building crowd. Parasols against the watery sun, ribbons, silks and satins, it seemed that the whole of polite society had descended upon the ruins of the ancient Camelot, gaunt against the breathtaking backdrop of sea and sky.

'Sholto?' Lestrade turned to the direction of the shout. It was Letitia Bandicoot, sitting on one of the tiers of seats in the nearest pavilion. 'What are you doing here?'

The policemen tipped their hats. 'Oh, no, you'll have to do better than that, you know,' Letitia taunted them, 'this is the Tintagel Tournament. Knights Errant are supposed to doff their caps and pledge undying love to their ladies.'

Dew's lip trembled for a moment as he thought of Mrs Dew, so many, many miles away.

'We're on official business,' Lestrade explained, crouching on the stairs beside her.

'Uncle Sholto!' Rupert and Ivo Bandicoot, resplendent in scarlet tabards, scrambled over their mother to pull the inspector's moustache and listen to the ticking of his watch. He ruffled their hair as their mother eased them back into their seats.

'They're so excited,' she said. 'They didn't sleep a wink last night, Nanny tells us.'

Little Emma, adorable in a hood lined with white fur and a long crimson cloak, squeezed past her brothers and gave Rupert a clout when he didn't move fast enough. She threw her arms around Lestrade's neck and hugged him. Letitia's eyes met his behind the girl's back and the look spoke volumes. He pulled the girl away and kissed the tip of her nose.

'How's my best girl?' he said, but her answer was drowned by a roar from the crowd nearby. Lestrade looked up to see a heavily armoured knight canter across the tilt yard towards the pavilion.

'Daddy!' Emma shouted.

The knight swung up his visor to reveal the beaming schoolboy face of Harry Bandicoot.

'Sholto,' he shouted, 'how do you like it? Knight of the Golden Chalice!' he announced himself.

'Very good, Harry,' Lestrade smiled.

To the roars of the appreciative audience, Bandicoot whirled his horse away to where other knights were taking position at the far end of the lists.

'What's he going to do, Letitia?'

'Shame on you, Sholto Lestrade. Have you no sense of history at all? This is a tournament, in honour of the coronation. Harry volunteered to take part at once. Look at my poor finger,' she held it up, 'it took me days to sew all those sequins onto his tabard.'

And I thought he made all his own frocks, thought Lestrade to himself.

'Business?' Letitia whispered in a dark brown voice in his ear.

'I do believe you're prying, Letitia,' Lestrade scolded.

'Right,' she confirmed.

Lestrade laughed.

A voice bellowed out that the festivities were about to begin. The wind successfully drowned the speech that followed it, made by the Lord Lieutenant of the county; a divine wind indeed thought those who knew him. His lady wife looked less than pleased, but then the wind was not blowing in her favour. One by one, the knights who were to do battle trotted before the Lord Lieutenant's pavilion and were announced to roars and cheers from the crowd.

'I hope it doesn't rain,' Letitia scanned the sky. 'Harry's grandfather fought at Eglinton in eighteen thirty-nine, you know. The heavens opened. It was a shambles, apparently.'

It would be impossible for Lestrade to get to the pavilion where he would find John Watson. He would simply have to sit it out until this nonsense was over. Another announcement punctuated by a blast of trumpets – the Marazion Brass Band doggedly wearing their modern braided tunics without deference to the occasion. The crowd cheered and clapped appreciatively as, to the 'oohs' and 'aahs' of the ladies and the restiveness of the gentlemen, the Queen of Beauty was brought down the lists in a gilded carriage. Historians might have winced that the vehicle was mock-Elizabethan, but to most of the company – Lestrade included – it was splendid.

'Good Heavens!' Letitia fixed her field glasses on the Queen, a beautiful girl with long tresses of hair, plaited and swathed over her cloth of gold cloak. 'It's Mercy Alabaster. I haven't seen her since her engagement. Isn't she ravishing, Sholto?'

'Indeed,' said Lestrade, 'particularly her hair.'

'Oh, that isn't hers,' said Letitia, 'she's dark really. Aumerle loved dark-haired girls, she told me once.'

'O'Merle?' Lestrade's ears pricked.

'Aumerle Holmes. Her fiancé. He's—'

'A cousin of the Great Detective,' Lestrade beat her to it.

'Do you know him?'

'We have met.'

'Such a shame. I think it's perfectly horrid the way Mercy treated him.'

'Really?'

'She left him, you see. Oh, I'm sure she was very kind about it. He was heartbroken, apparently. A year ago she married a shipping magnate. They say Aumerle hasn't mentioned her since.'

The Queen of Beauty took her place on the central dais. The trumpets sounded again. Letitia consulted her programme.

'Harry's on first, Sholto. Oh, dear. I do hope he's all right.'

'If I know Harry Bandicoot, Letitia, he'll clear the field. Who's he fighting?'

'William, Lord Dymoke, the King's Champion. I'm afraid he drew the short straw. William has rather a reputation as a *beau sabreur*. They say he killed a man in a duel in Germany.'

'Let's hope he's off form today then,' said Lestrade.

Harry cantered across to Letitia's pavilion and thrust his lance tip towards her. 'Your colours, my lady,' he boomed through the iron visor. Letitia felt her heart rise and her cheek blush as she tied her scarf around the ash pole. He nodded to her and wheeled his horse away, the children bouncing excitedly. Lestrade noticed Letitia's eyes wet with tears. 'You must think me silly, Sholto,' she said. He smiled and patted her hand.

Harry's horse was lurching down the lists, the man on its back hunched in the saddle to meet the shock of impact. His lance was level, his shield high, and he and Dymoke sailed past each other, woefully wide of the mark. A groan of disappointment escaped from a thousand lips. The tilters wheeled again and drove home their spurs a second time. This time Harry's aim was better and his lance shattered high on Dymoke's shield, the King's Champion being catapulted backwards over the crupper to land in an undignified heap on the grass. Letitia hugged her children to her and the crowd went wild.

'Bread and circuses,' said Dew to no one in particular. The man was definitely bettering himself.

Harry sat his caracoling horse, saluting the cheers of the crowd, when a solitary horseman galloped from nowhere, riding straight for him. The rider swung a sack which broke on impact and showered the Knight of the Golden Chalice with flour. It hit him with such force that he pitched forward out of the saddle. The rider then swung away, spurring towards the pavilion of the Queen of Beauty and proceeded to hurl another sack at Mercy Alabaster. Another perfect shot and the ravishing Queen stood sobbing hysterically, running with what appeared to be mud from the bottom of a river.

There were screams and shouts of panic. A dazed Harry

Bandicoot sat upright, coughing and spluttering, much to the amusement of William Dymoke who was grinning maniacally with a new-found gap in his teeth which the fall from his horse had given him.

'Catch him, Dew!' Lestrade shouted as the unknown assailant cantered past. The sergeant hacked his way with both arms flailing through the crowd and launched himself at the retreating rider. He mistimed it perfectly, snatching thin air as he leapt and bringing down two or three of the Marazion Brass Band, tuning up for the next bout. Lestrade's attack was better, although he had to use a few heads and shoulders as stepping stones to get there. He caught the horseman around the neck and both of them sprawled across the tilt yard. As he straightened, an army of burly constables encircled them and one of them snatched off the hood which covered the rider's head. The long auburn hair shook free.

'Emily!' Lestrade was truly astonished to see Miss Greenbush kneeling in the mud before him.

'It would have to be you, Sholto, wouldn't it?'

'Do I understand that you know this . . . lady, Lestrade?' the chief constable had arrived.

'In a manner of speaking, sir,' the inspector answered.

'What is the meaning of this outrage,' the chief constable rounded on her, 'ruining the enjoyment of these good people?'

'Enjoyment?' Emily looked at him levelly. 'This chivalric nonsense degrades womankind. It is a return to the bestiality of the Dark Ages. I am merely registering a protest.'

'You are disturbing the peace, madam.'

'If I may, sir, I'd like to deal with this,' Lestrade interrupted.

'Eh?' the chief constable looked irked. Still, this man *was* the Yard. No point in antagonising him. 'Oh, very well. Advise her on her rights, Lestrade.'

'Rights?' snapped Emily. 'Women have no rights. But you wait. The women of Britain will soon unleash such a campaign that every policeman in the country would be insufficient to cope with it.'

'Come on Emily,' and Lestrade dragged her out of the ring of policemen, towards the horse lines to the approving applause of the crowd. Out of sight of them, he swung her sharply round and she gasped. 'What the hell is all this about?' he hissed.

She shook free her wrist, 'Just because you share my bed from time to time, does not mean you can shake my resolve.'

'Resolve?' Lestrade repeated in disbelief. 'You sound more like Mrs Pankhurst every day.'

Emily stopped and looked at Lestrade. They both started to laugh. 'Do I?' she asked. 'God, how awful. I'm sorry Sholto, I've embarrassed you.'

'No,' he said, and brushed the grass from her riding habit. 'Have I hurt you?'

'No,' and she kissed him.

'The knight you hit with the flour is a friend of mine. I think I can persuade him not to press charges. But I'm afraid the Queen of Beauty may file a complaint.'

'It's all right, Sholto,' she whispered, stroking the gaunt cheek, 'I've been in prison before.'

A roar from the crowd told them that the jousting had recommenced.

'Dew!' Lestrade shouted.

'Sir?' the sergeant emerged inches from him, under a tent flap. It took the inspector unawares.

'You haven't heard this conversation, understand?'

'What conversation is that, sir?'

Lestrade slapped his back, 'Good man. Accompany Miss Greenbush to the edge of the field. We'll take her back to London with us. I'm going to see the Queen of Beauty and then John Watson. It's time we got out of this madhouse.'

The Queen of Beauty was sitting in an improvised shelter behind the pavilions, sipping cocoa. Around her fussed a number of attendants. Lestrade introduced himself and ascertained how the lady felt about the assault on her person. The attendants left at the Queen's command.

'I will settle for the cost of my gown,' she said, with a

materialism which surprised Lestrade. She pulled off the long blonde wig and combed out her own hair, 'But that harridan should be horse-whipped.'

'Quite so, ma'am. Oh,' Lestrade turned back in the doorway. 'I understand you are acquainted with Mr O'Merle Holmes?'

Mercy Alabaster opened her mouth, glancing hurriedly around her, 'I *was*,' she said.

'He was your fiancé, I gather?'

'Until his blindness, yes, he was. Why are you asking me these questions?'

'You ended your engagement because of his blindness?'

She paused. 'Yes, Inspector, I did. Does that shock you?'

She swept past him as regally as her damp clothes would permit.

'A lifetime with a blind man. Imagine it, Mr Lestrade. I am young, pretty. He is a wreck. I should, I know, feel for him, but I do not, not even pity—'

'And all for a moment's carelessness with a Hotchkiss,' mused Lestrade.

'A Hotchkiss?' she queried.

'It's a kind of gun, ma'am,' he explained. 'It blinded Mr Holmes in the veld.'

'I think you must have been misinformed, Inspector.'

'My dearest,' an armoured man rushed into the tent, 'forgive me, I could not get to you for the crowd. Are you all right? That beastly woman. Who are you?'

'Inspector Lestrade, sir, Scotland Yard.'

'Ah, good. You've got the slut, have you?'

'No, sir,' said Lestrade with an unusually tart reply, 'you have.' And he left.

He was crossing the field in a last determined attempt to find Dr Watson when the trumpets blasted in his ear. Recoiling from them, he overheard from men nearby what the signal meant.

'An Unknown Knight,' said one, 'what fun! Just like *Ivanhoe*, what?'

Lestrade had heard that name before, but he couldn't place it and turned to watch the knight trot onto the field. He struck the shield of Dymoke where it hung on a brightly painted pole.

'What's his device?' another man asked.

'Three feathers,' came the answer, 'that's Bohemia, isn't it? How odd.'

The Bohemian knight cantered to the far end of the lists and waited for William Dymoke to mount again and face him. The crowd watched, eager and hushed as the trumpets sounded. Then Lestrade saw it. It was having Harry Bandicoot's lance-tip so near to his face when Letitia had tied her scarf to it that alerted him. This knight's lance had an iron tip. And it was sharp. He rode over to where the Queen of Beauty had resumed her place.

'Your colours, my lady?' the voice boomed out, Irish and fierce through the breathes of the helmet.

Mercy Alabaster bowed and handed him her scarf. He wrapped it around his lance and rammed his spurs home. Something in the man's movements, something cold, ruthless, made Lestrade move. He found himself running across the field, deaf to the 'I says' and 'bad forms' crashing around him. Those level with the central pavilion saw it most clearly. They saw the Bohemian's lance come up at the last moment, away from the shield of his opponent and straight for his head. The very observant saw the iron tip slide with a sickening thud through the sights of Dymoke's visor and into bone and brain behind. The King's Champion dropped lance, shield and reins and pitched sideways, blood trickling over the dark steel casque. The Bohemian knight galloped on to the end of the barrier and then swung round to race for the gap in the crowd. People were on their feet, shouting, screaming. Children cried, women fainted. Lestrade tried to grab the horseman, his fingers snatching the stirrup for a moment, but the knight jabbed a short iron mace down on his shoulder and the inspector somersaulted across the hard ground.

Policemen were running towards the knight, who slashed them with the mace and wheeled away, the snorting horse lashing out with steel-shod hoofs. Time and again, he drove for the blue lines before turning again and disappearing through a gap in their ranks.

Lestrade, dazed and bleeding, stumbled into Sergeant Dew.

'Are you all right, sir?'

'Dew. Where's Bandicoot? I need his horse.'

Harry was there in a second, 'My de Dion's faster, Sholto. Can you stand?'

Lestrade waved aside the fussing and the policemen and the Knight of the Golden Chalice dashed for Bandicoot's horseless carriage. They all leapt onto the gleaming machine. 'What happens now?' asked Lestrade.

'Oh, sorry,' said Bandicoot and tugged off his helmet. 'Sergeant Dew, grab that.'

'Right, sir.' Dew grabbed the helmet.

'Not that, man,' said Bandicoot, 'the starting handle. On the floor.'

Bandicoot snatched the thing from Dew and disappeared below the blunt end. Lestrade and Dew sat willing the engine to start. Once, twice, Bandicoot's shoulder appeared above the front and the whole machine roared into life, Dew and Lestrade vibrating like unmoulded jellies. Bandicoot pulled levers and switches in all directions and the de Dion sped away as the Cornwall Constabulary hurtled past them in a Maria. Bandicoot soon outpaced them, leaning forward into the wind. The Bohemian knight was a speck bouncing on the horizon.

'He'll cut across country,' shouted Lestrade, his coat flying out behind him. 'Can this contraption follow him?'

'To the ends of the earth, old chap!' Bandicoot beamed with pride.

Dew was clutching his bowler with white knuckles, his eyes tightly shut. 'How fast are we going, Mr Bandicoot?' he managed to ask.

'Ooh, must be twenty miles an hour, Dew,' and he turned smiling to see the burly sergeant slip backwards over the seat in a dead faint. He hit the bank and rolled into the road. Bandicoot reached for the brake.

'Keep going, Harry. Dew will be all right. There isn't a road made that can make an impression on that skull. Besides, the Maria will pick him up.'

Lestrade glanced back in time to see the Maria swerve around the prostrate Dew and keep going.

'Determined, the chief constable, isn't he?' observed Harry.

'I think he's more intent on beating us than catching our murderer,' said Lestrade.

Bandicoot pushed his foot to the floor and the de Dion hurtled off the road, bouncing out of control across the fields and slewing across the furrows.

'If he reaches the woods, we're lost,' said Harry, 'I can out-distance a horse, but I can't out-manoeuvre one.'

Their quarry was clearly visible now, the knight still in armour from head to knee, lashing his lathered horse as he raced for the safety of the trees. The de Dion was rattling with a vengeance, the pursuing constables invisible in the spray of mud and smoke.

'Get the other side of him, Bandicoot. Have you got your sword?'

'Steady Sholto. Are you up to this?'

Lestrade gave the younger man a withering look and jerked free his broadsword. It wasn't sharp, but it was heavy and could no doubt do a reasonable amount of damage in the right hands. Were those, however, the hands of Lestrade? Time would tell. He stood up in the bouncing machine, bracing his knees against the front bit and steadying himself against the bit that stuck upright, extending his sword arm in practice. Bandicoot swung right to avoid a tumulus and Lestrade sat down again, jarring his spine.

'For God's sake, Bandicoot, you told me you could drive this thing.'

He struggled up again and waited until the de Dion was level with the horseman. He was using his left arm, never his best, and the knight was pulling away, but he swung wildly, smashing the high cantle of the ornate saddle. Leather and studs crunched under the blade's impact but it acheived nothing. Lestrade hacked again, higher this time in an attempt to hit the man. The knight parried with his mace and the two men traded swings, the steel ringing together as they reached the trees. Bandicoot was wrestling manfully with the wheel, missing trees by inches and crashing through bushes. Lestrade took a blow from the mace on his forearm and using two hands in a desperate attempt to unhorse his man, drove the blade deep into a silver birch. The impact made him lose the sword altogether and the de Dion spun out of control, tilted at a crazy angle, then plunged into a hollow.

At a safe distance, the Bohemian knight wheeled his tired horse and saluted with his mace. Lestrade knelt in the bushes, fighting for breath, wondering what lay behind the dark steel of that helmet. Then the Unknown Knight rode away. By the time the lumbering Maria came up, Bandicoot and Lestrade had freed themselves of the tangle of de Dion and undergrowth and clambered wearily on board.

'Bad luck, Lestrade,' said the chief constable, 'we've lost the blighter now for sure.'

'Get us back to the village, sir,' said Lestrade, 'we can still stop him. An armoured knight on horseback is likely to turn a few heads even in Cornwall. This *is* nineteen-o-two.'

But the Bohemian knight had other plans. Beyond the woods he unbuckled his armour, let his horse run free and climbed into the seat of his waiting Lanchester. It had all been so easy.

William Lord Dymoke lay in one of the pavilions, his helmet and accoutrements beside him. The crowd had gone now and it was almost dark. The Eglinton tournament had ended in a downpour. The Tintagel tournament had ended in murder. There was a bitter taste in everyone's mouth. Lestrade stood bareheaded beside the body. It was the eighth murder of its kind, and once again the pattern had been broken.

'So Mr Churchill was right,' Lestrade said softly to himself in the candlelight, 'there has been a death in the "Other Place".'

'What's that, Lestrade?' Dr Watson forced himself out of the silence he had maintained for some time.

'Nothing. Thank you for waiting, Doctor. I came to ask you a question and found, or nearly found, the man I'm after.'

'What question?'

'Do you have a key to Sherlock Holmes' room?'

'Of course.'

'Who has the other?'

'Other? Mrs Hudson, I suppose.'

'And have you lost or mislaid yours recently?'

'Why, yes, as a matter of fact, I have. It was, let me see . . . the night Hamilcar Waldo died. A day or so later Boscombe brought it back. I'd left it behind.'

'Boscombe?' asked Lestrade.

'Yes, you know, Mycroft's man at the Diogenes.'

The Devil's Feat

'You don't want to come here any more, do you Sholto?' Emily Greenbush looked up from her book.

Lestrade was staring at the evening sky, heavy and dark with unshed April showers. He looked at her.

'Why do you say that?' he smiled.

'Because it's true. Because the only reason you came here at all was to – what's the phrase you policemen use – keep me under surveillance?' There was no malice, either in voice or look.

Lestrade crossed to her. 'That was so,' he admitted, 'at first. Now—'

'Now you care?' The impassive smile played around her lips.

He nodded.

'But not enough,' she said. 'Geoffrey was the same. Oh, Sholto, don't you see how it is? For all your fondness, you don't approve of me. Of what I stand for. And I . . . I shouldn't care for you, either.'

'And you do?' he asked her.

She nodded.

He lifted her face in his hand and planted a single, gentle kiss on her lips. He felt an iron lump in his throat, but he took the Donegal and the bowler from the settee.

'Before you go,' she said, 'do one thing for me. That little girl of yours, Emma. Tell her about you, that you're her father. I think she'd want to know.'

'Perhaps,' said Lestrade, shaking his head.

She stood up, sniffing away her tears, determined not to cry. 'If I see you again, Sholto, when I'm chained to the railings outside Number Ten, Downing Street, I'll pretend I don't know you. I'll never embarrass you again. But one day,' she stood erect, proud in the lamplight, 'one day, we'll meet each other in the polling station, my cross next to yours.'

'I'm sure we will, Emily Greenbush,' he said and walked into the night.

Curzon Street was quiet for a Saturday. The theatre crowds were not yet abroad and the teeming thousands had gone home to sleep in the suburbs – the Surbiton secretaries and the Norwood builders. Yet Lestrade was aware somewhere behind him of a shadow. Not one, he realised, but two, and a third. He was still being followed. Ever since he had visited 221B Baker Street, he had known it. He ducked left into an alley and waited. A dark figure crept past, followed by a second. Lestrade waited for the third then grabbed the man's collar and swung him backwards into the wall. He rammed the prowler's arm hard behind his back and forced him down onto his knees.

'Right, laddie,' he hissed, 'who are you?'

'Find out, copper!'

Lestrade hauled him upright so that his face scraped every brick on the way up.

He spun round and struck a match near his face. A man in his mid-twenties, rough looking, unshaven.

'Wiggins,' a voice called from behind. Lestrade clapped his hand over the lad's mouth and dragged him down to street level again.

'Wiggins!' said the voice. 'Where are you? We've lost 'im.'

'No, you haven't,' said Lestrade and kicked Wiggins so that the other two went sprawling. They struggled upright, clawing free heavy coshes. Lestrade tried the old ploy and thrust his finger into the pocket of his Donegal, so that it looked like a pistol.

'Drop them!' he snarled.

The three men looked at each other, gripping their weapons, sweating.

'Any trouble here, gentlemen?' the gentle tones of a constable of the Metropolitan Police growled behind the three. They threw down their coshes and Lestrade picked them up.

'No thank you, officer, no trouble. Is there, gentlemen?'

The three men mumbled.

'Now, Wiggins, tell me why you've been following me,' said Lestrade as the policeman moved on.

'Orders,' said Wiggins.

'Orders? Whose orders?'

'Mr Holmes',' answered Wiggins.

'Sherlock Holmes?' Lestrade checked.

'That's right.'

'He's dead.'

'No, 'e ain't,' said another.

''E's alive as you are,' chimed in the third.

'Where?'

The three looked at each other.

'Dunno,' said Wiggins.

'How is it you know Mr Holmes?' Lestrade asked.

Another pause.

'We're his Irregulars,' said Wiggins. ''E called us so 'isself. The Baker Street Irregulars. I've been tailin' coppers and trassenos since I was so 'igh.'

'If Mr Holmes so ordered it?'

'Right.'

'And when did he give you these orders to follow me?'

''Bout a week back,' said Wiggins.

'You saw him, face to face?'

'Na. 'E's in 'idin', see. Moriarty's in England.'

This last was breathed in such reverence it was as though the King himself had just walked past.

'Is he now?' said Lestrade. 'So how did Holmes get the message to you?'

'A letter. We was to follow you until we 'eard different and report to 'im regular.'

'Where?'

Silence.

'Wiggins, I can get you and your friends two years apiece. And not even Mr Holmes can save you from that.'

The Irregulars conferred by a series of grunts and monosyllables.

'At the newspaper stand opposite of 221B.'

'And when do you next report?'

'Tomorrow night. Ten sharp.'

'All right. Keep your appointment. But I shall be there too. And Wiggins – all of you. One signal, one gesture and I'll have you inside so fast your arses won't touch the dock bench. Got it?'

'Yes, Mr Lestrade,' they mumbled and shambled off into the darkness.

'Roderick, love, can we have a word?' the disembodied voice whined in the darkness of the theatre.

Lestrade stumbled down the steps in its direction.

'It's no good, sweetie,' the producer was at his most acid, 'you're not getting it. The rugged quality of a policeman on the edge, a man hopelessly out of his depth. I just don't feel it. It's got to come from here,' and he patted Lestrade's waistcoat with his tapering fingers. 'And you *have* missed rehearsals, haven't you, Roderick?'

'What are you saying?' Lestrade asked.

'I'm afraid you're out, dear. I've given the part to Lewis Casson. Well, he's no Henry Irving, but he'll have to do. I'm sorry, Roderick. Don't send a telegram to us. We'll send one to you, dear.'

Lestrade wasn't sorry. That one line had given him more trouble than all the assassins and Bohemian knights put together. Besides, he'd had time during the endless rehearsals to ask questions and note responses. He was sure that no one here was impersonating Sherlock Holmes off stage as well as on it. Mr Roderick Lister, actor, could go back into the closet for a well-earned rest. And Lestrade swore he'd never touch a police revue again.

* * *

'I've got it,' the little man chirped, waving sheets of paper at Lestrade.

'I'm sorry to hear that,' the inspector emerged from a pile of paperwork. 'What have you got, and who are you?'

The little man looked crestfallen, 'Bloom: Codes and Cyphers. I've broken your code.'

The cryptic notebook of the late Ralph Childers; Lestrade had all but forgotten in the hurly-burly of the past months.

'About time,' he said. 'What does it mean?'

'Not much, I'm afraid. It's a series of meetings, weekend parties and so on. I've listed them here. These,' he pointed to page two hundred and twenty-one, 'are the initials of . . . who knows? Friends, acquaintances, colleagues? This one's interesting,' he quoted, '"Ghastly time at the Grange. Felt guilty about it." And this one, "Scars beginning to heal." Or this, "Galley slave routine tonight. Very enjoyable. New cat arrives tomorrow."'

'Yes, well, I don't think we need dwell on all this,' said Lestrade. 'Thank you, Mr Bloom. Better late than never, I suppose.'

The little man exited.

'Jones?'

'Inspector?'

'What do you know about John of Bohemia?'

'John of Bohemia?'

Lestrade was used to these delaying tactics. Dickens used them too. It was an excuse to give the photographic brain time to go into action.

'The name given by the Unknown Knight to the Marshal of Arms.'

'John of Bohemia.' Lestrade heard the brain click into position over the staccato tap of Dew's typewriter. His finesse was such he might as well have used his elbow. 'Elected by the German nobility and reigned from thirteen hundred and eleven to forty-six. He was Count of Luxemburg . . .'

'Yes?'

'Forgive me, sir, but about this stage in my giving of information you usually stop me.'

'For myself, I would,' said Lestrade, 'but between us, Sergeant Dew is hoping for promotion and he needs all the culture he can get. Go on.'

'Count of Luxemburg,' repeated Jones, 'married Elizabeth, sister of Wenceslas the Third.'

'Ah, yes,' said Dew, 'Good King Wenceslas; I've heard of him.'

'Congratulations, Dew,' said Lestrade.

'He was killed at the battle of Crécy in thirteen forty-six and it is said that from him the Black Prince took his device of three feathers and his motto of "Ich dien", "I serve".'

Lestrade rubbed his chin, 'And all he served was death on a plate. You look constipated, Constable. What's the matter?'

'There's something else, sir, about King John, I mean. But I . . . I just can't remember.'

'Never mind, Jones. You can't win them all. It can't have been very important. Dew, Dickens. We're going to meet Mr Sherlock Holmes.'

It was a waste of time. The three of them left the desk-bound Jones for the basement changing room of the Yard and got into coster clothes before catching a bus to Baker Street. They busied themselves in various ways. Lestrade muscled in on a chestnut-seller's stall. After all, he had done the man on four separate occasions for shoplifting. The chestnut-seller was glad to slope off into the warm, spring night. Nobody was buying chestnuts at this time of the year anyway. Dew barked something incomprehensible after the manner of newspaper vendors and Dickens blacked more boots than he had seen before in his life. At the appointed time, Wiggins and his Irregulars strolled along. They waited. And waited. No one came. No Sherlock Holmes. No man in a deerstalker, smoking a meerschaum. No King of Bohemia thundering along Baker Street.

At midnight, Lestrade called the whole operation off. He

might have guessed it was a fool's errand anyway. He glanced up at the windows of 221B. They were dark. Dr Watson and Mrs Hudson had gone to bed – together or separately made no odds. Three tired, dispirited policemen went home.

'You sent for me, sir?' Lestrade stood before Edward Henry.

'Sit down, Lestrade. Lemon tea?'

'Now, that's much better for you,' simpered Miss Feather-stonehaugh.

'That will be all,' Henry said to her.

'Mr Frost used to—'

'Become as irritated by you as I am,' said Henry.

The secretary stood up as though there were a rocket in her drawers and left the room with all the bonhomie of a mantis shrimp.

'That woman has to go,' grunted Henry. 'Now, Lestrade – the case.'

'It's as I thought, sir. Bradstreet and the commander were and are working on the assumption that the killer is a paid assassin. That these murders are political.'

'And?'

'And the death of "Uncle" Deering worried me. It didn't fit the pattern. Here was a man who was toying with entering politics. He was still a serving soldier. The death of Lord Dymoke has strengthened my opinion. *He* wasn't an MP in the accepted sense, either.'

'Where does that leave us?' Henry sipped his tea.

'With the notion of revenge,' answered Lestrade.

'The revenge of Sherlock Holmes?'

'The revenge of someone pretending to be Sherlock Holmes. The question is, who and why?'

Henry leaned back in his chair looking at the inspector.

'It's not a question I can let you answer, Sholto,' he said.

'Sir?' Lestrade sniffed conspiracy in the wind. He had most of the nose for it.

'You're off the case, Lestrade. From now, I'm putting

Gregory on as senior officer.'

'Gregory?' Lestrade almost choked on his tea.

Henry walked to the rain-lashed window. 'It's not my doing, Lestrade. I too have superiors.'

Lestrade could believe that. 'Mycroft Holmes?' he asked.

'Lord Lansdowne put pressure on the Home Secretary and hey presto . . .'

'Gregory pops out of the hat,' said Lestrade. He put his cup down. 'And if I refuse?'

Henry looked at him, 'Don't be an idiot. You've got a few years to go to your pension. What about that daughter of yours?'

'What indeed?' said Lestrade. And he went away to kick a few cats.

The Boers ceased to be beastly that May. An armistice was declared and, as the dust settled, accusations began to fly. Why hadn't the army been prepared? How was Krupp to be dealt with, supplying the enemy with all those guns? And who exactly *was* involved in the Army Remount scandal? Lestrade could probably have helped them there, but he felt disinclined to do so. The summer approached, warm and dry and all London began to buzz with the approaching coronation. Bunting by the mile fluttered from lamp post to lamp post. Ribbons and lace and flowers fluttered everywhere else.

No one thought of the maniac who had been reducing the elector's choice for the past months. No one except Tom Gregory, who was supposed to be catching him. And Sholto Lestrade who couldn't forget him. The Commander of the Special Branch had the Houses of Parliament sewn up, he said, as tight as a gnat's arse. Not a man of refinement, the commander. Miss Featherstonehaugh fainted when she heard it.

It was the night before the coronation that Lestrade received the summons. Two sober-looking men in top hats and scowls came to his bedside and spirited him away. It was urgent, they said. Of the gravest urgency. Two in the morning it may be, but he was to ask no questions and to go with them. Under the stars of the clear night, he saw the façade of Buckingham Palace loom as the carriage rattled down the silent Mall. In an hour, perhaps less, the crowds would begin to assemble, camping at the roadside. Bobbies patrolled the shadows already, ready for their stint of duty. It looked like being a long three days.

He followed the undertakers, for so they behaved, through a maze of silent corridors, gleaming in gaslight and electricity. He was shown into a hall of vast dimensions with painted ceilings and marble columns and told to wait.

'Lestrade.' A curt voice made him turn.

'Sir Frederick.' Lestrade attempted a bow and realised his pyjama jacket was dangling below his waistcoat. He tucked it in as unobtrusively as he could. A second figure, frock coat flying behind him, dashed into the room.

'Is this he?' he said to Ponsonby.

'This is Inspector Lestrade. Lord Esher.' There seemed no time for greater ceremony.

Esher grunted at Lestrade.

'Know why you're here?' Ponsonby asked.

'I haven't a clue, sir,' said Lestrade.

'That doesn't bode well,' Esher grunted at Ponsonby.

'Lestrade,' Ponsonby took the inspector by the arm and led him to a table in one corner of the room, 'what I am about to tell you is of the utmost importance. It concerns . . .' and he paused to look around him, 'the Highest in the Land.'

Lestrade looked at him quizzically.

'The King is gone.'

'God rest him,' said Lestrade. 'His heart?' He remembered the sudden demise of the overweight Nimrod Frost.

'No, no, Lestrade. He's not dead, man. He's been kidnapped.'

'Kidnapped?' Lestrade repeated dumbly.

'Are you sure this is he?' Esher checked with Ponsonby.

'Gentlemen,' a female voice rang from the dais.

'Your Majesty.' Ponsonby and Esher clicked their heels and bowed. Lestrade did likewise, but his slippers clicked but poorly. At least it gave him a chance to check his pyjamas again.

Alexandra, Queen of England walked noiselessly and as elegantly as her hip would allow into their presence.

'This is Inspector Lestrade, ma'am,' Ponsonby bellowed.

'There's no need to shout, Freddie, I am not deaf.'

Ponsonby looked suitably chastened. She turned to Lestrade and held out her hand.

'Inspector Despade. How good of you to come.'

'Charmed, ma'am.' Lestrade kissed the outstretched ring. Didn't that make him Prime Minister, he wondered?

'You will help us, Inspector? You see, my husband is so dear, to us all.'

He looked at the fine face, dignified and wise, the lip firm but the eyes glistening with tears.

'Fear not, ma'am. We'll find His Majesty,' he said.

She patted his hand.

'Best you retire, ma'am,' suggested Ponsonby. 'Leave it to us.'

The Queen looked a little surprised. 'I don't know, Freddie,' she said, 'it must be about half past two,' and she limped alone into the shadows.

'She's taking it very well,' whispered Ponsonby.

'I'll say this for Her Majesty,' said Esher, 'she certainly calls Lestrade Despade. Ha, ha!'

The others looked at him. 'I'm not sure this is a time for levity, Esher.'

It was Esher's turn to know his place.

'Gentlemen, forgive me. I'll have to have some details.' Lestrade was bewildered.

'Of course,' Ponsonby explained. 'You know there was a banquet here tonight? Royalty and aristocracy from the world over. His Majesty retired shortly after midnight, when all the speeches were done. Just after one I went to his chamber to escort Miss . . . to see if he needed anything. And he was gone. His bed had not been slept in. Miss . . . no one had seen him.'

'You have searched?'

'Of course,' Esher snapped. 'Good God, man, you don't think

we'd invent this business, do you? The whole world is waiting for a coronation in two days and there is no king to crown.'

'Besides,' said Ponsonby, decidedly the calmer of the two, 'there is this.' He showed Lestrade a piece of paper.

'It is the transcript of a telephone call made to me within the hour.'

Lestrade read it. '"I have the last of them. The big fish himself. If you wish to see Bertie again bring one million pounds in used notes to . . ."'

'Is that it?'

'The phone went dead. I tried to get him back, but it was hopeless.'

'What did the voice sound like?'

'An Irish accent.'

'What?' Lestrade rounded on Ponsonby.

'I said—'

'Yes, yes,' Lestrade began to pace the floor, 'I heard what you said.'

'Do you think it's a practical joke, Lestrade?' Esher asked.

Lestrade looked at the distraught courtiers. 'No, gentlemen. If I'm right, the man who made the phone call – the man who has the King – is the same man who has been murdering Members of Parliament in recent months.'

'God!' said Esher.

'So he *is* an Irishman? A Fenian after all?' asked Ponsonby.

'No, sir, I don't think so. That's merely a blind. The man is as English as you or I.'

'Well, I'm not so sure about you, Lestrade,' grunted Ponsonby. 'What the devil do we do?'

'Why did you send for me?' Lestrade asked.

'The Queen wished it,' Ponsonby explained. 'His Majesty often talks of you in the fondest terms. You were the natural choice.'

'Don't let it go to your head, Lestrade. Unless you can find him by morning, we'll all be out of a job,' Esher grumbled.

'That won't be possible,' said the inspector.

'God!' It was no more than Esher had expected.

The three men paced the room. 'What about ...' Lestrade began.

'Yes?' the other two asked.

'An announcement that the King is ill, appendicitis perhaps, something sudden. The coronation will have to be cancelled, of course. But it will give us time to think and to act.'

'What do you think, Freddie?' Esher asked.

'It's brilliant,' said Ponsonby, who by now was praying for an earthquake, an invasion, anything to avert the publication of the truth.

'Right, consider it done. We'll have to take the King's surgeon into our confidence, of course. We'll get a sick room set up. Only ourselves, Her Majesty and the doctor can come and go. Hourly bulletins and so on. That sort of thing. It *might* just work, Lestrade,' said Esher.

'It will have to,' said Lestrade. 'Now, to the matter in hand. How could anybody have smuggled the King out of the building without anyone seeing him?'

'God knows. He is rather large, when all's said and done,' said Ponsonby. 'It must have been the very devil of a feat.'

'Very little has been said and nothing has been done!' Esher snapped. A pause, 'You know it's the Browns, don't you?'

'The Browns?' Lestrade looked up for an explanation.

'The family of the Highland ghillie, John Brown.'

'The attendant of Her late Majesty?'

'Attendant? That's a polite way of putting it!' Esher said.

'The point is,' said Ponsonby, 'it's common knowledge in court circles that His Majesty detested Brown. When the old Queen died, he personally ordered that everything which smacked of Brown, every memento, every keepsake, should be destroyed.'

'So it stands to reason. The Browns are wreaking their revenge. That's where you'll find the King.'

'With respect, Lord Esher, the man who has the King is the same man who has been killing MPs for the past year.'

'Yes, yes, Lestrade. You said that. But where is your evidence, man?'

'The telephone call. The Irish accent. I received just such a call the night a colleague of mine was killed in the Houses of Parliament.'

'I remember that,' said Esher, 'Broadstreet, wasn't it?'

'Nearly,' said Lestrade.

'What's your plan?' Esher asked him.

'To get some sleep.'

'Good God, man, the King of England's life is at stake and you're going to bed!' Esher was purple.

'I may be all that can preserve that life, Lord Esher. And if I'm going to do it, I want to be at my best.'

'Lestrade,' Ponsonby took him aside, 'there's to be no going to the Yard with this. Who knows how this maniac will react with policemen all over the place. Not even the commissioner knows. And Edward Henry is totally in the dark.'

'His usual place,' mused Lestrade. 'I can call in sick this morning,' he said, 'but I will need a man. My sergeant, Walter Dew.'

'Very well. But you and he had better operate from here. I want no leaks. Come, Esher, we have much to do.'

Walter Dew's mouth was not seen to close for twenty-four hours. He moved as if in a daze through the wing of the palace set aside for 'the gentlemen' and intrigued footmen and flunkies of all shapes and sizes wondered who these two furtive looking men might be. To Walter Dew fell the hopeless task of sifting through the coronation guest list, in case one of them, having dined with the King the previous night, had then smuggled him who-knows-where in the most audacious plot in history. What Lestrade needed was a thousand constables and all the resources of the Yard at his back. Instead, for reasons of State of which Ponsonby continually reminded him, he had Sergeant Dew. That illustrious example of the Metropolitan Police Force pored over the names at his disposal: the Crown Princes of Russia,

Denmark, Portugal and Italy, Prince of Asturias, Prince Tsai Chen. When his crossed eyes alighted on the Japanese representative, Prince Akihito Komatsu, the memories of his experiences at the Strand Palace sent a shiver up his spine. When Inspector Lestrade asked him who he suspected, he said, 'All of them, guv'nor,' refusing to believe anything good of men with names like Ras Makunan, Mohammed Ali Pasha and Said Ali. When his guv'nor asked him which of them had butchered Ralph Childers, poisoned Hamilcar Waldo, shot Arthur L'Estrange, stabbed Reginald Cobham, gassed Geoffrey Manners and skewered Lord Dymoke and Major Deering with lances ancient and modern, the sergeant was at a loss for words.

Esher and Ponsonby had done their job well. The Houses of Parliament took the news of the King's acute appendicitis and the indefinite postponement of the coronation with a stoicism unusual in a collection of men damned by Nimrod Frost and Miss Emily Greenbush alike. The wires and the post office were flooded with letters and telegrams. Changes of plan, alterations of itinerary. Trains, yachts, liners and steam packets, not to mention trams, buses and hackneys, were in urgent demand. The invited noblesse were going home. No one had told the workmen, however, and they continued hammering nails and hanging bunting until the boys in blue, already exhausted with turning away crowds, sent them home too.

Frantic royal chefs fled this way and that and the palace was ringing with cries. 'What shall I do with two thousand five hundred quails?' Lestrade clapped a hand over Dew's mouth before he had a chance to answer. In the end, the bulk of the food was distributed in Whitechapel by the Sisters of the Poor. Lestrade and Dew got a chicken each and a bottle of exceptionally fine wine. Both of them declined the black stuff that looked like sieved rabbit droppings, and felt a lot better for it.

The King's surgeon came and went as though for a real operation and sent out bulletins with impeccable timing, being as non-committal as he could about the state of His Majesty's health. Then the letter arrived. It was addressed to Ponsonby.

'By now you will have called in Lestrade,' it read, 'I expected that. He really will do you no good at all. But he can serve a purpose. He is to bring one million pounds in used notes in a suitcase of your choosing to the Old Wharf, Shadwell, at midnight tomorrow. He is to come alone and unarmed. If any of these demands are not met or if anything should go wrong, the King must die. Do you see how clever I am?'

Lestrade saw. He knew the Old Wharf from his years with the City Force in his youth. There was one point of access now the new docks had been built – a narrow pass where one man could hold off an army if he wanted to. And beyond it, a labyrinthine maze of courts and alleys, running this way and that along and under the Thames.

'You think he has the King there?' Ponsonby asked him.

'If he has, it might take us months to find him.'

Lestrade reached Shadwell Stair with five minutes to spare. He carried a battered old suitcase as requested and took along nothing but his trusty brass knuckles with the switchblade. It was moonlight, the river bright and silver under the creaking timbers. He left the ghost of the Ratcliffe Highway behind and joined the water rats scampering and squeaking on the rotting jetties and green timbers. But he crept rather than scampered and he kept his squeaking to a minimum. A thin mist wreathed the river. He saw in mid-stream an anchored barge, laden with tarpaulins, roped and bound. There was a whistle along the quay, a signal he knew was used by the Bluebottles, the River Police. He ducked into the shadows and stopped breathing for a while. At least on the warm night air his breath was not visible. The last thing he wanted now was some oaf of a constable pursuing his enquiries all over Lestrade's beat. The whistle moved off and Lestrade heard the lapping waters and briefly saw a boat under the moon. Across the river the line of warehouses and wharfs looked dark and threatening. He kept his back to the walls and edged towards the Old Wharf.

'Hello, Lestrade,' the voice was cold in the warmth of the

night. As if in answer, a ship's siren whooped a mile away and there was a bark from somewhere, probably the Isle of Dogs.

'Who's there?' Lestrade's knuckles closed white around the Apache knife in his pocket.

'Don't you remember my voice, Lestrade?'

'Sherlock Holmes?' the inspector asked.

'It's been a long time,' the voice answered.

'Where is the King?' Lestrade was peering into the total blackness of the doorway, desperate to make out a figure, something to give him the direction of the voice.

'The King is dead, long live the King,' said Holmes.

'Why are you doing this, Mr Holmes?' Lestrade asked, 'Oh, I can understand you trying to kill Watson, even me perhaps—'

'You, Lestrade!' the voice hissed. 'You flatter yourself.'

'Bradstreet then. Why did you kill him? Because he repre-sented everything you are not? A good detective?'

There was a crash of timbers. Lestrade realised a block and tackle of heavy iron had splintered the wall behind him, showering him suddenly with brick and plaster.

'One of my many skills, Lestrade,' Holmes went on, 'is being able to see in the dark. Didn't Watson chronicle that in one of his infantile stories? Ah, I see you have the money with you.'

'It's all here.' Lestrade brushed himself down, rising to his feet now, but staying out of the moonlight. 'Why did you kill those men? Childers, Waldo, the rest? What were they to you?'

'Nothing to me, Lestrade. Nothing whatever.'

'And why the King?'

'That's my business. I have my reasons. But it's over now, Lestrade. Finished. And so are you. I have a Martini-Henry carbine pointed at your head. I want you to put that suitcase down on the jetty. No, to your right.'

Lestrade checked his position. He was still in the dark, the sharp shadow of the building was inches to his right. If he placed the suitcase where Holmes had told him to, he was in the moonlight, a standing duck.

'Now!' the voice bellowed.

'All right Sergeant,' Lestrade bluffed, 'call your men up. He's in there!'

A shot rang out as Lestrade rolled to the right. He saw, in that instant, where the explosion came from. The bullet grazed his forearm and he dropped the case, but the momentum of his roll had carried him too far and he somersaulted off the end of the jetty to splash into the water. He clamped his mouth shut. He knew a few gulps of this water was as deadly as the cyanide Sherlock Holmes had given to Christian Barrett. He let his limbs go loose and floated to the surface. He saw the moon and stars and kept his eyes open.

As the surface bobbed and the water in his ears drowned all sound, he saw as in a dream the Ulstered figure, tall and gaunt, saunter out onto the jetty. He saw the deerstalker and the rifle, cocked in one hand. Sherlock Holmes bent down and picked up the suitcase. Lestrade lay motionless, letting the rank water wash over him. He knew he was helpless in this position. That any minute, the late, Great Detective might finish him with a second shot. His only hope was to play dead, something Sherlock Holmes had done for eleven years. He gambled on the man's arrogance, that he could not bring himself to admit that he needed one more shot. He heard him laugh as he checked the suitcase and turn away. And there was something in his walk . . .

'You gave that maniac one million pounds?' Esher fumed as the royal surgeon patched Lestrade's arm.

'It's only a scratch,' the eminent man pronounced.

'Scratch be damned,' roared Esher, 'Lestrade, you've killed the King.'

'I don't think so, my Lord. And by the way, I gave that maniac three hundred and twelve pounds. The rest was paper.'

'What? You bloody idiot, you've signed His Majesty's death warrant!'

'What's this, Esher?' Ponsonby came in. 'Going for the record of saying the same thing several ways?'

'Ponsonby, you're damned casual! You know, of course, that Bertie's done for?'

'That's three,' said Ponsonby. 'Tell him, Lestrade.'

'Either His Majesty was dead before the ransom note was written, or he is still alive. That's the way with kidnappers.'

'But when he discovers he's been cheated?'

'We may call him a maniac, Lord Esher, but actually, he's very clever. He must be aware that even the Royal Family cannot raise one million pounds in used notes in twenty-four hours, not without telling the Bank of England and that's as good as shouting it from the rooftops.'

'What does he care for secrecy?' Esher bellowed. 'If the whole story is blasted over the country, why should that bother him?'

'Because if he wanted publicity, he would have gone to the newspapers. Northcliffe, Liesinsdad, somebody would have been informed. We know he's made such contacts before.'

'Then why—'

'Because he has the King in a public place. Oh, not the middle of Hyde Park, I'll grant you, but somewhere where he might be discovered, recognised.'

'I don't follow.'

'Put yourself in the shoes of a member of the public,' Lestrade explained. 'If you saw a stout, elderly gentleman with a grey beard and poppy eyes on the thirty-seven bus, would you assume it was the King?'

'Well, no, I suppose . . . Is it as public as that?'

'Not exactly.'

'You know where the King is, Lestrade, don't you?' Ponsonby suddenly realised.

'Let's say I have a pretty good idea. Sergeant Dew here carried out a great piece of detective work earlier. This paper . . .' Lestrade waved the ransom note, 'has a rather peculiar water-mark. Hold it up to the light, Lord Esher.'

'So?' Lord Esher saw nothing of portent.

'So it is the type used by the Foreign Office.'

'The Foreign Office? Good God.'

'Could that explain how the King was spirited away?' said Lestrade. 'Not unconscious, drugged, gagged and bound, but of his own volition, because of an urgent summons from the Foreign Office which, on the eve of his coronation, could not wait? Once outside and in a waiting hansom, it was too late.'

'Are you telling me—' Esher began.

'Gentlemen, my arm hurts like the very devil. I must catch a nap for an hour or so. Trust me. The King will be safe and I think I know where to find him. If I may take my leave?'

Ponsonby and Esher had more questions than answers, but they had little choice. If the King's secret and the King's life were to be safe, they *had* to trust Lestrade, there was no one else. As he dozed, the inspector tried to keep his arm as loose as possible. It was stiffening and whatever the surgeon's advice, he couldn't run the risk of it becoming useless. There was too much to do. He ran his eyes again over Ralph Childers' cryptic book and the boffin's translation which Dew had brought from the Yard. It was nearly dawn in the great grey gardens of the Palace and Lestrade suddenly saw it. The link that had been missing. He rang the bell by his bed furiously. Ponsonby staggered in moments later, in nightshirt and cap, bleary from the half hour's sleep he had snatched.

'Do you have a diary of the King's private functions? Shooting weekends and so on?'

'Of course, but I carry most of it in my head. Why?'

'I'm talking about nearly three years ago, now. December, eighteen ninety-nine. Where was he?'

Lestrade ran with Ponsonby to the Equerries' Office. Together, they threw open ledgers, riffled through papers.

'The Grange!' thundered Lestrade. 'I knew it! Ralph Childers was there too.'

'It's the Dymoke country seat,' said Ponsonby, hearing, as did Lestrade, pieces of the puzzle falling into place.

'What do these initials mean to you?' Lestrade found another deciphered page in Childers' notebook, 'Alongside the Grange entry. People? Who are they?'

Ponsonby read them out loud, 'CR, MG, WH, BC . . .' he paused, 'God knows!'

'Probably,' said Lestrade, 'and so do I. What about this one?' he pointed to the last on the list.

'HM,' read Ponsonby, 'His Majesty! But, no, the King was still HRH in eighteen ninety-nine—'

'Precisely,' said Lestrade, 'but turn the initials around and what do we have? CR: Ralph Childers himself; MG: Geoffrey Manners, Bart; WH: Hamilcar Waldo; BC: Christian Barrett. Need I go on? The names of all those murdered in the past months.'

'And HM?' said Ponsonby.

'Ah, yes,' said Lestrade, 'I shall take great pleasure in turning those initials round myself.'

Six men outside the immediate Royal Family knew that the stories of the King's appendicitis were lies. Two were royal aides, two were officers of Scotland Yard. One was the King's Surgeon Extraordinary. The sixth was the kidnapper himself.

And it was to him Lestrade and Dew made their way by hansom late that night. The clock was striking ten as they reached the Diogenes Club. It was in darkness and its imposing façade was encrusted with scaffolding.

'As I thought,' nodded Lestrade, 'a very convenient time for structural alterations.'

'Well, that's it then sir.' Dew was ready to go back to the Palace. It wasn't often a sergeant of the Metropolitan Police got to sleep in the same house as a king. But then, the King wasn't there, was he?

'The devil it is,' said Lestrade, dismissing the cabbie. 'We'll try the back.'

The back was as dead as the front, but there was a light burning in the attic of the building.

'Shoulder, Dew,' said Lestrade. 'I'd do it, but the arm . . .'

The sergeant had been here before. 'Yes, sir, of course,' and he stepped back onto the cobbles of the yard. He mentally measured the door in the moonlight and paced the run up to it. Then he took several deep breaths, lowered his head and charged. This was how he must have tackled the geisha, Lestrade imagined. Expecting the thud of a Metropolitan shoulder and the corresponding splinter of oak, all Lestrade heard in the shadows was the click of a latch and an echoing cry as the door·swung open as Dew reached it. Lestrade saw him disappear at breakneck speed down the darkened corridor and winced at the re-echoing clash of copper and aspidistrae.

'Can I help you, sir?' It was the cheery Boscombe, ever ready with a merry quip at times like these, who had opened the door at so untimely a moment.

'Perhaps,' said Lestrade, fumbling past the man and his candle, 'but first I think, my sergeant . . .'

Dew was groaning and bleeding profusely from a head-wound. It was nothing he hadn't received countless times from his mother-in-law.

'How are you, Walter?' Lestrade helped him to sit up.

'All right, sir, thank you. I'm just wondering where your twin brother came from.'

'Ah.' Lestrade pulled him back so that his head could rest against a wall. 'This is Sergeant Dew, Boscombe. Do what you can for him, will you? Why the candle? Are there no lights at the club?'

'All the power is off, sir, on account of the workmen. May I ask your business?'

'You may, Boscombe,' said Lestrade cryptically, lighting a second candle from Boscombe's, 'you may indeed. When Dew comes round, he will have some questions to ask you. And I suggest you are more forthcoming than I have been. Or is your three-word rule still in operation?'

'No, sir, not while the club is under reconstruction.'

'Good,' said Lestrade and, candle in hand, he made for the stairs. 'Who's up here?' he asked.

'Why, no one, sir. I am alone in the building. At least, I think—'

'When were you last in the attic portion of the club?' Lestrade asked.

'Not for a few days, I suppose. I suffer from vertigo, you know . . .'

At last Lestrade knew why he walked that way.

Boscombe was detained by Dew, manfully trying to clear his head.

'Now then, sir,' Dew fumbled for his notebook and pen, 'you were here on the night that Hamilcar Waldo was killed? True or false?'

'True,' said Boscombe.

'And you know the party who killed him. True or false?'

'False, Inspector Dew.' Boscombe was on his dignity.

'That's Sergeant, sir. Sergeant Dew,' he said and slumped forward in a faint.

Lestrade had visited the Diogenes only once before and in the dark orientation was particularly difficult. He passed the corner where Hamilcar Waldo had been silently stabbed to death, the room where he had talked with would-be witnesses to the murder. His hand slid along the polished rail, gleaming mahogany in the moonlight. The skylight bathed the stairwell in a lurid silver. All else was blackness. Below him, Lestrade could hear the ministrations of Boscombe, tending to the fallen sergeant. Above him, where every instinct told him his quarry lay, was silence. He took a leaf out of the book of Inspector Smellie whom he had met on the Childers case all those months ago. He remembered where he had seen the light in the attic and tried to navigate by the stars.

He found the door, the light shining beneath it, at the top of the house. The paint was peeling on the walls here. There was a smell of disuse, of decay. Perhaps even of death. Aware of Dew's débâcle downstairs he tried the door handle. It gave way under his hand and he kicked the door back. It crashed on its hinges and he ducked into the room. He found himself kneeling on bare boards. In front of him, a table, bare except for an iron helmet and a shield bearing the three feathers. But it was the figure beyond the table which held his gaze, silhouetted against the pearl of the night sky. The unmistakable outline of deerstalker and Ulster, the smoke ascending lazily from the ornate meerschaum.

'Mr Holmes?' Lestrade eased his right hand into the brass knuckles in his pocket.

No reply.

Lestrade rose to his feet, the candlelight dancing on the walls and ceiling. The figure beyond the table did not rise with him, as he had expected. He checked his position, the door still open to his left, the table and chair in front. Little room for manoeuvre. He could make out the gloved right hand in the lap but the left he couldn't see. What was in it? A pistol, cocked and aiming at the inspector's head? He decided there was no time to wait.

'Do you have nothing to say to me, Mr Holmes, after all these years?' He edged nearer the table. 'No cheery greeting? Not even a snarl?' And he suddenly hurled the helmet with all the force his arm could manage across the room. Somehow the candle stayed alight and the candlestick stayed in his grip and he saw the meerschaum fly to the left and the deerstalker to the right and the head pitch forward onto the floor.

For a second, Lestrade's heart stopped. He blinked in disbelief at the headless body slumped in the chair, then dropped to his knees again and let the candlelight play on the head. This was no dummy. There lay a skull, peat-brown, with gaping jaws and sightless eyes. Lestrade ran his fingers over the clothes in the chair and felt a fragile framework of bones. 'The body of Sherlock Holmes,' he said aloud. Nothing unusual in that. After all, he had been talking to himself for the last five minutes.

A sudden rush of air snuffed his candle. 'Damn.' He crouched in the darkness, the cranium that once housed the Great Brain, the grey matter so beloved of Watson and Conan Doyle and countless others, still cradled in his lap. He crossed to the window and looked out on the sleeping rooftops. He saw the silhouette of the Houses of Parliament, 'tight as a gnat's arse', and, by craning a little, the secret spires of the Foreign Office, lights still lingering under Lansdowne's regime. Had he been six stories higher he could probably have seen the round bastions of the Yard and the fleeting comfort of Curzon Street. He wondered, not for the first time in his life, whether he would see these things again, after tonight. There had been too many such nights. He checked the cobbles below. He had missed the room by feet. The one he wanted must be next to him. He pulled away from the window and chanced the naked corridor once more.

This time he did not bother with the candle. He had no means of relighting it anyway unless he could salvage something from the corpse's pipe. Better to trust to the wayward fancies of the moon. He gripped the knuckles again and let the blade click free in his pocket. He placed his boot against the door, prayed to his God for a second and then launched himself forward. The room was in darkness save for a single candle burning away to the right. It lit the rotund figure of His Majesty Edward, by the Grace of God, King of England etc. He was bound, gagged and blindfolded, but there was no mistaking the royal paunch and the astrakhan-trimmed coat. Even the Homburg was perched jauntily on his head. He turned, alarmed, to the direction of the noise, roaring as much as the tightness of the cloth would allow.

'You're late, Lestrade,' said a voice, 'and so discreet an entrance.'

Lestrade flung himself from the doorway. There he repre-sented too open a target. In the corner away from the King he might stand a chance. Then he saw the gleam of the gun's barrel jutting from utter blackness. 'This is a Martini-Henry rifle,' said the voice, 'and will blow your head off your shoulders, rather as you did to my brother next door, judging by the noise.'

'Mycroft Holmes,' said Lestrade, in as matter-of-fact a tone as possible while staring death in the face, 'I arrest you for the kidnapping of the King. We'll get to the murders later.'

'Later?' queried Holmes and chuckled. 'I'll be charitable, Lestrade, and assume you knew it was me before I mentioned my brother next door.'

'You left a trail a blind man could follow.' Lestrade was playing for time.

'Indeed?' Holmes seemed content to play that game too. 'For example?'

'For example, the reporting of the death of Hamilcar Waldo. Not the first time a murderer has trumpeted his own crime. Yours was the Irish voice your cousin O'Merle heard asking for Waldo – presumably when the reception desk was unattended, only your cousin of course wouldn't know that.'

'Quite right. Go on.'

The King struggled against his bonds. 'Shut up, Your Majesty,' snapped Holmes. 'I have no fear of adding regicide to the list of Lestrade's charges against me. Assuming, of course, that he can spell it.'

'Then there was your over-reaction to Watson's exhumation of your late brother.' Lestrade felt for the wall behind him. 'Of course you didn't want us to find out the man was really dead, because by that time you'd laid a clever trail – the deerstalker, the Ulster – your resemblance to Sherlock was of course a vital factor. But you'd been there before us, hadn't you, filling the coffin with rocks? I should have noticed the grave had been tampered with. But I still don't understand why the scene at the graveside. Once you'd removed the body, that was unnecessary, surely? Presumably, that was for the honour of the family and all that?'

'Oh, of course.'

'Then,' Lestrade was trying to catch the outline of the man behind the gun, trying to think of a way to duck the bullet he knew was inevitable, 'there was the muscle you showed in getting me removed from the case, the ransom notes on Foreign Office paper – very careless. Above all perhaps I sensed I was looking for a man whom nobody else would dream of looking for. Who better to kill a cavalryman with a lance, a brilliant games player with a ping-pong bat and a king's champion in the lists than a man noted for his lethargy? A man for whom the effort of walking to and from his club was widely known to be too great – and his only – exercise. And, of course, a Foreign Office employee could produce any number of special passes to enable him to spirit himself past any police cordon ever erected. Hence the bomb that killed Bradstreet – a particularly pointless flaunting of power, that, I thought.'

'Yes,' Holmes sniggered, 'wasn't it?'

Lestrade heard the bolt slide back.

'Tell me,' he gabbled, desperate now to postpone the next sound it was said the target never heard, 'isn't it usual to grant a dying man a last request?'

'Oh, come now, Lestrade,' said Holmes from the shadows, 'you can't want a cigarette, surely?'

'Never touch them,' the inspector said, 'but I am fond of answers.'

'Fire away.' He heard Holmes chuckle.

'How did you get into Ralph Childers' house without his man noticing?'

'His man was paid not to notice. I was a member of his fatuous Hell Fire Club. It amused me for a while, but it was about as titillating as a cycle ride without wheels. As for Miss Fifi Labedoyere—'

'And you battered him to death and walked home with blood-soaked clothes.'

'No, I brought a change of clothes with me. I knew Ralph's proclivities. That night I pretended to share them. The nauseating misfit. He deserved what he got. They all did.'

Holmes' voice was rising with anger now. He didn't sound himself.

'And you were the rider on the grey horse who rode to hounds with John Deering?'

'Of course. Uncle was an idiot. A lecherous old bastard who got his come-uppance. In fact, his amorous intentions nearly undid me there. I was poised behind a tree when he suddenly pounced on poor Lady Brandling. I had to wait.'

'Shame,' said Lestrade, but the rifle muzzle lifted in disapproval of the flippancy and he changed tack. 'Hamilcar Waldo I know about. Your arrogance was such that you had to call me to test my abilities as a detective. And you had the perfect witnesses – a blind man and an idiot.'

'Tut, tut,' Holmes clicked his tongue, 'what a way to refer to

Doctor Watson. He's truly fond of you, you know. I even did him the honour of calling myself Henry Baskerville after one of his characters.'

'I assume that's the gun you used on Arthur L'Estrange?'

'It was. A shame about Arthur. I really quite liked him. You realise of course that *I* was the waiter who poisoned Christian Barrett?'

'I know how you killed Barrett, Holmes,' said Lestrade.

'I was inches from you, man. You took the glass from my tray and looked straight through me. No one, not even an inspector of Scotland Yard, notices lackeys.'

'The cyanide gas in the ping-pong bat was clever.' Lestrade tried flattery to ease the trigger finger.

'Yes, wasn't it? Aumerle was kind enough to welcome me to his house in Jermyn Street, a mere ping-pong ball's throw from the home of Sir Geoffrey Manners. Geoffrey's face when I walked in was a picture!'

'Why the Japanese sword for Reginald Cobham?'

'A whim, nothing more. I saw these little yellow fellows going around and thought I'd litter the trail with a few more false clues. Like the letter from Switzerland. Actually, I wrote it in my office in St James's and smudged the postmark. Then of course there was the German stein. I thought it might send you racing off to arrest the entire staff of the Kaiser's embassy. Sure enough, you wasted time running up all those blind alleys.'

'And of course, you'd met the Japanese delegation in an official capacity.'

'Ah, yes,' said Holmes and gave an uncharacteristic brittle laugh. 'You're moving to the right, Lestrade. That won't do. You see, I'm going to kill you anyway. What matters is how slowly I do it. Move again and I'll blow off your kneecap. I'll have time to hit every limb and kill the King before anyone comes to investigate the noise. I, of course, shall be gone.'

'It was Childers, the very first one, who betrayed you, Holmes. He kept a secret diary. It contained the initials, reversed, of all the victims. It also contained yours. HM. And one final question,' Lestrade blurted out, seeing the muzzle rise again and hearing the tortured breathing of the King, now almost behind him, 'the obvious one, really. Why? Why these men?'

'Ah, yes,' said Holmes, 'I thought you'd get to that eventually.' He walked forward into the candlelight.

'O'Merle!' Lestrade literally staggered back as though from a punch.

'You see, Lestrade, my late cousin's opinion of you was justified, wasn't it? You *are* an idiot. Ironic really, you were actually on the right tack. You *were* looking for a man whom nobody would dream of suspecting. But not a smug, complacent lump like cousin Mycroft. Who would dream of a blind man committing the murders? And I led you like a lamb to the slaughter, Lestrade. The blind leading the blind.'

'So that explains Mycroft's indignation at Sherlock's exhumation.'

'Of course,' Holmes said, 'it was genuine. He didn't know I'd removed the corpse days earlier to give credence to Watson's obsession. A few appearances in Baker Street outside number 221B, the odd contact with those morons Sherlock called his Irregulars and the picture was complete. The cocaine syringe merely framed it. Sherlock Holmes was alive.'

'But can you see?' Lestrade squinted at the clear, blue eyes.

'Better than you, Inspector, so no tricks. I really don't want to prolong the end for you. Sorry to spoil all that nonsense of dear old Ralph's diary. The reversed HM was ingenious. If only Mycroft had been your man. Besides, had you delved deeper you would have found that Childers habitually referred to the Prince of Wales as His Majesty long before the Old Queen died. It was something of a private joke between them. Weren't there any other initials there? HA, for example?'

'Well, yes,' said Lestrade, 'I couldn't place them. Presumably someone you have yet to reach?'

Holmes laughed. 'Dolt!' he said flatly. 'Don't they teach spelling at the Yard? *I* am HA.'

Lestrade chose to ignore the slur. He had never seen the name written down and in any case, Childers had given no indication that there was anything special about Holmes' presence at the Grange. He was wondering what else he and the boffin from Codes and Cyphers had missed in the diary.

'And the motive?'

'Yes, the motive. I think perhaps you were right all along. Revenge, not the revenge of Sherlock Holmes, but of Aumerle Holmes. Mimicry was always simple for me,' he lapsed into the crisp, curt delivery of Mycroft, 'wouldn't you say?' And then the Great Detective, 'Eh, Lestrade? Eh? A three-pipe problem. I was a dab hand too at forgery. I knew Watson would be totally taken in by "Sherlock's letter from Switzerland". Oh, I *was* blind, Inspector.' He came closer. 'Can you know what that is like? Total, unutterable blackness? And these fine fellows, these bastions of society caused it. It was a weekend shooting party. I was home on leave from South Africa. His Royal Highness was there. The big fish himself. All of them, laughing and joking. The toast of the Conservative and Unionist party, and Uncle Deering who was about to join them. We were at Dymoke's place when it happened. Horseplay, they called it. Playing silly beggars with a Hotchkiss Dymoke had bought. I knew it was dangerous. Deering, as a soldier, should have known better. The thing blew up in my face as I tried to stop them. Blindness. Oh, they were all very sorry. Sorry!' He spat with contempt at the obese bundle of monarchy at Lestrade's elbow. 'I lost my sight, the girl I loved—'

'Mercy Alabaster,' said Lestrade.

'You know her?'

'I met her at the tournament,' he said. 'It's funny, she almost gave you away. When I mentioned you had told me you had been wounded in Africa, she said I must have been misinformed. I didn't listen.'

'You should have, Lestrade. Well, my sight returned. I fell downstairs one day when Blenkinsop was out. It was a miracle. A sheer bloody miracle. The jolt had somehow restored nerves the bang on my head had affected. And that very miracle gave me my chance. I couldn't have hoped for revenge as a blind man, but as a sighted man playing blind man's buff, well, it was easy! I got them all, Lestrade. You and Bradstreet got under my skin. So I killed him in a fit of pique. You, I was merely toying with. It amused me, just as it has amused me to go on playing the blind man for Blenkinsop and the world. As it amused me to choose the Diogenes, Mycroft's odd place, as the scene of your death. Because now you're going to die too. With the King dead, I will have had my revenge. Aumerle Holmes will leave the country after a suitable period has elapsed and take up a new, sighted identity elsewhere in the world. Which is precisely why I needed the ransom money. You owe me, Lestrade. But that's a debt I will overlook, because, you see, you won't be here to pay it.'

The muzzle came up for the last time. Click. Click. Lestrade's features were frozen in a maniacal grin. Holmes laughed his brittle laugh. 'Empty,' he said, 'how careless of me. And London's finest has been quaking here for half an hour under an empty gun. What would Mr Henry say?'

Lestrade lurched forward, only to come nose to tip with the rapier blade from Holmes' white stick. 'This, however,' Holmes hissed, '*is* loaded. The weapon that killed Hamilcar Waldo. You see, I *was* a cavalry officer, Lestrade. Lumsden's Horse, remember? You can keep your Martini-Henry, your cyanide. Give me the clean poetry of a blade. You see how clever I am.' He forced Lestrade back to the wall again and lapsed into the brogue which had haunted Lestrade almost since the case began. 'Goodbye, Inspector, darlin'.'

He lunged upward, the blade stabbing through Lestrade's collar, but deflecting on a stud and drawing a crimson line across his neck. In the same instant, the Apache blade ripped through Lestrade's pocket, up with a sickening thud into the pit of Holmes' stomach. The eyes rolled upwards and he hovered there, pinned to the wall by his sword stick. Then he pulled away, gurgling as he stumbled backwards. Lestrade fell back against the King and clutched out in vain as Aumerle Holmes crashed bodily through the moonlit window. All that was left in Lestrade's hand was a piece of torn cloth and the white-coloured lenses he had inserted under the eyelids – the perfect disguise for a man who could see in the dark.

He rushed to the sill and looked down. Five floors below, the body of Aumerle Holmes lay twisted awkwardly on the cobbles. Boscombe was already coming out to see what the commotion had been.

'That's for Edgar Bradstreet,' said Lestrade.

He staunched the flow of blood from his neck with one hand and with the other began to untie the King. His Majesty gasped and breathed in the chill night air with gratitude. When the feeling returned to his hands, he hugged Lestrade for all he was worth. Not many men could say they had been hugged by a King. Especially this King.

'Harlequin,' the older man growled, 'I owe you my life. Name your reward.'

Lestrade waved it aside. 'Every citizen's duty, sir,' he said.

'Lestrade, I'm going beyond the bounds of decency. You risked your life to save mine. And that's a lot. But I'm going to ask one thing more.'

'Name it, Your Majesty.' Lestrade stood to attention as well as the dizzying pain in his neck would allow him.

'Have you got a cigar?'

And the inspector and his King smoked together in the candlelight.

'I've got it, sir.' Constable Jones hobbled across to the bandaged inspector. 'Oh. You look as if you have too.'

'Thank you, Constable,' said Lestrade stiffly. 'I'll do the jokes. Now, tell me,' he collapsed gratefully into the worn old chair, 'what have you got?'

'King John of Bohemia, sir. There was something I couldn't remember about him. At last, it came to me. The man was blind. Does that help the case, sir?'

Lestrade glanced at Dew, 'Enormously, Constable, enormously.'

And he looked at Dew, Dee and Dum, a happy, smiling trio of coppers. And he started to laugh.

The rest is history. For his part in the case, Walter Dew was made a chief inspector. Never had there been so dramatic a rise at the Yard. Much to Abberline's disgust, Sholto Lestrade was made Superintendent. In addition, the King instituted a new order for him, the Order of Merit, and Lestrade was first to wear the ribbon. The reason for the honour was never made clear. To a world teetering on the brink, the news of the King's abduction could never be made public. When Lestrade returned from the palace, a gleaming new Lanchester awaited him. He called it Elsa. But old habits die hard. And at the King's coronation in August, as the feeble old Archbishop of Canterbury trickled holy oil down Queen Alexandra's nose, Superintendent Lestrade caused a scene by treading on Mr Balfour's poodle. He still had the feet of the unfortunate. Fame and promotion could not alter that.

'These are very popular now, sir,' said the anxious assistant in Hamleys toy shop, waving a pair of ping-pong bats.

'I'm sure they are,' said Lestrade, 'but I think this is what I had in mind.'

He picked up a lovely doll with a china face. Its hair was the colour of copper and its eyes were bright and clear.

'For a little girl, sir?' the assistant asked while wrapping it.

'Yes, my daughter,' said Lestrade. 'We haven't seen each other for a while. We're going to have a little talk . . .'

Lestrade and the Leviathan

Volume IV in the Sholto Lestrade
Mystery Series

M.J. Trow

A Gateway Mystery

REGNERY
PUBLISHING, INC.
Since 1947 • An Eagle Publishing Company

'. . .To Murder done by night,
To Treason taught by day . . .'

Rudyard Kipling

Contents

Chapter One

Beginnings

The little man on the park bench turned up his collar against the cold. He checked again the half-hunter cradled in his gloved hand. Half-past two. Where was she? He got up, paced up and down past the knot of children feeding the ducks, clicking his tongue at their squeals and chatter. He threw his feet out in his odd little walking style and tilted the bowler further forward on his head.

Again he flicked open the case. Two minutes had passed. Already he was framing the story in his mind, the story to tell Munyon's. There had been a collision. Nothing serious. A horse brought down, delaying the tram. Was that plausible enough? He stamped his feet and walked purposefully back to the bench. Mercifully the children had moved on.

Then there she was, approaching with that merry step of hers, light, jaunty, her hair strained back from the boyish face under the crown of her ribboned hat. He stood up, tipped his bowler and they linked arms. He reached up and kissed her. She smiled and told him to behave himself. They walked past the lake under the bordering elms. Her breath wreathed back as she chattered on absent-mindedly about this and that.

'Ethel.' He stopped her. 'She's threatening to go.'

The girl stopped, looking hard at him. 'She has before.'

'I know, I know. But this time I think she means it. She's going to take out our money. Our savings. It's all we've got in the world.'

'But that's yours,' Ethel said.

'Some of it, yes. Ethel, look, we'll have to . . . stop seeing each other for a while. I can't afford—'

'Peter, I'm your secretary,' she interrupted him. 'How can we stop seeing each other?'

'You know what I mean,' he said. 'I only get commission on my sales . . . the hotel bills—'

'Peter!' She whirled away from him sharply, the pitch of her voice startling the elderly couple on their afternoon stroll through the park. She came in closer, lowering herself so that their eyes were on a level. 'I'm tired of hotels. Of meeting like this. Of being treated as though I were some sort of leper. You've got to do something, Peter. It's got to be me or her.'

He faltered, the huge eyes blinking in the cold behind the gold-rimmed glasses. 'It's difficult . . .'

'You're a doctor, for God's sake,' she hissed.

'Well, I've never actually practised—'

'You haven't the leisure to practise, Peter. You've got to get it right first time.'

'Ethel . . .' He reached out for her small breasts under the folds of her pelisse.

'Oh, no, not until you've done something. I don't know what. I don't want to know what. But until it's done, Peter, you and I are merely colleagues. I'll type your letters and that's all.'

She swirled up the hill, away into the January mists.

He caught a bus, blindly, unthinkingly circling the streets until he realised where he was. Then he got off and walked past his office in Albion House, on to the premises of Messrs Lewis and Burrows, the chemists.

'I'm afraid we have none in stock, sir,' the chemist informed him. 'But we can get some in a couple of days. Not much call for hyoscine, you see. Will that be all right?'

The customer was miles away. 'What?'

'I said it'll be a couple of days. Would you mind signing the register now?'

'Register?' he repeated blankly.

'Yes, sir. The poisons register. Just a formality, you know.'

'Er . . . yes . . . yes, of course.'

And he steadied his hand as best he could to form the words – 'Dr H. H. Crippen'.

The nattily dressed gentleman sipped his umpteenth glass of tea in the warmest corner of the Warsaw Restaurant. Outside in Osborn Street the clutter of the Whitechapel day passed him by. Occasionally he would wave at a passing gonoph or smile and chuckle to himself at some inward joke or remembrance of happier times. He checked his waxed moustache in the little looking-glass he carried and hastily pocketed it in case any of his chavim noticed his vanity.

'Afternoon, Leon.' A voice brought him back to the present and a huge dark hulk blocked his view of the window.

'Steinie.' Leon extended a hand. 'It's been . . . weeks. Tea?'

'Why not?' Steinie sat down, an enormous, handsome young man, immaculate in grey suit and matching titfer.

'Nice.' Leon ran his hands over the cloth. 'Yours?'

'It is now,' beamed Steinie. 'So's this.'

He placed an object wrapped in paper on the table. The older man looked at him with his deep, dark eyes and easy smile. There was nothing there to trust, something there perhaps to avoid.

'What is it?'

'Leon, about the rent. . . .' The two men broke apart in their huddled corner as a third joined them.

'Sol, my dear,' Leon greeted him, with all the false bonhomie of a viper. 'It has been a while, you know.'

Sol crouched beside his landlord, submissive, like a feudal vassal paying homage. It was a posture the Jews had always managed without difficulty. 'I know, believe me, I know,' agreed Sol. 'But it's the business. Nobody's buying latkes these days.'

'Not at your prices they're not,' commented Steinie.

Sol's grin turned sour. 'Hello, Steinie. I didn't notice you there.'

'And I'm a rabbi's uncle,' said Steinie. 'Where's my three bob?'

'Three bob, he says,' Sol raised his hands to heaven. 'I'm on my knees and he wants three bob.'

'All right, Solly, you've got till Thursday.'

Sol groaned in relief.

'Only Thursday, mind you . . . or I'll send Steinie round to bend your neck.'

'You're a saint, Leon Beron, a saint.' Sol all but kissed his landlord's hand.

'What's this, a Gentile I'm turning into? Get out!' and Sol scampered for the door.

'Of course, he's got a pretty daughter,' said Leon, rubbing his well-waxed goatee.

Steinie shook his head and clicked his tongue. 'And you're old enough to be her grandfather.'

'Ah, you're never that old.' Leon poured them both more tea. 'What's in the parcel?'

Steinie's hand slammed down on the landlord's, jamming his fingers onto the brown paper. Leon's eyes widened in realisation. He pulled his hand away suddenly. 'It's a gun,' he whispered as though the words were choking him.

Steinie nodded. 'A Webley. With a box of forty-four cartridges. Want to count them?'

Leon leaned back from the table. 'What for should I want to count them? Why have you got that?'

Steinie leaned forward. 'The burglary business ain't what it was, Leon, old friend. The Bill's getting difficult. I'm not getting any younger. You mentioned a job in Lavender Hill . . .'

Leon snorted. 'That's out of your league, Steinie . . .'

The younger man raised a finger to his lips and dropped it to the package. He shook his head. 'Not with this, Leon.'

Leon shook his head sadly. 'You'll be the death of me, Steinie Morrison,' he whispered.

★ ★ ★

The removals men had been coming and going all day at the large, comfortable house at No. 63 Tollington Park, London N4. The new owner supervised their every move and expected his family to keep out of the way. It was nearly dark when they finished and the senior of the four men approached him on the pavement, cap in hand.

'That's it then, sir. All done,' and he coughed loudly.

His client looked at him. 'Are you waiting for a tip?' he asked in his clipped Lancashire accent.

'Well, sir, I . . .'

'Young man,' he began with clarity if not precision, for the removal boss was easily fifteen years his senior. 'I am district superintendent of the London and Manchester Industrial Assurance Company. I have worked for said company for over twenty years. And I haven't got where I am today by giving money to the likes of you. Do I make myself clear?'

'Perfectly . . . sir,' growled the Londoner and proceeded to tip the contents of an ash bucket on his client's doorstep.

'Come back 'ere,' screamed the new owner, his Lancashire broadening in his annoyance. But the removals men were on their cart and away, hurling abuse at the Northerner.

'Whatever is it, Fred?' His wife appeared in the doorway.

'Nothing!' Fred kicked the bucket as he passed it. A sign perhaps of things to come. 'Mind your business, Margaret. And where's that maniac of a maid got to?'

'Ssshhh, Fred, she'll hear you!' Margaret winced at her husband's lack of discretion.

'I don't care if t' whole bloody street hears me. Her brother and cousin are both you-know-where, chained to t' wall. And she'll be joining 'em before too long!'

'What's that?' A large, dishevelled-looking woman hurtled around the side of the house.

'Ah, there you are.' Fred relented a little, suddenly mindful of the need for dignity in his new abode. 'Clean this mess up.' He scowled at her.

She bobbed a curtsey and proceeded to start on the ashes with her fingers.

'Look at her,' he muttered to his wife. 'Mad as a hatter,' and he took her indoors.

'Well, my love' – the phrase hung in the air like ice – 'this is it. Fourteen rooms.' He strolled the hall surveying his new domain. 'The front basement I shall turn into an office. You may grow some plants in the conservatory. That big room upstairs at the back we'll partition off. Grandfather William can have one half with the boys – by the way, I must up their rent to six shillings. The little buggers eat like horses. The other half the girls can have together with that lunatic of yours.' He gestured to where the maid was still struggling on the doorstep.

'Which leaves the top floor. Four rooms. We would be able to get a few bob for that. And we needn't waste time getting them, neither. I'll place an advertisement in the *Standard* tomorrow.'

And he was as good as his word. It read 'Top floor tenancy now vacant. Four good rooms. All mod. cons. Would suit single lady. Must be well-to-do.'

His wife was surprised he had not complained to the newspaper of the cost of the advertising. He signed it 'Apply Mr & Mrs Frederick Seddon'.

Mr and Mrs Rose walked that afternoon in the hushed halls of the National Gallery. She knew little of paintings, but her husband did. She spent most of the time gazing rapturously at him. He was tall, gaunt almost, with high cheekbones and the heavy moustache of a respectable gent. It was his eyes that really held her. Cold, piercing, grey as a dreadnought and almost hypnotic. He smiled down at her, pointing now and again at the work before them, saying, 'Ah, now that I do like. Oh yes. Oh yes. Rubens.'

'Titian,' the strolling attendant corrected him.

'Bless you,' said Mr Rose through clenched teeth. And whisked his wife away.

'George?' she said.

'Yes, my dear?'

'You know I withdrew all my savings from the Post Office?'

'Yes, my dear.' He smiled benignly.

'And sold the little bit of Government Stock I had put away? You know, for a rainy day?'

'Yes, my dear.'

'Well, when are you going to buy that antique shop you talked about? I don't like the thought of that money lying about. Is it safe?'

'Safe as houses, dearest,' Mr Rose said. 'Do you like this one?' He tried to steer the conversation back to canvas.

'Oh, yes, I do. Who is it by?'

'Er . . . Rubens,' said Mr Rose.

'They've got a lot of Rubens here, haven't they?'

'Well, I expect someone got them as a job lot. Shall we get some for our antique shop, dearest?'

'Ooh, that sounds nice, George. "Our antique shop". That does sound nice.'

'Well, it won't be yet awhile, Sarah,' he said patiently, patting her hand. 'These things take time. And, as I told you, when my Aunt Lucy, the Dowager Duchess, settles on me, we'll have a chain of antique shops.'

'I don't want a chain, George,' Sarah Rose sighed, looking up at him. 'I just want you.'

He stooped to kiss her cheek. 'First we must get a few things for the house. A new bath perhaps?'

'What about one of those new shower contraptions? I hear they're all the rage.'

'Newfangled,' commented George. 'I'm an old-fashioned sort, dearest. I prefer baths.'

'Of course, dear,' she smiled. 'A bath it is.'

'Talking of which,' George hopped from foot to foot, 'I must pay a call, my love. Hold my hat, will you? I shan't be long,' and he pecked her on the forehead.

Sarah Rose, newly wed, so, so deeply in love for the first time in her life, wandered the echoing halls, cradling the shiny topper lovingly. George Rose, newly wed for the third time, took a bus to Clapham and sold all his wife's furniture and belongings.

Mrs Rose was still holding the hat when they asked her to leave at closing time. No, there was no one in the building other than Gallery personnel. No, they had checked the conveniences. Empty. The gentleman must have been called away. Sarah Rose wandered the streets, tears streaming down her cheeks. Through the blur, she happened to notice the name in the hatband. George must have picked up the wrong hat by mistake. The name read George Joseph Smith.

It had not been a good day for Alfred Bowes. He waited in the outer room of the Public Carriage Office for nearly two hours. His feet hurt and he was cold, despite the attempt of the coal fire to lend a glow to the cheerless room.

The tap of a pen on a counter top made him stand up.

'Mr Bowes?' the clerk enquired.

'That's me,' Bowes tried to sound as cheerful as he could, coming from Acton and all.

'I understand you have applied for a licence as a taxi driver.'

'Yes, I have, yes.' Bowes straightened his tie.

'I'm afraid it has been refused,' said the clerk.

Bowes blinked. 'Refused?' he said.

'Refused.' The clerk closed his ledger purposefully.

'Why?' Bowes became indignant.

'Why?' the clerk repeated. 'Why is it not possible for you to become a taxi driver? Because you cannot drive, Mr Bowes. You have not passed the test.'

'Nobody else has to pass a test,' snapped Bowes.

'Private individuals, no. Though, if I may say so, the day must come when they do. But if you wish to operate under licence in London you must satisfy the examiners . . .'

'What if I drive without a licence?' Bowes saw a way through the entanglement of red tape hedging him round.

'You will be arrested.' The clerk was patience itself, and only a few yards from the Monument, too.

'By whom?'

The clerk looked at him. 'By the police,' he said, concluding that the failed applicant was at best feeble-minded; at worst he might even be a Socialist. 'By Mr Edward Henry himself, I shouldn't wonder. These buildings were the premises of Scotland Yard. Take care you don't find yourself in the New ones.'

'Edward Henry? Who's he when he's at home?' The Acton man became cocky.

'When he's at home he is probably Edward Henry. But at his place of work he is Assistant Commissioner of the Metropolitan Police.'

'Is he now?' Bowes appeared far away. It came as no surprise to the clerk. 'Well,' he slapped his fist down on the counter, 'Mr Edward bloody Henry isn't going to stop me getting a licence. I'm going to stop him. You'll see!' he screamed as he reached the door. 'I'll stop him!'

Mr Edward bloody Henry clattered over the cobbles at Scotland Yard the following morning at his usual time. Ever-punctual, the dark-skinned little man belied his years, dismounting and running up the steps into the side entrance. A brace of constables saluted him, a gaggle broke up a cosy chinwag to let him pass and a positive parliament of them rushed to open the lift door.

'Not this morning, gentlemen. Mrs Henry says I'm putting on weight. The stairs.'

And, suiting his action to his word, he bounded up them two at a time. It was as well. For the lift that morning was jammed with the moribund hulk that was Superintendent Frank Froest, sweating in his attempt to beat his chief to his office.

'Late again, Frank?' was all he heard as a little brown whirlwind hurtled past him on the landing.

Froest slammed the ornate gates shut and met a wry smile floating along the corridor towards him, somewhere between a bowler and the upturned collar of a Donegal.

'Not a word, Lestrade,' Froest grunted. 'Not a bloody word.'

Lestrade raised his hands in submission. 'Frank,' he said, 'I wouldn't be so beastly. Anyway, it's your shout at the Horse's Collar at lunchtime. I wouldn't want to jeopardise that.'

'Meaning?' Both men continued to walk past and away from each other.

'Nothing. It's just that Sergeant Horner has been waiting since he was a rookie for a drink from you. He retires tomorrow.' Lestrade had vanished round a corner by the time Froest's bowler hissed through the air to hit the aforementioned sergeant squarely in the teeth.

Lestrade threw his bowler instead at a constable and followed it with his Donegal. 'Tea!' he roared.

A steaming mug of the said brew appeared at his elbow as he lowered himself over an in-tray that would have buried a weaker man. He looked at the constable.

'Are they here?' he asked.

'In your outer office, sir.'

Lestrade stared at the lad. If he'd listened to the old adage about policemen looking younger than you, he'd have retired years ago. Looking at the forms in triplicate, he wondered again why he hadn't.

'Right.' He snatched the mug, with its cracks and chips. Superintendent he might be, but only commissioners and their assistants got porcelain. Still, a saucer only cramped your style. It left no room to be expansive, to interrogate suspects and to lean on villains.

Lestrade had gone up in the world. His superintendent's office was on the third floor, as far away from Fingerprints and the sergeants' stews in the basement as it was possible to be, unless of course you counted the manic manifestations of Special Branch in the attic. He was convinced they hung chirruping from the rafters until twilight like a demented colony of bats, defecating on the buggers below.

'Gentlemen!' Lestrade liked to make sudden entrances. 'No, don't get up. It spoils concentration. My, my. How I enjoy these monthly chats of ours. Walter, you first, I think.'

Chief Inspector Walter Dew shuffled uneasily in his chair.

'Not a lot, sir,' he said. 'We're still watching those lads on the waterfront, but it's over to the bluebottles any day now.'

'Lady Whitridge?' Lestrade asked.

'Oh, she coughed,' Dew said. 'Asked for thirty-three other cases of armed robbery to be taken into account.'

Lestrade shook his head and clicked his tongue. 'And her only sixty-four,' he said.

'Well, it's the surprise,' said Dew. 'Nobody expects it.'

'Like the Inquisition,' the second man at Dew's elbow commented.

'I think we can leave your Roman Catholic analogies out of this, Eli. What's new?'

Inspector Elias Bower flipped open his file. 'Very little, sir. It looks as though we've lost Ambrose, but the Pinkertons will pick him up on the other side.'

'The Other Side? So you're a spiritualist as well as a Catholic?'

'Imagine,' chortled the next. 'Picked up by the Pinkertons. Tut. Tut.'

'We *are* jovial this morning, Alfred. What have you done about the Belmont diamonds?'

'Ah . . . .' Alfred Ward reddened as only sandy-haired men with a guilt complex can. 'I'm afraid we've drawn something of a blank there, sir.'

'We?' Lestrade's barbed banter had been learned at the assorted knees of Meiklejohn, McNaghten and Frost. Even 'Dolly' Williamson had acknowledged his debt to Lestrade in the early years. Only the fatuous scribblings of the good doctors Watson and Conan Doyle implied he was less than thorough.

'Very well, sir, me.'

'Ah,' echoed Lestrade. 'So the padre . . .'

'Was Benito Garcia, as you surmised.'

Lestrade placed his empty mug down complacently.

'And last, John,' he said. 'But by no means least.'

John Kane said two words before he was howled down by his fellow inspectors. 'Theocratic Unity.'

'Now, now.' Lestrade held up his hand. 'Don't ridicule conspiracies, gentlemen. Especially religious ones. One of them nearly did for me a few years back. Do you have anything new on them, John?'

Kane sighed. 'No, sir. Nothing.'

'Could be one for . . .' Lestrade pointed ominously to the ceiling ' . . .upstairs.'

There were universal rumblings of 'God forbid!', 'Never!' and 'Resign!'.

'Well, gentlemen.' Lestrade stroked his nose, searching vaguely as he always did for the missing tip. 'All quiet, then? You're promising me a peaceful one, eh? This Year of our Lord Nineteen Hundred and Ten? Let's hope you're right.'

It was a little before noon and Lestrade was less than a third of the way through his paperwork when the peace of the new year was shattered. The constable in the outer office opened his door.

'A Miss Bandicoot to see you, sir.'

Lestrade rose in surprise as a demure girl in claret velvet hurried into his office. She looked alarmed, her grey eyes wide with worry, but she checked herself as the superintendent dismissed the constable.

When he'd gone she ran into his arms, burying her face in his shoulder and sobbing convulsively.

'Sshh,' Lestrade comforted her, stroking her golden hair and her wet cheeks. 'Here. . . .' He rummaged for a handkerchief. 'Big blow now. Come on, that's the way. Constable!' he roared, 'a cup of tea for Miss Bandicoot. And one for me.'

'Very good, sir.'

Lestrade sat Miss Bandicoot down on the chair facing his. He lifted her chin and smiled at the huge grey eyes, the nose, reddened by the chill January air and the crying.

'You look more like your mother every time I see you,' he said. 'Now,' and he was professional once more, 'what's the matter?'

'Oh, Daddy.' Miss Bandicoot's lips quivered as she struggled with the words. 'Something terrible has happened.'

'I see,' said Lestrade. 'Then you'd better tell me all about it.'

Like what you've read so far?

Then turn the page for a special offer...

A STEAL OF A DEAL
LIKE WHAT YOU'VE READ SO FAR?

Or fill out the form to the right and send it in.

Yes, please send me _____ copies of *Lestrade and the Leviathan,* Volume IV in the Lestrade Mystery Series.

❑ Enclosed is my check for $15.95 per copy

or

❑ Charge my   ❑ *VISA*   ❑ [MasterCard]   ❑ [ ]   ❑ [NOVUS]

Credit Card#_____ Exp. Date _____ / _____

Signature _____

Phone _____

GSP003   LST3

Please indicate the address to which you would like your copy of *Lestrade and the Leviathan* sent.

Name _____

Street_____

City_____State _____Zip _____

MAIL THIS FORM TO:

Gateway Mysteries
PO Box 97199 • Washington, DC 20090-7199

OR CALL 1-888-219-4747 TODAY

Take Advantage of a Special Offer!

For only Four Dollars more, you can have a copy of *The Adventures of Inspector Lestrade*, the first book in the Lestrade Mystery Series, sent to a friend or a loved one.

❑ Please send a copy of *The Adventures of Inspector Lestrade* to the address below. I have enclosed an extra $4, along with payment for *Lestrade and the Leviathan*

Name _____

Street_____

City_____State _____Zip _____

Too good to be true? Take advantage before we change our minds!

she had drawn. Soon she began looking at me more often, casting her eyes up and then down, up and down, while the chalk moved back and forth, faster and faster, and I realized all at once that what she was drawing was a picture of me.

I kept my eyes down after that, and held very still, with my sneakers lined up and my head just right so she could copy my highlights and my gold chain and the M. E. on my T-shirt. Nobody had ever drawn my portrait before, and it felt nice, being examined that way, being reproduced, having a whole other *me* created across the street, right next to the girl I wanted to have as a friend.

I turned my lips up a little so that she would give my sidewalk face a smile, and then, after a while, I said hello, silently, thinking somehow that she could copy that, too, and make it speak from my chalk mouth. *Hello*, I said in my head, *I'm Mary Ella.* And I imagined the words rising out of the white powder to the girl across the street. *I've just finished sixth grade, but I'm a year younger than everybody else in my class because I skipped fourth grade. I go to the Agnes Daly School, which is this special private school for smart kids. I'm exceptionally smart, but I'm also quite nice, nicer than anyone else on Jefferson Place, and I've been told that I'm unusually sensitive for my age. That's what grown-ups always say about me. I won first prize in an essay contest once, and Mrs. Pierce . . .*

"Who's that?" Suddenly the girl across the street spoke, and I looked up, startled, thinking that she had actually heard the words I was trying to send over to my mouth on the pavement. But she wasn't looking at the picture at all, and she wasn't looking at me, either—the real me, that is. Her eyes were on the corner, and I saw now that all the public-school kids were coming home from school. *"Who's that?"* she asked again, and I knew at once that she had spotted Morton on his way up the street.

Morton is the dumbest kid on the block, and he is also the ugliest. Last year he was only one grade ahead of me, but he's three years older, and every summer he has to go to summer school to catch up with everybody else, but he never does. He always wears a dumb gray T-shirt with a peeling Mickey Mouse or Snoopy on it, and his socks are always sliding into his shoes so that his heels show. Actually, he isn't that ugly—his hair is a rather nice shade of red, and his eyes are large and dark. On anyone else, in fact, his face wouldn't look at all bad; on him, though, it looks ugly. His head hangs down on his chest all the time, and he shuffles his feet as though he's trying to pick up static on a carpet. Also, in winter, his hat comes down

to his nose so that he looks like a fire hydrant, and
sometimes when he loses his gloves he wears ugly
gray socks on his hands, which he waves around like
paws.

The other thing about Morton is that he is my
brother.

CHAPTER THREE

"Who *is* that?" the girl asked again, but I returned my eyes to the wet sun with its crooked rays and twisted rainbows, and pretended not to hear.

"Hey," she said, louder this time. "Who's that kid?"

"Who?" I answered, not looking up. That, after all, turned out to be the first word I spoke to the new girl across the street—"Who?"—and I said it into my knees.

"With the red T-shirt."

"Who?" I looked up quickly. "Oh, him. That's Charles." I finally looked into her face, giving her my friendly smile, the one that makes my eyes pinch together and my cheeks stick out.

"Cute," she said. "Who's the one in the back?" Morton always walks in the back, partly because his walk is so slow, but mostly because nobody wants to walk with him.

The wet rays were shrinking into the puddle now,

first one and then another, and I tried to stretch them out again with the end of the Popsicle stick.

"I said, who's the one in the back?"

I looked toward the corner again, squinting into the light and pretending, as I do when I misread a word on the blackboard in school, to be nearsighted. "Which?" I asked. As if there was more than one.

"In the Mickey Mouse shirt," she answered. "With the walk."

"Oh, that," I said, looking at my feet again. "Morton."

"What?"

"Morton," I said, louder this time, but not really loud.

"Morton? That's that kid's name? *Morton?* Who would give anybody a name like that?"

"I don't know," I said. "There's an Ezra on this block, too."

"So?"

I didn't say anything. I had always thought Ezra was a dumber name than Morton, but Morton was pretty bad, too. Morton.

Morton without the t. I had made that up once, a long time ago, but I had never told it to anyone, even though I thought it was pretty funny. Morton without the *t* spelled moron, and I couldn't understand why no one else had ever thought of it. Someday, probably, somebody would. Franklin, most likely. He was always thinking up things like that. Someday, he would shout down the street, "Hey, you know what? Take the *t* out of Morton and what do you get?" Then as soon as everybody else caught on, they would all start to laugh, and Franklin would get credit for something I had really thought up first. Still, I kept it to myself, because I knew everyone would immediately start calling Morton "Morton without the *t*," and I didn't especially want that, even though I had made it up.

"Dumb name," the girl across the street said.

In a little while, everyone would reach the awning, and in a little while after *that*, the new girl would belong to someone else—Deirdre, probably, or Justine. Maybe both.

"That's about the dumbest name I ever heard," she added, and in another minute she'd say something like "He's about the dumbest kid I ever saw."

"It's not really a first name," I said quickly. "It's his mother's maiden name."

There was a long silence. Then, "How come you know so much about him? How come you know all that, about his mother's maiden name and everything? Is he your boyfriend, or what?"

I stared at her. Did I look like someone who would pick Morton for a boyfriend?

"Is he?" she persisted.

"Is he what?"

"Your boyfriend."

I slipped the gold chain across my chin, letting its clasp dig into the back of my neck as I moved my head. "No," I answered.

"How come?"

"I have another boyfriend," I lied.

"Who? Ezra?"

"No. Someone who doesn't live around here. He goes to my school. I go to a private—"

"If he's not your boyfriend, how come you know all that stuff about him?"

I thrust my chin up quickly, and all at once the gold chain broke, spilling like a sudden stream of water into my hand.

"I bet he's your boyfriend," she said.

Everyone had reached the awning now, even Morton, but I didn't turn around to say hello. I felt them move about behind me and bump into each other like a bustle of pigeons, and I listened to the footsteps of those who continued up the street, but I looked only at the gold pool in my palm, stirring it with a finger.

"Hey, Morton," the girl across the street suddenly called out.

Don't answer, I said to myself, closing my eyes tight. *Don't answer, don't answer, don't answer.*

"What?" he answered.

"Come here. I want to ask you something," and I heard him shuffle across the street.

"Hey, Morton," she said. "Is that your girlfriend?"

"What?" he said. He always says "what," and once my mother took him to an ear doctor because she thought maybe he was deaf. "Hard of hearing" is what she called it, but there was nothing the matter with his ears. He says "what" to give himself time to think up something else to say, only the ear doctor didn't tell her that. He said my brother was faking. I think my mother was disappointed that Morton wasn't deaf. Hard of hearing is better than dumb.

Anyway, the girl across the street didn't get a chance to repeat her question, because just then someone behind me called out to her. "Hey," she cried. "You new here?" It wasn't Deirdre *or* Justine. It was Ina, and the next moment I opened my eyes to see all the girls on my block walking across the street toward the girl who was going to wait in the shed for my packages of grapes and mittens, who was going to repeat "awning" and "gold chain" after me, who was going to play hangman with me under the privet, who was going to be my friend.

CHAPTER FOUR

Pretty soon they were all telling their names—the new girl said hers was Polly—and their ages and what grades they were in and where they lived and which ones were sisters. They were all talking at once, and I couldn't tell who was saying what, but all of a sudden there was a pause and someone noticed the picture on the sidewalk. "Hey," she said. "Did you make that? That's a really good picture. Is it supposed to be you?"

"Me? No."

"Then how come it says 'ME' on it?"

"It's a picture of her, over there." Polly pointed with her chin. "With the writing on her shirt."

Everybody suddenly turned to look at me. "You mean Mary Ella?" "That's supposed to be her?" "Hey, Mary Ella, come and see what you look like." "Hey, it looks just like you, with the stringy hair and all, and those crooked letters on your T-shirt."

I half rose, wanting to join them, not wanting to,

wanting to again. But finally I sat down, knowing it was too late. They all belonged to each other now, and I somehow belonged with Morton, who remained, as I did, apart from the group. All the other boys had already gone home, and the rest of the street was quiet. It would have been a good time for Morton to get away, but he just stood there, as I knew he would, waiting for the new girl, for Polly, to notice him again and to ask her question: "Hey, Morton, is that your girlfriend?"

Morton never runs away from anything, no matter how dangerous, not because he's brave, but because he's dumb. Once, long ago, Franklin found an old baby carriage in his lobby, and he offered to give everybody a ride in it. All morning long he ran up and down the block with it, wheeling two, sometimes three kids at a time in its canvas sling and singing "Rockabye Baby" at the top of his lungs. Morton and somebody else were having their rides when the man who owned the carriage came after us, and everyone except Morton ran away. Morton just sat there, waiting, looking like a circus clown in a baby suit, until the man tipped him out onto the ground. I watched from behind a car, scared, as Morton was marched up the street by the collar, his head bouncing back and forth like a punched balloon, and I wonder even now what happened when the man finally led him into the shed down the block.

The girls across the street were still admiring the drawing on the sidewalk, putting their heads to one side and the other as they examined first the picture and then me. "You know what?" Justine said, taking Polly's piece of chalk. "You left something out," and she crouched over the pavement. "You forgot to put in her book bag." She began making big chalk strokes on the ground. "The Agnes Daly School book bag." "Daaaaay-ly," she pronounced it, letting her voice linger long and high on the first syllable.

"And put in the hat," Ina added. "Put in the Agnes Daly School hat with the worms."

They're not worms; they're laurel leaves, and they curl around the initials of my school on a little gold emblem that decorates my hat and the pocket of my blazer. It's the part of my school uniform that I like best, and I draw pictures of it all over the binding of my loose-leaf notebook, and sometimes in the dust on the hood of a parked car. They're *leaves*, I wanted to say, not *worms*. But I didn't.

Morton had edged closer to the group and was by now leaning over to look at the picture with everybody else, so that suddenly I was the only one who didn't belong. "It looks just like you," he said, repeating what

somebody had already said, "with the hat and all."
That's the way he talks lots of times—he says other
people's words as though he'd thought of them himself.

There was a long silence, and then I heard, "Hey!"
The voice was loud and sharp, and it took me by
surprise, even though it was my own. "Hey, Morton!"
I heard myself call, the voice seeming to float down
from a rooftop. "Hey, Morton, you know what?" I was
standing up now, one foot on the curb, one off, as
though I were about to run a race. "Hey, Morton!" I
yelled. "Take the *t* out of your name and guess what's
left!" And then, "Hey, Morton without the *t*!" and
all their faces blurred like paints in a dish of water as
they turned slowly to look at me.

Later, after everyone had gone home, I bent over
to examine the chalk picture on the sidewalk. Parts
of it had already been erased by being walked on, so
that one elbow was missing and the M. E. was smudged,
but the rest of it was still there. It looked just like all
those pictures of girls everybody draws—a fat U for a
face, a square hat, broom-straw hair, round eyes with
lashes like sunrays, and mittens instead of hands. No
highlights in the hair. No upside-down sneaker laces.
No laces at all, for that matter, and no sneakers either.
Each leg ended in a sharp point. And no gold necklace.

I stared at the picture a long time and then, uncoiling the broken chain from my palm, I carefully curved it across the chalk throat on the sidewalk. It looked nice there, glowing in the sun like real gold, and I felt good, as though I had given a present to someone poor. It's for you, I said into the eyes with their sunray lashes, and with the tip of my finger I stretched the chalk lips into a small smile.

Ina had been the first one in the group to catch on to my joke about Morton's name. Polly had been the last. "That's pretty good," Ina had said, looking over at me as I stood on the curb, and I smiled at her. "Morton without the *t*," she cried out to the others. "Get it? Morton without the *t*." She clapped her hands in time to the words.

Everyone else stood around, not understanding at first, looking at Ina, looking at me, and then finally catching on, but still not joining in. Not right away. Not until someone said, "But Mary Ella said it *first*. She made it *up*," and then they all took up the cry, flapping around Morton like a ring of hungry sea gulls.

Polly watched them from the iron fence along the privet, and I watched from the curb across the street. "Morton without the *t*!" they sang, over and over, until it became a chant—"Morton with*out* the *t*! Morton with*out* the *t*!"—and they locked hands, fencing Morton in. Suddenly Polly's mouth twitched a little and her eyebrows rose, and I knew that she, too, had finally caught on. At that moment I crossed the street and the circle opened up to let me in.

We all sang together after that—all of us except Polly, who stood at the privet and watched—and we sang as loud as we could, keeping time with our feet and pumping our arms up and down.

I sang the loudest of all. And although I didn't look at Polly, I felt her eyes on my back, and I liked knowing that she was watching me, that she was watching all of us—Ina and Deirdre and Justine and everybody—while we sang the song that I'd made up.

Morton never caught on to the joke at all. Instead, he looked around with that dumb expression he has, and tried to join in, which is another thing he does all the time. He joins in anything that's going on, even when it's directed against him, because he doesn't even know he's being kept out. "Morton without the tea," he called out, trying to break into the circle. "Morton without the coffee," and when everybody laughed, he laughed too, and said it again. Four times.

I rubbed out the face first, smudging the chalk with my sneaker sole until the lips with their twin peaks

spread into a pale egg and the eyelashes faded to powder. Then I worked on the hat, the tattered ME, the
book bag, and the pointy legs, until there was nothing
left on the sidewalk but a gray smear, shapeless as a
scrap of cloud, and the gold chain, tan now in the
dusk.

CHAPTER FIVE

When Aunt Sophia gave me the Easter egg that day long ago, she lifted it up to my eye and whispered, "Look inside, Mary Ella. There's a surprise in there," and she smiled at me in that way she had. "It's magic," she told me as I peered through its dark round window, and she was right. It *was* magic, and I caught my breath at the vision of a whole rabbit household in a sunlit room—with a mother rabbit, a father rabbit, and a child rabbit, all dressed in little clothes and seated around a table set with bowls of wooden eggs.

Off to one side was a fireplace with a paper flame in its hearth, and along the rounded walls were tiny pictures: of flowers, of birds, of other rabbits—a grandfather and a grandmother. At the far end was a little rabbit bed, big enough for the child rabbit, and across it lay a pale-blue spread.

I stood there a long time, gazing at it all and saying, "Oh, Aunt Sophia, look. Look at the table and the chairs and the pictures. Look at the bed. And the little eggs!" Look at this, look at that. "Look how tiny!" I wanted to break the glass with my finger and hop the little bodies about from chair to fireplace to bed. I wanted to roll the tiny eggs against my thumb and to fan the flame in the hearth until it leaped up.

"And the clothes, Mary Ella," Aunt Sophia said, so close to me I could feel her breath against my ear. "Look at the clothes. Look carefully at the father rabbit's jacket. Do you see what's on the left-hand side just below the collar? It's a *pocket*, and there's something very wonderful inside."

"There is?"

"Yes. It's a little gold coin. A rabbit coin, with a picture of the first rabbit president on one side, and the words BUNNY MONEY on the other. You can't see it, of course, but it's there all the same."

"How do you know?" I demanded. I didn't really care how she knew; I just wanted her to go on talking about the rabbits.

"Well, it *has* to be there, because that's the only pocket he has."

I held the egg in front of me and tapped at the little window, urging the rabbits to turn their heads, to look at me, to smile, to invite me in, to show me the coin— and that was how I began my game.

That night I pretended that my room was an Easter

egg, exactly like the one Aunt Sophia had given me, with a little bed and pictures on the walls and a fire-place and bowls of tiny eggs on the table. The Easter egg was held between the fingers of some giant girl whose eye filled my window, and I was the child rabbit she saw inside. "Oh, look!" she would cry, and she would watch me move about among my things, from table to fireplace to wall. "Look how tiny! Look at the little pictures and the eggs." Look at this, look at that. "Look at how beautiful the child rabbit is. Look at the highlights in her hair and her white dress."

Then she would start tapping at my window glass and calling to me. "Hey, Bunny," she would say. "Look at me," but I never would. I'd pretend not to know she was there, and I would struggle to keep from smil-ing while I felt her eye at the window, her lashes brushing against the pane.

I would feel her wishing things, too. She would wish she could reach through the window and move me about from place to place, to grasp me by the waist and bend my legs so that I would sit in my chair, or to straighten them out so I could be put on the little bed. She would wish she could cover my little rabbit body with a blanket and close my eyelids one at a time with her finger, saying, "Go to bed now, Bunny." But the window would be too small for her hand, and so she would just look in, filling the pane from top to sill with her dark, giant eye.

I would pretend that a father and a mother rabbit were in the egg room with me, and we would all sit together at the little table. "Happy Easter," I'd say to them every night, because it was always Easter Sunday inside the egg, and they would say "Happy Easter" back. "How pretty you look today," the mother rabbit would say, and I would smile, liking to hear that. Then we'd nibble at the little wooden eggs in our bowls, and later we'd take a walk around the room, just the three of us, with no brother rabbit or sister rabbit. First we'd stop at the pictures on the walls and say something nice about them: "Wow, look how blue that flower is," or "Hmm. Grandfather was some handsome rabbit," and we'd stop to warm our hands—our paws, whatever they were—at the fireplace.

Then I'd give the mother rabbit an Easter present—something nice, a flower maybe—and she'd say, "Oh, Mary Ella, this is the most beautiful flower I have ever seen. Look!" She'd hold it up for the father rabbit to see. "Oh, wow," he'd say, and he'd fasten it to the mother rabbit's hat. We'd all hold hands after that, liking the flower, liking each other.

Pretty soon the father rabbit would take out his paint set, and we'd all sit around the table and decorate the little wooden eggs in our bowls. We wouldn't speak. We'd just sit there, side by side, while dazzling little pictures took shape at the ends of our tiny brushes. Each night I'd paint a bowl of daisies on an egg. The bowl was a lovely blue and perfectly round, like a bubble, and the daisy petals looked cool and stiff, like real ones. "Exquisite," the mother rabbit would say, admiring it and shaking her head back and forth in disbelief. "Absolutely exquisite." She pronounced it the way Mrs. Pierce does in school: "*EX*quisite," she says. "Say it after me, boys and girls: *EX*quisite," and we do.

Finally, just before saying good night to me, the father rabbit would bend over and say, "Now I have something very special to show you," and that would be the best part of the game. With his paw he would reach into the little pocket on the left-hand side of his jacket and pull out the tiny gold coin. "Look!" he'd say, and he'd hold it up. Aunt Sophia was right: The head of a rabbit was on one side and the words BUNNY MONEY were on the other. But I knew something she didn't know: On the picture side was a little circle, so tiny you had to squint to see it, and inside were the initials M. E. The rabbit on the coin was *me*.

"Well," the father rabbit would say to me. "Tomorrow we will go out and spend it. What shall we buy?" And I would always answer, "Oh, Father Rabbit, don't spend it at all. Just keep it in your pocket so we can have it for always," and that is what he would do. He'd slide it back into his pocket and then kiss me good night, while the eye of the giant girl watched between the slats of the blinds at the window.

CHAPTER SIX

When my *real* family sits at the table, there are four of us, not three, and when we go for a walk, as we do every Sunday afternoon, I have to walk ahead with Morton, because the paths in the park are too narrow for four. My father never offers to buy me something with money from his pocket, and my mother never tells me I'm pretty, although I try to get her to. "Oh, Mom," I said to her once as she braided my hair in front of the mirror. "Look how ugly I am. Who will ever want to marry me?" and I waited for her to say, "Oh, Mary Ella, you're not ugly at all. You're beautiful," but all she answered was, "Plenty of ugly women get married," and she tightened the braid at my neck so that my skin pulled and I cried out.

Also, we never paint pictures on eggs. On *anything*. My mother doesn't like to paint, my father has no time, and all Morton knows how to draw is those dumb houses where the chimney juts out from a triangle roof and the windows and the door make a face.

I like to paint, though, and my pictures in school are so good, some of them, that they hang in the art room for weeks, but I don't ever paint when I'm at home. I don't want my pictures hung up on the refrigerator door with Morton's dumb triangle roofs. When I bring home a picture from school I roll it up in a drawer, where its ends crinkle like chapped lips and the paper gets less and less white.

And, when I give my real mother a present, she doesn't say, "Oh, how beautiful!" like the mother rabbit in the egg. All she ever says is "Very nice," even though she knows my present is quite wonderful. "Very nice," she says, because what I give her is a whole lot better than what Morton gives her, and she has to pretend to like them both the same.

In fact, she doesn't like to get presents at all. Once, when Morton asked, "What do you want for Mother's Day?" all she could think of to say was "Obedience." Obedience! For *Mother's* Day.

She complains a whole lot about how disobedient Morton is, but she doesn't mean disobedient, really; she means dumb. He isn't disobedient at all. He doesn't sneak off to the movies when he's supposed to be studying, the way Ina's brother does, and he doesn't smoke cigarettes on the roof, like Ezra. He isn't smart enough to do things like that. Instead, he puts his clothes on crooked and he forgets to wipe his nose. I think she talks all the time about how disobedient he is because that's what she wishes he really were— disobedient instead of dumb.

As it happened, Morton already had a present for her that Mother's Day, but he asked her what she wanted anyway, hoping she would say "bookends," which is what he was planning to give her—wooden bookends that he had made in school and that were shaped like cats. He had carved them out with a jigsaw, tracing around the patterns his shop teacher had pasted down on two slabs of wood, but the saw blade had slipped, and the cats didn't match. They didn't even look like cats; they looked like dinosaurs, and his teacher had given him a D on them, because everything was crooked and the nails showed through, but Morton wrapped them up for a Mother's Day present, anyway. "What do you want for your present?" he asked her that day, and he laughed his dumb laugh because he had a secret and he was excited about it. When she said "Obedience," he just looked at her.

"Why don't you *buy* her a present?" I asked him then, because I didn't want her to see the terrible bookends, and also I didn't want her to have to say that my present was very nice. I had picked out a necklace for her that year—a string of tiny seashells, so thin you could see your fingers through them when you held them up to the sky, and so brittle they let out a tiny chime when their edges brushed. "You could get her an African violet from the five-and-ten," I told him. "They come in all kinds of colors—purple and pink and everything. You could get her any color you liked."

"I don't have any money," he answered, which was true. My mother had stopped giving him an allowance when she discovered that he had been giving it all away to Ezra. So she got bookends from Morton that year instead of an African violet, instead of obedience, and she put them next to my necklace and said they were both very nice. "Very nice," she said as she stood Morton's wooden cats side by side on the table, and "Very nice" when she held up my beautiful row of shells. *Very nice!* Even though the necklace hung from her fingers like a flurry of blossoms and tinkled with the softness of a mouse paw on glass.

Next Mother's Day, Morton didn't remember to buy her anything at all. He had forgotten the date, and I purposely hadn't reminded him. In secret, I went out to buy her a present of my own—a little glass prism that spilled rainbows all over the room when it caught the light—and in secret I gave it to her early that Sunday morning.

"Oh, Mary Ella!" she said, and she swung the prism around by its string, making the rainbows race around the walls. I think she really liked it, although she didn't say.

When Morton saw it, though, he finally remembered the day, and he went through the house looking for something to give her. What he found was a library book—a *library* book!—that my father had borrowed for himself and that had been lying on the coffee table for about a month. Morton wrapped it up in my tissue paper, and he made her a card, copying out the verse from the one I had bought and coloring a border around it with red crayon. Then he wrote "To Mother From Morton" on it and stuck it under a fold of the wrapping. He spelled Mother wrong, though—"To Moter," he wrote—and he spelled From wrong, too: Form.

My mother said his present was very nice, and she even kept it a week after it was due, pretending to read it now and then, but in the end she had to take it back, and at the same time she stopped admiring my prism.

It still hangs at the kitchen window, splattering tiny rainbows each morning on everything in the room: the refrigerator, the cereal bowls, the bread, the sink— even, at times, our faces, tinting our skin with thin, watery colors: reds and greens and blues, pale as a bruise. But my mother doesn't notice it at all.

CHAPTER SEVEN

When I finally went upstairs that evening, after singing my moron song to Morton, everybody was already in the kitchen. My father and brother were sitting at the table, and my mother was at the stove, making circles in a pot with a wooden spoon. "There's a new girl on the block," I told her before she could ask why I was late. "Her name is Polly," I said, going over to the sink and splashing water loudly on my hands. "She's my friend now," I shouted over the noise.

I don't have many friends. Before this summer, I really didn't have any—not the kind, anyway, who call you up on the phone a lot and borrow your clothes. Once someone asked me, "Which would you rather have, one really good friend or lots of half-good friends?" I said I didn't know, but what I wanted was both: one really good friend to have fun with, and a whole bunch of half-good friends to make me look popular. Mostly, all I have is one half-good friend and then some people

I play with now and then: Ina, maybe, or Deirdre, but they are best friends with each other, not with me. Until this summer, I never had a best friend. I am the only girl in my class who doesn't have one in school, and when we have to pick partners in gym, I always end up with the teacher.

But I pretend to my mother that I have lots of friends, so I won't be like Morton, who has none. I tell her a lot about Wanda and Iris from school, and Rhoda and Linnet. Actually, Wanda is my friend from the class I used to be in before I skipped, and there isn't any Linnet at all. I just like the name. "Why don't you invite them over?" my mother always asks, and I say they live too far away. They don't, really. They live on Calvin Boulevard, and sometimes *I* visit *them*, but I don't want them to see where I live. I don't want them to know that we eat dinner in the kitchen and hang our wash from a ceiling rack over the bathtub. I don't want them to see Morton. And besides, they wouldn't come anyway.

"You're late," my father said, looking up at me from the table.

"I was with my new friend, Pop," I answered.

Pop. I began calling my father Pop a long time ago, because that's what Wanda calls *her* father, and I thought maybe he would get to be like Wanda's father if he had the same name. Pop: someone who knows how to play Old Maid and who asks knock-knock jokes and reads the funnies. I feel silly calling him Pop now, though. Father would be better, or Wilson, which is his first name, although everybody calls him Bill. Or even Mr. Briggs. "Hi, Mr. Briggs," I could say, as though he were a visitor.

Most of the time I call him nothing at all, which is what he calls me. Last year, I asked him to call me M. E. "All my friends are going to call me that now," I said, "so maybe you should call me that, too," but all he said was "Mmm." He doesn't call me anything because he doesn't talk to me very much. He calls Morton by his name more than he calls me by mine, but that's because "Morton" is *all* he says to him. "Morton!" he says at the dinner table, and that means use a handkerchief or close your mouth when you chew.

Once, a long time ago, I wondered if he remembered my name at all, or my birthday, or how old I was, or what grade I was in, and I even tested him. I wrote out a questionnaire and pretended it was a form he had to fill out. "My teacher wants you to answer these questions," I told him. "It's so I can get promoted," and I handed him a paper with lots of headings and blank spaces: NAME . . . SEX . . . BIRTHDAY . . . NAME OF SCHOOL . . . GRADE IN SCHOOL . . . NAME OF TEACHER . . . AWARDS. . . .

Things like that, but he didn't fill it out at all. "Silly girl," he said, handing it back after glancing at it. Silly girl, and so I filled in the word "girl" for him next to where it said SEX, and I signed his name at the bottom: Wilson F. Briggs.

"What are used oars?" Morton suddenly asked, bending over the newspaper at the kitchen table. He was doing the crossword puzzle. He does it every night, although he doesn't really *do* it. He just puts in S's where there are plurals, and then he asks us to tell him all the rest of the answers. If there are still some empty squares after that, he fills them in with any letters at all. Mostly M's, for Morton. "It's a house," he says about the puzzle, "with a whole lot of rooms, and the letters live there."

He's fourteen years old and he still does that.

"That's stupid," I tell him. "That's not what you're supposed to do with a crossword puzzle. You're supposed to put in the right words so they fit together when they cross. That's why it's called *crossword*. Get it?" But he doesn't. "CROSS WORD!" I shout, and he looks at me with his dumb look and says "*tss*," which is a sort of laugh he makes when people get mad at him. He never cries.

Except for once.

"What are used oars?" he asked my mother. She was still stirring the pot and the steam rose into her face, making a curtain on her glasses. On her ears, too, maybe, because she didn't answer.

"Used oars," he repeated, and when she still didn't answer, he said, "Five letters."

"I don't know, Morton," she finally said. "Put it away. We're about to eat."

"What do you *think* it is?" he insisted. "Used oars."

"I don't *know*, Morton. There's no word for that."

"It says it here," he said. "Five letters."

"You're reading it wrong," I said, turning to him from the sink. Water slid down my elbows and onto my stomach. "It's probably used *cars*," and I looked over to my mother so she would agree. So she would think I was smart. So it would be okay that I had sung that moron song to Morton on the sidewalk. He *was* a moron.

"Look what you're doing, Mary Ella," she said. "You're dripping."

"It's used *cars*," I said to Morton, wiping my elbows on my shorts.

"Oh," he answered. "Oh, oh, oh." He always says that when he makes a mistake, except it comes out like wo-wo-wo, as though he's talking to a horse. "Wo-wo-wo. That's what I meant. Used cars. What's a word for used cars?"

"Jalopies," I told him.

"What?"

"JALOPIES! Don't you even know what jalopies are?"

I have no idea why Morton gets to do the crossword puzzle and I don't. I'm the one who knows all about words and everything. I'm the one who knows how to spell. I'm the one who won first prize in an essay contest—not just first prize in my school, but first prize in the whole *city*. I'm the one who tells him most of the answers.

"How do you spell it?" he asked, and he put down the letters as I gave them to him. "It doesn't fit," he said. I already knew it wouldn't fit. "There are only five spaces," he said, and he rubbed at the page with an eraser worn down to its metal ring and smudged black.

I pulled the newspaper from his hand and sat down with it at the table. "Where is it, down or across?"

"Across. Where it says 'used oars.' "

"Used *cars*. CARS! There's no such thing as used oars. Can't you even read?" But then I saw that it said "used oars" after all, and I handed the puzzle back. "It's a mistake," I told him. "It's supposed to say used cars."

"Oh," he answered. "What's a word for used cars?" he asked my mother.

"I don't know, Morton. Put the puzzle away now."

"Five letters," he said.

"I don't *know!*" And then she said "Stubborn mule" into the pot.

"That doesn't fit," he said, bending over the page. "Five letters."

My mother said something else into the pot after that, but I didn't hear what it was. She wasn't really talking to the pot. She wasn't talking to herself, either. My mother doesn't talk to herself, although it looks that way. She talks to someone you can't see. Someone who moves with her from room to room and listens when she is angry at Morton. Someone who agrees with her a lot. Sometimes my mother calls Morton terrible things, but not to his face. She says them to her listener, who sits with her at the kitchen table or walks alongside her on the street and doesn't mind hearing that Morton is a stupid rat. Or brat, maybe; I can't always hear.

There was soup for dinner that night, pale-yellow soup that you could see your face in, and I blew ripples into it, making my hair dance in the bowl and my lips stretch into a broken grin. Suddenly I knew the right word for the crossword puzzle.

"I know what used oars is," I said.

"*Are,*" my father said.

"Is. It's 'rowed,' " I told Morton, waiting for him to misunderstand, to spell it wrong.

"It doesn't fit," he said, writing ROAD in the spaces.

"ROWED!" I yelled at him. "Like, he rowed a boat. Get it? He *used oars* to row the boat."

"Oh," he said. "Wo-wo-wo. How do you spell it?"

"How do you think?"

"Oh, now I know," he said, and he wrote down RODE.

"No, dummy! ROWED!" and my mother and father looked at each other across the table.

I know that look. It hangs like a little string between their faces and it means that I am smart and Morton is dumb. It means: Look at Mary Ella—three years younger and ten times smarter. It means that I make them happy and Morton doesn't, and sometimes it makes me feel good, sometimes not. That night it did.

"Put the puzzle away, Morton," my mother said. "You can finish it later."

"It *is* finished," he said. "I have to cut it out now."

That's what he does after he puts in all the S's and some words and fills the rest of the spaces with any letter at all. He cuts the puzzle out of the newspaper and adds it to his collection.

Morton collects things. He collects those little metal bottle caps with pleated edges that lie along the curb. He collects plastic spoons from lunch counters and he collects the paper sleeves from drinking straws. He used to collect the drinking straws, too, until my mother made him throw them away because of germs. He collects gum wrappers and the red cellophane strings from cigarette packs. He collects things that people throw away, and once my mother threw the *collection* away, and stuffed it into the trash can in the kitchen. "It's just a lot of rubbish," she said. "It will attract vermin," but he took it all out again and returned it to his closet. "You can come back now," I heard him say to a bottle cap. He collects things because he feels sorry for them—all those scraps and pieces lying at the curbstone or curling around the ketchup bottle on a lunchroom counter, things nobody wants.

"You can cut it out later, Morton," my mother said. "Finish your soup," but he had already gotten the scissors and was working them around the black margins on the page.

"Morton!" my father shouted, and Morton tucked the puzzle under his soup bowl. "Like a handkerchief," he said.

With my spoon I stabbed the soup in its middle, and my face broke into fragments that flew around in a circle and washed to the sides of the bowl. "My new friend just moved in," I said. "She comes from someplace far away."

"Where does she live now?" my mother asked.

"I don't know. Somewhere on the block." I put my spoon down and watched my face straighten itself out in the soup.

"No, she doesn't," Morton said suddenly. "She lives on the other block."

I looked at him. "How do *you* know?"

He was eating his soup now, and every time he put the spoon in his mouth it knocked against his back teeth. His teeth are always getting in the way. They bite into his glass when he's drinking milk and they crack against each other when he chews. I hate his teeth.

"How do *you* know?" I said again. "What other block?" It's not a good idea to ask Morton more than one question at a time. He ends up staring at you and not answering either one. "What other block?" I asked.

"Over there," he said, pointing. "Behind us."

"You mean Preston?"

"Yes," he answered. "Preston."

"How do you *know*?"

"I saw her move in," he said, and then he pushed his soup bowl away, knocking over his glass of milk, spilling it on the table, on the floor.

"Morton!" my father shouted.

"Wipe it up," my mother said in a quiet voice, not yelling. My mother is angry at Morton a lot, but she never yells and she doesn't hit him. She doesn't believe in hitting. Instead, she tells her listener about how *other* mothers would hit him if he were their child. "Any other mother," she always begins, "would take a wooden broomstick and lower it on his head." Then she talks about how lucky Morton is not to have any other mother, and after that she talks about how the trouble with her is that she's too nice. "I'm too easy on him," she says to an empty chair or to a space on the wall. "Any other mother would hit him with the morning paper." She gets very specific when she talks about what any other mother would do. *Wooden* broomstick, she says. *Morning* paper. Things like that.

Sometimes she tells about all the sacrifices she has to make for him. "All those sacrifices," she says. "The *money* I've spent on him, and the *time*. No other mother would have done as much." Long ago, when I first read about sacrifices in a mythology book, I thought the Greeks were buying lots of clothes for their kids and helping them with their schoolwork.

Meanwhile, Morton shuffles his feet around and says *"tss"* a lot. "Any other mother would put him in the hall closet," she said once, and I wondered why *that*? Why the *hall* closet, which has only a few coats in it and the vacuum cleaner, and really isn't such a terrible place to be? Why not their own closet, which is so small the sleeves of their clothes press into your face when you hide there and you have to stand on their shoes? Maybe that was why. Maybe she didn't want him close to her dresses, with his runny nose and all.

Morton's puzzle lay under a puddle of white, and he

stared at the swarm of bubbles that had collected in its center. "*Tss,*" he said when he finally lifted it up. The paper had turned gray and a picture from the other side showed through. "*Tss,*" he said again, and he stared at the penciled letters—the S's and the M's, soggy now and fuzzy in the tiny square rooms of their house.

Instead of being the child rabbit in my egg room that night, I was somebody else. I tied my hair into a big tail with a shoelace and I frizzed it up a lot so it would look curly. I put on two skirts, one green and long and the other yellow and short, so that together they would look like one skirt with stripes. I cut out a piece of paper and taped it to my forehead for a Band-Aid, and finally I colored my lips bright red with a lipstick that I keep behind the underwear in my drawer and that I'm not allowed to wear or even to own.

Then I made up a crazy dance: I waved my arms around a whole lot and closed my eyes, which is what Miss Frazier tells us to do in Interpretive Dance at school, and I added a folk-dance step I had learned in gym. The music was inside my head: It was the Morton-without-the-*t* song, and I sang it over and over to myself, while the giant girl watched at the window and wondered who I was.

Who *is* that? she whispered, and she pinched her fingers into a long beak, trying to seize me, to pick me up like a clothespin and dance me across the room. I whirled around faster then, and she withdrew her hand; I could hear her sigh rustle the edges of the curtains. Faster and faster I spun, until my skirts puffed out like a beach umbrella and my ponytail slapped my cheeks like a pennant in the wind. I never once looked at the window, but I felt the eye upon me all the time, and when suddenly my door flew open, I let out a small cry, thinking somehow it was the giant child, entering the egg at last. Instead it was Morton, and we stared at each other a long moment.

"Get out!" I finally screamed. "GET OUT!" and I slammed the door so hard the window, vacant now and dark, shivered in its frame.

"Mary Ella is wearing lipstick," I heard him tell my mother down the hall.

CHAPTER EIGHT

The first thing Polly noticed when I led her into my room, one week after everyone sang my song on the sidewalk, was my play orphanage. "Oh, wow, Mary Ella," she said, "these are neat," and she stared in wonder at the twenty-four little girls dressed in beautiful gowns and marching two by two across my windowsill.

They weren't real little girls. They weren't even dolls. They were the little glass bottles from the paint set I got two Christmases ago and never painted with. In fact, I never thought of them as paints at all. They had white metal heads and smooth shiny bodies and they stood side by side in their cardboard box like a row of little girls in colored gowns.

I took them out one by one that Christmas Day and arranged them in little clusters—in families, really—of purple sisters and red sisters and blue sisters, and I called them by their names. They all had beautiful names printed on labels across their stomachs: Marigold, Ecru, Heliotrope, Mauve. *Mauve!* That was the most beautiful name I had ever heard. "Hey, Mauve," I said, hopping the little bottle on the floor. "Come meet Heliotrope," and I tapped their metal heads together as they made friends.

After that they became the twenty-four girls in an orphanage. They lived in the cardboard box, standing waist high in separate round holes, and I let them out each morning just before I went to school. "Good morning, Eggshell," I'd say, standing her on the windowsill with Ebony at her side. "Good morning, Marigold. Good morning, Umber. Good morning, Violet. Good morning, Taupe," and I'd march them two by two to their classes on my desk.

The two most beautiful colors of all stood to one side, their liquid gowns as thick as syrup and flecked like a sunbeam with sparkling dust. They were the teachers, Miss Gold and Miss Silver, and they lived apart in their own waist-high spaces, square ones this time, because, unlike the orphan girls, their bodies had corners.

The school the girls all attended was just like Agnes Daly, except that they didn't have to wear uniforms, as we do, because their dresses were all different colors, and there were no boys. Everything else was the same— they had art class and Interpretive Dance and something called Free Expression, and chapel once a week.

Chapel, just like in Agnes Daly, wasn't really chapel at all. It was what other schools call assembly, and in it the orphans had to listen to the headmistress give a lecture, just like Miss Rice's, on how lucky they all were to attend such a wonderful school and to have three meals a day and good warm clothes and a roof over their heads. "Where else would it be?" Topaz once whispered to Taupe. "Under our feet?" And the headmistress punished them both, just as Miss Rice had when Iris whispered that to Rhoda. "Sit in this chair," the headmistress told her orphan girls, "and think about the consequences of offending the feelings of your fellow human beings," which is what Miss Rice had said to Rhoda and Iris that time. Then the head-mistress would talk about children on other parts of the globe—she always said globe instead of world—who wore rags and ate scraps from the street and had no roof over their heads at all.

I was the headmistress.

Each day, when the teachers entered their class-rooms, the girls would all rise. "Good *morning*, Miss Silver," they would sing together, tilting their heads forward. Or "Good after*noon*, Miss Gold." I made that part up. We don't do that at Agnes Daly, but I wish we did.

At the end of every day the orphans would meet,

one by one, with the headmistress in her office, to discuss what they had learned.

"I learned about the Mojave Desert," Ebony would say.

"That's not the way to pronounce it, Ebony," and I would tell her how.

"Yes, Miss Briggs," she would answer, and she would repeat "Mojave" after me, saying it right.

"What did you learn about the Mojave Desert, Ebony?"

"That it's very old, and it's very dry and hot."

"That's not enough. Tomorrow you must show me where it is on the map and tell me who lives there."

"Yes, Miss Briggs," she would say.

Then I would ask Miss Gold and Miss Silver for a report on everyone's behavior. "Crimson wrote words on the mirror," Miss Gold would tell me, "and Violet spat."

I'd be very angry at that and take both girls into my office and knock their hard white heads together. I made that part up, too. Then I'd tell them they would have to stay home that night and miss the ball.

Every night there was a ball, where the girls danced to music and spun around in their lovely gowns. I would help them all get ready for it, making sure that each girl looked her best. "Let me straighten your dress," I would say to Marigold, to Indigo, to Emerald, to Mauve, and I would hold each one in my fist, shaking her gown into a shimmer, into a sheen, into a liquid glow.

Sometimes all the orphans would get sick at the same time and have to lie in a dark room, side by side, for days and days, but I would make them better. "Get better," I'd say, wetting a finger with my tongue and touching each head. "Get better," and they would, all at the same time.

Sometimes, too, they'd all get kidnapped and be taken to a cave with walls cold and green with slime, but I'd pay a huge ransom and bring them safely home.

Once in a while I would take them for a walk in town. Town was my Monopoly board, and I would move them from street to street, past the little green houses and red hotels and around the jail and the parking lot. They would all take turns walking on the boardwalk, and then I would take them to visit the poor children.

The poor children were the marbles on my Chinese checker board. There were red poor children, blue poor children, and yellow poor children; green, black, and white, and they sat in their classrooms at each point of their star-shaped school. When the rich orphans came, the poor children would look at them from their little round holes and wish they could be rich, too, with gowns of ebony, taupe, and mauve. The orphans would twirl around in front of them and talk about their parties and balls. "Too bad you can't come," they'd say, or "See how my dress sparkles in the light," like Cinderella's stepsisters, but then I would tell them to stop.

I would feel sorry for the poor children in their triangular classrooms, with their drab dresses all alike. "Stop it, Heliotrope," I'd say. "Don't talk like that." "But they're so dumb," Heliotrope would answer. "It's not nice to call people dumb," I would tell her. After that the orphan girls would not say anything at all, and I would march them all back to their house in the cardboard box.

When I couldn't think of anything else to do with them, I would call them all out of their house, one at a time, just so I could recite their beautiful names: "Vermilion? Topaz? Marigold? Mauve? Hurry up, Magenta; stop *dawdling*. Indigo? Scarlet? Taupe? *Taupe?* Where *are* you, Taupe?"

"Here, Miss Briggs."

"Why don't you ever paint anything, Mary Ella?" my mother always asked. "You have a beautiful paint set and you haven't even opened the bottles." That wasn't true. Now and then I *would* open the bottles, unscrewing the caps and peering into the liquid gowns, just as sometimes I would lift the dress of a doll to see what was underneath. But that was all. I would put their little metal heads back on and line them up again for their next class.

"I'm going to," I'd answer my mother. "I'm waiting for some good ideas of what to paint. Maybe tomorrow," but I knew I never would. Even if I had wanted to paint at home, and Morton didn't get in the way, I would never have used those paints, because by then they weren't paints at all. They were my orphan girls, and I loved them more than I loved anything in my whole life. More, even, than the Easter egg.

"Oh, wow, Mary Ella," Polly said when she saw them all lined up, two by two, on my windowsill, on their way to recess. "These are neat. Let's paint."

CHAPTER NINE

I hadn't invited Polly over. I hadn't even seen her since that day when we had all danced around Morton. She had gone away then without ever learning who I was, without saying good-bye. She didn't even know that Morton was my brother.

She wasn't my new friend at all.

When I answered the doorbell and saw her in the hall, I thought she had come to the wrong apartment, and I waited for her to notice her mistake, to say, "Oh, hey, this isn't where I wanted to be," to go up another flight of stairs, to go back down, to leave.

Kids from the block don't come to visit me very often. They don't come at all, in fact, unless I invite them, which I usually don't do. They don't especially like me, really, because I go to private school, because I'm snooty, because I have better stuff than they have, because I can never think of anything to say, because

I'm not like them. Because of Morton, too, maybe.

Once, Ina came to the door and I thought maybe she had stopped being best friends with Deirdre and wanted to be best friends with me. I asked her to come in and I began to tell her about my new Monopoly set, but she hadn't come to play with me at all. She was collecting money for heart disease and she was ringing all the doorbells in the building. I felt silly then, with the words of my invitation hanging in the doorway, so I got two dollars out of my allowance and put them in her envelope. That was all the money I had at that time, and they were the only dollar bills she had gotten. Everything else in her envelope was nickels and dimes. Some pennies.

So when Polly came to the door, I didn't say anything at all. I just waited for her to say she was looking for someone else or to ask me for money. Instead, though, she asked, "Where is everybody?"

"Where *is* everybody?" I repeated, and I looked at her for a while. "They're still in school," I finally said, and then I added, "My school's finished. I go to Agnes Daly. It's a private—"

"No, I mean here. Where's everybody here?"

"Here?" I looked at her some more. "You mean besides me?" She nodded. "My mother's at the hospital and my father's at his bookstore." I didn't mention Morton.

"What's the matter with her?" she asked, walking past me into the apartment.

"With who?"

"Your mother. How come she's in the hospital?"

"Nothing. She works there."

"Oh. Let's see your stuff," she said.

She didn't look much different from the way she had looked the week before. A Band-Aid still stretched across her forehead, and her hair was still tied together with string. Her clothes were still too long, too wrong—everything was crooked and nothing matched. I was glad of that. If she wore crazy clothes, then maybe no one else on the block would like her or want her for a friend, and she could belong to me alone.

I led her carefully through the apartment, so she could see all the things that make my building the best on the block: the metal blinds on the windows instead of paper shades, the refrigerator with a real freezer on top, the piano, and the ceiling light that turns on from a switch and not a string. "Do you want to go to the bathroom?" I asked, hoping she would, so she could see the tiles, which are pink instead of just white, and the bathtub that rests flat on the floor instead of on feet with crooked toes. It didn't matter about the clothes rack on the ceiling. Everybody around here has one of those. It's only my Agnes Daly friends who dry their clothes in secret, where no one else can see.

When we got to Morton's room, I closed the door, so she wouldn't look in and ask whose it was. So she wouldn't say after that, "Oh, I didn't know you had a *brother*," which is what the girls in school always say. "Is he cute?" So I wouldn't have to answer, "No, he's a pest. He's a big pest," which is what I always tell the girls in school, and which is what I wish he really were: a pest like everybody else's brother. "My brother's a pest, too," they answer, "but my parents like him best, anyway." They say that all the time: "My parents like my brother best," or "My parents like my sister more than me." Nobody ever says, "My parents like me best."

I never say it either, even though it's true.

It was two o'clock then. At three-thirty, Morton would be home from school, and at three I would tell Polly she had to leave. "I have to go to my piano lesson," I would tell her. Or to the dentist or to the supermarket for my mother. "So you'll have to go now."

But Polly didn't notice Morton's room at all. She didn't notice the freezer either, or the blinds or the light switch or the bathtub. All she noticed in the whole house, in fact, was my play orphanage.

"Let's paint, Mary Ella," she said. "These are neat colors. Where's the brushes?"

"I'm not sure," I said. "I don't think I have any. They're probably all—"

[76]

"Here they are," she said. "They're in this box."
She had found the cardboard house where the orphan
girls lived, and she was already removing the six brushes
from their little elastic loops. "Oh, hey," she said,
running the bristles across the back of her hand. "Feel
of *that*! They're so soft, it's like they're just whispering
into your skin." She had a funny way of talking. "Suh
soft," she said, and "jist" for "just." "Feel of that."
Where did she come from, anyway? Nobody around
here talks like that.

"Let's get started," she said, placing the tip of a
brush into her mouth and sucking it to a fine point.

"We can't," I said. "We can't play with those paints,"
and then after a while, I added, "I just got them."

I just got them. That's what Wanda or Iris or somebody like that from Calvin Boulevard says when they
don't want me to play with something. "I just got
them," they say.

"Can we play with these paper dolls?" I'll ask, lifting
up a booklet with two punch-out girls in their underwear on the cover and pages of lovely dresses inside,
and Iris or Wanda will take it away and say, "I just
got them," which means no.

"I just got them," I told Polly again, but I don't
think she heard me at all.

"Hey, look at this purple," she said, grabbing Violet
by her neck. "Purple is my favorite color. Every time

I look at it I get this taste in my mouth, like a smooth sourball, and my ears ring, too. I hear this big fat noise. Let's start with purple, Mary Ella."

"No," I said. I took Violet back and put her in her special space in the house. "I'm really not allowed to use these paints at all. They're not mine."

"Whose are they then?"

"My mother's."

"Your *mother's*? Your mother plays with *paints*?"

"She doesn't play with them. She uses them. She's an artist."

"I thought you said she was a nurse."

"I didn't. I said she worked at the hospital."

"She's an artist at the hospital?"

"No. She does other stuff there." I was putting all the other orphan girls away now, too, as fast as I could, tumbling them down from the windowsill and cramming them into spaces that weren't their own. "She paints when she comes home," I said.

Don't worry, Emerald, I whispered in my head. *Don't worry, Taupe. Don't worry, Vermilion and Ivory. Don't worry, Marigold, Eggshell, Topaz, Mauve. I'm your head-mistress, remember. Miss Briggs. I'll take care of you. Stop crying, Ebony. Remember when you were all kidnapped and I rescued you? Remember when you all got sick and I made you better? Stop crying!* I pressed Miss Gold and Miss Silver into their little square holes. *You're in charge*, I told them. *Make sure nobody worries. Especially Ebony. Look after her. She's frail,* and I pushed the roof onto their house.

"You want to play Monopoly?" I asked Polly. I slipped the orphan house under my bed. "I have this really nice set." It *is* nice. Not as nice as Wanda's, but nice just the same. Wanda has the deluxe set, with wooden houses and hotels and a real metal shoe and car to push along, while mine has just plastic things, but no one else on my block has a Monopoly set at all. "You want to play?"

"No," she said. "I don't know how. Let's paint, Mary Ella. What's your favorite color? We can do that after we do purple."

"I don't have any. And anyway, nobody calls me Mary Ella. My friends all call me M. E."

"Okay, Emmy. Let's get started."

"Not Emmy. M. E. Look," and I showed her the initials embroidered in red on my T-shirt. "See? M. E. It's my initials. For Mary Ella. Get it?"

She stared awhile at my chest. "I thought that said 'Me.' "

"No. It's M. E. It's kind of a dumb name, but everybody's called me that for years."

M. E. It would be nice to have someone call me that, I thought. "Hey, M. E.! You want to go to the movies?" "You know what, M. E.? You're the best friend I ever had." Maybe if Polly started calling me that, other people would call me that, too. Maybe everybody would. Maybe if everybody called me M. E. I wouldn't be Mary Ella anymore. Maybe I'd be someone else. Someone everybody liked.

"Okay, Mary Ella," she said. "Where's the paper?" She was still holding the paintbrushes, and they fanned out from her fist like flowers in a vase.

"I don't have any," I told her, although that wasn't true. I had a whole stack of nice paper in my desk drawer. It had come in a special portfolio, and my mother had given it to me, along with two pens, after I won that essay contest. She thought I was going to become a famous writer—not when I grew up, but right away—and I needed a lot of paper to get started.

"It's all used up," I told Polly, but I knew she would find it anyway, and she did.

"Hey, it's right here," she said, reaching into the drawer. "Look at it all!" She held the portfolio over her head and let the paper float like leaves onto the floor. "Look at it go!" she cried. "It's like magic rugs flying around in the air. Millions of magic rugs!" The pieces came to rest in little drifts against our feet and they curled like tiny waves along the walls. "Pick as many as you want," she said, as though it were *her* paper, not mine.

She was on her hands and knees now, sliding the

orphan house out from under my bed. "Oh, wow, Mary Ella," she cried, removing the lid. "Look at this one. It glitters. *Look* at it! It's gold! Wet gold!" She began to unscrew Miss Gold's head.

"Don't do that!" I shouted, but it was too late. She had already plunged a brush into the bottle and was spreading Miss Gold's beautiful gown into a broad smear across a sheet of the paper that I was supposed to write more essays on, so I could become a famous writer someday soon.

CHAPTER TEN

The essay I won the prize for was about Elizabeth Cady Stanton, the suffragist, and I wrote it because Mrs. Pierce gave it as an assignment, not because I wanted to. Also, *I* didn't send it to the contest—my mother did. I'd never even heard of Elizabeth Cady Stanton before, and all I could find out about her in the encyclopedia was her birthday and the names of some books she had written. So I made up a lot of stuff about how if she were alive today she'd be so happy to see women voting and being lawyers and not bothering to get married. It was a terrible essay. Probably it won because nobody else had entered the contest. The prize wasn't very good either—a little medal and a certificate with my named spelled wrong: Mariella. No money. But when the letter came telling me I had won, my mother got all excited and called up all her friends, reciting the name of the award very carefully: The Francis Bacon Essay Society Award, as though it were the Nobel Prize or something, and she had won it herself.

The medal was attached to a little purple-and-yellow ribbon, the kind with ridges to bump your fingernail along, and it was engraved with my initials—M. B.— and the date. It came in a little box with fuzzy cardboard that was supposed to look like velvet, and it lies, with the certificate and a newspaper clipping— where my name is also spelled wrong—in my mother's bureau drawer, not mine.

"This is a crummy color," Polly said, tilting her head to one side as she examined the stripe she had just painted on my writing paper. "It isn't gold at all. It's mud. They put mud in this bottle and made it look like gold."

She was right. It *was* the color of mud. Outside Miss Gold's glass body, the paint had no shine at all, and the sunbeam flecks lost their glint. Mud and bits of grit was what it was like. I looked at Miss Gold standing on the floor with her head off and her dress dripping down around her neck, and I reached out for her. *Miss Mud,* I said, tightening her head back on and wiping her shoulders with my thumb. What would the orphan girls sing out now, I wondered, when she entered their room? Good *morning,* Miss Mud, probably, and Vermilion would laugh. *Shut up, Vermilion,* I said in my head.

"Watch this now," Polly said, and she began to pull all the orphans out of their holes and to drop them in a heap on her lap.

"Stop that!" I yelled. "STOP THAT! Put them back in their house! Box, I mean. Put them back in their *box!*" But she moved away from me and began scrambling the orphans all around, knocking their bodies together as she searched for something. Finally she found what she wanted, and she put Violet's head between her teeth and twisted it off. "I'm starting with purple," she said.

"No, you're not!" I pulled Violet away and screwed her head back on.

"Red, then," she said, picking up Vermilion. "You want to see something?" She undid Vermilion's head and stirred her dress around with a paintbrush.

"No! No, I don't. I don't want to see something. I want to see you put that back. That's what I want to see." My teachers in school talk like that, and I talked like that, too, sometimes, to the little orphans when they said fresh things. "*Stop* that!" I yelled. "You're ruining her *dress!*"

"Ready? Watch." She folded down the top joint of her thumb, and on its smooth, shiny knuckle painted a little red face, with O's for eyes, an L for a nose, and a shallow U for a smile. "Now look," and she straightened out her thumb, wrinkling the skin into the face

of an old man, a monkey, a bulldog, a crying baby—
a what? I couldn't tell. Something ugly. The next
instant she smoothed it out again and it smiled up at
me like a face on a balloon.

"Don't do that!" I yelled again, and I grabbed Vermilion from her hand, spilling some of her red dress
on my wrist. "Look what you did! She's getting all
messed up!" I put Vermilion's head back on. *Stop
squealing*, I whispered to her. *Your dress just got a little
torn around the shoulders. It's* okay. *Don't* worry *about
it. I'll make it better. I'll fix it.* "This stuff costs a lot of
money," I told Polly. "Wait till my mother comes
home. She's going to be really mad."

"Look," she said. "Now I'll do a green one," and
she dipped the same brush, still dripping with the red
of Vermilion's dress, into Emerald's satin gown.

I tried to grab her arm this time, but she was too
quick. A scarlet swirl floated for a long moment on
the green surface like a goldfish in a pond. "Don't," I
said, watching now as the red spread and darkened to
gray, to brown, to black, but my voice was so tight I
could barely hear it myself.

I watched in silence after that as Polly painted the
knuckles on all her other fingers with the dresses of
my orphan girls—of Marigold, Ebony, Indigo, Taupe,
mixing them up, streaking them in their glass bodies:
black on blue, yellow on red, green on white.

"Now I'll do yours," she said, squeezing my hands into fists and making little features on each of my knuckles with the colors of ten different girls. I tried at first to twist away, but her hold was hard, and I finally sat still, offering my hand quietly, as I do in the school infirmary when the nurse bandages a cut.

Be still, Sapphire, I said. Listen to me, Topaz. Listen to me, all of you. I have something to say. This is a dream that you're having, okay? It's a terrible dream that you're all having at the same time. Pretty soon it will be morning and you'll wake up and see that it was all a bad dream. But I wondered what I would tell them the next day when they saw that their gowns were still streaked with crazy colors and torn at the shoulders and neck.

"Now," Polly said, raising first her right fist and then her left. "This hand is the boys and this one is the girls. Look, they're kissing," and she brought her two rows of knuckles together so that their painted lips touched. "Now let's give them names. Boys first. The thumb is Tony, and the others are Donald, Angel, George, and Max."

How did she think those names up so fast? I wondered. Angel. *Angel!* Max. It used to take me weeks to name my dolls, when I played with dolls, and even then I'd never be sure I had chosen the right ones. Fancy names they would be, out of books, mostly—

Daphne and Belinda, things like that—and then I'd keep them all secret, because they sounded dumb when I spoke them aloud. "What is your dolly named?" my mother's friends would ask, and I would answer, "Sally."

"What're yours named?" Polly asked. "Start with the girls."

I peered into the little faces smiling at me and then frowning as I smoothed and shriveled my skin. Maybe, I thought, *they* could be my orphan girls—these little painted faces on my hands. Maybe they would stick to my knuckles forever, and would trail alongside me wherever I went. Ten little orphan girls lined up in rows, smiling and frowning at home and at school. They would go to Agnes Daly instead of the classroom on my desk, and they would learn about the Mojave Desert from Mrs. Pierce instead of from Miss Silver and Miss Gold. For recess they would curl around the jungle-gym bars and for chapel they would listen to Miss Rice. At night they would still go to lovely balls, creating their own music as they ran up and down the piano keys, and later they would sleep among the folds of my pajama sleeves instead of in the circles of a cardboard box. Maybe it would be better if they were fingers instead of bottles of paint. For them, for me.

"Give them names," Polly said.

"Okay," I answered. "This one is Heliotrope," and

I touched the purple-blue face on my thumb. "And this one is Topaz."

"What?"

"Heliotrope and Topaz. And these are Marigold and Umber and Eggshell."

Polly stared at me. "What kind of names are those? Toe pads? Eggshell? *Eggshell?* You can't name anybody that. Pick a real name."

"I can't think of one," I said.

"Yes, you can. Everybody can think of a name."

"Sally," I said, straightening out my thumb and staring into its old, wrinkled face. "This one's Sally." After that I picked names of kids from my class at school. "This one's Rhoda," I said, "and this one's Iris."

"Okay," she said when they were all named. "Let's play that they're gangs."

"Gangs?"

"Yeah. My gang against your gang," and she suddenly pressed her knuckles so hard against mine I let out a cry.

"Who was that?" she asked. "Which one cried?"

I looked at the row of faces smiling up at me from my hand. "Sally," I said. "She always cries," and I pressed back, crushing the smooth little smiles on Polly's fingers.

The two gangs fought for a long time after that, boys against boys, girls against girls, their faces all smiles when they tightened for a blow, wrinkled into frowns when they stopped.

"Let's do knees next," Polly said, pausing for a moment. "Me first," and she rubbed a paintbrush on the inside of Sapphire's neck.

Stop it, I yelled at Sapphire in my head. *Stop crying like that. And you, too, Taupe. Stop crying, all of you! Ebony! Umber! Be still,* and I closed my eyes because I didn't want to look at them, because their heads were knocked off, because their gowns were in shreds, because they were, in fact, no longer orphan girls at all; they were ordinary bottles of paint, with streaks of color hardening down their sides and collecting in the ridges of their necks.

It hurt, banging our knees into each other, but neither of us cried out. I tightened my hands into fists when our bones were set to strike, and the little knuckle faces smiled with every blow.

"Hey," Polly said. "Look what you just did when you wiped your face. You made a green face on your nose!" and she pushed me in front of the mirror. "Scrunch it up and make it holler."

I stared hard at my reflection. Streaks of color spread across my cheeks like the patterns on a cow, forming no design, but the three green spots on my nose made a perfect face: an eye, an eye, and a mouth. I wrinkled them into a scowl.

"Oh, wow," Polly said, and she painted a face on her nose, too. "Watch *this*."

We stood side by side after that, stretching our lips, pulling our cheeks, making faces on top of our faces, and staring at them in the mirror. We looked funny like that, and suddenly I thought: This is what best friends do. I bet this is what Ina and Deirdre do when they play together, and Iris and Rhoda, too. This is what it's like to have a best friend, and I looked again at our faces in the mirror and began to laugh. Big laughs burst from my mouth, taking me by surprise. Real laughs, the kind that come from your stomach somewhere and that you can't help—not those little laughs that you make up when somebody tells a joke that you don't get. Laughs with tears, even; little rivers of water began to spread around my eyes and turn purple as they hit my painted cheeks.

Purple laugh tears. They were my first laugh tears ever, and I blotted them onto a tissue. I stared into the soft, wide splotches that they made. Polly was right, purple did have a taste—I could feel its sudden smoothness on the edges of my tongue—and it had a sound, too—deep, like the gong Miss Rice strikes at the start of every chapel when she wants us to be silent and think important thoughts.

Later, when Polly wasn't looking, I folded the tissue over its own purple dampness and put it into my dresser drawer, to keep. I had never laughed like that before, and I thought it really didn't matter that I didn't have my orphan girls anymore. Polly was going to be my best friend.

"Let's do our elbows," I said, out of breath. "Let's paint them all the colors in my whole paint set." I had just dipped a brush into a bottle of blue when somebody said, "What are you doing?" and we both turned around.

Morton was standing in the doorway.

CHAPTER ELEVEN

He looked as dumb as ever.

My mother always makes Morton wear his door key on a shoelace around his neck, and the lace was in his mouth now, stretching from ear to ear like a thin white grin. Also, his shoes were untied. *Shoes!* Morton wears real shoes all the time, even to school, even in the summer, although he has perfectly good sneakers. "I'm keeping my sneakers for when I have to climb something," he always said. "Climb what?" I'd ask, and he'd answer, "I don't know. Maybe a fence."

His Mickey Mouse shirt was tucked inside his underpants, so that a band of gray elastic showed above his belt, and sticking out from the elastic was a long white envelope.

"What are *you* doing here?" I demanded. I could still pretend he wasn't my brother. I could say he lived downstairs and had come up to play with my things. Or he got the apartments mixed up and wandered into mine by mistake. Or he was the delivery boy, bringing groceries. Something.

"What?" he asked, staring at me.

"What are you *doing* here?" What *was* he doing there, anyway? It wasn't even three o'clock yet and he never got home before three-thirty. Then I remembered—today was the last day of school. The last Friday of June. That was why he was home early, and that was why he had an envelope. It contained his report card.

"I don't know," he answered. "I'm just here. Where's Mom?"

"Who?"

"*Mom.*"

"I don't know," I said. "I don't know where your mother is. Why don't you go away where you belong? I don't have time for you. I'm playing with my friend now."

He looked at me the way he always does when he doesn't understand—his eyes stayed the same but his lips got puffy. I put my face up to his. "I said, why don't you go *away* now," and he did. He walked into his room, tripping on his shoes as he went and chewing hard on the shoelace in his mouth.

I turned to Polly and shrugged at her so she, too, would wonder what Morton was doing at my door, but she brushed past me and followed him down the hall.

"Hey, Morton," she said, "come here. I want to ask you something," and I suddenly remembered her words of the week before: *Hey, Morton. Come here. I want to ask you something.* And then, when he crossed the street, *Is that your girlfriend?*

That's what she still thought—Morton was my boyfriend, not my brother. My *boy*friend! And he had come to my apartment to be with me, to talk to me, to play, to—whatever boyfriends do.

"Polly!" I called after her. "*Polly!* Wait! I have to tell you something," although I didn't know what I would tell her. "Polly, come *here.*"

"Morton," she repeated, "I want to ask you a question," and then I thought of something else. Maybe she really didn't care who Morton was. Maybe she didn't care if he was my boyfriend or my brother or anything. Maybe she just saw him there and decided to play a trick on him, which is what everybody does when they see Morton. "Hey, Morton, come here," they say, just as Polly had. "I want to ask you something." Or tell.

"Hey, Morton," Ezra will suddenly call from down the block. "Come here. I want to tell you something. It's a secret," and he'll blow a whistle into Morton's ear.

"Hey, Morton, come here. I want to tell you something. Shake," and a hand will reach out to buzz a little shock into Morton's palm.

"Hey, Morton, come here. You know what?" This was the longest trick of all. "There was a guy around here from Western Union. He had a telegram for someone named Morton Briggs who lived in your building, but I told him there was no one there by that name."

Morton stared at him for a long time. "That's me," he finally said. "Morton Briggs."

"It is? That's your name? I thought it was Morton Diggs or something. Anyway, when I told him there was nobody around here named that he just tore the telegram up. It was something about winning a lot of money."

I never say anything when somebody plays a trick on Morton. I just stand and watch, waiting for it to be over.

Sometimes I play tricks on him myself.

"Come here," Polly said. "I want to ask you something."

Morton turned around. "What?" he said.

Don't play a trick, I said to myself. *Don't, don't, don't. Best friends don't play tricks on each other's brothers.*

"Where are your trains?" she asked.

"My trains?"

"Yeah, the electric ones. With the station and all. Where are they?"

His trains? His train set? How did she know about *that?* . . . *Nobody* knew about Morton's train. What kind of trick was this, anyway? Morton's train set had lain under his bed in its big flat box for more than a year. Nobody had touched it since the time Lenny from his class had come over that day long ago and played for a whole afternoon, all by himself, while Morton watched from the sofa. "What train?" I asked. "How do you know about his train?"

"He told me," she said.

"Who? Lenny?"

"No, *him.* Your brother."

"What brother?"

"How many do you have? That one. Morton."

"Morton told you about his train? When did he tell you that?" How did she know he was my brother?

"When he came to my house."

I stared at her. What *was* this, anyway? "Morton came to your house?" I turned to him. "You went to her house? When did you go there? How come you never said so?" My voice was growing loud and high. "What were you doing at her house?" *When she's supposed to be* my *friend*, I thought.

"It's not her house," he answered. "It's her grandma's." He slipped his report card out from his belt and propped it up on his dresser, in front of the clock. His name had been written on the envelope in fancy script, with extra tails dangling from the capital letters and little g's that looked like 8's. The kind I always try to copy, but can't do right. "She lives with her grandma," he added.

"I know that," I said, although I didn't. "I know she lives with her grandmother. When did you go there? What were you doing? What was he doing at your house?" I said to Polly.

"Playing," she answered.

"Playing what?"

"Dress-up."

"She showed me her grandma's clothes," Morton said. "We tried them on."

I stared at him. "You tried them on? You played dress-up in her grandmother's clothes? At *your age?*"

"She had a whole bunch of hats," Morton said. "And shoes that you needed a hook to put them on, like long ago."

I turned to Polly to see if she was laughing, but she wasn't even listening. "Where are they, Morton?" she asked. "The trains with the station?"

Morton pulled the train box out from under his bed and turned it upside down. "Hey, look out!" I cried, as a rush of silver track crashed around his legs and train cars slid about like little mice.

"Is this it?" Polly had the transformer in her hands. "Is this the station?"

"No," Morton told her. "That's the thing with wires you attach. *This* is the station." He held up a little plastic platform with a tiny slatted bench and signboards at the edges of the roof. ORCHARDTOWN, they read. "That's the name of the town where the train goes," Morton explained. "Look." He balanced the station on his knees. "This is Orchardtown, and my legs are all the streets," and he laughed his dumb laugh.

"Look at *this*," I said quickly, before he could say any more dumb things, and I held up the transformer. "This is where they keep all the volts and watts. I can explain how it works, if you want. I can show you how to set it all up with the wires. I know all about how to do it. It's really very complicated. You have to do it just right or it won't work. You need a scientific mind to figure it out," I added. "My teacher is always telling me I have a scientific mind." She isn't really. She says Iris and Joseph have scientific minds. I have a literary mind.

"Let's see the station, Morton," Polly said, holding out her hand. "Let's *see* it," and I finally understood what her trick was going to be. "Let's see it" is what everybody says to Morton when they want to take his stuff away and keep it for themselves. "Let's see it," they say, and he gives them whatever is in his hands or his pockets. For good.

"Let's see your money," Ezra said one morning, a long time ago, as Morton and I stood beneath the awning.

"What?" Morton asked, blinking a little.

"Your *money*. You know, money? Coins? Round silver things? You buy stuff with it?" He was wearing a pair of mirrored sunglasses, even though it was winter, and our whole street, tiny as a peep show, lay inside their lenses—the sidewalk, the cars at the curb, the awning frame, Morton, me. Two whole streets, really—one at each eye. Everything was double; I raised my arm in a brief wave, and two small snowsuit arms waved back. "Let's see your money, Morton," he said, turning the double street from side to side.

"Wo-wo-wo-wo-wo," Morton said, catching on, and he groped about in his pocket for the two quarters from his allowance.

"Let's *see* them," Ezra said, putting his hand out.

Morton held up the two coins by their rims and turned them back to front. "See?" he said.

"Very funny," Ezra said. His hand was still out.

Finally I spoke up. "He doesn't mean *look* at, dummy," I said to Morton. "He means *hold*," and I looked over to Ezra and smiled. I wanted him to know that I wasn't dumb like my brother. I wanted him to know that just because I had a dumb brother, that didn't mean I was dumb, too. "He means give them to him," I said, and I plucked the two quarters from Morton's fingers and handed them over, waiting for Ezra to say something nice to me.

"Thanks," is what he said. He tossed the quarters one at a time into the air and slapped them on the back of his other hand. "Thanks a lot," and he disappeared around the corner, taking the whole street in his sunglasses along with him. Double: double Morton, double awning frame, double sidewalk, double cars, double me.

After that, Morton understood what "Let's see it" meant, so that one day when some kid no one had ever seen before came up to him and said, "Let's see your bicycle," Morton just gave it to him.

"Why'd you do that, Morton?" Franklin had asked. "Why'd you let him ride it, anyway?"

"What?"

"Why'd you let him get on your bike like that and just ride it away? You didn't even *know* him," he said. "He just *took* it. He took your bike and you let him. You just *let* him."

Morton pressed the palms of his hands together and spun them around each other, making one finger wiggle up and the other down, like a clapper toy that you shake on New Year's Eve. He had just learned that trick and he did it all the time. "Look," he'd say, wiggling his fingers in my mother's face. "A bird." Once he scratched her eye doing that.

"Why'd you let him?" Franklin insisted.

"He wanted to see it," Morton explained.

And now Polly.

"Let's see it," she said, reaching for the little plastic station on Morton's knee.

"No!" I shouted. "It's Morton's!" But he gave it to her, anyway.

"Look," she whispered, stroking the roof as though it were some kind of pet animal. "Look at the little signs with the name of the town on them." She flicked them with her fingernail and made them swing. "And the billboards. Look how tiny." She was like the giant girl at the window of my egg room. "And the little bench," she went on.

"You could sit on it if you wanted," Morton said, "and wait for the train to come."

"Yeah, sure," I said, and I smiled so Polly would think Morton was just making a joke.

"You could grow down to be small," he went on, "and then when the train came you could get on. You could have a little ticket, too, to give to the conductor."

"You want to see how the train can go?" I asked Polly. "I can show you how," but she didn't hear me. She was listening to Morton.

"I could be the conductor," he said. "I could get small, too, and wear a blue uniform with a cap to put on my head. All aboard!" He waved his hand back and forth. "All aboard, everybody! We're going to Africa!"

I waited for Polly to laugh, to say that was dumb—you can't take a train to Africa—but she just stroked the roof some more and finally, after a long while, she placed the station very carefully on Morton's knee.

"Or Australia, maybe," she said, and I stared first at her and then at Morton.

CHAPTER TWELVE

When Morton first got his electric train, I didn't believe it was his. I thought it was for me.

It was lying in an enormous box on the coffee table one evening when I returned home from visiting Wanda, and Morton and my mother and father were all looking down at it as though it were a new baby.

"What's that?" I asked, and Morton moved aside so I could see. My breath caught in my throat for a moment. "Oh, wow," I whispered. It didn't seem to belong in our living room; it was too new, too wonderful, with the tracks in perfect stacks of silver arcs, and the cars all gleaming in a row. "Oh, neat," I said, and neat is what I meant—the *tidy* kind of neat, where everything is in its own special place.

"There's a light in the engine that goes on," Morton told me, "and pills to make smoke."

I lifted up a little car and stood it on my palm. It was the color of a buttercup, and bright-red letters spelled a name on either side: Chesapeake & Ohio, they read, beneath the drawing of a cat. I skidded the wheels against my arms and watched as they spun on and on. "It looks so real," I whispered, stopping the wheels all at once with a finger. *Everything* looked real. The doors on the boxcars slid back and forth, and the windows on the passenger cars were thin and clear. A tunnel made to look like brick and stone stood in one side of the box, the little plastic station in the other. ORCHARDTOWN, said the letters on its signs.

"It's beautiful," I whispered.

"It's for me," Morton said, and I stared at him.

"Is that true?" I asked, turning first to my mother and then to my father. "Is that *true*? This is for *him*?"

"We got you a writing set," my mother answered. "Let me show it to you. A lovely writing set in a portfolio, with special paper and two gold pens. Because you won the essay contest," she added, and she handed me a thin package wrapped in pink.

I opened it on the sofa, where I could still look at the train set, and I dropped all the wrappings at my feet. The special paper wasn't really that great. It didn't have lines on it, and it wasn't for writing essays at all. It was for writing letters, and it came with matching envelopes and a little address book. And the pens were gold *colored*.

"It's very nice," I said, closing the portfolio on my knee. I still couldn't believe it. *I* won the essay contest, and all I got was a bunch of paper, that you couldn't even write an essay on, and a couple of pens? While Morton got the most wonderful train set in the whole world? With pellets to make smoke and a real light bulb in the nose of the engine? *Morton?*

He *never* got presents better than mine. Never. At Christmas we always got one present each, and mine was always better. The year I got my Monopoly set he got a bedspread, and when I got my paint set all he got was gloves and a scarf. Stuff he needed anyway.

I looked into the train box and then up to my mother. "It's not even his birthday," I said. "How come he got that?"

"He's never had a train set before," she answered.

"So?" Neither had I.

He wouldn't even know how to use it, I thought. He wouldn't know how to attach the wires to make it go. He wouldn't know how to put the tracks together to make a circle. He wouldn't know how to plug it *in.* He wouldn't even like it.

It was a while before he touched anything in the box, and when he did it was only to lift out two pieces of track and try to fit them together. They got stuck halfway, and when he pulled them apart, one of them bent. *"Morton!"* my father shouted, and my mother whispered something to the lamp.

"Here, Morton," I said. "I'll show you how," and I unpacked all the pieces of track and spread them out on the floor. There were curved pieces and straight pieces and double pieces that made X's and Y's. The picture on the lid showed a huge figure eight inside an oval, with a siding leading off from one edge, and I began to copy it, piece by piece. "Look," I explained to him. "It's easy. You start with this piece that looks like an X, and then you add all the other pieces until it's like the one on the picture."

Meanwhile, my mother and father were connecting wires from the transformer to a little metal plate and moving the sofa so they could reach the outlet on the wall. Morton sat on a chair the whole time and watched. "It looks good," he said, when everything was all set up. "It looks very good," and it did. It looked wonderful.

I had hooked all the train cars together and placed them exactly in front of the platform, so passengers could step right onto the cars without falling, and I had set up the tunnel on the other side, halfway through the train's journey. The track covered almost all the living-room rug, and parts of it ran in and out of the legs of tables and chairs. When I narrowed my eyes I saw a real countryside, with a long silver track running through fields of flattened flowers and trees of dark-stained wood.

"Make it go," Morton said, and he leaned forward in his chair. "Make it go fast," and I turned on the switch.

The bulb on the engine turned a quick, sharp white, and a motor hummed. The train moved slowly at first, pulling itself carefully away from the platform, but it picked up speed after that and worked its way along the tracks, in, out, around—in, out, around—through the tunnel, out. None of us spoke. Suddenly I turned the speed dial as far as it would go, and the train flew around in crazy loops, so fast I could no longer read the letters on the cars. Banners of smoke burst from the chimney and a sudden whistle sounded—whispery, low, and full of warning.

Finally I drew it to a stop, and lowered two fingers onto the roof of a car. They were the new passengers, going to their grandmother's house, and they'd never been aboard a train before today. In and out they went, in and out, past some cows, a pond, a windmill, a school, the house where their grandmother waited at the door. "We're here!" one of them shouted.

"Give Morton a turn now," my mother said. "It's his train, after all."

"Oh, sure," I said, pulling the passengers away and turning off the switch. "Here, Morton. It's your train. *Here*," and before my mother or father could say anything, I pulled all the tracks apart and scrambled them around on the rug. "It's all yours," I said, and I disconnected the train cars, too. "Now you can put it together all by yourself. Go ahead, Morton. Go *ahead*. Just copy the picture on the box. It's easy. Look, you can make a siding and everything," I added, knowing he didn't even know what a siding was. "Anybody can do it. A baby, even."

He picked up two pieces of track and carefully fitted them together, nicely this time. "That's fine, Morton," my mother said. Then he added more pieces, and some more after that, making a crazy zigzag that wandered all over the living-room floor and didn't join together end to end. Finally he picked up the yellow car with the red writing on it and tried to run it along one of the curves, but its wheels kept sliding off the track, and after that he just pushed it up and down his outstretched arm.

"*Rum-rum-rum,*" he said, while the wheels slid silently along his sleeve, "*rum-rum-rum,*" and my mother and my father exchanged that look.

I carried my new writing set into my room and drew out the top sheet of paper. "Stupid brat," I wrote with one of the gold-colored pens. "Stupid brat, stupid rat, stupid brat," I wrote, but not with the writing end. With the other end, so no one could see—no one but some private reader, invisible and silent as the listener who always sat by my mother's side and agreed with her whispered words.

CHAPTER THIRTEEN

Two weeks after Morton got his train set, I found out why he had been given it in the first place.

"Morton," my mother said to him one morning, "why don't you ask one of the boys in your class to come over and play with you sometime? You never invite anyone home. Why is that? You have a nice train set now," she said, "and lots of boys would like to play with it. I bet no one in your class has a train as nice as that."

And that was why: He had been given the train set so he could make friends, and every day after that, when Morton came home from school, my mother would ask, "Morton, did you ask one of the boys to come and play with your train?" and he would say no, he forgot.

In the end, though, someone did come.

Not because *Morton* invited him, but because my mother did. We were all walking back from the supermarket one afternoon, and Morton was pulling the grocery cart, when some boy passed and said hello to him. "The boy said hello," my mother said, and she offered the smile that Morton didn't give. The next minute she was calling him back and telling him about Morton's new train set and asking him to visit, while Morton pulled the groceries up the street.

My mother does things like that. Even with me. When we go to the beach in the summer, she always finds some girl my age and brings her over to me. "I found a nice girl for you to play with," she says, and all of a sudden I am looking into the face of someone I will hate. Someone in a bathing suit that is either a whole lot nicer than mine or a whole lot worse. "Her name is Amanda and she's just your age," my mother says, and she waits for me to smile, to say hello, to be friendly, to be liked, to be not the same as Morton.

"Come tomorrow afternoon," she said to the boy on the sidewalk, and I hoped that when he said no he would offer a really good reason. Not just "No, I have a lot of work to do," but "No, I'm moving away," or "No, I have to get my appendix out." Instead, he said yes.

When we opened the train box the next afternoon, we found a dead moth lying in the corner. Morton lifted it up and looked at it, and then settled it carefully in the bottom of the yellow car. It was a passenger, he said. It was Mr. Moth and he was going to work. "Mr. Moth is going to his bookstore."

Lenny looked at him for a while. "What do you want that for?" he asked "What do you want with a dead bug in the coal car?" He pinched its body between two fingers and blew the silver dust into the air.

"Tss," Morton said, and then he picked up the little car and held it out. "You want to see something? You want to see what I can do?"

"Wait," I said, so Morton wouldn't make the car go rum-rum-rum on his arm in front of this new boy. "I need that!" But Morton didn't answer. "Look," he said, and he wheeled the car up the length of his arm and down again. *"Rum-rum-rum,"* he said, and then he let it roll down his thigh.

Lenny took the car from Morton and attached it to the engine. "You want to know what gauge this train is?" I asked him.

"I already know," he said. "It's H-O. Where can we set it up?"

"On the rug," I answered. "I'll show you how."

My mother had told me to be in charge until she came home. "You're the hostess, Mary Ella," she had said that morning. I was to serve cookies and milk when they came in after school, and then help set up the train. "And then go to your room. Lenny isn't coming to play with you," she said. "He's coming to play with Morton," although that wasn't true; he was coming to play with the train.

I set out the cookies and milk on the coffee table. My mother had baked the cookies herself, for Morton and his new friend, and they were very fancy, like holiday cookies, with different shapes and colored icing and sugar sparkles, even. Too fancy, really. I messed them around a little to make them look plain.

"I'll set the tracks up now," I said, and I took them all out of the box. "I can make them look just like the ones on the cover. You want to see? You start with this X piece, and then you make a figure eight, and after that—"

"Never mind," Lenny said. "I can do it myself." He knelt on the rug and slipped all the track pieces together, one after another, without even checking the picture on the lid. He was finished in two minutes.

"You want me to show you how to attach all the wires?" I asked.

"No," he answered, setting up the transformer. "I can do that, too."

When he had all the cars hooked up and in place on the track, I told him about the smoke pellets for the engine. "They make real smoke," I said, "and the engine lights up and blows a whistle."

"I know," he answered.

After that I stood aside and watched him play with

Morton's train. Morton watched, too, from the sofa. He had taken a glass of milk and was drinking it as he always did, lifting the bottom too quickly so that a wave of liquid washed over his upper lip, leaving a stripe, and swallowing with the noise of a frog.

"I'm going to my room now," I said. "Let me know if you need anything," but neither one of them answered.

I sat alone on my bed for a long time after that, listening to the hum of the train motor and the rustle of wheels on tracks. Now and then there was the sound of Lenny's voice. "Is there anything to eat besides these cookies?" he asked once, and then, later, "What other stuff do you have?" I heard their footsteps go into Morton's room and, soon after, the rattle of things in boxes—puzzle pieces, probably, or wooden Bingo numbers. Later, a rush of something spilling on the floor.

"Don't you have anything else?" I heard, and finally, "Is this all?" There was silence for a while, and then came Morton's voice. "You want to see something else?" he said. "Something really nice?" and once again I followed the sound of their footsteps.

This time they led to my mother and father's room, and I sat up straight and still on my bed. A drawer slid open, and there was silence. He's showing Lenny her jewelry, I suddenly thought. He's showing him the string of pale-pink beads that used to be her grand-mother's and her good earrings with the tiny specks of sapphire. He's going to show him the bracelet with the green stones and the cameo pin that has a carving of a lady with peach-colored hair. Lenny's going to look at it all and then he's going to say, "Hey, let's see that. Let's just see that stuff," and he's going to slip it all into his pocket and go home. I ran out of my room and down the hall.

"Get out of there!" I yelled. "What do you think you're doing in here? GET OUT OF THEIR ROOM!" And then I stopped still. Both boys were bent over an open drawer, and Morton was showing Lenny my box of prize essay things: the certificate in its fake leather folder, the newspaper clipping and, pinched between his fingers like a struggling butterfly, the little silver medal on its gold-and-purple ribbon.

"My sister won this," he was saying.

"Get out of there," I said again, but this time my voice was just a whisper, and I don't think they heard me at all.

CHAPTER FOURTEEN

Lenny never came back, and the train set had lain under Morton's bed ever since. Sometimes my mother would threaten to give it away, but she never did. "It's a shame," she would say, hitting the box unexpectedly with the vacuum cleaner brush. "Such a nice train set and nobody ever touches it. Why don't we give it to someone who would appreciate it, instead of leaving it on the floor week after week, collecting dust?"

Sometimes I thought that in some strange way she was *glad* that he never played with his train, that he didn't know how, that no friends came. So she could be angry.

"Collecting dust?" Morton asked. "The train collects dust?"

"Not that kind of collect," I told him quickly. "Not like collecting bottle caps. She means it gets dusty."

"I'm sure there are lots of boys who would be glad

to have a train set like that," she would go on. She is always saying how everybody would be glad to do things. And then she would say she was going to speak to his teacher. "Miss Carroll probably knows of some poor boy who could use a good train set. I'll have to go in someday and ask her."

Then Morton would say he was going to start playing with his train very soon. "Tomorrow, maybe," but he never did.

"Why don't you give it to me?" I asked her once. "I know how to play with it. I know all about what gauge it is and everything, and how to make figure eights," but she didn't answer, and the train remained under Morton's bed, collecting dust.

Until the day Polly came.

"You want to see how it can go?" I asked her again. "You want me to make it run? Sit up on the bed and I'll show you. Look. This is the track," I said, laying all the pieces out on the floor, "and these are the cars. The doors really open and the windows are made of glass. It's H-O," I added. "That's the gauge," and I waited for her to say, "What's that, gauge?" but she didn't say anything at all. "This is the engine," I told her. I dropped a little pellet into the chimney, but not so she could see—secretly, so she would be surprised when it suddenly began to smoke. "And here's how to work the transformer." I fastened all the wires together, making them look more complicated than they really were.

"Now watch." I felt like a magician about to put on a show. "I can make the train go wherever I tell it to. Ready?" I turned on the switch, and with my fingers on the dial, I gave it commands: *Go here, go there. Cross over. Go inside. Go outside. Go fast.* It was nice doing that, making the train follow my orders while Polly watched from the bed. "Look at the smoke!" I cried, as soft puffs of white lifted into the air. I twisted the dial all the way to the right and the cars flew around and around and in and out, and then I brought them to a perfect stop, exactly in front of the station. "Everybody off!" I said. "Last stop!" I turned to Polly. "Isn't that wonderful? Isn't that the best train you've ever seen?" I asked, although I knew it was probably the *only* train she'd ever seen.

"That's it?" she said. "That's all it can do? Just go in and out like that, and around?"

"I can make it do something," Morton said. "You want to see?"

"Don't do that, Morton," I told him. "That's bad for the wheels," but he didn't listen. He removed the train from the track and unhitched the little yellow coal car. "Watch this," he said. "Watch what I can do." He curled the fingers of his left hand into a fist and stretched out his arm to make a track. Then he ran the little car along his vein, back and forth, back and forth. *"Rum-rum-rum,"* he said.

"You'll ruin it," I said, "doing that."

"Look what else," he said. "Watch out, Mary Ella. Watch out of the way."

I didn't move.

"Move back, Mary Ella. I want to do something. Mary Ella?"

"What?" I finally said, as though I were just waking up. "Oh, are you talking to me? How come you're calling me *that*? You know nobody's called me Mary Ella in years."

He stared at me.

"M. E.," I told him.

He stared at me some more and then he said, "Wo-wo-wo-wo-wo. I forgot."

"I don't even answer to Mary Ella anymore," I explained to Polly. "Nobody calls me that at all."

"Ina does," she said.

"Move out of the way, Mary Ella," Morton said. "I want to show how I can do something," and this time I moved.

He sent the coal car crashing down the ramp of his thighs and onto the floor. Polly laughed. "Let me try that," she said, and she rolled it down her thighs, too. "Neat," she said. "This is really neat. Now watch *this*."

She ran the car along the floor, as though it were a piece of chalk, and then up Morton's bed, onto its spread, over the headboard, up the wall, around the picture, across the radiator, and back along the floor to its box. *"Rum-rum-rum,"* she said, and she rolled it over to Morton.

"Rum-rum-rum," he said, sending it back. *"Rum-rum-rum,"* they said together, rolling the car into each other's knees.

I stared at them both. What was happening here, anyway? Morton was the dumbest kid on the block, and the ugliest, too. He even had a dumb name, and here was Polly playing with him as though she actually *liked* him—going rum-rum-rum with him and everything, and listening to all that stuff about Africa. He'd even been to her house once—when?—and played dress-up. What was the *matter* with her?

She was looping the coal car through the air now. "Watch it go!" she cried. "It's a bat!" I wondered suddenly what my mother would say if she came in at that moment and saw what had happened now that someone had finally come again to play with Morton's train. She'd be home soon, I thought, and I glanced up at the clock on the dresser, but instead of its face I saw the flat white envelope that held, like a secret message, Morton's seventh-grade report card.

"What's in the envelope?" Polly asked, following my eyes.

"My report card," Morton answered.

"Your report card? What did you get?"

"O," he said. "I got O in conduct."

"What's that stand for, O?"

"Outstanding," he told her. "I got outstanding in conduct. Because I'm good."

Morton always gets O in conduct, and instead of being happy about that, my mother gets angry. "I can never understand," she says to her listener on the kitchen chair, "why it is that he is so obedient for his teachers in school and so ill-behaved at home." My father gets angry, too. "Why can't he get O in something that matters?" he asks.

"In my school," Polly said, "we get number marks, and we call it deportment, not conduct. I always get about fifty-five. Once I got fifty-nine. The teacher said I was doing better, but I wasn't good enough to pass."

"In my school we don't get marks in conduct at all," I said. "If we don't behave, we get invited to the headmistress's office and she sits us in a chair and talks about respecting our fellow human beings. I go to a private school."

"What's in your closet?" Polly asked Morton, getting up and opening its door. "Hey, what's all this? What's in all these bags?" She had discovered his collections.

"Trash," I said quickly. "That's where we keep the stuff we're going to throw out."

"They're my *things*," Morton told her. "They're my things that I find and I keep them."

Polly pulled a handful of bottle caps from one of the bags. "Oh, hey, look at these!" she cried. "Look at all of *these*!" and she let the little metal disks fall between her fingers like a bunch of loose beads. "This is the best stuff! Hey, watch what I can do!" She lifted up a blue bottle cap and held its sharp edges against her palm until it left a prickly ring on her skin. "Look! It makes designs! Here, Morton, give me your arm," and she pressed the cap up and down the arm where moments before the train had run. Little pleated circles like piecrusts sprang up along his skin, turning white and then red. "Isn't this great?"

"It's like flowers," Morton said, examining the rings on his arm.

"You have good stuff, Morton," Polly said. "You have really good stuff." She was back in the closet. "Hey, what's *this*?" She sank her hand into another of Morton's bags. "Oh, it's spoons! Look at all these spoons!" and she spilled them onto the floor. "Morton, you have the best stuff," she said again, lifting a plastic spoon and rubbing her tongue on the inside of its bowl. "What's in this bag here?"

"Special papers and things," Morton answered. "Candy papers and paper strings that I save. Nice red string from cigarette packs."

I didn't know Morton had collected so many cellophane strings. I didn't know there were so many strings to collect. There were more than Polly could hold in both hands. "Hey, we can make rain out of these," she said. "Watch this! Red rain!" She stood on Morton's bed and released a cellophane shower, slippery and red, onto the bedspread, the floor, the train, while Morton reached his hand out, and his tongue, too, to catch the drops before they fell. "Red rain!" he cried, flinging it all up into the air again. "Red rain!"

"Morton," I said. "You'd better clean that up before Mom comes home."

"I have the best stuff," Morton said, and he laughed out loud—too loud, which is how he always laughed whenever somebody said something nice about him. Aunt Sophia, usually.

"It's not *that* good," I told him, making my face stiff and blank, with no laugh in it at all, so he would know he wasn't as great as he thought.

"It's just junk," I said to Polly, "all that stuff. It's just old torn-up paper and a bunch of spoons that you get with your ice cream at the five-and-ten and that you're supposed to throw out. And anyway," I added, "we never finished doing our elbows. With my paint set. Let's have an elbow fight. We can make an elbow gang and give them names. This one will be Miranda," I said, crooking my arm at her face, "and this one is her twin sister Fanny." I don't know how I thought up those names. They just came to me, and I liked saying them in front of Morton, knowing he wouldn't understand. It was like telling a secret, not behind his back, but right out loud, and I felt him wondering, *What elbows? Who's Miranda?* "My sisters against your sisters," I went on. "Let's go back to my room and get the paints."

"No," Polly said. "I'm tired of that now." She picked up the coal car and spun its wheels hard against her palm. "Let's take this upstairs," she said. "To the roof." She spoke to Morton, not to me. "It will go on a trip up there," she went on. "To Africa."

"The roof!" I cried. "The *roof?* You're not allowed up there, Morton." He was already following her out of his room and into the hallway. "YOU'RE NOT ALLOWED UP THERE!" I shouted, but in another moment I heard the door of the apartment open and then close, and I realized all at once that Polly had not come to play with me at all. She had come to play with Morton, and she was going to be his best friend, not mine.

CHAPTER FIFTEEN

I picked up all the cellophane rain from the floor and put it back in its bag. Then I nested the plastic spoons together, bowl into bowl, and put them away, too. I collected the bottle caps from the bed. I pressed one against my own arm and watched as a little scalloped pie shell turned red on my skin. I put all the train things back, and after everything was cleaned up, I walked around Morton's room, looking here and there, and pausing finally in front of the envelope against the clock. With a finger I traced the long curves of the M and B of his name, and then I lifted it from the dresser all at once and opened its flap.

When Morton started school last fall, my mother bought a special arithmetic kit so she could help him with math and he wouldn't be left back again. He was left back in third grade and again in fifth, because he was dumb, mostly in arithmetic. The new kit was part of some special method that was supposed to be good for dumb kids. Slow learners, they were called. Every evening, my mother would sit down with Morton at the kitchen table, and he would take all the things out of the box, one by one.

There were lots of things to take out. First came the instruction booklet that told you how to follow the special method. Then came a pack of flash cards held together with a rubber band, and then came a whole bunch of wooden sticks painted different colors. They were the best part—smooth and shiny, with nice straight edges so that they stood up tall, like a row of little men in suits of red and green and blue.

"Each red stick represents one hundred units," the booklet said, although that was not how you were supposed to explain it to the slow learner. "Each blue stick represents ten units, and each green stick represents one unit. Place ten green sticks in the student's left hand and one blue stick in his or her right hand. Then say, 'The green sticks are like pennies and the blue stick is like a dime. Ten green sticks are worth as much as one blue stick.' " On the next page the booklet showed how to combine the blue sticks and the green sticks to teach Number Concepts. "Reinforce this learning," it said, "with the accompanying flash cards."

"One blue stick and two green sticks make what number, Morton?" my mother would ask, and Morton would think awhile. "Twelve," he would say; he would get that right, because, although he's dumb, he's not that dumb. Then she would show him how to make more twelves out of the blue and green sticks, and when he had made four twelves, she would bring out the right flash card and show it to him: $4 \times 12 =$

"Four times twelve equals. Say that, Morton."

"Four times twelve equals."

"Now say, 'Four times twelve means four twelves.' "

"Four times twelve means four twelves." He would slip the rubber band from the flash cards over his fist and run it up and down his arm. Suddenly it would pop off and fly across the table. "Look at *that* one," he'd say, laughing his dumb laugh.

"*Listen* to me, Morton." My mother's voice would grow quieter instead of louder. Then she would recite the next phrase from the booklet. "Ask yourself: How many blue sticks in *one* twelve? How many green sticks? Ask yourself that, Morton."

"I just did."

"Out *loud*. Ask it so I can hear. Nice and loud."

"I forgot what to ask."

"How many blue sticks in *one* twelve? How many green sticks? Ask yourself that. Out loud."

"How many blue sticks in *one* twelve?" His voice would go way up on "one." "How many *green* sticks?"

"Now answer it. When you ask yourself a question,

Morton, the next thing to do is answer it. How many blue sticks in one twelve?"

"One."

"How many green sticks? *Count* them, don't play with them."

"Look," he'd say. "I made a blue M. For Morton."

After a while they'd have all the sticks arranged in the right number of rows, and she'd ask the last question: "Now. Four times twelve equals what?"

"Four twelves," he would answer.

"Morton! Four times twelve equals," and she would wait for him to answer something else dumb.

"Forty-eight."

"Be quiet, Mary Ella. I asked Morton."

"Forty-eight," he would say.

When half an hour was up, Morton would say, "Time's up," and he would put all the pieces of the kit back in the box, smoothing the rubber band over the flash cards and straightening the sticks into rows, so that everything looked nice and neat. I think he liked the arithmetic kit.

I slipped the report card out of its envelope and turned it over in my hand. Morton did get an O in conduct, and it hung like a little moon at the top of the page. He had a few S's too, in things like "Works Well With Others" and "Shows Respect for School

Property," but mostly he had N's for "Needs Improvement" and U's for "Unsatisfactory." At the bottom, next to where it said "Grade Placement for Next Year," his teacher had written the number seven, with one of those fancy lines through its stem, in black ink. Seven, not eight. For the third time since he began school, Morton was going to be left back. Retained, they called it.

When school started again in the fall, he and I would be in the same grade.

CHAPTER SIXTEEN

The little painted faces on my knuckles and knees had smeared by now into tattered streaks, and I went into the bathroom to wash them off. The colors floated away when I lowered my hands into the sink, and I watched them swirl around in the water—red, green, yellow, blue, stretching out like scarves in the wind. I stirred them around with my wrist, and all at once they were my orphan girls again—Vermilion, Emerald, Topaz, and Sapphire, dancing all together at their ball.

Round and round they went, their gowns flying smoothly from their throats and rustling as they brushed each other's hems. "Dance," I said into the sink. *"Dance!"* and they whirled around some more—faster and faster until they became no color at all, like pictures on a child's top: clowns and tigers and balloons that melt into a streak of gray when you push the plunger down. I pulled out the plug then and watched them rush away—all of them—down and away, down a darkened stair, laughing and whirling, to someplace I would never know. "Good-bye," I said to them, and then I washed my face and knees and wandered back into my room.

In an hour or so, my mother would come home, and she would ask where Morton was.

"He's with his new friend," I would tell her, but I wouldn't say where.

"New friend?" She would look pleased. "I didn't know Morton had a new friend. Who is he?"

"She. It's Polly."

"Polly! The new girl?" She would look disappointed now. "But I thought she was *your* friend."

"She was. Now she's Morton's." Would I be able to say that? Probably not.

Later, my mother would ask where Morton's report card was, and I would tell her it was on his dresser, leaning against the clock, but I wouldn't say I had already seen it myself. I would hold very still then and listen as she went into his room, and I would feel her eye running over the page until it came to the bottom where the seven stood, slanting like a garden hoe about to topple down. There would be a moment of quiet and then a sigh. A gasp, maybe. Then she would whisper something to her listener. "Stupid," or "impossible," she'd say, or "slow," the *s*'s hissing like water running into the sink, and although the words would be about Morton, I would feel as I do at Agnes Daly when the secrets in the hall are about me.

When I first began to hear my mother speak to her listener in the other room, I would go to the doorway and wait until she noticed me. "Tell me what you just said," I'd demanded one night, knowing she wouldn't. The girls in school never tell me their secrets either, even when the secrets are about somebody else. "Not meant for babies," they say, moving away and carrying their whispers with them. "Not for your ears," my mother had said then.

Now, though, I just stand still, wherever I am—in my room, in the hall, behind the bathroom door— and I listen all alone. I *make* myself listen, just as I make myself look when there's a dead bird in the street, or a squashed squirrel, so I can know how bad it is, all at once.

The little glass paint bottles still lay this way and that on the floor of my room, and I placed them one by one in a row along the desk. They were just a bunch of paints now—smeared-up paints with crazy names that didn't match. Eggshell was green; Ivory was blue.

Two colors only remained untouched: Crimson and Silver, and I twisted open their white metal caps. I lifted a sheet of paper from the floor and brushed a stripe across its face, thick and wet and red. It looked nice, like a lipstick streak, and I sat down at my desk to paint a picture, the first I'd ever painted out of school. It was the very same picture I made every night when I sat beside the rabbits in my Easter egg room: daisies in a bowl. This one was done on paper, though, not on little wooden eggs, and it wasn't quite as perfect. But it was lovely just the same—the bowl was almost round and the petals of the daisies were like silver insect wings, brittle and thin. I wrote "To Mother" across the top when I was through, but I was going to show it to my *real* mother this time, not a make-believe rabbit, and while she wouldn't say, "Oh, *exquisite*," she might say it was lovely. "Oh, lovely," and she would suddenly be very, very happy. So happy, in fact, that she wouldn't mind at all that Morton had a seven on the bottom of his report card instead of an eight, and that next fall he would be in the same grade as me, even though he was three years older.

CHAPTER SEVENTEEN

I put on some clean shorts after that and a nice white blouse—the one my mother liked best and that I wore last year when she took me—*just* me—to the ballet. Then I went up to the roof.

I'd never been up there before, and I put my foot over the doorsill cautiously, as though I were stepping into a cold lake. The floor was soft in the hot sun, and it gave way a little under my shoe. I couldn't see Polly and Morton anywhere, and I called out to them, but there was no answer.

Off in one corner, a line of clothes dried in the sun: shirts, fastened wrist to wrist, and underwear, too, hanging there for everyone to see. They rose, suddenly, all together, as though in alarm at the sound of my voice, and then fell. At the same moment a row of pigeons flew up from the branch of a TV antenna, their wings touching tip to tip, like the sleeves of the shirts, and then they, too, fell back and were still.

After that, nothing moved at all.

"Morton!" I called again. "Polly!"

It was scary up there, so far from where things were attached to the ground—far from the basements of buildings and the roots of trees—and I kept my eyes away from the sky. Stretching all around me was a field of tar, smooth and wide as a meadow, and as flat. It could have *been* a meadow, really, but one no longer green. Antennas stood along the walls like blackened trees, and chimney pipes, chipped and brittle, clustered like charred toadstools at their feet.

"Morton! Polly!" I moved away from the door and slid my feet along, as though I were nearing the edge of a cliff. *"Morton!"* And then I saw them on the other side of the roof, across the courtyard, heads down, walking slowly together. Like best friends.

When they got closer, I could see that Polly was pushing the coal car along the floor with her foot. "You're going to ruin that," I called out to her. "It's going to break if you do that." She picked the car up then and flew it around like a plane, making it dive and rise and do loops in the air. "And anyway, Morton, we're not supposed to be up here. We're not allowed."

"Why not?" Polly asked.

"Why do *you* think why not? Because we might fall off."

"How can you fall off? There's walls all around up

to your waist. You'd have to climb over them and jump, in order to fall off."

"Well, you could lean over or something and fall off that way. You could lose your balance."

"That's dumb. When you lean over a wall on the *ground* you don't lose your balance, do you? Hey, Morton, you want to make a shadow tower?"

"What?"

"A shadow tower. You want to make one? Look. See my hand's shadow? Now you put your hand's shadow on top of that. Then I'll put my other hand's shadow on, and then you put your other hand's shadow on, and then I'll put my head's shadow on, and we'll keep piling on a lot of shadows until we have a shadow tower."

Morton looked at his hands. "Which one?" he asked.

"This." She took his left hand and placed it above hers so that its shadow blotted out her own. "Now do this one."

"Don't do that, Morton," I said. She was going to play a trick on him after all. She would make him do crazy things with his arms and legs and then she would laugh when he fell down. People do things like that at Agnes Daly—to third graders, mostly. "Don't do it, Morton," I said. "It's a trick."

"It is," Polly said. "It's a shadow trick. It really works, too. You get a whole pile of shadows one on top of the other until there's a big tower, and then you jump in the middle of it like a haystack."

"That's dumb," I said. "That's the dumbest thing I ever heard." It *was* dumb. Not just silly dumb, but *dumb* dumb. Dumb like Morton, and suddenly I understood what was the matter with Polly: She was dumb. That was why she liked Morton. Because she was as dumb as he was. "Don't do it, Morton," I said. "You can't pile shadows on top of each other."

"You can so," Polly said. "We're doing it right now. Now do your head, Morton, on top of my head. How many shadows do you think it will take to make a tower three feet high?"

He looked up as he did when my mother asked a question from the arithmetic kit. "A hundred?" he guessed.

"Maybe. Look, let's make shadows from these shirts." She undid some of the clothespins on the line and held the drying wash up high so that it made a single dark map on the floor.

"You're not allowed to do that!" I yelled. "That's somebody else's clothes, and anyway, that's stupid, what you're doing. If you put one shadow on top of another it just makes one shadow." I was glad she wasn't my friend. She was even *dumber* than Morton.

"It does not. One shadow and one shadow makes two shadows, right? One and one is two, dummy."

"But not with *shadows!*" My throat hurt all the way up to my ears from yelling. "If you put one shadow on top of another it just *disappears*, sort of." Nobody had ever called me "dummy" before.

"Well, where does it go, then?" she asked, and I couldn't answer.

She took a piece of chalk from her pocket, and crouched down with it. "Look," she said, and I thought she was about to draw a diagram to explain how shadows added up, but she wasn't addressing me at all. "Look, Morton," she said, and she began tracing around the shadow of a chimney pipe, making the outline of a toadstool on the floor. She had forgotten about the shadow tower altogether. "Leave that there," she said. "Then, tomorrow morning when the shadow comes back, it will know where it's supposed to go."

Morton stared at the chalk outline. "Comes back?"

"Yeah. Shadows go away at night. They go up into the sky. That's what makes the dark. Didn't you know that?"

"Yes," he said.

"It does not," I shouted. "It does *not!* That's not what makes the dark. The sun goes down, that's what."

"Stand still, Morton," she said. "I'll do your shadow next." Morton stood with his hands and feet apart while Polly outlined his silhouette, moving the chalk up and down the tar to make arms and legs, and in and out to make fingers. "Don't move," she said, as the chalk traveled around his ear, his hair, his other ear, his neck, his shoulder, the little notch his sleeve made.

"There. Now take your shadow away." Morton stepped aside, pulling his shadow with him, and we all stared down at the empty outline sprawled flat on the roof. "Next time you come back," Polly told him, "your shadow will be waiting for you. It will know just where to go."

Morton grinned.

Suddenly, I wanted her to do my outline, too, even though she was dumb, or whatever she was, and I stood very straight, holding my shadow still on the tar, like a large paper doll colored black. *Do mine*, I whispered in my head. *Do mine, do mine, do mine*, but all she did was pick up the coal car and rub it across her palm. "You know what?" she said to Morton. "We could make real coal for this thing. You want to see?" She pulled another clothespin from the line and crouched with it over the floor. Overhead, two shirts swung by one arm apiece, like a pair of monkeys on a branch, and the underwear bounced. "Watch," she said, and I saw now that the tar floor really wasn't smooth at all, but puckered all over with fat black blisters. "Here's a nice juicy one." She plunged a leg of the clothespin into the tar's crust and a thick black liquid sprang out, making my mouth suddenly—surprisingly—water.

"Look," she said. "The roof is bleeding," and that made Morton laugh. Everything Polly said made him laugh. "That's a good one," he said. "The roof is bleeding."

"It is not," I told him. "That's just tar. Roofs don't bleed. Only people."

"Let's put a Band-Aid on it," Polly said, and she peeled off the strip on her forehead. I looked away at first, not wanting to see her scab, but there was nothing on her skin at all.

"What do you do that for?" I asked, suddenly curious. "Why do you wear a Band-Aid if you don't have a cut or anything?"

"I don't wear it," she answered. "I just keep it there in case I need it." She settled the gauze carefully on the broken bubble and pressed the ends out on the floor. "If I kept it in my pocket it would lose its stick."

"Hey, Mary Ella," Morton said, "the roof is bleeding," as though he had just thought of that himself, and with a finger he burst a whole cluster of bubbles, making them ooze. "The roof is bleeding," and he laughed his dumb laugh some more.

"Yeah," Polly said. "That's how they get coal. From roof blood," and she pulled the wet tar into a long string, sticky as licorice. "Watch." She molded a little ball between her palms and carefully dropped it into the hollow of the coal car. "Real coal. Let's make a whole lot."

They looked like two children in a sandbox, stooping side by side like that, messing with their hands. "Morton," I said, leaning against the wooden clothesline frame, "you'd better clean up your hands before you go downstairs. Mom will be mad if she sees you like that."

I thought about my mother suddenly. She'd be home by now, I realized, and she'd already have walked through all the rooms, wondering where we were, calling our names. She'd have walked into the kitchen, too, and seen my picture propped up on the table. I imagined her pausing at the kitchen door and drawing in her breath. "What's that?" she'd ask, hurrying in, and she'd lift it up carefully and carry it to the window. "Why, it's a watercolor," she'd finally whisper. *Watercolor*, she'd say, not picture. "By Mary Ella. What a lovely, lovely thing," and she'd hold it to the light. Then she'd stand it against the napkin holder and step back to see it better, the way people do in museums, putting her head to one side. "Look at how round the

bowl is," she'd say aloud, "and how red. Crimson."
She'd speak out loud, even though she was alone, and
not to her listener either—to *herself*.

"Mom will be mad," I said to Morton, and he stared
into his palms for a moment and then wiped them
across the front of his Mickey Mouse shirt. "Morton!"
I yelled.

"Oh, look," Polly said. "You drew a picture of a
fish. Wait, I'll give him an eye," and she stuck a little
dot of tar in the middle of Morton's stomach. He
laughed at that and then he said, "Mickey Mouse has
his own fish to eat now."

Polly added some more wads of tar to the pile in
the coal car, and then stood up. "Let's take it all for
a ride," she said.

"Let's take it to Africa," Morton said.

"Trains don't go to Africa," I told him.

"Yeah," Polly said. "Let's take it to Africa."

"And we can get on it," Morton said. "We can get
small."

"We can shrink ourselves. I know how, Morton.
You know why? Because I'm magic. I can shrink whatever I want. I can shrink all my clothes and everything,
and a whole bunch of food. Bananas and stuff. I can
shrink my grandma's icebox, too, to keep the food in.
I can even shrink my grandma, so she can come, too,

to wash our clothes and everything. I can shrink my chalk."

"And don't forget your toothbrush," Morton said. "So you can brush your teeth."

"Yeah. Except I don't have a toothbrush." She used the top of the roof wall for a track and ran the car along its edge, while Morton trailed behind, saying *"Rum-rum-rum."* Sometimes Polly said *"Rum-rum-rum,"* too. They went around all four sides of the building like that. I stood beside the clothesline and watched them go. "Morton!" I called out now and then, "don't get so close to the edge!" But he didn't answer, and after a while I stopped watching. Anyway, how could he fall over? Polly was right. The wall was too high.

Across the roof two pigeons sat, side by side on the branch of an antenna, not moving, and I squeezed my eyes open and shut at them, making them jump, making them double. A moment later, a third joined them, and they stood in a perfect row, like X's on a tic-tac-toe. They looked nice there, all three together, belonging to each other, and with a finger I drew a winning line through their bodies. *Stay,* I whispered to them. *Stay there,* and I held them down with my finger, but Polly suddenly shouted and they all flew away.

"Hey, Morton!" she called out. "Something's up ahead on the track!" They were on the right-hand side of the building now, away from the clothesline, away from me. The coal car was still between her fingers, zigzagging along the wall. "Look out! It's a cow or something! The car can't stop in time! It's going to hit the cow! It's going to derail! *Wham!*" and the little yellow car flew out of her hand and over the side of the roof.

CHAPTER EIGHTEEN

We all leaned over the wall, motionless as the three pigeons, and stared down at the next-door roof, one story below. Two, maybe. Even now I'm not sure.

The coal car had disappeared. "Where'd it go?" Polly asked.

"To Africa," Morton said. "That's Africa down there."

"It is not," I said. "That's a roof and your coal car is lost. It's gone. You're never going to get it back," and although I looked at him, it was Polly I really spoke to.

"Hey, look at all that stuff," she said. "There's lots of neat things on that roof."

There *were* lots of things down there: a long gray sock pressed flat into the floor, a scattering of clothes-pins, a comic book, a shoe. A shoe! How did a shoe get there? How did any of it? From some other roof or from the sky, because there was no door or stairway to the building underneath. Just a black glass skylight lying flat against the tar.

"*There* it is," Polly said suddenly, and she pointed to a spot in the corner where the tiny coal car lay, its wheels spinning into the sky like a turtle struggling to its feet.

"I see it," Morton said. "Look, Mary Ella. Over *there*."

"I *know*, Morton. I have eyes, don't I?"

"It's upside down," he said. "Look, you can see its underneath," and he laughed, as though he were looking up somebody's dress.

"I told you," I said to Polly. "I told you it would fall over."

"No, you didn't," she answered. "You said Morton would fall over. You said the coal car would just break or something."

"I didn't say Morton would fall over. I said he *could*."

"Well, he didn't. Just the coal car. And anyway, I can climb down and get it."

"No, you can't. It's too far down. And besides, there's no way to get back up."

"I know what," Morton said. "Use a rope."

"Very smart," I answered, sounding like Mrs. Pierce at Agnes Daly. "How's the rope going to hold her?"

"Not her," he said. "The coal car. The rope can get the coal car up."

"Hey, good idea," Polly said.

"Dumb," I said. "How's it going to stick?"

"Put tar on it," he said.

"That's the dumbest thing I ever heard."

"Let's do it," Polly said.

It took two clotheslines tied together to make a piece of rope long enough, and Polly had to take down all the rest of the wash to get at them. She scrubbed one end of the rope around in a broken tar blister until it was thick with goo, and then she lowered it slowly over the side.

"Hey," she called out to the coal car, "here's a nice fat worm." She twitched her wrist as though she were fishing. "Come and grab ahold!" The fuzzy tip bounced along the ground like a frightened insect, sticking nowhere. "Come *on!*" she yelled, and this time she swung the rope out as far as it would go, but it didn't hit the coal car at all.

"See?" I said. "It doesn't work. Nothing will. Your coal car is gone, Morton. You're never going to get it back. It's going to lie there forever. Even when you're all grown up, it's going to keep on lying there. Even when you're *dead.*"

"No, it won't," he said. "I can jump down there and get it. You want to see? I'll put on my sneakers with all the rubber on the bottom. They're my climbing shoes. I can climb down things in those sneakers. And then I can climb up again. My sneakers stick to things."

"They do not," I said. "It's gone, Morton. Your coal car is *gone*."

"Look at the rope *now!*" Polly cried. She was still swishing it around, shaking it, making it shiver. "It's a skinny lady dancing on her toe. Look at her shimmy," and she rubbed it back and forth between her palms like a string of clay. "Now watch! She's doing that thing where you click your feet together in the air. You know? Like those people in the movies? What do you call that, Morton?"

"*Entrechat*," I told her, but she didn't look at me.

"Mom's going to be plenty mad," I said to Morton. Mrs. Pierce always says that: Plenty mad. "That train set cost a whole lot of money," I said. "You weren't supposed to take any of it out of the apartment. You weren't supposed to bring it up here. You're not supposed to be up here at all, in fact. Mom's not going to like it."

She *wasn't* going to like it. She was going to tell her listener a whole lot of things when she found out. She was going to say that Morton had no sense. She was going to say that he was stupid and disobedient and clumsy. She was going to say, "He would." That's what she always says, even when things happen to him that could happen to anyone else—to other kids in his class, to kids on the street, to me. "He would," she says when he gets sick or his jacket gets taken from his locker. "He would," when someone in the supermarket steps on his foot.

"He would," she said the day the toy sailboat was stolen, even though I was with him at the time and it was as much my fault as his. "He can't keep anything for more than five minutes," she said when we both stood before her in the kitchen, with nothing in our hands but a wet roll of string.

"It was more than five minutes," Morton corrected her. "It was a whole lot of hours."

It was, too. We had taken the boat to the park right after lunch that day and had sailed it in the lake all afternoon. It wasn't until the sky had turned the color of its own gray clouds and the tree reflections had darkened and grown heavy in the lake that the boat was carried off by some hands we never saw.

It had been a lovely boat, with a tiny steering wheel, a wire railing around its varnished deck, and a cloth sail that traveled up and down when you pulled a little string. It wasn't even ours. It had belonged to my father when he was little, and the only reason he let us have it was that I was the one who had asked, not Morton. "We'll just take it to the lake in the park," I had told him. "I won't let anything happen to it. I promise. I'll take really good care of it," but it was Morton who was blamed when we came home with our arms hanging empty at our sides.

I had carried it through the streets myself that day, holding it down under my elbow as though it were a large bird, a fat goose or something, about to fly away. It was late October then, and the rowboats in the park were all chained together near the boathouse for the winter, so the sailboat had the lake all to itself. We tied it to a roll of kite string my father had given us, and we watched it wobble out to sea—what we *pretended* was sea—sometimes here, sometimes there. "All aboard!" Morton said when it reached the opposite shore, and at first I laughed, imagining a crowd of tiny foreigners climbing to its deck, but it's always a mistake to laugh at anything Morton says. He just says it over and over again after that, and that's what he did this time. "All aboard," he kept saying, even when the boat wasn't near the land at all. Finally I told him to stop. Once, it paused at a spread of lily pads and the tip of its sail leaned way over, pecking at the rim of a wide, flat leaf. "Look," Morton said. "It's getting a drink."

"No, it's not," I said.

Sometimes, when the wind fell, the boat would rest on the surface of the lake like a flower planted in water, while Morton tried to blow at it from the shore. Sometimes a sudden puff from somewhere would topple it over and it would wash, like a broken-winged gull, to our feet. Then we'd stand it up again and push it back out with long sticks, trying to steer it to the lily pads, to the other shore, to the big black island in the middle of the sea. But it followed private trails of its own. "Go!" I shouted at it. "Over *there!*" while it darted back and forth, sometimes too far, sometimes not far enough. "No, dummy! *There!*" I stretched my arms out wide to embrace the lake, to *tilt* it, like a puzzle where you roll tiny balls into the eyeholes of a face. "Go!" But the sailboat wandered where it pleased.

It must have been after five when the wind grew suddenly strong and the sailboat swept away like some wild living thing—a loon, maybe, or a swan—toward the crowd of wooden rowboats that huddled by the boathouse like a herd of sleeping cows. It bounced from boat to boat, and then rounded a bank where we couldn't see it at all.

"Last stop!" Morton called out. "Everybody off!" The roll of string spun out swiftly from his hand and then—surprisingly—the cardboard cone jerked away and hopped about on the ground. "Wo-wo-wo!" he cried, and I caught it under my heel, but the string continued to tug even after that, and a sudden sound of laughter came from somewhere far away.

The string grew quiet then and trailed loosely in the

water once again, gentle as seaweed. We watched it for a while, and then Morton began slowly to wrap it around the cone. "Come along, little boat," he said, pulling and winding, pulling and winding, but when he pulled the last of it from the water there was nothing tied to its end at all.

"He would," my mother said as we stood there in the kitchen, holding in our hands the coil of string, gray now and swollen with the wet of the lake. "He *would*," she told the light bulbs on the ceiling.

And now the coal car.

"Hey, Morton," Polly said, dancing the rope around some more on its fringed toe. "Look at her now. She's doing leaps. She can fly, even. Watch this!" The rope streamed out for a long moment and hung in the air like a bird, before falling back against the wall with a quiet slap. Morton laughed. "She bumped her head," he said. "The lady bumped her head on the wall."

"Yeah," Polly answered. "She bumped her head. Now she's going to jump way up in the air, about a hundred feet. Watch her go!"

Morton leaned over the wall and peered down. "That's good," he said, laughing again. "A jumping lady, like in the circus." He wasn't thinking about the coal car at all anymore.

"Hey, that's right, Morton. That's what she is—a circus acrobat. Now she's going to do her best trick of all. Ready?" Polly pulled the rope up and wound it around her hand to make a loose circle. Then she sailed it out like a Frisbee onto the roof below. "Look at her spin!" she cried.

"What did you do *that* for?" I shouted, looking down at the rope sprawled like a script S on the tar. "Why'd you do that? We could have used that rope. We could have gotten the coal car up with it, maybe. We could have figured something out. And anyway, it wasn't even yours. It belonged to the lady who hangs up the wash. That wasn't your rope!" I yelled.

"It's not a rope. It's an acrobat."

I leaned far over the wall and stared at the rope and the coal car. They would both lie there forever now, the coal car here, the rope there, belonging more to each other than they ever would to us. Forever. In the rain, in the snow, year after year. The make-believe coal would harden in the cold and ooze black blood in the sun. Ten years from now, twenty, when I was grown up, I'd come back up here, and the car would still be lying out of reach, its buttercup sides grown dark and its wheels turned to rust.

I decided to go downstairs after that, and I stepped over to the clothesline frame to fix myself up, so my mother would like the way I looked. I reached my hand up into my shorts to pull down my blouse, and I made comb teeth out of my fingers to smooth my hair. She wouldn't have to know where I'd been, or who with. "I was playing with a girl I know. Outside," I'd tell her, not lying. "How do you like my picture?" and she would look first at me, in my nice white blouse that she liked, and then at the picture still in her hand. "It's wonderful, Mary Ella," she'd say. "Just wonderful."

"*Rum-rum-rum,*" I heard all of a sudden, and I snapped my head around, thinking maybe Polly had gotten the coal car back after all, but she was only running her bunched-up fingers along the edge of the wall, making a toy car out of them. "*Rum-rum-rum,*" she said again, and then Morton made a toy car out of his fingers, too. "*Rum-rum-rum,*" they said together, and they crashed their hands one against the other. "*Wham!*"

Somehow, Morton had gotten tar on the back of his Mickey Mouse shirt, as well as on the front, and I knew all at once that my picture wouldn't make my mother happy after all. Nothing would. She'd be standing in the bathroom, not the kitchen, right now, and she wouldn't be exclaiming, "Oh, how lovely!" She'd be crying. The bathroom is where she always goes to cry; it's the only room with a door you can lock, and you can wash your face in the sink when you're through. I hear her in there sometimes, pretending to be coughing and letting the water run a lot. She'd be looking at her face in the mirror now, at her cheeks all splotched red and her eyes made narrow inside their lids. "Left back," she'd be saying to a towel, to the sink. "For the third *time*."

She'd be there still when I went downstairs, and when she finally came out later, she'd find Morton standing in the living room with tar all over his shirt. He wouldn't notice her face, and he wouldn't notice his report card, either. Instead, he'd tell her that the little coal car from his train set had fallen onto the next-door roof and you could see its underneath.

He and Polly were running their finger-cars over the side of the wall now, down toward the next-door roof, and Morton was leaning so far over I could no longer see his head. I didn't tell him to be careful, though. I didn't tell him anything at all. I just stood there for a long time, watching him, watching Polly; and then, suddenly, I did a dumb thing.

Even now I'm not sure why I did it. Maybe it was to make Polly like me more. Or my mother like me less. Maybe if my mother liked me less, she'd like Morton more. Maybe if Morton and I did the same dumb things, she'd like both of us the same. Anyway, instead of telling Morton not to lean over so far, instead of going downstairs, I crouched down and plunged all ten fingers into the black blisters on the roof floor. Then I dragged them across my chest, painting a blaze of stripes across my blouse—two rows of five stripes each, like staffs of music, on my nice white blouse, the one my mother liked best.

"Hey," I called out, standing up again. Polly and Morton raised their heads. "Look at me!"

Morton dropped his hand, spilling his make-believe car into the air, and stared at me. "Why'd you do that for?" he finally said. "Why'd you do that to your nice blouse?"

But Polly only laughed. "Hey, Mary Ella," she said. "Hey, M. E. That looks neat. It's like a picture. Of waves in the ocean or something. And that little spot there could be a boat."

"Mom will be mad," Morton said. "Your best blouse! Mom will be plenty mad." And he was right. My mother *was* going to be mad, plenty mad, and this time not at Morton, but at me.

CHAPTER NINETEEN

During the first few days after my mother found out that Morton was going to be left back, the house was very silent. No one spoke, and we passed one another on our way from room to room the way, in my school plays, people known as "passersby" crossed on the stage, pretending to be strangers.

It was a silence that comes over us whenever something terrible happens and Morton and I are not supposed to know. Up until then only two really terrible things had happened: My father's bookstore closed and he had to work for somebody else, and Aunt Sophia died. I was nine when she died, and my mother thought I was too young to hear news like that, so she didn't tell me, although I had been allowed to know all along that she was sick. "How's Aunt Sophia?" I used to ask during those long weeks, and my mother would sigh a lot and say, "Not well." But when she died, there were no words at all, and that was how I knew.

I had to pretend, though, not to know, so that when both my parents put on black clothes that hot summer morning and said they were going to a luncheon, I pretended to believe them. "Have a nice time," I called out, and I pretended even to myself that what they had said was true. I pictured them seated at a long table with a bunch of aunts and uncles, all eating their lunch—their luncheon—all wearing black. Aunt Sophia was there, too, at the head of the table, eating soup with a dainty spoon and talking first to the guest on her right and then to the one on her left, and finally to my mother and father down the table.

For a week after that, for two weeks, the house stayed silent, and once, to show my mother that I hadn't guessed her secret, I asked again, "How's Aunt Sophia?" But this time she answered, "Oh, she's better. She's all better," and that was the last time we ever mentioned Aunt Sophia's name. I never even got to cry for her, because she wasn't supposed to be dead, but I wish I could have, because she was my favorite aunt.

Now the house was silent again, and this time, too, I tried to let my mother think I didn't know her secret. "When Morton goes to eighth grade," I said one day, "he's going to have Miss Pines, who everybody on the block hates," and she answered, "We'll see." When would she tell me? When would I be allowed to know?

I never saw the report card again, and I don't know where it is even now. Hidden in a drawer somewhere, probably, or thrown out. It had stayed propped up against the clock on Morton's dresser all that afternoon and all that night, too, because, as things turned out, my mother never got to see it that day at all. She didn't even discover it herself; Morton showed it to her at breakfast the next morning.

Nothing, in fact, turned out as I expected it to that day. My mother didn't learn about the lost coal car until weeks later, and she didn't even see the tar on my blouse. She wasn't crying in the bathroom when I went downstairs, and she wasn't staring at my picture of daisies in a bowl. She wasn't even there. She was late coming home, and my painting still stood where I had left it on the table.

I picked it up and looked it over. It really wasn't so great. Pictures never are the second time you look at them, and anyway I didn't want her to see it at all by then. So I tore it up. I made a long crooked rip through the middle of the page, cracking the crimson bowl and splintering the daisies with their slender silver wings. Then I put the pieces in the wastebasket and sat down in the living room where my mother would see me first thing when she came home, with my ears sticking out of my hair and the black tar streaked across my blouse like tire tracks on snow.

Where she'd see that *I* did dumb things, too. Not just Morton.

But when she finally came home, she didn't look at me at all. "Where's Morton?" she demanded, and I suddenly realized it had grown late and Morton and Polly hadn't come back downstairs. "Why didn't he meet me at the barber's?" she went on. "Where *were* you? Why didn't anybody answer the phone?"

"He was supposed to meet you at the barber's?"

"You knew that, Mary Ella. Where *is* he?" She walked past the couch and into his room.

"He's not there," I said, following her. "He's outside. Playing with Polly." I didn't say where.

"Who's Polly?"

"The new girl. I told you about her. She lives on Preston Street with her grandmother. She's Morton's friend," I added, wanting her to know that, to know that Morton had found a friend, although he had lost his train car and had tar all over his clothes and was being left back in school for the third time.

"Where are they? I didn't see them on the street."

"They're around," I said. "I'll go find them," and I walked right past her with my ruined blouse.

＊　　＊　　＊

"Morton?" I called from the doorway of the roof. "Mom wants you. You were supposed to have a haircut."

Everything seemed different up there now. The air was strangely cool and very still. Nothing moved. The wash was all taken down and the pigeons, too, were gone, as though, like the laundry, they'd been carefully unpegged and folded flat and smooth into a drawer. Only the chalk outline of Morton's body seemed the same, sprawled like a clothesline on the floor. If I waited long enough, I wondered, would his shadow creep back in, as Polly had said, and fill up all the space?

"Polly?" I called.

Nobody answered.

"Morton!" I raised my voice this time. "It's getting late!" and my words floated like bubbles through the air. "Polly!" Where were they, anyway? My eyes wandered over to the wall on my left, and suddenly I felt a shiver dart through my body. A *hot* shiver. The coal car lay on the other side of that wall, one story below—two, maybe; anyway, it was far—on a roof that had no door. I could go over and look if I wanted, but I didn't move.

"There's walls all around up to your waist," Polly had said. "You'd have to climb over and jump, in order to fall." Morton's waist, too? I tried to measure from where I stood. Anyway, when you lean over a wall on the *ground* you don't fall off, so why should you fall off up here? Polly had said that, too, but what if they didn't fall by mistake? What if they had tried to *climb* down there? To Africa, where Polly had wanted to go, and Morton, too.

"I can climb down there in my climbing shoes," Morton had said, and then what had *I* said? Had I told him no, he couldn't? I tried to remember. Had I told him no, he couldn't in his *sneakers*, but he could in his regular shoes? I shook my head to rattle the thought away.

"MORTON!" I shouted, and his name broke against a chimney pipe, making a small ring.

It was a long time before I stepped over the sill and onto the tar, and when I finally did, it wasn't to go over to the wall. Instead, I walked around the opening of the courtyard and over to the front of the building. *They're probably down on the street*, I thought. *Playing or something*, and I leaned way over to look.

Right down below me, in a straight line under my nose, stretched the top of the awning, looking strange from so far up—flat as a strip of tape and no wider than the space between two fingers.

People were down there on the sidewalk: Franklin, Ina, Henry, Charles. I knew them from the tops of their heads. They moved around as fish do in a pool, slipping back and forth—here, there, in, out—never touching. Polly and Morton could be down there, too, I thought. They could be just inside the doorway, out of sight, like minnows in the shadow of a rock. With the drop of a pebble I could startle them into view.

I lifted a chip of broken chimney and held it out high above the canvas. In a moment—longer than I thought—I heard its tiny plop, and I caught my breath, watching, waiting for two shapes to dart into the sun, but nothing stirred. I finally turned back and walked around the roof, high above the courtyard, until I came to the wall where the coal car lay.

I shut my eyes when I got up close. I kept them shut until my toes bumped against the wall, and then I lifted them little by little, as I would lift a page in a scary book.

Morton's coal car lay quietly on its back in the puddle of its own shadow, looking small, and Polly and Morton were nowhere to be seen.

CHAPTER TWENTY

"They're missing," I said, liking the alarm of the words. "They were up on the roof," I explained, "and now they're gone." I looked from Ina to Deirdre to Justine.

"Polly and *Morton?*" Ina asked. "Polly's playing with Morton?"

"How come she's doing that?" Deirdre asked.

"I don't know," I answered. "He has this train she likes."

"Weird. What's that stuff on your blouse?"

"It's tar," I told her. "From the roof."

"From the roof? What were you doing on the roof?"

"Nothing much. Playing. With Morton and Polly. She's his friend." And then, all of a sudden, I remembered something Polly had said up on the roof. I didn't *remember* it, exactly; I *noticed* it, for the first time. "Hey, Mary Ella," she had said, and she had laughed as I showed her the tar on my blouse. "Hey, M. E.

That looks neat." For the first time ever, somebody had called me M. E., and I turned to Ina and Justine and Deirdre and gave them my biggest smile. "She's my friend, too," I told them.

"You were up on the *roof?*"

"Yeah. It's nice up there. There are pigeons and things and these bubbles you can break to make the roof bleed."

They all looked at me after I said that, and then Ina asked, "Does your mother know?"

"No. But anyway, she wouldn't care. She lets me do whatever I want." That's not what I tell my friends at Agnes Daly. I tell them my mother doesn't let me do anything at all, so they'll think I'm rich, like them. Wanda's mother doesn't even let her walk to school by herself, even though she lives closer than I do, and Peggy's mother makes her wear long underpants until the end of April, so her legs will keep warm. You can see them when she walks up the stairs.

"So if you were up there with them, how come you don't know where they are?" Justine asked.

"Because they stayed up there some more after I went home."

"Maybe they fell." It was Ina who said that.

"How could they fall?" I said. "The walls are up to your waist all around. People don't fall over walls like that when they're on the ground, do they? And anyway, I looked." Except not everywhere, I suddenly remembered. Not in the courtyard.

Pretty soon everyone on the block was looking for Polly and Morton, and by then I had begun to hope that something terrible really had happened to them, so that Deirdre and everybody wouldn't feel cheated, going to all that trouble for nothing. We really didn't know where to look, and so we looked in a whole lot of dumb places—under cars, in the sewer, in trash cans, behind the hedge—as though it were a stray jack ball we were tracking, and not two people with legs that could take them far away.

"Maybe they were kidnapped," someone said.

"Them? Who would want to kidnap *them?*"

"Maybe someone stole them, to sell somewhere."

"Maybe they fell," Ina said again. "Maybe they're lying in some alley somewhere. All broken up."

"I told you," I repeated. "You can't fall. There's walls all around."

"So? Maybe they were walking on top of the walls. Polly does things like that."

"Yeah," Henry said. "She's crazy. She does crazy things. Yesterday she took this piece of chalk she always has and she drew a line around the whole block— one long line on all the buildings and on the fences and on the bushes even, and when she got back to where she started she drew a bow, like she was tying up a present or something in a ribbon."

"She eats leaves, too. Every day she eats leaves from those bushes."

"She wrote a note on a piece of paper and mailed it in the sewer. She said she knows somebody who lives down there."

"She hung on the back of a bus and rode it for a whole block. I saw her."

"Maybe that's where they are now. On the back of a bus."

"Maybe they're running away. Maybe they're running away to where she comes from."

"Where does she come from?"

"I don't know. Someplace far away. She talks funny."

"She talks crazy."

"She *is* crazy."

"I bet they fell off the roof."

Maybe they were right: Polly was crazy. Not dumb, *crazy*. Maybe that was why she liked Morton. Somebody who ate leaves and mailed things in the sewer would be crazy enough to like Morton. Maybe that was why she liked me, too—because I put tar on my blouse and she thought it was nice.

And then all of a sudden there she was, walking up the street, chewing on a piece of bread. Alone.

"Hey, Polly!" someone shouted. "How did you get down?"

"What?"

"Where's Morton?"

"Who? Oh. I don't know. Still at the movies, probably," she answered through a wet crust. "Hey, M. E.," she said to me. "You want to play jungle?"

"At the movies!" I stared at her. "Morton's at the movies? What's he doing there?" Morton never goes to the movies. I don't go much, either. My parents think movies are bad for your eyes, and anyway, they never want to spend the money.

"Where'd he get the money?" I asked.

She pulled the piece of bread out of her mouth and I saw that it wasn't really bread at all. It was a thin white sock bunched up in a ball. "What money?"

"To get in," I said. "To the movies." But by then I realized that they had gone in without paying at all. "How come he's still there and you're not?" I asked.

"I'd already seen that movie. Do you want to play jungle, M. E.? We can be apes."

"No." I wanted to go upstairs. I wanted to tell my mother that Morton had done a wonderful thing. I wanted to tell her that he had gone to the movies with a friend, without telling anyone where they were going, when he was supposed to meet my mother at the barber's, and that they had sneaked in without paying. I wanted to tell her that Morton, for once, had done something disobedient—really disobedient, like other boys—and not just dumb.

"Did you find him?" she asked when I walked through the door.

"Yes," I said, "and don't be mad." That's what Ezra's sister says to *her* mother when she explains where Ezra is or what he's done, but what I really wanted to say was, "Be mad. Not mad the way you usually are, whispering to your listener in the kitchen or telling about what any other mother would do, but really mad. Like any other mother. Like Ezra's mother, who shouts a lot and says that Ezra has the devil inside him."

"He went to the movies," I said. "He and Polly went to the movies and they sneaked in without paying. Like Ezra. Ezra does that all the time. And Franklin, too, sometimes." Then I stood back and waited for her to be secretly glad that at last Morton had done something like other boys on the block.

"Good," she said, and for a minute I thought she *was* glad. "Good. Wonderful," and then I knew she wasn't. "When he was supposed to meet me at the barber's. When he could have been outside. A beautiful day like this and he spends it at the movies. Ruining his eyes. He has as much sense as a toad," she said to the kitchen clock.

A toad? Is that what she had said? A *toad*? I'd never heard her say that before. As much sense as a toad, and suddenly I thought of Morton crouched on a seat at the movies, all wet and shriveled and the color of mud, blinking at the screen with eyes that bulged from each side of his head—a toad—and something inside me wanted to cry. Instead, though, I thought of something.

"Look what I did to my blouse," I said. "I got tar on it. I was playing up on the roof, and I got this tar all over my best blouse, and I don't think it will wash out ever."

JULY

CHAPTER TWENTY-ONE

The strange thing is that, except for the beginning, when Morton got left back, and the end, when everything went wrong, this was the best summer I'd ever had.

It used to be that all my summers were the same. As soon as my parents left for work and Morton left for summer school, I'd go into my room and look for something to do. First, maybe, I'd try to read some hard book that I'd gotten out of the library to make the librarian think I was smart, and then I'd play with my orphan girls for a while. Or I'd write a letter to Wanda at camp and tell her what a wonderful time I was having. Then I'd put my face up close to the mirror and practise different smiles. Sometimes I'd take all the socks out of my drawer and make a parade, but mostly I did nothing. I'd just stay in the house all day until my mother came home from her job and told me it was a crime to be indoors on such a beautiful day.

"A crime," she would say.

"But there's nothing to do outside."

"How can there be nothing to do?" and she would list all the things she would do if she were young and had no responsibilities. "I'd take a good long walk somewhere," she'd say, putting out her chest as though she really *were* taking a walk. "I'd take a book to the park and read it on a bench. I'd get together with a whole group of friends and plan a picnic." When she was my age she always had a whole group of friends who did things together. Outdoors. "I'd organize a game."

"Nobody is around," I would tell her. "Everyone from school is at camp, and everyone on the block is doing something." Playing with each other, was what.

"Why don't you go downstairs and call for someone?" she would say, not listening.

Call for. That's what her friends did all the time when they were young. They would call for each other, ringing each other's doorbells, and then they'd go outside together and organize nice games.

Finally she'd say what I waited for her to say every day and hated to hear: "Why don't you call for Audrey?" Audrey was the daughter of one of her friends. She lived six blocks away and was almost three years older than I was. "She'd be glad to have someone to play with, Mary Ella."

"She's too old," I'd tell her.

"But you're used to older girls. You have loads of friends in school and they're all older than you."

"But Audrey's in high school, practically."

"She'll have a lot to teach you, then. Call for her, Mary Ella. She's a lovely girl."

She *was* a lovely girl—smart in school, pretty. Besides that, she had good manners. She said, "How are you, Mrs. Briggs?" when she passed my mother on the sidewalk, and she helped people pull their shopping carts home. When I see people's mothers coming up the street I bend down to tie my shoe.

"Call for her, Mary Ella," my mother always said, and one day I did.

I stood in front of her apartment door for about ten minutes before I managed to ring the bell, and it took her a long time, too, to answer it. She looked a little rumpled when she finally appeared, and at first she didn't know who I was.

"Do you want to go for a good long walk somewhere?" I asked, putting out my chest.

She squinted at my face in the dark hallway. "What?"

"Do you want to take a walk? To the park or something? We could take a picnic along. Or we could play a game."

"Oh, it's Mary Ella. I'm sorry, Mary Ella. I'm busy

now." And then I saw she already had a friend with her. A boy.

"She already was playing with somebody else," I told my mother when I returned home.

"Well, why didn't you ask them *both* to go with you? They would have been glad to get out in the fresh air on such a nice day."

This summer, though, everything was different. Suddenly, for the first time ever, I had a best friend and we played together every day. Sometimes we went to her grandmother's apartment and sometimes we came to mine. Sometimes we went to the park, and sometimes, on hot mornings, we just sat on the sidewalk in front of her building, letting its shadow chill the backs of our legs. All morning long we would sit there, not doing anything, sliding slowly back along the shadow as it moved from curb to front step, until it disappeared entirely, like a letter slipped under a door, and we knew it was time for lunch.

Sometimes we didn't bother with lunch at all, and after a while we didn't bother to wash either, even before dinner, even after we'd floated privet leaves in mud for an hour.

It was nice, being dirty. I liked rubbing the sweat on the inside crease of my arm to make black crumbs, and I liked scraping at the dark stripes, thick as crayon wax, that filled the spaces under my fingernails. I liked the new things I could do with my hair, now that it was sticky—tie it into little knots that stayed for hours and paste it against my forehead in flat rings. I liked letting my nose run and, like Morton, licking off my wet upper lip with my tongue. Also, there was a heavy smell, like a warm cage, under my arms, and I liked that, too.

It was nice doing a lot of things Polly and I did together. Wherever we went she took her chalk with her and marked up places where we'd been. Sometimes she just ran it along the sides of a building as we walked, so that a thin strand of white uncurled behind her like a trail of spider silk. Sometimes she paused and drew a picture on the sidewalk—of a face, a cat, a bug. Or she'd write her name, outlining the letters so she could color them in, and giving them a bar to stand on when she was through.

Sometimes she would add LOVES POLLY to a name already written on a wall: BOB LOVES POLLY, she would make it say, or POLLY LOVES BOB. Even when somebody already loved someone else, she'd add her name: STEWART LOVES JILL AND POLLY it says—still, to this day—on the inside of a tunnel in the park.

* * *

A week after Morton's school closed, it opened all over again, for summer-school kids. Morton had to get up early every day, just as he did the rest of the year, and walk the same seven blocks, carrying the same lunch and the same books to the same dark building behind the same wire fence. "He mustn't be allowed to neglect his *skills*," the principal told my mother, as she tells her every summer, even though this time he wasn't going to be promoted and summer school wouldn't do him any good. Every summer it's the same. He spends the mornings doing arithmetic and reading, so he won't neglect his skills, and the afternoons doing Creative Recreation, which means making lanyards out of plastic strings and bug cages out of Popsicle sticks.

This summer, though, was different for Morton, too. For the first time ever, instead of spending the afternoons alone in his room when he came home, he'd go to Polly's house or she'd come to ours, and then I'd stay alone in my room, because I wasn't the only best friend Polly had. Morton was her best friend, too, and she played with us one at a time.

"Where's Morton?" my mother asked one day when she found me alone.

"Playing."

"Playing where?"

"At his friend's."

"What friend's?"

"Polly's."

"Polly's! I thought Polly was your friend."

"She is. She's both of ours."

My mother was silent for a while. "What kind of girl is that who plays with you and with Morton, too?" she asked.

"I don't know," I answered. "She likes us both. And anyway, we're not that different, Morton and me."

And by that time we weren't.

CHAPTER TWENTY-TWO

"Look at the twins," I heard someone say, and I looked up to see.

It was a Sunday and we were all in the park together—Morton, my mother, my father, and me. I was walking side by side with Morton, matching my step to his, sliding my feet the way he does, tripping sometimes and moving so slowly that my mother and father, far behind us to begin with, soon caught up, and my mother stepped on the back of my shoe.

"Walk *ahead,*" she said. "Move faster, Morton."

"Come on, Mary Ella," Morton said. "Don't walk like that," and for a while we quickened our pace.

It was the hottest day of the summer so far. The sky was the color it gets on days like that—the color of steam—and imaginary puddles kept springing up in the roadway far ahead—wide, rippling pools of black that flattened out to nothing when we got up close. I kept my head down, like Morton's, and looked at things along the road: a spilling of Crackerjacks, some-times a whole boxful, here and there, and Styrofoam cups stained brown along the rim. Morton picked up a cup and dropped cellophane strings into it for his collection, and I dropped things into a cup, too—matchbooks, because by then I had started a collection of my own.

"Look, Mary Ella," he said, tightening a cellophane string around his fingertip. "My finger has a sunburn." I laced a string around my own finger and watched the tip grow red, liking the ache it sent into my hand.

"Look at the twins," someone said from a bench, and I lifted my head to see.

I liked looking at twins. I liked to see two people exactly alike, with the same hair and the same clothes and the same face. The same walk, and maybe even the same talk, too—the same words coming out of both mouths at the same time.

I always used to wish I could be twins.

"Let's pretend we're twins," I said to Wanda one day last year. "Let's go to the park and fool people."

"Twins?" she asked, staring at me. "How can we do that?"

"We'll dress alike and make ourselves look alike and everything. You want to?"

"Okay. Who'll be the real one and who'll be the twin?"

"What?"

"Which do you want, you be my twin or me be yours?"

"I don't care," I answered, although I did care. *I* wanted to be the real one, the one with the double, and I wanted her to copy my clothes and my face and make her hair like mine, with the red highlights and all. "Which do you?"

She looked me over for a long moment, examining my T-shirt, which that day had a little hole just under the collar, and my face, which was all red and streaked from a cold. "You be mine," she said. "We can wear my camp clothes, which are all alike, and you can wet your hair to make it straight."

Wanda's hair is light and smooth, and when she shakes her head it moves all in one piece, like the fringe on a curtain. Now and then she takes a strand between two fingers and slides it behind her ear, and I tried that now, with a piece of my wet hair. It felt lovely, with the air sudden and cool against my ear, and I could see why she wanted me to be her twin and not the other way around.

We gave ourselves twin names—Jeanie and Janie— and we went to the park, wearing our matching shorts and shirts and keeping our feet in perfect step.

"This is nice," Wanda said, "being twins. If my sister and me were twins we could wear the same clothes all the time and do everything together and be in the same class. That would be neat."

"Yeah," I said.

"And then my mother wouldn't like her best anymore. She'd like us both the same."

We stayed in the park all day, walking along the paths, waiting for someone to notice. When no one did, we called each other "Twin." "Oh, look, Twin," I shouted, pointing into a tree, "I see a sparrow," and she shouted back, "Oh, yes, Twin. I see it, too."

"Come *on*, Mary Ella," Morton said. "Don't do that."

"Don't do what?"

"What you're doing. Walking funny and everything."

"How funny?"

"*You* know. With your head like that and all. Walk normal, like you always do," and I realized all at once that the twins those people saw were really Morton and me.

Two dumb twins. Walking alike, looking alike, *being* alike. Picking stuff up off the ground alike and wearing clothes alike, too; we both had on our shirts with the tar streaks, and our socks had slid into our shoes.

Someone even liked us both the same.

CHAPTER TWENTY-THREE

"I could tell you belonged to Morton the minute you walked through that door." Polly's grandmother was wearing an apron that reached to the floor, and she looked over at me from the kitchen sink. "You have the same walk, the same look in the eye. You hold your head the same, too," she said, putting her chin down to her chest, copying Morton, copying me. "Odd," she said.

I was visiting Polly's apartment for the first time, in the beginning of July, and I stood at the kitchen door a long time, looking in. *Squinting* in, really, because although the morning sun shone heavily on the sidewalk outside, the light that came through the window was an evening light, thin and gray, and it took me a while to see.

There were things in there that nobody ever puts into a kitchen: a dresser with a mirror and the kind of chair that belongs in a living room—big and stuffed and covered in something green. A pillow of spotted fur lay in its corner. Everything looked old.

Polly's grandmother looked old, too. Her face was like the charcoal drawings we do in art class, where we sketch in lots of lines, sharp and thin, and then rub them to a shadow with the edges of our hands. Her hair was like her face—all lines and shadows— but her hands were strangely pink and shiny bright. Big pink hands she had, clinging to her hips and dripping suds, and then I saw that she was wearing rubber gloves.

"Odd," she said again. "So very odd," and I could tell that *she* belonged to *Polly*. Not from the way she walked or held her head, but from the way she talked. "Suh very odd." She turned back to the sink, and I noticed then that she was wearing Polly's skirt—the one with the stripes that Polly had worn the day we met, and the shirt was Polly's, too. How come Polly let her grandma wear her clothes? I wondered.

She lifted something slowly from the sink—something long and fat—and grasped it at its center, wringing hard. Tighter and tighter she twisted until it kinked into a loop, and then, with a snap that made me jump, she shook it loose. It was another one of Polly's shirts, and her grandmother hung it on a rack with wooden arms. "There now," she said, buttoning the collar and smoothing out the sleeves. "All dressed," and she stepped back to admire the rack that stood now like a scarecrow in the middle of the floor.

"You even dress the same," she said, looking me over some more, and I glanced at my clothes. I had put on one of Morton's Mickey Mouse shirts that morning, a gray one with black borders at the sleeves and collar. "How come you're wearing my shirt?" he had asked me. "Mom, Mary Ella's wearing my shirt." He wasn't angry; he was disappointed. "Why don't you wear something nice?" he had asked.

"I always wear my brother's clothes," I told Polly's grandmother, liking the way that sounded. The girls in Agnes Daly wear their brothers' clothes, too: big gray sweatshirts with the name of some high school printed on their fronts, and, in the winter, long striped scarves, maroon and gold. Not Mickey Mouse shirts.

"Even down to your shoes," Polly's grandmother added, although my sneakers were my own. They were just untied.

How did she know, I wondered then, what Morton's shoes were like? How many times had he been here, anyway? "What do you do here," I asked Polly, "when Morton comes?"

"Nothing much. Play games. Mess around."

Still, I wondered. The only time anybody had ever invited Morton to their house, it was to play a trick on him.

"Hey, Morton," Henry had once said. "Come to my house tomorrow at three o'clock. I'm having a party."

"Where do you live?" Morton had asked.

"Down there," and he laughed as he pointed into the stairway that led to a cellar. Nobody went into the cellar. Rats lived down there and old men, too, sometimes. Justine had seen someone in a torn shirt come up the steps one day and blink at her in the glare. And once, in its doorway, we had found a single shoe. "Where'd this come from?" Ina asked, picking it up, turning it over, swinging it by its lace. She held it to her ear for a moment, as though, like a seashell, it held an echo of where it had been, but then Franklin said, "It's the old man's," and she dropped it on the stairs while we all ran away.

Morton didn't try to go to Henry's house, but he did go to Justine's once when she and Ina and Ezra invited him. I never found out what had happened, because he never told, and they didn't tell either, but one time I heard Ina say, "Remember when Morton came to Justine's?" and everybody laughed.

"*How* mess around?" I asked Polly.

"I don't know," she answered. "We just do stuff."

Suddenly the fur pillow on the chair began to move in its corner, and I jumped back.

"Here, kitty, kitty," Polly said, and the pillow jumped

down to the floor. "Come here," she said to it, and she stooped down to drag a finger through its hair.

"Is that a cat?" I asked. "I mean, is that yours?" I moved back some more.

"Yeah. She has fleas. You want to see? I can make them come out. Hey, flea!" she shouted, and she snapped her fingers. "Come make friends with M. E. Sit still, kitty, so the flea can shake hands. SIT!" But the cat walked out of the room.

"What's its name?" I asked, watching it go.

"Kitty. I already said that."

"No, I mean its real name."

She stared at me. *"Kitty."*

"Kitty? That's all you call it?"

"What's wrong with that?"

"I don't know. That's what people call cats that don't have a real name."

"They do so have a real name," Polly's grandmother said from the sink. "It's Katherine. Kitty is what you call *anyone* who's named Katherine. It's a nickname. Didn't you ever know that?" She turned around to stare at me. *"Didn't* you?" she repeated, when I didn't answer.

"No. I mean I didn't know it about cats."

"Well, you do now." She turned back to the sink.

"Let's play, M. E.," Polly said, and she led me through the kitchen into the living room.

The living room was dark, too, darker even than the kitchen. Polly pulled at a hanging string and a little cluster of bulbs lit up on the ceiling. There wasn't much to see: a table with a radio on it, a picture of a pyramid and a camel taped to the wall, a couple of wooden chairs. But there were two sofas instead of one, and the room looked crowded.

"You want to watch bugs?" Polly asked.

"Bugs? Fleas, you mean, from your cat?"

"No, a different kind. These live on the ceiling."

I looked up. "You have bugs on the ceiling?"

"Yeah. They come out after the light goes on. Lie down and we can watch them. They do tricks and everything, like at the circus."

Polly lay down on the wooden floor, and after a while I lay down, too. I didn't see any bugs at all—just little spider strings hanging like stray hairs on a chin or joining one light bulb to another.

"Are they spiders," I asked, "the bugs?"

"No. They're bugs. They'll come out in about a minute, first one and then the other. They go over to each other like they're about to kiss, but then they change their minds and they move away."

We lay there for a long time staring at the ceiling and at the ring of lights, but no bugs came. When I closed my eyes, a circle of blue disks clung to my lids, and I watched them brighten and fade. Maybe that's what Polly thought were bugs. Eye spots.

I didn't care, though. It was nice lying there, with a real friend, and I tried to think of something to say to her. What? Mostly, at Agnes Daly, friends say something like, "You want to trade sweatshirts for keeps?" and they go into the bathroom and come out wearing each other's clothes. Or they trade spit. "Let's be spit sisters," they say, and they spit into their own hands and rub each other's palms. Sometimes they say things about someone they hate. Me, usually. Standing by the lockers or against the washroom door, I will catch a sudden whisper and I'll stop to tie my shoe or wipe my nose. Mostly, all I hear is lots of *She's*. *She, she, she*, rustling like two fingers at my ear. But now and then my name will come: Mary Ella, I will hear, each syllable floating down the hall like a balloon and exploding at my shoulder with a pop.

What could I say to Polly?

And then I thought of something.

"Polly," I said, "do you think it can happen"—and I turned my eyes from the ceiling so I could look into her face—"that games come true?"

"What?"

"Not the Monopoly kind of game. The other kind, where you play that something happens. Something bad. Do you think that?"

"Games come true? Like what?"

"Like broken leg or scarlet fever? Make-believe games? Somebody told me that once. If you play you're poor you get poor, and if you play that somebody dies they really will. Do you think that—that games come true?"

"I don't know. Anyway, so what if they do? What's so terrible about that?"

"Well, what if you get to be poor or somebody dies or something or you break a leg, just because you played it once?"

Suddenly, that sounded like a dumb thing to believe, but I believed it anyway. Lots of times I believe things even though I know they're not true. "If you touch stone, you turn to stone," Wanda used to say, and even now, sometimes, I keep my hands against my side when I walk beside a building made of stone instead of brick.

"So?" Polly said. "I'm poor. And somebody died. The only thing, I didn't break a leg. But it wouldn't be so bad if I did. I'd get out of helping my grandmother in the house and going to the store for her all the time."

I was silent for a long while after that, and finally I said, "Somebody died?"

"Yeah. Two people. First my other grandmother and then my father. That's why I'm here. Because my mother couldn't afford to keep me and my sister both. So she sent me up here and she kept my sister Irene, and anyway, she likes my sister best."

She didn't seem to mind very much that her mother liked her sister best. She didn't whine about it the way everybody else I know does. "She likes your sister best?" I asked.

"Yeah. My father did too," and then I said something I'd tried out before only in my head. "Me too," I said. "My parents like my brother best." The words made a little echo in my ear. It was a nice thing to say to a friend, even though it wasn't true.

"Probably because he's nicer," Polly said, "like with my sister."

"Yeah," I answered. "Probably," but I thought about that. Morton was nicer? He was? I had always thought *I* was nicer. I do lots of nice things for people. I let people get in front of me in the supermarket line if they have only one thing to buy, and once, in the park, I read the newspaper to an old lady who couldn't see. Also, I helped a little kid find her mother once, and in school sometimes I let people copy my answers on spelling tests. Morton never does things like that.

But maybe Polly didn't mean that kind of nice. Maybe she meant that Morton never argued back.

CHAPTER TWENTY-FOUR

"Hey, look!" Polly cried out. "There's one," and she pointed into the air. A tiny brown spot had emerged from a hole at the top of the wall, and it began to move across the ceiling like a bead on a string.

"That's a bug?" I asked. "*That?* Where's its legs?"

"It doesn't have any. It just slides on its stomach. Look, here comes the other one."

From the same hole another brown spot appeared and slid slowly toward the first. Then, just as their noses were about to touch, they suddenly pulled away, like the wrong ends of magnets.

"How come they do that?" I said. "How come they go up to each other like that and then move away?"

"That's how they say hello. They're going to kiss, but they change their minds because their breath smells bad. Look, they're dancing."

They did seem to be dancing—sliding back and

forth together, twirling around. "What makes them go like that?" I asked.

"There's wax up there," she said. "They're sliding on the wax."

"Wax! Who put *wax* up there?"

"I don't know. Somebody. Lots of people wax their ceilings. Like they wax floors."

I never know what to say when people tell lies like that. Usually I just pretend to believe them, but sometimes I try to argue. "Nobody does that," I said.

"They do so. There's this special wax that people use on their ceilings. Kings mostly. My teacher said. She read us a story once about this king who had a whole bunch of ceiling wax and all and he was always using it. For the bugs, probably, so they could dance."

"Kings don't wax their ceilings, and anyway, they don't have bugs." This wasn't what I wanted to be saying to my friend.

"This one did. My teacher told us. He had this special ceiling wax and he kept it in a little pot on his desk."

"A *king?*" I stared at her. "Oh, *sealing* wax, you mean. Polly, that's dumb. That's the dumbest thing I ever heard. You're thinking of sealing wax."

"Yeah. That's what I said."

"But not *that* kind of ceiling. The other kind. For sealing letters and stuff."

"They're both the same. Ask my teacher. Hey, M. E., I have an idea. You want to play bug race?"

"Bug race? What's that? You mean like potato race?"

"Potato race! There's no such thing. Potatoes can't run. Bug race is like horse race, except you don't use horses. Here's how we play: I pick a bug and then you pick the other one and whichever gets to the light first wins. You want to play?"

"I don't know. What happens if you lose?"

"*You* don't lose, the *bug* loses. You feel sorry for it, is all. We'll wait till they get lined up and then we'll start. I'll take that one and you can have the other one. Okay, GO!" she shouted, and somehow the two bugs began to move toward the light.

"What makes them go there," I asked, "to the light like that?"

"I don't know. They think it's the sun. They go there every day and just lie around without any clothes on, getting warm. That's how they get so brown. Then they go home. Hey, bug, MOVE!"

This time I didn't argue with her.

"MOVE!" she yelled again.

"I'll move when I please." Polly's grandmother was standing in the doorway behind us. "Get up off your back, Polly, and go to the store for me. I need more soap."

I lifted my head to look at her. She had taken her

apron off and she stood there in Polly's blouse and skirt. They fitted her better than they did Polly, and I realized all at once that they weren't Polly's clothes at all. They were her grandmother's. It was Polly who wore her grandmother's things. Not the other way around.

"POLLY!"

Polly didn't stir.

"Get up like I told you."

"Later," Polly said, but she spoke to the bugs on the ceiling. Her grandmother remained in the doorway for a while, and I thought she would yell, but she didn't. She didn't even sigh. She just turned back to the kitchen.

"She's always making me do stuff that she doesn't feel like doing herself," Polly said to me.

"Maybe it's because she's old," I said.

"Yeah. Old people are terrible, don't you think? They shouldn't let old people be born."

I turned to her and smiled, happy to be there, happy to listen to the things she said, happy to have her as my best friend. She didn't tell lies, really. She just said crazy things. Or dumb ones. It didn't matter which. "When this is over," I said, "let's go to your room and you can show me your things."

"I don't have any things," Polly said. "And anyway, this is my room."

"This? I thought this was the living room."

"It is. It's my bedroom, too, and my grandma's."

I looked around. "Then what's that down the hall?"

"The bathroom."

"That's it? That's the whole apartment?"

"Yeah. It's crummy, but it's better than where I used to live. I used to have to share a room with my sister. She always had the best bed and everything. All her stuff was better than mine. Here I have the best bed."

"Where is it?" I asked. "Your bed?"

"Over there. With the red pillows," and she pointed to the sofa behind us. It was like the bed Wanda and I might have had when we played poor children—hard-looking and full of lumps. "That's nice," I said. "That's a nice bed," and that was a nice thing to say to a friend, too.

CHAPTER TWENTY-FIVE

All the girls at Agnes Daly, except me, have what they call outside friends. An outside friend is someone who doesn't go to your school and is a better friend than anyone else you know. When you play with her you think up things to do that would never occur to you with your ordinary friends. In fact, you don't even think them up. They just happen.

"I had this really great time with my outside friend yesterday," Rhoda will say, and then she'll describe an afternoon that could have happened to nobody else in the world. "I was visiting her in this enormous house where she lives, and all of a sudden we decided to be Siamese twins. Just like that." That's the way things happen with outside friends: just like that. "So we dressed up in her father's huge T-shirt and her grand-mother's long skirt and we tied our inside legs together and hopped all around the block. One kid thought we were for real." And I will listen and wonder why things like that never happen to me.

Now, though, I had an outside friend. "My outside friend and I did this wonderful thing," I could say to Rhoda or to Iris some day when I went back to school. "She lives with her grandmother in this really funny place where they have huge old sofas for beds and there are these special bugs that stick to the ceiling. They put on shows, and we were watching them for a while, when all of a sudden we decided that they were racing bugs. We spent the whole morning just lying on our backs picking which one would win."

"You better yell at your bug," Polly said, "so it'll move."

It *was* moving. It was within an inch of the light bulbs, in fact, while Polly's was far behind. Anyway, I felt silly, yelling at a bug. "I'll yell in my head," I said.

"Morton yells out loud."

I sat up. Morton? "Morton plays this? Morton plays bug race with you? I thought you just made this up." *That's* what they did? Lay here on the floor, just as she and I were now lying, and raced bugs? Did she tell him about ceiling wax, too, and about how bugs said hello and got brown in the light of a bulb? "Who wins?" I asked. "You or him? His bug, I mean, or yours?"

"Mine."

"All the time? Yours always wins?"

"Yeah."

"How come?" I asked, although I already knew how come: Morton never wins anything. Not even Bingo, where you don't have to be smart. Not even War. I never have to cheat to win when I play with him, because no matter what happens, he loses all the time. "Think about what you're doing, Morton," my mother says to him, even when we're playing War and thinking doesn't do any good. Then she says "He would" to her listener when he loses all his cards.

"Because I can make bugs do whatever I want. I'm magic. GO!" she yelled, and suddenly her bug moved away from its spot on the ceiling and began to catch up with mine. "GO!" I yelled at my own bug. "MOVE!" but it stopped in its path and remained fixed, like a pin stuck through paper, while Polly's glided past and bumped its head on the ring of bulbs.

"See? He won! My bug won!" She got to her feet and jumped up and down. "Good bug. GOOD BUG! See, M. E.? I told you I was magic."

"You are not. It's just luck. And anyway, I don't care. It's just a game," but I did care. I felt sorry, just as Polly said I would, for my bug, standing still up there, too dumb to move. And I felt sorry for myself;

usually I won things. I felt sorry for Morton, too, who lost all the time.

"Put the seven green sticks in one bundle," my mother was saying. "No, *seven*. Count them out. Now make another bundle just like that one. Make six bundles in all."

They were sitting at the kitchen table, and although it was still early evening the overhead light was on, because the sun came into the room only in the morning. I walked around them on my way to the window, and Morton looked up as I passed him, but my mother didn't.

"You now have six bundles of seven. Six sevens. That means six times seven. Six times seven equals what, Morton?"

A tree grew up from the courtyard below, and in the summer you could lift up the window screen and touch its leaves. I did that now, pulling leaves off one after another and letting them float away like paper planes. No one ever went into the courtyard, because there was no way to get inside except through the cellar, and besides, everybody from the building could look down at you once you were there. Still, there were two benches facing each other, and now and then pigeons rested on them—fat, silent pigeons in dark-gray coats, who tipped their heads to one another and left thick white stains when they flew away.

"I can't hear you, Morton."

One leaf landed on a bench, making no sound.

"Six times seven equals," he said, and I felt his eyes on my back.

"Equals what, Morton? Equals *what*? Count the bundles. Count by sevens. Ready? Begin. Seven. Fourteen. Now, what comes after fourteen?"

In another moment, Morton was going to say something dumb and my mother was going to say "Stupid" to her listener on the wall.

"Hey, guess what." I turned around from the window before Morton had a chance to answer anything at all. "Guess what happened today? I was playing this game with Polly and I was ahead the whole time and then something happened and I lost. I lost the whole game."

My mother looked up at me. "That's too bad, Mary Ella," she said. "What game was it?"

"It was a race, and I lost. I lost the whole race."

"Well, try harder next time. Count by sevens, Morton. Seven. Fourteen. What comes after fourteen?"

"Fifteen."

"Be quiet, Mary Ella."

"Fifteen," Morton said.

CHAPTER TWENTY-SIX

Ever since Aunt Sophia died, I think about how surprised she'd be if she came back all of a sudden and saw all the changes that have happened in the world since her funeral. Like those fancy new buses with the bodies that bend, and those toothbrushes that play music when you scrub them on your teeth. Sometimes I pretend that she's with me when I walk down the street, and I show her things that have changed. "Look at the new cars, Aunt Sophia," I tell her, "with those funny bumpers and everything. And we have these new streetlights now that go on by themselves when it gets dark. And look at these TVs," I say, pausing at a store window. "You can play games with them and everything." I can feel her eyes grow large as she watches. "Imagine that," she says. "Who would have thought?"

Mostly now, though, she'd be surprised at the changes in *me*.

"Look out, Mary Ella," my mother cried out, and she pushed her chair quickly from the table.

"She spilled her milk," Morton said in surprise, as a white puddle spread from plate to plate, soaking the napkins and coating the spoons. "Mary Ella spilled her milk!"

"I don't know how it happened," I said, jumping up. "It went over so fast," but that wasn't true. It had taken me a long time to knock it over. I had started very slowly, leaning the edge of my hand against the glass until it began to travel a small path across the table. The milk splashed in waves from side to side, but it wouldn't spill out. Why was it so hard to knock over a glass of milk? I bumped my plate into it once, and when that didn't work, I picked it up and dropped it on its side.

"Look out!" my mother cried.

"Mary Ella spilled her milk!" Morton had never seen that happen before. "Look what it's doing. It's making a big J. Look what Mary Ella did, Mom. The milk is getting all over the table."

"It was an accident, Morton," my mother explained. "We all have accidents," and my father rushed over with a rag to catch the spreading puddle before it hit the floor.

I didn't spill my milk every night, but I spilled it a lot after that, and soon I got so I could spill it without even trying. Sometimes even when I was trying not to.

"Be careful tonight, Mary Ella," my mother would say. "Don't spill," and I *would* be careful, picking up the glass with both hands, holding it tight, fastening my eyes on its rim, the way Morton does, and lifting it slowly to my mouth. Then, just as it would reach my lips, my elbow would twitch or my wrist give out, and a sudden splash would hit my lap and trickle, strangely cold, between my thighs.

Once, Morton and I spilled our milk at the same time. I pushed my glass across the table as I saw his go down, and they toppled over together, like a couple of clowns, rolling side by side in a fat white ring.

"Mary Ella, don't do that," but it was Morton who spoke, not my mother or my father. "You're not supposed to do that."

The thing was that although I did a lot of dumb things this summer—one dumb thing after another until I became just like Morton—my mother didn't seem to mind or even to notice. "Soak it in the sink awhile," she had said when I showed her my blouse with the tar on its front. And when I brought it to her again the next morning, she didn't say anything at all.

By then, though, she had seen Morton's report card. "Look," he had said, coming in to breakfast. "I have something to show you," and he handed her the envelope with his name written in beautiful script. "I got O in conduct."

"Very nice," she said, slipping the report card into her hand. "Very nice," and then she saw the seven at the bottom of the page, and after that she said nothing at all, not even to her listener.

The silence that fell over her passed from one of us to the other like a bad cold, and like a cold, it stayed with us wherever we went: to the Laundromat, to the supermarket, to the park where we took our Sunday walk. All summer long she was angry at everything he did, even though by then I was doing the same dumb things.

Dumber, even.

Every day before I went upstairs for supper, I would stretch out the front of my T-shirt and fill it with matchbooks picked up from the street, or from trash cans or the stream that ran along the curb. They were dirtier than the things Morton collected, and more dangerous, too: Some had rows of matches tucked inside—unstruck matches, their pink heads rough against my thumb.

When I got them to my room, I'd dump them on my bed and sort them out. The restaurant ones went in one pile, the supermarket ones went in another, and the animal and flower ones went in a third. "Look," I said to my mother. "I'm starting a collection. It's going to be of matchbooks," and I waited for her to tell me that they were dirty, that they were dangerous, that I could start a fire, but she didn't say any of that. "Oh, look, Mary Ella," she said, lifting one up. "Did you see this? It's from a place in England," and she put it carefully beside the others, in the right pile.

And when I didn't get her a present for her birthday, it didn't seem to bother her at all.

"What are you going to get her?" Morton asked one day. He was holding something behind his back and he sounded excited as he stood in my doorway.

"Get who?"

"*You* know, Mary Ella," he answered, sounding impatient. "It's tomorrow. I'm getting her this lanyard I made in Creative Recreation. It could be for a belt."

For two weeks now I had been making myself forget my mother's birthday, just so I could see what it was like to wake up one morning and suddenly remember, too late, that I had nothing to give. I had tried to mix the days up in my head, so I wouldn't know when July nineteenth came, and I made myself think of other things all day, but it really didn't work. Two years ago I tried to forget my own birthday, so I'd be surprised when it finally arrived, but my mother spoiled it by telling me every day, "In six days"—or five, or four— "you'll be nine years old, and by then I will expect you to wash your hair by yourself instead of having me do it for you." Probably, though, I would have remembered anyway. Nobody forgets their own birthday. And besides, you can't make yourself forget anything. The more you try, the more you think about it; I knew as soon as Morton came to my room what he would say.

"*You* know, Mary Ella. It's tomorrow."

"I don't know what you're talking about," I said, and I closed the door before he could tell me.

I gave my mother a handmade card the next day, and that was all. It was a terrible card, with a picture of a girl standing in front of a house. The crayon went out of the lines all over the place, and the house was the kind that Morton draws, with a triangle roof and a tilted chimney. I put it on the kitchen table next to Morton's present so my mother would see them both when she came in.

"Very nice," she said, picking up the card and putting it down again. "Very nice," she repeated, and she began to unwrap the lanyard.

"Oh, my!" she said, and she held it up so it dangled from her fingers. "Isn't that nice!"

"You're supposed to wear it," Morton told her. "It's for a belt." He looked happy.

"Yes, I see," she said, and she tied it around her waist. "It's very pretty, Mary Ella."

"It's from Morton," I told her. "I just gave you the card."

"You did? Oh, I thought . . ." She picked the card up again and studied it carefully. "Why does it just say 'From me' on it?"

"It doesn't. It says M. E. That's what people call me now."

"Oh, I didn't know. It's a very nice card, Mary Ella," she said, even though it was terrible.

"I didn't remember to get you anything else," I said. "I forgot your birthday was today."

"No, you didn't," Morton said. "I told you."

"I didn't hear."

"It's all right," my mother said. "The card is really very pretty, Mary Ella. I like the colors." She held it out in front of her and looked at it for a long time, holding her head to one side, the way I had wanted her to look at my picture of the daisies. "It's just *lovely!*"

she said, at last sounding like the mother rabbit in the egg. "Lovely," she said, for the first time ever, but she said it because she was sorry for me, because she thought I had forgotten her birthday and had made the card in a hurry. Not because the card was lovely at all; it was terrible.

Only Morton was disappointed. "Why didn't you give her something nice?" he asked later. "You always give nice things."

The tar never came out of our shirts, Morton's or mine, and in the end my mother took them both away. She dropped mine into the clothing bin outside the supermarket, because poor children would be glad to have it, and she turned Morton's into a dustrag. A floor mop now wears the gray Mickey Mouse shirt with the tar fish on the stomach, and once a week it slides around under the bed, along the baseboards, up on the ceiling even, collecting things that no one else wants: dust puffs, pins, and cobwebs sticky with grime.

CHAPTER TWENTY-SEVEN

"You want to be in my club?" Polly asked one day.

I turned to look at her. "Be in your club?" Nobody had ever said that to me. The girls in my class are always asking each other to join clubs that they make up, but they never ask me. They have a lunch club and a walking club and a hair club. All they do at the lunch club is sit at the same table in the lunchroom, and all they do for the walking club is walk to school together. For the hair club they meet in the bathroom and comb their hair at the same time. And although I sometimes sit at the lunch table with them or comb my hair in front of the same mirror in the bathroom, I'm not in any of their clubs.

"What kind of club?" I asked Polly. We were sitting side by side under the awning, on the same curb where, in the beginning of the summer, I had sat alone, pretending the new girl would be my best friend. Now she was.

"No kind. It's just a club."

"Who else is in it?"

"No one. I just started it."

"Well, but what's it for?"

"It's so I can be president. You can be vice president if you like, in case I'm absent."

"But what do you *do?*" I asked. "I mean, do you walk somewhere or comb your hair, or what?"

"We don't do anything. We're just *in* it. You want to join? Morton's joined."

I looked at her again. "I thought you said no one else was in it."

"He's in my other club. I have two clubs."

"Who else is in that one?"

"No one. I just started that one, too. Last week. You want to join? All's you have to do is a trick I make up, and then you're a member."

I waited a long moment before answering. "What trick? An initiation, you mean?"

"A what?"

"Initiation. That's a trick you do to get into a club."

"There's a name for that? Well, your initiation could be you steal something."

"No."

"My sister did. We had this club once and she had to steal a beach chair from the five-and-ten. It was easy. She just walked in and put it on top of her head and walked out again. Nobody said anything. They thought it was her hat. It was a nice chair, with a thing to put your feet up on and everything. We used it for the president. You could steal a chair, if you wanted, and then you could sit in it when the president was absent."

A thin stream of water was running along the street against the curb, and I put my finger in it to make a little dam.

"You want to?"

"No."

"Then *what*? You want to climb something? That fence across the street? You want to climb that? You could walk on top of it for a little ways, and then pick a leaf from the top of that bush and eat it. That could be your trick."

"Polly, that fence has *spikes* on it."

"Yeah, well. How about that tree, then, down at the corner, with the pollynoses? You could climb to the top and put a pollynose on and climb back down again."

"No."

"Well, what then? This awning? You want to climb this awning? All's you have to do is slide on your stomach until you get to the wall. Then stand up and write your name under that window with some chalk and walk back, no fair using hands. It'll be easy. You can climb up there from that car roof."

I tilted my head back and looked up at the gray-green canvas stretched tight across its frame. It was thin and frayed, and here and there little points of light shone through its holes, like stars on a paper chart that you hold against the sky. Walk on *that?* "There's nothing to hold on to," I said.

"Yes, there is. Hold on to those bars, with your feet."

"With my *feet?* That's crazy. And anyway, you're not supposed to write on that wall. It's against the law or something."

"No, it's not. I write on walls all the time and nobody ever put me in jail. Besides, it's nice, writing on walls. When you go away, it's still there. It's like leaving yourself behind, for everyone to see."

"You're not supposed to," I said again, and after that we were silent a long time. I lifted my finger from the running stream and let some drips trickle down my leg and collect at the top of my sock, turning it gray, and then I thought of something. "Hey," I said. "What about *you?* What trick are you going to do for initiation?"

"Me? Nothing. I'm already *in* the club. Come on,

M. E. Then you can be a member. Like Morton. You can use this piece of chalk. It's brand-new."

I thought of something else: "What did Morton do," I asked, "for his trick?"

She paused a while before answering. "He went into that cellar. The one over there, with the little door."

I stared at her. Morton had gone in *there*? Where the old man lived and the rats ran around? So he could be in Polly's club? "What did he have to do when he was down there?" I asked, "Write his name, or what?"

"He had to find something and bring it back."

"What did he find?"

"I don't know. A glove."

"A glove! Whose glove? The old man's?"

"Yeah, I guess. It was old. The tops were gone and everything so his fingers showed through."

Morton had gone into the cellar and never told. I thought about that. Morton had pushed his way through the black down there, with his hands held straight before him, as though he were blindfolded for a game, and his chin down low on his chest. Noises had come, from the rats and the old man, and smells, too, from rotten things. After a while his toe had bumped against something soft and flat, and he had patted the cellar floor with his hands so he could pick up whatever it was and take it back to Polly to show he had been there. How long had it been, I wondered, before he had brought it out into the sun and found it was only a glove he held and not the body of a rat? He had put it on, too, even though the wool smelled of rot and was stiff with dirt. He had slid his hand into its cuff and watched as his fingertips, like five bald heads, pushed through a row of raveled collars. "Look," he'd said, making them nod. "People."

"Let's see the chalk," I said, holding my hand out to Polly.

CHAPTER TWENTY-EIGHT

The edge of the awning frame reached only to my chest when I stood on the car roof, and Polly had to push against my feet to get me up the rest of the way. The chalk in my pocket pressed into my hip, and I shifted to one side so it wouldn't break. It *was* new, as she had said, still flat at each end and silky smooth.

"You're almost there!" Polly shouted, although I hadn't begun to move. "Write your name on the wall nice and big, so everyone can see it. Write M. E."

The wall at the other end was far away, farther than I had imagined—a mile or more—and I quickly lowered my head to gaze instead into the canvas that for the first time ever I could feel against my skin. Its color, so close to my eye, turned out to be not green at all, or even gray, but black, and its smell was not of canvas but of something else. An old coat, maybe, or a closet, and it settled in my mouth like a taste.

I held my eye for a moment to one of the holes and

peered down at the sidewalk. Spread on the shadow of the awning was the shadow of my own body. A shadow on top of a shadow, like the tower of shadows Polly had said you could make that time on the roof. One shadow and one shadow made two shadows, after all. If Polly stepped on it, I wondered, would her foot sink in, just a little?

I closed my eyes then and began to move. Inch by inch I went, like a blind lizard, bending my knees, straightening them again, scratching at the cloth with my nails, rubbing my chin. On and on, for a mile. More. I didn't know I had reached the wall until I hit it with my head, and then I didn't know what to do next.

"Stand up!" Polly shouted from wherever she was. "Go ahead, M. E. Go *ahead!*"

In science class at Agnes Daly we watch a movie every year about evolution, where slimy things swim through a pool of water, and then, when they reach the shore, sprout legs and begin to crawl onto the land. After a while they rise up on their hands and knees, and finally they walk on their hind legs like apes. At the end a man in a bathing suit stands by himself on the beach. That's how I got up from my stomach, except at the end I wasn't on a beach. I was pressed against a wall of brick with my forehead at the sill of a second-story window.

"Hey, you made it!" Polly's voice came from far away. "What's it like up there?"

"Fine," I whispered into the brick.

"Write your name now. Write it just under the windowsill, where everybody can see it. Make it big."

A window slid open somewhere above and a shout was thrown from it. "You! YOU! You GIRL there! GET OFF THAT!" I pressed my hands into the wall. I had never noticed before how jagged brick was, or how full of color. All over there were patches of pink, or orange—purple, even. Black.

"GET AWAY FROM THERE!"

I flattened myself into my own shadow, stretching my neck, and suddenly I was looking into a living room. A stranger's living room, with furniture against the walls and things on the tables. Magazines and stuff. An open book. Lamps. A banana, halfway peeled, on a plate. There were shoes on the floor—somebody else's shoes, and I caught my breath, feeling like the giant girl who peered through my window each night. "Look!" I could say. "Look at the real sofa and the chairs. And the banana on the table." I could squeeze my arm through and move things around. Slip the shoes under the sofa, where they couldn't be seen. Pull the peel the rest of the way off the banana. Turn on the lamp.

At any moment, though, someone could walk in.

Someone—the lady who lived there—would remember the banana on the plate or the open book and, walking in, suddenly see my eyes over the sill. What would she do?

"What's she doing there?" someone cried out. The lady! A jump ran through my body. "How come she's up on the awning?" Someone had joined Polly on the sidewalk. A boy. Henry, probably. Then more voices came.

"How'd she get up there?"

"How's she going to get down?"

They spoke as though I couldn't hear them, and I felt like a performer in a show. At the circus, it could be, on the high wire.

"She's spying on someone, I bet. She's spying on those people who live there's apartment."

"She's going to climb in."

"She's going to rob them. Hey, Charles, look what Mary Ella's doing! She's going to rob that apartment."

"She's got something in her pocket."

"A gun!"

"No, it's a cigarette. She's going to smoke up there."

"It's a piece of *chalk*. Hey, she's writing something," and they began to call out the letters as though they were watching an airplane trail a message in the sky.

"T."

"H."

"I."

"S . . . This."

"Is."

"This is . . ."

"M."

"E."

"Apostrophe S. This is Me's . . ."

"A."

"W."

"N-I-N-G."

"This is Me's awning." They waited to see if there would be more.

"*Me's* awning?" somebody asked.

"She's crazy."

"No, she's not." It was Polly's voice now. "She's being initiated."

There was a silence.

"What?"

"Don't you know what initiated is? It's what you do to get into a club."

"What club?"

"Mine."

"She has to stand on the awning to get into a club? What kind of club is that?"

"HEY, GIRL. IF YOU DON'T GET OFF THERE I'M GOING TO CALL THE POLICE!"

"Somebody's going to call the police."

"She better get down."

"Look, she's turning around now. There she is. You can see her face."

"Look how dirty she got. Her clothes are all black."

"And her legs."

"Everything. Look at her *face*."

My back was against the wall now, and from the side of one eye I could see a crowd of faces. Everybody I knew was down there, but I didn't look at them long. I fastened my eyes instead on a wash bucket on the fire escape across the street. "*Spot!*" Miss Frazier always yells in Interpretive Dance. "Spot, and you won't fall."

"How's she going to get down?" somebody asked.

"Jump, probably."

"From *there?*"

"No, she's not," Polly said. "She's going to walk. Those are the rules. You have to walk to the front of the awning, no fair using hands, and then climb down."

"She's crazy." That sounded like Ezra.

"She's dumb." Justine. "Dumb like her brother."

CHAPTER TWENTY-NINE

Always, just before I fall, I can see the whole accident, even though it hasn't happened yet. I can see my ankle catch in the jump rope and my knees turn bloody even before it's my turn to jump, and I can see my hand miss the last rung of the monkey bars before I'm half-way across. Now, as I pressed my back against the brick wall, I could see my leg give way at the sound of some sudden noise—a car horn down the street or a window slamming shut—and I could see my body crash to the ground. I could hear it, too—I could hear the squawk of canvas as it ripped beneath my leg, and I could hear the hum of metal as my shoulder hit a bar.

I would end up like the girl in my make-believe game: in a wheelchair. I would be wheeled through the park with my legs wrapped in a blanket, even in summer, and a muffler at my neck.

Except this time, instead of saying, "She's gravely

ill," my mother would explain that I had broken my bones in a fall. "She had a terrible accident," she would say, but she wouldn't add that I had fallen from an awning or that I had gone up there because—because why? Because my best friend said I should. Because I did a dumb thing my friend told me to do.

Me, not Morton.

"Why doesn't she *move?*"

"She's too scared. Look at her leg shake."

"Come *on*, M. E. They're going to call the police."

"The fire department, too, I bet. They'll have to get her down with a ladder. Or one of those basket things."

"They don't send the fire department just to get somebody off an awning."

"They send them to get cats out of trees."

"No, they don't. That's just in baby books."

Or I would die. When I fell to the ground I would hit my head hard and then lie very still while everyone stood around me, afraid to come closer, afraid to move away. Later, the doorbell would ring, and my mother, answering it, would find Ina standing there, or Deirdre. There would be a tiny silence and in that moment my mother would know something terrible had happened. Morton, she would think, and Ina would say, "Mary Ella's hurt."

"Get down from there!" Somebody's mother was

coming up the block across the street. "Get down from there before you break your neck." It was Justine's mother, and I could see her now, from the side of my other eye, pulling a shopping cart loaded with bags. "Get down from there this *minute!*"

"She can't," somebody said. "She's too scared."

"Get off that thing," Justine's mother continued, "or I'll call your mother."

I held my head still, as though I were posing before a camera, and I kept my eyes on the wash bucket. "She's not home," I answered, lying, and I sent my words, one behind the other, over to the wash bucket, too. Even so, I swayed a little, and that's when the sudden noise came.

Justine's mother, seeing me sway, suddenly let go of her shopping cart, and a bag full of tin cans and jars hit the street like an explosion. My leg faltered, as I had known it would, and I pitched forward a little. The next thing I knew I was on the sidewalk.

"Look what you made me do!" Justine's mother was still shouting. Cans from her cart were rolling down the street, and a broken jar of something gray lay at her feet. Applesauce. "I'm going to tell your mother!" she yelled again, but I knew she never would. She didn't even know who my mother was, and besides, there was nothing to tell because nothing had really happened. The crash of the shopping cart had pushed me like a spring away from the wall and sent me stum-bling across the whole length of the awning. On my *feet!* I hadn't crashed through the canvas. I hadn't fallen to the ground. I hadn't even touched anything with my hands. When I reached the front end of the awning I had jumped down to the car and then to the sidewalk. I had followed the rules. I could be in the club. "Hey, Polly!" I shouted. "I did it! I did it, I did it, I did it! I'm *initiated!* I wrote my name up there and I walked all the way back, no hands! I can be in the club!" I looked around. "Polly?"

"Hey, Mary Ella," Deirdre said. "How did you do that?"

"I don't know," I answered. "Where's Polly?"

"I thought you were going to fall." She sounded disappointed. They were all disappointed; as soon as I landed on the sidewalk they began moving away.

"Me, too," I said, apologizing. "I thought I was going to fall, too. It was an accident, sort of, that I didn't. Where's Polly?" I asked again.

"I don't know. She was here before. I guess she went home."

"Where's that glove you found?" I asked Morton.
"What?"
"You know," I said. "The glove from the cellar."
"The glove?"

"The glove you found in the *cellar!*"

"What?"

"THE GLOVE FROM THE CELLAR SO YOU COULD BE IN POLLY'S CLUB!"

"Oh," he said. "Wo-wo-wo-wo-wo," and he went to the hall closet. "You mean this one?" His voice settled into an overcoat, and in a moment he returned with a glove my father used to wear before he lost its mate. "You mean this?" he asked, handing it to me.

Probably I had known all along that Polly had made that up, about Morton and the cellar. There really was no glove. There was no club either, for Morton or for me. Polly had finally played a trick. Not on Morton, but on me, and I twisted the glove around in my hand for a long while. Then I did something I had never done before. I hit him. I hit Morton with the glove. Its fingers swept through the air and spread out like a real hand, covering his face with their slap. Then they curled into a little fist on the floor.

That was the one time I saw Morton cry.

AUGUST

CHAPTER THIRTY

And then, at last, my mother began to notice, and to mind. "What happened to your forehead?" she asked one afternoon.

"What forehead?"

"Why are you wearing that Band-Aid? What did you do to yourself?"

"Nothing. I just keep it there in case I need it for something. If I kept it in my pocket it would lose its stick."

"Take it off, Mary Ella. It looks ugly."

"I don't care. I like it."

I had been sitting alone on the living-room sofa, arranging my matchbooks in my lap, when she came home from work. "Where's Morton?" she asked next.

"At Polly's."

"Again? Day after day he plays with that girl."

"No, he doesn't," I told her. "He wasn't there Monday."

"Why does she play with him all the time, Mary Ella? She's *your* age."

"No, she's not," I answered. "She's younger."

There was silence for a while, and then, "Why are you just sitting here? Why aren't you doing anything?"

"I am doing something. I'm fixing up my matchbooks. Look," I said, holding one up, "a kangaroo."

"Throw those away, Mary Ella. It's dangerous to keep matches around the house. You could start a fire."

"I'm not collecting the matches. Just the covers. Look at this one. It's of a flower."

"Throw them away. They're dirty. You don't know where they've been."

"Yes, I do. They've been on the street."

"Throw them *away!*" Her voice rose a bit. "We have enough dirty things brought in here from the gutter."

"Some of them are from the sidewalk," I told her. I stood them in a row along the sofa arm. "I'm making a parade."

There was some more silence and then she said, "It isn't wholesome for a girl your age to sit around the house all day, not doing anything."

Our sofa is the kind that's made of plush, and it darkens when you draw your finger along it. I made a thick, fuzzy M alongside my thigh. "I didn't sit around all day," I answered. "I played with Polly in the morning."

"Why don't you spend some time on your writing?" *Your* writing, she always says. "You used to do such nice writing."

"I *am* writing," I answered, drawing the three bars of the E. "See?"

"Stop that, Mary Ella. That's bad for the upholstery. Why don't you write another essay? You wrote that lovely essay about Susan B. Anthony. Why don't you write another one? You could win another prize."

"It was Elizabeth Cady Stanton."

"Mary Ella, what's the *matter* with you? Why are you behaving like this all of a sudden? Spilling your milk and wearing dirty clothes. Letting your nose run. Not doing anything. Making yourself ugly."

"I don't know," I answered. "I don't know why I'm so ugly and everything." I drew another line across the sofa.

"*So* ugly," she corrected. "Don't say 'suh.' It sounds ignorant."

"*So* ugly. But you said once that it didn't matter if I was ugly. You said lots of ugly women get married."

"Stop being *fresh*! And pick your head up. Don't sit that way. You look just like your . . . STOP THAT, MARY ELLA!" I'd never heard her yell before. "You never used to behave like this. What's the matter with you?"

"I don't know," I said again.

I waited for her to say something else, but she just moved off into the hallway, and when I heard her speak at last, it wasn't to me at all. "Nasty brat," she said, or "rat." She was speaking to her listener, and for the first time ever she wasn't telling about Morton.

She was telling about me.

CHAPTER THIRTY-ONE

"Mary Ella?"

My mother had come into my room so quietly her voice made me jump.

"Mary Ella, I want to talk to you." She sat on my bed, which is something she never does. It makes the mattress sag, she says, and it wrinkles the bedspread.

"What about?" My matchbooks were spread all over the floor. I was taking out the doubles to give to Morton, and I was making a parade out of all the rest, standing them up on their edges, like tents, in a careful row against the wall.

"I thought I told you to throw those away. Look how dirty they are."

"I'm giving some of them to Morton. He's going to start a matchbook collection, too. Just like mine. So we can be twins."

"Never mind," she said, which isn't what I expected her to answer. "I didn't come to talk about that," she went on, but she didn't say what she had come to talk about. She just sat on my bed, where no one is supposed to sit, and stared down at my parade.

"Mary Ella," she finally began, "your father and I have been noticing your behavior lately, and we've been very dissatisfied with what we see. You've altered a lot since—since the beginning of the summer."

Since Polly came, is what she meant, and I waited for her to go on.

"So we've decided to . . ." She touched a matchbook with her toe, toppling it.

"To what?"

"To make some changes."

There was silence for a long time.

"Like what?"

"Mary Ella," she began again, "your father and I have given this a lot of thought." That's how she talks when she's about to say something terrible. "Your father," she says, instead of Daddy or Pop, and "We've given this a lot of thought," which means there's no use arguing. "We feel there is such a thing as a bad influence, and we have decided that it is time that you two were separated."

I looked up at her quickly. "Who two?" I asked, although I already knew. Polly was the bad influence. She got me to put a Band-Aid on my forehead when

I didn't need one, and to say "suh" instead of "so." She made me wear dirty clothes and spill my milk at the table. She tricked me into climbing the awning, although I didn't know if my mother knew about that. She made me look ugly. Now we weren't going to be allowed to play together, and I wondered if that meant Morton couldn't play with her anymore, either.

"Morton, too?" I asked.

She looked at me as though she were trying to make out my words. "Stop being fresh, Mary Ella. That's just the kind of behavior I'm talking about."

"I'm not being fresh. Can't Morton play with Polly either?"

"Polly? I'm not talking about Polly. I'm talking about you and Morton." She smoothed the bedspread alongside her lap. "Mary Ella, you are together too much. Your father and I both feel that you should be separated for a while."

Separated? Morton and me? *Separated?* Separated was what happened to kids in school who got into fights and Mr. Healy had to pull them apart. Separated was what happened to Iris and Rhoda when they talked too much in class. Separated was what happened to kids who had friends. "I'll have to separate you," the teacher says, as though they're Siamese twins, and Iris ends up having to sit next to me.

But Morton and I already were separated. We had separate rooms and we went to separate schools. We sat on separate sides of the kitchen table and we even played with Polly at separate times. "How separated?" I asked my mother, but when I looked at her I saw that she was crying—right out there in the open, not in the bathroom in front of the sink—and I suddenly understood what she meant.

She was going to send me away somewhere, to get me away from Morton. Because I gave him dirty stuff for his collections. Because I told him the wrong answers to his arithmetic problems. Because I was fresh and he could become fresh, too. Because I hit him in the face with a glove and made him cry.

Because *I* was the bad influence.

"You need to be apart, Mary Ella. For a little while."

Where would they send me? To a boarding school? To a *reform* school? Somebody on Polly's street had been sent to reform school last year, only they didn't call it that. They called it some kind of home.

"Where?" I asked now. It was the only word that came out of my mouth.

"We've found someplace nice, Mary Ella." She kept saying my name when she spoke to me. "It's a farm."

A farm! A *farm?* I was going to live on a farm with cows and things? With *chickens?* Instead of going to Agnes Daly in the fall I was going to live on some place with a bunch of animals? I gave my matchbook parade a kick with my toe and sent it sprawling across the floor.

"It's a very nice place," my mother went on.

"I don't want to hear about it," I said. "I DON'T WANT TO HEAR ABOUT IT!" I shouted so loud that she drew back on the bed, wrinkling the spread even more.

Each year in June, when Agnes Daly closes for the summer, all the girls buy new autograph books and pass them around for everyone else to sign. Mostly they write little puzzles, with numbers and letters instead of words: "2 SWEET 2 B 4-GOTTEN." Things like that. I made up a puzzle message of my own once, although I never got to put it in anybody's book because nobody asked me to sign. It went "I hope 2 C U in the fall." and I really did hope that, because I never knew in June whether I would return in September.

Each year, I have to wait until the middle of summer to see if I am going to get another scholarship, and some years, even if I do get my scholarship, I'm not sure I'll be going back. The summer after my father had to sell his bookstore there wasn't enough money for all the things the scholarship didn't pay for, and Aunt Sophia had to help. Now she's dead, though, and so I worry every year.

This year especially, because this was the year I most wanted to go back. I was going to be a lower senior, which is what they call a seventh grader at Agnes Daly, and that means lots of privileges. You get to work on the school paper, for one thing, and you get invited to tea once a week with Miss Rice, but best of all, you go to different rooms for some of your classes, instead of staying all day with one teacher, and your gym teacher is a man. Mr. Healy.

I don't know why I love Agnes Daly so much. I don't have any friends there, except for Wanda, and she isn't even in my class. She barely speaks to me, in fact, on the playground or in the lunchroom, and she sometimes even calls me "baby" to her friends, even though I'm a grade ahead of her. She's nice to me only when we're not in school. Also, I think you learn more in public school. Ina and Deirdre know a whole lot of things about geography and grammar that I never heard of, and Justine's arithmetic book is way ahead of ours, but I love Agnes Daly all the same.

I love the uniform and I love the classrooms and I even love Miss Rice and her lectures about the roof over our heads. I love the building, too. It's made of gray stone, and it has turrets and balconies and lots of stairways. It also has a hidden dumbwaiter that leads nowhere.

Joseph discovered the dumbwaiter one day when he came upon its only doorway in a storage closet off the art room. "Look at *this*!" he cried out, and we all left our easels to watch him tug at the small wooden door. Inside was a wooden shelf that moved up and down on ropes through a tower that smelled of old things. "It goes to a secret room," Iris said, and we all caught our breath. "There's a crazy man who lives up there," Rhoda said, "and this is how he gets his food."

We put a note on the dumbwaiter the next day and sent it up into the darkness, scalding our hands on the rope as it whizzed by and chilling our noses with the damp. "Here's a special message!" we shouted into the dark. The note was still on the dumbwaiter when we brought it down the next day, and it contained no reply, but that didn't matter, really. I was just happy knowing that our school had a dumbwaiter that no one had ever seen before, and a crazy man, maybe, who lived in an unseen room.

That's what I love about Agnes Daly, and that's why each summer I hope I won't have to go to P.S. 53, with its bare tile walls and linoleum floors.

Now I wasn't going to go to either one. I was going to a farm.

"When do I go?" I finally asked.

"Go where?" My mother looked into my face.

"To the farm."

"Oh, Mary Ella," and this time her face looked as I'd never seen it look before. As though someone had hit it. "It's not you who's going. It's Morton."

CHAPTER THIRTY-TWO

It was Morton, after all, who was the bad influence.
Not Polly. Not me. Morton.

"You'll get good, wholesome food there," my mother
told him the next day, "and farm-fresh milk. And
you'll learn all about how a farm works. Mrs. Floyd
will teach you how to milk cows and feed chickens,
and you'll get to ride around in a tractor, maybe. It
will be like going to camp, Morton." She made it sound
like some kind of reward or something. "Would you
like that?"

"Yes," Morton said.

"You'll go as soon as summer school is over. In two
weeks. And of course we'll come and visit you whenever we can, and you'll come home for holidays, and
in the meantime we'll write to you and you can write
to us. You'll get lots of mail, Morton. Won't that be
nice?"

I'd never heard her talk to him like that before.

Usually when she wants him to do something he doesn't want to do, she just tells him to do it and he does.

"And there'll be a special school for you to go to, Morton, where the work will be a little easier for you, and there'll be other children your age who also have problems with their schoolwork."

A dumb kids' school.

"And then in January we'll see how you like it, and if you want to stay longer you may."

Two weeks later, all his clothes were set out in little piles on his bed: the Mickey Mouse shirts, the underwear, the socks, the shorts, the pants—all laid out in a big oblong, following the border of his bedspread. "Look, Mary Ella," he said. "Look, Mom. I made a design."

On the pillow were his three bags of collections.

"You can't take those with you," my mother said. "Mrs. Floyd isn't going to want all that junk in her house."

"But I need them," he said.

"No, Morton. There won't be room."

"I'll keep them under my bed."

"No. Find something else to take. Something small."

"What?"

"I don't *know*, Morton. *Find* something. A picture

would be nice," and that evening the bags of collections were back in Morton's closet.

"Morton's going away tomorrow," I said to Polly. We were both lying on the floor, watching the bugs on the ceiling. They were moving in straight, steady lines away from the light bulbs, and they looked like cars seen from a tall building. "He's all packed and everything. My mother's going to take him to the bus tomorrow at six o'clock in the morning." I had to whisper because her grandmother was asleep on the sofa.

"Six o'clock in the morning? That's when the bus leaves? Six o'clock in the morning is still *night*."

"Yeah. It has to leave early because it's a long trip."

"Hey, M. E., let's give him a going-away present," Polly said. "Let's give him those bugs to take with him. They can be his pets. He can put them on his ceiling and he can talk to them at night when everybody else is asleep."

"Polly, he can't do that," I said, but I wondered all the same. Bugs were small. Morton could take them instead of his collections. He could put them on the ceiling, as Polly had said, and talk to them while he lay far away in the dark of a room he had never seen before.

"Okay," I said. "Let's."

Polly brought in a broom from the kitchen and, holding it upside down, swept both bugs into its bristles.

They did have legs after all: short, whiskery threads that thrashed around when we held them upside down in our palms. "Look," Polly said, nudging one with a fingernail. "They're ticklish."

"Who's that?" Polly's grandmother woke up suddenly and turned to us.

"It's me," Polly said.

"No, the other one."

"That's M. E."

"Who?" She sat up slowly.

"Mary Ella. Morton's sister."

"Oh, her. Hello, Mary Ella. It didn't look like you at first, all dressed up like that. You going somewheres, to a party or something?"

"No."

"Then why is your hair combed?"

My hair *was* combed, and I was wearing clean clothes, too. I had started taking baths again, and I wiped my nose when it ran. Also, I had stopped spilling my milk. Maybe, I thought, my parents would decide that Morton wasn't a bad influence on me after all. Maybe they wouldn't send him away.

"What do bugs eat?" Polly asked her grandmother.

"Depends what kind you have. Some eat sweaters. Some eat houses. Some eat behind your ears."

"These." Polly held out her hand.

"What do you want to feed *them* for? They already ate. Look how fat they are."

"We're giving them to Morton for a present," Polly told her. "He's going away tomorrow. To a farm. To live."

"A bug farm?"

"No, Grandma. A farm with cows and chickens. I told you that already. What do these bugs eat?"

Her grandmother poked at them with a finger. "Gingersnaps," she said. "Gingersnaps is what they like. Lots of spice."

Polly punched some holes in an empty Jell-O box and dropped the bugs into it, along with some gingersnap crumbs. "Maybe they're the kind of bugs that carry messages," she said. "You know? You tie a note on their leg and they fly home with it? Morton could send us special messages and stuff."

"That's pigeons. And anyway, these bugs can't fly."

"Crawl, then."

Morton wasn't home from summer school when we got back to my apartment, and we stood in the doorway of his empty room for a while, holding on to the Jell-O box and looking at the suitcase that lay open on his bed. It was all packed now, and the clothes made a smooth mound, like somebody's stomach, under a Snoopy shirt. His school shoes lay on the floor, one upside down, one on its side, trailing their laces behind them.

"Let's put the bug box on top of his clothes," I said, "so he'll see it as soon as he comes in," but Polly didn't seem to hear. She was walking around his room, picking things up, putting them down again. Looking for something. In another moment she was on her hands and knees, sliding Morton's train box out from under his bed.

"What are you doing?" I demanded. The lid was off now and I stared into the box. All the train cars were tucked into their special cutouts, except for the coal car, whose space lay empty and full of shadow.

"Let's take the bugs for a ride," she said. "We'll get them used to traveling so they won't throw up tomorrow in the bus, like I did." She lifted out a red boxcar from the train box and slid open its door. "Let's put them in here. What's that mean, C & O?"

"Chesapeake & Ohio."

"Okay, that'll be their names. This one is Chesapeake," she said, dropping one of the bugs inside, "and this one's Ohio." She closed the little door and wheeled the car back and forth across the floor.

Someone across the courtyard was listening to a ball

game, and a cheer suddenly floated from a window and into Morton's room. "That was a home run," Polly said. "Everybody yells like that when there's a home run, even when it's not their team. It makes them happy, like it's their own home and somebody's come back to it, all safe."

"Yeah," I answered, but I really wasn't listening much. "Polly," I said, and I asked something I had been wanting to ask for two weeks. "Are you sorry Morton is going away? Will you miss him?"

"Me? No. I never miss anybody."

Not even me? I wanted to ask. Would you miss me, if I had to go away? Instead, I said, "Not even your mother? Or your sister?"

"No." She opened the boxcar door again and looked in. "Hey, Chesapeake's doing exercises in there. Look, M. E., he's lying on his back and making his feet move up and down."

"Do they miss you?" I persisted. "Do they write to you?"

"Sometimes. They moved to a new place. My sister has to go to a new school. You know what? Where they live now it's an hour earlier than it is here."

"That's how far away they live?"

"Yeah. Anything that happens here, it doesn't happen there until an hour later. Like that home run. Where my mother lives, it won't happen for another hour, because it's only a quarter till four there," she said, looking at Morton's clock, "instead of a quarter till five."

"Polly, that's dumb. That's really dumb. That home run has already been *made*."

"Not where my mother lives. It has to wait another hour. Also, sometimes it isn't even today there. It's still yesterday."

And then suddenly, something she had just said made me stop still. "Polly," I whispered. "It's a quarter to five? A quarter to *five*?" I stared at her awhile. "Where's Morton? How come he's not home?"

CHAPTER THIRTY-THREE

We tried the movie theater first. After that we went to the candy store and the five-and-ten and the barbershop. Places he never goes, but I couldn't think of where he *did* go. Finally, we went to his school, looking into doorways along the way, and asking kids if they had seen him. I felt funny telling them that he was missing again, scaring them for nothing, like the last time, and so I pretended that he wasn't missing at all; we were just looking for him.

Ina thought she had seen him, but she couldn't remember where, and anyway she wasn't sure if it was yesterday or today. Franklin saw him right then. "There," he said, pointing to a small figure two blocks away, but it turned out to be somebody else. A small old man.

The school building was quiet and still, like those photographs of famous monuments where, mysteriously, nobody is in sight, even though it's daytime. I knew from a block away that the doors would all be locked and the windows closed tight. Polly and I stood at the bottom of the steps a long while, looking into their silence. A name had been spray-painted near the door: RODNEY, it said, in white letters all crowded together and puffed out like pillows. Polly ran up the stairs to write LOVES POLLY under it with her chalk, and then she surrounded both names with a heart. She stepped back and smiled at the door. "Look, M. E.," she said. "He loves me. Rodney loves me."

"Polly, where *is* he?"

"I don't know. I've never even met him."

"No, I mean Morton. Where did he *go?*"

"Morton? I don't know. Somewhere. He's getting something, probably."

"Where were you?" My mother was waiting for me in the doorway. She was wearing the slippers she puts on sometimes when she comes home, and her hair was wet with sweat. She looked messy. "I wanted Morton home early today so he could get ready. Where is he?"

"I don't know," I answered. "He didn't come home from school." The words, coming suddenly into my ears, made my head shiver. "Polly and I just came back from looking for him," I added, so she would know it wasn't my fault. "We went to his school and the movies and everything."

"He didn't come home from school?" I don't think she heard what I'd just said.

"No." And then I said, "He's probably hiding someplace. He does that. Remember that time?" He *had* hidden once—behind a tree in the park while we were all sitting on the grass. After a while he came out and said, "Surprise!" but none of us had noticed he'd been away.

"Hiding! Hiding from what?"

"I don't know. Maybe he felt like it," and suddenly I began to believe that myself. "Maybe he doesn't want to go to the farm tomorrow."

She didn't seem to hear that, either, and in the next moment she was out the door. She was still wearing her slippers.

Maybe he was hiding right there in the apartment, behind a door somewhere, in a closet, in *his* closet. "Morton?" I called into the hall. "Morton?" I said into his room. "I know you're there," I whispered into his closet door, just as I do when I'm "It" in hide-and-seek: *I know you're there*, I say through a door, and the next moment, among a tangle of clothes and shoes, I see the arms and legs and face of someone I know.

I pulled on the knob. Morton's three bags of collections stood on the floor, one beside the other, and a little puff of dust scurried by. Otherwise, the closet was empty. His clothes had all been packed away.

I walked back into the kitchen and stared into the courtyard. "Morton?" I called, blowing his name through the window screen. "Morton?" although I knew he wasn't there. Who would hide in the courtyard, where everyone could see?

Dinner was already cooking and something from a pot sent down trickles that sizzled on the stove. I lifted the lid and looked inside. Chili. We never had chili in the summer, but that was Morton's favorite supper. Maybe my mother was making it just for him, because it was his last night home, and I wondered if she was sorry he was going away.

I stirred the pot awhile with a spoon, and suddenly I knew Morton would come back. If his dinner was there, then *he* would be there, too, to eat it. He was coming up the sidewalk right now, in fact, with my mother. She was a little ahead, hurrying in her slippers, and he was sliding his shoes along behind her. Past the fire hydrant, past one doorway, past another, another, another. Now they were at the awning, and my mother was getting out her key. I counted their steps across the lobby floor and then up the first flight of stairs, the second, the third. They were coming to our own door now, and I waited for the key in the lock. When I didn't hear it, when I didn't hear anything at all, I started them again from the sidewalk, farther back this time.

I'll set the table, I decided. I'll set the table for Morton and everybody, and I'll set it very slowly—fork by fork and spoon by spoon—and as soon as I'm through they'll be back. "You were right," my mother would say. "He was hiding." Morton would be pale from staying in the dark so long, and his clothes would be wrinkled. He'd look at me on his way to the bathroom. "Mom still has her slippers on," he'd say. Maybe later, when we were all at the table, we would laugh, the way I do sometimes when I'm scared about something, and then I'm not anymore.

I set Morton's place at the table very carefully, running my finger an extra time along the crease in his napkin and then resting a fork in its exact center. Next to that I put his dinner plate, turning it so that the big flower on the border was where the twelve would be if it were a clock, and I set his milk glass right above that. I set all the other places, too, nicely. Then, the moment I put down the last glass, the door opened, just as I knew it would, and someone came in.

"Where is everybody?" It was my father. "Why are you here alone?"

"I'm setting the table," I said, "while Mom gets Morton. He's hiding."

"Hiding!" He looked into my face, at my mother's empty chair, at Morton's. "What do you mean, hiding?"

"He does that sometimes," I said. "Remember that day in the park?"

"Where is he? Hiding where?"

"I'm not sure. Somewhere. Mom went to find him."

"How long has he been gone? When did he leave?"

"I don't know." And then, "He didn't come home from school." And because the words didn't come out at first, I ended up saying them too loud, shouting them, almost.

"He didn't come home from school? Where *is* he? Why didn't you call me? Why didn't you call the police?"

The police! The word made something squeeze the sides of my head.

"Why didn't you?"

"I don't know." I didn't want to tell him I hadn't noticed until a quarter to five that Morton was late coming home from school. "He's just hiding," I said. "Mom's bringing him back. His place is all set at the table and everything, and his supper is waiting."

My father walked through the living room and into

Morton's room. "His shoes are here," he called out. "How did his shoes get here if he didn't come home from school?"

"His shoes?" I asked, following him.

"What are his shoes doing here?" He was shouting now, and he looked angry.

I looked at the two brown shoes, the ones Morton wore to school every day, with the scratches at the toe, and the laces that came untied all the time.

"I guess he took them off," I said, and I bent down to line them up neatly, one beside the other, and tuck their laces inside. "He just put them here after he took them off," I said, looking up at my father, who was pulling at his hair now.

And then the front door opened and my mother came in. Alone. She looked at us both without speaking.

"His shoes are here," my father said.

"His shoes?" My mother stared down at the floor. "Who put his shoes here?"

"*He* did," my father shouted. "Who else? He came home after school and he took his shoes off. Then he went out again."

"But where would he go without his shoes?"

"NOWHERE!" I had never heard my father shout like that before. "He put on some *other* shoes."

"What other shoes?"

"How should I know? How many pairs of shoes does he have? Sneakers or something."

"But why would he do that?" She was beginning to shout now too.

"I DON'T KNOW!"

It was a long time before I finally spoke, and when I did it was in a whisper. "I know," I said, not looking at either of them. "I know where he is," and I ran past them out the door.

I had known all along.

I, too, had seen his shoes. I had seen them when I first entered his room with Polly, and all afternoon, walking with her to the movie theater, to the five-and-ten, to the barbershop, to the school, I knew somewhere inside my head or my stomach or wherever it is that you know things like that, that Morton had gone up to the roof in his sneakers so he could climb over the wall. Polly had been right—he had gone to get something. He had gone to get his train car so he could take it with him to the farm. Instead of his collections.

I stood still a moment and tried to catch my breath before I reached the top step. It was twilight by then, and the sun, deep orange now and flat, shone through the open door. It rested on top of the far wall like a coin on edge. With one finger I could have sent it rolling to the corner and crashing over the side.

The floor glowed orange in the light, and ripples I had never seen made shadows on the tar. Chimney pipes made shadows, too—long black shadows, flat as paint. I stood a long moment in the doorway, looking at the sun, at the shadows, at the ripples on the floor. *I know you're there!* I whispered to myself. *I know you're there!* I said when at last I sank my foot into the warm orange tar. *I know you're there!* when I edged very slowly to the wall on my left. "I know you're there!" I shouted as I reached the edge of the roof, and there he was.

CHAPTER THIRTY-FOUR

What is it like, I wondered, to be unconscious? "What's it like?" I asked the nurse. "Does he know I'm here? Can he hear me? Can he feel my hand?" I pushed aside his hospital gown and pressed a dent into his shoulder, as though it were a lump of clay. "Can he feel that?"

"It's like being asleep," she answered—but it's not. When you're asleep and someone presses a dent in your shoulder, you open your eyes, and when someone calls your name you answer "What?"

When you're asleep you wake up.

"Does he dream?" I asked. "If it's like being asleep, does he have dreams? Is he dreaming now?" Was he? I wondered. Was there, behind his closed eyelids, a whole crowd of things making a story he could watch? Did the sounds of the room—the rattle of bottles in the tray beside his bed, the rustle of my clothes as I walked across the floor—occur inside his dream as something else: bottle caps or trains or sailboats on a lake?

"Morton," I said aloud, "it's me. Mary Ella," and I wondered if, in his dream, my words became those of someone else—a beautiful lady, maybe. "Here's some pretty flowers," I said for her, and I fluttered my fingers at his face. "They're for you," and I waited for the figure in the dream behind his lids to press a bowl of roses to his nose.

Or did he dream, instead, about his fall? Did he, as he lay there so still, watch the accident happen over and over again? Did the rattles and the rustles in the room become the wings of startled pigeons and the sound of his very own scream?

"Morton?" I reached out and touched his lashes, and then I did a crazy thing. "Let me watch with you," I said, and I lifted up his lids so I could look inside, so I could see, with him, that afternoon on the rooftop when he tried to get his coal car and he toppled from the wall.

"Look out!" the nurse cried. "What are you doing?" and I dropped my hand.

"Does he dream?" I asked.

"Don't do that to him."

"Does he?" I insisted.

"We don't know," she finally answered. "Probably not."

What was it *like*? What was it like not to know that it was day, that it was night? That the sun was on your face, that it wasn't? That sometimes a man in orange coveralls hung outside your window and wiped it with a cloth?

I thought all at once of the princess in that fairy tale, the one who snagged her thumb on a spindle or something and went to sleep for a hundred years. A hundred *years* she lay asleep! while everything around her stirred and changed. Vines, for instance. Long vines, like quiet thieves, crept under all the window-panes, entering rooms where they had never been allowed, fingering things that weren't theirs. And trees. Trees grew where there had been no trees at all, making new shadows on the floor and dropping leaves on doorsills that had till then been bare. Cobwebs, too—sticky threads ran here and there, weaving cat's cradles from wall to wall and across the arms of the chairs. And all the time the princess slept. Slept, slept, slept, with the spindle at her side, the thumb blood on its tip no longer red.

"Hey, Morton," I said from the window. "Guess what! It's raining outside," I told him, so that maybe, if he heard me, he would know. So he wouldn't be like the princess. "It's raining really hard and there's a whole bunch of cars down there on the street. There's a big traffic jam or something and everybody's honking their horns and there's this cop waving his arms around like a maniac and blowing his whistle."

And then I thought of something else about that princess.

I had never kissed Morton before, although people were always urging me to. "How about a big birthday kiss?" they would say as somebody posed us for a photograph. Or, "Aren't you going to kiss your brother good-bye?" when my class went on a week-long trip. Who would want to kiss *him*? I'd never even kissed him with an X on the bottom of a birthday card. If I gave him a birthday card at all.

Still, it had worked on the princess, and so I pushed my lips out as though I were sucking on an egg, and I slowly lowered my face over his. "That was a kiss," I told him, so he would know, and I stepped back, licking off the taste of his skin. A small, moist circle clung to his forehead, and I watched it fade.

Then I waited to see if, like the princess, he would wake up.

CHAPTER THIRTY-FIVE

So the make-believe game—the *good* make-believe game—that came true in the end was not Blondie or First Lady or movie star or rich girl.

It was Easter egg, where I played I was a bunny in a bright plaster room. But it didn't come true the way I played it.

My mother and my father and I all got to sit around a little table, like the rabbits in the game, and we each were given little colored eggs. Sort of colored eggs. There were pictures all around us, too, as there were inside the egg, and my father, like the father rabbit, reached into his pocket every evening for a coin.

But the table was in a hospital waiting room with fluorescent pipes along the ceiling, not in an egg with a porthole full of light, and the walls were hung with posters from the zoo. My father took a quarter from his pocket, not a coin with a rabbit on its face, and the little colored eggs were M&M's. Still, though, there were only three of us, and when we got up to leave at seven-thirty each night, we would walk out together, side by side, like the three rabbits in the egg—a mother, a father, and one child.

Every evening was the same. My parents and I would get to the hospital—a big hospital, not the one where my mother works—and wait downstairs in the lobby until a bell rang and visitors could see the patients. We would sit in the same places—on three pink chairs around a table that sometimes had magazines on it, sometimes not. If it did, I would turn the pages one after the other and not read anything. After a while my father would get up and walk over to the candy machine. He would study all the packages in their little windows, as though he were trying to make up his mind, but in the end he always pulled the same plunger and a bag of M&M's would drop into the tray.

Then my mother would get up and look at the zoo posters, moving slowly from one to the other and studying their scenes as though they were famous paintings and she'd never seen them before.

Morton was allowed only two visitors at a time, and at seven o'clock, when the bell rang, my parents would go up in the elevator together while I ate my M&M's one by one, green first, yellow last. I'd hold each one between two fingers, licking its hard shell and feeling the color come off on my tongue. When I got down to the chocolate, I'd float it carefully in my mouth, not moving it at all, so it would keep a long time. The yellow one would just be turning sticky and warm when my parents would come out of the elevator and it would be my turn to go upstairs.

Always when I entered his room, I'd say the same thing: "Hello? Hello, Morton?" as though he were far away and I were speaking to him on the phone. Then I'd sit in the chair beside his bed and watch him breathe. His face was the only part of his body that I could see, although his feet and knees made cones beneath the spread. An upside-down bottle dripped something through a tube, but I couldn't tell where it went. I'd sit there for about five minutes, staring at Morton, staring at the tube, staring at the labels on the bottles next to his bed. I'd pick out a word from one of them—"sterile," maybe—and make little words from its letters: list, tire, tile, else, steel, trile. I played a game—if I could make six words or more, then Morton would wake up. Trile probably wasn't a real word, but I let it count anyway.

A television set, mounted on a shelf near the ceiling, tilted its black, blank screen toward Morton's bed. I would stare at it a long time, pretending that the figures deep inside its glass were the brother and sister in a family show and not just the reflections of Morton and of me.

Then, after another five minutes—ten, maybe—I'd get up and walk to the window. Two stone birds were carved into the corners of the building across the street, and I'd watch them as though they were real. Their wings were spread wide, and their claws were pulled up against their chests. In another moment they would maybe fly away.

If you touch stone, you'll turn to stone. Wanda used to say that, and I imagined now that long ago two real birds had flown by mistake into that big stone wall and been frozen into its corners ever since. Now and then a pigeon would approach, and I would wave my hands to warn it off.

When visiting hours were over, I'd say good-bye to Morton. "Good-bye," I'd say out loud, and I'd keep my hands behind my back as though he, too, were made of stone, and by touching him I'd harden like a statue on the floor. "Good-bye. I hope you feel better," which was a dumb thing to say, because he didn't feel anything at all. Then I'd go back down in the elevator.

Once, returning to the waiting room, I saw two old people in the pink plastic chairs where my parents had been sitting before, and I stopped still. Then I saw that they *were* my parents, looking old, looking worried and scared, and I wondered something: Were they secretly glad, I wondered, that such a terrible thing had happened to Morton, so that at last they could love him and want him to live?

CHAPTER THIRTY-SIX

"Don't stare," my mother said, and I snapped my eyes straight ahead. We were walking through the hospital corridor and I had been looking into rooms at all the people in their beds. It was Thursday, my mother's day off, and we had come, just the two of us, to see Morton.

Four more doors and we would be at his room. I closed my eyes for a moment and pretended something: When we reached his door we would find him wide awake. He'd be sitting up in bed, with his knees bent into a hill and his eyes all the way open. He'd be staring into the blank television screen high up on the wall, and the first face he'd see after his long sleep would be his own; he would think, maybe, that it belonged to someone else—someone in a show.

I pretended something else: When he woke up he wouldn't be dumb anymore. He'd be smart. The fall would have unclogged something in his head, the way kicking a broken toy makes it run again, and he'd understand all his arithmetic and spelling. He'd get promoted to eighth grade when he went back to school, or to ninth or tenth, and he'd look different, too. When the girls at Agnes Daly asked me if my brother was cute, I'd say yes he was.

"Will he be different when he wakes up?" I asked my mother.

"How different?"

"I don't know. His brain, I mean. Will it be different?"

"Damaged, you mean? No, Mary Ella. Don't worry about that. The doctor says he'll be just the same as before."

"No, I meant . . . Oh, that's good," I said. "That's good, he'll be the same."

Somebody with a stethoscope hanging out of her pocket bumped my shoulder and hurried along the corridor. Then a whole bunch of people in white clothes ran by, going somewhere. Something was happening at the end of the hall; carts rattled and uniforms swished. Somebody shouted; I couldn't tell who. Maybe somebody had died in one of those rooms. Maybe somebody had died just that minute. People did die here. Only the day before, some doctors had come out of a room very slowly and closed the door behind them, holding the knob all the time so it made no noise at all. I twisted my neck now to make sure Morton's door was open.

Someone had moved him in his bed; he was lying on his side, not on his back, but his eyes were still tight shut. If he did wake up, the two stone birds across the way would be the first faces he would see.

I walked to the window and looked out. They were really pretty ugly, those birds. Their heads jutted out on long stone necks and their beaks hung down like hooks. What were they doing there, anyway, far, far up from the street, where no one but me could see?

"What did he *do* it for?" my mother asked from somewhere in the room. She was speaking to her listener, who had followed her through the door and settled on the wall. "What *for?*"

"To get his coal car back," I answered into the window. "It was on that other roof where it fell."

I had already told her that.

I had told her a million times.

I had told my father.

I had told the policeman when he came to our apartment the morning after the accident. "He was trying to get this train car back from where it fell on the next-door roof," I had told him that day.

No policeman had ever been in our house before,

and I gasped when I saw him at the kitchen table, all that blue filling the room. Before then, I had never even spoken to a policeman. Not aloud, anyway. I spoke to them all the time, though, in my head. *See how good I am,* I would say as I passed one on the street, and I would straighten my spine and make my face look nice. *See how I'm not stealing anything or crossing on a red light or writing bad words on walls,* and I would feel his eyes on me, liking me because I was good.

"Come in, Mary Ella," my mother had said, although I already was in. She was sitting across from the policeman, and she looked small. My father was there, too, leaning against the refrigerator door. Standing while the policeman sat. "The officer wants to ask you some questions." Officer.

I looked at him again. He was too big for the table, too big for the room, and anyway, he didn't belong in our apartment at all. He belonged outside, with cars and trucks and sidewalks, not among our dishes and cups and the little glass prism throwing rainbows on the floor. Still, I smoothed my hair back when he told me to sit down, and I pressed my knees together, and my ankles, too, the way I do when I talk to Miss Rice in her office and I want her to think I'm nice.

A thick notebook lay on the table and he smoothed

a page with the flat of his hand. "Did he always play on the roof?" he asked.

"Just that once," I told him. "The second time he wasn't playing."

"Never," my mother said. "They weren't allowed up there."

The policeman leaned over and wrote something down. Which answer, I wondered, did he pick? He looked as though he was doing schoolwork, with his forehead pressed into his hand, and once he raised his eyes to the ceiling, trying to remember the spelling of a word.

"How did the object fall?" he asked.

"The object?" I thought he meant Morton.

"The toy."

"It just fell," I told him. That's the kind of answer grown-ups hate, so I went on, wanting him to like me, to like my answers. "We were playing this game," I said, "and it fell, but not the same day Morton fell. At the beginning of the summer. When he fell he was all by himself."

"Where is the object now?" and again I thought he meant Morton.

"It's still there," I finally told him.

"It was a very expensive train," my mother added, and the policeman wrote something down then, too.

"They took an expensive toy up to the roof and threw it over the side," she went on, but she wasn't speaking to him anymore. She was speaking to her listener on the clock.

"We didn't throw it, Mom. It *fell*. We were playing that the wall was the track and there was something up ahead that the coal car bumped into. A cow," I added, and the policeman wrote something else in his book. Maybe about the cow. "And then he wanted it back. To take to the farm, because he couldn't take his collections."

At that time, that's what I really thought.

"What collections?" my mother asked.

"In those bags. Those paper things that he kept, and the bottle caps. His plastic spoons."

The policeman kept writing in his notebook, even though we weren't talking to him anymore.

"Those? That's ridiculous, Mary Ella. He didn't want to take that with him. That's just junk. He understood all that. I'd already explained to him that Mrs. Floyd wouldn't have tolerated it in her house. No other mother would."

I thought she was going to tell about how any other mother would have thrown all that stuff into the trash can, and the policeman would write that down, too, but she didn't.

"It makes no sense," she said, and my father leaned on his other foot.

He hadn't said anything the whole time.

"It makes no sense," my mother said in Morton's hospital room. "Why would he take an expensive toy up to a place like that and just throw it over the wall?"

I turned around now to look at her. "Mom," I said, "it wasn't his idea to go up there and put the train on the wall. It was Polly's. And he didn't make it fall. She did."

I hadn't told her that before, because I knew what she would answer. In fact, she answered it now. "That's why he did it? Because somebody told him to? Somebody told him to take an expensive toy like that up to the roof and drop it over the edge, and he did?" And then she asked the other thing I was afraid she would ask. "What else did he do because somebody told him to? Climb over the wall and try to get it back?"

It was a long time before I said anything.

"Yes,'" I finally answered. "Yes, he did."

CHAPTER THIRTY-SEVEN

I had found that out myself only the day before, and I hadn't meant to tell it to my mother at all.

I had found it out because I'd gone back up to the roof, which was another thing I didn't want my mother to know about, and it was Polly herself who had told me.

I'd gone up there to see the coal car, to say good-bye to it or something, or hello; I'm not sure which. *I'll go there just this once*, I'd said to myself, *and never again*, although I wasn't sure of that, either.

It had rained that morning, and flat black pools lay scattered on the tar. In one I could see, for just a moment, the white-and-purple wings of a pigeon over-head; in another the edges of a cloud. I touched the cloud with my toe and made it wobble.

Everything looked as it had the very first day I'd gone up: the chimney pipes, the antennas, the drying shirts that dangled like a stretch of paper cutouts from the line. The pigeons.

But the sun was high in the sky and the chimneys made no shadows on the tar. Also, something smelled funny. Paint, maybe, or that stuff they clean the bathrooms with in school. It nipped at the corners of my eyes, and its taste slid down my throat like a cough drop. Another thing: An empty stretch of rope, brandnew, was coiled around the crosspiece of the clothesline frame. I took it down and carried it to the wall.

The coal car lay upside down in a puddle, like a tiny shipwreck, so dark it made no image in the water. I couldn't even find it right away.

"Hey," I said, swinging the rope out to it. "Hey, wake up," as though, like Morton, it had settled into some strange, deep sleep.

I swung the rope out a few times more, and then, all at once, I felt it touch. The kiss of rope on plastic traveled like electricity into my hand and I jumped back. At the same moment a voice spoke behind me— "What smells up here?"—and I whirled around. "It smells like needles in your nose."

It was Polly.

That was the first time I'd seen her since the accident. I didn't know where she'd been all that time, and no one on the block knew, either. "I think she ran away," Deirdre said, and Ezra said she was in jail.

I wasn't sure I wanted to see her at all. I liked being up there all alone, just me and the coal car. Anyway, I couldn't think of anything to say. I didn't want to talk about Morton, but I didn't want to *not* talk about him, either.

"What are you doing here?" I finally asked.

"I don't know. What are you?"

"Nothing," I said. "Looking."

"Me too," and that's all we said for a long time.

A small puddle of rain had collected in the little hollow between the coal car's wheels, and it shimmered like dew. "Look," Polly said. "You can see its underneath."

"Yeah," I answered, and that was how we finally talked about Morton.

She bunched her fingers together after that and ran them along the top of the ledge. *"Rum-rum-rum,"* she said.

"Rum-rum-rum," I said, too, making a finger-car of my own and sliding it along after hers.

Rum-rum-rum, and together the two cars ran back and forth along their single track, smoothly, not bumping into each other, not crashing into cows, not flying over the side.

"Last stop!" Polly walked her finger-car into the air and puffed it away.

After that we just stood there side by side, leaning over the wall as though it were the railing of a boat and the tar a stretch of sea.

A small flock of pigeons tumbled down from somewhere and arranged themselves in a crooked row, a foot or so from the coal car. "Hey, look, M. E.," Polly said, pointing down at them. "Look at those pigeons. They're going to *sing* for us. They're all lined up, like on a stage in school, and we're the mothers who came to watch. They're going to sing 'My Country, 'Tis of Thee.' " She said "Tizzathee," like kids in kindergarten. "Which one do you want to be yours, M. E.?"

"I don't know. Maybe that one, with the neck that turns green and purple."

"Mine's the gray one on the end."

"That one?" I said, looking. She had picked a pigeon that had no colors on it at all—no stripes, no bands, no green-and-purple shimmer on its neck. All it was was a plain gray bird. "How come you want *that?*"

"I like the way it walks. It's wearing this gray cloak thing that's all tight around its ankles, and it has to take these little steps." She showed me with two fingers how it walked.

It did walk that way, sort of, but still I wondered. What was so great about that? And I wondered once again about Polly. Was she dumb or crazy or what?

How come she picked the ugliest bird in the row to be her own?

"I'm magic," she said, and I wondered if I had spoken aloud.

"What?"

"I can make pigeons do whatever I want. Watch. *Dance!*" she shouted down at them, and they all bounced off the ground. "See?"

We stood there for a long time, watching the pigeons, not saying much, and then suddenly I asked something. "Polly, remember when we were playing bug race and I told you about this kid I knew who said that make-believe games came true?"

"No."

"She said someone inside you listens to bad wishes in your head and makes them happen?"

"So what about her?"

"Well, she was right, sort of. I used to play this game a lot, just for fun, and then it came true, but all wrong."

"What game? You mean bug race?"

"No, not that kind. The kind you make up. In your head."

"You played bug race in your head?"

"*No!*" Why didn't she ever understand anything I said? "I made something *up*. And later it came true."

"That's dumb. Nothing comes true. Things just happen, no matter what. Hey, look now, M. E. The gray pigeon is bowing. It's *bowing.* The others all forgot to do that, but mine didn't. Come on, M. E. Clap for it. *Clap.*"

Things just happen, no matter what. I tightened my ears, so the words would stick inside my head and not leak out, and I touched Polly's hand for an instant so that what she had just said would stick to my skin, too, and keep.

"Clap!" she said again, but I didn't—I was still thinking about what she'd said. "What did you make up?" she asked after a while.

"Something." And then I told her. "I made up that I lived with a mother and a father all by myself. Without a sister or a brother or anything. And now that's true, sort of."

"That's dumb. How could somebody fit inside your head? And besides, if they did that for everybody, then all the wishes would get mixed up." Suddenly, for the first time ever, she seemed almost smart. "Like, suppose *I* played that I lived with you and Morton, and *you* played that you lived with me and my grandmother. How could they make both wishes come true?" and she gave me a smile she sometimes had, where her lips stretched out wide, like a string of gum, and her eyebrows disappeared beneath her hair.

I loved her then. I loved the way she looked and I

loved the way she smiled and I loved the way she thought it was dumb that make-believe games came true.

"Let's see that," she said, taking the rope from my hand.

"Don't throw it over," I warned her, "like last time."

"I didn't throw it over last time. It jumped. It was an acrobat. This one's a snake." She wriggled the rope along the wall. "It's a poisonous snake and it could bite my hand, but it won't, because I'm magic. I'm a snake charmer, and all's I have to do is stare into its eyes and it will go to sleep. Go to sleep, you," she shouted down the wall. "SLEEP!"

The row of pigeons suddenly took flight above our heads, holding their wings straight out and sweeping around, going nowhere, looking like the kids in Interpretive Dance when they're supposed to be airplanes. "Look," Polly said, raising her head to watch them. "They're going crazy. They probably smell that stuff and they can't hold their noses because their feet won't reach. What *is* that smell, anyway?"

"I don't know," I said. "Polly, do you think we can get it back, the coal car? With the rope?"

"No. Anyway, it's not a rope. It's a snake. Come on, snake, give me a kiss," and she rubbed the fuzzy end against her mouth. "Hey, look, M. E." She was leaning far, far over the wall now, and suddenly she stopped swinging the rope. "Look! *That's* what that smell is: *paint.* On that ladder there. Orange paint. I knew it smelled orange. Orange always smells like needles."

"What ladder?" I leaned far over, too. So far over, my toes lifted off the ground and my hands slid out along the wall. "I don't see a ladder." But then I did.

CHAPTER THIRTY-EIGHT

Fastened against the wall and sticky still with bright orange paint was a row of iron rungs. It was a fire escape ladder, and it led from our roof to the rooftop down below.

"Hey," Polly said. "Where did that come from?"

I didn't answer her for a long time. "It didn't come from anywhere," I finally whispered. "It was there all the time. Attached to the wall."

"It was? That ladder?"

"Polly, it wasn't orange then. That's why we didn't see it." Even the ambulance men had missed it. The roof was dark when they had arrived, and they had used a ladder made of rope.

"What color was it then? Purple?"

"*No.* It was no color. It was—I don't know. Polly," and my face felt suddenly hot. "He could have gone down that ladder!"

"They should have painted it purple. A purple lad-der. My favorite color."

"Polly!" I repeated. *"He could have climbed down that ladder!"*

"Yeah," she said. "Like this. Watch." She flung her leg over the wall and lowered herself backward down the orange steps.

"POLLY! HE COULD HAVE DONE THAT, TOO!"

"Yeah. Hey, it's still wet!" and she held out a hand stained orange on the palm. "Look! It's like mud. Orange mud. Look at *this*." She pressed both hands against the tar floor to make two perfect prints. "You know what, M. E.? We can have another club. You can be the president of this one and I can be initiated. First I have to climb down here and then I have to leave a picture of my hand on the floor. Then I have to get the coal car," she added, walking over to the puddle.

"Don't touch it!" I yelled, and she turned to look up at me. "You'll get paint on it!"

"No, I won't," and she rubbed her hands, as I knew she would, on her skirt.

Our foreheads nearly touched as we both peered down at the coal car huddled like a bird in the creases of her hand.

"Look, M. E.," she said, rocking it back and forth. "Look at the yellow. It's gray. And the red cat is brown," but I didn't speak at all. I didn't even breathe, as though the smallest stirring of air would make it lift its wings and fly away. In a little while I would hold it myself, enclosing it in my own hands like a pet mouse, and I would carry it downstairs to the box in Morton's room. I would fit it into its own special cutout and I would say, "Look who's back," to all the rest of the cars. It would wait there for Morton to wake up so he could finally take it with him to the farm, instead of the bugs. Instead of his collections. For now, though, I didn't want to touch it at all.

"The wheels don't go," Polly said, rubbing them against her thumb. "Still, it will make a good going-away present."

"Yeah, well, he won't be going away now for a while."

"Who won't?"

"Morton. He has to get better first and everything."

"I don't mean Morton. I mean *me*. *I'm* going away."

At first I thought she meant—I don't know what I thought she meant. That she was going to camp, maybe. Fresh-air camp, or she was going to visit someone. "Where are you going?"

"Back home."

"Where back home? You mean to your grandma's?"

"No. *Home* home. To my mother's."

"To your mother's? That far? Where it's yesterday sometimes? That's where?" I couldn't believe her. "When are you coming back?"

"I'm not."

"But I thought she didn't have enough money. I thought she liked your sister best. I thought you were going to stay here." And be my best friend, I wanted to say.

"Yeah, well, I'm not." She looked down once more at the coal car in her hand. "Hey, you know what, M. E.? I could fix this up, maybe, and then it could go places. All's I have to do is teach it to turn its wheels again. It forgot how, is all. Then when I make it better, it can go all over. It can go to Africa. Or Australia."

"Polly." I reached my hand out and held it open. "Let me have it now. It's Morton's coal car."

"No, it's not. It's mine. He said I could have it."

"Come on, Polly."

"He did."

"He did not. He can't even talk."

"No, *before* that, he said I could. Before he fell."

"When before?" I stared at her. "*Just* before? Polly, were you there when he fell? WERE YOU?"

She stared back. "No. How could I be? I was with you. Getting the bugs ready. Remember?"

"When, then? When did he say that?"

"I don't know. The day before, probably. The day before he fell. He said I could have it if I wanted it."

"He did not, Polly. He wanted it for himself. So he could take it with him to the farm. Instead of his collections. That's why he tried to get it."

"Oh, M. E. That's not why."

"Then why? Why did he? WHY?"

"Because I told him to."

A cloud covered the sun just then, and everything turned gray: Polly's face, her hands, the row of drying shirts, everything that should have been white. "Polly," I said, and my voice came out in a whisper. "All that afternoon, when we were waiting for him to come home from school, and then when we walked through the streets looking for him—at the movies and everywhere—did you know all along that he had gone to the roof to get the coal car? *Did* you?"

"Yeah," she said. "I didn't know he fell, though. I thought he was waiting somewhere. To surprise me."

CHAPTER THIRTY-NINE

"Polly told him to climb down that wall?" My mother stared at me. "And he did? Because she told him to?" She looked away from me now and said what I was waiting for her to say: "He would," she said to her listener on the wall. "He *would*."

For a while there was a great silence, and then suddenly the whole room was filled with the sound of a voice. Mine. "That's not true!" I yelled. "That's not true what you said—that he would. *I* would, too." I moved forward and my words shot out into her face across Morton's bed. "It could be *me* lying here, not him. It could be ME!" I had never yelled like that at my mother before, and I felt dizzy, a little. The words came out of my mouth by themselves, as though I were throwing up, and my head began to shake. "You know what I did once? I climbed up on the awning, on that awning in front of our house, and I almost fell. The only reason I didn't was it was some kind of accident.

I could have broken my neck. Justine's mother said so. Ask her. Ask anybody. My name is up there, even. I wrote my name up on the wall in chalk. And you know why? Because Polly told me to. She played a trick on me." My eyes were closed tight now, and my words came from some dark tunnel. "IT COULD BE *ME*! IT COULD BE *ME*! NOT *HIM*. *ME*!"

Somebody had grabbed hold of my wrists and I opened my eyes. It was my mother, standing close to me, making me stand still, making me shut up. "Be quiet," she whispered in a voice I had never heard from her before, and I was afraid of what she might do next. Kill me or something. "Be *quiet*, Mary Ella. Stop that yelling. *Stop* it! The nurses will hear you."

"Let them!" I yelled back. "Let them hear me!" My throat ached and something far inside my ears stung as each word struck. "*All* of them!"

"Mary *Ella*!" My mother's voice was getting loud too. "Be *still*. Don't yell like that. They'll think . . ." but she fell silent: She didn't know how to finish. "They'll think . . ." and she stopped again. What *would* they think, anyway, all those nurses listening to me make all that noise while they glided so softly along the hall?

"They'll think there's a *cow* in here!" my mother yelled.

"Cows don't yell in hospitals!" I yelled back, and

then my voice dropped and so did hers. We just looked at each other and the next thing I knew she was laughing. *Really* laughing. The way Polly and I had laughed when we made faces on our noses in the mirror that day. With tears. They washed over her cheeks and got her hair all wet and her ears too.

I'd never seen her laugh like that before. I'd never seen her laugh much at all, in fact, and I wanted the moment to last. "Cows don't yell in hospitals," I said again, although I wasn't sure she was laughing at that. I wasn't sure what she was laughing at, really, but suddenly I began to laugh with her. Tears burst from my eyes too—laugh tears—and then, because we didn't want to look at each other with our faces all wet like that and twisted up, we hid ourselves on each other's shoulders. For a long time we stood there, together, shaking and sniffing, holding on—hugging, sort of— while our faces grew wetter and wetter.

"Visiting hours are over." Someone in a pink uniform pushed a mop into the room. "Hi, Big Boy," she said to Morton. "How's it going?" and she pushed the mop out into the hall again. She hadn't looked at my mother and me at all.

After a while we both quieted down, but we still held on to each other, not moving. "Mom," I whispered when my voice came back. "Don't be mad at Morton. Be mad at me, too."

"I'm not mad at either of you," she whispered back. "I love you both."

We didn't move after that, and her head lay on my shoulder for a long time.

"Time to go!" somebody called through the door, but we stayed where we were, holding each other for a long, long time.

"They said we have to go," I said finally, and I slipped out from her arms. I took a tissue from the box next to Morton's bed and wiped my tears. I'd dried my eyes too, when Polly and I had laughed together, but that time the tissue had turned purple and I'd saved it for always in my drawer. It lies there even now; I see it every day when I go to get my socks.

My mother wiped her face and nose, too, but not on a tissue. On the back of her hand, like Morton. "Mom," I said. "We should go," but she just went over to Morton's bed and leaned over him. Then, making scissors out of two fingers, she grasped a piece of his hair and slid it back and forth as though it were a strip of satin or of seaweed; as though it were smooth and slippery and she liked the way it felt. Suddenly she began to speak to him. Tiny sounds came from her lips, and she tilted his head to one side so he could receive them into his ear. They fell, one by one, like pennies dropping into a jar. "Morton," I heard her say, "listen to me. *Listen*," and I turned back to the window, because the words were just for him.

A bird—a real one—flew over to the stone head across the way and settled on the beak. *Look out*, I whispered in my head, *you'll turn to stone*, but it didn't. It shifted about from foot to foot for a while, as though it were dancing on hot sand, and then it lifted itself into the sky. I followed it until it was just a speck.

My mother continued to murmur behind me, pretending that Morton could hear her, just as she used to pretend, when she spoke to her listener, that he could not. Suddenly, her voice grew loud, making me jump. "Listen to me, Morton! *Listen!* You're going to get better, do you hear me? Do you? You're going to get better and you're going to come back home. We're all waiting for you there."

He wasn't going to the farm after all. He was going to come home. He wasn't a bad influence on me; I wasn't a bad influence on him. We were going to be a family, like the one in the egg, except the child rabbit now would have a brother.

If he woke up.

SEPTEMBER

CHAPTER FORTY

They took the awning down today. It was up when I left for school in the morning, down when I came home. Sky was stretched across its frame now, instead of canvas, and I stood with my head back for a while, looking between the long skinny bars.

Summer is over.

Not only that. Today was the first day of school. Agnes Daly always opens on this day—the last Wednesday of September, weeks after everybody else has gone back.

All the kids were standing around talking when I walked into my new classroom, but they fell silent as soon as they saw me, so I knew right away that they had all heard about Morton.

I was hoping they hadn't. I was hoping they didn't even know I had a brother at all. Mostly, I was hoping they hadn't heard how the accident had happened. Falling from a roof was a poor kids' thing to do, not a rich kids', and I didn't want them to think I was poor. Rich kids didn't fall from roofs. Rich kids didn't go up on roofs in the first place. Rich kids played where there was lots of grass and trees, like at camp. Rich kids were *watched.*

I didn't look at anybody as I went to my new desk and sat down. One of the wonderful things about being a lower or upper senior at Agnes Daly is that you get a real desk, like the kind teachers use, with big drawers on the sides for your papers and a nice blue blotter on top. Our names were printed on folded strips of cardboard, as though we were the president of a company or something. Iris's name was on the desk next to mine, and I tried to see whose name was on the one next to hers. Rhoda's, probably.

I ran my hand across the new blue blotter, smoothing it, and then I opened each drawer, pretending to look for something. I put my pen in one and my notepad in another. After that I sat very still, with my eyes on the front wall, as I do at a play when the curtain is about to go up. Soon the new teacher would come in and everyone would be quiet. Quiet because of *her,* and not because of me.

Later, though, when I thought everyone had forgotten I was there, Iris sent me a note. It bounced across my blotter like a lame bird and fell into my lap. "I heard about your brother," it read. "Love, Iris." I stared at it a long time, wondering whether she was being mean or not. "Love," it said. "Love, Iris." Why would anyone who was being mean write "Love"? Unless it was some kind of trick. Something she and Rhoda had thought up together, but when I looked around I discovered that Rhoda wasn't at any of the desks. Maybe she didn't go to Agnes Daly anymore. Maybe Iris was looking for a new friend. I read her note again and looked up at her. She gave me a smile.

"I heard about your brother." What, I wondered, had she heard? That he had fallen on his head while trying to get a toy from the next-door roof because some girl had told him to, and that he had lain unconscious in a hospital bed for days?

Or that one day, three weeks ago, while he lay there, a strange thing had happened that no one at the hospital could explain?

It was the day before Polly left for good, and I was walking down the hospital hall, holding a box in my hand and rehearsing in my head what I would say to Morton when I sat beside him in his room.

I had started visiting him in the afternoons then, by myself, going there on the bus and coming back before my mother got home from work. There was nothing to do at home by then; everyone else had gone back to school and I didn't feel like seeing Polly anymore. Besides, I liked to talk to Morton, even though he couldn't hear me. *Because* he couldn't hear me.

"Guess what," I was going to say to him this time. "Your coal car isn't on that roof anymore. Polly got it back. Morton, there was a ladder up there that went from our roof to the one next door. It was there all the *time*, only we didn't know about it, and Polly climbed down and got your coal car back."

Somebody was wheeling a bundle of something on a long cart, and I stepped aside to let it go by. After it passed, I realized the bundle was a person, stretched out straight and still under a sheet.

"But Morton, this is the bad part: She's keeping it for herself. She says she needs it for something. She says she has to have it, even when I told her it was yours and everything. Even when I told her it cost a whole lot of money." In fact, that was all I had told her that afternoon. That and, "Polly, you can't do that," but of course she could. She'd already done it.

Another cart hurried by, making a little breeze, and I held the box close to my body so it wouldn't blow away. "She says it's magic," I was going to tell him, and I felt myself begin to cry, as I had up on the roof that day when Polly snapped her fingers over the coal car and ran with it down the stairs. "She says it has special powers. I don't know what she says. Morton, she really isn't my friend anymore, and anyway, she's going away. She's going back to live with her mother, where it's yesterday sometimes, and we won't see the coal car again, or her, either."

Then I was going to tell him about the present I had brought him. "But I brought you something else instead, Morton," I was going to say, and I would open the box right in front of his face. "Look," I'd say, even though his eyes would still be closed. "This is for you."

I held the box up to my ear then and gave it a small shake, liking the click I heard against the cardboard. It would be a good surprise, and I wondered if somehow in his deep, deep sleep, Morton would know that I was there and had brought him something nice.

More carts rolled by and people were running along the hall. Something was going on down there—something bad, probably—and all of a sudden I saw that, for the first time ever, the door to Morton's room was tightly shut.

I stood still as a stone.

Up until that moment I had thought that nothing worse could happen to Morton than what had already happened. He would go on forever, I thought, asleep in his bed, like the princess. Or he would wake up.

I closed my eyes. *Don't let anything happen to him*, I whispered. *Don't let it, don't let it, don't let it.* And then I walked up to his room and faced the door.

Everything was silent on the other side, and I stood

there a long time, listening, not hearing anything, staring at the number—435—on the polished wood. Four three five, I read to myself, as though it were a message left especially for me. Four hundreds, three tens, five ones. Four red sticks, three blue sticks, five green sticks. Say that, Morton. Say it after me. *Say it!*

Suddenly, on the other side of the door I heard something. *Scratching*, it was, and I called out, "Who's there?" thinking—I don't know what I was thinking. That Morton was trying to get out, maybe, or someone else had already moved in. "Who's *there?*" and all at once the door swung open and I stood face-to-face with Polly.

She was wearing her grandmother's skirt and blouse again, and in her hand she held a piece of chalk.

"What are you doing here?" I finally asked. I had meant to whisper, but a half shout had come out instead. "What happened to Morton?"

"Nothing." I didn't know which question she was answering, but by then I saw that Morton was still lying in his bed, breathing in and out, the same as always, with his eyes tight shut. A paper bag, squashed flat like a sweet potato, lay at his feet. Who put that there? I wondered, but I didn't ask. I didn't say anything. I turned my back to Polly and closed the door.

"Hey," I said suddenly, staring at the door. "You're

not supposed to do that! You're not supposed to write your name on things in a hospital! You can get germs all over the place that way. Look what you *did*! You put chalk germs all over his door." I began to rub the P with my fist.

"What's in the box?" she asked, but I didn't answer. I didn't even turn around.

"I said, what's in the box?"

"Nothing." The chalk wasn't coming off, and I wet it with a finger.

"Hey, Morton," she said, and I could see from the edge of my eye that she was moving over to his bed. "Morton, you know what? You look like a fish, with your mouth open like that. Doesn't he, M. E.? Look at him. He's just like a fish."

What kind of chalk was that, anyway? It didn't even *smear*.

"Hey, you know what, Morton? I brought you something. Guess what it is." She was reaching now for the bag at his feet. "Here, open it," but she was holding it out to me, not to him, and in another moment she was standing at my side. "Take it, Mary Ella," she said. She had opened up the bag and was putting something cold in my hand.

For a moment I didn't even recognize it. It had been painted shiny orange, and a brand-new cat—a circle with whiskers, a circle with spots, and a long, looped tail—had been drawn in Magic Marker on each side. The wheels were polished clean and they spun when I pushed them with my thumb.

"Go ahead, M. E.," Polly said. "Give it to him," and in a moment I was walking across the room to his side.

"Morton," I said. I reached under the covers for his hand. "Hey, Morton. This is for you." I spoke the words I had rehearsed in the hall, to go with the present I had brought. "Look." Then, carefully, carefully, as though the lines across his palm were a stretch of silver track, I settled each wheel in place.

"Hey, Morton, you know what?" I said. "We can go somewhere in this now. All of us. We can all go to Africa. You and me and Polly. Or Australia. We can make ourselves really small, and we can shrink all our stuff, too, and take it along. You can be the conductor, Morton, and collect all the tickets. Oh, and guess what else," I added, remembering. "I brought two other passengers."

"Oh, hey!" Polly cried out as I emptied the little box into my hand. "The bugs! Where'd *they* come from?"

"They were in the bathroom," I told her. "Next to the tub, except I don't know how they got there." How *had* they gotten there, anyway? The last I knew they were in the boxcar. "Maybe they pushed the door open," I began to say, "with their . . ." but then I stopped. Something had suddenly changed in the room, and Polly and I both leaned forward from either side of Morton's bed, to stare down into Morton's face.

"Look, M. E.!" Polly whispered.

One day last spring, right out in the yard at Agnes Daly, a baby bird tumbled from its nest and landed on a patch of dirt beneath a tree. Joseph was the one who saw it first. "Hey, look!" he called out. "A broken bird! Let's fix it up and keep it for a pet." But by the time we all collected around it, it had stopped moving, and Joseph said, "Never mind. It's dead."

It wasn't, though. Someone touched its body with a stick, and all at once its wings began to stir. Slowly, very slowly, they began to lift from its body, to *peel*, really, like skin from an apple, and to stretch farther and farther into the air, until at last they pointed to the sky and carried the bird off the ground.

And that was the way Morton's eyelids moved when suddenly they lifted from his eyes that afternoon: They *peeled* open, like the skin from an apple, like the wings of that bird. Polly's head and mine nearly touched as we bent across his bed, watching, and we matched our breathing to each other's, to make less noise. Tiny breaths they were, coming both together, and once, when Morton's eyelids stiffened and we thought they'd shut again, we even gasped together, in a single small sound like a half-swallowed cry.

And then, all at once, his lids were up, all the way up, with his lashes reaching almost to his brows. His eyeballs wobbled slightly, like marbles coming to rest, but finally they locked into place, and the first thing Morton saw after his long, long sleep was not his image in the screen or the pair of stone birds on the wall across the way.

It was Polly and me.

I can't remember how long it took, but suddenly the room was filled with people—people in white, people in green, people in pink. Someone had a thin paper mask across her mouth, and it puffed like a balloon at every word she spoke.

"It's the strangest thing," she said.

"It's a miracle."

"All they did was put that thing in his hand."

"It's magic."

Morton was propped halfway up on his pillows by then and his eyes were still wide open. He held the little coal car in his hand and slowly, very, very slowly, he moved it across the white spread, leaving thin trails. His lips moved a little, as though he were kissing the air or sipping at a straw.

"He's saying something," someone said. A nurse.

"What's he saying?"

"Nothing, just sounds. That happens sometimes."

I looked across to Polly and she looked back at me. Together, with Morton, we whispered to each other.

"*Rum-rum-rum.*"

CHAPTER FORTY-ONE

I didn't know what to write back to Iris. The only answer I can ever think of when someone says something nice to me is "Same to you." "Same to you," I reply when people say "Have a nice summer" on the last day of school, and "Same to you" when they say "Good luck on your midterm." Once I even said that when someone wished me happy birthday.

But I couldn't say "Same to you" to someone who told me she'd heard about my brother. Even if she meant to be nice. Besides, I still wasn't sure that she *was* being nice. So all I wrote back was "He's better now." I signed it M. E., and I left out the "Love."

"That's good, Mary Ella, that he's better," she said to me at yard time. We had both been tagged out of dodgeball, and we were sitting on a ledge, waiting for the game to be over. "I didn't even know you had a brother until my mother said."

"No. Well, I do."

"How old is he?"

"Fourteen."

"Fourteen? Is he cute?"

"No. He's funny-looking."

"Is he nice, though?"

"Sort of. Yeah. He does things that are nice sometimes."

"Like what?"

"I don't know. He thinks up nice things to play."

"What grade is he in?"

I paused for just a moment. "Seventh."

"*Seventh?* He's fourteen and that's all he's in? The same as you? How come?"

"I don't know. It takes him a long time to learn things."

Other kids were getting tagged out, too, and they lined up next to us on the ledge.

"Who?" Peggy asked. "Who takes a long time to learn things?"

"My brother."

"You mean because he fell and everything?"

"No. He was always like that."

We sat there for a while and then Iris said, "I'm starting a club, Mary Ella. You want to be in it? It's a makeup club. We meet in the bathroom and we put on lipstick. You want to join?"

*   *   *

I put my new books down in a careful pile under the awning and swung on the V-shaped legs at the curb. If I leaned way back I could see, or I *thought* I could see, a few pale flecks where I'd chalked my name on the brick. THIS IS M. E.'S AWNING, it had said up there once. That was the first time I'd ever written on a wall, and I remembered how the chalk crumbled on the bumps, making pale-blue dust that fell like tiny snow. That was the first time I'd ever written on *anything* where you weren't supposed to write, and I thought then that it would be the last.

But as it happened, it wasn't.

Just before Polly and I left Morton's room, that afternoon when he first opened up his eyes and all those people in their white and pink and green hospital suits crowded around his bed, I took the piece of chalk from Polly's hand and I wrote something underneath her name on the door.

LOVES M. E. AND MORTON is what I wrote, and I enclosed it in a long, uneven heart.

A row of pigeons had settled on an antenna on the roof, and I stared at them, upside down, from the awning bars, just as I had stared at Polly back in June when she first walked down the street. From where I watched, they all looked alike—gray and plain, like the one Polly had picked to be her own, with stiff dark cloaks that narrowed at their feet.

I stared at them so long that when I closed my eyes they sprang up inside my lids, pale pink now and flat as paper—five birds pasted on a green paper sky. I held them there until they faded away, and I thought about Polly and her favorite pigeon and about how she liked it best because it had a funny walk. And then, suddenly, I understood what Polly was all about.

She wasn't dumb and she wasn't crazy.

She was magic, just as she had always said.

Not the kind of magic that can shrink things or make bugs win a race. Not the wand kind, or the trick kind either. Not that. The *other* kind; the kind of magic that can make things wonderful. She made the pigeon wonderful. She made Morton wonderful. Maybe she made me wonderful, too.

I slid my heels out into the street and brought my shoulders down low so I could see the pigeons even better, and then, all at once, for the first time ever and without even trying, I turned a somersault. Just like that! One minute I was leaning back to see a row of birds, and the next I had twirled over, with my feet behind me and my arms stretched backward on the bars in a sudden, perfect flip, quick and neat and wonderful. I had been wrong about how you're supposed to lean your head way back and look at the sidewalk. The trick is, you have to look up at the roof.

I heard voices coming from the corner after that; the public-school kids were on their way home, but I didn't turn my head. I wanted them to see my somersault, but I didn't want them to *know* I wanted them to see it. So I just flipped over, back and forth, looking like Ezra and Charles when they stand around sometimes and swing key chains. As if I didn't care.

"Hey, look," I heard someone say. "Look at Mary Ella! Look what she can do!" It was Morton, and I straightened up so I could see him.

Today was *his* first day back at school, too, three weeks late. I looked down the block, but I couldn't find him right away. He was walking behind some other kids, but not *way* behind, and his clothes were like everybody else's. He was wearing the new jeans my mother had bought him and a new shirt with a football number on it. She had bought both of us new clothes for school—nice clothes. We got to pick out what we wanted, and his were as nice as mine. Also, he was talking to someone, but I didn't see who.

"Hey, Mary Ella," he said when he reached our front door. "That's nice, the way you do that," and I turned one more somersault—quick and neat and perfect— just for him. So he could watch me and like what I could do.

our understanding of filial therapy while simultaneously improving clinical practice.

REFERENCES

Abidin, R. (1983). *Parenting stress index manual*. Charlottesville: University of Virginia Press.

Achenbach, T. (1991). *Manual for the child behavior checklist and 1991 profile*. Burlington, VT: University Associates in Psychiatry.

Andronico, M. P., & Guerney, B. G., Jr. (1969). A psychotherapeutic aide in a Head Start program. *Children, 16*(1), 14–22.

Axline, V. M. (1947, 1969). *Play therapy*. New York: Ballantine Books.

Beckloff, D. (1997). Filial therapy with children with spectrum pervasive developmental disorders. *Dissertation Abstracts International, 58*(11), 6224B. (UMI No. 9816128)

Belsky, J., & Nezworski, T. (Eds.). (1988). *Clinical implications of attachment*. Hillsdale, NJ: Lawrence Erlbaum Associates.

Bratton, S., & Landreth, G. (1995). Filial therapy with single parents: Effects on parental acceptance, empathy, and stress. *International Journal of Play Therapy, 4*(1), 61–80.

Bratton, S., Ray, D, & Rhine, T. (2002). What the research shows about filial play therapy. Retrieved June 15, 2002, from http://www.a4pt.org/research.html#meta_analysis

Chau, I., & Landreth, G. (1997). Filial therapy with Chinese parents: Effects on parental empathic interactions, parental acceptance of child, and parental stress. *International Journal of Play Therapy, 6*(2), 75–92.

Clark, K. E., & Ladd, G. W. (2000). Connectedness and autonomy support in parent–child relationships: Links to children's socioemotional orientation and peer relationships. *Developmental Psychology, 36*(4), 485–498.

Cohen, N. J., Lojkasek, M., Muir, E., Muir, R., & Parker, C. J. (2002). Six-month follow-up of two mother–infant psychotherapies: Convergence of therapeutic outcomes. *Infant Mental Health Journal, 23*(4), 361–380.

Cohen, N. J., Muir, E., Lojkasek, M., Muir, R., Parker, C. J., Barwick, M., et al. (1999). Watch, wait, & wonder: Testing the effectiveness of a new approach to mother–infant psychotherapy. *Infant Mental Health Journal, 20*(4), 429–451.

Costas, M., & Landreth, G. (1999). Filial therapy with nonoffending parents of children who have been sexually abused. *International Journal of Play Therapy, 8*(1), 43–66.

Figley, C. R. (1989). *Helping traumatized families*. San Francisco: Jossey-Bass.

Ginsberg, B. G. (1997). *Relationship enhancement family therapy*. New York: Wiley.

Ginsberg, B. G. (2003). An integrated holistic model of child-centered family therapy. In R. VanFleet & L. Guerney (Eds.), *Casebook of filial therapy* (pp. 21–47). Boiling Springs, PA: Play Therapy Press.

Ginsberg, B. G., Stutman, S. S., & Hummel, J. (1978). Notes for practice: Group filial therapy. *Social Work, 23*(2), 154–156.

Glover, G., & Landreth, G. (2000). Filial therapy with Native Americans. *International Journal of Play Therapy, 9*(1), 57–80.

Guerney, B. (1964). Filial therapy: Description and rationale. *Journal of Consulting Psychology, 28*(4), 303–310.

Guerney, B. G., Jr., Guerney, L., & Andronico, M. (1966). Filial therapy: Historical introduction. *Yale Scientific Magazine, 40*, 6–14.

Guerney, B. G., Jr., Guerney, L., & Andronico, M. (1969). Filial therapy: Historical introduction. Reprinted in B. G. Guerney, Jr. (Ed.), *Psychotherapeutic agents: New roles for nonprofessionals, parents, and teachers* (pp. 461–465). New York: Holt, Rinehart & Winston.

Guerney, B. G., Jr., Stollak, G. E., & Guerney, L. (1970). A format for a new model of psychological practice: Or, how to escape a zombie. *The Counseling Psychologist, 2*(2), 97–104.

Guerney, B. G., Jr., Stollak, G. E., & Guerney, L. (1971). The practicing psychologist as educator—An alternative to the medical practitioner model. *Professional Psychology, 2*(3), 276–282.

Guerney, B. G., Jr., & Stover, L. (1971). *Filial therapy: Final report on MH 18264-01.* Unpublished manuscript, Pennsylvania State University, University Park.

Guerney, L. (1975). *Follow-up study on filial therapy.* Paper presented at the annual convention of the Eastern Psychological Association, New York, NY.

Guerney, L. (1983). Introduction to filial therapy. In P. Keller & L. Ritt (Eds.), *Innovations in clinical practice: A source book* (Vol. 2, pp. 26–39). Sarasota, FL: Professional Resource Exchange.

Guerney, L. (1997). Filial therapy. In K. O'Connor & L. Braverman (Eds.), *Play therapy: Theory and practice* (pp. 131–159). New York: Wiley.

Guerney, L., & Guerney, B. G., Jr. (1994). Child Relationship Enhancement family therapy and parent education. In C. E. Schaefer & L. J. Carey (Eds.), *Family play therapy* (pp. 127–137). Northvale, NJ: Jason Aronson.

Guerney, L., & Guerney, B. G., Jr. (2002). *Filial therapy bibliography.* Bethesda, MD: National Institute of Relationship Enhancement. Retrieved June 15, 2002, from http://www.nire.org/filbib39.htm

Harris, Z., & Landreth, G. (1995). Filial therapy with incarcerated mothers: A five-week model. *International Journal of Play Therapy, 6*(2), 53–73.

Horner, P. (1974a). *Dimensions of child behavior as described by parents: A monotonicity analysis.* Unpublished doctoral dissertation, Pennsylvania State University, University Park.

Horner, P. (1974b). *Filial problem list.* University Park: The Pennsylvania State University Individual and Family Consultation Center.

Jang, M. (2000). Effectiveness of filial therapy for Korean parents. *International Journal of Play Therapy, 9*(2), 39–55.

Johnson-Clark, K. (1996). The effect of filial therapy on child conduct behavior problems and the quality of the parent–child relationship. *Dissertation Abstracts International, 57*(4), 2868B. (UMI No. 9626460)

Joseph, J. (1979). *Joseph preschool and primary self-concept screening test: Instruction manual.* Chicago: Stoelting Co.

Kale, A., & Landreth, G. (1999). Filial therapy with parents of children experiencing learning difficulties. *International Journal of Play Therapy, 8*(2), 35–56.

Ladd, G. W., & Ladd, B. K. (1998). Parenting behaviors and parent–child relationships: Correlates of peer victimization in kindergarten? *Developmental Psychology, 34*(6), 1450–1458.

La Greca, A. M., Silverman, W. K., Vernberg, E. M., & Roberts, M. C. (Eds.). (2002). *Helping children cope with disasters and terrorism.* Washington, DC: American Psychological Association.

Landreth, G. (1991). *Play therapy: The art of the relationship.* Muncie, IN: Accelerated Development Press.

Landreth, G., Homeyer, L., Bratton, S., Kale, A., & Hilpl, K. (2000). *The world of play therapy literature* (3rd ed.). Denton, TX: The Center for Play Therapy.

Landreth, G., & Lobaugh, A. (1998). Filial therapy with incarcerated fathers: Effects on parental acceptance of child, parental stress, and child adjustment. *Journal of Counseling and Development, 76,* 157–165.

Muir, E., Lojkasek, M., & Cohen, N. J. (1999). *Watch, wait, & wonder: A manual describing a dyadic infant-led approach to problems in infancy and early childhood.* Toronto, Canada: Hincks-Dellcrest Institute.

Oxman, L. (1972). The effectiveness of filial therapy: A controlled study. (Doctoral dissertation, Rutgers University, 1971). *Dissertation Abstracts International, 32,* 6656.

Porter, B. (1954). Measurement of parental acceptance of children. *Journal of Home Economics, 46,* 176–182.

Ray, D., Bratton, S., Rhine, T., & Jones, L. (2001). The effectiveness of play therapy: Responding to the critics. *International Journal of Play Therapy, 10*(1), 85–108.

Sensue, M. E. (1981). Filial therapy follow-up study: Effects on parental acceptance and child adjustment (Doctoral dissertation, Pennsylvania State University, University Park), *Dissertation Abstracts International, 42,* 148.

Smith, N. R. (2000). *A comparative analysis of intensive filial therapy with intensive individual play therapy and intensive sibling group play therapy with child witnesses of domestic violence.* Unpublished doctoral dissertation, University of North Texas, Denton, TX.

Stinnett, N., & DeFrain, J. (1985). *Secrets of strong families.* New York: Berkley Books.

Stover, L., & Guerney, B. G., Jr. (1967). The efficacy of training procedures for mothers in filial therapy. *Psychotherapy: Theory, Research and Practice, 4*(3), 110–115.

Stover, L., Guerney, B., & O'Connell, M. (1971). Measurements of acceptance, allowing, self-direction, involvement, and empathy in adult–child interaction. *Journal of Psychology, 77,* 261–269.

Sywulak, A. E. (1978). The effect of filial therapy on parental acceptance and child adjustment. (Doctoral dissertation, Pennsylvania State University, University Park, 1977). *Dissertation Abstracts International, 38*, 6180–6181.

Tew, K. (1997). The efficacy of filial therapy with families with chronically ill children. *Dissertation Abstracts International, 58*(3), 754A. (UMI No.9727806)

VanFleet, R. (1994). *Filial therapy: Strengthening parent–child relationships through play.* Sarasota, FL: Professional Resource Press.

VanFleet, R. (1999a). *Introduction to filial play therapy: Video workshop.* Boiling Springs, PA: Play Therapy Press.

VanFleet, R. (1999b). *Introduction to filial play therapy: Video workshop manual.* Boiling Springs, PA: Play Therapy Press.

VanFleet, R. (2000). *A parent's handbook of filial play therapy.* Boiling Springs, PA: Play Therapy Press.

VanFleet, R., & Guerney, L. (2003). *Casebook of filial therapy.* Boiling Springs, PA: Play Therapy Press.

Youngblade, L. M., & Belsky, J. (1992). Parent–child antecedents of 5-year-olds' close friendships: A longitudinal analysis. *Developmental Psychology, 28*(4), 700–713.

V

FINAL COMMENTS

13

PRESENT STATUS AND FUTURE DIRECTIONS FOR EMPIRICALLY BASED PLAY INTERVENTIONS FOR CHILDREN

TARA M. FILES-HALL AND LINDA A. REDDY

The goal of this book is to offer a comprehensive reference that highlights empirically validated interventions that use play as an integral component in treating an array of childhood disorders and problems. The highlighted programs are a sample of the many innovative play interventions that are available.

This chapter has three objectives. First, we critically review the current outcome literature on play interventions. We conceptualized the outcome literature, including the interventions in this book, as the "first generation" of play interventions. Second, new frameworks for designing the "second generation" of play interventions and conducting outcome assessment are proposed. Finally, directions for future research and training are presented.

CURRENT STATUS

This review identifies play intervention studies that represent rigorous design and data analytic methods. To do so, an exhaustive computerized bibliographical search was conducted to identify published empirically validated play intervention studies in the past 15 years. The terms play therapy and play-based interventions were searched across four age groups (i.e., infant, preschool, child, and adolescence) in six databases (i.e., PsycLit, ERIC, PsycINFO, Medline, Sociological Abstracts, and CINAHL). Studies that used control groups or treatment comparison groups, data analytic methods, and pre–post standardized outcome measures were reviewed.

The review of outcome literature revealed that the number of well-designed and controlled play intervention studies is growing. The majority of the investigations included preschoolers or elementary school age children. The interventions were conducted in a multitude of settings, including the clinic, hospital, school, and home. Interventions were delivered in an individual, group, or family context. In addition, a wide range of treatment agents were included, such as psychologists, social workers, teachers, psychiatrists, occupational therapists, physical therapists, nurses, parents, and paraprofessionals.

Play interventions prevent and treat emotional and behavioral difficulties. For example, play interventions have successfully treated children who have disruptive behavior disorders, including attention-deficit/hyperactivity disorder (ADHD; e.g., Reddy, Spencer, Hall, & Rubel, 2001) and oppositional defiant disorder (ODD; e.g., McNeil, Capage, Bahl, & Blanc, 1999). Overall, play interventions reduce child externalizing behavior and parental stress and increase child compliance and social skills. Children with developmental disorders such as autism (e.g., Restall & Magill-Evans, 1994), pervasive developmental disorder (e.g., Rogers & Lewis, 1989), and cognitive impairments (e.g., Kim, Lombardino, Rothman, & Vinson, 1989) have shown significant improvement in symbolic play, social–emotional functioning, perceptual–fine motor skills, and language after participating in play interventions.

Hospitals and medical clinics have effectively integrated play interventions into practice. For example, positive outcomes have been found with children who require hospitalization (e.g., Rae, Worchel, Upchurch, Sanner, & Daniel, 1989; Zahr, 1998) or have chronic illness (e.g., Johnson, Whitt, & Martin, 1987), burn injuries (e.g., Melchert-McKearnan, Deitz, Engel, & White, 2000), sensory integration difficulties (e.g., Case-Smith & Bryan, 1999), and cerebellar dysfunction (e.g., Yaggie & Armstrong, 1999).

Play-based prevention programs have promoted children's social and emotional health. For example, play-based prevention programs have helped at-risk children (e.g., Cowen & Hightower, 1989; Nafpaktitis & Perlmutter, 1998), children of divorce (e.g., Pedro-Carroll, Sutton, & Wyman, 1999), child witnesses of domestic violence (e.g., Kot, Landreth, & Giordano, 1998; Tyndall-Lind, Landreth, & Giordano, 2001), and child victims of abuse and neglect (e.g., Fantuzzo et al., 1996).

Although much progress has been made, play interventions for a number of childhood disorders and problems have not been fully examined. For example, there are prevention programs that treat bereavement (e.g., Griffin, 2001; Masterman & Reams, 1988), children infected and affected by HIV/AIDS (e.g., Leavitt, Morrison, Gardner, & Gallagher, 1996; Willemsen & Anscombe, 2001), and children of substance dependent parents (e.g., Carmichael & Lane, 1997; Cwiakala & Mordock, 1996). However, the majority of these prevention programs are not well controlled or empirically validated.

Gold-Steinberg and Logan (1999) reported in a case study that the behavioral and psychopharmacological treatment of obsessive–compulsive disorder (OCD) was enhanced by the addition of play therapy, but further investigation in this area has not been conducted. The additive effects of play interventions in multimodal intervention programs for other internalizing disorders, such as generalized anxiety disorder, major depressive disorder, and bipolar disorder have yet to be investigated. Finally, some have recommended that children with schizophrenia be treated with a multimodal treatment approach that includes play therapy (e.g., Sikes & Kuhnley, 1984; Wundheiler, 1976). However, outcome studies do not currently exist.

In the following section, we offer a new framework for designing future models of play interventions.

FRAMEWORK FOR PLAY INTERVENTIONS

The 11 chapters in this book illustrate the range of empirically validated play interventions for children. Each program reflects a strong theoretical basis, empirical support, and use of innovative play-based approaches. These programs highlight some of the key treatment ingredients for developing future play interventions. We recommend that future creators of play intervention models include (a) comprehensive outcome assessment approaches; (b) psychometrically sound and clinically sensitive outcome assessment instruments; (c) multimodal intervention approaches; (d) cognitive–behavioral techniques or home/school contingency management plans; (e) structured, time-limited interventions; (f) directive or nondirective play interventions; (g) interventions tailored to the developmental level of the child; (h) interventions that target functional behaviors and competencies in children or parents; (i) the assessment of quantifiable behavioral goals; (j) parents as agents of therapeutic change; (k) varied treatment agents (e.g., psychologists, psychiatrists, nurses, physical therapists, occupational therapists, social workers, teachers, parents, paraprofessionals); (l) different treatment settings (e.g., clinic, shelter, school, home, medical facility); and (m) outcome success defined by statistical and clinically meaningful methods (e.g., effect sizes, Jacobsen and Truax method).

We suggest that future play interventions broaden the *scope* and *focus* of interventions and programs. The *scope* of new play interventions should incorporate children from infancy through adolescence. As mentioned, the vast majority of the outcome literature includes children 10 years of age and younger. New models will also profit from broadening the type of intervention agents (e.g., nurses, peers, siblings) and service delivery settings (e.g., school, camp, home) used.

It would be beneficial to expand the *focus* of play interventions in the context of the individual child, family, and school. For the individual child, interventions could focus on the improvement of symptoms (e.g., hitting, noncompliance, anxiety, depression), difficulties related to psychosocial stressors (e.g., death, chronically ill family members, separation or divorce, sexual or physical abuse, natural disasters, substance-dependent parents), and adaptive behaviors and competencies (e.g., asking for help, self-control, eye contact, self-expression, creativity). For the family, intervention could focus on enhancing family cohesion, resiliency, communication, coping, relationships, flexibility, and adaptability. For the school, interventions could focus on increasing problem solving, cooperation, rule following, safety, and sense of belonging.

As outlined by Pfeiffer and Reddy (1998), it is recommended that the spectrum of mental health interventions in the home, school, and community be expanded to include prevention, intervention, maintenance, and health promotion/wellness services and programs. This book outlines several play prevention and intervention programs. However, maintenance play interventions and health promotion/wellness play interventions are significant, yet often overlooked, modes of intervention. Maintenance interventions are designed to aid in the retention of clinical gains achieved during a prevention or treatment intervention. Maintenance play interventions are particularly useful for preventing relapse among children during high stress periods (e.g., parent separation, relocation, natural disasters, remarriage, reunification). Health promotion/wellness interventions are designed to improve overall well-being. The goals of health promotion/wellness interventions are to enhance empowerment, resilience, enjoyment, and efficacy in children and families (Cowen, 1991). Play serves as a natural, powerful vehicle for accomplishing these objectives.

When developing new play intervention models, it is imperative to answer four questions. First, who will implement the interventions (e.g., a teacher, nurse, psychologist, social worker, parent, older peer)? This decision should be made carefully as it will affect the transfer, maintenance, and generalizability of gains to the targeted and nontargeted settings. Second, what specific play interventions will be implemented? Third, when will the interventions be introduced into the treatment process? Interventions should be carefully timed so that they occur at the appropriate developmental points in the children's lives. Fourth, where will the interventions be delivered? As discussed, interventions can be implemented in a number of settings (e.g., home, school, clinic, hospital). Each setting can uniquely affect the transfer and maintenance of gains.

It is essential that future play interventions are well conceived and use comprehensive outcome assessment approaches. The following section provides a framework for outcome assessment.

FRAMEWORK FOR OUTCOME ASSESSMENT

Psychometrically sound outcome instruments are essential to assess the efficacy of play interventions. Given the array of play interventions, it is difficult to propose a core set of outcome instruments. In general, it is recommended that comprehensive evaluations be conducted that incorporate a variety of assessment instruments, settings, and informants to observe children's adaptive and maladaptive functioning. The instruments used should be highly reliable and valid, as well as sensitive to clinical change, social, gender, linguistic, and cultural differences, and developmental factors and timing.

Future outcome assessments should include adaptive behavior scales, direct behavioral observation methods, the assessment of the home and school context, and behavior rating scales. Also, the inclusion of play-based assessment would be beneficial. For a detailed review of standardized play-based assessment instruments, see Gitlin-Weiner, Sandgrund, and Schaefer (2000).

Adaptive behavior scales or strength-based assessments offer an important addition to play intervention investigations. Strength-based instruments are designed to assess the unique strengths, social competencies, resources, and daily independence living skills observed in children. Two well-researched strength-based assessment instruments are the Behavior and Emotional Rating Scale (BERS; Epstein & Sharma, 1998) and the Social Skills Rating System (SSRS; Gresham & Elliott, 1990).

The use of direct observation methods of children's behavior and their interpersonal interactions in the home and school offer an impartial view of behavior that is not filtered by an informant. The Behavioral Assessment System for Children–Student Observation System (BASC-SOS; Reynolds & Kamphaus, 1992) and the Child Behavior Checklist–Direct Observation Form (CBC-DOF; Achenbach, 1986) are two well-known empirically validated observation methods. The Structured Observation of Academic and Play Settings (Milich, Loney, & Landau, 1982) is another valuable method for assessing academic and play behavior in both structured and unstructured settings.

Two noteworthy play-based observation methods are the Transdisciplinary Play-Based Assessment (TPBA; Linder, 1993) and the Parent-Child Interaction Play Assessment method (P-CIPA; Smith, 2000). TPBA provides a holistic approach to assessing children's level of social–emotional, cognitive, communication and language, and sensorimotor development. TPBA is family inclusive in that parents are key members of the assessment team before, during, and after the assessment process. Children (i.e., 6 years of age and younger) are observed playing in four contexts (i.e., alone, with his or her parents, with a play facilitator, and with a peer). Normative tables indexed by age are provided to aid professionals in determining the developmental level of the observed behaviors. The TPBA provides information on children's lowest, highest, and most typical range of functioning that can be used in designing interventions. The TPBA can be implemented in the clinic, hospital, school, or home and has strong reliability and validity indices (Linder, 2000).

When assessing children, it is imperative to obtain an understanding of the parent–child relationship, which can be done, in part, by observing child–parent interactions. One way to accomplish this objective is by using the P-CIPA (Smith, 2000). Parents and children are observed as they interact for two 15-minute periods. The first period is unstructured. The second period is structured, and the parent is directed to issue three commands, which are often resisted by the child. Following the observations, the parent is given a brief interview to determine how characteristic the child's behavior and interactions were. The observer rates the interactions quantitatively and qualitatively on the P-CIPA recording form. The scores can also be graphed on the profiling sheet. Favorable interrater reliability and criterion-related validity studies have been found.

It is important to assess the social context of the home and school (Baker, 1998; Ollendick & Hersen, 1998). Family factors can influence the development of children's psychopathology and personality (Ollendick & Hersen, 1998). The family environment can significantly influence children's emotional and behavioral functioning. Four empirically validated measures that assess the family environment are the Family Environment Scale–Second Edition (FES; Moos & Moos, 1986), the Family Adaptability and Cohesion Evaluation Scales (FACES III; Olson, Bell, & Portner, 1985), the Family System Test (FAST; Gehring, 1998), and the Parent Stress Index–III (PSI-III; Abidin, 1995).

The FES is based on family systems theory. The FES provides a comprehensive assessment of children and parents' perceptions of family functioning in three areas: relationships, personal growth, and systems maintenance. The FACES III is a 40 item rating scale that assesses parents' perceptions of their family's cohesion (i.e., degree that family members are separated or connected to their family) and adaptability (i.e., the ability of a family system to alter its power structure and roles in response to developmental and situational stress). The theoretical basis of the FAST is structural family systems theory and developmental family psychology. The FAST is designed to collect information from family members (6 years of age and older) in an individual or group context on how they perceive the family from a typical, ideal, and conflictual viewpoint. The FAST is designed to analyze biopsychosocial problems and family structures for planning and evaluating interventions (Gehring & Page, 2000). The PSI-III is a parent rating scale designed to assess parents' level of stress and stress attributed to parenting their children. The PSI-III contains a total score and 13 subscale scores divided into two domains: the Child Domain (i.e., Adaptability, Acceptability, Demandingness, Mood, Distractibility–Hyperactivity, Reinforces Parent) and the Parent Domain (i.e., Depression, Attachment, Role Restriction, Competence, Isolation, Health, Spouse).

Assessment of the social context of the school would enhance future play interventions. Roeser, Midgley, and Urdan (1996) reported that students' perceptions of school as a secure and caring environment are crucial to school completion, satisfaction, and social integration. Two measures that assess children's perceptions of classroom and school social climate are the Psychological Safety Index (PSI; Hinman, 1993) and the Multidimensional Student Life Satisfaction Scale (MSLSS; Huebner, 1994). The PSI assesses children's perceptions of teacher attributes (e.g., "My teacher is patient"), interpersonal interactions (e.g., "My teacher really cares about me"), and classroom norms (e.g., "In my class everyone gets a chance to play"). The MSLSS measures students' sense of wellness and cognitive appraisals of school satisfaction.

Childhood problems and disorders can be assessed through narrowband (e.g., Reynolds Children's Depression Scale, Multidimensional Anxiety Scale for Children, Brown ADHD Scales) and broad-band (e.g., Child Behavior Checklist, Devereux Scales of Mental Disorders) behavior rating scales completed by children, parents, or teachers. Although numerous behavior rating scales are available, play-based assessment linked to the *Diagnostic Statistical Manual of Mental Disorders—Fourth Edition, Text Revision* (DSM–IV–TR; American Psychiatric Association, 2000) and childhood disorders are limited (Gitlin-Weiner et al., 2000). One assessment instrument that has achieved this is the Kiddie Formal Thought Disorder Rating Scale (K-FTDS) and Story Game (Caplan, Guthrie, Fish, Tanguay, & David-Lando, 1989). The K-FTDS was designed to assess the four *DSM–III* criteria for formal thought disorder (i.e., loose associations, illogical thinking, incoherence, and content of speech). The 20- to 25-minute Story Game was designed to provide professionals with speech samples of latency age children. Videotapes of the Story Game are then viewed and rated for formal thought disorder using the K-FTDS. The K-FTDS and Story Game are being adapted for use in clinical practice and have been demonstrated to be reliable and valid for the assessment of formal thought disorder (Caplan & Sherman, 2000).

Professionals are encouraged to evaluate the efficiency and cost-effectiveness of their interventions. In general, cost-effective interventions are those that can be conducted in the shortest amount of time and offered in a group, rather than individual, context. Professionals should consider whether their interventions can be delivered, at least in part, by parents, paraprofessionals, or peers. Finally, a comprehensive cost-analysis that measures resources used and outcomes produced would be beneficial (Reddy & Savin, 2000).

The new frameworks for play interventions and outcome assessment approaches offer directions for future research. In the next section, we discuss directions for future research.

DIRECTIONS FOR FUTURE RESEARCH

We hope the architects for the "second generation" of play intervention programs will incorporate the new frameworks proposed in this chapter. It is critical that future research based on these programs carefully document all aspects of each study. LeBlanc and Ritchie (1999) and Ray, Bratton, Rhine, and Jones (2001) asserted that many studies fail to indicate basic information, such as the participants' age, gender, ethnicity, and presenting problem(s). Some studies also failed to report the level of training of the intervention agents and included incomplete protocol and research procedures. It is imperative that researchers provide (a) descriptions of the participants' characteristics; (b) details of the play interventions; and (c) inclusion and exclusion criteria. Moreover, the development and use of manualized play interventions would be beneficial to practitioners and researchers. This information will enhance the interpretation of outcome results, refinement of interventions, and replication and transportability of interventions to other settings and populations.

Research has indicated that interventions that are rated as more acceptable by clients are implemented more often (Reimers, Wacker, Cooper, & DeRaad, 1992). The effectiveness of an intervention is also mediated by the treatment agent's acceptability of that intervention (e.g., Dunson, Hughes, & Jackson, 1994; Greene, 1995). Thus, it would be useful to use measures of treatment acceptability (e.g., The Behavior Intervention Rating System; Von Brock & Elliott, 1987) in future play intervention studies. The success of interventions is also influenced by the extent to which treatment agents implement the interventions as planned (Springer & Reddy, 2004). Therefore, measuring treatment agent's adherence to and efficacy in implementing play interventions is warranted.

Research initiatives offer priorities for training. Outlined below are directions for training.

DIRECTIONS FOR FUTURE TRAINING

Professionals who design and evaluate new models of play interventions require a broad range of skills and competencies. The following are some directions on what is needed for training.

- knowledge of developmental psychology, emphasizing normal and atypical developmental factors;
- advanced training in neuroscience and neuropsychology focused on neurocognitive processes and pathways of childhood disorders;
- comprehensive assessment skills and knowledge of empirically validated treatments for childhood disorders and problems;
- understanding the role that play has on normal development, and in the assessment, prevention, and treatment of childhood problems;
- skills in designing prevention, treatment, maintenance, and wellness/health promotion play interventions;
- ability to evaluate the success of interventions from statistically and clinically meaningful approaches;
- didactic and practical experience in collaborating and consulting with various professionals (e.g., physicians, nurses, teachers, occupational therapists, physical therapists); and
- applied training in various treatment settings, such as the school, home, clinic, or medical facility.

FINAL COMMENTS

This chapter critically reviews the outcome literature on play interventions. Well-designed play interventions have effectively prevented and treated emotional and behavioral difficulties. However, there still remain a number of childhood disorders and problems that have not been fully studied. The success of future play-based interventions rests on the thoughtful integration of intervention methods and outcome assessment.

The 11 chapters in this book highlighted some of the key treatment components for developing future play-based interventions. In this chapter, these components are outlined and suggestions for broadening the scope and focus of future play-based interventions are offered. The efficacy of new play-based interventions lies, in part, on the use of comprehensive outcome assessment. A new framework for outcome assessment is provided that includes the use of adaptive behavior scales, direct behavioral observation, the assessment of the home and school context, behavior rating scales, and play-based assessment instruments.

Guidelines for future research in this area are presented. It is suggested that all aspects of studies be carefully documented to aid in the interpretation of the results and the replication and transportability of interventions to other settings and populations. It is also recommended that manualized treatment programs be developed and treatment acceptability and adherence be measured for program development efforts.

Finally, directions for professional development and training are proposed. Priorities for training include training in child development, childhood disorders, neuropsychology, program development, program implementation, and statistically and clinically meaningful approaches to program evaluation.

REFERENCES

Abdin, R. R. (1995). *Parent Stress Index—Version three*. Charlottesville, VA: Pediatric Psychology Press.

Achenbach, T. M. (1986). *Child Behavior Checklist—Direct Observation Form* (Rev. ed.). Burlington: University of Vermont.

American Psychiatric Association. (2000). *Diagnostic and statistical manual of mental disorders* (4th ed., text revision). Washington, DC: Author.

Baker, J. A. (1998). The social context of school satisfaction among urban, low-income, African American students. *School Psychology Quarterly, 13*(1), 25–44.

Caplan, R., Guthrie, D., Fish, B., Tanguay, P. E., & David-Lando, G. (1989). The Kiddie Formal Thought Disorder Scale (K-FTDS): Clinical assessment, reliability, and validity. *Journal of American Academy of Child Psychiatry, 28*, 408–416.

Caplan, R., & Sherman, T. (2000). Kiddie Formal Thought Disorder Rating Scale and Story Game. In K. Gitlin-Weiner, A. Sangrund, & C. Schaefer (Eds.), *Play diagnosis and assessment* (pp. 169–209). New York: Wiley.

Carmichael, K. D., & Lane, K. S. (1997). Play therapy with children of alcoholics. *Alcoholism Treatment Quarterly, 15*(1), 43–51.

Case-Smith, J., & Bryan, T. (1999). The effects of occupational therapy with sensory integration emphasis on preschool-age children with autism. *American Journal of Occupational Therapy, 53*(5), 489–497.

Cowen, E. L. (1991). In pursuit of wellness. *American Psychologist, 46*(4), 404–408.

Cowen, E. L., & Hightower, A. D. (1989). The Primary Mental Health Project: Thirty years after. In R. E. Hess & J. DeLeon (Eds.), *The National Mental Health Association: Eighty years of involvement in the field of prevention*. New York: Haworth Press.

Cwiakala, C. E., & Mordock, J. B. (1996). Let's discover health and happiness in play groups: A model of psychoeducation of young children with parents in addiction recovery. *Journal of Child and Adolescent Group Therapy, 6*(3), 147–162.

Dunson, R. M., III, Hughes, J. N., & Jackson, T. W. (1994). Effect of behavioral consultation on student and teacher behavior. *Journal of School Psychology, 32*(3), 247–266.

Epstein, M., & Sharma, J. (1998). *Behavioral and emotional rating scale: A strength-based approach to assessment—Examiner's manual*. Austin, TX: Pro-ed.

Fantuzzo, J., Sutton-Smith, B., Atkins, M., Meyers, R., Stevenson, H., Coolahan, K., et al. (1996). Community-based resilient peer treatment of withdrawn maltreated preschool children. *Journal of Consulting and Clinical Psychology, 64*(6), 1377–1386.

Gehring, T. M. (1998). *The Family System Test*. Seattle: Hogrefe & Huber Publishers.

Gehring, T. M., & Page, J. (2000). Family System Test (FAST): A systematic approach for family evaluation in clinical practice and research. In K. Gitlin-Weiner, A. Sangrund, & C. Schaefer (Eds.), *Play diagnosis and assessment* (pp. 419–445). New York: Wiley.

Gitlin-Weiner, K., Sandgrund, A., & Schaefer, C. (Eds.). (2000). *Play diagnosis and assessment*. New York: Wiley.

Gold-Steinberg, S., & Logan, D. (1999). Integrating play therapy in the treatment of children with obsessive-compulsive disorder. *American Journal of Orthopsychiatry, 69*(4), 495–503.

Greene, R. W. (1995). Students with ADHD in school classrooms: Teacher factors related to compatibility, assessment, and intervention. *School Psychology Review, 24*(1), 81–93.

Gresham, F. M., & Elliott, S. N. (1990). *Social Skills Rating System*. Circle Pines, MN: American Guidance Service.

Griffin, R. E. (2001). Playing the unspeakable: Bereavement programs. In A. Drewes, L. Carey, & C. Schaefer (Eds.), *School-based play therapy* (pp. 216–237). New York: Wiley.

Hinman, G. (1993). [The psychological safety index]. Unpublished scale.

Huebner, E. S. (1994). Preliminary development and validation of a multidimensional life satisfaction scale for children. *Psychological Assessment, 6*, 149–158.

Johnson, M. R., Whitt, J. K, & Martin, B. (1987). The effect of fantasy facilitation on anxiety in chronically ill and healthy children. *Journal of Pediatric Psychology, 12*(2), 273–283.

Kim, Y. T., Lombardino, L. J., Rothman, H., & Vinson, B. (1989). Effects of symbolic play intervention with children who have mental retardation. *Mental Retardation, 27*(3), 159–165.

Kot, S., Landreth, G. L., & Giordano, M. A. (1998). Intensive child-centered play therapy with child witnesses of domestic violence. *International Journal of Play Therapy, 7*(2), 17–36.

Leavitt, K. S., Morrison, J. A., Gardner, S. A., & Gallagher, M. M. (1996). Group play therapy for cumulatively traumatized child survivors of familial AIDS. *International Journal of Play Therapy, 5*(1), 1–17.

LeBlanc, M., & Ritchie, M. (1999). Predictors of play therapy outcomes. *International Journal of Play Therapy, 8*(2), 19–34.

Linder, T. W. (1993). *Transdisciplinary play-based assessment: A functional approach to working with young children* (Rev. ed.). Baltimore: Paul H. Brookes Publishing.

Linder, T. W. (2000). Transdisciplinary play-based assessment. In K. Gitlin-Weiner, A. Sangrund, & C. Schaefer (Eds.), *Play diagnosis and assessment* (pp. 139–166). New York: Wiley.

Masterman, S. H., & Reams, R. (1988). Support groups for bereaved preschool and school-age children. *American Journal of Orthopsychiatry, 58*(4), 562–570.

McNeil, C. B., Capage, L. C., Bahl, A., & Blanc, H. (1999). Importance of early intervention for disruptive behavior problems: Comparisons of treatment and wait-list control groups. *Early Education and Development, 10,* 445–454.

Melchert-McKearnan, K., Deitz, J., Engel, J. M., & White, O. (2000). Children with burn injuries: Purposeful activity versus rote exercise. *American Journal of Occupational Therapy, 54*(4), 381–390.

Milich, R., Loney, J., & Landau, S. (1982). The independent dimensions of hyperactivity and aggression: A validation with playroom observations. *Journal of Abnormal Psychology, 91,* 183–198.

Moos, R. H., & Moos, B. S. (1986). *Family Environment Scale Manual—Second edition.* Palo Alto, CA: Consulting Psychologists Press.

Nafpaktitis, M., & Perlmutter, B. F. (1998). School-based early mental health intervention with at-risk students. *School Psychology Review, 27,* 420–432.

Ollendick, T. H., & Hersen, J. (1998). *Handbook of child psychopathology* (3rd ed.). New York: Plenum Press.

Olson, D., Bell, R., & Portner, J. (1985). *FACES-III: Family Adaptability and Cohesion Evaluation Scales.* St. Paul: University of Minnesota, Department of Family Social Science.

Pedro-Carroll, J. L., Sutton, S. E., & Wyman, P. A. (1999). A two-year follow-up evaluation of a preventative intervention for young children of divorce. *School Psychology Review, 28*(3), 467–476.

Pfeiffer, S. I., & Reddy, L. A. (1998). School-based mental health programs: Present status and a blueprint for the future. *School Psychology Review, 27*(1), 84–96.

Rae, W. A., Worchel, F. F., Upchurch, J., Sanner, J. H., & Daniel, C. A. (1989). The psychosocial impact of play on hospitalized children. *Journal of Pediatric Psychology, 14,* 617–627.

Ray, D., Bratton, S., Rhine, T., & Jones, L. (2001). The effectiveness of play therapy: Responding to the critics. *International Journal of Play Therapy, 10*(1), 85–108.

Reddy, L. A., & Savin, H. (2000). Designing and conducting outcome studies. In H. A. Savin & S. S. Kiesling (Eds.), *Accountable systems of behavioral health care* (pp. 132–158). San Francisco: Jossey-Bass.

Reddy, L. A., Spencer, P., Hall, T. M., & Rubel, E. (2001). Use of developmentally appropriate games in a child group training program for young children with attention-deficit/hyperactivity disorder. In A. A. Drewes, L. J. Carey, & C. E. Schaefer (Eds.), *School-based play therapy* (pp. 256–274). New York: Wiley.

Reimers, T. M., Wacker, D. P., Cooper, L. J., & DeRaad, A. O. (1992). Acceptability of behavioral treatments for children: Analog and naturalistic evaluations by parents. *School Psychology Review, 21*, 628–643.

Restall, G., & Magill-Evans, J. (1994). Play and preschool children with autism. *American Journal of Occupational Therapy, 48*(2), 113–120.

Reynolds, C. R., & Kamphaus, R. W. (1992). *Behavioral assessment system for children—student observation scale*. Circle Pines, MN: American Guidance Services.

Roeser, R. W., Midgley, C., & Urdan, T. C. (1996). Perceptions of the school psychological environment and early adolescents' psychological and behavioral functioning in school: The mediating role of goals and belonging. *Journal of Educational Psychology, 88*, 408–422.

Rogers, S., & Lewis, H. (1989). An effective day treatment model for young children with pervasive developmental disorders. *Journal of the American Academy of Child & Adolescent Psychiatry, 28*(2), 207–214.

Sikes, V., & Kuhnley, E. J. (1984). Multimodal treatment of a child with schizophrenia. *American Journal of Psychotherapy, 38*(2), 272–285.

Smith, D. T. (2000). Parent–child interaction play assessment. In K. Gitlin-Weiner, A. Sangrund, & C. Schaefer (Eds.), *Play diagnosis and assessment* (pp. 340–370). New York: Wiley.

Springer, C., & Reddy, L.A. (2004). Measuring adherence in behavior therapy: Opportunities for research and clinical practice. *The Behavior Therapist, 27*(4), 1–9.

Tyndall-Lind, A., Landreth, G. L., & Giordano, M. A. (2001). Intensive group play therapy with child witnesses of domestic violence. *International Journal of Play Therapy, 10*(1), 53–83.

Von Brock, M. B., & Elliott, S. N. (1987). Influence of treatment effectiveness information on the acceptability of classroom intervention. *Journal of School Psychology, 25*, 131–144.

Willemsen, H., & Anscombe, E. (2001). Art and play therapy group for preschool children infected and affected by HIV/AIDS. *Clinical Child Psychology and Psychiatry, 6*(3), 339–350.

Wundheiler, L. (1976). "Liberty Boy": The play of a schizophrenic child. *Journal of the American Academy of Child Psychiatry, 15*(3), 475–490.

Yaggie, J. A., & Armstrong, W. J. (1999). From the clinic: The use of play therapy in the treatment of children with cerebellar dysfunction. *Journal of American Kinesiotherapy Association, 53*(4), 91–95.

Zahr, L. K. (1998). Therapeutic play for hospitalized children in Lebanon. *Pediatric Nursing, 23*(5), 449–454.

AUTHOR INDEX

Lobaugh, A., 254, *263*
Logan, D., 269, *277*
Lojkasek, M., 244, *261, 263*
Lombardino, L. J., 268, *278*
Loney, J., *165*, 271, *278*
Lorion, R. P., 28
Lotyczewski, B. S., 24, *29, 30*
Love, B., 124, *141*
Lowenfeld, M., 3, *10*
Lucka, G. W., 192, *209*
Lumley, V. A., 174, *189*
Lynch, E. W., 238
Lynch, N. R., *119*
Lyytinen, P., 3, *10*

Maccoby, E., 175, *190*
Madden, N. A., 193
Magill-Evans, J., 268, *279*
Mahler, J., 54, 70, *75*
Mallory, R., *166, 190*
Mangual, J., 25, *29*
Manikam, R., 231, *235*
Mannarino, A. P., 81, 82, 83, 84, 86, 87, 90, 95, 99, *102*
March, J., 80, 86, 91, 92, 98, *101*
Margolin, G., 32, *47*
Marin-Hertz, S. P., 108, *121*
Marlowe, H. A., *71*
Martin, B., 107, *120*, 268, *278*
Martin, J., 136, *140*
Martino, T., *47*
Maruyama, G., 193
Mash, E., *163, 186, 190*
Masten, A. S., 55, *73*
Masterman, S. H., 269, *278*
Matarazzo, R. G., 178, 179, *188*
Matheson, C., 3, *10*
Mathews, K. A., 192
Matson, J., 231, *235*
Matthews, W. J., *120*
Mattlinger, M., *237*
McBurnett, K., 147, *166*
McCarthy, G., 52, *73*
McClelland, D. C., 170, *188*
McCue, K., 126, 127, *141*
McCune, L., 3, *10*
McDonough, L., 217, *237*
McEvoy, R., 217, *237*
McFarlane, A. C., *103*
McGaw, B., 158, *164*
McGee, R., 146, *165*

McGinnis, E., 150, *165*
McGrath, J. M., *191*
McGrath, P., 111, *121, 147, 166, 190*
McIntosh, D. E., 181, *189*
McKee, D. H., 125, 129, *140*
McLanahan, S., 53, *73*
McLeer, S. V., 81, 86, 99
McMahon, R. J., 153, *164*
McMillan, I., 4, *10*
McNeil, C. B., 169, 170, 171, 174, 177, 178, 179, 180, *187, 188, 189, 190, 191*, 268, *278*
Mearns, N., 33, *48*
Mehta, P., 55, *74*
Meichenbaum, D. H., 86, 94, *101*
Melchert-McKearnan, K., 268, *278*
Meller, P. J., 25, *29*
Melton, G. B., 182, *189*
Mercer, J., 146, 147, *164, 165*
Meredith, R. L., *100*
Messer, D., 216, 217, *237*
Meyers, R., *277*
Midgley, C., 273, *279*
Mijangos, L. B., 27, *29*
Milich, R., 271, *278*
Miller, S. M., 130, 131, 132, *141*
Mills, A. R., *29*
Minassian, D., *100*
Mireault, G., 64, *73*
Moersch, M. S., *238*
Monteiro, L. M., 147, *164*
Monteiro, M. L., 146, 147, *165*
Montes, G., 64, *74*
Moos, B. S., 272, *278*
Moos, R. H., 272, *278*
Mordock, J. B., 269, *277*
Morris, R. J., *140*
Morrison, D. R., 53, *75*
Morrison, J. A., 269, *278*
Mroueh, A., 85, *102*
Muir, E., 244, *261, 263*
Muir, R., 244, *261*
Mundy, L., 216
Mundy, P., 218, *236, 237, 239*
Murdock, T., 93, *100*
Murphy, C. M., 32, *48*
Murphy, H. A., 194
Murray, M., 91, *101*
Muskin, P. R., *101*
Mussen, P. H., *74*
Myer, R., 52, *72*

SUBJECT INDEX

Minnesota, Primary Mental Health
    Project in, 26
Misconceptions, clarifying of (CODIP),
    60–61
Missouri Children's Picture Series
    (MCPS), 134, 135
Mistrust, and PTSD, 88
Modeling, in CAMP children's program,
    150, 152
Mother–Child Play Interaction Scale, 223
MSLSS (Multidimensional Student Life
    Satisfaction Scale), 273
Multicultural adaptations, of filial therapy,
    247
Multidimensional Anxiety Scale for
    Children, 273
Multidimensional Student Life
    Satisfaction Scale (MSLSS), 273
Musical chairs, cooperative, 197, 200

National Institute of Relationship
    Enhancement, 250
National Mental Health Association, Lela
    Rowland Prevention award of, 23
Native Americans, filial therapy with, 256
New York State, Primary Mental Health
    Project in, 26
  in New York City, 25
New York State Sharing Successful
    Programs, 23
Noncompetitive games, 52. *See also at*
    Cooperative games
Noncontingent attention (NCR), as
    aggression treatment, 194
Nondirective play therapy with children,
    83–84
  and bearing witness, 96
Nondirective supportive therapy (NST),
    for sexual abuse victims, 90
Nonoffending parents of sexually abused
    children, filial therapy with, 255

Obsessive–compulsive disorder (OCD),
    and play therapy, 269
Operant conditioning, Hanf's two-stage
    model of, 170
Oppositional defiant disorder (ODD), 268
Outcome assessment framework, for
    empirically validated play
    interventions, 271

Outcome evaluation
    for CAMP, 157–160, 161–162
    for Children of Divorce Intervention
        Program, 65–71
    on Primary Mental Health Project,
        23–24, 52
        evaluation designs for, 24–26
    and posttraumatic play therapy,
        97–98
Outcome evaluations
    on cooperative games, 197–204
    on Denver model, 223–227
    on filial therapy, 250–257
    on guided fantasy play, 110–114
    on PCIT, 169–170, 177–179
    and play therapy with hospitalized
        children, 133–138
    See also Research studies
Overlearning, in CAMP children's
    program, 150

Pain reduction, imagery for, 117–118
PAM (Parent Adherence Measure), 162
Pantomime, and autism, 217
Paraprofessionals, child associates as
    (Primary Project), 15, 17–18
Parent(s)
    as agents of therapeutic change, 175
    children's advice for, 63
    in cooperative games intervention,
        198
    in filial therapy, 242, 242–243, 243,
        244–245, 247 (*see also* Filial
        therapy)
    and guided fantasy play, 110
    intensive play therapy carried out
        by, 45
    and outcome of play therapy, 5
    in play therapy with hospitalized
        children, 132–133
    in posttraumatic therapy, 81, 87
    in Primary Mental Health Project, 21
    See also Children of divorce; Divorce;
        Family(ies)
Parent Adherence Measure (PAM), 162
Parent–Adolescent Relationship
    Development program, 244
Parental consent, for Primary Mental
    Health Project, 19
Parental role, child's perception of
    (sibling play therapy), 36

ABOUT THE EDITORS

Linda A. Reddy, PhD, is an associate professor of psychology, founder and director of the Child/Adolescent ADHD Clinic, and former director of the Center for Psychological Services at Fairleigh Dickinson University, Hackensack, New Jersey. She has published two edited books, *Innovative Mental Health Interventions for Children: Programs That Work* and *Inclusion Practice in Special Education: Research, Theory, and Application.* She has published over 30 book chapters and articles. She specializes in the assessment and treatment of children with disruptive behavior disorders, family–school interventions, test validation, behavioral consultation, play interventions, and treatment outcome evaluation. She maintains her practice in New Jersey. She received her BA (1986) in psychology from Boston University and her MA (1989) in educational psychology and PhD (1994) in school psychology from the University of Arizona. She completed postdoctoral research and a clinical fellowship at the Devereux Foundation Institute of Clinical Training and Research.

Tara M. Files-Hall, PhD, completed her predoctoral internship in clinical child psychology at St. Luke's Roosevelt Hospital Center in New York and her postdoctoral fellowship in the School District of Hillsborough County, Florida. Her clinical and research interests include disruptive behavior disorders, play therapy, early intervention, family–school assessment and intervention, group-based intervention, consultation, and program development and evaluation. She received her BA (1997) in psychology from the University of Central Florida and her MA (2000) and PhD (2003) in clinical psychology from Fairleigh Dickinson University, New Jersey. She maintains her private practice in Sarasota, Florida, and is employed as a school psychologist in Tampa, Florida.

Charles E. Schaefer, PhD, is a professor of psychology and former director of the Center for Psychological Services at Fairleigh Dickinson University, Hackensack, New Jersey. He is the cofounder and Board Member Emeritus of the International Play Therapy Association. Dr. Schaefer is the founder and codirector of the Play Therapy Training Institute in New Jersey. He has published over 40 books and numerous articles and book chapters on play-based interventions. He has over 30 years of experience working with young children and parents. Dr. Schaefer coordinates an annual international play therapy study group in England. He earned his BA from Fairfield University and his MA and PhD in clinical psychology from Fordham University (1967).